Year by Year with the Early Jesuits

Year by Year with the Early Jesuits (1537–1556)

*Selections from the "Chronicon"
of Juan de Polanco, S.J.*

Translated and annotated by

John Patrick Donnelly, S.J.

St. Louis

THE INSTITUTE OF JESUIT SOURCES

No. 21 in Series 1: Jesuit Primary Sources
   in English Translation

The Institute of Jesuit Sources
3601 Lindell Boulevard
St. Louis, MO 63108
   tel: [314] 977-7257
   fax: [314] 977-7263
e-mail: ijs@slu.edu

Library of Congress Control Number: 2004110571
ISBN 1-880810-57-3

CONTENTS

v

PREFACE

A uthors always run up many debts in producing a book. Here I wish to thank those who have helped me with this project. I have had the support of many members of my Jesuit community at Marquette University in the course of this project, especially its rectors, Fathers Eugene Merz, S.J., and Thomas Krettek, S.J. From its inception Father John Padberg, S.J., director of the Institute of Jesuit Sources, has encouraged this project, and Father John McCarthy, S.J., edited and polished the manuscript and guided it through all the stages of its production. Father Thomas Caldwell saved me from numerous problems with my computer. Three research assistants in the History Department of Marquette University, Melissa Prickett, Jason Hostutler, and Jason Feucht, proofread parts of the manuscript and suggested which sections of an overlong manuscript could be eliminated.

John Patrick Donnelly, S.J.
Marquette University
Milwaukee, Wisconsin

March 1, 2004

INTRODUCTION

The Purpose of This Book

As will be argued shortly, Juan Alfonso de Polanco's *Chronicon Societatis Iesu* is one of the most important sources for the history of the Jesuits during the life of St. Ignatius of Loyola, but one that is largely inaccessible to most readers for three reasons. First, it is written in Latin, a language that most younger Jesuits and many scholars can no longer read or read with facility. Second, the only printed edition was published at Madrid from 1894 to 1898 as part of the Monumenta Historica Societatis Iesu series; it is safe to say that most libraries, including many good scholarly libraries, do not have copies. Third, Polanco's chronicle runs to some forty-five hundred pages, a prospect that many may find intimidating. This book makes available selected passages from the *Chronicon* in a modern English translation.

This volume aims to serve three groups of readers. The first group comprises Jesuits who are interested in their family history—how the early Jesuits under the guidance of Loyola thought and worked and why they were so much praised and blamed. Worth recalling is the Second Vatican Council's recommendation that members of religious orders examine the foundation experience of their orders in seeking renewal of their charism.[1] The second group includes scholars who are working on early Jesuit history. This collection is designed to give them, in a user-friendly form, an introduction to and a sample of what they are likely to find in the full six volumes of the *Monumenta* edition. Finally, there is the average reader, who can find here not only abundant information on what the Jesuits did but also on how they saw themselves and understood their ministries.

Juan Alfonso de Polanco, 1517–1576

It has been claimed that the six most important early Jesuits were Ignatius of Loyola, Francis Xavier, Francis Borgia, Diego Laínez, Jerónimo

---

[1] *Perfectæ Caritatis,* in *The Documents of Vatican II,* ed. Walter M. Abbott, S.J. (New York: Guild Press, America Press, Association Press, 1966), no. 2(1) (p. 468).

Nadal, and Juan Afonso de Polanco.[2] There are recent biographies in English of them all except Polanco, who remains relatively unknown. Who was he, and why is he important?

Polanco was born in Burgos, Spain, December 24, 1517; his father was a wealthy and prominent merchant, who sent him at age thirteen to the University of Paris, where he studied classical languages, literature, and philosophy for nine years and earned a master's degree in 1538. His family then secured for him the post of apostolic notary in the papal curia. He was on the fast track for a position in the papal curia or possibly back in Spain. But at Rome he met Laínez, made the Spiritual Exercises under his direction and decided to enter the Jesuits in 1541. The next year he was sent to Padua with Father André des Freux to set up a Jesuit *collegio* (understood in those days to mean a Jesuit community for students) and to study theology at the University of Padua, then regarded as the finest in Italy. Polanco spent four years there. His studies at both Paris and Padua influenced the legislation on schools in the later Jesuit *Constitutions*.[3] Laínez visited the Padua community in 1545 and wrote short evaluations of each of its members; here is his entry on Polanco: "about thirty years old, short in stature, not very imposing, weak eyesight but otherwise healthy and hardworking."[4]

In 1546 he was ordained a priest at Padua and was sent to do some pastoral work at Bologna, Pistoia, Pisa, and the other Tuscan towns. More eventful was his work at Florence with Duke Cosimo dei Medici and his wife Eleonora de Toledo, to whom he sent a letter of spiritual advice that seems to have displeased both of them; this and Polanco's ministry to men opposed to the Medici may have contributed to the waning interest of the duke and duchess in financing a Jesuit college. Worse still, Polanco encountered his brother Luis, a successful merchant at Florence, who shared his family's disgust with Juan's

---

[2] Richard H. Dowling, "Juan de Polanco: 1517–1576," *The Woodstock Letters* 69 (1940): 19. In addition to Dowling's article (pp. 1–20), there is an overview of Polanco's life and work by Cándido de Dalmases in *Diccionario de la historia de la Compañia de Jesús,* ed. Charles E. O'Neill, S.J., and Joaquin M. Domíngues, S.J. (Rome: Institutum Historicum Societatis Iesu [IHSI]; Madrid: Universidad Pontificia Comillas, 2001), 4:3168 f. Arturo Codina, in his introduction to the first volume of *Polanci complementa* (vols. 52 and 54 of the series Monumenta Historica Societatis Iesu [MHSI; Madrid, 1916–17]), gives a short biography of Polanco (pp. vi-xxi) and an overview of his writings (xxi-xxviii).

[3] Polanco's Padua years are studied by Angelo Martini, "Gli studi teologici di Giovanni de Polanco alle origini della legislazione scolastica della Compagnia di Gesù," *Archivum Historicum Societatis Iesu (AHSI)* 21 (1952): 225–81.

[4] László Lukács, "La catalogue-modèle du Père Laínes (1545)," *AHSI* 26 (1957): 64.

entering the Jesuits. When Luis could not persuade Juan to leave the Jesuits, he had him imprisoned in his home. Juan escaped through a window and down a rope and fled to Pistoia and the palace of his friend, the local bishop. But Luis used his influential friends at Florence to have Juan arrested and returned to Florence. Loyola, however, intervened with Duke Cosimo and had Polanco sent to Rome.[5]

Ignatius then appointed Polanco secretary of the Society. Juan spent most of his next twenty-five years at Rome as secretary of the Society under the first three Jesuit generals, Ignatius of Loyola (March 1547–July 1556), Diego Laínez (July 1558–January 1565), and Francis Borgia (July 1556–October 1572). Polanco may have been an ineffective fund raiser at Florence, but at Rome he was the perfect fit as secretary. Somehow amid his other duties Polanco managed to find time for several ministries while at Rome; in the *Chronicon* (vol. 1, §168) he tells us that he used to hear confessions and preach in the nearby church and teach catechism. He even worked in the kitchen and dining room at humble tasks. Later he accompanied Laínez to the Colloquy of Poissy in 1561 and even served with Laínez as a papal theologian in the last sessions of the Council of Trent in 1563, where he made a presentation on the sacrament of holy orders. During 1571 and 1572 he was Borgia's companion on a journey to Spain, Portugal, and France for important dealings with the kings of those three countries.

Polanco governed the Society as vicar-general from the death of Borgia in October 1572 until the Third Jesuit General Congregation met in April 1573. Polanco probably would have been elected the fourth general of the Jesuits, but there were outside interventions by powerful rulers. A Portuguese delegate, Leon Enriquez, presented a letter from the Portuguese king objecting to the election of anybody of Jewish descent. Polanco seems to have been the target here, although it is far from clear that he was of Jewish ancestry. More critical were two interventions by Gregory XIII, who urged the delegates to elect a non-Spaniard, because the previous three generals had all been Spaniards. The congregation elected Everard Mercurian, a Belgian subject of Philip II, so the Spanish king was unlikely to object to the choice. Mercurian made Antonio Possevino secretary of the Society because he had worked closely with Possevino in France. Polanco spent two years, early 1573 to February 1575, at Rome

---

[5] Dowling, "Juan de Polanco," 7.

dictating his *Chronicon* to an unknown amanuensis.[6] In 1575 Mercurian appointed Polanco visitor to the Sicilian Province. There he was seriously sick several times and returned in broken health to Rome, where he died December 20, 1576.

In addition to the *Chronicon,* Polanco was a popular writer of spiritual tracts. His most notable short works were a directory on how to make a good confession (*Breve directorium ad confessarii et confitentis munus rite obeundum concinnatum* [Rome, 1554]), which emerged in some forty editions in Latin, and his tract on the art of dying, written to help priests carry out this ministry (*Methodus ad eos adjuvandos qui moriuntur* [Macerata, 1575]), which went into twenty Latin editions. Both these works were also republished many times in vernacular translations. His *Monita vitæ spiritualis* was written sometime between 1562 and 1575, but was published posthumously at Cologne in 1622. He also wrote an early directory on how to give the Spiritual Exercises.[7]

It is hard to exaggerate the importance of Polanco's work as Loyola's secretary. Two of the best recent historians of the early Jesuits, Mario Scaduto and John O'Malley, have called Polanco Loyola's alter ego. Loyola's enormous correspondence fills twelve volumes in the section of the MHSI series called the *Monumenta Ignatiana.* There are only 152 letters before March 1547, when Polanco took over as secretary; thereafter, the Monumenta edition contains 6,590 letters. Polanco was a more skilled writer than Loyola, especially in Latin and Italian. Often Loyola dictated the outline of a letter; Polanco would write the text, Loyola would make some corrections and then sign it. Often Loyola had Polanco write letters to Jesuits *ex commissione:* "Dear Father X, Father Ignatius has commissioned me to tell you to do this or that." The work of Polanco as Loyola's secretary has been studied in detail by Clara Englander.[8]

---

[6] The manuscripts of the *Chronicon* are discussed in vol. 2 of the *Fontes narrativi de S. Ignatio de Loyola et de Societatis Iesu initiis,* ed. Candido de Dalmases, vol. 73 of MHSI (Rome: 1951), 30*–33*. They are in the Roman Archives of the Society of Jesus located in the Jesuit Curia in Rome. The main set of manuscripts is in folio and is listed as *Hist. Soc. 67, 68 I-II* and *69 I-II. Hist 67* covers 1549 to 1551. *Hist. Soc. 68 I-II* covers 1552 to 1554. *Hist. Soc. 69 I-II* covers 1555 to 1556. The life of Ignatius and the *Chronicon* for 1537 to 1549 are found in *Hist. Soc. 5.*

[7] For a description of Polanco's spiritual writings, see Jean-Francois Gilmont, *Les Écrits spiritueles des premiers Jésuites* (Rome: IHSI, 1961), 196–208. For the various editions of his works, see Carlos Sommervogel, *Bibliothèque de la Compagnie de Jésus* (Brussels and Paris, 1890–1932; reprinted Héverlé-Louvain, 1960) 6:939–47.

[8] Clara Englander, *Ignatius von Loyola und Johannes von Polanco: Der Ordensstifter und sein Sekretär* (Regensburg: Pustet, 1965).

Polanco played a considerable role in helping Loyola write the Jesuit *Constitutions* and made the official Latin translation of the original Spanish text. The interaction of the two in drawing up the *Constitutions* has been described thus by Arturo Codina in his long introduction to this document in its MHSI edition: Loyola was the author, Polanco was the redactor.[9] Polanco's own correspondence and minor writings are found in the *Polanci complementa* (see n. 2 above). The second volume of the *Complementa* contains Polanco's short chronicle of Jesuit history covering the period 1564 to 1573.[10]

Polanco's *Chronicon*

This brings us to Polanco's *Chronicon*.[11] Its importance as a source for Jesuit history is best illustrated by a decision of the editors of the MHSI: the six massive volumes were published from 1894 to 1898; they are volumes 1, 3, 5, 7, 9, and 11 in the series that already counted 151 volumes by the year 2000, and other volumes have been added subsequently. No earlier religious order has so detailed an account as Polanco's *Chronicon* from somebody who knew so well the early history of the order. Not only did Polanco know more intimately than anybody else the correspondence coming into and going out of the Jesuit headquarters—even better than Loyola himself for the years after 1547—he also personally knew all the main early Jesuits except Xavier.

The administration of the Jesuits was more centralized than that of previous religious orders. This centralization was partly due to the fact that the Jesuits were international from their start—the first Jesuit companions were five Spaniards, but also included a Portuguese, a Frenchman, and a Savoyard. Among the first Spaniards, Loyola, Laínez, Salmerón, and Bobadilla spent most

---

[9] "De labore Polanci," in *Constitutiones II* (MHSI no. 64 [1936]), clxiv–cxcii, especially cxc–cxci. Polanco's role in writing the *Constitutions* is also discussed in *Ignatius of Loyola, The Constitutions of the Society of Jesus,* ed. and trans. George Ganss, S.J. (St. Louis: The Institute of Jesuit Sources, 1970), pp. 49–55. Polanco's role has been the subject of controversy, which Ganss summarizes with bibliographic references (55).

[10] "Commentariola Polanciana," 635–723.

[11] The full official title of the six volumes in the Monumenta series is *Vita Ignatii Loiolæ et rerum Societatis Iesu historia.* Volume 1 begins with Polanco's life of Loyola (pp. 9–74), which seems to have been written after the *Chronicon* itself. It was not printed until 1894, but Polanco's short biography did not go without influence. The first and most popular biography of Loyola for centuries was that of Pedro de Ribadeneira, the quasi-official life, but not all Jesuits were pleased with it; so Mercurian commissioned Giampietro Maffei (1538–1603) to write a new life. His elegant Latin work, *De vita et moribus Ignatii Loiolæ, qui Societatem Iesu fundavit* (Rome, 1585), used Polanco's *Vita* as its major source.

of their Jesuit years in Italy. Xavier worked in Asia. Letters tied them together. Loyola also ordered every Jesuit community to send a report to Rome every four months starting in November 1546.[12] Polanco handled that correspondence. He also supervised sending out reports of these activities to Jesuits around Europe and the production of the sixteenth-century equivalent of promotional brochures for benefactors. When he sat down to dictate his *Chronicon* at Rome, he drew on this knowledge and had access to many of the written sources that he had assiduously gathered and filed over the years.

Specifics of this edition

The purpose of this book is to make the *Chronicon* more available and user friendly. Polanco did not plan to publish the *Chronicon;* he wrote it as a source book for later historians. Even though the *Chronicon* has been used extensively by Jesuit historians from Niccolò Orlandini to John O'Malley, still, other scholars have often overlooked it.[13] Recently André Ravier's *La Compagnie de Jésus sous le gouvernement d'Ignace de Loyola (1541–1556): D'apres les Chroniques de J.-A. de Polanco* (Paris: Descleé de Brouwer, 1991) has made Polanco's work more accessible. Ravier, a respected Jesuit historian, prints extracts from the *Chronicon* year by year with his own intervening paragraphs of explanation or transition. He has chosen to translate paragraphs illustrating the careers of Loyola's first companions along with Borgia, Nadal, and Peter Canisius. His volume runs 389 pages in all, considerably shorter than this work. The present translation does not give special attention to the activities of those key early Jesuits, partly because passages in Ravier's translation are more available to readers than the Latin edition. The goal of this book is to give readers a sample rather than a systematic guide to the *Chronicon* as a whole.

Since this book translates only about 8 percent of Polanco's text, choosing which passages to translate presented obvious problems. One problem is the uneven distribution of materials in Polanco's own text, which can be compared

---

[12] The *Litteræ quadrimestres* (vols. 4, 6, 8, and 10 in the Monumenta series) cover the period November 1546–December 1556—almost exactly the same years as the last five volumes of Polanco's *Chronicon.* They were probably his most important single source. Unfortunately, precisely because the *Chronicon* was the first work published in the Monumenta series, the editors did not have available the volumes of the series that would be published later, which they could have used for cross-referencing. In general, the scholarship of the *Chronicon* volumes is excellent, as are the indices.

[13] Niccolò Orlandini, *Historia Societatis Iesu,* pt. 1 (Rome, 1614); John O'Malley, *The First Jesuits* (Cambridge, Mass.: Harvard University Press, 1993).

to a pyramid. He starts in 1537 and goes down to 1556. The narrow top of the pyramid is the decade from 1537 till Polanco's appointment as secretary in 1547. Only 128 pages are devoted to the years 1537 to 1547. The years 1547 to 1550 are covered in 285 pages. But the pyramid expands sharply as it goes downward. Thus volume 5 covers 1555 and has 731 pages. Volume 6, covering 1556, has 839 pages. Moreover, Polanco's paragraphs (or numbered sections) tend to be shorter and more numerous, more factual and less pious, in the later volumes. Thus the first volume has only 551 numbered sections, while the sixth volume has 3,581.

Several reasons lie behind the pyramidal distribution of space and pages. Polanco's knowledge of the Society's history was obviously much better after he took up his position at the center of affairs in 1547. His reorganization of record keeping, illustrated in the enormous increase of extant letters of Loyola after his appointment as secretary, meant that he had richer sources to draw on for the years 1547 to 1556. Also the Society of Jesus was growing rapidly in these years, so there was more history to record. This translation will also be pyramidal, but will give relatively more attention to the early years. For the last thirty years the translator has been the house historian of the Marquette University Jesuit Community and so is painfully aware of how repetitious such histories are. Polanco's chronicle is largely a composite of house histories, so there is little need to keep repeating roughly the same material.

Polanco had a systematic mind. His arrangement of material largely follows the same pattern year after year. He starts with Rome, then Italy proper, then Sicily (where the Jesuits rapidly became more numerous), then Germany and the Netherlands, followed by France, Spain, Portugal; finally, he chronicles missionary activity outside Europe. In each country he moves from city to city, community to community; but he often inserts sections devoted to the special work of prominent Jesuits, for instance, Nadal's activity in promulgating the *Constitutions* and Borgia's as commissary of Spain. Jesuit growth during these years was much slower in France, Germany, and the Netherlands than in Italy, Portugal, and Spain. Poland, England, and Scandinavia get only passing references. A case could be made to rearrange Polanco's material geographically rather than chronologically, thus pulling together all the sections with Italy, Spain, Portugal, and the other countries into separate chapters, and arranging each chapter by city, for instance, Rome, Padua, and Messina. Yet following Polanco's own arrangement seemed a better way to give a feel for his chronicle.

Readers who want to trace the history of a given community can do so by using the index as a guide.

Arbitrarily perhaps, Polanco's treatment of events o˙ˋside Europe have been excluded. Polanco's sources for this material were slimmer; his most important source was the letters of Francis Xavier, which are now available in English.[14] Both the MHSI series and research in English have given relatively more attention to Jesuit missionaries than to Jesuits working in Europe.

Given the sheer size of Polanco's work, this book had to highlight certain contributions of the Jesuits. Loyola and his companions did not at first plan to work in schools; by 1600 schools were the main Jesuit ministry. The roots of Jesuit education at Gandía and Messina and elsewhere deserve special stress. So does the early use of Loyola's Spiritual Exercises. Today there are roughly eighty publications annually on Loyola, better than half of which deal with the Exercises; so it is important to show how the early Jesuits used the Exercises. The first Jesuits were also pioneers in advocating frequent confession and Communion, weekly Communion, that is, and their advocacy earned them many enemies. This ministry too is stressed.

During the last thirty years, interest in women's history has grown enormously. Unlike most other religious orders, the Jesuits tried to avoid starting a branch for women. Yet Polanco notes repeatedly that Jesuit preaching and sacramental ministry enjoyed more success with women than with men. Sections on Jesuit dealings with women should be made available, especially those dealing with Princess Juana, the daughter of Charles V, sister of Philip II, and the widowed mother of King Sebastian of Portugal. She was regent of Spain during Loyola's last years, while her father and brother were in northern Europe. Given her power, Loyola and his advisors had to yield to her request to become a Jesuit. They kept this a secret, referring to her in their correspondence by a male code name. She died as the last woman Jesuit. She was of enormous help to the Jesuits in Spain, but she was both very devout and very strong willed. For practical purposes, she ordered Loyola not to allow her favorite preachers, Francis Borgia and Antonio Araoz, to leave her court without her permission. Her vows as a Jesuit were kept secret from Philip II. She was also

---

[14] *The Letters and Instructions of Francis Xavier,* ed. and trans. M. Joseph Costelloe, S.J. (St. Louis: The Institute of Jesuit Sources, 1992).

beautiful and young, and the Jesuits at Rome lived in dread that Philip might want her to enter yet another dynastic marriage. Here it is worth recalling the famous couplet: "Let others wage wars; do you, O happy house of Austria, contract marriages" *(Tu, felix Austria, nube)*. Watching Polanco dance around this secret situation, of which he was fully aware, has a special fascination.

The MHSI edition of the *Chronicon* prints the short biography of Loyola that Polanco wrote after finishing the *Chronicon*, perhaps because Father Ignatius (as Polanco always calls him) seems a bit neglected in the *Chronicon* proper. This translation gives special attention to Loyola's role in making decisions and in crafting "our way of proceeding." No religious order has been as highly praised or bitterly condemned as the Jesuits, so its friends and enemies deserve extra attention. The early Jesuits had to cultivate powerful benefactors. Academics know that running colleges costs money. Because the Jesuit Constitutions forbade charging tuition, the early Jesuits had to cultivate support from both individual benefactors and administrators who could divert church and city funding to the new Jesuit colleges.

Their strongest supporters were King John of Portugal and Juan de Vega, the Spanish viceroy in Sicily, together with his wife. Charles V and Philip II were lukewarm, but Ferdinand I was more supportive. The Duke and Duchess of Tuscany promised much, insisted on much in return, and gave grudgingly. The Jesuits were chronically short of money; and often they had to turn away fine candidates to the Society because money was lacking for their support, as these selections from the *Chronicon* show.[15] The early Jesuits were abundantly supplied with enemies. Protestant enemies do not loom large in Polanco's account, probably because he takes them for granted. Ecumenists were rare in the sixteenth century, and Polanco was not one of them. His narrative and this translation give more attention to Catholic enemies, such as the University of Paris, Melchor Cano, Cardinal-Archbishop of Toledo Juan Silíceo and Mary of Hungary, the regent of the Netherlands.

Polanco's account tends toward triumphalism, but that is understandable. When he was writing his chronicle in 1573 and 1574, the Catholic Reformation was gathering momentum. The Council of Tent was finally finished, and its

---

[15] The number of references to financial problems and transactions in Loyola's correspondence grew sharply in his last four years: see the graphs on this in *Landmarking: City, Church and Jesuit Urban Strategy*, by Thomas M. Lucas, S.J. (Chicago: Loyola University Press, 1997), 136 f.

reforms were slowly being implemented, for instance, by Saint Charles Borromeo in Milan. The St. Bartholomew's Massacre (1572) had destroyed much of the Huguenot leadership in France. The forces of Philip II seemed to be making headway in the Netherlands. Late in life, Polanco could look back on the rapid growth of Jesuit numbers and impact on Catholic Europe. At Loyola's death there were roughly one thousand Jesuits; on the death of the second general, James Laínez, in 1565 there were three thousand, and their numbers and influence kept growing. Many Jesuits felt that Catholic losses to Protestantism in Europe could be, indeed were being, made up for by converts in Asia and the Americas.

Still, Polanco does not hide Jesuit failures and shortcomings. The biggest disaster in Loyola's lifetime was the meltdown of the largest Jesuit province, Portugal, where more than half the men left or were expelled. Polanco discusses this at length, putting much of the blame on Jesuit leaders in Portugal, notably Simão Rodrigues and Diego Miró.[16] Polanco was also much dismayed by the ignorance of rural Catholics about their faith. This comes through especially in his description of Jesuit work on Sardinia. Even more pessimistic is his appraisal of Catholicism in Germany, where many nominal Catholics had adopted Lutheran attitudes on many points. The sections chosen for translation in this book record both victory and defeat. Finally, colorful vignettes have been included to add spice or illustrate the cast of mind of the early Jesuits. Not all of them mirror the approved image of the Jesuits, then or now.

Polanco did not live to revise the manuscript, which remained unpublished but not unused until the 1890s. He did add a two-page preface in Italian shortly before his death, which is reprinted in the first volume and describes the composition. He tells us that he has set down "alcuni successi et cose non edificative." He also notes that because he had not read it over since dictating it, there are many errors, as well as things that could have been added, but the substance is solid.[17] Many of the errors are misspellings. Often the editors of the Monumenta series add a footnote to correct these slips. These corrections have

---

[16] For a different interpretation of Rodrigues's role in this matter, see José Vaz de Carvalho, S.J., "The Rehabilitation of Simão Rodrigues," in *The Mercurian Project: Forming Jesuit Culture, 1573–1580,* ed. Thomas M. McCoog, S.J. (St. Louis: The Institute of Jesuit Sources; Rome: Institutum Historicum Societatis Iesu, 2004), 421–59.—ED.

[17] Pp. 7 f. Polanco was fussy about minor slips. Gilmont observes with amusement that when his book on helping dying people was published, Polanco was enormously upset over its typographical errors (*Écrits spirituales,* 206n34).

been silently incorporated into this translation. The translator has inserted material that seemed needed for clarification in square brackets ([ ]). Thus the text often refers to people by only their first or last name. The missing part of a name has been put into brackets when having both names seemed helpful to readers. The names of people have also been inserted in brackets when Polanco's pronouns or the subject of sentences needed clarification. The Latin names have usually been translated into their vernacular spelling, thus Juan (not John) Polanco; but sometimes the English form of a name has been used when it seemed more familiar, thus Francis Borgia rather than Francisco de Borja. The deletion of one or more sentences in a section is indicated by four spaced periods (. . . .), the deletion of part of a sentence by three spaced periods (. . .). Polanco does not call members of the Society *Jesuits,* but rather *nostri,* which is here translated by *Ours.* In referring to days of the year, Polanco sometimes uses the Roman calendar, for example, *quarto Calendas Septembris,* which translates as August 29. Other times he gives a saint's feast day, after which this translation inserts the appropriate day and month in brackets.

All the sections in the *Chronicon* are numbered. Volume 1 (1539–1549) numbers all the sections consecutively from beginning to end. Volume 2, however, numbers 1550, 1551, and 1552 separately, each year beginning with the number 1, as do all subsequent volumes. These traditional numbers have been retained to help readers check the original text, but also to let them know whether the translated sections are continuous or not, and if not, how many sections have been skipped. The translator has given each section a title in italics. Usually the title indicates the place where the events related were taking place. Several times in volume 6 Polanco indicates that he planned to continue his chronicle beyond 1556, but his assignment to Sicily and his death cut his plan short.

The Latin style of the *Chronicon* is usually straightforward, though not without its complications. Like many authors writing in Latin, Polanco is fond of double negatives: "Father Laínez's preaching enjoyed no small success." The translator has often (but by no means always) eliminated the double negative: "Father Laínez's preaching enjoyed considerable success." Likewise, many connectives (for instance, *itaque, autem, enim*) have been left untranslated, and a good many of his long sentences have been broken up and other adaptations made so that the text could resemble modern English more closely.

Chronology of the Houses of the Society Founded during the Years Covered by the *Chronicon*

Ph = Professed house; H = House; C = College for Jesuits and other students; R = Residence for Jesuit students studying at a university; M = Mission; N = Freestanding novitiate

1538
Rome, Ph

1540
Paris, R

1541
Lisbon, Ph

1542
Coimbra, R
Louvain, R
Padua, R

1543
Goa C, M

1544
Cologne, C,R
Valencia, C,R

1545
Gandía, C
Valladolid, R

1546
Alcalá, R
Barcelona, R
Bologna, R
Comoran, M

1547
Salamanca, R
Zaragoza, H

1548
Bassein, M
Cochin, M
Messina, C
Molucca, M

San Tomas, M
Socotora, M

1549
Ingolstadt, H,R
Ormuz, M
Palermo, C

1550
Bahia Salvador, M
Borgos, C
Espirito Santo, M
Messina, N
San Vincente, M
Tivoli, H, C

1551
Chorão, M
Évora, C
Ferrara. C
Florence, C
Medina del Campo, C
Oñate, C
Palermo, N
Porto Seguro, M
Rome, C (Romano)
Venice, C
Vienna, C

1552
Bungo, M
Gubbio, C (†54)
Modena, C
Naples, C
Perugia, C
Rome, C (Germanico)

1553
Lisbon, C
Monreale, C

1554
Amanaguchi, M
Argenta, C
Coimbra, N
Córdova, C
Cuenca, J
Genoa, C
Loreto, C
Placencia, C
Roma, Villa
Syracuse, C
Zaragosa, C

1555
Ávila, H
Granada, H
Murcia, C
Simancas, N
Seville, H
Tournai, H

1556
Aymeries, C
Billom, C
Bivona, C
Monreal, C
Prague, C
Samanca, N
Siena, C

Selections from the *Chronicon*

of

Juan de Polanco, S.J.

THE YEAR 1539

■ **Italy**

9.   *First ministries of the Society*

During 1539 our fathers energetically accomplished the Lord's work in many holy activities, in reconciling conflicts, and in directing several important men (among them were Cardinal Contarini and Doctor Ortiz) through the Spiritual Exercises, with the result that the good repute of Ignatius and his companions became widespread. In view of this, the services of two of them were requested at Siena, so that they could devote themselves to reforming a certain well-known monastery. Undertaking this mission were Father Paschase [Broët] and Father Simão [Rodrigues]; by their ministry, especially that of Father Paschase (who remained there longer), the divine Goodness marvelously recalled the whole aforesaid monastery to a holy way of life worthy of its profession. Other people too in that city made great spiritual progress through the endeavors of Ours.

10.   *Estrada at Siena and Montepulciano*

Among those who joined our ranks at this time was Father Francisco Estrada. When he left Rome for Naples, he met Father Ignatius, who was returning from Monte Cassino (where he was helping Doctor Ortiz with the Spiritual Exercises). Estrada enlisted in the militia of Christ; he then returned to Rome and lived with us for a while. About twenty years old at that time, he was assigned to accompany Fathers Paschase and Simão when they were sent to Siena. Although he had studied only Latin literature in school, he so impressed the Sienese by his pious conversation and by the example of his life that not only did they themselves profit from speaking informally with him but, as his reputation spread, the

---

This translation is based on the Latin text found in *Vita Ignatii Loiolæ et rerum Societatis Iesu historia*, by Juan Alphonso de Polanco, S.J., 6 vols., nos. 1, 3, 5, 7, 9, and 11 of the series Monumenta Historica Societatis Iesu (Madrid, 1894–98). This work is known as the *Chronicon* of Juan de Polanco, S.J.; hereafter, it will be abbreviated to *Chron.*, followed by the volume number and the page or paragraph number as needed. Vol. 1 contains the years 1539–49. The headings introducing each section were added by the translator.—ED.

citizens of Montepulciano wrote to him a number of times, inviting him to visit them. When he went there in 1539, several Sienese followed him; and after he had assisted them with the Spiritual Exercises and heard their general confessions, remarkably benefiting their souls thereby, they went on to enflame the souls of those who had invited Estrada to [their town]. As a result, not only did many persons (among them several doctors) themselves profit from the Spiritual Exercises, but, despite all that he could do to resist their importunities, they piously urged this young man to give public lectures on the Gospels and then to deliver sermons—and this even though he did not know Italian adequately and had not yet devoted himself to academic pursuits. He gave these lectures before such a large and enthusiastic audience of all classes of people and met with so much success that both men and women undertook a serious reformation of their lives and behavior. [As a result,] the poor who were in the greatest need were given help; confraternities were set up for teaching disadvantaged boys and girls and for other worthy purposes; and the frequent use of the sacraments of confession and Communion was introduced. . . .

12.   *Favre and Laínez at Parma*

    . . . Finally, on weekdays, even in the evenings, those fathers [Favre and Laínez] gathered in the harvest through the sacrament of penance. They began to give the Spiritual Exercises to some men and selected women. Those who had once gone through the Exercises directed others in them, so much so that a hundred people were engaged in making them at the same time and were achieving singular benefit [to themselves]. Besides the pastors and other priests, who shared with other people the spiritual training they had received, no small number of very promising young men were called by the Lord to the Institute of the Society. Among them was Father Jerónimo Doménech, at the time a young man and a canon at Valencia as well, who, when passing through Parma, met the aforesaid fathers in their hospice. Persuaded to [make] the Spiritual Exercises, he decided to enter the Society and immediately started to be of assistance to many other people by means of these Exercises, achieving singular success. In addition, Father Paolo Achille, who was already a priest, also joined our number; he began to dedicate himself wholeheartedly to [hearing] confessions and giving the Spiritual Exercises. Elpidio Ugoletti and Battista Viola next followed [him into the Society].

THE YEAR 1540

■   **Italy**

13.   *Further ministries at Parma*

Early in 1540, as these same fathers kept working in the Parma vineyard, through general confessions leading to the frequent use of penance and Holy Communion; and through the Exercises, now given to larger numbers of people (some assisting others by means of whatever skills and abilities were theirs); and through teaching Christian doctrine, which many Jesuit-trained priests and schoolmasters do on behalf of the people and their own followers in the city and in the suburbs—through all [these means] the Lord mightily increased the spiritual fruit [produced]. The entire city yearned to reform their lives through sermons and the aforementioned works of devotion. Once they had been disposed by sermons, the Spiritual Exercises, and general confessions, the nuns of two convents went on to make remarkable advances in their religious life, ever growing in fidelity to their Institute and to zeal for still greater perfection. Although toward the end of Lent preachers attacked the frequent use of the sacraments of confession and Communion as a novelty at that time, they achieved absolutely nothing, because at Parma and in the ten or twelve surrounding villages (in which Father Laínez stirred up the people even by one sermon and all the while made himself available for confessions), observers could note progress and improvement in the lives of many of the people who communicated frequently; the lives and pious deaths of these frequent communicants made their spiritual progress so obvious that the evidence of their own eyes refuted the preachers [who disparaged frequent Communion], without Ours' having to say a word.

■   **Portugal**

20.   *Simão Rodrigues and John III of Portugal*

In part owing to the good reputation of the Society that had reached Portugal and in part owing to the recommendation of Doctor [Diogo de] Gouveia, the serene king of Portugal, John III, reached the conclusion that our priests would be of great use to him by leading to the faith of Christ the people in [that part of] east India subject to him and instructing them in it. Acting through his ambassador, Don Pedro de Mascarenhas, he obtained from the supreme pontiff Paul III a mandate that two of those Jesuits should be sent to him, whomever Ignatius would designate. The first of those chosen for this mission was Father Simão Rodrigues, one of the first ten [companions of Ignatius], who had long been aflame with a consuming desire to spread Christ's name among unbelievers. After being recalled from Siena in the spring of 1540, even though suffering from quartan malaria, he took ship from Civitavecchia and reached the port of Lisbon in a few days *[sic]*.

After [Simão] had rested several days outside the city in a house of the aforesaid ambassador, the King, who wanted to speak with him and would brook no delay, ordered him to come into the city whether he was well or ill, so that his malady could receive proper attention. Joined by the Queen, his wife, the King summoned Simão to their presence and greeted him very kindly. Enjoying a lengthy conversation with him, one that he found consoling and edifying, he ordered [Simão] to enter the hospital and undergo the medical treatment he required. But when Simão pressed the King to allow him to gain his livelihood by begging, [His Majesty] finally gave way; and so [Simão] lived for a time on alms, even though he was suffering from malaria. At times hearing confessions and at other times giving the Spiritual Exercises, he began to throw himself energetically into work that was of notable benefit to the city and the royal court; moreover, he carried on other pious activities resulting in the salvation of souls.

21. *Xavier goes to Lisbon*

Nicolás Bobadilla was chosen to be the second man on the mission [to the Indies], but it did not seem wise to assign him to such an arduous mission, in view of his sickness (as we mentioned above). So, the day before he had to depart, Father Ignatius notified Francis Xavier (who had no inkling of this change of plans) that he would have to undertake this province [of the Indies]. The announcement brought him [Xavier] great joy, for he had long and intensely desired to convert the Gentiles. The next day he set out on his journey with the [Portuguese] ambassador and his family, and he persuaded them to frequent the sacraments of penance and the Eucharist and kept them occupied with practices of Christian devotion. They reached Lisbon three months later.

. . .

22.   *Royal support for the Jesuits in Portugal*

After three days both [Jesuits] were summoned to the King. With the Queen also present, they discoursed at length about matters relating to the Society, especially about the persecutions being undergone by their companions. The monarchs listened with pleasure to this narrative and gave heartfelt approval to what they had heard. The King then entrusted them with the education of the young nobles, whom he wanted to go to confession once a week on Fridays, so that as they grew older they would continue to abide by their habits of devout living. By the sacrament of penance they elevated more than a hundred young nobles of the Court to a better style of living, as well as many others of greater maturity, both from the nobility and other social classes, with such exceptional success that, after experiencing the spiritual benefits that others gained from pious activities, there was now talk of abandoning the mission to India and retaining them in Portugal. . . . They began to accept food from the King, setting aside only two days a week for begging, so that they would not lose sight of this humble practice. They made it their custom to donate what they collected by begging to a certain hostel for the poor.

23.   *Further ministries in Portugal*

Since everything was prospering and [Rodrigues and Xavier] were achieving edifying successes and enjoying good health, Father Francis was greatly troubled because he was experiencing no persecutions in his life; but he consoled himself with the hopeful anticipation of those he would suffer in India. Frequently he used to declare that to go a long time without them was not being a faithful soldier of Christ. Four other men joined the Society with them, so now there were six in all. At the request of Prince Henry, the grand inquisitor, they daily visited those confined in the prison of the Inquisition, and by exhortations and instructions they brought them to a clear recognition of their sins and to sorrow over them. Meanwhile, through administering the sacraments and giving the Spiritual Exercises, they daily continued to deserve well of the leading and more illustrious men of the court. The King was greatly pleased with our Institute, but he was especially keen on [having the Society] erect colleges. Because it was not yet certain that apostolic letters approving our Society had been issued, he pledged his complete support and, if need be, offered to send letters to the Emperor and the King of France. But through the favor of God, by this time the letters had already been issued, so he began to work toward founding a college and seeking students of the Society.[1]

■ Germany

25.   *Favre at Worms*

Toward the beginning of this year, 1540, when Protestants and Catholics met together at Worms [in Germany], the illustrious Cardinal Morone was present as legate of the Apostolic See, and the Supreme Pontiff sent Doctor Ortiz there together with other people. At the same time the men of the Society also began to come to the attention of the Germans. Father Pierre Favre was sent from Parma; although he was not allowed to have any dealings with the Protestants, he diffused the good aura *[odor]* of Christ there by helping many prominent men both of the imperial Court and others, including the legate himself, through [hearing] confessions and uplifting people with the Spiritual Exercises. He asserted that in his heart he frequently felt powerful transports of love for Germany and of hope that someday she would be assisted through the ministry of the Society.

---

[1] The first Jesuit college for non-Jesuit students was founded at Messina, Sicily, in 1548. Until that time, when Polanco refers to a "college" he means a residence where young Jesuits lived while studying, usually at an established university.

THE YEAR 1541

■ **Italy**

26.   *Ignatius is elected General*

While the divine Goodness through these few fathers was scattering certain seeds in various places of Italy, France, Spain, Portugal, and Germany that were later to mature into a rich harvest, at Rome Father Ignatius manned the rudder of this little ship. But even though he was the father who had begotten them all in the spirit and to whose prudence and charity all gladly deferred, officially he did not have any legitimate power. Already in September 1540 the Society had been confirmed by apostolic authority; but in that year no superior had been appointed. Although, after many prayers and sacrifices, [Ignatius] had already worked out the basic outline of the Constitutions, he summoned the companions scattered throughout Italy both to give their approval to what he had done and to elect a superior for the Society. Jean Codure and Alfonso Salmerón were present and were engaged in cultivating the Roman vineyard to the extent that their fragile health allowed. Father Paschase [Broët] came from Siena and Father Jay from Brescia. Father Laínez came from Parma after reaping there a harvest of souls by preaching in some convent of nuns and in the cathedral church of Reggio; indeed, he brought several candidates to Rome with him. Great distances or papally assigned missions prevented the other four [original companions from coming]; but by documents written in their own hands, these four had approved in advance the decisions regarding the Constitutions that would be made by those who had reached Rome. But for the election of a superior, those who were in Portugal and Germany sent in their own sealed ballots.[1]

After the six who were present had placed their signatures on the afore-said Constitutions, they set aside three days to ponder and commend to the Lord the election of a superior. When that time was up, each of them placed his written and signed vote in a box. Three days later all gathered again to discuss and open the ballots. It turned out that Father Ignatius was unanimously elected

---

[1] Paragraph breaks such as this one have usually been introduced by the editor for the sake of easier reading and are not found in the original Latin text.—ED.

superior. But out of humility he declined this responsibility and urged them to reconsider their action. After three more days the fathers who were present held a second election, but with the same result. Ignatius submitted the matter to his confessor (at the time a certain Friar Teodosio, a Franciscan), who warned [Ignatius] against resisting the Holy Spirit. Finally he accepted the office and gave directions that on the Friday after Easter (which in 1541 was on April 22), they should all go together to the seven [pilgrimage] churches of Rome and then in the Church of Saint Paul should make their profession. Thus, when Ignatius was celebrating Mass, he made his vows before Communion; he then turned to the five companions who were attending the Mass, and before their Communion they too in loud voices pronounced their solemn vows one by one into the hands of Father Ignatius himself. They then received Communion. . . .

27.   *Vocations to the Society*

Although the rest of these fathers were sent to different destinations, that summer Father Laínez stayed in Rome, engaged in hearing confessions and preaching. Father Ignatius [remained also, for he] wanted to set an example by teaching Christian doctrine in accord with his professed vow; through the days of Lent, he explained that doctrine very effectively in a church, to the great benefit of his listeners. Margaret of Austria, the serene duchess of Parma and daughter of Emperor Charles, along with her retinue, and others made good use of [Laínez's] help in spiritual matters. Through the Spiritual Exercises he led several people to follow the counsels of Christ by means of the Institute of the Society; among them was François Turrianus, an upright young man born in Bruges. We were companions and friends, and I [Polanco] followed his example in making the Exercises and entered the Society the same summer that he died [1541]. That same year André des Freux was admitted, a man outstanding for his talents and learning but even more outstanding for his piety. Fathers Jean Codure, Paschase [Broët], and Salmerón were present during this year and the previous one, when twelve other men—some priests, some laymen—enlisted at Rome in the militia of Christ.

Although they lived in a rented house, they already had their own church, which they used for confessions, teaching catechism, and sermons, even though it was narrow and ill adapted to their purposes. Outside [this church] they devoted themselves in an edifying way to many other works of piety. That year Father Codure, one of the original ten, died on August 29; he was the first after Ignatius to make his profession. We piously believe that he was the first of the professed Society to enter heaven, for his integrity of life and charity in helping his neighbors and his holy death bear witness to that.

28.   *Jay at Faenza*

During 1541 after having stayed in Rome for several weeks after his profession, Father Claude Jay was sent to Faenza, where he introduced the pious and salutary practice of receiving the sacraments of confession and Communion weekly. He accomplished this by the example of a holy life, friendly conversations, and private exhortations, and by actually administering these sacraments. He also consoled many sick people both in the hospital and in their private homes. After the office of vespers at the cathedral church, he gathered an even more abundant harvest by delivering lectures in which he explained the articles of the Christian faith; moreover, he frequently gave sermons to the people. . . .

Those he led to frequent Communion elected from their group one doctor to be an advocate for the poor, another to defend them in legal cases, and another (a most prominent medical doctor) to care for the poor—all of them offering their services free of charge. Some eagerly made efforts to help the doctors, some to gather orphan children together and clothe them, some finally to perform other works of piety. The number and devotion of these women converted [from prostitution] increased, and many vendettas were settled peacefully; in sum, spiritual progress was increasingly observable. Then [Jay] received a mandate from the Supreme Pontiff bidding him under obedience to go to Germany. Toward the end of the year, he went there (after delaying for some time at Bologna while awaiting his companion, gathering in a spiritual harvest meanwhile).

■ Germany

29.   *Favre in Germany*

Father [Pierre] Favre was at Worms and from there traveled to Speyer and finally to Regensburg, accompanying the court of Charles V. He did no preaching, but accomplished so much by the ministry of the sacraments of penance and the Eucharist, by holding private conversations, and, most important of all, by giving the Spiritual Exercises that Germans as well as Italians and Spaniards, even men outstanding for their authority, dignity, nobility, and learning, exerted themselves to change their lives. Some among them helped others through the same Spiritual Exercises. Among the others, [John] Cochlaeus stood preeminent for his fervor.[2] As he used to say, he rejoiced that teachers of affectivity had been found; and once he had been helped by the Spiritual Exercises at Regensburg, he either brought many other Germans to Favre to be guided through the Exercises or he himself gave them the Exercises. Favre himself added that no one who had confessed to [Cochlaeus] or had savored the delights of the Spiritual Exercises under his guidance ever returned to his old ways or ceased to hold him in esteem. [Cochlaeus] admits that he had a wonderful opportunity to cultivate [spiritual] fruits.

At Nuremberg (a city which was then totally Lutheran), [Favre] was called to help a certain Florentine who at the time had lost his ability to speak; during the [patient's] lucid intervals, Favre tried to get him to make signs that would show his contrition. When [the patient] died, Favre struck so much fear into a member of his family that he requested to return to the Catholic religion and to be reconciled to it by Favre himself through the sacrament of confession (which he had neglected for the last seven years). After this, two other merchants imitated his example. Two Moors whom he had catechized received baptism. Although the harvest there was abundant, on July 27, in response to an order of holy obedience, [Favre] left Regensburg for Spain, together with Doctor Ortiz. This is why Father Claude was sent to Germany in his place.

■ France

30.   *Jesuits in France*

Meanwhile, in France Father Jerónimo Doménech was not idling away his time in leisure (for Father Didaco [de Equia] had returned to Rome).[3] He was guiding certain persons through the Spiritual Exercises: immediately thereafter and with exceptional effectiveness, these people poured forth upon others what they themselves had gained. Among the first was Father Diego Miró, who, after making great progress in his studies at Paris, decided to complete them. But he fell in with Father Jerónimo and enlisted in the militia of the Society. As he was carrying out the usual exercises of humility and mortification, with fervent charity he helped a group of three Frenchmen make the

---

[2] Cochlaeus (1479–1552) was among the earliest defenders of Catholicism against Protestantism and especially Luther. Among his many polemical works was the first biography of Luther.

[3] De Eguia was the previous superior at Paris.

same meditations from which he himself had profited. One of them was an apostate [from his religious order], who not only returned to his order but won back some others from the heresy with which they were infected. Through these same means as well, a remarkable change of life took place in certain other people, and day by day a door began to open wider [for our ministries]. Doctor [François] le Picart, outstanding among the preachers at Paris, began to be so influenced by Ours that he would have joined our order—so he declared—had he not been afflicted with a defective shin.[4] Doctor [Pierre] de Cornibus, famous among the Franciscans, defended our interests against the assaults of others.

■ **Portugal**

31.   *Relations with John III of Portugal*

At the beginning of 1541, day by day the good repute of Francis Xavier and Simão Rodrigues and of the companions who joined them increased, as did their success. King John began to think seriously about setting up a college of the Society at Coimbra and another house at Lisbon and enlisting our fathers to build them and to help his kingdom.[5] He also requested that scholastics be sent to him. When Ours had made this known to Father Ignatius (who had embraced with fervent desires the Pope's mission to India), he wanted to refer the whole question to Paul III, the supreme pontiff. The Pope granted free authority to the King of Portugal to use the work of those fathers as he saw expedient. Ignatius wrote to Ours about the acquiescence of the Pontiff, so that they might obey the will of the King without fear of retreating from their earlier [command under] obedience. Nonetheless, he added his own view, namely, that Father Francis should go out to India and Father Simão should remain in Portugal and continue to reap the harvest that had been prepared in that Kingdom, and that he should take charge of spreading the Society in the same kingdom by setting up a college at Coimbra. Thus, in accord with the mind of the King, many men might be sent to India from there, as from a seed bed. Embracing Ignatius's plan, the King kept Simão [in Portugal], and on April 7 of that same year, 1541, he sent Francis Xavier to India along with two companions, namely, Father Paolo [of Camerino], an Italian whom [Xavier] had brought with him from Rome, and Francisco Mansilhas, a Portuguese. . . .

---

[4] Le Picart's life and preaching are discussed by Larissa Taylor in her *Heresy and Orthodoxy in Sixteenth Century Paris: François Le Picart and the Beginnings of the Catholic Reformation* (Leiden: Brill, 1999).

[5] As we observed earlier, "college" in Polanco's account often means a residence for Jesuit students at a university.

THE YEAR 1542

■ **The Society in General**

36.   *Overview of the Society in 1542*

As the year 1542 began, the Society had three established communities; namely, at Rome under Ignatius, at Paris (where Ours did not have a house, but rather they lived at the Lombard College) under Jerónimo Doménech, and at Lisbon under Simão Rodrigues. The other [Jesuits] cultivated the Lord's vineyard on missions. At Rome there were the usual ministries, whose purpose was to help souls and assist pious works (in the eyes of the Apostolic See, however, and of all those who flocked to that nurturing city from the various nations, these [works] shone like a candle mounted on a candlestick). In addition, Ignatius had to care for whatever affected the common good of the Society itself and of the Christian commonwealth. So when the Supreme Pontiff wanted to employ our services in Germany, not only were Pierre Favre and Claude Jay sent there (as was noted above) but also Nicolás Bobadilla from Calabria, where he was laboring fruitfully. After he had made his profession in Rome, he was then dispatched to Germany. Five of the nine professed companions, including Paschase [Broët] and Salmerón, were now working in northern regions. During April [Ignatius] also sent some men to the Paris community in France. Among them was Pedro de Ribadeneira, still a young man, who had been admitted before the [papal] confirmation of the Society; like the others, he set forth on foot. At the same time [Ignatius] designated three men for Portugal to lay the foundations of the future college of Coimbra, namely, Martin Santacruz, along with Guillaume Codure (brother of the deceased Jean) and someone else; at the same time there were others with orders to stay in Lisbon. Two Italians who were to go on to Francis Xavier in India accompanied them, namely, Antonio Criminali (several years later a martyr of the Lord) and Nicolò Lancillotti.

■ **Italy**

37.   *The community at Padua*

That same April of 1542 the fourth house of the Society had its start at the University of Padua. When Father Ignatius assigned André des Freux and me to complete our studies there, Girolamo Otello, who was already a learned and devout young man, immediately joined us. Stefano Baroello, who was returning from Portugal, was also added to our number. Accordingly, we began to have a fixed residence there (although we were in rented quarters the first year). Apart from the time demanded by his studies, André des Freux, who was already a priest, began imparting spiritual help there through his holy example and efforts.

■ Ireland

38.   *Broët and Salmerón in Ireland*

Those apostolic nuncios who had set out for Ireland the previous year, after encountering many dangers from the sea and the English, passed through Scotland and from there pressed on to Ireland on the second day of Lent; there they stayed for only thirty-four days. They perceived the devastation prevailing there as regards both the Christian religion and the political situation. So great was the fear of the secular princes, whom Henry VIII had called on to accept him as supreme head in things spiritual and temporal after Christ, that they did not want to see or speak with the nuncios, far less to promise them protection or even funds to help them return to Europe. Also, in the time they remained there, they had to flee from one place to another, in order to escape the hands of certain Englishmen who were trying to capture them in exchange for the reward that had been offered. Those who dared to harbor them put their lives and fortunes in obvious jeopardy and made themselves subject to charges of treason. To [the nuncios] it seemed best in the Lord for them not to stay any longer on that island, especially considering the instructions they had received bidding them to return to Italy if they saw that it was not safe for them either to enter or to remain there.

Therefore, during those few days they administered the sacraments of confession and Communion to certain men, bringing them singular consolation and profit; moreover, they imparted a plenary indulgence and made use of their faculties to give dispensations to certain persons, either free of charge or for a modest fee, which was to be devoted to repairing churches or supporting poor widows or virgins and other pious works. Finally, after winning the people's utmost admiration and offering them powerful edification and after having their patience tested to a remarkable degree—they could find none of the amenities of food, drink, lodging, or security—they gave up all desire of completing their mission and returned to Scotland. When they had begun to discuss arrangements allowing them to meet the [Scottish] king and promote the business of the Catholic religion in his kingdom, they found that the door to helping that nation was closed because of the faction of many nobles and powerful people who had deserted the true faith.

After crossing over to France and landing at Dieppe, a port in Normandy, they arrived in Paris. There they receive new letters in the form of a brief entrusting them with the office of apostolic nuncios in the kingdom of Scotland. But when, on wise advice, they decided that, before undertaking the task involved in this new legation, they should first alert the Supreme Pontiff about the state of religion in the kingdom. [Soon] they received the answer from Rome that they should return to Italy, leaving Scotland behind. Therefore, the humble nuncios undertook their journey on foot after leaving Francisco Zapata with Ours at Paris to devote himself to studies. At Lyons they were thrown into prison as spies, but when Cardinal [François de] Tournon and Cardinal [Nicholas] da Gaddi recognized them, they were set free. Accepting the horses offered to them, they returned to Rome.

■ **Germany**

39.   *Claude Jay in Germany*

Those sent to Germany did not work in one place. Father Claude Jay moved every stone at Regensburg in his effort to bear some fruit to the Lord's honor. . . . But when the cross and danger threatened them on all sides, it is marvelous to what a degree Christ filled his servant with spiritual consolation. To some who threatened that they were going to throw him into the Danube, he answered that he could go to heaven as easily by water as by land. Some people tried to get rid of the man by poison, others to eject him from the city. Still, many Catholics, among others the bishop, loved him and rejoiced because he so heroically pitted himself against evil men. In patience, by the example of his life, holy conversations, and private discussions, he achieved a success that left no grounds for regret. . . .

■ **Austria**

40.   *Bobadilla in Austria*

While Ferdinand, the King of the Romans, and his children were staying at Innsbruck, Father Bobadilla was at work there as well. Although physically in poor health, he kept busy there in the ministry of the sacraments of confession and the Eucharist and in discussions with many leading men. Later, when the court moved to Vienna, he spoke with King Ferdinand, who warmly received him and invited him to discuss more at length things pertaining to devotion. He did not take advantage of the nuncio's very pleasant residence, but preferred to stay at the hospice for the poor. With the approval of leading men, he occupied himself now in public sermons, now in [hearing] confessions, now in lectures on the Epistle to the Romans, sometimes in instructing catechumens who discarded the false belief of the Turks and Jews and embraced the faith of Christ, and at other times in treating of spiritual matters with the King (whose royal favor he secured for Ours who were at risk in Regensburg).

■ **France**

42.   *The Jesuits in Paris are forced to flee*

This year, 1542, the sixteen of Ours who were living in Paris and devoting themselves to studies along with works of devotion were for the most part dispersed. Francis, the king of France, decided to make war on Emperor Charles V, and in July an edict was published at the University of Paris to the effect that all who were subjects of Charles must leave the country within eight days under pain of death and the confiscation of their goods. When our students consulted the president of the Parlement and Cardinal [Anthony de] Medon and the Cardinal of Bourbon, [these dignitaries] gave them no promise of protection or delay; so Father Jerónimo Doménech with seven Spanish brethren hastened toward Belgium on foot, leaving behind the others not affected by the edict. Hearing reports at that time that the army of Martin van Rosem, fighting under the authority of King Francis, was attacking Louvain, [Doménech] led his men to Brussels. But when the [French] army withdrew, Ours gathered at Louvain toward the beginning of autumn. Pursuing the study of philosophy that they had begun at Paris, they laid the foundations for [our] college at Louvain.

■ **Italy**

43.   *Laínez at Venice*

In 1542 the Supreme Pontiff sent Father Laínez to Venice at that republic's own request to promote certain works of devotion. He gave sermons in many places, sometimes even twice in the same day. Three times a week he delivered sacred lectures explaining the Gospel of Saint John; a very large audience, a mixture of nobility and ordinary folk, attended. Among them he gathered a rich harvest, both by his sermons and especially by his lectures, as he refuted the heresies that had begun to spring up rapidly there. . . . Through the Spiritual Exercises, he gathered in a larger and longer-lasting harvest among some people who seemed more suitable. Through [the Exercises] and private conversations, some were healed of the plague of their heresies and restored to the Catholic Church. Others followed the counsels of Christ, and so day by day the good reputation of the Society pervaded that very large city. Also Andrea Lippomano (who almost from the start had extended the hospitality of his home to Father Laínez), once he had become more supportive of our work, began to give thought to discuss with Father Laínez [the possible] establishment of colleges at Padua and Venice.

■ **Portugal**

45. *Ministries in Portugal*

This same year Francisco de Villanova was sent from Rome to Portugal; afflicted as he was with ill health, he came to Alcalá for a change of air. There he began to devote himself to studying letters; but his spiritual conversations and the Spiritual Exercises brought many benefits to prominent men. Even though he had almost no companions there for close to two years, our house at that university traces its beginnings to him. As the number of our workers in Portugal increased at Lisbon, our harvest also increased and spread out over a wider territory day by day. The majority of the nobility often came to the church of Saint Anthony for confession and Communion, so that they might receive [these sacraments] every eighth day or, what was less common, once a month. By now this was not regarded as an innovation at the royal court, for it had become customary. Many made progress by using the Spiritual Exercises, and some sought and obtained admission to the Society. The King sent five Saracens (who had come from Mauritania to accept the religion of Christ) and two Jews to our house, so that we could instruct them. Among the Saracens there was one who was held in high esteem among his people because of his nobility.

By now there were twelve scholastics, some of them sent from Rome and Paris and others admitted [in Lisbon]; all of these Simão [Rodrigues] had put up for a time at Saint Anthony's Church. At length, at the King's command he led them in June to Coimbra, where the King had set up an illustrious university and had decided to augment it with a college for Ours. Turning over to them a rented house, Simão looked about for a suitable site for building a college (as the King had commanded); and after setting up for Ours a library and other necessities, all supplied from the royal bounty, [Simão] returned to Lisbon. These were the initial stages of our college at Coimbra, which was the fifth residence of the Society. Day by day it grew larger until it reached the number of students that it enrolls today. Louvain (discussed above) was the sixth residence to be established, begun in August of the same year. The King was considering setting up another house or college at Évora, and his preacher first went there to inspect the site and the design of the building to be built; but the completion of that work was deferred for a time.

THE YEAR 1543

■ **Italy**

48.   *Ministries at Rome*

At Rome early in 1543, among the usual ministries proper to our Institute—preaching, administering the sacraments of confession and Communion, teaching catechism, giving the Spiritual Exercises, bringing peace to quarreling factions, and carrying out other similar pious works—our charity toward catechumens was preeminent. A good number of converts from Judaism to Christianity used to be fed and instructed at our house. But through the efforts of some of those who were already reborn in Christ and enjoyed a solid reputation among the Jews, others and then still others came over to Christ. When, at Ignatius's request, the Supreme Pontiff granted a concession that those who were converted from among the Jews should not deprived of their temporal goods, contrary to what had been the practice previously, the belief was that a larger number of such people would come forward to embrace the faith. Because our house could not, without grave inconvenience, offer facilities for instructing so many or for accepting so many temporary guests, Ignatius began to take steps to set up a special house for instructing catechumens. That pious work was begun this year, and under Julius III an endowment was set up, with the synagogues of Italy also making contributions according to their ability.

With the help of Father Ignatius, a house for orphan boys was built, and another one for orphan girls. Likewise, another one was set up for the young women known as "the unfortunates" *[miserabiles],* a very creditable work in the city [of Rome]. Also efforts were expended to have the holy decree of Innocent III *Cum infirmitas corporis* (which had fallen into disuse) reinstated through the apostolic letters of Paul III. According to its terms, doctors of the body were not to visit sick people until doctors of the soul had freed them from their sins through confession

49.   *Buildings at Rome*

As regards the whole Society, since the divine Goodness was calling many to its Institute and deigned to use it for helping souls everywhere in its gradually widening ministry, the proposal was made to the Supreme Pontiff that he abolish the restriction on our numbers (which he had wisely set up at the beginning on a trial basis), and that he freely confirm our way of life and offer the opportunity of admitting to it all who seemed called by God. This Paul III did willingly. . . . Also this year, besides the Church of Santa Maria della Strada, which had been given to the Society toward the end of 1540, the Church of San Andrea della Frata was handed over to the Society. It was almost deserted, and therefore the Pope had decreed that the church there should no longer be used for divine worship. This church was very conveniently located, adjacent as it was to the garden of Sancta Maria. That same year construction began on what was to become our professed house, all expenses being covered by alms.

50.   *Broët at Foligno and Salmerón at Modena*

After Father Paschase, who had returned from Ireland, had stayed in Rome for some time, he went to Foligno . . . where the bishop had requested his services through the Cardinal of Santa Croce [Cervini];[1] there he began to devote himself to works of piety. When he learned that many were shamefully befouling themselves with concubinage, he called them aside one by one and thus rescued twelve men from that sin. Five of them were married, and some of them had been ensnared in the net of this evil intimacy with women for a dozen years. When one of the women wished to confess to him, he refused to hear her confession until she had first moved out of the house in which she had been sinning. She agreed and separated herself from that house where she had been offending God for thirteen years; later she asserted that it had been as if an angel sent from heaven had aided her to abandon this house. There was also a priest who had put aside clerical garb, donned secular clothes, and gone around in public with his concubine seeking a living by doing some manual *[mechanico]* labor. After being admonished and warned in a brotherly way, he sent his woman away; then, after obtaining absolution and a dispensation, he returned to his clerical state and garb. . . .

At almost the same time Father Salmerón was sent to Modena at the request of Cardinal Morone; after he worked there in the vineyard of the Lord for several months and preached strenuously against the heretics who were

---

[1] On Cervini see William Hudon, *Marcello Cervini and Ecclesiastical Government in Tridentine Italy* (DeKalb, Ill.: Northern Illinois University Press, 1992).

sowing tares, he was recalled by Father Ignatius. With the cooperation of that cardinal, who was the bishop of Modena, Ignatius also arranged to have the decree about medical doctors, which we mentioned above, observed in the Modena Diocese.[2]

■ Germany

52. *Jay at Regensburg*

Father Claude Jay was at Regensburg early in 1543, and there he strove to help religious and secular priests as well as some lay people through the Spiritual Exercises of the First Week, climaxing in the general confession. This work was of benefit to more than a few people. Among them was a man who had defected from the religious life but was induced to return to it. After trying with great diligence to recall some people from their errors, Jay experienced how closely one should embrace that counsel of Blessed John *[sic]:* "As for a man who is heretical, after admonishing him once or twice, have nothing more to do with him because he is perverted."[3] The wonderful judgment of God manifested itself in two of these cases. One was a lay professor who persuaded the Senate that Communion under both species should be accepted. Tortured for two hours by intense pain, he died suddenly. The other, a professed Franciscan, a church of the wicked engaged as their pastor. He then took a wife, but within fifteen days he was tortured severely in that part of his body by which he was violating his vow of chastity and was swept away by a horrible death. Claude went to the bishop of Regensburg (who was outside the city) to urge him to reform certain evils that were the source of other grave dangers. He also wished to secure the promulgation of the jubilee that the Apostolic See had recently issued. Both of these requests were granted. . . .

The constancy in our religion displayed by the Duke of Bavaria was something to behold; when he had observed the downward plunge that the Catholic religion was taking in Regensburg, he prohibited his subjects under pain of death from entering that city until it recovered its senses. When the enemies of the faith were said to be threatening war against him, he said, "We would sooner suffer the loss of our life, homeland, and status than allow our

---

[2] Morone was seldom in his diocese of Modena because of his work at the papal curia or as a legate. No Italian city, with the possible exception of Lucca, had such a flourishing Protestant movement as Modena.

[3] This is actually an allusion to Titus 3:10.

people to slide into Lutheranism." When the apostolic nuncio, the bishop of Caserta, passed through Regensburg on his way to the diet being held at Nuremberg, he ordered Claude to follow him after several days. But since things were wrapped up there in a short time and the diet was dissolved, Jay went to Ingolstadt, where during that summer he cared for Catholics and even for some persons holding suspicious doctrines, successfully giving them the Exercises and encouraging them privately. Later, following the advice of the archbishop of Armagh and the pleas of the professors at the University of Ingolstadt, he began to lecture publicly, so that his efforts might produce results that were more extensive.

53.   *Bobadilla in Germany*

Nicolás Bobadilla accompanied the same [archbishop], coming from Vienna, where, at the King's command and in the presence of six professors, he had disputed with a certain professor, a nobleman by birth who had once been a royal counselor. When Bobadilla had denounced fifty and more errors in his teaching and refuted the man in a disputation, the King ordered that man to be bound by chains and incarcerated in a monastery. There he stabbed himself with a small knife; but when he did not die immediately, he is said to have converted to the Catholic faith and died after receiving the sacraments. At Nuremberg [Bobadilla] dealt kindly with the head of the Lutheran synagogue, who had corrupted Regensburg, and did not despair of leading him back to the path of the truth or at least recalling him from undergoing such severe penalties [in the next life].

Among those for whom he gained forgiveness through the sacrament of confession and whom he restored [to spiritual health] by the Eucharist was a man of the upper nobility who because of a public sin had abstained from the sacraments for many years. Neither the King nor other nobles could persuade him to avoid this sin. When the King sent the bishop of Passau to Speyer to take his place at the diet, Bobadilla was forced to accompany [the bishop] because [the former] was said to be well known both among Protestants and Catholics. When the bishop completed his task there and returned to his diocese, Bobadilla went to Vienna; there he requested and obtained from the King many permissions necessary for gathering a richer harvest in the vineyard of Passau. He absolved and reconciled to the Church some Christians who had abjured their faith and had been circumcised when among the Turks, and he restored some noblemen by the sacraments of confession and Communion.

54.   *Pierre Favre in Germany*

Meanwhile in this same year, 1543, Father Pierre Favre was exerting himself strenuously for the Church of God at Mainz and Cologne. At Mainz he explained the Psalms and helped now one person, now another, by hearing confessions and giving the Spiritual Exercises. But when he had to discontinue his lectures for a while, he visited the cardinal-archbishop of Mainz at Aschaffenburg, in order to transact with him some things contributing to the glory of God. [The archbishop] received him very kindly; when consulted about a certain reformation that [the archbishop] had decided to make, [Favre] also had a fine opportunity to inform the prelate about the nature of our Institute, which he was greatly pleased [to hear about]. When he was soon to return to Mainz, the archbishop asked him to deliver Latin sermons on Sunday in addition to his lectures; he promised to do so, God willing. By the sermons and personal conversations he went on to help many people. When he judged that he should go to Cologne to promote some very important works in favor of religion, he stayed on [in that city] for some time, busy in these projects, so that when he visited the apostolic nuncio [Giovanni] Poggio at Bonn, he gave him an account of what was happening, and especially the case of the archbishop [Hermann von Wied], whom no one had the courage to oppose even though he held positions against the faith or, with the exception of [Favre himself], to warn those who should be alerted to his activities. Thus, it seemed to [the nuncio] that he should not leave Cologne for any reason.[4] He promised that he would satisfy the Cardinal of Mainz by means of letters, so that he would accept [Favre's] absence with equanimity.

Among the other things that Favre did there for God's glory and Germany's profit was that through the Spiritual Exercises he won Peter Canisius for the Society.[5] [Canisius] was then already noted for his zeal in defending and

---

[4] In 1542 Wied tried to introduce Lutheranism and had Martin Bucer write a doctrinal statement for implementation. Had Wied succeeded, four of the seven imperial electors would have been Protestants, with enormous implications for the election of emperors and for Catholicism in Germany. Faced with opposition from many quarters based on economic and political grounds as well as religious ones, Wied was eventually deposed by the cathedral chapter.

[5] Here is Canisius's own reaction to Favre and the Exercises: "To my great good fortune I have found the man I was seeking—if he is a man and not an angel of the Lord. Never have I seen or heard such a profound theologian nor a man of such shining and exalted virtue. . . . I can hardly describe how the Spiritual Exercises transformed my soul and senses, enlightened my mind with new rays of heavenly grace, and I feel infused with new strength"

spreading the Catholic religion against the sectarians, and doing so with learning, eloquence, and outstanding piety. However, while there [Favre] received a letter from Father Ignatius instructing him to go to Portugal with his companions. So after a few days he set out for Antwerp, from which he was going to sail to that kingdom. . . .

■ France

56. *The Community at Paris*

. . . But when Father Ignatius, to test the hearts [of Ours at Paris], inquired whether they were prepared to obey if they were ordered to continue their literary studies at Paris, although they would have to gain their living by begging, or if they were ordered to go to Portugal or to Rome or to another place, whether by land or by sea. They answered unanimously that they were eager to go to any country, even India, with bare feet and begging their way if need be. If they had to stay [in Paris] and lacked the necessary resources, they would be most eager to beg for food and to continue their studies as best they could. They were mindful that they had offered up their liberty to the Lord through holy obedience. . . .

■ Portugal

58. *The Jesuits in Portugal*

In Portugal, meanwhile, the situation of the Society and, through it, the glory of God and the assistance of souls were flourishing. As 1543 got underway, Father Simão [Rodrigues] visited Coimbra at the King's command, so that he could pick a suitable site for building a college. He found a very healthful and beautiful spot in an elevated part of the city, one very suitable for students. Already by that January twenty-five students were living in a rented house, but the King wanted to build a residence suitable for accommodating one hundred men. Meanwhile the royal liberality supplied everything our men needed.

Besides these [students] there were six doing pastoral work in the Lord's vineyard. A certain man came from Castile to Portugal that year to bring his brother back from the Society, to which he had been admitted; but after thoroughly investigating our Institute, he began to favor it enthusiastically. He

(Otto Braunsberger, ed., *Beati Petri Canisii Societatis Iesu Epistulæ et Acta* [Freiburg i. B.: Herder, 1896–1923], 1:76 f.).

followed his brother into religion, as did his nephew who had accompanied him. Both are now outstanding preachers. . . .

59.   *Rodrigues and John III*

When it was decided that the daughter of King John should be given as wife to Prince Philip of Spain, Simão suggested to the King that it would be to God's glory if one of Ours should be sent to Castile with the aforesaid daughter. His presence and activities could help the Society to take root in that kingdom. The King was greatly pleased by this advice and ordered Simão to obtain from Ignatius one or other of the first fathers for this task. This is the reason why Father Favre, even though he was quite profitably occupied in Germany, as we described above, received the order under obedience to sail for Portugal. When he was detained, first by sickness, then by the order of the Supreme Pontiff delivered through the nuncio, Father Antonio de Araoz was sent. But both finally reached Portugal the following year.

61.   *Ministries at Coimbra*

Meanwhile at Coimbra the harvest was increasing day by day through preaching and the sacraments of confession and Communion. While the college was being built ([the King] sent an industrious man to relieve Ours of any worries regarding its construction), the King added to our living space by buying up other houses for Ours. God called some men to the Society; among those admitted two were distinguished by noble blood but even more by their great piety, namely, Gonzales de Silveira, whom God later glorified with a martyr's crown in the kingdom of Monomotapa. The twenty-two-year-old son of Count de Silveira, he was endowed with mature and quick judgment. He edified Ours by his humility and love of Christ's cross; his example also offered no little inspiration to lay people. Following him was Rodrigo de Meneses, son of the governor of Lisbon. Their entrance upset their parents, who were very distinguished in that kingdom, but the young men's constancy easily settled all opposition. After the usual spiritual meditations, the novices were tested by pilgrimages and exercises in humility, and thus they were approved in the Lord and made progress.

Among those who were admitted at this time were Melchor Carnero, Melchor Nuñez, and Luis de Grana, who rendered great service to God in the Society. Among the others was Father Ponce [Cogordan]. Although he was engaged in studies, he was a priest and devoted much time to confessions and pious works; he strove to bring back more than a few erring women and to reconcile a number of those at odds with one another. Father Simão devoted much effort to having certain monasteries fitted up to receive these fallen women and lead them back [to virtuous ways]. He directed that those women should receive instructions that would help them make progress in the spirit. Five or six coadjutor brothers were admitted to do household tasks, which were occupying too much of our scholastics' time.

■   **Italy**

66.   *Ignatius and the Inquisition*

This is how the Society carried on its affairs during the year 1543, but we must note that when at Modena certain secret sectarians, as we reported above, dared to infect some people with the plague of their heresies, Salmerón made efforts to offer a skillful refutation of their errors from a pulpit in that city. Ignatius, judging that he should seize this opportunity, took care to call the matter vigorously to the Pope's attention, resulting in the establishment of the Holy Office of the Inquisition, an institution so salutary for all Italy against heretical depravity. Paul III established it at that time and entrusted it to the most respected cardinals; it clearly gained greater importance day by day as it strove to cleanse Italy of errors and preserve it in the true religion.

THE YEAR 1544

■ **Italy**

68.   *Developments in Rome*

Already as 1544 was beginning, through the charity of Ignatius a different pious work was begun at Rome called [the House] of Saint Martha. It was set up for erring young women who wished to recover from a shameful lifestyle but who could not be accepted among the *conversæ,* either because they were married or because they were not so gifted in spirit that they wished to be cloistered and remain forever in a convent.[1] The House of Saint Martha accepted these women, kept them away from sins and their wicked habits, and trained them in what would contribute to their salvation until they were restored to their husbands (after being reconciled with them), or else had dedicated themselves to the religious life through perpetual vows, or had contracted a respectable marriage. Because our house was laboring under conditions of dire poverty [and so could not be of financial assistance to St. Martha's], Ignatius first offered one hundred gold scudi (obtained from selling certain jewels) to assist this house in its early stages; for he knew that those who had already refused to be the first to contribute to this work had to be persuaded to do so by the example of someone else. Other people then offered their financial support, and a wonderful and helpful work was begun that in a short time achieved great growth.[2] Faithful to the purpose of our Institute, those at Rome devoted themselves to things contributing to spiritual edification both inside and outside our church. The community of the house was increased by a number of those called by God; when our own house had been built somehow, Ignatius along with his men moved into it during September, leaving behind their rented [lodgings].

---

[1] The *conversæ* were a sort of "lay sisters" or women who entered the convent at a mature age, e.g., widows. [Often, especially in Spain, the term also applied to reformed sinners who wished to live a penitential life in a convent. This seems to be Polanco's sense of the word.—ED.]

[2] The House of Santa Marta all'Arco Comigliano was a halfway house for prostitutes who wanted to reform their lives; by 1552 some three hundred women had passed through it on their way to living more respectable lives.

70.   *Laínez at Padua and Brescia*

At the same time, by his exhortations at Padua Father Diego Laínez also persuaded another convent of nuns badly in need of reformation to return to common life and the observance of their rule. Some young women also consecrated themselves to God in convents. Some of those men living in the college exerted themselves to help others, especially by directing some of them in the Exercises and carrying out the ministry of confession and Communion. Some men were also called to follow our Institute. But when Father Laínez, at the command of obedience, went to Brescia, after bidding farewell to his friends in Venice and Padua, he influenced for the better those he left behind as he traveled by river boat and by land, and others whom he encountered while staying at inns. Among them was a man who was hurrying off to kill somebody; moved to compunction, he swore he would not do it and promised to confess his sins in a nearby town.

After Laínez had twice preached effectively in a certain town, he arrived a Brescia on February 18. Although he would have preferred to give exhortations in convents and hospitals and to teach catechism (and this is what he asked permission of the vicar to do), nonetheless, he had to preach on the Sundays of Lent in the cathedral church, and he continued with that same daily task throughout Lent. As his audience grew larger day by day, so too through the grace of God did his harvest increase. The Lord gave him strength to preach the word of God on Saturdays to women converted from sin and on two other afternoons a week to a crowded audience in hospitals. He did not refrain in the meantime from hearing the confessions of the large number of people from both the upper and lower classes who came to him.

After Easter he preached on Sundays and feast days in the cathedral, but the vicar wanted him to lecture three times a week to the people on a subject taken from the Holy Scriptures; the other three days he preached in convents of nuns. This steady labor resulted in a gratifying harvest. For, as the vicar and other trustworthy persons testified, the people who were somewhat dubious about their faith were so confirmed in the Catholic truth that more than a thousand of his hearers said that they were prepared to undergo martyrdom for the faith of Christ. Very many people came to Father Laínez in person and at his direction burned their heretical books. . . .

■ **Belgium and Germany**

74.   *Favre and Estrada at Louvain and in the Rhineland*

Pierre Favre returned to Cologne after the nuncio Poggio, acting on the authority of the Apostolic See, had prevented his sailing to Portugal; but before leaving Louvain he gathered in part of the harvest that Father Estrada had planted by his sermons and he himself had cultivated by informal conversations. When the rumor spread around Louvain that [Ours] were going to leave for Portugal, some of the students were inflamed with a desire to follow them, among them [someone else named] Peter Faber, a bachelor in theology, who had preached through Advent. Eight other students besides decided to leave everything behind, enter the Society, and set out for Portugal with [Fathers Favre and Estrada]. The very day of Epiphany, when they informed Father Favre about the desires they had conceived in the Lord, they were admitted [to the Society]. Five of them were masters in liberal arts, a sixth was a bachelor in theology, and a seventh had given public lectures on ethics. One was a canon of the principal church. One also had studied a year of theology and another had studied law. But they were all very adept in Latin literature. It was something to behold the consolation that each of them claimed to perceive in his soul with regard to his vocation. All of them, before setting out on the journey, confessed the faults of their past lives, received holy Communion, and opened the secrets of their hearts to Father Favre; the lack of time, however, did not allow [Father] to present the Spiritual Exercises to them.

The parents of two of the students tried to block the vocation of their sons—indeed, one threatened imprisonment and the like—but both parents departed contented after considering the matter more thoroughly. The [father], who had made the threats, tearfully and on bended knees begged pardon from Francisco Estrada for having wanted to turn his son away from such a holy commitment. Certain men of great authority in the university itself attempted to turn away another of these students, but when they found him adamant, they yielded to a vocation from God. So they all set out from Louvain and came to Antwerp and then to Zeeland; they were twelve in number: namely Estrada, Oviedo, with Father Jean and the nine [students] picked up at Louvain. They sailed to Portugal with the archbishop of Compostella, who showed great kindness to them.

But Favre himself, with Aemiliano de Loyola [a nephew of Ignatius] and a certain bachelor in theology (by name Lambert Castrius, from Liège) who entered the Society with the others, went to Cologne.[3] At Saint Trund he preached in Latin three times to monks, canons, and other priests and left the hearts of the men wonderfully affected. At Liège, where he preached twice, he found a harvest greater than can be explained. Very many from both Louvain and Liège promised to come to Cologne to make the Spiritual Exercises. Maastricht and Aachen also opened their doors wide to them, but Favre, hastening on to Cologne, did not stay there. He was undecided [what to do] because, after Ignatius had sent him an order under obedience to go to Portugal, the Sovereign Pontiff had countermanded this order and bidden him stay in Germany. All the while he had received no letters from Ignatius himself.

At Cologne Aemiliano devoted himself to many works of piety, giving much edification. He went to Cologne to participate in a disputation—a task at which no student was ever found to equal him. Master Lambert was still working at theology together with Master Peter Canisius, who was busy setting up a house for the beginnings of a college, of which the zealous Carthusian prior greatly approved. Nothing was more in the forefront of Father Favre's prayers than that he would see a firm foundation for the Society in Germany. Although he did not doubt that the young men previously mentioned could make greater intellectual and spiritual progress elsewhere, he admitted that he could not resist the interior impulse from God to keep them in Germany. A richer harvest could be hoped for from them in that region, even though he acknowledged the contrary argument that, things being as they were in Germany, it seemed that nobody should stay there, except under obedience. But the divine consideration won out, for it rested upon a hope grounded in God according to which he would have wished a considerable part of the Society to live there, where they might win God's mercy for that nation by their prayers, tears, and cries. . . .

■ Portugal

80.   *The Louvain Jesuits in Portugal*

The twelve who had set out from Louvain arrived in Portugal in early spring. Francisco Estrada began to preach on the feast days of Lent with singular spirit and grace, even twice a day. Since our house could not as yet

---

[3] This Jesuit is the same as Lambert Duchateau, noted by James Brodrick as Canisius's co-worker in Cologne (*Saint Peter Canisius, S.J., 1521–1597* [New York: Sheed and Ward, 1935], 53, 57, 59, 200).

hold so large an audience, [Estrada] had to move to the royal palace, which was the largest gathering place for students at Coimbra. Antonio de Araoz heard him preach and could not marvel enough at the spirit of the speaker, the size of his audience, and the abundance of fruit that he gathered in. With the addition of these [twelve], sixty [Jesuit] students were now devoting themselves to studies at the college in Coimbra, and so many asked to be admitted that careful selectivity was required. Only those more advanced in their studies and demonstrating excellent talent were admitted, and some also sought the backing of leading men to get themselves admitted. Among others, Louis, the King's brother, recommended a man who had already completed the course in philosophy and was a nephew of the master of his household. Among the exceptional talents of the scholastics we have to mention those of Rodrigo de Meneses: after hearing an entire sermon, he repeated it word for word, including all the citations to authors, and gave Father Araoz a written copy of sermon that he had heard him deliver.

82.   *Missionaries to India*

This same year two men from the college at Coimbra were sent to India. One of them was Antonio Criminali; when Simão [Rodrigues] called him in and told him he was going to India in two days, he embraced the command with great delight. When Simão tried to sound out the inclinations of his heart and questioned him whether he would prefer to return to Italy rather than sail off to India, he could get no answer from him except that in his heart he was prepared to be sent under obedience to India or Turkish territory or to any other place, provided only that he was doing God's will. Therefore, along with Father Juan de Beira they set off for Lisbon, where they were to board their ship.

■ The Society in general

85.   *Overview of Jesuit Communities*

This year the Society started with houses in nine places. Three new ones were added this year, namely, Cologne, Valencia, and Alcalá, to the six noted previously, namely, Rome, Paris, Lisbon, Padua, Coimbra, and Louvain. None as yet had an income; those living in the places mentioned above sustained themselves by means of alms or gifts received from certain private persons. But the next year, namely, 1545, the generosity of the honorable Lord Andrea Lippomano, who, as has been said, held *in commendam* the priorate of the

Lambertines at Padua, brought it about that the college established at Padua would have a stable income.[4] When that man, who was kind to all and extremely supportive of the Society, indicated that he would give that priorate if the Supreme Pontiff would grant it to be united [to the Society], Father Ignatius, who was going to take up several other important negotiations with the Supreme Pontiff on behalf of the King of Portugal, went to Montefiascone, where the Pontiff was staying at the time, and obtained [permission for] the aforesaid union, along with the other things he requested.

------

[4] In a situation of this kind, the person holding this abbacy enjoyed the revenues of his abbey without bearing the responsibilities of a regular abbot.—ED.

THE YEAR 1545

■ **Rome**

87.   *Activities at Rome*

At Rome, meanwhile, in our church and elsewhere Ours delivered lectures on the Sacred Scriptures and preached the Word of God for the people's benefit, and they also made efforts to convert the Jews. In its beginnings Father Ignatius had to sustain the pious work of Saint Martha's [House] (which had already admitted nearly forty women), providing them with food for body and spirit. Nonetheless, he saw to it that a confraternity of pious men was organized to take over this responsibility and free our Society from such a heavy burden.[1] Our house at Rome now had more than thirty [Jesuits], but all were so occupied in religious tasks that they were left with no leisure at all. The work load was increasing because some pious and devout women requested and obtained from the Supreme Pontiff permission to live under obedience to Father Ignatius.[2] This certainly did not seem good to the aforesaid father. Because the Society by its Institute ought to occupy itself in matters related to the common good, he regarded this sort of commitment as obstructing the greater good. Still, God's providence seems to have allowed this at the beginning, so that experiencing how troublesome this burden was might teach the Society to be more diligent hereafter in keeping the door closed to this sort of activity. (At the proper time we shall narrate how this was accomplished.) Novices were admitted and were trained [in the Society's ways] both within and outside our house by pilgrimages and by serving as hospital workers.

Among the other novices a certain Guillaume Postel, a Frenchman rather famous for his learning (especially in mathematics and languages), was admitted to probation. But he thought, said, and wrote many things that in his eyes flowed from the spirit of prophecy but that, in the judgment of Ignatius and other Jesuits, were untrue and not conducive to fostering edification and unity in the Society. After many remedies were tried in vain, he was dismissed. Apart

---

[1] The Confraternity of Grace enrolled more than one hundred prominent Roman men and women.

[2] The women were Isabel Roser, her maid Francisca Cruillas, and Isabel de Josa. Roser had been Loyola's principal benefactor when he was a student at Barcelona.

from this flaw, he was a devout man and endowed with good morals, if only he had learned to think more humbly and subject his judgment to the service of faith and obedience.[3] . . .

The amenity [of the professed house] was enhanced this year by a garden and by dwellings contiguous to the church (after the death of the person who had possession of them while he was still alive). This provided us with a more healthful and slightly more spacious living quarters. This year some men were sent out who increased the number [of Jesuits] at the Padua college and others from various nations who augmented the Valencia college community. A document was requested and granted in the form of a [papal] brief giving Ours very ample faculties for administering the sacraments of confession and Communion, preaching the word of God, and carrying out some other very useful activities, so that the Society, equipped with spiritual arms, might bend its efforts more effectively to helping our neighbor.

89.   *Laínez and Salmerón are sent to Trent*

The Council of Trent had already been convoked almost three years ago, but it finally got underway toward the end of 1545. Because the learning and piety of Fathers Diego Laínez and Alfonso Salmerón were already well enough known to the Supreme Pontiff and the leading cardinals of the curia at Rome, both were sent in the course of this year to Trent as the Supreme Pontiff's theologians.

90.   *Broët at Faenza*

At Faenza, meanwhile, Father Paschase [Broët] devoted all his energy to helping his neighbors, at first by weekly visiting sick paupers, who were very numerous in that city. When he noticed that they were not receiving spiritual or even bodily assistance in their need, with the kind permission of the vicar he began to discuss with many devout men the establishment of a confraternity, to be called the Society of Charity. As it began taking shape, he gave [it] a plan, drawn up in a short, comprehensive document, for living and a way of practicing devotion. The duty of members was to inquire about and visit sick and suffering paupers everywhere in the city and at first urge them to confession and Communion, then provide them both with the food they needed for as long as

---

[3] Guillaume Postel (1510–1581) wrote Europe's first comparative study of languages and a treatise on how to convert Muslims. His interest in the Cabala and apocalyptic views alienated the Jesuits and later led the Roman Inquisition to declare him mad.

their sickness lasted, and also with a doctor and medicine. His energetic dedication also did much for other persons of both sexes through the sacrament of confession. Because certain preachers, especially Bernardino Ochino, had sown some seeds of Lutheran teaching in that city, he employed great vigilance to head off any discussions about the infectious teaching of such sectarians, typical of what usually takes place in artisan-class taverns, so as to ensure that the memory [of these heresies] would be totally blotted out.[4]

In the church of the converted women [that is, former prostitutes], he began to explain Christian doctrine at the beginning of Lent. He also gave the same converted women some written rules and a formula for spiritual living and took care that they observed [them]. As a result, they lived like religious without [personal] property, even through they were bound by no vow. After Easter he saw to it that they learned from memory the articles of the faith, the precepts of the law, the seven spiritual and corporal works of mercy, and other matters related to spiritual progress. He also taught the same lessons in Christian doctrine in seven schools for boys and made them learn them from memory, to the great edification of both the students and their parents. They declared that this was the subject matter that lads everywhere should learn. A marked improvement in the boys' behavior manifested itself; and although the abuses of swearing and blasphemy had been very prevalent among them, not only did they correct them but when some such thing erupted because of their former bad habit, they came to Paschase, accused themselves, and asked for penance at Easter time. There were about four hundred such boys.

[Broët encountered] a certain man who had left his wife and kept a concubine in his house for four years, and led him back to his wife; and the concubine returned as well to her husband, who, avenging himself on his faithless wife, had taken a concubine himself. [Broët] gave useful service to other people involved in concubinage of this sort. By seeing that members of the Society of Charity came to monthly confession and Communion, he helped them in the Lord. Among the confessions that he heard in the city, many of them were general confessions, resulting in a great emendation of life there. Owing to his efforts several prostitutes gave up their shameful kind of life and were admitted to the convent of converted women. Every Sunday he gave an

---

[4] Bernardino Ochino (1487–1564) was the former general of the Capuchins and the most famous Italian preacher of his era. Gradually he was won over to Protestant doctrines. Actually his teachings were more Calvinist than Lutheran; Polanco designates all Protestants by the term "Lutheran." Ochino fled Italy for Geneva in 1542.

exhortation based on an explanation of the Gospel, thus exerting a considerable influence on the listeners who came to the church of the converted women. He frequently visited the hospitals to hear the confessions of the sick, to console them, and to bolster their patience and endurance; moreover, he encouraged those ministering at the hospital to exert greater care and charity toward the sick.

In Faenza as in the other towns in Emilia, vendettas and factions were so long-standing that some had perdured for more than a hundred years and frequently resulted in murder and other grave evils. Reflecting on a remedy that would induce some of the leading families to enter into concord, [Broët] began to deal with some suitable men who could bring their authority to bear on this project. Working under the inspiration of God's goodness and grace, he reconciled more than one hundred men with one another amid great solemnity in the cathedral church, and he brought them to forgive one another for murders, injuries, and the harm ensuing from these vendettas. After this public reconciliation, he added an exhortation in which he explained the good effects resulting from peace and contrasted them with the evil consequences of discord. He also performed the same service for other families. He heard about certain people who denied the existence of purgatory, did not pray to the saints, and did not observe the Church's fasts. By fraternal correction and friendly explanation of the truth, he induced them to make resolutions to adhere to the teaching of Holy Mother the Church. In exhortations held on Sundays for many lay people, he discussed the Ten Commandments and led his listeners to a life worthy of Christians.

■ Germany

91. *Jay's work in Germany*

At the start of this year, 1545, Father Claude [Jay] was working at Worms, where an imperial diet was being held. When he saw that the study of theology, especially Scholastic theology, was almost dead in Germany, he sought, urged on by Father Ignatius at Rome, to establish colleges in that [country], where indigent students might devote their efforts to this subject. Conditions in Germany had made the name of anything religious so hateful that wealthy students no longer wanted to devote themselves to studying theology. The bishops of Salzburg, Eichstätt, and Augsburg showed that they were prepared [to support] this good work. When the bishop of Salzburg urged Claude to return to Ingolstadt and after Claude had remitted a decision on this matter to superiors, Father Ignatius suggested four theologians (Claude himself included among them). He then asked [Claude] to indicate whom he judged most suitable for the post of theology professor. He answered that in his view he himself was unequal to the task, but if [Ignatius] as his superior required this of him, he would obey out of blind obedience. He judged that of the three others whom the Society proposed, Father Alfonso Salmerón and also Father Diego Laínez were qualified, as long as the young age of [Salmerón] did not detract from his standing among the German students. Although he felt that the task of lecturing in universities was not appropriate for professors of our Society, still he judged that it would be very useful for the glory of God and the restoration of that land, given the devastated state [of religion] in Germany. . .

While [Jay] was staying at Worms during Lent, he preached before [Ferdinand] the King of the Romans on Sundays and at other times. At his last sermon, which he delivered on the feast of the Most Holy Trinity, His Imperial Majesty Charles V was also present at the invitation of his brother, Ferdinand (who took great delight in sermons of this sort). But before [Claude] climbed into the pulpit he was unsure of himself and rather fearful, more so than he had ever been before; but the moment he began to preach, the Lord made him so animated that (as he himself said) never had he so freely proclaimed the word of God; and, as a nobleman of the Emperor's household asserted, the [Emperor] himself praised his sermon as very useful and erudite.

Extending [the range of] his preaching still farther, the Cardinal of Augsburg decided to send [Jay] to take his place at the Council [of Trent] itself. When [Jay] had received generous alms from Cardinal Farnese, he devoted most of it to help the brethren at Cologne and the rest to other pious works.

94.   *Bobadilla as chaplain to the imperial soldiers*

This year, when Father Bobadilla was accompanying the King's court and military camp and the war of Charles V against the Lutherans broke out, he was not remiss in wielding the arms of our militia, namely, the word of God and the sacraments.[5] The throng of those suffering from sickness in the camp and those, too, who were in good health usually were in great need, both spiritually and temporally, of these acts of charity.

---

[5] Polanco is speaking of the First Schmalkaldic War, won by Charles V.

■ Portugal

98.   *Rodriguez and the Jesuits in Portugal*

This year, writing from Portugal, Father Simão Rodrigues urged Father Ignatius to recall him to Rome from that kingdom and to request the King's permission for this. Ignatius made this request, but it was not granted. Since the King was very given to piety, he wanted his son the prince to be given an equally devout upbringing. He assigned Simão as his tutor in place of the bishop of Coimbra, who had once been his preacher. After accepting a bishopric, this man could not be absent from his church. Although the Society, in accord with the humility of its Institute, ought to refuse such exalted tasks, when the King informed Simão of his wish, Simão referred it to Father Ignatius, declaring that the inclination of his heart was toward humble things rather than tasks of this sort. Still, it seemed good to Ignatius, to whom the King had written about the matter, that it was not possible to refuse the request of a prince who had done so much good for the Society and was so zealous for the common good. Meanwhile, Simão, along with many other priests, was kept very busy giving useful spiritual help to many people.

The whole city followed the sermons of Francisco Estrada with excellent results. Although many came out of the Spiritual Exercises with considerable profit, still, only a few select persons among them were admitted to the Society. A certain other priest serving the Count of Feria made the Exercises in Portugal prior to celebrating his first Mass. After celebrating it, he preached with so much ardor that those present were edified to a remarkable degree by something no one could have hoped for. Because he was already a theologian, there was hope that he would be a very useful worker for the kingdom, for he had already decided to enter the Society. So many asked to be admitted to the Society that within two months almost thirty men were pressing their applications. Among those who had made the Spiritual Exercises with great profit was Luís Gonçalves de Câmara, son of the governor of the islands called the Madeiras. He had studied letters at Paris and was renowned for his nobility no less than for his talent and erudition. He was well versed in Latin, Greek, and Hebrew literature. Among the many applicants who applied to [enter the Society], some were [chosen] who had finished the philosophy course and others who had long experience in canon law.

99.   *New recruits in Portugal*

More than sixty students were living at the Coimbra college; Father Favre asserted that there was no one among them who did not seem to be working to [achieve] perseverance and to progress in spirit each day. And he was aware that they were all going forward in great peace and brotherly love, in humility and obedience. While studies in that university were flourishing and famous professors were drawn there from everywhere, the studies carried on at home in our college were making splendid progress. . . .

Among the others admitted to the Society was Antonio Gomez, considered one of the most talented persons in the city of Coimbra and quite learned in philosophy and canon law; moreover, he dedicated his considerable patrimony to pious works. João Nunes, already a priest, after leaving behind a certain abbacy and after finishing studies in philosophy, canon law, and also part of theology, entered the Society.[6] He was patriarch of Ethiopia, noted for his virtue both before and after his entrance. The same year Manuel da Nóbrega was admitted; he too was a priest and was related through his brother to the chancellor of the kingdom; he was very respected for his virtue and skill at canon law. Very fortunately for our students, it happened that the university, which used to hold its literary exercise of lectures, disputations, and meetings in one part of the city very remote from our college, moved them to the upper part [of town] close to where we lived. In every faculty Ours stood out among the other students by their erudition. They did not omit their literary exercises in order to fulfil their spiritual ones, or vice versa. Father Favre's private conversations with each one of them contributed greatly to their progress and left them better instructed and more eager for spiritual progress. Nonetheless, Favre also preached on feast days and Sundays either in the cathedral church or in monasteries of monks or elsewhere; he heard many confessions, and he also gave the Spiritual Exercises to certain people in his usual way. . . .

■ **Spain**

102.   *Araoz's Work in Spain*

When Father Araoz was ordered to leave [Salamanca] and bade farewell to the people in a last sermon, the news was so unwelcome to his listeners that they tried through their prince to block his departure. Francisco de Villanova, the rector of the principal college at Alcalá, indicated that he would appreciate

---

[6] Almost certainly the abbacy was a benefice *in commendam.*

it if some of Ours would come to Alcalá, in order to help him set up the college. Since a college had to be established for [future] teachers of theology, allowing them time to devote to the Sacred Scriptures, it seemed to Doctor Medina that it would be more useful if it were to be turned over to the use of the Society. Araoz went there to find out what needed to be done next about this project. Although he did not bring the negotiations about that college to a conclusion, through the goodwill of certain important people it was arranged that several students of the Society were assigned to Villanova. . . .

THE YEAR 1546

- **Italy**

114.   *Developments at Rome*

As the year 1546 got underway, with the Society's growth in membership and residences, Father Ignatius's anxiety over his ministry of governance increased as well. But this gave him no excuse either to omit his usual edifying activities in Rome or to become lukewarm about missions consistent with our Institute and related to the glory of God. At Rome he gathered in a not insignificant harvest through preaching and administering the sacraments of penance and the Eucharist, as well as through [teaching] Christian doctrine. Not a few Jews and Turks were baptized in the house accommodating the catechumens. Young girls, badly brought up and exposed to the scandalous example of prostitutes, and now brought to the very verge of a precipice, as it were, found themselves snatched from the devil's maw and placed in a pious environment. Some women already living in a less-than-reputable manner were led to repentance and received into the House of Saint Martha. Among them was one with whom Matthias, the chief of [the papal] messenger service, was passionately in love; he was a vigorous man who had gained high favor in the papal household. He stirred up malicious talk against Ignatius. For the sake of the Society, whose good reputation was damaged by such calumnies, Father Ignatius wanted the situation to be put to rights by a [judicial] sentence. Thus he was not only freed of suspicion but highly praised, and in this way he slammed shut the mouths of calumniators. Matthias himself also reformed [his life]; he had a son by the wife he had married and converted his hatred into friendship and goodwill. . . .

116.   *Ignatius and Jesuit poverty*

Although questions relative to the Society and other pious works [carried on] outside it were dealt with at Rome, Ignatius judged that neither he nor Ours at Rome should be involved with applications for ecclesiastical revenues and other similar matters that people usually regard as temporal rather than spiritual affairs. Hence, when something of that sort from Portugal was recommended to his good offices, Ignatius insisted that the King himself should refer even our own [temporal] affairs to the official who handles such business for him.

Ignatius held that spiritual affairs were proper for Ours but that it was inappropriate for Ours to involve themselves with temporal affairs, even those of greatest importance. Some questions of this sort he did not allow even lay people to handle [on our behalf], because he felt that they did not accord with the purity of our Institute. Thus, Doctor Ortiz, out of his love for the Society, sought to gain the authorization of the Holy See to arrange for one of the professed [fathers] of the Society to be in charge of souls at a certain parish with a very rich income, but with the stipulation that the income [from this parish] would be devoted to supporting our scholastics at Alcalá. [Ignatius] petitioned the Pope not to approve this arrangement despite our distressing lack of money. He wrote back, however, and thanked the good doctor for his devotion; but he insisted that our professed fathers should be diligent in preserving poverty.

He was convinced that the professed of the Society should not for any reason whatsoever accept the three or four bishoprics which had been offered [them]. But [at that time] King Claudius of Ethiopia begged the Serene King of Portugal to request the Supreme Pontiff to send a patriarch to those regions, one appointed from among the professed of the Society. The King of Portugal passed on this request to Father Ignatius, specifically requesting Father Favre [for this mission], for he knew of his integrity and learning. With tokens of his affection, the King urged Ignatius to take to heart the salvation of those regions. Ignatius did not shrink from accepting this sort of dignity, provided the Apostolic See ordered it, because he considered that accepting this office would be equivalent to accepting, not leisure, honors, and wealth, but labors, hardships, and death itself for the religion of Christ and the salvation of souls. To such a degree did he convince himself that this mission to Ethiopia would be for the honor of God and the propagation of the Christian religion that if others refused to undertake it, he would offer himself for this work if the Society did not prevent him [from going]. Still, he thought that Father Paschase [Broët] would be a suitable choice instead. But this establishment of the patriarchate and mission was postponed for many years for other reasons.

118.   *Jesuits are assigned to the Council of Trent*

When circumstances surrounding the Council of Trent improved toward the beginning of this year, the Supreme Pontiff ordered Ignatius to choose some of Ours to attend the council as theologians of the Apostolic See. He therefore chose three, namely, Pierre Favre, Diego Laínez, and Alfonso Salmerón. Since the latter two were working in Rome, they were sent off at once to Trent. This year Laínez, before going to Trent, also preached at Bassano with remarkable success (his good reputation preceded him to Trent, which was a two day's journey distant). But it was only with greater difficulty that Favre, who was working with several companions at the court of King Philip and wanted to [gather in] the rich fruits of an abundant harvest, could be torn away from Spain. Still, such was the power of obedience that Favre thrust aside all the hindrances and had no fear about entering Rome even during the dog days. But the divine Goodness called Favre to the council of heaven rather than to the Council of Trent; loosed from the chains of an earthly life, he rose to the freedom of heavenly life on the very day of Peter's Chains [August 1].

120.   *Polanco at Pistoia*

This same year Fathers André des Freux, Girolamo Otello, and I completed our theological studies at the college in Padua; from there we arrived at Venice on September 4 and shortly thereafter at Bologna, from which two of us went on to Rome. One of us [Polanco himself], after staying [at Bologna] awhile and beginning to work at preaching, hearing confessions, and performing other pious works, was sent under obedience to several other places and carried out the same tasks successfully, until finally he came to Pistoia. The bishop had dealt with Father Ignatius and had obtained what he deeply desired, that he could employ somebody from the Society in things pertaining to himself and his diocese. When the bishop had devoted himself to spiritual meditations and requested that something be written for him about the proper administration of his office, this was done. This [bishop], who was already a good man but now became even more fervent, diligently set himself to preaching (which bishops at that time did only rarely) and to performing the other duties of his office.

In the city [Polanco, speaking in the third person] began to nurture the townspeople and several convents of nuns with great care by preaching sermons; he strove as well to improve some priests with the Spiritual Exercises. There was a certain confraternity in that city to which, as the bishop saw it, the best men of the town belonged. Here their purpose was to carry into practice all the works of piety and to come together every day in a chapel, where they would devote part of one hour before supper to hearing an exhortation and the rest to prayer. When he preached to this confraternity and began to instruct and encourage them, those who perceived that they were making progress elected him director of their confraternity without our priest's being at all aware of their action. When a good number of them had gathered at the bishops's palace and made him their intercessor [with Polanco], they decided that [Polanco] should undertake to care for [their spiritual needs]. The bishop seconded this request.

But our man took time to commend their request to the Lord. The next day he replied that he lived under the obedience of Father Ignatius, to whom he referred all things. But the confraternity persistently wrote to Father Ignatius, [only to hear that] this type of activity was not appropriate for priests of the Society. Still, for a time [Polanco] carried on his work for them both by exhortations and [hearing] confessions, thus bringing them consolation and profit. Nonetheless, he also preached in many [other] places, sometimes two or three times the same day. The canons of the cathedral church also asked him to preach to them occasionally.

He was involved in setting up a house and college at Pistoia. At the same time he also preached first in the city square and then in the main church at Prato (which is no insignificant town, located some ten miles from Florence and Pistoia). He was also busy in the other villages of the Pistoia Diocese, greatly benefiting the people who thronged to the sermons. Some there also were in Pistoia who desired to give themselves totally to God and the salvation of their neighbors, especially in India.

121.   *Polanco in Tuscany*

When Duke Cosimo of Florence revealed to a friend of the Society that he would welcome it if our Society were to open some sort of college at Florence, [Polanco] went to Pisa to better sound out the duke's mind; and when the duke confirmed what he had said earlier, he went to Florence. After inspecting the various properties that were shown him, he preferred a place with its own church over the other possibilities.

It happened that he discussed with several devout men the many young women in Florence who reportedly did not have the dowries that were necessary for entering a convent or getting married. Because of this, these women did not put into execution many inspirations and holy desires and, what is worse, they subjected their bodies to unseemly practices because of their poverty. Therefore, these men deliberated about how to find a remedy for this evil. Finally, it seemed that the most effectual way would be if some place were set up similar to the convent established at Rome for wayward girls. There such girls could for a time be kept busy with work and training until they could be placed in either marriages or convents. After [Polanco] had inspired such men by a sermon delivered in a certain monastery and had set forth the rationale for establishing this work, some men in the audience then and there offered their support and part of their resources for this project. Standing right in front of him, one offered a house, another offered a farm, and a certain matron offered a thousand ducats and [promised to] work in the home. Some pledged other things, and thus the project for helping many young women took root and grew. He also preached in Florence and then returned to Pistoia.

123.   *Establishing a community at Bologna*

Among those who were receptive to the seed of God's word at Parma was Father Francesco Palmio, who at that time was working and helping many people at the parish of Santa Lucia in Bologna. He kept urging Father Ignatius to send three or four of the Society [to him]. Because many of both sexes had listened to some of the Society's first fathers as they preached or had made progress by confessing their sins to them, they begged that a college be started where Ours might reside permanently. Some wanted to make the Spiritual Exercises and reach some decision about their state of life. Lady Violante Gozzadina, a noblewoman of great piety, was one of those making this request. Therefore, Father Alfonso Salmerón was sent during the spring before he was to leave for Trent, and he preached there during Lent. Not only did he preach in the morning but also sometimes in the afternoons in convents of nuns; and he had to hear so many confessions that he hardly had time to prepare his sermon. But the kindness of many people gave promise that the scholastics to be sent there would lack for nothing.[1] He introduced the practice of frequent confession despite the complaints of some who objected to the novelty of this practice. He continued delivering sermons from Easter till its octave; then the next Tuesday [Salmerón] set out toward Padua and from there moved on to Trent. . . .

Finally, Father Jerónimo Doménech with some of our scholastics arrived in Bologna following the feast of the Ascension and laid the first foundations of that college or community of Ours. Father Francesco Palmio had not yet entered the Society but was doing outstanding work and collaborating with another priest in helping the neighbor just as those belonging to the Society do. After

---

[1] Bologna was the site of a famous medieval university. [The "scholastics" were Jesuits studying in preparation for ordination.—ED.]

Father Salmerón's sermons the number of those receiving monthly Communion climbed to two hundred, and there were nearly thirty weekly communicants. He personally took charge of providing food for Ours from alms.

Thus did Ours begin to live in Bologna at the Church of Santa Lucia, where Father Jerónimo devoted himself to both preaching and hearing confessions. Although the episcopal vicar invited him to the [Cathedral] Church of Saint Petronius, [Doménech] preferred to continue his sermons at Santa Lucia, where he had begun, for he hoped for greater success there. Nonetheless, at the request of this vicar and in his presence, he began to preach in convents of nuns to the great consolation and approval of the vicar, to whom the convents owed obedience. At their request he gave the Spiritual Exercises to certain noblewomen who came to him from a very distant part of the city. Later some of them came weekly for confession and Communion. So ardent were the desires of many women that they did not spare him even when he was sick, thus delaying his recovery. There was a woman who came thirty-six miles to make a general confession; she previously had made the First Week of the Exercises.

The sermons also produced another happy result: breaking with custom, members of other religious orders began to preach on Sundays and feast days in their monasteries. Some men after [making] the Exercises inclined their souls toward the Society. Efforts were made to establish a confraternity of those ladies who had made spiritual progress; its goal would be to found a convent for converted [prostitutes]. Some noblemen also met together at another location for the same purpose. Leaving their shameful way of life behind them, some women had already prepared themselves to enter the aforesaid building, [bringing] along household furnishings from their homes and their own possessions. On Christmas Day itself almost fifty came to Communion. They occasioned considerable edification when they remembered not to accept the alms they were offered.

125.   *Toward a community at Pisa*

Father Ignatius gave indications of his earnest hope that some colleges might be set up in certain leading Italian cities in which Ours might do literary studies (where they would not be teaching other people). Therefore, when Fathers Laínez and Salmerón were sent from Rome to Trent, Laínez took care of this through a certain philosophy professor at the University of Pisa, which Duke Cosimo of Florence had established. The arrangement was that four or five scholastics would be given food and lodging at [the university]. The secretary of the duke, who was in charge of the university, was very happy to handle the details of this negotiation. The duke was pleased that Ours were coming to that university. But at that time the project came to nothing. At Ferrara, too, a certain friend of the Society in the household of Duke Ercole attempted the same thing when the aforesaid fathers passed through there; but if a community of Ours were to take up residence there, it seemed necessary for one of our Fathers to go there and render the heart of the duke more pliable by his sermons.

126.   *Jay, Laínez, and Salmerón at Trent*

From the start of this year, Father Claude Jay was occupied at Trent. After the Cardinal of Augsburg recalled [from Trent] his companion on this legation, [Claude] came to be admitted to the general sessions and was also active in the frequent particular sessions.[2] Moreover, he was also kept busy holding private conversations with many prelates about numberous aspects of the council. On May 18 Fathers Laínez and Salmerón finally reached Trent after devoting themselves to preaching and the other ministries of the Society in their usual way at Venice and elsewhere. After Salmerón had given his last sermon at Bassano, in which he urged his hearers to frequent Communion, more than a hundred persons began this pious practice. When they arrived at Trent, not only did they find Father Claude enjoying great favor among the prelates and enhancing the good reputation of the Society, but they were themselves also kindly and warmly received by the legates del Monte and Santa Croce (who were later [to be elected] popes) and by the other council Fathers.[3]

Cardinal Santa Croce generously offered them lodging and the other necessities of life, but they preferred the quarters that Father Claude had prepared for them at Saint Elizabeth's House which was better suited to carrying on the tasks of our ministry. Claude also wanted to move to the same place and tried to get permission from the Cardinal of Trent, who at the time was at Regensburg.[4] Before leaving Trent, the cardinal had granted him faculties to

---

[2] The particular sessions were discussions and presentations by theologians, whereas general sessions involved discussions and voting by the bishops.

[3] Cardinal Giovanni Maria Ciocchi del Monte was Pope Julius III from February 8, 1550, till March 23, 1555. Marcello Cervini, known as Cardinal Santa Croce from his titular church, was Pope Marcellus II from April 9, 1555, till May 1, 1555; he was a strong supporter of the Jesuits.

[4] Cardinal Christopher Madruzzo (1512–78) was prince-bishop of Trent.

preach and conferred on him all his own power to administer the sacraments, as well as the authority to delegate this to others whom he judged suitable. He made assiduous use of this faculty during Lent and especially during Holy Week.

On Thursdays the cardinal liked to practice charity toward the poor and wanted to have Claude assist him; the cardinal himself, with head uncovered, waited on the poor for whom he had prepared a banquet in a certain private room, and after the dinner he also poured water on their hands and gave each of them a new coat and a purse with a gold coin. After he had given them a short exhortation, he then took his meal alone with Claude and conversed with him about spiritual matters.

127.   *Jesuits discuss doctrine at Trent*

After Fathers Laínez and Salmerón had at the command of the legates expressed their views in the congregation of theologians on the subject of justification, with the help of God they handled themselves so well that they won the admiration, favor, and respect of the legate and all the prelates and theologians. The Spanish bishops especially, who previously did not willingly see [Ours] speak before they themselves did, were so favorable toward them that it seemed they could not get enough of their company. Many of the prelates also consulted Ours about their voting; indeed, some of [the bishops] carried with them the opinion [of Ours] in writing.

131.   *Preaching at Trent*

Even though certain theologians belonging to religious orders requested permission to engage in public preaching, they were denied this office; but it was granted to Ours. So Father Laínez performed this office every Sunday and feast day with edification and indeed before a large audience of eminent men at the Church of Blessed Mary. On the feast of Saint John the Evangelist, Father Salmerón preached a Latin sermon before the fathers of the holy council; the bishops warmly approved of what they heard, so much so that they induced him to have it written out and printed. Father Laínez gave the Spiritual Exercises to several bishops; and as the days passed, the example of their lives, their teaching, and the fruits of charity extended their reputation still more widely.

132. *Ignatius and dubious teachings*

When somebody among the leaders of the council voiced some opinions that were valid and reasonable but nonetheless new, Father Ignatius wanted to acquaint Ours with his own view on such opinions.[5] It was his judgment that even if equally good arguments could be mustered from here and there, still he considered it preferable that no opinion should ever be made public which seemed to lean toward or be similar to the opinions of the heretics or of those supporting innovations. This stance should be maintained as long as the Church had not decided for one side or the other.

133. *Helping returning soldiers*

When many soldiers returned from the war in Germany and were suffering from sickness as well as from a lack of material necessities, like clothing and food, Cardinal [Cervini] of Santa Croce turned this charitable work over to Ours. Our men, who even before receiving the command of the cardinal were inclined to perform this task, collected money from the bishops with great diligence and edification, so that those soldiers could return to Italy well clothed (which was extremely necessary during wintertime) after recovering their health.[6]

134. *Trent's decree on justification*

The legates relied heavily on the contributions of Ours in formulating the decree on justification. They entrusted to our men the task of gathering in summary form all the Lutheran heresies (except those pertaining to original sin and justification). Our men did this, but not without great labor.

136. *The bishop of Clermont and Jesuit colleges in France*

Along with the other French bishops, Guillaume du Prat, bishop of Clermont, who was favorably inclined to the Society, came to Trent. He discussed aspects of our Institute first with Father Claude and then with Father Laínez and began negotiations aimed at setting up two colleges, one in Paris and the other in his own diocese. When for reasons of health he went to Venice and

---

[5] Cardinal Reginald Pole (1500–1558), one of the papal legates at Trent, was sympathetic to a theology of justification with affinities to Luther's teaching.

[6] Paul III sent a large contingent of Italians to help Charles V fight the Lutherans in the First Schmalkaldic War, 1546–47.

then on to Padua, he observed our college; at Rome he also requested and obtained from the Supreme Pontiff permission to donate [to the Society] the episcopal residence of Clermont, which was on the rue de La Harpe in Paris and seemed well suited for a college; he had definitively made up his mind regarding this proposal.[7] He held such an exalted opinion of the Society that he hoped that Christ would accomplish much toward the reformation and consolation of the Church through its ministry.

■ Germany

137. *Bobadilla in Germany*

At the beginning of this year, Father Bobadilla was exercising his ministries at Cologne. . . . He traveled to Speyer and then to Regensburg, where a very important diet was to be held; he worked with Catholics and Protestants and strove to help both in the Lord through private conversations. . . . But at the Regensburg Diet Charles V determined to bring the Protestants into submission; for he had been unable to compel them, either by the authority of the council or by his own, to live according to their [religious] duty. Because the Supreme Pontiff had sent Ottavio Farnese there as well as Cardinal Alessandro Farnese, the apostolic legate, both accompanied by an excellent army of Italians, Bobadilla had to accompany the imperial and papal camp.

. . . When the war broke out, he had to serve in the imperial camp by ministering to sick Spaniards and providing them with confession and the other sacraments. When the papal army arrived there, his work and its good effects increased immeasurably. Cardinal Farnese put him in charge of the hospital for the Italians. Many were wounded by enemy cannons, which were almost countless. His daily sermons abundantly increased this harvest. Even though while carrying on these labors he himself was sorely tried by sickness, he still strove to perform his duties with a joyous spirit; for he realized that this remedy of war was the only way to bring Germany back [to the faith]. He also suffered from the plague, but with God's help he came out unharmed.

When he returned to Regensburg, once again in good health, he fell victim to robbers who, besides robbing him, struck him more than once; but when three Italians appeared, the thieves turned their attention to them. He reached Regensburg healthy and happy, naked except for his undergarments.

---

[7] The rue de La Harpe is on the Left Bank and runs from the place St. Michel to the Hôtel de Cluny.

The King of the Romans discussed sending him to Trent; other missions of significant importance presented themselves as well; but he felt obliged to return to the camp. There, besides having to sleep on the ground, at one point he was also wounded in the head; and if he had not been protected by rather thick headgear, his life would have been in danger.[8] . . .

■   **Spain**

138.   *Borgia's Early Contacts with Jesuits*

Doctor Michael de Torres left Rome in September.[9] . . . He visited the Duke of Gandía and was deeply impressed by his profound humility, abnegation, and purity and by his zeal for total perfection. Ever since the death of the Empress, the divine Goodness had begun to bestow a large share of its gifts on the duke, Francis Borgia; after the death of his wife, who fell asleep in the Lord in May of this very year, he had devoted himself with his whole heart and energy to the pursuit of perfection. Using these Spiritual Exercises, by which he stirred up within himself humility and self-contempt, he wrote a small book. Master de Torres considered that this book would be extremely useful for any person who hoped to make progress in the spirit, and he supported its publication. But [Borgia] embraced the advice of Father Ignatius with so much reverence and submission of heart that even if he had earlier thought otherwise, he submitted without difficulty his own judgment to [Ignatius's] view.

This [spirit of submission] was not only evident in the college at Gandía but also in another work of piety. Lady Juana de Meneses had decided to grant an endowment toward building a convent for poor women and had entrusted its administration to the Society. But after pondering the reasons that Ignatius wrote and other suggestions regarding the administration of this institution (arrangements that would not require the ministry or work of the Society), the duke immediately acquiesced in the judgment of Ignatius and adopted his advice. Even though he and many others had completed the Spiritual Exercises with singular consolation and progress of soul, he hesitated somewhat. He believed that some approval of the Apostolic See should be sought, for fear that they may be [condemned] as a [dangerous] novelty. With the approval of Father

---

[8] For Bobadilla's own account of his close brush with death, see the letter he wrote Claude Jay from the Emperor's camp dated August 17, 1546 (*Nicolai Alphonsi de Bobadilla . . . gesta et scripta,* vol. 46 of the series Monumenta Historica Societatis Iesu [MHSI; Madrid, 1913], 104).

[9] Torres later served as provincial of Portugal and of Andalusia.

Ignatius, he obtained from the Supreme Pontiff an indult that all who made the aforesaid meditations followed by a general confession would receive a plenary indulgence.

140.   *The college at Gandía gets underway*

That same year the course in philosophy began in the college at Gandía. The professor was a Frenchman, François Onfroy. Previously for three days he had so skillfully defended theses in logic, physics, metaphysics, ethics, and theology before the duke, a certain bishop, and other learned and noble listeners that he seemed a paragon of talent, learning, and modesty, as well as an inexhaustible font of edification. All this, augmented by a Latin oration by this [professor], so pleased the duke that he wanted him to defend a second set of theses before the bishop of Valencia, whom he expected to arrive soon. This was done on the feast of Saint Francis [October 4] in the Church of Saint Clare with no less edification and satisfaction.

The students from among Ours were noteworthy for their talent and outstanding progress in the virtues. The duke wanted to increase the number of Ours at Gandía so that at least twelve would be engaged in studies. When Father Miró at Valencia directed certain learned young men through the Spiritual Exercises and saw that some of them were interested in the Institute of the Society, he wrote Gandía to inquire whether some of them could be sent there. The duke answered thus: Let him make every effort to send them, for Gandía would always have room to receive them. In addition, [Francis] wanted to have some [students] at Alcalá supported at his expense, and he sent a very polite letter to Silíceo, archbishop of Toledo, asking that, just as he had shown favor toward one of his sons to win his goodwill, he would direct the same gracious dispositions toward assisting the scholastics of the Society of Jesus at Alcalá.[10]

. . .

141.   *Using the Spiritual Exercises in Spain*

At this time the work of God was progressing at Gandía, and Father Andrés de Oviedo was directing some noblemen and even important women in spiritual meditations. As he wrote [to us], so great was the reputation of these exercises that when they were proposed to one group, others who were waiting for the same thing were disappointed that they had to wait their turn. [Oviedo]

---

[10] Silíceo was initially friendly toward the Society but later became its bitter enemy.

directed twelve or fourteen people at one time, and they all made general confessions. Some also turned their minds toward the Institute of our Society. Among others was a monk, a preacher and teacher of theology, who wanted to be exercised in humility, so he too made great progress in the Exercises. . . .

145.   *Araoz at Alcalá*

When Araoz visited Alcalá, in the college (called the Greater College), he preached with notable applause and success, as the confessions that followed clearly demonstrated, as did the Spiritual Exercises that were requested and the edifying public reforms of life that were observed. Among the college students were some who, without Father Araoz's knowing it, went around barefoot, carrying a sack and begging alms. Given their nobility and reputation, this did not arouse any scandal; indeed, it edified many who witnessed it. . . . When Araoz was in attendance at the death of the vice-chancellor of Aragon, the dying man demanded that [Araoz] spend many hours with him (nor did [Araoz] want to leave him); several important people who were with him there were so moved by the exhortations and other means by which he helped the dying man that some of them expressed their desire to yield up their souls into his hands. . . . Among them was a certain leading merchant who faced beheading; he insisted that [Araoz] be present at his execution. Otherwise, if anything should happen to him other than what was supposed to, Araoz should know that he would have to take the blame. . . .

156.   *Nuns and Muslims in Sicily*

. . . Father Jacob Lhoost was the first of the Society sent to Sicily. . . . He visited the hospitals and encouraged the sick to make their confessions, and he heard many confessions of the sick and others. He encouraged some slaves of Christians to accept the Christian religion, nor were his attempts at this in vain with all of them. Along with the vicar he encouraged reform among nuns who had been living on their own resources without religious discipline. He tried to accomplish this by sermons and confessions and individual conversations. One of these convents abandoned personal ownership and submitted to reformation. While he accompanied the vicar of the diocese on his visitation, he occupied himself in preaching, and he strove to instruct and exhort the poor in the hospitals to the right manner of living. It happened that in a certain home of Muslims, after hearing the confession of a sick old man, he exhorted the Muslims to convert to the Christian faith. They admitted to him that they could not gain eternal life without the faith of Christ, but they asserted that they were not yet ready to be baptized.

157. *Reforming Sicilian convents*

From there [Lhoost] went to Sciacca. While visiting the sick, he encouraged bystanders to a life worthy of Christians. Along with the vicar he devoted himself to reforming three convents. Because he began by hearing the confessions of certain nuns, he was hoping for a good and successful reformation.

Above all he encouraged individual nuns privately to lead a life without possessing anything individually. Along with the vicar he also did considerable work in examining the priests and encouraged them to live in a Christian manner and to perform their duties faithfully; other people as well [he urged] to receive the sacraments. He exercised the same ministries in various localities, both for the benefit of the clergy and the convents. He led one whole convent to a complete reformation. In another convent, a large one, he achieved a partial reformation; only some of the nuns surrendered all their private possessions. In another convent also deep divisions hindered its advance [toward sanctity]. He persuaded the abbess to resign her office. Thereafter, all were in harmony: young lay women were excluded from the convent, and a man was given the responsibility of receiving, distributing, and selling the handiwork that the nuns produced on their own. With cloister now observed, the nuns were led to a splendid reformation. He carried on similar activities when he came to Bivona; and when a whole convent would not accept reform, he urged individual nuns to make a start at reformation by resigning their personal property over into the hands of the abbess. This proved successful.

THE YEAR 1547

■ **Rome**

167.   *Loyola labors at Rome*

At the start of 1547 and throughout its course, the Society did much at Rome and everywhere else to increase the glory of God and expanded her ministries considerably. Its glowing reputation was very much enhanced. Because many places urged Father Ignatius to send men into the Lord's vineyard, he was able to retain few men at Rome, but those few with God's favor carried out simultaneously the tasks of many men. Father Ignatius now freed himself of the burden of Saint Martha's Convent by setting up one confraternity of men and another of leading Roman women to take charge of this charitable work. Father André des Freux began to preach at our church; Girolamo Otello, who had not yet been advanced to the priesthood, also began to employ his talent for preaching, manifesting a wonderful sincerity of heart and simplicity as well. [He preached] in the Convent of Saint Martha, in the hospital for the incurables, and elsewhere; so often did he preach that in one week he gave seventeen sermons.

It happened that when he was going to preach to the nuns in the Convent of Saint Anne, he divided his sermon into two parts. In the first of these, he encouraged the sisters to practice sincere poverty and give up all personal possessions. When he saw that he had now inflamed them to make this sort of renunciation of property, he added: "In the meantime, while I rest a little bit to prepare for the second part of the sermon, go to your rooms and carry to the feet of the abbess whatever private funds you have, because you now have recognized that if you keep one needle as your own property, it can lead you down to hell." They quickly got up, went to their rooms, opened their cabinets, and carried all they had there to the feet of the abbess; only then did they listen to the second part of the sermon. Girolamo did not actually witness this, because as usual a curtain blocked his view of the nuns. After the sermon was finished, the abbess summoned him and with great spiritual joy related what had happened.

168. *Polanco's own activities*

The secretary of the Society [Polanco] devoted himself to hearing confessions and also gave a sermon in the morning and an afternoon lecture in the church. He did not in the meantime cease serving in the kitchen and working in the dining room. He was also functioning as the procurator general and explaining Christian doctrine. At the beginning of this year, he stayed in Pistoia and preached every week in eight convents of nuns and took charge of leading them to [make] spiritual meditations—all this with not inconsiderable good results. But on feast days he preached in one of the main churches of the town (which the bishop wanted to give to the Society). He did not neglect, meanwhile, the exhortations and spiritual instructions that were given in one of the confraternities described above. Because many persons, both ecclesiastics and laypeople, met at the confraternity in pursuit of spiritual progress, and because it was reasonable to hope that [the confraternity would have] considerable effect in that city, he labored to formulate constitutions for it, so that [the members] themselves would make progress and help others by pious works. After he had dealt privately with the duke and duchess [of Tuscany] about some works of charity for their own spiritual advantage and that of their subjects and had preached in many parts of Florence, Father Ignatius called him to Rome in March because his blood relatives were causing the former a great deal of bother.[1]

169. *Steps toward a community at Salamanca*

. . . Cardinal [Francisco de] Mendoza, then bishop of Coria and later of Burgos, loved Ignatius and his companions warmly and wanted to have some help from one of them in the Spiritual Exercises, so he began negotiations aimed at setting up a college of the Society at Salamanca. But the report that Doctor Miguel de Torres had entered the Society and could be sent to Salamanca came as very welcome news to the cardinal's ears. He loved and supported learned men and had made much use of his friendship with the aforesaid

---

[1] Polanco's family bitterly opposed his becoming a Jesuit. At Florence Polanco encountered his younger brother Luis, a prosperous merchant there, who tried to encourage him to return to their hometown of Burgos. When Juan refused, his brother replied by locking him up in a room at his home, from which he escaped by climbing out a window and down a rope and went on to Pistoia. But Luis made use of his connections at Pistoia to have Juan brought back to Florence as a prisoner. Ignatius used his influence to have Juan freed and ordered him to come to Rome (Richard H. Dowling, "Juan de Polanco, 1517–1576," *The Woodstock Letters* 69 [1940]: 5).

Doctor Miguel de Torres at Rome. [De Torres] was said to be forty-six years old when he joined the Society at Rome, confirming this step with a vow; but because he had been sent by the so-called Greater College at Alcalá to Rome for important negotiations, he was not able to openly reveal this decision about his life until he had returned to Alcalá and rendered an account of how the negotiations had turned out. But this year that business was finished, and he indicated that he was ready for ministries under obedience. Therefore, as a favor to Cardinal Mendoza, Doctor Miguel de Torres was entrusted with managing the initial stages of a college at Salamanca this year, even though he did not travel to Salamanca till the next year.

172.   *Should there be women Jesuits?*

Right at the end of the last year and the beginning of this one, in compliance with the wish of the Supreme Pontiff, a handful of devout women came under the obedience of the Society. But because Ignatius was so involved in negotiations about more important matters and because he foresaw that such a burden would not be appropriate for the Society in the future, he secured from Pope Paul III that, even if such women were nuns or could adduce any other considerations, they should never be admitted under obedience to Ours (whether they wished to live either in communities or as private persons). That was granted this very year on May 20.

173.   *Further developments at Rome*

The vicar of Rome [Achinto] kept urging Ignatius to appoint some person from the Society to examine the men who were being promoted to holy orders. Although the work was clearly pious, Ignatius judged it inappropriate for our Society. But he could not wholly refuse this request of the vicar, who had greatly befriended the Society; accordingly, he added this condition: Ours were not to specify which ones were judged suitable or not; they would only report back to the vicar or his substitute what they found out about the person who had been examined. [Ignatius] also added that those to be promoted must first make a general confession to one of Ours; after that, if they wished to be examined, a different person who had been assigned to this [task] would examine them. . . .

Also at this time one of Ours made a presentation to the city's pastors about the responsibilities their ministry entailed. In his audience was the man who was substituting for the vicar; he suggested imposing a penance on those who without reason had avoided this presentation. Expositions of Christian doctrine and children's confessions were continued as usual. This same year a certain religious, a very devout man, attempted to unite a certain congregation of priests, known in Lombardy as the Somaschi, with our Society, constituting thereby a single body. But Father Ignatius modestly suggested that he did not see how this would advance God's glory. Hence, [the Somaschi] were united with the religious order of clerics regular that takes its name from the Theatine cardinal.[2]

174.   *Electing superiors at Valencia and Gandía*

We have already stated that communities had been started at Valencia and Gandía, but no superior had yet been installed to hold the office of rector among Ours. So Father Ignatius wrote letters to both communities and advanced many arguments demonstrating that they needed a superior whom they would obey like Ignatius himself and who would preside with the same authority that Ignatius would exercise if he were present. If anybody did not want to obey this sort of superior, he should leave the Society. But at that time [Ignatius] wanted the procedure for choosing a rector to be the same as the first Society had used in electing the general. He wanted this to be observed until something different was enacted through published constitutions. He himself approved in advance whomever they would elect this way; also, he added, this method was to be followed as long as no professed [father] was living there.

176.   *Training novices at Rome*

There was no separate house of probation at Rome. Still, those who were admitted, besides receiving careful training in the Spiritual Exercises, were nonetheless employed at hospitals in both spiritual and corporal ministries. They begged alms in the streets and much frequented places in the city and preached at street intersections. This they did to overcome in other ways their self-esteem and solicitude for their own honor. But when men otherwise quite respectable had done this a first, second, and third time, Ignatius did not allow them to continue it further. By permitting such things at the beginning, he brought it about that, once they had overcome their desire for prestige, they won for themselves a greater freedom in the Lord, joined to humility; and where it was

---

[2] The Somaschi were founded in 1534 by St. Jerome Emiliani (1481–1537) and approved by Paul III in 1540. Their union with the Theatines was short-lived, lasting from 1546 to 1555. The Theatines got their name from Chieti (Teate in Latin), the diocese of their cofounder, Cardinal Gianpietro Carafa (later Paul IV), who was no friend of St. Ignatius.

necessary, they would turn this foolishness in the eyes of the world into edification, lest what they were doing would seem very hard and difficult. This same
year Ignatius established the practice of writing every fourth month and other
devices that would contribute to unity in the Society by means of an interchange
of letters.

■ Italy

177.   *Further Jesuit activities at Trent*

Those living at Trent when the year began were by no means idle, since
two meetings were held daily, in the morning on moral reformation and in the
afternoon on the dogmas of the faith. The session on justification was held on
January 13 of this year. This subject completed at last, discussion about the
sacraments began. The legate, Cardinal [Cervini] of Santa Croce, charged Ours
with compiling the errors of the heretics, as was said above. As Ours collected
and organized them, so they were presented to the congregation by the legates—
first errors concerning the sacraments, second those concerning baptism, third
those concerning confirmation. These fathers [of Ours] stated their opinions on
all of these [questions], gaining everyone's approval. Father Canisius writes
thus: "Putting aside all my affection, I can swear with sincerity that there are
here many very learned theologians all around, whose judgment is acute,
careful, and wise about crucial questions; but among all of them there are none
more universally beloved and admired than these two, Laínez and Salmerón.
When the space of a single hour remained for a few [theologians] to speak, I
think that the presiding cardinal himself gave three hours and more for Father
Laínez to speak."

These [Jesuits] were commissioned to set down the places in the holy
councils, the decrees of the Supreme Pontiffs, and the writings of the holy
Doctors where errors of this kind were condemned. Again, just as Ours gave
these to the legates, so they were proposed to the theologians for examination.
Despite this, Laínez kept on with the task of preaching. Father Ignatius notified
Father Laínez that he should go to Florence, but the Cardinal of Santa Croce,
legate of the Apostolic See, wrote back to [Ignatius] that he was going to keep
[Laínez] for the sake of the greater public good, because he had given [Laínez]
the task of assembling the things just mentioned above. He asked Ignatius to
accept with equanimity that he was going to retain [Laínez] even a bit longer.
Nonetheless, he promised to send Laínez on at the first sign of Ignatius's will,
even if [Ignatius] should wish that the work there be left incomplete.

When Ignatius realized that these occupations were of great importance and when the papal vicar Archinto, who had also labored at Trent, asserted that nowhere among the nations could Ours labor more successfully, in that their work was being put to use every day, [Ignatius] judged that he should not call Ours away from there while the council was in session. On the third day of the following month of March, the seventh session was held on the sacraments, and on the eleventh of the same month the Supreme Pontiff in a *motu proprio* decided to transfer the council to another city [Bologna] because of the danger from disease-laden air. . . .

178.   *Broët and Palmio at Montepulciano and Bologna*

This year Father Francesco Palmio, who previously had been a disciple of the Society and had worked with several devout persons to set up a college, consecrated his whole self to the Society in the month of June. From this the man who had striven to enhance the Society's standing among others attained the same grace of a vocation from the Lord along with them. Father Paschase came to Bologna from Faenza (leaving behind an excellent reputation and a great longing [among the townsfolk] for his return); he also worked very usefully throughout the whole of Lent of this year in [hearing] confessions and [giving] the Spiritual Exercises in the Lord's vineyard. Even the legate, Cardinal [Cervini] of Santa Croce, made a weekly confession to him. But by working too hard he contracted headaches; at the advice of this cardinal, he went to recover his health at a certain spa near Montepulciano, where water trickling over his head made him feel much better.

Still, he was not wholly idle; he took care of finding clothes from the alms of other people for several poor young girls who were undergoing a similar treatment. In the villa of the cardinal's brother, which is called "Vivum," he gave the Spiritual Exercises to both this brother and his wife and heard their general confessions. He then went to Montepulciano, where he was of great help to many people. Among them were three sisters of the Cardinal of Santa Croce whom he introduced to the Spiritual Exercises.[3] After hearing many confessions, not a few of them covering whole lifetimes, and leaving many trained to make spiritual meditations and seriously devoted to reform according to their state [of life], he returned to Bologna, where during that whole year he was occupied with gathering in a very abundant harvest.

---

[3] One of the three sisters was the mother of St. Robert Bellarmine.

His efforts opened up for persons of both sexes the Spiritual Exercises, especially the First Week, which was followed by a general confession. Sometimes he was engaged in [giving] this version of the Exercises to twelve people at the same time. He also provided a useful service to nuns of a certain convent who were disrupting it with discord, to the scandal of the city. Meantime, Father Francesco Palmio was preaching and devoting himself [to hearing] many confessions.

Father Salmerón was occupied day and night in matters pertaining to the council. Even though no sessions were being held, still the smaller groups continued to meet; besides the discussions devoted to the sacraments, they also dealt with indulgences and purgatory.[4] Father Salmerón sometimes exercised the power that he had received from the legate, [the Cardinal of] Santa Croce, and absolved some of those who had fallen into the errors of the Lutherans. The divine Goodness called some of them back to a sounder attitude. Over a two-day period, Salmerón presented his view of the sacrifice of the Mass, to the great satisfaction of his hearers. . . . At the suggestion of Father Ignatius, they searched for some place that would be suitable for the Society, but they found none that was in accord with our Institute, even though the Cardinal of Santa Croce himself offered to help them. Meanwhile, at the Church of Santa Lucia they administered the sacraments to so many people that almost six hundred received Communion on Christmas. Not a few people were restored to the unity of the Church after having secretly lived in heresy or been entangled in serious excommunications for reading heretical books. Nor was there a lack of leading noblemen who drew profit from the Spiritual Exercises.

189.   *Ministries in Bassano*

One of those who left the college [at Padua] this year was Father Elpidio [Ugoletti], who had been in charge of the others; complying with Father Ignatius's orders, he left the Flemish father Peter Faber as superior in his place.[5] Another person who left that college was Father Stefano Baroello, who went to Bassano, where Father Laínez had preached one or two times and sown not a few splendid seeds of God's word on the rich soil [found there]. Stefano

---

[4] The council had been transferred to Bologna because of the threat of plague at Trent, but Charles V objected to the transfer; many of his bishops refused to go to Bologna, which delayed final decisions on issues.

[5] This Peter Faber De Smet (born at Brussels in 1518, died at Padua in 1548) should not be confused with Loyola's first companion, whose name we give in its French version.

devoted himself both to preaching and to hearing confessions. He strove to help a large group of boys in things spiritual. He presented the Exercises greatly benefiting many people thereby. He had two hundred or more communicants for the holy sacrament of the Eucharist. He administered the sacrament to the Confraternity of Saint Vitus, who were performing outstanding service in charitable works. He also devoted himself to helping nuns. What contributed to edification above all was that when he himself was suffering from great poverty in all things material and had many opportunities to accept money, he never accepted anything, not even from the things that were sent to him at his residence. He tried to improve monasteries and individuals not only by sermons but also by friendly conversation and by offering some written descriptions of how to live an upright life.

So great was the affection of many people to whom he had given spiritual instruction that they followed him around, blessing the father and mother who had procreated him. With tears and vows made to God (one of them promised to go about barefoot for a year), some nuns tried to get him to become their confessor. They had lived previously in that convent without observing poverty and had not gone to the sacraments for some time; but after they had confessed to him, God so opened their eyes and changed their hearts that they began to abound in the great gifts of God. Regretting their past life with sighs and tears, they were renovated in spirit and, casting away all their personal possessions, they then made great progress in spirit. . . .

194.   *Doménech urges reform in Sicily*

Father Jerónimo [Doménech] also advised the viceroy [Juan de Vega] that he had discovered other convents of that city [Palermo] very badly in need of reform. When the viceroy ordered several devout and prominent men to meet with Father Jerónimo and discuss applying a remedy, [the upshot was that] Father Jerónimo was given charge of examining the rules of the convents and visiting them, accompanied by the vicar. Although Father Jerónimo fell sick and so had to postpone his efforts to lead the convents back to a better state, still, when he had recovered his health, he carried out this pious task. His labor was not in vain, because Father Ignatius got help from the Apostolic See, just as he had done for convents in Catalonia. The viceroy Juan de Vega had written and requested [Ignatius] to do this. For, as the viceroy himself wrote, toward the end of the year two convents of nuns at Palermo were reformed through the work of Father Jerónimo.

In addition, that decree of Innocent [III] was promulgated at Palermo, according to which doctors should not visit sick people unless they had previously made their confession. This came about with the help of Doctor Ignacio Lopez and at the command of the viceroy, who was prompted [to do so] by the piety in his heart. Now one could see everywhere that the holy sacrament was being carried to the sick, and the doctors had coat pockets filled with written testimonials that sick people had made their confession. It was only with great effort that the confessors were able to satisfy so many sick penitents. The promulgation of the edict through the whole kingdom was then put into effect; this was very useful, for people in many places were embarrassed to confess in public. One hundred letters signed by the viceroy with the edicts attached were sent out through the hands of Father Jerónimo. Thus, finally, the edict came to be promulgated in all parts of that island.

195.   *Caring for orphans in Sicily*

Moreover, a home for orphans of both sexes was set up in Palermo. The viceroy wrote to Rome about this and wanted the help of Father Ignatius. Because they had found a house and church suitable for this purpose and because the city possessed more than two thousand scudi in annual revenue for orphan girls, it was less difficult, with help by the viceroy's authority and the charity of Lady Eleonora [his wife], both to start this very admirable work for boys and girls and to keep it going. Meanwhile, Father Jerónimo was working out a peace between certain confraternities, something of great importance. He contributed much to bringing tranquility to a certain city, namely, Trapani. Finally, Father Jerónimo also devoted himself to similar works of piety, prompting Lady Eleonora to thank Father Ignatius for having sent him to Sicily.

197.   *Helping prisoners*

When Father Jerónimo visited the public jails, he observed many poor people being held there on account of small debts. Therefore, he encouraged the viceroy to earmark a sum of money from fines to freeing twenty of these poor debtors—some of them had been held in jail for one year and some for two, to the considerable detriment of their wives and children. He arranged for fourteen others to go out under guard to a certain public work (namely, a fortified bastion), so that by their labor they might gain some earnings wherewith to free themselves [from debt and prison]. In the Spiritual Exercises he moved a certain man to excellent deeds. With the same means he also trained two priests in spiritual matters. One of them taught the orphans. The other went to Messina to set up a confraternity of clergymen to teach boys throughout the whole kingdom free of charge. His companion also helped at this. On the following Sundays and feast days, [Jerónimo] also began preaching at some of the main churches in Messina.

198.   *Doménech and the Exercises at Messina*

At Messina [Doménech] found many people who wanted to advance spiritually and learned that a certain priest who had made the Spiritual Exercises had achieved great progress himself and had gone on to share the [Exercises] with many others and to direct twelve people in them. A remarkable change could be seen in all of them. More than the others, a young merchant gave visible and extraordinary evidence of his progress. Father Jerónimo himself directed three men at the same time, among them a clergyman who was a baron's son. When his father could not tame him, he held [him] for three months on a galley ship; this man then changed marvelously for the better. A man called the Count of Candia made great progress through the same Exercises. Two other noblemen wanted to do the same; so did a certain convent of nuns and many others. But one [director] could not satisfy them all, especially when [Doménech] was preaching weekdays in various convents of nuns in addition to giving sermons on Sundays and feast days. Orphan boys who received the Exercises under his direction registered great spiritual progress, making evident to many observers what they had gained through the Spiritual Exercises.

199.   *Correcting irreverence in Church*

Through a great abuse at Messina, men had been accustomed to stroll about the churches during the sacred services, thereby giving considerable offense to God. But Father Jerónimo brought it about with the authority of the viceroy that this abuse was abolished throughout the kingdom. At Messina an edict against men of this sort was published, and then the vicars were ordered to promulgate it through the whole island.

201.   *Preparations at Messina for the first Jesuit college for lay students*

At the suggestion of Ignatius Lopez, a medical doctor, and with the support of Lord Didaco de Cardona, the syndic of the kingdom, serious negotiations about setting up a college at Messina got underway. The viceroy and his wife warmly encouraged this project. The viceroy judged that colleges could be set up not just at Messina but also at Palermo, Catania, and Calatafimi; but he wanted the city of Messina itself to make a request before he wrote to Father Ignatius. The proposal easily gained approval when Lord Didaco brought it before the city council. . . . When the request was made to the city [authorities], they quickly consented to give an appropriate residence and church and a fixed and secure annual income of five hundred gold [scudi] toward establishing the college.

The city gave thought to setting up a *studium generale* or university at Messina and required the Society to provide only four teachers. Of them, one would lecture on grammar, the second on philosophy, the third on Scholastic theology, and the fourth on cases of conscience. A certain confraternity of noblemen, which had a chapel dedicated to Saint Nicholas with a house attached, gladly offered their quite beautiful and spacious church to advance the good of the city and of such a worthwhile project. It was on one of the city's main streets and in a healthful location, with a garden and a residence well suited to studies and sufficiently quiet. At length the city magistrates came to the viceroy, Juan de Vega, and easily obtained his consent (which was necessary) and letters requesting both Father Ignatius and the ambassador of Emperor Charles V at Rome to obtain from the Supreme Pontiff whatever authorization was necessary for a university. At this time they were already thinking about expanding the college, and they decided to ask for one of the rather numerous abbeys in Sicily [whose income] was sometimes applied to hospitals and charitable works. Therefore, the city and Lord Juan de Vega wrote to Father Ignatius requesting that a college be set up at Messina, which would be of great benefit to the city. This petition Ignatius gladly granted at the start of the next year. Their request was made toward the end of 1547.

■ **Germany**

202.   *Bobadilla in Germany*

Emperor Charles V brought the war in Germany to a close during the first months of this year, 1547, and kept with him in captivity the Duke of Saxony along with the landgrave.[6] Father Nicholás Bobadilla was in that area

---

[6] The climactic Battle of Mühlberg (April 24, 1547) effectively ended the first Schmalkaldic War. John Frederick, elector of Saxony, was captured during the battle and

and spent the beginning of the year with the bishop of Passau, who entertained great goodwill and esteem for him. In that city Bobadilla preached Lenten sermons in Latin and engaged in other works of piety. Later he did the same at Regensburg when he went there after Easter. He did not labor there in vain, even though the town council as well as much of the city was corrupt. Among other things, he brought about a public ceremony or solemn procession to celebrate the Emperor's victory against the Lutheran princes, and he took care that there were other public ceremonies according to the Catholic rites, which had been abandoned in that city for some years. His reputation and authority were great with the prelates and princes of Germany, but above all with Ferdinand, the king of the Romans. As a result, the bishops of Vienna and Bratislava and many other men of great authority used his influence with the aforesaid king in their ecclesiastical negotiations. Taking into account the times and places, he gathered in no meager fruit from the sterile vineyard of Germany.

■   **France**

207.   *Developments at Paris*

A few of Ours were living in Paris this year, with Father Paolo de Achille in charge. Among them were Battista Viola and Father Jean Pelletier. They gave the Spiritual Exercises to certain individuals and weekly administered the sacraments of penance and the Eucharist at the Carthusian [monastery]. When the bishop of Clermont [Guillaume du Prat] returned to Paris from the Council of Trent, he greeted them through [the person of] his vicar, whom he sent to the Lombard College. When they came to see him, he received [them] with great humanity and kindness and recounted many things about the success that was due to the work of the Society, especially at the council; he related how a speech of Father Salmerón had brought many people to tears. He asserted that he intended to build a college of the Society—indeed, in Paris—adding that he would soon show his inner intention by taking prompt action in Paris. This year several men decided to enter the Society, among them one Father Robert Claysson. Some other Flemings—and these were students of theology—made the same decision, even though they did not carry it out at this time. . . .

Landgrave Philip of Hesse surrendered to Charles V in its aftermath.

■ Spain

208.   *Overview of the Society in Spain*

Toward the beginning of this year, Father Antonio Araoz returned to the court of Prince Philip. Father Ignatius had given him charge of Ours then living in Spain, and he was second in authority after Father Simão [Rodrigues], the provincial of Portugal. All of Spain was then his province: its territory was quite extensive, but its Jesuit residences were few in number; even the men subject to the Society were not many. As we saw in the preceding year, the Society began with five small communities: one at Coimbra where eight or ten men lived this year; a second at Pintia (called Valladolid), where three or four lived; the third and fourth were at Valencia and Gandía, where eight or ten, more or less, lived in each [community]; the fifth was at Barcelona, where there were three or four. In addition, there were a few at the royal court and others on missions.

At Toledo a noble matron, Lady Isabel de Silva, offered [Ours] a house and had at her disposal a large sum of money in the form of income to serve as an endowment for the college; but she hoped that orphan boys would live in one part of the house entrusted to the care of the Society. Because this was not in accord with the rationale of our Institute, Father Ignatius decided that we should not accept the gift of Lady de Silva, even though having a college at Toledo was much to be desired. Other people too were motivated to ask for colleges of the Society, and they were prepared to help [support them], for instance, in Seville, Zaragoza, and other places. The marchioness of Pliego wanted to pay the expenses of several students at Seville, and several others [were willing also] if a college could be set up at Cordoba. But the scarcity of workers did not allow the Society to expand [its operations].

211.   *Francis Borgia and the college at Gandía*

Meanwhile, the Duke of Gandía, Francis Borgia, who was living in his town of Gandía at the start of the year, was watchful in overseeing preparations for his college and university. With the help of Father Ignatius, he had obtained [approval for the college] that very year at Rome. This was the first university that the Society possessed. Granted that it was a tiny college, it was the first in Spain to have a solid endowment.

At the urging of the duke [of Gandía] that the *Exercises* of our Society be approved by the authority of the Apostolic See, the supreme pontiff Paul III handed them over to be examined by Juan de Toledo, the cardinal-bishop of Burgos, who was the inquisitor of heretical depravity; to Filippo Archinto, vicar for the city of Rome; and to Friar Egidio Foscharari, master of the Sacred Palace. With a solid consensus they all approved them and [sent] along a commendation of the two Latin versions, one of which is circulating in print. But when the duke [of Gandía] wrote to Father Ignatius a courteous request to have a colleges started at Zaragoza and Seville, [Ignatius] was not well enough informed about the Society's situation in Spain to be able to decide anything for certain. . . . Nonetheless, he gave permission to open a college in Zaragoza; it was tiny, but still it was the only college begun that year in Spain—indeed, in the whole Society. . . .

213.   *Ups and downs in Spain*

Father [Diego] Miró was giving the Spiritual Exercises to a large number of retreatants at Valencia. One of them, a certain Master Vincente, a doctor in theology and an outstanding preacher, was admitted to the Society. But because he showed so much tender affection toward his relatives and did not seem to hold his vocation in high enough regard, when Father Ignatius was consulted, he ordered the man to be dismissed from the Society, despite our great scarcity of workers. When our community at Valencia was suffering from a lack of temporal goods, the Duke of Gandía wanted to help them with a subsidy of a thousand ducats. As it happened, they ran into various obstacles in Valencia. Still, the scholastics made excellent progress in their studies.

Noble women were helping the work of Ours. A very prominent noblewoman named Lady Juana de Cardona, aided spiritually by Father Miró and others of our men, made admirable progress in the way of the Lord; had the Society allowed it, she would certainly have put herself under the obedience of the Society. In her zeal for penance, mortification, and charity, she had so progressed that she wanted to give her whole self to serving sick paupers in a hospital, and with great devotion she used to kiss the sores of the poor. She used to spend five, seven, or nine hours at a time in prayer, always on bended knees, and she dampened the ground with her perspiration. Although her husband had been killed long ago, after she had drunk in the spirit of the Lord, she went to the house of her husband's murderer to dine there; and to conquer herself even more, she wanted to take food from the hand that had stabbed her husband. In the same [hospital in which she had labored], she died, leaving behind a great reputation for sanctity.

Already at this time the Society received an invitation from Majorca to establish a college there, and the citizens wanted to support a number of scholastics there in their studies.

■ Portugal

214.   *The explosion of vocations in Portugal*

This year, 1547, the Society flourished notably in Portugal. At the King's court and at Lisbon, Ours made progress in the activities that we described when writing about the previous years. Father Estrada preached to the King, giving great satisfaction. The prince, who had Father Simão [Rodrigues] as his teacher and confessor, made progress. The usual works of charity were performed. When Father Ignatius wrote that some scholastics should be sent to him [in Rome], Father Simão easily sent six and offered even more if [Ignatius] wanted them. At Coimbra so many presented themselves to the Society that it was impossible to house them all. At the beginning of this year one hundred and fifteen [of Ours] lived at the college, of whom ninety-two were scholastics. Each year the King spent three thousand ducats to subsidize them. . . .

215.   *Emmanuel de Nóbrega's unique ministry in the villages*

Father Emmanuel de Nóbrega also showed his zeal through the villages and towns that are near Guardia by teaching those living there, drawing them away from mortal sins and calling them to chastity and a life worthy of Christians. Among these people were some priests who lived with their concubines as if they were their wives. Sometimes, with his feet bare and in great poverty, [Emmanuel] devoted himself to charitable pursuits, such as occurred in the town of Gabugal, where his preaching and teaching catechism resulted in a bountiful harvest. He lived by begging alms door-to-door and turned down offers of fine food and comfortable quarters.

He threatened the wrath of God against those who did not desist from their public sins. In one sermon, carried away by the fervor of his spirit, he promised that if sinners did not give up their manifest sins of this sort, he would go to each of their houses and with loud cries invoke the justice of God against that house. Such tactics induced terror in the people and drove them to amend their lives markedly. In another town riven by internecine factions and rivalries among the townsfolk, after giving his sermon he came down from the pulpit and knelt before them and humbly begged them with great fervor to restore mutual concord. He asked certain ones by name to pardon others and those others to pardon the first group. The result was that all his listeners on bended knees begged pardon of one another. Therefore, in this place and in all the other places where he stayed, he led many people to harmony.

But sometimes he was insulted in public, so that he would not fail to enjoy the prerogative of apostles, "to suffer dishonor for the name of Jesus."[7] In another town, when he arrived worn out and hungry, he nonetheless began to preach immediately; but because his speech was halting due to fatigue, everybody drifted away as he spoke. But when he requested the pastor to notify the people that he would be preaching in the afternoon, [the pastor], aware of the previous day's faltering performance, told the people, "That stammering clergyman will be preaching in a certain church; you can listen to him, but I fear you will draw little profit from him, because in the end he will say nothing of value." Still, the listeners came and received so much consolation from his sermon that they tried by every means to keep him in their town, even by petitioning the King for this favor, and they promised that they would all go to weekly confession. . . .

216.   *A sermon attracts a larger audience than a bullfight in Portugal*

. . . But when Gonzalvo [Vaz] was preaching in the morning in a certain town and a bullfight was scheduled for the afternoon, Gonzalvo announced that he would preach in the afternoon as well and observe who were the servants of the world and who were the servants of God, and promised that he would not cancel his sermon even if only one little old lady was listening. The people were so moved that nobody wanted to attend the bullfight; on the contrary, to show they were servants of God they filled the church before the time of the sermon and summoned the preacher to announce the word of God to them. These people marched down the path of the Lord with a wholly admirable fervor of spirit.

---

[7] Acts 5:41.

THE YEAR 1548

■ Rome and Spain

229. *Paul III approves the* Spiritual Exercises

As stated above, this year Paul III, the supreme pontiff, gave the Cardinal of Burgos (the inquisitor), Filippo Archinto (vicar of the Supreme Pontiff), and Egidio Foscharari (master of the Sacred Palace) the *Spiritual Exercises* for them to examine. They approved them with a laudatory testimonial. On July 31 that Pontiff in his apostolic letter confirmed and commended them, at the same time encouraging the faithful to make use of them. Hence, the mouths of those who censured the *Spiritual Exercises,* while knowing little about them, were clamped shut by the authority of this Holy See, so that from that time onward they could find in them nothing to calumniate.

Because in many places, and this year especially at Salamanca, the Institute of our Society was bitterly attacked by religious men of the Order of Preachers and the patience of Ours was tried in no small measure, Friar Francisco Romei, a man much respected and the Master General of the aforesaid order, sent letters patent urging that religious of his order stop vexing the Society; moreover, by the authority of his office, in virtue of the Holy Spirit and obedience and under penalties to be assessed at his discretion, he forbade his religious to dare to malign the Order and Institute of our Society whether in public lectures, sermons, meetings, or in private conversations—if I may use his words. On the contrary, like fellow soldiers they should strive to defend it against its attackers. Lord Francisco de Mendoza, cardinal-bishop of Coria at that time, took charge of these letters and also added his own out of his love for our Society and zeal for the common good.

■ Italy

230. *Ignatius works on the Constitutions*

At this same time Father Ignatius devoted his efforts to both the Constitutions and the rules; relying partly on prayer, partly on careful reasoning, and partly on experience, he gradually crafted what he later promulgated as the basic law of our Institute.

231.   *Origins of the college at Messina*

Toward the beginning of this year, the viceroy of Sicily and the city of Messina diligently took action, sending letters to the Supreme Pontiff and to Father Ignatius about a college at Messina. And so it turned out. Colleges of this sort came to be established in these regions when Ours undertook the responsibility of teaching there, although Ours had already begun to teach at Goa in India and Gandía in Spain. Before those destined to inaugurate this college had left Rome, Father Ignatius asked all members of the community to give their replies to four questions and required an answer from everyone. First, were these individuals prepared and ready to go to Sicily or not, and would they embrace with greater enthusiasm whatever role the superior, who held the place of Christ, would assign to them? Second, would the person who would be sent there be prepared for any external ministry (if he should be uneducated); and if he should be educated, would he be prepared to interpret texts in any discipline as he was commanded under obedience, whether it be in Scholastic theology or Sacred Scripture or philosophy or the humanities (for these were the four areas in which lectures were to be delivered)? Third, would a person sent as a student devote himself to whichever discipline [Ignatius] wanted, according to the command of obedience? Fourth, besides being obedient in carrying out what they had been commanded, would they regard whatever the superior would indicate to them as the better course by submitting their own judgment and will to holy obedience?

When all gave the proper answers, he designated those who were to be sent. Among them was Father André des Freux, a Frenchman; Father Peter Canisius, a German; Father Benedetto Palmio, an Italian; Father Jerónimo Nadal, a Spaniard; and Annibale de Coudret, a Savoyard.[1] Thus did charity and obedience join very diverse nations together. There was a problem about the teaching methods of some of those being sent. [Ignatius] wanted this handled in his presence. Finally, he wanted to bring the [future faculty] before Pope Paul III, who received them kindly and sent them off with an apostolic blessing and a fatherly exhortation, in which he responded to a very deferential address of Peter Canisius.

---

[1] On Nadal's role in the early Society, see William J. Bangert and Thomas M. McCoog, *Jerome Nadal, S.J.: Tracking the First Generation of Jesuits* (Chicago: Loyola University Press, 1992).

233.   *Laínez at Florence*

. . . That city has the praiseworthy practice of bringing to the cathedral church sinful women on the day when the Gospel about the sinful woman who approached Christ in the Pharisee's house is the theme of the homilies, so that if God has touched the hearts of some of them, they may turn away from their shameful life. A huge crowd made up not only of this class of women but also of the [ordinary] citizens gathered on that day. From them seven or eight who repented were welcomed into the homes of respectable women, so that they might find help in entering upon an honorable way of life.

The canons and other citizens indicated their eager desire for a college of Ours and promised to contribute a large part of their revenues to support our men. The duchess pledged her help in setting up a college at Pisa, perhaps to keep Laínez from leaving there. At the request of the commander of the citadel, he preached in Spanish on Palm Sunday to the garrison of soldiers, much to the consolation of his listeners.

[Laínez] received a letter in which the duchess summoned him to Pisa so that she could listen to his sermons and make use of his services in hearing the confessions of her household and confer with him about her spiritual concerns. Therefore, he substituted Father Jerónimo to preach in the cathedral church while he was gone. Once arrived in Pisa, he began to move souls to piety by preaching, by private conversations, and by hearing the confessions of important people at that court; among them were the daughter and the sons of the duke, who were still young boys. Tearing himself away from them, he returned to Florence, for the duchess put the common good ahead of her own consolation. Thus he concluded his sermons at Pisa and resumed the earlier ones at Florence. Although Father Jerónimo did his task most competently, there was no other way to satisfy the great desire for Laínez himself. . . .

When Father Ignatius ordered [Laínez] to go to Venice, [the latter] left Florence and went there to deal with the arrangements involved in taking possession of the priorate, which was united to the colleges at Padua and Venice. (Ignatius anticipated considerable difficulty in this matter.) Although Duke Cosimo had promised to provide Ours with a place [to live] and financial aid to support some of our scholastics at Pisa, the matter remained in suspense either because of Father Laínez's departure or because Father Ignatius did not think it good to press the matter at that time.

234.   *Negotiations at Venice and Padua*

Father Claude Jay along with his companion arrived at Venice on April 18, where they found the prior of the Holy Trinity [Andrea Lippomano] animated by a paternal affection for the Society but not at all confident that he could obtain permission from the senate [to transfer ownership of his priory to the Society] unless they could find help elsewhere. They went to Padua and publicly took spiritual possession [of the priory] on the sacred feast of Saint Mark [April 25]. Then, returning to Venice while the negotiations were carried on, they began devoting themselves to declaring the word of God to the people, as was the Society's custom, and to other spiritual ministries. But Father Claude had to return to Ferrara when that negotiation was further protracted. Some of our noble friends proposed this negotiation in the chamber of the [Venetian] Senate, presenting also the apostolic letters; at first the senators commended the proposal and addressed many kind words to the prior for having done something that was so pious and contributed so much to the common good. But meanwhile some difficulties were raised (by the prior's relatives, it is believed) when the question was taken up in the Great Council . . . forcing the matter to be deferred. . . .

236.   *Salmerón at Bologna*

From the beginning of this year till Easter, Father Alfonso Salmerón was working at Bologna. The Council [of Trent], which had been moved to Bologna, had not yet been dissolved even though it had enacted nothing important during this year, and gradually some prelates went off to Rome, while others went elsewhere. Nonetheless, Salmerón continued performing the works of the Society at Bologna. He presented the Spiritual Exercises to a certain prelate and to other leading men; he heard the confessions of various noblemen.

Still more varied was the work of Father Paschase [Broët], who presented the Exercises very successfully to many of both sexes—among others, to more than thirty noble women. These women, who put aside various worldly pomps and devoted themselves to reforming their lives, taking care of their families, giving alms, and praying, made great progress in the way of the Lord. Some men among those with whom he worked turned their heart toward the Society. Not a few young women made progress in the same way and decided to enter the religious life. He added to the Spiritual Exercises the practice of frequent confession and Communion, so that they might be more efficacious.

. . .

238.   *Salmerón at Verona*

As we wrote above, Father Salmerón went to Venice. When the business involved in [our] taking possession of the priorate at Padua was completed, he went on to Verona, in order to satisfy Bishop Luigi Lippomano, who had been of much help in [the Padua acquisition]. As long as he lived in that city, he was occupied on Sundays and feast days with lectures on the Sacred Scriptures, namely, the Epistle to the Romans. He also helped some convents of nuns by preaching the word of God. As his lectures continued, he drew a larger and more noble audience, whom he left very satisfied and edified. The vicar of the bishop wanted him to visit all the monasteries subject to the ordinary, but at the start he undertook only half of them, leaving the rest for later. Among the good results of his ministry at Verona were that many of those in possession of heretical books burned them and that those who had doubts about the Catholic faith and were inclined to the sectarians were confirmed in their Catholic religion and abandoned their errors. Arousing deep emotions in the vicar and others, Father Salmerón departed, called elsewhere by obedience: he had to pull himself away from there because the Duke of Bavaria had asked for and received from the Supreme Pontiff his assignment to Germany. Before this he preached the upcoming Lent at the city of Belluno.

243.   *Starting the college at Messina*

Father Jerónimo Nadal with the others mentioned earlier left Rome for Sicily as spring drew near. On their journey they moved many souls to devotion, sometimes by preaching, sometimes by hearing many confessions. They also tried successfully by disputations or private conversations to bring to a sounder state of mind some people who did not think as they should about the faith. They finally arrived safely at Messina right on the octave of Easter of this year, 1548. They were welcomed with every evidence of humanity and charity, displayed not only by the viceroy and Lady Eleonora, his wife, a woman of lofty virtue, but also by the city itself, which evinced the strong support in their hearts for the foundation of this college. Although the Church of Saint Nicholas and a house were set aside for Ours, they nevertheless lived in a rented house for some months because much construction was required to bring proper decorum to the church and to furnish our dwelling and the schoolrooms. While [Ours] opened the school and began zealously to benefit their neighbors, a nearby house was purchased and a garden acquired and the surroundings of Saint Nicholas were suitably arranged at considerable expense to the city. This year it disbursed almost twenty-five hundred gold scudi over and above the five hundred in annual income for supporting Ours that had been allocated by the unanimous consent of the city council and ratified by the viceroy. A public ceremony was also held in the presence of the viceroy himself in which the land of Saint Nicholas was turned over to the Society.

The city entrusted a certain nobleman with the care of the building, and he in turn employed an outstanding architect and built six interconnected classrooms outside the dwelling place of the college. Although the citizens needed no persuasion to be in favor of this project, the authority and support of Didaco de Córdoba, syndic of the kingdom of Sicily and of the viceroy himself encouraged them not a little. Almost beyond belief was the unfailing warmth with which the viceroy embraced our Society. The number of [students] who attended the classes for beginners was large enough right from the start; fewer were those who came to the upper classes—as is usual. The college offered not just the lessons [in those subjects] that the city had requested in its letters but taught many others out of charity or to help the young men.

The teaching method of the University of Paris was gradually introduced there. Father Nadal assigned three teachers for grammar: Father Benedetto Palmio was in charge of the first class, Annibale de Coudret of the second, and Giovanni Battista [Passeri] of the third. Father Canisius taught the art of oratory, Master Isidoro [Bellini] taught dialectic, Father André des Freux taught Greek literature, and Father Nadal [taught] Hebrew, but left the prelections to Father André; for although [Nadal] was occupied with the administration of the college, he also taught Scholastic theology in the morning and gave lessons on cases of conscience in the afternoon.

248.   *Our ministries in Sicily expand*

Many other works of religion were carried out in the Kingdom of Sicily through the zeal of the viceroy, Juan de Vega, and at the persistent suggestion of Father Jerónimo Doménech; for instance, [caring for] groups of orphan boys and girls, reforming convents occupied by nuns, setting up the teaching of Christian doctrine, doing other good works benefiting the poor people kept in prison, and also generously distributing alms even beyond the confines of the Kingdom itself. Thus, the Convent of Saint Martha at Rome profited from the charity of the viceroy. Because Father Jerónimo Nadal had a great reputation for learning, many noble people trusted his judgment when they had to make decisions, even involving matters of great importance; and indeed the most respected men of the city and those holding offices in the administration hurried to get his advice.

250.   *Convent reform in Sicily*

Among the other convents of nuns that received spiritual help from Ours, there was one at Messina where almost all the nuns were aroused to devotion through the Spiritual Exercises and were led back to the frequent use of confession and Communion—on Sundays, that is. Through the exertions of Father Jerónimo Doménech, another convent at Agrigento accepted common life and the observance of poverty by getting rid of private funds, or rather by contributing them to the common purse. Through sermons, the Spiritual Exercises, and general confessions, Father Stefano Baroello likewise so influenced a third [convent] at Palermo that those [nuns]—or certainly some of them—who previously were rather obstinate and did not want to make detailed confessions, threw themselves at his feet and showed themselves prepared for surrendering their private caches of money and for reformation in all aspects [of their lives].

251.   *A boy preacher and vocations at Messina*

A certain thirteen-year-old boy came to Messina with his paternal uncle. By a special gift of God, he had begun preaching at age five and had so persevered in this work that he stirred up great astonishment among the people, especially because of the incredible grace and freedom with which he presented the word of God. When the viceroy's wife, Lady Eleonora, heard him preaching, she began to show him great kindness and asked Ours rather insistently to accept him into our house, so that he could mature [toward greater] perfection. She zealously requested this in a letter she wrote to Father Ignatius. But it seemed better that [the child] get his education among the orphan boys at Messina and make frequent visits to Ours, so that he might make progress in his [spiritual] life and learning.

Because a large number of students aspired to the Institute of our Society, it seemed good to Father Nadal to give the Spiritual Exercises to the more select ones and carefully choose whom to admit to the Society. Still, he did not want any of the students to be persuaded to enter the Society; rather, he wished them to go to the sacraments frequently, so that, if God should be pleased to call them, they would be better prepared to hear his call, even as this had [already] begun to happen.

■ Germany

256.   *Bobadilla in Germany and the* Interim

While these things were going on in Italy, Father Nicolás Bobadilla was working in Germany, accompanying the courts of both Emperor Charles V and of [Ferdinand] the King of the Romans and making useful contributions to matters affecting the common good and also that of private individuals. . . . At Augsburg he wrote many tracts relating to the religious reform in Germany; these he decided to send to Cardinals Farnese and [Cervini] of Santa Croce.[2] . . . If there was ever a time when this task would be useful, he was convinced that this was the year when it would be of the greatest use; for now that Charles V had recently achieved victory and held the Duke of Saxony and the landgrave [of Hesse] in captivity, many prelates, princes, and people even in Saxony were beginning to turn their hearts to the old religion.[3] Seeing that the Germans are regarded as rather sluggish and cold by nature, it seemed even more essential that some people would try to win them back to the Catholic religion.

Although the Emperor was of the opinion that he could go forward in this business only gradually, he still wanted some men whose efforts and preaching would cause the Germans to glow with spiritual warmth. [Bobadilla] asserted that it was amazing how many returned to the true religion, despite the Emperor's silence and the small number of workers in the Lord's vineyard at Augsburg. As is certain from the letters sent from Germany at that time, the electors of the Palatine and of Brandenburg along with their territories had been led back to the bosom of the Church; for when the aforesaid princes were at Augsburg, they joined their wives in participating with great devotion in all the Lenten services. Duke Maurice [of Saxony] was also thought to have been led back and to have sent men to the people under his jurisdiction to encourage them in his name to do likewise. Brandenburg also commanded his subjects to abstain from eating meat during Lent and to confess and receive Communion in the old Catholic way, and that very year he promised that he wanted to restore to the Church all that he had taken away from it; and when on Holy Thursday a procession of flagellants (as they call those who whip themselves) was to take place according to Spanish and Italian custom, the Germans were greatly

---

[2] Alessandro Farnese was the grandson of Paul III and perhaps the richest and most influential cardinal at Rome. He was a supporter of the Jesuits and later underwrote much of the cost of building the Gesù.

[3] Actually it was the elector of Saxony that Charles held captive; Duke Maurice of Saxony had fought on the Emperor's side in the First Schmalkaldic War.

impressed when they did not cancel the event in view of the danger presented by the snow and frigid temperatures.

When the nobles (as was their custom) carried about a great number of blazing torches and returned to the hospice from the church and passed in front of the house of the mark [marquis] of Brandenburg, he began to weep profusely when he along with his wife gazed on the blood that [the flagellants] had shed. When some of the Lutherans murmured that they did not believe it was true blood oozing from their bodies, he took care that some bloody undergarments be brought to him and a whip as well, so that he could know for certain whether it was blood.

At Ulm many confessed and communicated in the Catholic way—more than seven thousand Germans, it is said. The sacrifice of the Mass and the sacrament of the Eucharist began to be restored in Germany. Negotiations were started in the hope of reaching some sort of religious agreement until a general council should determine what must be held. This agreement they called the *Interim*. But when Bobadilla assessed this sort of agreement (the *Interim*) as quite useless for promoting religious negotiations and made every effort to oppose it in word and writing, the ministers of the Emperor, who wanted the agreement to be completed before the Emperor left for Flanders, ordered him in the Emperor's own name to leave Germany, even though many in the court of the princes had great affection for him. . . .

■ **France**

259.   *The Jesuits at Paris*

In France the only residence our men possessed as yet was in Paris. Father Paolo de Achille left there and worked for a time in Rome. Father [Giovanni] Battista Viola was in charge of our men while he and our collegians devoted themselves to studies. Meanwhile, through the Spiritual Exercises and the ministry of confession and Communion, he cultivated some students who seemed like future workers in the Lord's vineyard. Among those who entered the Society this year was Everard Mercurian, now the general superior of the whole Society. Since he had made great progress the previous year in the Spiritual Exercises, he went to Liège to put his household affairs in order and dispose [of his property]. This was the time when those mentioned earlier were going to leave Belgium for Rome. He returned to Paris and was admitted to the Society, for he had previously studied philosophy and theology. He quickly won extraordinary praise among Ours who were at Paris for how he dealt with people's souls and advanced their spiritual progress.

260.   *Melchor Cano attacks the Jesuits*

. . . There was a certain religious [Melchor Cano is meant here] of the Order of Preachers in the illustrious College of Saint Stephen; famous for his learning, as erudite in his writings as he was renowned for his preaching, he lectured from the magisterial chair (called that of the *first hour*). He persuaded himself that the end times were already at the door and that the Antichrist had been born. For various human reasons, he was hostile to Father Ignatius, whom he had known at Rome. The conviction that both Ignatius and his companions were the precursors of the Antichrist began to take root in his heart and could not be eradicated. He wanted to make the signs of the Antichrist and his ministers apply perfectly to our men. Hence, he began to brandish these spears [his accusations] against the Society, its Institute, and its members both in private conversations and in his Lenten sermons, to such an extent that almost all his hearers recognized that he was speaking about our men. So great was his reputation and his influence on the people that they pointed their fingers at our men whom they saw walking down the street and warned one another to beware of their tricks, because they feared that [our men] were servants and supporters of the Antichrist.

Respected men, many of whom Doctor Torres consulted, did not approve of the zeal or prudence of this sort of preacher. [Torres] had greeted the preacher himself politely before he attacked our men. Nonetheless, [Cano], both by his own efforts and those of another preacher of his order whom perhaps he had won over to his viewpoint, wanted to harass our men, who had not yet set foot in Salamanca. When Doctor Torres finally met with him face to face and politely asked him to restore the besmirched reputation of the Society, which the Apostolic See had approved, he did not persuade him to take a more balanced attitude toward Ours; on the contrary, [Cano] began to make this and that objection, asserting that the people should be forewarned so that they would not allow themselves be deceived. He also said that nothing displeased him more than that Doctor Torres—a man he said he thought well of—was one of Ours. He asked a certain famous preacher of his order, who is called Juan of Segovia, to join him in attacking the Society. After [Cano] had spoken at length to convince him, [Juan], prudent man that he was, smiled and answered with a single word that it was not appropriate for him to condemn that Institute before the Church had condemned it.[4] . . .

261.   *Opposition to the Jesuits at Alcalá*

. . . So that they might appear to have great skills at divination, some people who from the outset had not thought well of our Institute boasted that the Society would soon be destroyed. Moreover, the archbishop of Toledo [Silíceo], who showed himself less than fair toward Ours, threatened that he was going to come to Alcalá and examine both our lives and our ceremonies and Institute. . . . Moved by these [anti-Jesuit vituperations], as we have said, the rector called in Francisco de Villanova [the Jesuit superior]; he satisfied the [university] rector by explaining everything in detail and asked him to convoke a meeting of the Theology Faculty and look into all the causes of this rumor and of the whole disturbance and then make a list of those points about which they [the faculty] wished clarification. [Villanova] would be most grateful if the truth were sought out with the greatest rigor and that, if it pleased the rector, this examination should be entrusted to those who had showed themselves the most opposed [to the Society]. This last suggestion delighted the rector, and he turned the affair over to the three doctors who had in public shown themselves more jealous of the Society than the others. Villanova went to them and satisfied all their doubts concerning both the Spiritual Exercises (about which they had harbored many false notions in their hearts) and the rest of the things pertaining to our Institute and our way of proceeding.[5] . . .

262.   *Juan de Avila fosters vocations to the Society*

At this time there were a number of priests in Andalusia who were stirred to devotion by a venerable man and outstanding preacher of God's word, Master [Saint Juan de] Avila; they were well enough trained in what relates to prayer and zeal for souls. Although he had given thought to setting up a congregation consisting of such men, he discovered great difficulty in carrying this plan out; he noticed, meanwhile, men of our Society in Spain aiming at the same goal. Persuading himself that the divine Goodness had already accomplished through Father Ignatius what he had in mind, he decided to give no

---

[4] For an account of Cano's attack on the Jesuits, see Antonio Astráin, *Historia de la Compagñia de Jesús en la asistencia de España* (Madrid: Razón y Fe, 1912), 1:321–40.

[5] For opposition to the Jesuits at Alcalá and to the Spiritual Exercises, see ibid., 1:341–84.

more thought to founding a new congregation but determined to send his
disciples to the Society.

And so at various times many came to it, distinguished by outstanding
gifts of God. One of them was Master Gaspar Lopez, who had taught several
young men of outstanding talent in the town of Jerez in the diocese of Seville
and had begun to found a college there in which philosophy and theology were
taught. Leaving everything behind, he joined the Society; but because his city
had gathered a group of its townsfolk together [seeking education], it took
serious umbrage when he departed before completing his theological lectures.

[The city] sent a messenger after him and asked Father Master Avila to
send Gaspar back to [the town], at least for a time. The city made sweeping
assertions about [how much] his work promoted the affairs of the college for
God's honor; but they promised that once the course in theology would have
been finished, he could finally go to the Society. It seemed to God's glory that
he should accede to the city's desire in this matter, and after shedding many
tears Master Gaspar returned there. He was thinking that he would later increase
the Society not only by joining it himself but by leading many of his students as
well [to join]. But meanwhile he humbly sought to be admitted to the Society
and begged to have one of Ours sent there who would have authority over him
and the others.

267.   *Controversy over frequent Communion at Valencia*

Our men at Valencia acquired a fairly large and comfortable house with
a spacious garden, as well as a newly acquired adjoining house that would serve
as a church in which to preach. Our brethren who were engaged in studies there
attended classes in the public academy with great edification; the professors too
admired and greatly commended their learning, and their modesty as well, as
they pursued their degrees. . . . Among the other things that helped considerably
to diffuse our good reputation extensively among the people was that a certain
pious and wealthy man gave Father [Diego] Miró a large sum of money to be
distributed among the poor. He personally undertook this labor of distributing
these funds, fearing that otherwise this charitable work would be neglected. He
sought out poor people through the parishes of the city, especially those who
were ashamed to beg in public and yet were hard pressed by poverty. But it was
not proper to carry on this task for a long time because for good reasons it
seemed better that people other than Ours should distribute alms of this sort.

The Jesuits formed friendships not only with the nobility and men of the religious orders but also with the professors and those who held the first [chairs] in the university. On Saturdays and Sundays [our men] heard many confessions. They arranged dowries for some orphan girls and, finally, they busied themselves with other kinds of charitable works, thereby contributing to the edification of the city.

Among their major achievements was fostering frequent confession and Communion. The devil resented these developments and led some people to have doubts [about them]. Thus it happened that one preacher recommended their frequent use, and another attacked it. As a result, a mighty uproar erupted among the people over this controversy. When the archbishop became aware of this, he called together nearly all the theologians of the city during the Lent of this year, in order to settle this question after he had heard their opinions. Shortly afterwards he had an announcement proclaimed throughout the city that he himself would preach in the cathedral church on the Sunday after Easter and would explain what should be held in this controversy. He forbade others to preach elsewhere on that day, and he himself preached for two hours. As he was a man not only of piety but also of learning and endowed with a special gift for speaking, he fulfilled his duty magnificently. To conclude, he praised the frequent use of Communion and granted general permission to everybody to communicate every Sunday. If some wanted to communicate daily, they should not do so without consulting him; taking into account their desires, he was not going to deny permission when it contributed to the glory of God and their own advantage. . . .

270.   *Using the printed* Spiritual Exercises *at Gandía*

This year [Ours] at Gandía received the *Spiritual Exercises* as they had been translated into Latin, confirmed by the Apostolic See in the attached apostolic letters, and printed at Rome. They received them at Gandía with so much consolation and heartfelt devotion that all of Ours, from first to last, wanted to meditate on one exercise each day in place of their morning prayer. The duke [Francis Borgia], too, and his aunt, Lady Francisca, followed this devotion of theirs. This year some men at Gandía also decided to enter the Society, and several of them were admitted. . . .

271.   *The college at Gandía*

Construction of the college at Gandía had already been completed this year, but our men had to wait awhile until [the mortar] dried out. At length, on the vigil of the Lord's Ascension of this year they moved into the living quarters of the new college, and on the day of the Ascension itself they celebrated the sacrifice of the Mass for the founder in the new church—as our Constitutions prescribe—using our customary style of singing. That same day they placed the most holy Sacrament in that church, dedicated to Saint Sebastian; and after the lunch (during which the duke with his children and many others honored us [with their presence] in the new refectory), a theological disputation was held with Master François Onfroy defending and Father Diego Miró, who had come from Valencia, presiding. . . . There were thirteen of Ours who that day began to live in the new college. Ten neophytes, sons of Muslims, were housed in a certain remote part of the college.[6] At that time the income was almost five hundred ducats, more or less; the following year it was almost eight hundred, and shortly afterwards there was hope that it would reach a thousand; that would be adequate to provide for twenty-five collegians in addition to the neophytes.

Since the university had already been built and confirmed by the authority of the Apostolic See—indeed, with the privileges granted to other universities—the rector of our college was also the future rector of the university. Thus, the first rector of the first university possessed by the Society was Father Andrea de Oviedo, although subordinate to him another of Ours had the responsibility of training and directing the neophytes. This year the more complete [curriculum of] studies began in all the faculties, even though during the preceding [year] Ours had studied logic, had attended lectures on ethics on feast days, and had theses presented and held disputations every Sunday afternoon; there were also some lectures on theology. . . .

272.   *Ignatius limits long prayers and physical penances*

It happened that the inclination of both Father Andrea de Oviedo and François Onfroy toward the internal practice of things spiritual was so powerful that Father Ignatius felt it absolutely necessary to apply moderation. Father

---

[6] In some quarters, especially in eastern Europe, this term (*Agarenus*) has been used to designate North African Muslims; in western Europe it has also been used sometimes to refer to Gypsies. The first sense seems more likely in this context, even though Latin has other more obvious words available to translate "Muslim."—ED.

Andrea himself wrote that over and above the time he spent in reciting the Divine Office, he devoted at least three more hours daily to prayer and, depending on the number of official duties that demanded his attention on a given day, he spent more than three additional hours in this practice. As regards inflicting penances upon his body, he beat himself three times a day with a whip for the sake of the specific and general needs of his neighbors. Such a quantity of tears flowed that he had to employ considerable effort in holding them back since they were harming his eyes. . . . Sometimes his inclinations (which now perhaps seemed to be more properly an impulse from the tempter rather than from God) reached such a stage that he no longer wished to have any dealings with his neighbor if he could help it, except insofar as obedience or God's inspiration or at least right reason obliged him to engage in them; the rest of his time he desired to give to contemplation and prayer.

Father François Onfroy, as the duke himself wrote to Rome, began at midnight and devoted seven continuous hours to prayer. The situation finally reached the point that, motivated by a great impulse of the spirit, they both aspired to retreat to a desert. So Father Andrea wrote Father Ignatius in both their names and asked permission for this, adducing many reasons. But Father Ignatius, who was endowed with a singular gift of God in discerning spirits, wholly disapproved of this as something alien to our Institute because it would impede not only progress in studies but also helping our neighbors. Indeed, he ordered Father Andrea to come to Rome unless something else seemed better to the Duke of Gandía. . . .

274.   *Borgia secretly takes vows*

Already during the previous year a permission (the name of the beneficiary not being specified) was obtained from the Supreme Pontiff (as has been said often) for the Duke of Gandía to make his profession, but on condition that he retain the administration of his duchy and all his goods for three years, to be counted from May of this year, so that he could make arrangements for his daughters and make provisions for his sons' futures, and also bring to completion the college and other pious works already started. After the duke had received this permission, he immediately summoned the provincial, Father Antonio Araoz; but when [Aroaz] on the day of the Purification of the Blessed Virgin [February 2] was hindered [from being present] by sickness or business, the duke on the very day of the Purification made his solemn profession in secret, and he performed this pious exercise with great consolation of heart. . . .

Already at that time, after his wife had died and he had made the Exercises, he had consecrated himself to God by taking simple vows; now he daily made great progress in all spiritual virtues. As we have written about Father Andrea, so too Francis Borgia himself seems to have gone somewhat to excess, driven by a holy fervor, in the time [devoted] to prayer, in abstinence, and in mortifying his body by hairshirt and whip.

275.   *Loyola cautions Borgia about prayer and mortification*

When he consulted Ignatius about these practices, he replied as follows. (A copy of the letter still exists in which Ignatius replied to his appeal for advice.) What he had done so far, Ignatius wrote, was absolutely to be attributed to God; but while some spiritual and bodily exercises are appropriate for one time, different ones are appropriate for another time. It seemed quite enough if he cut in half the time he gave to prayer (his prayer was, however, very protracted) and devote [that time] to studying letters, so that he might strive to serve God and be of help to his neighbors not merely by learning infused by God but also by learning acquired [by his own efforts]. He said that [Borgia] could obtain greater virtue and grace from God and he could better serve him anywhere by [performing] various duties rather than only one duty, even if that one were prayer. As regards fasting and abstinence, since by the grace of God he already possessed a flesh free from the more serious temptations and sufficiently subject to the spirit, he should not abstain to such a degree that his stomach's capacity to digest was weakened, as had already begun to happen. On the contrary, his natural powers should be strengthened by appropriate foods. [Ignatius] greatly hoped to persuade him of this: Because the soul and body belong to God, care must be given to render God an account for them both; he must not allow his sound body and its vigor to waste away, lest he make his soul itself less useful for its tasks. . . .

■ **Portugal**

278.   *Overview of Spain and Portugal*

Here was the situation in Spain.[7] The Society was making steady progress in Portugal, thanks to God's grace. The Society resided in three places that year, although one of them was not altogether stable; namely, the royal court, where Father Simão [Rodrigues], the provincial, resided in order to fulfill his

---

[7] In Polanco's usage the term *Hispania* embraces the whole Iberian peninsula.

office as tutor to the prince, [which brought] great spiritual advantage to that dignitary, who made his weekly confession to Father [Simão]. Since [the prince] earlier seemed to be of a very different disposition, his inclination to piety aroused everybody's admiration. Simão also had great influence with the King and the other leading men of the Kingdom; this influence he used to promote many works of devotion and to help many people. . . .

He wrote to Father Ignatius with warm feelings, declaring that he was finding no consolation in his labors except when he mulled over fulfilling his desires to go to India. Thus, he urged Father Ignatius to use this opportunity to snatch him from [the spiritual] care of the King of Portugal, because he despaired of getting free of it by any other way. If what he was requesting did not succeed, he thirsted for Brazil, which the Portuguese had recently discovered at that time and [found to be] inhabited by cannibals. But something else pleased divine Providence, by whose help Father Simão was so successfully promoting the causes of the Society and of the common good in Portugal.

280.   *The huge community at Coimbra*

At this time more than ninety of Ours (in addition to some who served them) lived at Coimbra. Many of them, including not a few noblemen, were endowed with virtue, intelligence, and other wonderful gifts of God. The generosity of the King provided what was needed for supporting more than one hundred men. The future college building was also being constructed at the expense of the King; indeed, it would have the capacity to hold two hundred students. Father Simão visited them occasionally, and by spiritual documents and helps he encouraged them to everything that was best, so that they would be prepared not only to work and labor but also to lay down their blood and lives for Christ's glory. He admonished those who did not believe that their hearts were ready for such things to leave the college.

At the beginning of this year, he appointed a rector and used this approach: he said that he wanted to mortify some one person. He singled out Father Luis de Grana and ordered him to be rector, and he gave the honor of being the cook to Father Luís Gonçalves, who had been the rector the previous year. When somebody asked Father Simão which of those two should be regarded as being the one who had been mortified, the question was considered something that needed no answer; this is because humble offices clearly make for maximum consolation and quiet, whereas important offices make for labor and mortification. The scholastics took their duties seriously, both the things that pertain to literary studies and those that contribute to spiritual progress. . . . At the time there were already thirty theologians besides the philosophers and those studying humane letters. On Sundays theses were defended at the college in the presence of a professor, yielding beneficial results; and meanwhile with the promotion of now some, now others, to the priesthood, the number of workers in the Lord's vineyard increased.

285.   *God strikes down a blasphemer*

But when Manuel da Nóbrega, who had very successfully performed the ministries of the Society in various places, entered a church, he heard men and women singing there and making music most inappropriate for such a place; he warned the people to stop the music, but they paid him little heed and kept on with their merrymaking. One of them, who more than the others wanted to let him know how little he cared about this rebuke, began shouting blasphemous words against God. He did so because he thought that he would displease Manuel with this impiety. But Manuel knelt down in front of him to ask God not to turn his wrath against the man. But he was not heard. The unlucky blasphemer left the gathering and went off elsewhere with some others. A thunderbolt from heaven suddenly split in two both him and the horse he was riding, while it touched nobody else in the group surrounding him. This greatly terrified the townsfolk, so that they listened to [Manuel's] preaching with considerably improved attentiveness and amenability.

THE YEAR 1549

■ **The worldwide Society**

328.   *Overview of the Society in 1549*

As 1549 began, this was the state of the Society: only two provinces had been established, the first in Portugal and the other in Spain, with two provincials, Father Simão [Rodrigues] and Father Antonio Araoz. In India this year Father Francis Xavier was made provincial of India, as is evident from the letters patent sent to him. Those working in Italy, Sicily, Germany, and France were governed by Father General Ignatius himself, although Father Diego Laínez as visitor in Sicily was in charge of the other men on that island.

329.   *Jesuit residences*

The Society resided in twenty-two places, namely, in Rome, where the professed house also included a house of probation. In Padua, Bologna, and Messina, colleges were in their earliest stages rather than actually functioning; the same was true of Cologne, Louvain, and Paris; in the Portuguese Province Ours in Lisbon came closer to the definition of a house rather than a college; at Coimbra there was an established college; some [of Ours] were attached to the royal court, but because the court often remained in Lisbon, this was not counted as a separate residence; in Spain Ours resided in Alcalá, Salamanca, Valladolid, Valencia, Gandia, Zaragoza, and Barcelona. In India they had residences in Goa, Bassein, Comorin, Malacca, and the Moluccas. But only a few lived in each of these places except for Rome, Coimbra, Lisbon, Gandía, Padua, and Messina. Ours had their own residences only in Goa, the two places in Portugal, in Spain only at Gandía, in [continental] Italy at Rome and Padua, and in Sicily at Messina. There were no residences in France and Germany. Their income was almost nothing, except at Coimbra, Gandía, Padua, and Messina.

333.   *Progress in writing the Constitutions*

Many of the surviving First Fathers had submitted their written agreements to the Constitutions that had been written or were being written by Ignatius himself; but the Constitutions were not promulgated because, as

Ignatius thought, rather many of the fathers from diverse places were going to come together [on the occasion of] the jubilee [scheduled for] next year.

■ Italy

336.   *Colleges are founded at Palermo and Tivoli*

This year pioneers came from Rome to establish two colleges, one at Palermo and the other at Tivoli. Although some men were sent to Ingolstadt, among them Father Peter Canisius, who was called to this assignment from Sicily, still that college had not yet begun. These colleges and missions seemed to be only in their earliest stages, so Father Ignatius did not worry about beginning a college at Pisa in accord with the promise of Duke Cosimo of Florence. Neither did the people at Termini in Sicily, who wrote letters begging Father Ignatius to found a college there, have their wishes granted. Father Ignatius judged that burdens of this sort were not to be evaluated precipitately, just as those whom the Lord sent [to the Society] were to be tested gradually before they were sent out to undertake the work of ministry.

Meanwhile, Ignatius, shouldering the concerns about the places and persons of the whole Society, took charge of many things at Rome, improving them greatly thereby. Among other things, he gave his attention to erecting a university or *Studium generale* at Messina; this would be set up by papal authority and placed under the direction of the Society. As we have said, at the end of the previous year the Supreme Pontiff granted this authorization with the strong support of the [papal] Signatura.

When the apostolic letters were sent to Messina this year, a great difficulty arose from men both in Messina itself and in Catania who did not accept with equanimity that their university, in which they were going to become medical doctors and lawyers, would be under the rector of our college. Earlier, in the presence of Juan de Vega, the viceroy, the magistrates of Messina had agreed to this, but they later changed their mind. . . .

345.   *Nuns at Messina make the Spiritual Exercises*

A certain convent of nuns (called Holy Mary on High *[dell'alto]*) wanted our assistance in things spiritual. When Father Ignatius was consulted, he answered that our Institute permitted Ours to hear their confessions once only, but that it would be more helpful for their future progress if they were prepared by the Spiritual Exercises to make a good confession. Therefore, the Exercises of the First Week were presented to three of the prominent nuns, so that they [in turn] would present them to the other [nuns]. Thus did a great number of the nuns make their confessions—indeed, general confessions—and draw great profit therefrom. Father Cornelius [Wischaven] performed this work to their great advantage. Other noble women, listening to these same Exercises in a church, made great progress in the Lord.

348. *Mutual respect between Jesuits and Dominicans in Sicily*

When the Dominicans, as was customary during their provincial chapter, defended theses in public over eight days in their own church and the cathedral, Ours were invited to the disputation. Father Jerónimo Nadal with Fathers Canisius and des Freux attended; so did Master Isidoro [Bellini]. The disputation went so well (in the debates they came out in first place or among others in first place) that divine Providence seemed to have brought it about and imparted to them such powers and grace in debating that the reputation of our college regarding the humanities was wonderfully enhanced among the people and even throughout the island. The [Dominican] religious in that province were re- nowned throughout their whole order, and still Ours were recognized to have performed so well as to have won the applause of both the learned and the unlearned; Father Nadal claimed that they had never executed that task better than at that time. . . .

350. *The college at Messina goes forward*

Since the lowest class enrolled a considerable number of students, Father Nadal judged that it should be divided and for the greater progress of the students a new class, an intermediate one, should be added between the lowest and the second-lowest classes. Thus, grammar began to be taught in five classes. At that time Father [Benedetto] Palmio taught rhetoric in the top class. This took place when classes began to meet in the fall. At this time Father André des Freux undertook teaching logic with good results (it seemed good to start a class of philosophy each year); he continued this till he had a successor. For during this second year Master Isidoro [Bellini] continued with natural philosophy. Father Antoine Vinck Durandi took over Scholastic theology. Nadal himself taught three different subjects, namely, Euclidian mathematics and various Greek and Hebrew literary authors.

In accord with a regulation of Father Ignatius, they had to write every week in detail and inform him even about the number of students in every class.

Thus, during November Father Nadal writes that there were seventy-eight students in the lowest class, fifty-six in the second lowest, forty-two in the third class, fourteen in the fourth class (which is called humanities; Father Annibale [Coudret] had charge of this class), and fifteen or sixteen in the fifth class, that is, rhetoric. Father André [des Freux] had sixteen in logic, Isidoro [Bellini] had thirteen in philosophy, and Father Antoine had only three in Scholastic theology (since there was almost no mature student among the lay students, and the religious were not as yet coming to our schools). Father Nadal had ten for his Greek course and three or four for Hebrew and ten or twelve for mathematics. Presentations were added to the individual lectures, following the Paris method, so that the college seemed to have some appearance of a university. God preserved the health of the teachers despite these considerable labors protracted from dawn to dusk.

351. *Public presentations to start the school year*

This reopening of classes, carried out in October, was preceded by three days of public disputations involving all the disciplines that would be taught later. This was conducted to the great edification of the spectators and increased the enthusiasm and ardor of the young men who were about to take up their studies. The more advanced courses were delayed somewhat until negotiations with the university were completed; at that time these arrangements had not as yet been concluded in the viceroy's presence. (This official was attending the disputations along with the judges and all leading men of the city, and he heard the orations and poems related to the resumption of studies). Shortly thereafter the negotiations were completed.

352. *Other religious orders follow the Jesuit example*

Among the successes flowing from the exertions of Ours at Messina, not the least was that our example inspired persons of other religious orders, especially of the order of Saint Dominic, to teach cases of conscience and comment on the Epistles of Saint Paul (as Ours were doing on Sundays and feast days).

355. *Toward the first novitiate*

Because the number of those who either had been admitted to our Society or who had asked to be admitted was growing, Father Nadal began to think about taking over a [separate] house for their probation. It would be at some remove from the college and directed by two or three of Ours, so that these men could be transferred to our college after spending one year there or as much time as sufficed in exercises of humility, obedience, and prayer, while keeping their own [daily] order. After he had discussed this [idea] with some of the leading men and won their praise, he brought it to Father Ignatius. Even though this was not put into practice this year, I did not want to pass over it in silence, for this was the first time mention was made of such houses of probation.

357.   *Helping poor priests and prisoners*

The inquisitor had a great love for Father André [des Freux] and always wanted to have him around; he even [wanted des Freux] to direct him in the Spiritual Exercises, and his vicar as well, who was also his nephew, if his schedule of visitations would allow this. Since the bishop himself would be coming to Messina shortly, it seemed possible to satisfy his desire there. That inquisitor and the bishop held the Society in high regard, and [des Freux] meanwhile sent spiritual writings to some of [the bishop's] household, to their great profit. Because the priests of that diocese were so very poor that they could not live without laboring with their hands, in the sermons he gave to the people Father André urged them to plant temporal seeds in [the priests], so that they might reap a spiritual harvest. . . .

He preached to every group of people that the bishop was visiting and consoled the impoverished who were kept in prison and strove to hear their confessions. Finally, he served them well in the things pertaining to both spirit and body. He successfully requested that a poor man be liberated who had been unjustly thrown into prison, to the great detriment of his family.

365.   *Converting prostitutes*

Because the viceroy had commanded women who were public sinners to attend [Doménech's] sermons on the day when the Gospel about Magdalene is read and because they were also present for what followed, many of them were converted to the Lord. This was certainly the case for sixteen of them. Lady Eleonora, the viceroy's wife, received them graciously into her home with her usual charity. She took care of arranging that some of them contracted marriages (after dowries had been provided), and that some entered convents for the converted [sinners]; some of them she kept in her own household.

366.   *Converted prostitutes decide to become nuns*

There were nine women who at the request of the viceroy's wife and in her company went to a convent to live there [behaving as she had promised they would] until they could contract a marriage. As soon as these women were led to the convent, they swore that they wanted to be religious. But it happened that on the second day of Holy Week, they were assisting at the office of compline along with the nuns; but because they were laughing and making noise there, the nuns ordered them to get out of the choir. When compline was completed and the nuns had entered a darkened room for the flagellation, which they call the discipline, about the second hour of the night, one of the converts who had been expelled from the choir and the room where the discipline was taken—and who showed herself to be more headstrong than the rest and who, moreover, was holding a grudge because she had been expelled—stood next to the door, which remained open a little bit. Moved by curiosity, she wanted to peek inside, even though the room was dark. As is believed, God caused a certain radiance to fill the room, by which she could see both the nuns and their whips. At the same moment as she had seen this external sight, the Lord so touched her inwardly that, with great sorrow mixed with consolation, she cried out that she wanted to be a nun.

She shared this with her companions, and when one of them did not believe her (nor perhaps did the nuns), she suddenly cast off her head veil, removed the ear rings from her ears, and asked the bystanders to cut off her hair and clothe her in a nun's habit. When another of her companions saw this, the same spirit stirred her to do likewise. Three more followed her forthwith. The nuns took off their habits, clothed the women, and, shedding abundant tears of devotion, they began praying before an image of the Blessed Virgin. With joyful hearts the nuns sang the "Te Deum laudamus." When they informed the viceroy's wife of this development, sending along their shorn locks of hair and requesting nuns' habits for the new converts, she gladly took charge of having them made.

So that the facts of this matter might be established more indisputably, the viceroy sent a judge with a notary to the convent. They made it a public action, in which [the viceroy] wanted Fathers Laínez and Jerónimo involved. They witnessed it with great consolation and tranquility of heart. Two more women imitated the other women, so that there remained only two of the nine who were still waiting to be married.

374.   *Raising alms for women with incurable diseases*

When the home for the converted women had been fairly well enclosed, the number of nuns increased, leading to their being excessively crowded (for besides those already mentioned, others came forward to undertake the same regimen, and the one among them who stood out was a woman who had been the cause of great offenses against God). Father Jerónimo Doménech took care to have the building enlarged from alms [he had gathered].

Here is how planning a hospital for the incurables was subsequently handled: On May 1 the wife of the viceroy assembled the most important ladies at Palermo; they then established a kind of consorority with this as their objective: every month each one of them would contribute a certain amount in alms for the support of the incurables. She wished Father Laínez to give a sermon to them proposing the project and urging them to meet monthly and, moreover, to visit the women patients at the hospital for the incurables. At least this much he accomplished: they came together to contribute alms. The money was deposited with the viceroy's wife and another one of those ladies; they began making that contribution right from this very day forward. During the next month, when Father delivered another exhortation, not only did they contribute the alms but many of them gave a lump sum for the whole year.

376.   *Enforcing Trent's decree on cloister for nuns*

Under Father Jerónimo's supervision and with the viceroy's support, cloister was established in accord with the council's decree and the nuns' own religious Institute, and gradually progress was made toward their complete reformation.

378.   *An unworthy abbess resigns and her convent is reformed*

Although Father Diego Laínez preached on feast days and Sundays in Palermo after Lent, still he traveled to Monreale on other days and zealously carried out the visitation entrusted to him by Cardinal [Alessandro] Farnese. Because in many places controversies had long raged between monks and the [diocesan] clergy, he employed remarkable diligence in settling them. He also wanted to read documents that were locked away in the archives of a great monastery, in order to gain a clearer understanding of the background and so make progress [toward reconciliation]. Thus, he wrote about all these things to the cardinal, and he developed the basis for effecting a reconciliation that seemed worth implementing. . . .

At a convent of nuns badly in need of reform, the abbess in charge of the other [nuns] was a very noble lady, but she promoted reformation [of her convent] neither by the example of her own life nor by the prudence of her government. Indeed, she wholly opposed any sort of reform. Arrangements were made for her to depart from that convent and enter another one in Palermo; in addition, she was prevailed upon to renounce her previous office [as abbess]. At first her conscience reproached her for her earlier way of life and inclined her to take this step; but later, because of her female inconstancy or because of her ambition, she denied that she had wanted to resign. Father Laínez began to get information about her actions. She was of such a sort that even the nuns who had favored her, when they understood that she would otherwise be exposed to disgrace and by rights deserved to be expelled from her office in any case, persuaded her to resign. And so she abdicated her office of abbess, to the decided advantage of the convent and the edification of the people. While these things were going on at Palermo, Laínez, after hearing the confessions of the whole convent and after giving the nuns several exhortations, left the nuns desirous of a complete reformation. . . .

381.   *More on reforming the Palermo convent*

Father Laínez put a suitable vicar in charge of the nuns, and they returned to observing the common life in accordance with their Institute. The necessities of life that previously did not suffice for a few days now lasted for many days, as they learned by experience and confirmed by their testimony. Silence was observed, all participated in the Divine Office, cloister was diligently observed, they went to monthly confession and Communion, and finally, with a great renovation of their souls, they began to live up to the ideals of their Institute exactly—something that had never happened since the foundation of their convent.

402.   *Silvestro Landini's youth group at Foligno*

The number of young people who under [Landini's] leadership went to weekly confession greatly increased and by now counted almost eighty; the more mature among them communicated, to the great joy of their parents and of the bishop. Those who came frequently to the Sacrament, especially among the young students, met toward evening for prayer at an oratory designated by the bishop. This confraternity of young men gave itself the name of our Society, and so fervently did these adolescents devote themselves to these pious practices that the son of a certain respected professor, when his father refused him permission [to join this confraternity], joined it anyway—a decision his father later gladly approved.

406.   *Landini attacks salvation by faith alone*

At Reggio Emilia, which is a province under the Duke of Ferrara, where the leader of the Modenese militia is stationed, some men had spread heresies; and when some infected priests and medical doctors found out that Father Silvestro was coming, they branded him a Pelagian (this is what they call Catholics who hold that good works are necessary for salvation). They went to him, presenting themselves as friends, and spoke with him about justification; but when he asserted that good works done in charity were necessary for baptized adults, they began to grow furious and threaten that if he were to preach that doctrine in Reggio Emilia, they would see to it that he was regarded as a wild beast. Fifteen days later Silvestro came to Reggio Emilia and preached to its people for a whole week. On the first day he struck such terror into the heretics that a medical doctor fled the city so rapidly that his mount nearly collapsed on the road. . . .

407.   *Silvestro Landini stops vendettas in Correggio*

Through letters [Silvestro] encouraged the parish priests to persevere in the things that they had begun so well. In some places where the most holy Sacrament was not reserved in the parishes, he took care that not only would it be reserved [from then on] but lamps would always be kept burning; and [he urged] people to frequent Communion. . . .

He then came to a large town called Correggio, where he was so badly received at first that when he was preaching some people left the church and then threw stones against the door, thereby disturbing his audience. But he preached for eight straight days, sometimes twice on the same day. Not only did people stop throwing stones, but right at dawn they came to his sermons with great devotion. The vendettas in that place were so prevalent that forty-five people, three of them priests, had been killed. Armed men would come right up to the altar. These factions had two opposing leaders who came to Father Silvestro for confession, something they had avoided for many years; and they indicated that they were ready to make peace and do whatever he ordered them to do. Although they had instilled terror into others, after listening to the daily sermons, they bore themselves with great humility. Before vespers a herald proclaimed to the public that early in the morning everybody should come to hear God's word or incur some specified penalty. . . . . Previously [someone could be seen receiving] Communion there scarcely once a year; now it was a daily occurrence. On Sundays they came to church armed and heard barely half the Mass; now they came unarmed not to just one [Mass], but to as many as were being said in the church. . . .

The leaders of the opposing factions finally submitted their controversies to Father Silvestro's arbitration, and he was hoping that an edifying and far-reaching peace would ensue. And so peace was forged, and it was the more welcome because the opposing factions had been fighting among each other for thirty years with bitter hatred and great cruelty. Not only did they neglect confession and Communion, but because of their vendetta they also caused enormous losses in temporal goods.

Here is the approach he used: when he preached before a large congregation, after the word of God had softened the hearts of factional leaders, he called one of the two leaders by name—his name was Giovanni Corso. He answered [Landini], "My Father, what do you want me to do?" Silvestro said from the pulpit, "That you should forgive all your enemies, and beyond this, you should ask for pardon from all those you have offended and, second, that out of love of God you grant them all peace." He immediately threw his weapons on the ground, prostrated himself, and began to call in a loud voice, "Peace, peace." The rest of the men from both factions begin to say, "Peace, peace." Then Silvestro came down from the pulpit and said, "May you also do what I am going to do." He began to embrace the men and give them the kiss of peace. They then also embraced their enemies and began kissing them with convincing signs of love, and indeed they shed so many tears in their joy that they thoroughly drenched one another in the course of their kisses of peace. Old and young, men and women made the whole church resound with [cries of] "Peace" amid their tears. Those hearts, which a few days before thirsted like lions for nothing except vengeance and murder, became lamblike, touched by a gentle and mutual love; and from then on they began to compete with one another in deeds of charity. . . .

418.   *Ignatius and a sick superior*

Father Elpidio Ugoletti was rector of our college at Padua but he was suffering from bad health, and there was question of transferring him from Padua to a place with a milder climate. Father Ignatius ordered him to write and tell him frankly how he was inclined. Finally after consulting his doctors, [Ugoletti] himself judged that he should stay there but use more care in protecting his health.

421.   *Jay's preaching at Ferrara*

On feast days [Jay] continued the lectures he had begun the previous year at the Church of Santa Anna, and many of those who listened experienced an increasing warmth as they carried out works of devotion. The practice developed that at the end of his lecture he would immediately come down from the pulpit to the place where confessions were heard; he could not get himself free until he had heard many confessions. On one Sunday in the month of January, he skipped the lecture because of heavy snow and great cold, for he did not think that anyone would come to hear him. He found out he had guessed wrongly: the people came as usual. When they saw that their preacher was not coming to the church, many of them went to his room and, instead of his usual lecture, they asked him to teach them how to draw up a plan for living lives worthy of Christians. He did this gladly and gave them a spiritual exhortation. Due to the pressure of other listeners, he was not allowed henceforward to skip a public lecture; but he had to be available for them without fail, even when the cold was at its fiercest. . . .

426.   *Salmerón at Verona*

At the start of this year, Father Alfonso Salmerón was at Verona, where he lectured on the Epistle to the Romans before such a large audience that, although there were lectures on Sacred Scripture in three or four other churches at the same hour, he had to leave his teaching chair and climb into the pulpit, from which he usually preached, so that his voice might carry better. He preached in convents of nuns and in certain churches, and any number of good results flowed from his labor. Many of those belonging to the Catholic faith were helped, although some people also branded him a toady of the pope and of the Roman See and grumbled that he knew the truth but was unwilling to state it forthrightly. But people like this were very few and, in any case, already dammed because of their heresy, so his listeners heard him with great attention and consolation. Moreover, he showed charity and compassion to the sectarians even while he strove to heal their wounds.

427.   *Salmerón at Belluno*

. . . Some who were hardly Catholic in their thinking about matters of the faith regarding, for instance, purgatory, holy works, confession, and other things, were illumined by the light of God's word, so that they entirely abandoned their errors and doubts and returned to the bosom of the Catholic Church. They burned many Lutheran books and other suspect ones, and asserted that in the future they did not want to argue or ask questions, for they were certain of the Catholic truth. Among them was a man who, following Lutheran practice, had confessed in a general way the previous year that he was a sinner, but did not want to descend to the particulars of his sins; this Lent he went to the same confessor so that he might confess his specific sins and receive the confessor's absolution. Many who were accustomed to ignore Lenten fasting and [abstinence from certain] foods, after listening to four or five lectures fulfilled their obligations right to the end of Lent.

Hatreds and discords, which were widespread in that city and, indeed, prevailed everywhere, were so dormant and extinct that no signs of factions were observed; for the preacher had inveighed against these with special emphasis. As a sign of this, the bishop's vicar testified that almost a thousand more people had come to confession and Communion this year than had done so the previous year. Among the young women too, whom their mothers usually allowed to live with great abandon and licentiousness, from which stemmed any number of amorous conversations, clandestine marriages, and other scarcely upright activities, so great was the change from this dissolute manner of living to a more honorable and [spiritually] safer pattern of life that it rightly seemed that the Lord had done this. . . .

■ Germany

433.   *Jay, Salmerón, and Canisius arrive at Ingolstadt*

Leaving Munich on November 12 and accompanied by two guides to show the way, they arrived at Ingolstadt the next day and were received with great honor by the university (to which the Duke of Bavaria had earnestly recommended Ours). On the very day that Ours arrived there, the chancellor of the university, the professor of Sacred Scripture, the bishop, and all the doctors and professors came to their inn to welcome them. One of them gave a congratulatory oration in their presence. . . . Our older fathers delegated to Father Peter Canisius the task of responding, who went on to deliver an elegant address, even though he was speaking extemporaneously. . . . The next day they led Ours to the main college of the university (they call it the Old College) and assigned each of them very comfortable lodgings fully equipped with furniture and books and all the necessities; they saw to it as well that Ours could live in a religious and Italian manner, without the customary German-style banqueting.

434.   *Starting to teach at Ingolstadt*

Chancellor Eck had written to the university about the theological lectures that were to be given at Ingolstadt:[1] first on the Gospels, second on Paul's Epistles, third on David's Psalter, fourth on the Master of the Sentences [Peter Lombard]. The chancellor and the bishop were to lecture on the Gospels; Father Alfonso Salmerón was to explain the Epistles, Father Claude the Psalms, and Father Canisius the Master of the Sentences. On November 26, at the beginning of the lectures, Father Canisius gave a learned oration instead of an introductory lecture, partly to praise theology and partly to encourage his hearers to study it diligently. On November 29 Father Alfonso Salmerón . . . began to interpret the Epistle to the Romans, just as Canisius began with the fourth book of the *Sentences*. Many men, together with the chancellor, Doctor Eck, asked that these orations be printed for wider circulation. . . .

435.   *Problems at Ingolstadt*

. . . The Duke of Bavaria had secured from the Supreme Pontiff permission to collect a tithe from his ecclesiastical subjects for three years, to be used to establish this University of Ingolstadt. In the first year he collected more than twenty-four hundred florins; the belief was that he was using at least part of this sum to feed the theologians. Because the students did not have a foundation in philosophy and because Scholastic theology itself was quite bitterly detested, it was impossible to expect that the lectures of Ours would enjoy much success if the regular students did not have a suitable preparation in one or several colleges set up either by the duke or by local bishops. . . .

436.   *A Jesuit college at Ingolstadt is proposed*

After commending the question to God, Ours judged that the erection of a college of our Society at that university should be proposed to Chancellor

---

[1] This was Leonard Eck, who died in 1550; he should not to be confused with Johann Eck, the famous Catholic polemicist and professor of theology at Ingolstadt, who died in 1543.

Eck. When Father Claude [Jay] made the proposal, it greatly pleased the chancellor, for it seemed that [such an institution] would be very useful for the future of all Bavaria. Moreover, he declared that he had been thinking about this plan for the last two years; and after discussing it with the duke, he had no doubt about [the duke's] desire. But [he urged] that it seemed good not to use tithes to build such a college, for fear that this might seem to be taking something away from the university; rather, the building should be constructed [with funds] from some monastery devoid of monks or some vacant church benefices, with the approval of the Supreme Pontiff. So now, for the first time negotiations got underway preparatory to establishing a college of the Society in Germany, even though other [colleges] had been planned earlier, but due to delays for various reasons, [they had not been undertaken]. The arrival of Ours at the university greatly enhanced the standing and influence of Father Claude among the bishops of Germany.

■ **France**

439. *The Jesuits at Paris*

During 1549 Father Battista Viola was in charge of Ours at Paris, and the Italians elected him superior in the Lombard College. Since Ours did not have their own house, some of them obtained a number of burses, as they are called, in that college because they came from regions in Italy some of whose natives could be admitted in accord with the ancient regulations of that college. They concealed that they were religious, but others of the Society lived on their own as boarding students or persons to whom rooms were rented for their use. Father Viola carefully watched over them all and, with the help of Father Everard Mercurian, he upheld religious discipline (as far as the situation of time and place allowed; for in those days we had to tolerate hindrances and inconveniences rather than live according to any constitutions and rules). Some of these inconveniences arose because our living conditions required us to share quarters with lay persons residing in the same college; moreover, [Ours] did not dare to openly admit their membership in the Society, or they would have been expelled from the college. Thus, it seemed that it would be a great advantage for the glory of God and of the Society if Ours were to have a house of their own where they could live by themselves like religious and have a chapel in which to hear the confessions of those lay people who came flooding in and to administer the most holy Sacrament to them.

When Father Viola visited the bishop of Clermont [Guillaume du Prat] and conferred with him on this problem, [the latter] approved the plan and offered six hundred gold pieces in alms toward purchasing a house. Other friends and two of the novices actually transferred [funds] or promised a contribution toward purchasing such a house. With great diligence they searched virtually everywhere near the university for some suitable house, but they found none that could be purchased at a moderate price; even if they had found one, the Society could not yet have [legally] possessed any real estate in France until it had successfully petitioned the Most Christian King for the sort of permission that they call "naturalization."

440.   *Setting up a Jesuit house in Paris*

The hostile remarks of some men of considerable authority (for they were professors of theology) rendered the bishop of Clermont less eager than he had been to establish a college of the Society, and he judged that he ought rather to turn his attention to the spiritual good of the people in his diocese. As a man of a devout disposition, he could not back away from his previous commitments to such an extent that he did not want to help the Society acquire a house at Paris. After much thought he proposed the plan of giving us a certain house belonging to the bishopric of Clermont in which to live. It was on rue de La Harpe and was quite suited for our purposes. Meanwhile, until a more ample house was purchased, Ours would live by themselves there and observe the Society's norms. He also urged that a letter be written in his name to Father Ignatius [asking him] to send one of the professed to Paris not merely to carry on the usual ministries of the Society there but also to be able to accept things that were donated to the Society with authority granted by Father Ignatius himself. . . .

441.   *The Paris community*

Although this year passed with some domestic trouble because of the situation [at the College] of the Lombards, as we have described; still, Father Everard [Mercurian] and Father Jean Pelletier, freed from these annoyances, devoted their diligent efforts to the works of piety. Father Ignatius admitted Father Battista [Viola] to [the rank] of spiritual coadjutor (for the other men were still novices) and conferred on him the faculties of the Society through letters patent; he took care to send on these faculties to the two aforesaid (Everard and Jean) also, so that they could answer those who might ask on what authority they were administering the sacraments of confession and Communion to many. At the urging of the colleges in Sicily and elsewhere, Father Ignatius asked whether some support [in the form of] men to teach Hebrew and especially Greek literature might be sent from Paris. Thus, at the start of autumn four men from the Paris college were sent to Rome; all had master's degrees in the Faculty of Arts, and two of them were trained in theology. . . .

442.   *Ministries at Paris*

The aforesaid fathers went to [the church of] the Carthusians on Sundays and feast days, where Ours partook of the most holy sacrament of the Eucharist; moved by their example and also by their encouragement, many other students, sometimes exceeding six hundred, came there to receive those sacraments. But other people also of both sexes were assisted in spiritual matters through the efforts of Ours and were quite ready to support works of the Society. [Ours] offered the Spiritual Exercises to a considerable number of [those of] French and Flemish [nationality]; a certain Spaniard, who carried letters of recommendation from Father Estrada, also came to seek entry into the Society, inspired by these Exercises. Professor [François] le Picart very sincerely and lovingly seconded our undertakings by his advice, prestige, and everything he could do.

443.   *Opposition to the Society at Paris*

Ours at Paris were not spared a test of their patience. Many, especially from the ranks of the theologians, harassed them with remarkable persistence. Among them a professor enjoying an excellent reputation asserted that the Society would not last [for long], so alms should be given to other poor people rather than to them. Another discouraged this and that person [from becoming] familiar with Ours and would not have any dealings with Ours himself. A third man, who had made the Exercises under Father Ignatius when he was at Paris, asserted that all of Ours, if they were going to be treated according to their merits, should be publicly scourged through the streets with whips because they were seducers of youth. He adduced as evidence that Ignatius caused him to spend thirty days in a little room pondering spiritual matters.

A certain Talpin, who was learned in Latin and Greek humane letters and trained in philosophy and theology, spread similar rumors. When Father Paolo Achille was helping him make the Spiritual Exercises, caught up by spiritual fervor he had made a vow that he would join the Society if he were admitted. It happened that (although Father Paolo was totally ignorant about what he was doing) he wrote out our vows in the blood which by chance was flowing from his nose. But he was of an unstable frame of mind, and as time passed he regretted his vows. So he consulted several professors about whether he was bound by this kind of vow, one that he had written in his own blood. They thought that Father Paolo, who actually knew nothing about the business, might have been behind his making the vows and writing them in his own blood. [The professors], therefore, attributed to the Society [the practice] of encouraging men to make rash vows and write them in their own blood.

By spreading these rumors they dissuaded a certain woman who had decided to donate a house to Ours. They induced the bishop of Clermont to adopt a colder attitude toward the Society; but he had known Ours at Trent and in Italy and could not completely reverse his well-founded conviction, although for a time he behaved more tepidly. Father Ignatius took care to have letters sent to the papal nuncio and the Cardinal of Mâcon.[2] . . . [This cardinal] insisted he would not help the Society in any way, but rather would dissuade the King from helping it because under the cloak of religion Ours were eating the bread of the poor. He averred that it would be far better if Ours and many other religious were to turn themselves to digging ditches, and that he knew who had started this religious order, a certain Ignatius, a Spaniard. . . .

■ **Spain**

445.   *Developments in Spain*

In Spain the situation in the Society improved considerably, especially at Salamanca and Alcalá. At the beginning of 1549, in order to lay a more solid foundation for humility, Father Torres (who held a doctorate) worked as janitor, cook, or waiter in the dining room; he himself carried out the garbage, made the beds for all who lived there, swept the house, and performed all the more lowly tasks. He took the lowliest place at table and, in short, by his example no less than by his words invited the brethren who were his subjects to self-abnegation. An opportunity for humility came from another source: on the feast of the Epiphany [January 6], a religious and famous preacher of the Order of Saint Dominic said in his church, among other things, that those founding new religious orders were hypocrites because inwardly they are different from what they outwardly profess; that God's Church has enough approved religious

---

[2] The editors of Polanco's text in the MHSI point out that the bishop of Mâcon was not a cardinal.

orders; and that quiet hideaways *[anguli]* should not be sought out.[3] His audience easily recognized that these words referred to the Society, but this sort of
talk by now made little impact on their minds, while Ours at home aspired to
imitate Christ by the example of their rector and also were gaining practice by
privately delivering exhortations to their community.

447.   *The growing popularity of the Jesuits at Salamanca*

In a short time all this changed for the better, so that now hardly anybody dared to speak against the Society at Salamanca. People who previously
did not risk dealing with Ours, even though they loved us, now came for
confession and Communion every Sunday; and others came to discuss their
affairs, and the Lord planted in that city [the seeds of] a wonderful goodwill,
esteem, and devotion for the Society, so that these far surpassed the nagging
suspicion, contempt, and hatred which the devil tried to sow at the outset, and
the tranquility that followed was much greater than the storm had been. Observing the fruit, many men who were distinguished for their reputation and learning
very affectionately gave glory to the God who had deigned to illuminate them
with the light of his truth when they were blind and to guide along the path of
salvation those who were disgusted by their perverse former lives.

449.   *Helping prisoners at Salamanca*

Besides the sermons Father Estrada delivered at a number of churches in
Salamanca, the various pious works to which Father Torres devoted himself
resulted in much edification, especially among the learned men who knew him
better. Among his good works was preaching every Sunday in the city's public
prison; there he heard the prisoners' confessions, and he accompanied those
about to undergo the death penalty to the place of execution, remaining until the
very moment of death and helping them to die well. He took pains to provide
necessities also for the poor who were imprisoned there, so much so that the
prisoners, the prison guards, judges, and even the chief warden regarded him as
a father and went to him for confession. His hard work enabled him to find a
remedy for the afflictions of many people and he successfully requested that
punishment (either fines or prison time) be reduced or even canceled for them.

---

[3] Meaning, perhaps, that new religious orders should not seek out pleasant sinecures in
the Church.—ED.

The noblemen, too, who were numerous at Salamanca, flocked to Doctor Torres, so that he could make peace among them. . . . One nobleman said that if Ours secured a site, he would personally take over the responsibility of soliciting alms [from the citizens] to be used in building the college. . . . Many people brought alms to Ours for distribution to the poor and to good causes. When one or two of Ours fell sick, even seriously sick, not only did two medical doctors provide their services free but, moved by great charity, others also brought what was needed, both food suitable for the sick and also medicines.

455.   *Renting a retreat house*

There were a considerable number of people who wanted to make the Spiritual Exercises; but because the house was so small, they encouraged Ours to rent a bigger building as long as they did not already own one that was adequate. Many men also hoped to be admitted to the Society, but in vain, because neither the house nor the resources were adequate for supporting so many people.

456.   *Opposition from the Dominicans at Salamanca*

. . . Nonetheless, some religious of the Order of Preachers, with a zeal that was perhaps not evil but was poorly informed, kept attacking Ours; and it is certain that they tried to encourage the ministers of justice to visit our house to check on what books Ours owned. There was also a man who in his preaching viciously attacked certain clerics who were regarded as holy. His statement was understood as applying exclusively to Ours. They achieved little, and Rome sent some support, bringing papal authority to bear against such troublemakers; and, as we said above, letters patent from the [Master] General himself of the Order of Preachers imposed silence on detractors belonging to his order.

461.   *Cano returns to the attack*

One of the most prominent and noble ladies of that city, who regarded Ours with a great deal of love, was just on the point of giving her daughter, who had a dowry of fifty thousand ducats, to a certain count when the daughter proclaimed that she did not want to marry anybody. So exasperated was the mother, who suspected that [her daughter] had reached her decision after listening to what Ours were teaching, that she began to think evil of and even speak out against Ours.

That same religious of the Order of Saint Dominic [Melchor Cano], who on our first arrival warned people to avoid Ours like minions of the Antichrist, when he was about to leave Salamanca for the general chapter of his Order, in his last lecture warned his listeners repeatedly to be on guard against new teaching, conveyed not only in writing but also in one's behavior. So God wanted Ours always to have some people who would expose them to trials, to keep them from having their heads puffed up by prosperity and success and thus to allow them to draw benefit from contradictions.

463.   *Giving the Spiritual Exercises at Alcalá*

Nowhere did the power of the Spiritual Exercises shine more brilliantly than during this time at Alcalá. Precisely because there was no preacher or confessor belonging to our Society there, the spiritual fruit from the Spiritual Exercises and familiar conversations gradually grew, and no sooner had some people completed the Spiritual Exercises than other people were striving to take their place. Among them was the governor, who asserted that he wanted to relinquish his other occupations completely in order to make the Exercises. While they were engaged in their studies, not only Francisco de Villanueva but also Manuel Lopez were giving people the Spiritual Exercises with admirable spiritual effect.

Among those who profited greatly in this way was Doctor Alfonso Ramirez de Vergara, a man of great prestige and learning and no less piety, who thought that he might be called to the Institute of the Society because in his heart he was much inclined to it. But partly because he was promoted to a canonry at the church of Cuenca and partly because he had decided to start a college of the Society and endow it as much as he could with his goods, which consisted mainly of ecclesiastical revenues, he put off his entrance for so long that, with old age coming on, he was by then rendered unsuited for the labors of our Institute. This same year he sent documents of authorization to Father Ignatius at Rome, so that some of his ecclesiastical revenues might be applied to the college of the Society at Alcalá. Toward the end of that year, he bought the [original] building for the Society in which our college was set up, although it was to be augmented later by other adjoining buildings.

467.   *A Franciscan helps the Jesuits*

A member of our Society named Pedro de Sylva died at Alcalá; he was the only priest among Ours stationed at Alcalá. The poverty of Ours was so great that they did not have the garments with which to clothe him properly (the vestments in which dead priests are clothed are usually very inexpensive). But a religious of the Order of Saint Francis, who marveled at the mutual charity of our brothers (when he chanced to have contact with them), without anybody asking this of him, spontaneously provided both vestments and other things needed for burial. . . .

482. *Francis Borgia follows Ignatius's advice*

At Gandía when Francis Borgia understood the desires of Father Ignatius, he followed his advice with excellent resignation of will and consolation for his own spirit regarding both his way of praying and his physical mortification. So that he might work more diligently at theology (for he had already long ago done his other studies), he came to our college on the first day of Lent. Master Perez, who had lectured on theology for many years, was teaching theology there. He started his presentation right after Epiphany of this year. His audience was quite large, comprising in part our men, ten of whom were theologians who diligently devoted themselves to their scholastic studies, and in part extern students, among whom some were learned and some were preachers. Thus that new academy began to flourish in no small measure. . . .

486. *The dispute at Valencia over frequent Communion continues*

I will not fail to report that, as we have written, despite a dispute the previous year at Valencia over whether frequent Communion was advantageous—a dispute that the archbishop settled in a devout sermon in which he declared that weekly Communion was permitted for everybody—even so, many churchmen and a good number of learned men clung to their viewpoint and resisted this teaching at that time. The people, however, day by day kept coming to Communion more often.

■ Portugal

487. *Problems in Portugal*

Meanwhile, the state of our Society in Portugal was improving, in that our numbers and resources to support them were increasing; but because the Constitutions had not been promulgated, the same plan or method of proceeding desired by Father Ignatius was not being observed, especially as regards government and some matters related to spiritual progress. [Ignatius], therefore, considered putting Father Doménech in charge of that province. Because Father

Simão Rodrigues greatly desired to come to Rome, Ignatius leaned even more toward this [change of assignment]. So that he could withdraw Father Doménech from Sicily, he ordered Father Diego Laínez to sound out the mind of Lady Eleonora, the viceroy's wife. If, however, [Laínez] noticed that she and her husband were opposed to it, [Ignatius] warned [Laínez] not to proceed in any way with this plan. But the possibility of sending [Doménech] was dropped [from consideration] when the viceroy's wife seemed rather downcast at the first mention of this proposal and also when the viceroy expressed his fears that notable fruit would be lost through [Doménech's] absence.

488.   *Problems with the Portuguese nobility*

. . . There were two considerations preventing Father Simão from coming to Rome (even though he had by now obtained a temporary permission from the King [to do so]). The first was that Father Ignatius did not summon him in writing until the following year. The second was that a storm against Ours had arisen because of Lord Teutonius, brother of the Duke of Braganza, whose house was second in importance in that kingdom, next to the royal house. He was studying at Coimbra and was much attracted to the Society's Institute; shortly after midnight he climbed over the walls of a certain college in which he was living and came to our college and was admitted into the Society at his own insistence.

His blood relatives, especially his sister, Lady Isabella, took umbrage at this and requested the King and Queen to restore him to them. The King, however, extremely pious as he was, would not allow compulsion to be used; but so powerful was the ensuing attack brought to bear by the leading men that the status of the Society was put at considerable risk, as Father Simão himself wrote. He was of the opinion that he should remain in Portugal for a while to calm these towering waves that [the Braganzas] had stirred up. That young man remained in the Society for a while but did not persevere in it; neither did the son of the Duke of Aveiro, who was discussed above. This year, however, Ignacio de Acebedo entered the Society; he also was of noble blood, but much more noble in virtue; eventually he became a martyr of the Lord.

489.   *Portuguese candidates for profession*

Father Ignatius wrote that, from among those who were working in Portugal, Father Simão should nominate some men suitable to make their profession. He nominated only eleven, although he had been writing that there were far more suitable men in that province. [The candidates] seemed to be learned in theology and endowed with virtue and prudence. [Rodrigues] also proposed a twelfth man, Doctor Antonio Gomez in India. But this year none of them was admitted to profession, although in good time the majority of them made their profession.[4]

■ Italy

545.   *Broët at Bologna*

At Bologna Father Paschase gave the Spiritual Exercises to some students, among them a priest, and some of them joined the Institute of the Society. Among them was a canon who began to serve God and left behind his canonry and other church benefices. He gave the same Exercises to the noblemen, much to their spiritual profit, and also to many young women, sometimes to twelve or thirteen at a time; and the Lord moved some of them to [enter] the religious life. He began to explain Christian doctrine in a confraternity on Sundays and feast days. During those days Father Francesco Palmio preached to a rather large audience, giving much edification and satisfaction; and through his devout work they made great progress in the Lord. He spent not just the day but sometimes a part of the night in hearing confessions, and many of the Bolognese nobility and of the senate itself made use of Father Paschase's work in the ministry of this sacrament.

548.   *At Bologna three Jesuits take quick doctorates*

As was said above, Father Salmerón arrived at the city of Bologna in September, coming from the city of Belluno and from the Veneto. Father Canisius came from Sicily, and somewhat later Father Claude [Jay] reached there from Ferrara (after obtaining leave for several months from Duke Ercole). Because the Bolognese knew that plague was raging at Ferrara, they watched carefully so that nobody coming from there would be allowed entrance; thus, it required skill to get Father Claude into the city. Two of Ours went out to a suburban area, and Father Claude, having dressed in the kind of clothing worn by city dwellers, joined them. Together with them he entered Bologna.

Father Ignatius thought it good that these three Fathers, who were going to teach theology at the Ingolstadt university, should take the doctoral degree at Bologna, for that was a requirement for anyone exercising that office in Ger-

---

[4] At the death of Ignatius only 3 percent of Jesuits were professed fathers.

many. At the time, Cardinal del Monte, who was shortly thereafter elected pope and called Julius III, was at Trent. He commissioned Ambrogio Catarino, bishop of Minori, along with two other professors of the same order to examine them.[5] On the first day he proposed points on which they would lecture and answer [questions the following day]. After they were examined the next day, both the bishop and the other professors reported to the cardinal how greatly pleased they were by the [candidates'] erudition; accordingly, [Ours] were promoted to the doctorate on the day sacred to Saint Francis [October 4]. The letters testifying to this were composed and forwarded to them in Germany, and they did not have to wait for them [to arrive].

---

[5] Ambrogio Catarino Politi, O.P. (1484–1553), was a leading controversial theologian noted for his attacks on Luther and Bernardino Ochino. In 1546 Paul III appointed him bishop of Minori in the Kingdom of Naples.

THE YEAR 1550

■ Overview of the Society

1. *Status of the Society in 1550*

At the beginning of 1550, the status of the Society was as follows: There were only three designated provinces with three provincials—East India under Francis Xavier, Portugal under Simão Rodrigues, and Spain under Antonio Araoz . In France, Germany, and Italy, there were no designated provinces at that time, nor had any provincials been assigned, although somebody was in charge of the individual communities, all of which corresponded from wherever they were with Father Ignatius (who carried out the task of both general and provincial), and he governed all those territories by means of letters.

3. *The residences of the Society in Portugal and Spain*

The province of Portugal, although it increased in numbers and also in resources, enabling it to support its members, had residences in only two places, namely, Lisbon and Coimbra, just as had been the case in the previous year. In Spain the Society resided in the same seven places as the year before, namely, Alcalá, Salamanca, Valladolid, Valencia, Gandía, Zaragoza, and Barcelona. Only this year, 1550, did those at Alcalá and Valladolid begin to have their own houses.

4. *Other cities*

Ours began to reside in other places, first at Tivoli and then Palermo. In the other places, namely, Rome, Bologna, Padua, Cologne, Louvain, and Paris, things were similar to the previous year except that at Rome and also at Bologna the buildings for our residences were gradually expanded.

With this year begins *Chron.,* vol. 2. This volume covers three years—1550, 1551, and 1552. The sections are numbered separately for each year, beginning each time with no. 1, unlike the first volume, covering 1539–49, which numbered the passages continuously for all ten of those years.—ED.

■ **Rome**

At the start of this year, there were almost fifty men in the Roman community, even though more than twenty had been missioned to various places the previous year. A great many aspired to the Institute of the Society, some of them already living in Rome and others coming to Rome from other places seeking admission; thus it was that the places of those being missioned was immediately occupied by their successors. Among those admitted were some who had been trained in various literary skills; some were less advanced but gave hope that they would acquire learning and would communicate it to their neighbors in a helpful way. Out of his goodness the Lord did not allow our temporal resources to fail us.

6. *Novices at Rome*

Although the house of probation was not yet distinct from the professed house, still, the novices received special attention, and both they and the veterans [their older brethren] were engaged in whatever pertains to denying self-love, to obedience and the other virtues, and to praying to attain them. The good reputation of this house spread throughout Rome, and the Society was well regarded by both the Supreme Pontiff, who died the previous November, and by the cardinals, other prelates, and those of the laity enjoying greater authority. This was clearly evident when the College of Cardinals, while it was still in conclave, received a request from these men for something that cannot usually be easily obtained. Not only was this granted with unanimous consent, but the [cardinals] added many expressions of commendation and approval of the Society. . . .

7. *Ignatius wins back a heretic*

There was a lad who had been brought up in heresy from his earliest years and not only clung tenaciously to his errors but also taught them to other people. He was denounced to the cardinal inquisitors; but when they saw how talented and specially gifted he was, they successfully beseeched Father Ignatius to keep him in our house for a time and to devote efforts to recalling him from his errors. Ignatius gave his consent; the youth was at our house hardly eight days when he returned to the bosom of the Church, abandoning the opinions of the sectarians and abjuring them in public. When somebody asked him what influenced him the most in this transformation, he said, "Not just their arguments but also their example and behavior moved me to believe that those men, whose lives, so worthy of Christians, I was observing, held a sound faith." As a result he not only began to aspire to the Catholic religion but also to a more perfect state of life.

8.   *Two converts at Rome*

There was another man, a Jew, whom the other Jews stationed at Rome as their representative; after he had been led to the faith of Christ, the cardinal protector of the catechumens requested that he be welcomed into our house when it was time to teach Christian doctrine. He hoped to learn not merely what he was to believe but also how one should live as a Christian. There was another person, an adolescent and a Christian, but of such a difficult personality and wayward behavior that there was no way to keep him faithful to his duty. As a last resort, he was placed in our house; in just a few days, he was changed into another person, to such an extent that even the smallest defect could barely be found in him.

10.   *Dealings with Julius III*

When Pope Julius III had been legate at the Council of Trent, he was very friendly to Ours, and after assuming the supreme pontificate he showed his constant benevolence toward the Society in both words and deeds. Father Ignatius went to him and successfully requested that the grace of the jubilee be granted to Ours wherever they might be, whether in Portugal, in India, Brazil, the Congo, or Africa, and begged that the same be granted also to neophytes living in places beyond the seas and, finally, to all Christians living there, adding this qualifier: "if it seemed good to His Holiness." The Supreme Pontiff granted this with a joyous heart, saying that he wanted to add a restriction. This was that he had communicated his whole authority to [members of] the Society in this area, so that they might use it in granting the jubilee insofar as they judged it expedient in the Lord.

When Father Ignatius went on to narrate what they were doing in the most remote countries for the glory of God and the benefit of souls, the Pope was unable to restrain his tears, tenderhearted as he was; he confided that what he had heard brought great consolation to his heart. Even though Father Ignatius sought only spiritual favors, the Pope spontaneously made mention of temporal matters, and ordered one of his assistants to remind him of this. He also enjoined Father Ignatius, even binding him under obedience, to come back to him whenever our house was in need of something.

15. *Plans for a meeting of the First Fathers*

Even earlier Father Ignatius himself and others of the First Fathers hoped to meet at Rome during this jubilee year to deal with certain matters of greater moment pertaining to the Society. But when Father Simão [Rodrigues], who had asked for this very thing, could not be easily pulled away from the court of the Portuguese king, Father Ignatius wrote to this king and asked him earnestly if, without losing his good favor, Father Simão might be allowed to come to Rome with the other Iberian Fathers. He also wrote Father Simão to make serious efforts that, even though his presence [in Portugal] seemed quite necessary, he nevertheless could partake in the [Roman] consultation on matters that affected the whole Society, once he had acquired sufficient information [in Rome] about matters pertinent to all the parts of the Society. But if the King seemed unwilling to allow this absence even for a short time, then Simão should send some men in his place who had accurate information about that province, specifically, Father Luís Gonçalves [da Câmara] with Father Jorge Morea.

16. *Jesuits and Francis Borgia come to Rome*

This year there came to Rome from Spain Francis Borgia (who was still regarded as the Duke of Gandía) and Fathers Antonio Araoz, Francisco Estrada, Diego Miró, and Andrés de Oviedo. They were accompanied by Father Francisco de Rojas and by Master Manuel de Sa, who was not yet a priest. Francis Borgia had taken care of his family matters, not only giving his daughters in marriage, one to the marquis of Denia (the Count of Lerma, that is) and the other to the marquis of Alcagnices; but he also found a wife for his eldest son, called the Marquis of Lombay, and left him well prepared to administer the duchy and afire with a great desire to serve God.

Toward the end of August, when there were eight months still to go before the predetermined time for him to abdicate his duchy, [Francis Borgia] began his journey to Rome along with all those of Ours whom I have mentioned. Not traveling like a poor man of Christ (even thought he had vows), he set out on his journey with twenty-five or thirty horsemen as if he were somebody seeking the grace of the jubilee, but in reality hiding his heart's decision and even his profession [of vows]. As he traversed parts of Spain, France, and Italy, he left behind a great reputation for virtues and the edification of his piety. . . .

17.   *Borgia reaches Rome*

When [Borgia] reached Rome, the ambassador of Emperor Charles and Lord Fabricio Colonna along with servants of various cardinals and a crowd of horsemen welcomed him outside the city and led him right to our house. Although several cardinals made him very loving offers of hospitality, still he preferred to live in a little corner of our house rather than in palatial accommodations elsewhere. The Supreme Pontiff welcomed him very graciously, and all the cardinals and prelates showed him the utmost regard. Many men came to visit him at our house, not yet having discovered his profession [of vows], even though, beholding the remarkable aura of humility and other virtues that he could not conceal, they suspected that he would join our Society sometime.

18.   *Ignatius and Borgia*

Father Ignatius granted him a part of the Roman house that was adjacent to the church and divided from the living quarters of the others by a garden. It had its own separate entrance through which laypeople could be let in or out of his quarters without disturbing the quiet of our house. Nonetheless, [Borgia] could have close daily contact with Ignatius and others, and he really offered to all, even to veterans in the religious life, a wonderful demonstration of his abnegation and obedience and solid virtues. However, that he had already made his profession, or even his intention to do so, was as yet unknown to all in the house, even though some signs in his face and words out of the abundance of his heart gave indications of this. . . . After dinner, when [Borgia and his son] wanted to come into the refectory and even into the kitchen to wash dishes, Father Ignatius suspected what they had in mind and gave orders to the minister of the house that he along with others should cut them off in the walkway leading into the refectory and ask them to wait; meanwhile he and other community members were to crowd together and block the exit of the walkway, thus preventing them from breaking through into the kitchen and compelling them to come back and have dinner in the room of Ignatius. . . .

25.   *The First Fathers approve the* Constitutions

Father Ignatius presented the *Constitutions,* which he had written and carefully commended to the Lord, to the senior fathers so that, if something came to mind that should be added, deleted, or modified, they would suggest it to Father Ignatius. But the fathers strongly approved them [as they were]. Not all the senior fathers still living were present, because they were detained in various regions and occupations; besides, they had already entrusted to Father Ignatius their role in making [the *Constitutions*], as is clear from their signatures on them. Therefore, neither Father Claude [Jay] nor Father Alfonso Salmerón was summoned from Germany, nor Father Paschase [Broët] from Bologna, nor Father Bobadilla from Calabria. Father Simão came from Portugal not during this year but during the following one; and both he and the other absent ones approved [the *Constitutions*] after they had seen them, just as did those who were present.

26.   *Ignatius considers resigning*

Because he was in rather bad health, Father Ignatius had been thinking about resigning his office of superior general, and this consideration among other things may have moved him to call the First Fathers of the Society to Rome. When all those who were at the house had gathered, he sent them a letter written in his own hand, asking that somebody else be elected as superior and declaring that he had simply and absolutely resigned the office of general and that he had permitted the professed to summon anybody, even the non-professed, to consult about this matter. But if they could not agree among themselves, he begged those who had the right to make decisions on this business to diligently commend this question to God. But all of them without exception judged that they should not accept his resignation and that the father should be asked to continue to carry this burden for the common good of the Society. At this time he became seriously ill, but through the kindness of God he shortly recovered his usual health (which, however, was far from strong).

29.   *A Polish impostor bilks the Jesuits*

In the course of the first months of this year, a certain Florian Rolis from Warsaw, an extraordinarily clever impostor, made the Society more cautious thereafter. This fellow, Polish by nationality, learned in the humanities and quite eloquent, indicated that he wanted to join the Institute of the Society. But he first went to confession and, all things considered, he seemed very suitable, so he was admitted. He suggested that he enter not at Rome but elsewhere because, as he indicated, he was fearful that his own blood relatives, who were of the high Polish nobility, would bring trouble to the Society. This was especially true of a bishop, his paternal uncle, who enjoyed the friendship of Cardinal Farnese.

Letters directing that he should be admitted were therefore sent to the rector of the college at Palermo. Because he had some letters [of credit] from some Antwerp merchants unknown to me that entitled him to receive a considerable sum of money, and because no one could be found at Rome who would pay out the money to him (unless he wanted to reveal himself to some important people, which was not expedient), it seemed to me that he should seek his travel money elsewhere, which he could recover later from an Antwerp merchant. He, however, was an extremely crafty swindler; he went not to Palermo but to Spain, pretending that a storm had blown him off course. Since he showed the letters he was carrying to Ours in various places in Spain and Portugal, he inflicted no small harm on Ours in carrying out his deception. Still, he taught [us] that henceforth, when dealing with unknown men, we should not be so credulous as to lend them money.

35.   *Opening a school at Tivoli*

Ours began to open a school for the use of the city, and almost seventy boys were coming to our church outside the walls of Rome, and thirty-eight of them were going to confession weekly. Their purity brought Father Miguel [Ochoa] great consolation. But the citizens of Tivoli involved themselves in transferring the school inside their city for the convenience of their sons, and they offered Ours a certain church located in the middle of the city. There was a woman of a prestigious family and a religious of the Third Order of St. Francis who gave the Society a garden with a cottage right inside the city. Her name was Lucia Cynthia. A certain nephew of this Lucia got into a quarrel with other people, and his blood relatives wanted to get him out of town, so they brought him to Father Miguel and asked him to try to convert him and keep him at [our] house till the tumult cooled down. Miguel agreed to this proposal and decided to help him through the Spiritual Exercises. In a few days he was so changed into another person that it was regarded as a miracle. . . .

37.   *Helping poor women at Arezzo*

While [Stefano Capumsacchi], a native of Arezzo, was in that city, he saw that several young women could not be admitted to a convent because they lacked dowries. He saw to it that while [the young women] were still in their parental homes, two devout older women undertook instructing them in what would contribute to their souls' advancement; he also arranged for the matrons to visit the young ladies at set times and thus speed them along the path of piety on which they had embarked. Accordingly, he received a written report while he was at Milan that these young women were making good progress in the frequent use of the sacraments and in piety and that some of them desired to enter a strictly cloistered convent called the "convent of the walled-in *[murata-rum]* women."

50.   *Landini helps reform the Modena Diocese*

When Father Ignatius, as a favor to the bishop of Modena [Giovanni Morone], sent Father Silvestro [Landini] to Modena, which was near those places [where he was working,] the bishop commissioned him to visit the whole diocese and entrusted him with the task of instructing all the pastors on how to preach to the people about material contained in the First Week of the Spiritual Exercises. When the *Spiritual Exercises* were being approved by the supreme pontiff Paul III, he was the bishop who was given two copies of it in different translations; he was the first to write a strong recommendation [of it]. Father Silvestro also taught catechism and preached daily and wrote instructions for the pastors on what was to be done for their own reformation and that of their people. He was able to present this with the authorization of the bishop and the duke. He engaged some people to watch over the teaching of Christian doctrine. He also continued with other pious works, as he had done earlier in other places, for instance, introducing frequent confession and Communion. He did the same things in the city of Modena, too, after returning from his visitation, which included hasty stops at 137 places. Sometimes he visited six or seven different places in a single day and preached in each of them, and the devotion of the people caused his charity to wrench exertions [from him] that exceeded his bodily strength. The whole household of the bishop himself was also led to weekly confession and Communion.

51.   *More on reforming Modena*

Already by this time the bishop of Modena hoped to have some men from our Society reside at Modena, even though he did not dare ask Father Ignatius for this, perhaps aware of his lack of funds. But Father Paschase [Broët], who was residing at Bologna, revealed his desire [to Ignatius]. For Father Silvestro was not equal to the work of confession, Communion, and the Spiritual Exercises; and even though bad health confined him to his room, necessity or devotion [drove] many people to burst in on him. Meanwhile, the number of people going to frequent confession or Communion at Modena increased wonderfully; and in the home of the bishop, [Silvestro] daily presented one lecture on one of the Lord's commandments and another one explaining the catechism to converts. The bishop took great delight at the harvest in the city and from the reports that reached him describing the visitation of the diocese.

54.   *Reforming the clergy and marriage in Apulia*

During autumn of this year, Doctor Cristóbal de Madrid, even though he was then exercising [his ministry] in the household of the cardinal of Trani, was still completely attached to the Society in his heart. That cardinal sent him as visitor to the diocese of Trani. In the first eight days he gave one or two exhortations to the clergy in the chapter house and had some private conversations with certain of them. Eleven priests left their concubines. He also gave [the concubines] an explicit command not to approach the residences of those priests; they obeyed this injunction, much to the edification of the whole city. Finding that the priests were wearing military rather than priestly garb, he also easily led them to care for their bodies in a proper manner and to wear the tonsure. He also earnestly exhorted laymen to leave their concubines; some of them did leave them, and others promised to do so.

Observing that many had become engaged but then had gone on living with their spouses fifteen or twenty years without receiving the sacrament of marriage and the blessing of the Church, he had a public proclamation made that he would supply the sacrament and the blessing of the Church that they had not received, once they had confessed their sins. This they were happy to do, and they came forward by twos and threes to receive the blessing of the Church, thereby bringing much consolation to the city.

A good many members of religious orders, adducing fictitious reasons, had requested and obtained apostolic letters permitting them to remain outside their monasteries. Cristóbal took care to have these men brought back to their monasteries after investigating and exposing the falsity of their claims or demonstrating that they no longer represented these men's actual situations. Then, at the end of this year he went off to visit the [entire] diocese, which was all too befouled with public sins.

56.   *Opening a first novitiate in Sicily*

The initial steps toward setting up a house of probation were put into effect during the first months of this year. Efforts were made to rent a house suitable for this purpose and near the college, but Satan was envious [of the foreseeable success] of this pious work and threw up many obstacles. The viceroy Juan de Vega had provided official letters to the nobleman who owned the house, but Father Nadal did not think it wise to use them for fear that the owner of the house might complain that pressure was being brought to bear against him. But God supplied another house, nearer and more suitable, for this work; and on the first day of Lent several novices who had been admitted from among those who aspired to the Society began to use that house. This turned out to be the first of the houses of probation. Father Cornelius Wischaven was also the first master and taught ten or eleven novices in spiritual matters so effectively that they made uncommon progress and edified the city no end. This year it seemed good to admit only so many and no more because of the shortage of temporal things; all these were admitted with their parents' consent. Joining [Wischaven] were two or three veterans who were put to work in administering the house. Although this house was separate from the college, still it was virtually adjacent, so that the rector of the college could go there as if to a different part of the college itself; moreover, it had no porter or entrance of its own.

57.   *Problems in setting up a university at Messina*

This year negotiations about a university were long and contentious; and in the larger council, composed of Messinans, the decision was finally made to apply revenues of fifty-five hundred scudi toward setting up the aforesaid university. Apostolic letters obtained at Rome subjected the whole university to the rector of the [Jesuit] college of the university, and thus the Society took over possession of it. The documents drawn up by the viceroy facilitated this matter. The inauguration of the university was magnificently proclaimed throughout the city with the blare of trumpets and a thunderous discharge of cannons. The next day lectures in law and medicine began.

But the people of Messina resented having the professors of law and medicine subject to Ours, so Father Nadal, with the assent and approval of Father Ignatius, arranged for separate faculties, so that one branch offering courses in theology, philosophy, and humanities was under the control of the Society, whereas another branch was established comprising the Faculties of Canon and Civil Law and Medicine and functioning under its own rector. This arrangement the people of Messina welcomed so gratefully that it seemed almost impossible for them to commend Father Nadal's solution highly enough, and they kept calling him a lover and father of the city.

But when it came to dividing the revenues, actions spoke louder than words: four thousand scudi were assigned to the other faculties; they applied only fifteen hundred scudi of the annual revenue to our college, which bore the burden of having fifteen teachers. Indeed, this money was to be paid by the officials of the city itself, with the entire sun to be paid at the discretion of the city. Since the meager income and the conditions seemed intolerable, it was obvious that in their hearts the citizens were angry with the viceroy, whom they blamed for these arrangements. When the affair was brought to Father Ignatius, it seemed to him that these conditions were completely unacceptable. He judged that a reasonable solution would be to demand that the revenues should be divided evenly between those two bodies. If a larger contribution could not be obtained, the Society would be obliged to send fewer teachers. And if what the Society desired could not be obtained, it was preferable for the college to remain as it was, with the donation remaining at only five hundred scudi, rather than have it take on such heavy burdens with only modestly increased revenues.

Because the viceroy was already preparing himself for the expedition to Africa, the question of the revenues was postponed until his return, and so this year gradually ran out. Dealing with this business was rendered considerably more complicated because some of the magistrates, whom they call the sworn ones *[jurati],* had been thrown into prison, and some of the previous sworn ones had been sent into exile. Ours never gave their assent [to the agreement], but in accord with the mind of Father Ignatius they referred the whole business to the viceroy. After he had set out for Africa, he wrote from a certain island that Ours should obtain from the city what they could, but [the city officials] would not contribute anything.

59.   *Helping the military; devotions during Carnival*

Master Isidor [Bellini] devoted useful work to preaching to the soldiers at the castle, to judge from the confessions they made and the marriages they entered into with their concubines. In the trireme, which was the only one left there, Ours helped the chained-up oarsmen to purge their consciences through the sacrament of confession. Rather than allow instruction to cease, by order of Father Diego Laínez, the visitor, during Lent sermons were delivered, not daily, but only on Sundays and feast days. Even during Carnival time steps were taken to ensure that dissolute behavior, which was customary during that season, did not hinder many from coming to confession and Communion and gathering in large numbers to hear sermons. This afforded much edification to the city, because things that were usually done in Lent were taking place during Carnival season.

72.   *Nadal and the Inquisition*

The bishop of Pavia, the inquisitor against heretical depravity, wrote to Father Nadal granting him authorization to carry out some functions pertaining to that holy office; but because it required [engaging in] criminal proceedings, Father Nadal did not accede to the request. The inquisitor wrote back to him expressing his surprise that Nadal had refused a task whose objective it was to uproot heresies, and insisting that no valid privileges existed excusing one from collaborating in the suppression of heresies. Still, because of his love for the Society, he allowed Ours to be excused from some aspects of this task; but when it was a question of verifying whether books were heretical or not, he indicated that he wanted the help of Ours now and we could not justly refuse to comply. Therefore, the inquisitor was gratified that we examined such suspected books. So, on the basis of the judgment of Ours, many books found in bookstores were burned without anyone from our Society's incurring shame or a loss of reputation. The inquisitor also gave them authority to absolve anybody who owned such [heretical] books. The belief is that the use of this concession produced significant fruit.

75. *The college at Palermo grows*

This year the state of our college at Palermo recorded a great increase [in enrollment]. The number of students climbed to 380, although there were fewer students in the upper classes of rhetoric and logic than in the other classes, in which the students increased in numbers as they diminished in age. Amid their strenuous labors, Ours drew great consolation from the outstanding progress their students made in letters. Some students had spent three or four years in other schools without laying a solid foundation in grammar. But now they themselves confessed that in these few months while they were attending the new college, they had made more progress than in all the previous time, crediting it to the orderly teaching, the diligence of the teachers, and especially to the help of God. . . . All went to confession monthly and some did so every other week; they attended the sacrifice of the Mass daily and also sermons on Sundays; in the afternoon many of them came to their teachers, who discussed with them spiritual matters and those related to virtue. . . .

77.   *Helping prisoners*

In the public jails, besides the confessions of many people, Ours arranged for twenty debtors to be set free, made possible by collections from the viceroy and other alms. Because many of them were sick and even dying and because there was danger that their baneful fever might infect others, Ours made great efforts to have them transferred to the hospital for care. The prisoners claimed that this is why they survived. But there was danger that some of those brought to the hospital might escape, even though they were under guard; but if they were left in the prison itself, death threatened many of them who were sick. Therefore, Julian, a Belgian and one of our brothers, besides bringing them the spiritual consolations of the word of God and the sacraments and the corporal consolations, including alms from the palace, began to build some small huts for the use of men imprisoned like these. But while he was working among them, performing acts of charity toward the sick, he himself contracted the sickness and thus, we hope, he exchanged his temporal life for an eternal one. Not only those confined to prison but almost the whole palace of the viceroy and many others with whom he had been acquainted took his death hard. . . .

Perhaps with his help [from heaven], the viceroy completed what [Julian] had begun and ordered fairly comfortable huts equipped with beds and other necessities to be prepared for the sick, and he employed two men to care for them; finally, he decreed that medicines and whatever else was needed should be supplied for them. So that this pious work would continue, the viceroy summoned the public notaries and urged them to undertake this charge of caring for those kept in prison; and he sent them to Fathers Diego Laínez and Jerónimo Doménech for advice on how they might promote this pious work. When they had done this and received their recommendations, the notaries, who numbered more than fifty in Palermo, set a time and place to meet, wrote up constitutions, and in accord with them elected ministers, each of whom would fulfil his own function in this holy work. . . .

79.   *Helping orphans at Palermo*

Efforts were made to promote and stabilize work with orphan children, because no organization or confraternity had assumed their care. In his sermons, which the viceroy and the whole city attended in large numbers, Father Laínez promulgated apostolic letters dealing with orphans and earnestly commended such a pious work. Then, on orders from the viceroy, two of the leading men urged the other nobles of Palermo to organize a confraternity to take care of the orphans. Within a few days more than fifty men of considerable authority were inscribed on the [membership] rolls of the congregation, constitutions were drafted, and officials were appointed who strove to keep up and expand the work that had begun.[1]

89.   *Helping prostitutes and converted prostitutes*

The convent of the reformed [prostitutes] was experiencing considerable want, so to help them and open the path of salvation to such women, this plan was implemented. A public edict prohibited women of this kind from wearing mantles *[pallia]* (the type of outer garment women are accustomed to use at Palermo), so that they might thus be distinguished from upright women. The prostitutes were ashamed to go about without the mantle and did not want to go out in public or attend Communion or religious services. Another difficulty arose: many people mistook poor women, otherwise respectable, for prostitutes because they could not afford to buy themselves mantles. To take into consideration both groups of women and at the same time help the convent of the converted, steps were taken to promulgate another public edict [stipulating] that those prostitutes who wanted to be granted the right to wear mantles should gather on the first Saturday of each month at a certain church, there to listen to a sermon aimed at their conversion and have their names recorded. Moreover, each of them would contribute every month two royal coins as alms for the converted [prostitutes].

Therefore, the first Saturday of May four leading women of the city and with them Fathers Diego Laínez and Jerónimo Doménech met together, bringing along the priest of the church and a notary. That same day seventy prostitutes came and listened to the sermon very attentively, shedding many tears; then they offered their alms. Each day some among them began to be led back from their shameful life to respectability. The alms were intended not only for the use of the converted but also as dowries for the poor women among them, so that they could be joined in marriage. Nonetheless, the confraternity that had been organized prescribed a certain sign to distinguish these sinful women from respectable ones.

---

[1] The Latin text has *alvo* (womb or belly), for which I read *albo* (a tablet).

93.   *Ignatius helps soldiers bound for Africa*

When the expedition to Africa was being prepared, many noblemen and other soldiers came forward for the sacrament of confession; since it was a jubilee year and this expedition was being undertaken against infidels, it seemed to Father Diego Laínez that it would decidedly benefit the expedition if the Supreme Pontiff granted a jubilee indulgence to those who confessed the sins committed while they were in the army or before they had enlisted. When [Laínez] conferred with the viceroy about this matter, the latter strongly approved [his proposal]. Not only would the souls of those dying be consoled thereby, but the soldiers would be inspired to fight bravely and fearlessly. So the viceroy wrote Father Ignatius and asked him to beg the Supreme Pontiff in the viceroy's name to grant that those who were engaged in this war and could not come to Rome might also acquire the grace and indulgence of the jubilee. This Father Ignatius obtained, and he transmitted to Africa (for which the army had already departed) duplicate copies of a testimonial letter signed with his own hand and bearing the seal of the Society.

102.   *Novices at Palermo leave the Society*

At that time Ours were twenty in number. Every Sunday, [while holding] disputations the scholastics defended propositions, and on class days they also posted letters and poems [where others could read them] and held similar scholastic exercises at home for the sake of practice. Because many young men wished to be admitted to the Society, [Ours] opened a house of probation, as they also did at Messina, but without the same success. In a short time, all the novices left except one. This was attributed to two causes: first, there was no one with the responsibility of taking care of them, someone especially skilled at giving spiritual direction in such circumstances; second, they pursued their studies even though they were engaged in the early stages of a novitiate and did not lay a solid foundation in the abnegation of their own inclinations, with the result that when some exercises of humility were imposed on them, they would not accept them, comparing them unfavorably with the studies that had so captivated them. Still, one of them returned and persevered with great edification in the Society as an outstanding worker in the Lord's vineyard.

113.   *Young nuns at Bologna inspire the old nuns*

Many people, both men and women, were engaged in the Spiritual Exercises with singular progress and afterwards set up a new plan for living according to God; and many of them found themselves inclined to a religious institute. Among the young women who entered convents, this was noticed: they served God with so much edification and devotion that the veteran nuns were awe struck when they saw novices able to teach, by their word and example, women who had been in the religious life for a long time—something hitherto unheard of.

122.   *Setting up a confraternity for visiting the sick*

One of our priests, as one of his probations, brought much consolation and assistance to the poor in a Bologna hospital and no less edification to the city. After he left there, several men and also women of noble blood were encouraged by Ours to form themselves into a confraternity and promise that each week some of their number would visit a hospital and bring consolation and aid to the sick.

123.   *Growth of Eucharistic devotions at Bologna*

On the Sunday within the octave of Corpus Christi, Father Francesco Palmio gave a Latin sermon to the priests and students on the dignity of this sacrament and the advantage of receiving it frequently. The sermon elicited satisfaction and warm plaudits from the audience, and more than six thousand people participated in the procession held that same day. When Ours introduced the custom in their Church of Santa Lucia of having a procession in honor of this Sacrament on the first Sunday of every month, almost all the other parishes in Bologna imitated the same practice; their rectors became more diligent in God's worship, and their parishioners visited their churches more frequently than usual. They began to sing vespers, which had not been done previously, and to teach Christian doctrine. They also took to decorating their churches more elegantly and to making more precious tabernacles *[vasa]* in which to keep the holy Sacrament and to arrange lamps to burn perpetually before it. When the most sacred Sacrament was taken to the sick, it was attended with great honor and many people accompanied it with lighted candles (which was hardly the case earlier). The sick too, contrary to custom, asked to receive the sacraments of both confession and Communion in good time.

133.   *No private funds for Jesuit scholastics*

I will not omit mentioning that, although Ours at Padua experienced a shortage of temporal possessions, when Father Ignatius learned that one of our scholastics was receiving money from his relatives for his private use, he forbade the practice henceforward. Even though Ours were suffering some inconvenience because of the furnishings of the house, out of love for poverty they gladly endured this.

■ **Germany**

145.   *Disappointing harvest in Germany*

Meanwhile in Germany Fathers Claude Jay, Alfonso Salmerón, and Peter Canisius were laboring in the Lord's vineyard, a sterile one, indeed. As far as theology courses were concerned, because even the young men studying in Germany were very corrupted [by heresy] and as yet had available no colleges in which they could study theology, the harvest from among those listening to our lectures was meager, especially considering that the harvesters could have used their talents elsewhere and probably reaped fruit in richer abundance. There was almost no progress this year as far as founding a college at Ingolstadt was concerned. This is not at all surprising, for William, Duke of Bavaria and a most energetic defender of the Catholic religion, reached the end of his days on March 6. Although Albert was his successor and the heir to both his father's dominion and his piety, still he could not suddenly grow into his role, especially since the new pope, Julius III, revoked the concession his predecessors had granted to the Duke of Bavaria about collecting tithes. . . .

147.   *Claude Broët at Augsburg*

When [Broët] was working at Augsburg, where many princes were attending the diet, he devoted himself to hearing numerous confessions and performed excellent work for Cardinal [Otto Truchsess] in everything that could contribute to God's glory. But he was able to improve the state of the Society in Germany more fully. Hence, Ferdinand, the king of the Romans, who loved Father Claude dearly and had already seen the exemplary work performed by [our] theologians who had been sent to Ingolstadt, wrote the Supreme Pontiff and asked for two theologians of the Society, in order to set up a college at Vienna in Austria. He also wrote Father Ignatius and explained the reason for his proposal, namely, so that a seminary for workers might be prepared there for both our Society and the province of Austria. While the affairs of the college were being settled, he asked for two theology professors from our Society who would in the meantime prepare the hearts of the people for the new college.

But the elector [archbishop] of Trier began to work toward establishing a college in that city of his; and although there were detractors who were lodging many false charges against the Society, when he at length recognized that these were contrary to the truth (on this matter the bishop of Eichstätt performed a splendid function of charity), he absolutely made up his mind to found a college at Trier. [Broët] also sounded out the elector [archbishop] of Mainz and instructed him regarding the Society's Institute, but [the archbishop] informed them that without the consent of his chapter no college could be founded.

151.   *Canisius at Ingolstadt*

Father Peter Canisius was made rector of the University of Ingolstadt, so when he preached to the people on feast days, he found an opportunity to admonish and chide the students in his [official] capacity. He settled their quarrels and restrained the contentious, pugnacious, and drunken [students], and with God's help he made his office useful for many people. As a result, greater modesty and better discipline began to obtain among the students. This was most welcome to the bishop of Eichstätt and to the chancellor of Ingolstadt University, to whom Canisius secretly submitted a summary account of abuses needing reformation. . . . The professors and students were unanimous in their praise of Father Canisius; while he vigilantly provided for the common good, they asserted, he still made it his major concern that no hatred or envy of the Society would erupt and that the door would not be closed against any future college [of Ours].

154.   *Successes and problems at Ingolstadt*

Although the student body at Ingolstadt was sparse and had little capacity to absorb instruction on more subtle material, still, our teachers carried out their duties with marvelous satisfaction and applause from both the university and the environs. As this year began, some students, contrary to custom, came to the chapel of our college to confess [their sins] and receive Communion; and Ours encouraged them to do this every month. In order to aid people to make progress in spiritual things, Father Canisius gave them private instruction in his room; for [Ours] were finding that in Germany there was need for a more solid foundation in matters pertaining to the faith, even among Catholics. Hence, Canisius concluded that they needed to be instructed at our house. These people turned in their copies of books written by Luther, Bucer, and Melanchthon; but the consolation this aroused partly evaporated when the pastor began to complain that our professors were getting mixed up in spiritual matters. Also not a few among those who had turned in their heretical books asked to have them returned after the feast days were over, so it was fairly obvious that they were strongly attracted to reading such books. . . .

155.   *Distaste for theology at Ingolstadt*

At the beginning of the year, Father Claude [Jay] began lectures on the Psalms after delivering a very learned inaugural lecture before quite a large audience, allowing for the German coolness toward the study of theology. When Lord Leonard Eck, [the Bavarian chancellor], had listened to some lectures by Ours, he drew from them great consolation and satisfaction of soul; and when he began to discuss founding a college, he indicated that it was the mind of the duke [of Bavaria] to found [the college] by applying to it [income] from certain monasteries no longer inhabited by monks. Ours indicated that if the college were founded, two professors of theology and one of philosophy would be available from our Society; for in Germany there was a great lack of such professors, and unless such a college were set up, hardly any hope remained of reviving the moribund theological studies. This was the case because German students were, on the whole, disgusted with the Theology Faculty and had little background in logic or philosophy. This proposal greatly pleased the chancellor; and as soon as Julius [III] was elected pope, [Eck] sent his legate to offer in his name the usual obedience both to the Pope and the Apostolic See. He commissioned his legate to see to it that certain monasteries were attached by papal authority to the college of the Society at Ingolstadt, and he sent the same number of letters about this proposal to eight cardinals.[2] . . .

158.   *The sad condition of German Catholicism*

Father Peter Canisius both had experience of and deplored the wretched state of religion in Germany because among Catholics divine worship had been cut back to some emotionless preaching on feast days. For them Lent was a mere word; there was no fasting, few attended Mass, and when it was celebrated in the college chapel, one could hardly bribe Catholics to attend it. It seemed very hard for Catholic men, especially learned men, to give up their heretical

---

[2] Polanco then goes on to relate how the deaths of Duke William of Bavaria and Chancellor Eck within two weeks of each other, combined with other pressing business, prevented any progress toward establishing a Jesuit college at Ingolstadt during the pontificate of Julius III.

books, partly because the reserved cases named in the bull *Cœna Domini* had not been promulgated there, partly because they insisted that it was not the Pope's intention to excommunicate learned men for possessing heretical books in order to refute them. Because people also shrank in revulsion from vows and the evangelical counsels, it distressed Canisius that men were not moved [to join] the Institute of our Society, although Master Lambert Auer at this time consoled them by entering the Society. Auer at the invitation of the pastor began preaching in German at a parish on Lætare Sunday; that first German sermon enjoyed considerable success, and contrary to what people expected, the Germans understood it the right way.

181.   *Canisius as rector at Ingolstadt*

Father Canisius did not cease from preaching in both German and Latin because he had taken on the office of rector. But he did find the burden of being rector rather taxing and perhaps not worth the effort he expended on it. These were the rector's responsibilities: inscribe new students, force debtors to pay their creditors, listen to the complaints and accusations of the townsfolk against the students, admonish drunken [students], jail those wandering around the streets at night, occupy the first place at banquets, meetings, and presentations. Rectors normally did not play a role in reforming studies and religion because they left office after six months. . . .

■ **France**

207.   *Setting up a Jesuit house at Paris*

This year after Easter Ours moved into the house of Clermont that the bishop [Guillaume du Prat] had turned over to Ours as a residence. After a porter was hired and a bell installed that those seeking entrance could ring, Ours began to have the external structure of a religious house. Meanwhile, three of the brethren remained at the Lombard College; they had what are called *bursæ,* namely, annual incomes for their sustenance. Thus, in Clermont House everything was organized on the pattern of our house in Rome, so that when the bishop visited us, he observed with a joyous heart how the beds, poor but clean, were set up for each person in separate small rooms, also how a certain suitable room was converted into a chapel, and how all things were in order. He decided to give the house to the college not only for its use but as its own property. Indeed, he was thinking about leaving to our collegians also its revenue, although he did not say this explicitly. He kept saying that henceforward those attacking the Society would be wasting their words on him. Day by day his affection toward the Society was growing, and the letters that recounted edifying accomplishments in various places, sent to wherever the Society was laboring, inflamed it still more. He was also wonderfully moved by the letters Father Ignatius wrote to him, which he said were full of the divine Spirit. . . .

208.   *Relations at Paris with the bishop of Clermont*

Father Ignatius could easily provide for what related to assigning a professed father to Paris. He sent letters patent to Father Battista Viola, so that he could make his solemn profession into the hands of some prelate, since there was no professed [father] in that kingdom. He sent the formula of profession and urged that [Viola] make it into the hands of the bishop of Clermont. This and many other things that displayed his goodwill toward and confidence in the bishop greatly touched his heart, especially Ignatius's determination that, as far as possible, everything appertaining to the foundation of the college and the house was to be undertaken at the discretion and with the approval of the bishop. . . .

209.   *Ineffectual efforts to gain legal standing in France*

It was more difficult to gain the legal status that they call *jus naturalitatis,* on which depends the right to have stable goods and revenues. But this year the path toward this was opened somewhat. The Cardinal of Guise was still at Rome after the election of the Supreme Pontiff; he began to be known as the Cardinal of Lorraine that same year (because the other cardinal of the same name, his relative, had died). Father Ignatius greeted him and called his attention to the affairs of the Society. Later this cardinal and three other French cardinals visited our house and had close and friendly discussions with Father Ignatius. Just as Father Ignatius had desired, the [Cardinal of Lorraine] offered to be the protector of the Society in the kingdom of France. . . .

Father Battista asked him to make efforts to obtain for us the *privilegium naturalitatis.* . . . But a few days later, after he had discussed this matter with King Henry [II] and the Most Christian King had indicated verbally that he was pleased with the proposal, the cardinal reported to Battista his success in obtaining what he had requested. But it was not as easy to obtain the document that would bear witness to the privilege as it was [to gain] the King's consent. The approval of the Royal Council was needed before the chancellor affixed his seal and, finally, the matter had to be referred to the Parlement of Paris. . . .

211.   *Toward a college at Billom*

The bishop hinted that he had another building at Billom, a city in the diocese of Clermont, where a tiny school had been established which he planned to give to the Society if he saw that the college at Paris was making good progress. He said that the superior of our college at Paris could send some men each year to Billom to devote themselves to teaching the humanities and philosophy in that school; and he wished to have this desire of his forwarded to Father Ignatius.

218.   *The Origins of the name* Jesuit

At this time a certain Carmelite preacher, while explaining in the Church of Saint Severinus the Pauline expression "brothers in Christ Jesus," began at this point to attack our Society because at Paris and Rome they had usurped for themselves the name "Jesuits," as if they alone were brothers in Christ Jesus. He urged the people not to make much of this title, since sometimes a book has a catchy title but contains nothing worthwhile inside. Therefore, just like that preacher at Salamanca [Melchor Cano], he urged his listeners, among whom were many professors, to be wary. Our friends thought it worthwhile for Father Battista to meet with him, but he thought it better to combat such words with patience.

220.   *Sinners become religious*

When three young men who were slaves to the flesh and the world, living with great license and making hardly any use of the sacraments, saw our students going to confession and Communion at the Carthusian church, they came to Father Battista. His exhortation to make a general confession of their whole lives had moved them. They made their confession to him, expressing great hatred for their past life. When they went to weekly Communion, you would believe that they had been changed by a marvelous metamorphosis into wholly different men. A fourth one, after persevering in frequent Communion fairly long, entered the religious order of the Minims (whom the Parisians call "the good men"). The other three made the Spiritual Exercises very fruitfully and decided to embrace the counsels of the Lord. One of them, a Belgian, who was twenty-six years old and a graduate of Louvain in philosophy, decided to enter the Society. Another joined the family of St. Francis. The third, who lacked an education, decided to serve the poor in a hospital as long as he would live.

■   **Spain**

235.   *Helping the country folk around Gandía*

One of our fathers preached to the Confraternity of the Blood of Christ, noted above, which was begun this year. Another preached to the neophytes [living] in the nearby countryside. Others performed this task in other places. Except for four preachers who had finished their studies, our brothers who were studying theology spread out on Sundays, visiting the villages in which the neophytes lived and scattering the seed of God's word in many places. In the College of Gandía, confessions covering many years and sometimes a whole lifetime were heard with great fruit. So many women from these people flocked there [to confession] that the student priests often had to put helping their neighbors in this matter ahead of their classes.

236.   *Helping the poor at Gandía*

Father Bautista de Barma was so caring in seeking out indigents even in the hospital to hear their confessions that by now more people came than he could hear. Hence, Father Jean Couvillon joined him as his companion to [share] this ministry, and they heard many people every day. Father Bautista also added the task of seeking alms and food that his poor penitents needed for their sustenance, and he himself carried a pot to the hospital for their food. This greatly edified not just the poor themselves but other people as well. So devoted was he to helping the poor that once, when an important man asked him to hear the confession of his daughter, Father Bautista answered that he would first allow the poor people to come to him [for confession], and then he would go to his daughter. The father mentioned this with satisfaction to the duke. This Father also saw to it that clothing was made for the use of impoverished sick people when they were able to leave their beds. And he revived the long-abandoned pious practice of taking weekly turns serving at the hospital. Thus did the hospital make progress while being administered in an orderly way, and the sick paupers received consolation and help. . . .

252.   *The Jesuits at Barcelona*

Meanwhile, those Fathers did not stop looking to buy a suitable house. In addition to being engaged in hearing confessions, they attended the theology classes that were being taught there and encouraged the students by devout conversations to [make] the Spiritual Exercises; and they directed some of them in the Exercises with great spiritual success. Four of those students decided to enter the Society, but Father Jean Queralt admitted only one of them, whose work around the house was needed; three succeeded in being admitted after obtaining letters from the provincial. More students besides these conceived wholesome desires and waited until they saw that the others were accepted. [Ours] admitted another man who was learned in philosophy and gifted with great talent; but his father searched out the viceroy and obtained from him [an order] that his son should be restored to him. For several months [the son] took his meals and slept at home, although he associated with Ours in the meantime. Thus, because the authentic privileges of our Society had not been sent there, the secular power interfered in this way with our affairs. But eventually the privileges were sent. Meanwhile, the young man, named Juan Oliva, remained fixed [in his vocation] and for greater stability made the vows of the Society, [copies of] which he sent along with his letters to Father Ignatius at Rome.

280.   *Establishing our way of proceeding at Valladolid*

This year a few members of the Society also lived in our house at Valladolid, [proving themselves] excellent servants of God and useful workers; but because they had not lived in a fully established college, they had very little knowledge of our Institute and even less about how our practice applied to community behavior. This was not surprising, for up to this time Ours were living by a tradition rather than written constitutions or rules, for those had not as yet been promulgated. When Father Torres passed through Valladolid and noticed that this was the situation, reflecting that the care of Ours in Spain had been handed over to him by Father Provincial, who was leaving for Rome, he sent Father Pedro de Seville from Salamanca to take care of the house at Valladolid and ordered Father Juan Gonzalez to come to Salamanca, where he took charge of the others. . . .

287.   *Difficulties at Alcalá with the archbishop*

Since many people were influenced by our sermons and frequented the sacraments of confession and Communion, and other people after making the Spiritual Exercises wanted to make their general confessions, a scruple occurred to Ours because all faculties had ceased because of the jubilee year. The archbishop [Silíceo] added to the difficulty by prohibiting anybody from receiving the sacrament of the Eucharist more than once a year. But Father Ignatius removed every scruple by obtaining from the Supreme Pontiff a confirmation of our faculties even in a jubilee year and by transmitting this communication to [authorities] wherever the Society was exercising its ministries.

292.   *Winning the cooperation of St. Juan de Avila*

When Father Ignatius recognized that many of those who had followed the authority of Master Juan of Avila were suited for the Institute of the Society, he dispatched a letter to Father Francisco de Villanova, bidding him to act in his own name and not that of Father Ignatius in dealing with Father Avila himself about incorporating these young men into the Society, or rather leading them to its Institute. Because he would not be able to carry this out until after Easter of the following year, in the meantime he turned this matter [about the young men] over to a friendly ecclesiastic from Toledo who was going to Father Juan de Avila, in the hope that he could make [Avila], who was already rather well disposed [to us], still more favorable. When he himself got together with Master Juan de Avila after Easter, it was [now] with less difficulty that he accomplished what Father Ignatius judged to be right.

300.   *Estrada's preaching is too popular*

It was remarkable how distressed was the University of Alcalá at the departure of Father Araoz and Father Estrada and how glowing was the reputation of the Society that they left behind and especially how eagerly the local residents desired a preacher of the same Society to follow up on what had been so well begun. Father Estrada had preached in the Church of Saint Alfonso, which was the main church of the university, to such a large audience that people who wanted to find a seat had to get up rather early in the morning. Those who could not find room in the church furnished so many listeners to other preachers that the size of their audience was larger than it had been before Father Estrada began preaching. Everybody claimed that never in that university had hearts been so moved.

Nor was it easy to satisfy the people and the university at the same time. When he was preaching during Advent in the Church of Saint Alfonso, the rector and the professors tried to persuade him to preach the following Lent in the same place. But agreeing to this meant that the other churches which had made the same request had to be denied. As a result, the vicar and canons of the main church at Alcalá complained to the university and rector, alleging that they had been harmed, and they induced Father Estrada to preach at least one day a week in the largest church.

312.   *Miguel Torres calms dissension at an Avila convent*

When [Torres] had come to Avila on business recommended to him by a nobleman, something that would result in God's great glory, he was asked to strive to bring peace to the nuns in a certain noble convent of that city; these numbered more than 120 and had long suffered from deep-seated dissensions. He went to the convent; and after he had delivered only one sermon, the sword of God's word so penetrated the minds of the nuns that, beginning with the abbess, they all prostrated themselves and begged pardon from one another, responding to a powerful impulse toward a union of charity. This and other works of piety that Doctor Torres performed there so moved the hearts of many that no one could remember anything similar ever having happened in that city. They began to ask for some men from the Society, offering them a house and everything they needed.

313.   *Torres restores broken marriages*

Ours taught children Christian doctrine and preached to the people in the environs of Salamanca. When a man found his wife pregnant [in the aftermath of] adultery and so was of a mind to kill her, one of Ours went and upbraided the man; and the Jesuit's words so calmed and mollified the dishonored man that he forgave his wife. Both of them, after making their confessions, agreed to live together in peace. Another brought charges against his wife, who had been caught in adultery. When a death sentence threatened the [sinful pair], Father [Torres] obtained from the offended husband what a leading citizen and many religious could not obtain, namely, that he granted pardon to both his wife and her partner in adultery; and [Torres] brought it about that both the husband and wife went to confession, and then on that very day her injured husband accepted his wife back into marital union.

■   **Portugal**

317.   *The Society in Portugal*

As this year began, Father Simão [Rodrigues] had decided to go to Rome, bringing with him several men, in compliance with instructions from Father Ignatius, who hoped that [Simão] would shed more light on the affairs of that province. So he sent ahead five priests who were to await him at Valencia or Gandía. . . . When these had said goodbye to their brothers, with tears flowing freely all the while, they entered Castile and began to beg alms in the vicinity of the city popularly known as Cuidad Rodrigo. They went to the hospice, and many of the leading men visited them and carried on pious conversations until midnight. The next day Father Gonzalez [de Silveira] preached right in the hospice, and a certain marchioness who was staying there with her mother heard him, as did a great crowd of the nobility. Many confessions ensued, and without exception the priests were kept busy with them. That marchioness manifested a wonderful regard for the Society, and Ours were barely able to escape the multitude of gifts that were somehow being urgently pressed upon them.

320.   *Establishing a house of studies near Coimbra*

This year many men—as many as 155 scholastics—were admitted into our Society at Coimbra. Many missions, moreover, were undertaken in various dioceses of Portugal, where the divine Goodness accomplished many things through those men for the edification of souls. Because they lived in more crowded conditions at Coimbra (the house not yet having been completed) and some men were suffering from bad health, and because experience had taught that Ours enjoyed good health near San Fins (an abbey now united to the College of Coimbra by apostolic authority), Father Simão judged that those of Ours who had begun the course in philosophy the previous year should be sent to San Fins, even though the house was thirty-six leagues distant from Coimbra.[3] Thus, he looked after the health of the sickly without detracting anything from the studies of the young men, who did not attend the public classes. Those who remained behind lived more comfortably, and the spiritual work Ours accomplished was meanwhile very advantageous for the people near the monastery of San Fins.

321.   *Moral theology at Coimbra*

This year a second course in philosophy was begun at Coimbra, and fourteen of Ours were assigned to it from among those who already had training in Latin and Greek letters. The exhortations that the collegians used to give were reduced in number this year so that they would not hamper progress in studies. The theologians engaged in frequent disputations. Thirteen priests read cases of conscience at home, a subject that, it would seem, should not be a part of the theology or philosophy curriculum. These men became very skilled at

---

[3] The text has *leucis,* which is not a Latin word; I read *leugis,* which means a league, a distance varying between 2.4 and 4.6 miles.

hearing confessions partly from these readings, partly from holding discussions in common *[collationibus]*, partly [from analyzing] the decisions of professors at the university, which were available to them. . . .

322. *Developments at Coimbra*

Those who were admitted to the Society were tested by various exercises in abnegation. Worth noticing was the zeal for humility of one man who had been greatly honored when he was a layman. He wanted to be taught by the lowliest members of the Society. He was sent to buy some pigs outside Coimbra; although he could have gone out by a less frequented route, he wanted to leave through the public road, not wearing a cloak, carrying a rope in one hand and a stick in the other. On his return he herded the pigs, tied together by the rope, right through the middle of town and up to the college. He did many other things that way.

All of Ours had keen hopes of receiving letters from our Father Ignatius that would contain instruction coupled with encouragement, and they requested them with great eagerness. Because Father Luis de Grana had been moved away and Father Urbano [Fernandez] was made prefect this autumn at the College of Coimbra, he earnestly asked Father Ignatius for rules and procedures to serve as a norm according to which he could govern all the spiritual and temporal aspects of the college. He also requested a visitation, so that [Ignatius] might know and guide his sheep. If [Ignatius] was too beset by administrative problems to come, could he at least provide it with written directives so that all might walk together in one spirit. They knew that hitherto they had been following provisional norms; but if Father Ignatius should send other instructions, they would accept and observe them. In his own time Father Ignatius did both: for he sent the *Constitutions* and the rules there, and also a visitor, as we will see later.

323. *Activities of Ours at Lisbon*

Since Father Simão was absent, Master [Luís] Gonçalves [da Câmara] was in charge of the other men at Lisbon and was constantly occupied in hearing confessions and participating in other pious exercises. There were fourteen of Ours in that house, but the number increased from time to time as men accompanied the fleet to India or Brazil or the other places where Ours were usually sent. Even though this house at Lisbon was at the time designated with the name of a college, still the house of the professed did not carry out the [usual] duties of a college; for Ours devoted their efforts to the ministries undertaken by the Society and not to studies. Every day many people were refreshed by the sacraments of penance and the most holy Eucharist in our church, which was dedicated to St. Antonio.[4] If the priests had been numerous enough, we believed that the greater part of that city would have flocked to them. . . . The Spiritual Exercises were presented to many married people, who serve God by examining their consciences, practicing mental prayer, frequently receiving the sacraments, and performing other pious activities with great purity. Those mentioned above who met at our house on Fridays for a flagellation made progress with great fervor; one of Ours began with a sermon, and the litanies and other prayers followed the flagellation. Although this took place at night, the Queen and the prince wanted to see it, because they recognized that it contributed greatly to stirring up piety and devotion.

---

[4] St. Anthony of Padua was born near and raised at Lisbon.

THE YEAR 1551

■ Overview of the Society

1.   *The European Society*

At the beginning of 1551, the state of the Society was not changed as regards its provinces. There were only three provinces as such, namely, India, Portugal, and Spain. In the other areas of Italy, Sicily, Germany, and France, there was no provincial; the superiors received instructions, help, and encouragement by means of letters from Father Ignatius himself. The Society resided in the same places as at the start of the previous year, but the communities were withdrawn from two places, namely, from Venice in Italy and San Fins Abbey in Portugal. . . .

■ Italy

4.   *Francis Borgia's humility at Rome*

Let me return to the duke [Francis Borgia]: before he departed from the Roman house, he left remarkable evidence of his solid abnegation, obedience, and profound humility. . . . Before leaving, he obtained from Father Ignatius permission to take his food not only in the refectory but also at the "little table," which was situated in the middle of the refectory and served for penitential purposes. . . . On the day of the Purification itself, that is, two days before his departure, he brought out supper in the refectory for everybody who was in the house and, along with his son, he waited on table without any headgear, and this right to the end [of the meal]. On his departure, after receiving the blessing of Father Ignatius, he wanted to embrace all the brethren individually with singular charity and devotion. In those final days it was his desire to assist a certain cook by sweeping the kitchen and washing the dishes. Because his son, Lord Juan, who was his father's companion in all these exercises, accidentally broke a clay dish, [Borgia] ordered him to say a *culpa* from the lectern.[1] . . .

---

[1] Little table and saying a *culpa* (i.e., confessing a personal fault to the community, usually at the main meal) remained in use as a Jesuit form of penance until the 1960s. Those eating at little table usually knelt on the floor during the meal.

10. *Salmerón preaches at Naples*

[Salmerón] returned to Naples and stayed eight days at the Hospital of Saint James because there was no opening at the cathedral church, a certain preacher having taken over his work there. He decided to give lectures in the Church of Saint Mary Major, as it is called; Father Diego Laínez preached there when he was present during advent time. Thus, four or five times every week [Salmerón] lectured during the afternoons on the Letter of Blessed Paul to the Galatians, starting the second Sunday of the month. Day by day his audience grew larger, as did the goodwill of those who came. In the hospital for the incurables, where there were usually six hundred or more poor people, he preached and brought the benefit of spiritual consolation to the indigent. Devout men considered the fruit of his lectures all the more impressive because, with great spirit, learning, and truth, he refuted the errors of the heretics that had infected many at Naples, thus dispersing the dark clouds of such errors with the blazing light of truth.

11. *Salmerón returns to Rome*

He also preached in a convent of the converted [prostitutes] and in some other convents. But because, at the urging of Emperor Charles, the Supreme Pontiff had again called the Council of Trent into session, scheduling it to convene the coming May; and because the Pope [Julius III] had got to know our men well while he was legate and while at Bologna, he informed Father Ignatius that he wanted to avail himself of the services of Fathers Diego Laínez and Alfonso Salmerón in the forthcoming council. A written message was [sent] to Father Salmerón that he should return to Rome after Easter time. But when Father Salmerón told his hearers about this, they received the news with no small resentment, for he had begun to be both marvelously welcome and helpful to the Neapolitans. Striving to keep him at Naples at least for a time, his friends wrote various letters, [stressing] that his presence was advancing the business of a college, while his absence could slow it down and impede it. Regardless, he said goodbye to his friends and returned to Rome. He was even more in a hurry lest Father Simão, who was preparing to return to Portugal, should leave before they could have the pleasure of conversing with each other.

12. *Ignatius dismisses a Jesuit*

Father Giorgio Morera made some serious charges at Rome against his companion on the journey, Father Simão. But because Father Ignatius earnestly wanted to shed light on the question, the accuser himself ended by recanting his charges.[2] For this and other just reasons, he was dismissed from the Society (he was not yet professed), even though he was otherwise a very learned man and a preacher. Simão, after completing the business he had come to Rome to do, left that city and returned to Portugal before the oppressive heat began.

13.   *Salmerón gains new faculties for Jesuits*

Before Father Salmerón left Rome for Trent, he spoke to the Supreme Pontiff, Julius III, with whom he was acquainted.[3] He successfully requested from him some faculties for the use of the Society; they authorized Father General, either in person or through others to whom he communicated this faculty, to absolve in those cases of heresy reserved in the bull *Cœna Domini* and to dispense those who were under his obedience in the matter of both fasting and the choice of foods. Because few people had come to the council in the month of May, [the day when the fathers were to] convene was postponed till September; so it seemed that [Salmerón] should be freed from the pledge he had given to the bishop of Verona about returning to him after he had participated in the meeting at Rome. But Marcello [Cervini], the Cardinal of Santa Croce, who later was pope, was going to Gubbio that summer, so he obtained from Father Ignatius permission to take Father Salmerón with him [so that he could] enjoy his companionship for thirty or forty days.

14.   *Salmerón's pastoral activities at Gubbio*

. . . The cardinal gave Father Salmerón three main tasks. The first was to instruct the canons of the cathedral church and other churchmen and exhort them to live in accordance with their state of life. The second mandate was that he preach at convents of nuns under the bishop's jurisdiction, instructing them in what pertained to their institute. The third was that at home he give a daily lecture on a reading from Saint Paul, at which the cardinal himself and many of his household were his audience. The cardinal also brought up other things in private with Father [Salmerón]; and as long as he remained there, that is, up to the feast of St. John [December 27], he was engaged quite fruitfully in these occupations. So that he could more gently tear [Salmerón] away from the

---

[2] In Latin "recantaret palinodiam." This could reasonably be understood to mean "he recanted his recantation," which might make Ignatius's action even more understandable.—ED.

[3] Before his election Julius III had been legate at Trent while Salmerón was a theologian there.

cardinal, who treasured him greatly, Father Ignatius undertook to have letters written to both Cardinal Santa Croce himself and to Salmerón, ordering the latter in the name of the Supreme Pontiff to set out along with Father Laínez for Trent at the first opportunity. Therefore, the cardinal gave him travel money and sent him off lovingly, sending a letter of thanks to Father Ignatius.

21.   *Laínez reforms a convent at Pisa*

He preached on weekdays at four convents in that city (the only ones in Pisa under the archbishop's jurisdiction). All of the [nuns], contrary to the institute of their vows, owned [private] property. But thanks be to God, in three of the convents—actually, according to the nuns, in all of them—they were led back to a common life that was in keeping with their profession of poverty; and in one, which excelled the rest in the number and nobility of its nuns, the reformation was more striking. It was near the palace of the duchess, so she sometimes came to hear the sermons of Father Laínez. In it each of the nuns had been accustomed to dine by herself, and as soon as the bread was baked, the nuns divided it among themselves. Thus they seemed to retain not even the shadow of [being in] a religious order. Neither the archbishop nor their confessors were able to persuade them to observe their rule; but by the grace of God working through the word of [Laínez], not only did they return to the observance of their rule and common life on this matter [of poverty] but they made great progress in all aspects of their institute and in perfection of spirit, so that this was recognized as entirely the work of God. After Easter he continued his lectures on the Ten Commandments, to the consolation and delight of those who heard him; they all greatly desired for the Society to have a permanent place at Pisa.

24.   *Alms for the nuns at Florence*

At the urging of the same father [Laínez], the Duchess of Florence gave some alms to the poor and provided the nuns with much help, some of it money, some of it other necessities of life, so that they might live in common according to their institute. During his leisure Father Laínez reread some of the holy Fathers . . . ; he did this at just the right time, insofar as this year he was going to Trent for the council at the command of the Supreme Pontiff.

26.   *An unsuitable site for a college at Pisa*

[Laínez] judged as unsuitable the site that the duke and duchess wanted to assign for the promised college at Pisa, seeing that it was in a remote and unhealthful place. Although the duke and duchess were favorably disposed toward the Society and toward Father Laínez in particular, the latter could talk with them less than he wanted because they were very preoccupied with hunting and fishing.

29.   *Helping the poor and starving at Florence*

[Laínez] also continued to preach on Sundays and feast days; in the second part of his sermon, he urged his very large audience to give alms. This produced much assistance for the poor, who were suffering greatly this year from famine, even though Duke Cosimo had ordered that one loaf of bread be given daily to every poor person in all the cities under his authority on which the poor converged from nearby areas. This largesse supported more than a thousand poor people at Florence, who could find scarcely any other alms all day. Father Laínez spent his weekdays hearing the confessions of the poor and in giving them Holy Communion, and he took care to provide some extra alms for those who went to confession. By means of these sacraments, he also restored [to grace] some of the important men of the city. On Fridays he began to preach—with good reason hoping for considerable success—to those who were being held in the public prisons, who were many and had much to endure.

31.   *Laínez at Florence*

[Laínez] very frequently heard the confessions of the sick confined to the hospital of San Paolo, where he himself was living. But on the octave of Saint John the Baptist [June 31], he preached this year also to a very large and attentive congregation; at the end of the sermon, he urged all of them to join in a prayer, which he himself led. [To find] a good place to preach he was forced to leave the hospital mentioned above and move to a church near the archbishop's house. And so the days he spent at Florence before he went to Trent were passed with great spiritual advantage even though negotiations over the college went forward at such a lethargic pace that they considerably taxed Father Laínez's patience.

Finally on July 10, when he was just about to leave with Father Salmerón for Trent, he wrote an account of his dealings these days with the duke and duchess. It came down to this: at least a college at Pisa was going to be started at this time. The duke himself would give two hundred gold scudi for the expenses of [our] collegians, while the duchess [would give] from fifty to a hundred; finally, they promised to give what was needed to support a dozen collegians, taking into account that those at Pisa would have grain and wine from annual rents. They agreed that they would also give a residence and that the collegians would be sent there in time for the beginning of classes.

But [Laínez] himself thought that somebody should be sent ahead to prepare the residence and what was needed for those who were coming, and he suggested that Father Elpidio [Ugoletti] would be suitable for this. Father also encouraged the duchess to write to the Supreme Pontiff or to her ambassador, bidding him to talk with the Pope and also with Father Ignatius. The duchess indicated that she wanted to obtain apostolic letters also forbidding Father Laínez to leave their jurisdiction without her permission or that of the duke. And thus, after receiving travel funds from the duchess, [Laínez] set out for Trent with Father Salmerón and thus did not need to make use of the travel funds that Father Ignatius had offered.

32.   *More problems at Florence*

When Father Elpidio came to expedite this business, he found out that it was the wish of the duchess that the college not be inaugurated until Father Diego Laínez returned. She indicated clearly her reason for founding the college was so that she would have Father Laínez in her jurisdiction. Thus Father Elpidio returned to Padua with the project unrealized.

33.   *Loyola's response*

Father Ignatius easily understood the strategy of the duke and duchess and saw that as a result of it a project useful for God's glory and the salvation of many souls was being either impeded or delayed. . . .

37.   *The duchess proves difficult*

The duchess then wanted to talk with Cristóforo [Laínez] alone, and she told him that she had written to the Supreme Pontiff to have him send her Father Diego [Laínez]. Then she inquired how many of Ours had come and how many of them were Spaniards. When she found out that there were twelve [Jesuit collegians] in all and only two Spaniards, and that the others were some of them Italian, some French, and some Flemish (who nevertheless spoke

Italian), she asked: "Why do you send Frenchmen here? What are you doing, sending these Flemish here? Why not send them to their own countries?" She said more of the same. She next added, "You sent me some priest whom I do not know, and he does not know me." She then went on to say that she very much hoped that there would be a college at Florence; but in the meantime, until a suitable place at Florence was agreed upon, the Jesuits should live at Pisa for a time. . . .

40.   *The humble start of a Jesuit college at Florence*

At roughly the same time the Church of Saint Joseph, which belonged to some confraternity, was offered for the use of the college; but because it was far removed from the busy section of town, the house was tiny, and the air was unhealthful, it was not accepted. The enthusiasm [to have] Ours [in Florence] grew so unrestrained that people were saying that more than three hundred or four hundred students would be ready as soon as classes began. Father Louis [Coudret] had doubts whether such enthusiasm could be sustained, for some of the twelve had been sent only to teach grammar and humanities.

The college at Florence had such a humble beginning that Master John, a guest of the Society and its friend, did not hide in his letters what he thought, namely, that in such a famous city not all [of Ours] should be young men. He also wrote that he had hoped for men endowed with greater knowledge and skill at preaching, because that city was filled with learned and talented men, both religious and laymen, whom neither the sermons nor the lectures of Father Louis could satisfy. But laying a humble foundation seemed good to Father Ignatius, so that gradually a spiritual edifice might be built up. Besides, at that time the Society did not have more suitable men who could be sent.

41.   *Starting a college at Ferrara*

That same year the college at Ferrara opened its doors before those at Naples and Florence. For the Duke of Ferrara, as he had promised more than once, showed himself favorable to founding a college. Since he was greatly devoted to Father Claude [Jay], . . . he seemed not to have taken it with much equanimity when later he found out that [Jay] had been summoned to Vienna by Ferdinand, the king of the Romans. But even so he did not desist from founding the college. Nonetheless, he designated the site of San Luigi that Ours did not consider a suitable location in which to carry on the functions of a college. . . .

Our friends rented a house and furnished it with furniture they had donated. But the duke himself promised that he would give two hundred gold scudi every year. Although he showed Father Paschase [Broët] that he was well disposed toward the Society, he did not offer more than this sum; moreover, he ordered that the college teachers be summoned, among them as many priests as possible, men outstanding not just for their lives but also for their learning. He declared that he wanted to use their efforts for things of great importance. Still, Father Paschase showed the duke that it might be difficult to send many men, for they had to be sent to many other places as well; but he assured the duke that Father Ignatius would do what he could to gratify him because he acknowledged that right from the beginning the Society owed a great deal to [the duke's] goodwill and generosity. Meanwhile, Father Paschase informed Father Ignatius that seven or eight men and not more should be sent, among them some priests. . . .

42.   *Problems arise for the college at Ferrara*

Father Ignatius therefore sent seven men from Rome whose leader was Father Jean Pelletier, who had been superior at the Roman College for a few months. He also wrote Father Paschase that he would send Father Francesco Palmio or, if not, that [Paschase] himself should go to Ferrara and take charge of the college as its superintendent. But when [Ignatius] sounded out the mind of Father Francesco Palmio, that man, excellent though he was, was subject to melancholy; he was so disturbed after he had been informed of this [assignment] that he fell into a fever that lasted for some days. . . . The duke in his letters indicated to Father Ignatius that he was grateful for the arrival of our men, which he hoped would redound to the spiritual advantage of his people. . . .

47.   *The first stages of the college at Ferrara*

The number of our students began to increase daily and climbed to almost one hundred and twenty. Since the grammar students had not laid solid foundations in the rudiments, it required a great deal of work to instruct them in these things. Little boys came who did not know how to read or at least how to write. But Father Ignatius ordered that such students should not be admitted in the future. Even though it was a meritorious work, Ours could not carry out this elementary instruction on their behalf without great inconveniences.

On Sundays and feast days one of the brethren or an extern student gave a presentation on some virtue. Performed in the presence of the extern students, this kind of exercise proved very gratifying to the parents of the young people. A lesson in Christian doctrine followed at which a good number were present in addition to the students. Every day the students heard Mass in a nearby church; going and coming, they all prayed before a statue standing in the school. Finally those who were students of our college were easily distinguished from other students by their piety and good behavior. . . .

49.   *A Jewish man and woman are baptized*

A Jewish man and woman were instructed in Christian doctrine, and the woman was baptized in the cathedral church; but the man fell into a serious sickness and was baptized while lying in his bed, and after receiving the last anointing there that same day, he departed for a better life.

64.   *Devout women at Bologna*

[Paschase Broët] has such spiritual impact on many young women that some of them eagerly sought to enter a religious order. Some aspired to [a life of] virginal purity, and some after careful deliberation bound themselves to this by vow. Paschase declared that their devotion and progress in prayer, to which they applied themselves day and night, defied description. They fasted several times a week and chastised their bodies in other ways, so much so that they needed a bridle to keep them from going beyond [reasonable] limits. Among the other virtues, their obedience shone forth, for they did not want to deviate from the advice of their spiritual father by the width of a fingernail, as the expression goes. There were also widows who strove to imitate Anna, who was dedicated to prayer and fasting; the chaste Judith; and Tabitha, who was very devoted to works of piety.[4] They gave themselves over to prayer and fasting and proved themselves mothers to the poor; you might see them in the morning praying fervently before the holy Sacrament for two hours; when some left, others took their place at the Church of Saint Lucy, so that some were at prayer in the church at almost every hour of the day.

Many married women, including some from the city's nobility, also frequently approached the sacraments of confession and Communion. They were a source of admiration and edification for all in their bearing and dress, for they had put aside their pearls, silk dresses, necklaces—in short, their ostentatious adornments. In that city, where vast sums were lavished on vain and superfluous

---

[4] The allusions are to Luke 2:37, Judith 13:16, and Acts 9:36.

finery, their [new-found simplicity] was even more beneficial. This development greatly pleased the menfolk, who no longer were burdened with having to pay for their wives' extravagances, as hitherto had been the case. As a result of this, the men themselves encouraged their wives to a spiritual mode of living. The men did not come to confession and Communion as often, but many of the nobility and students also made progress in piety and spirit. . . .

74.   *Silvestro Landini at Modena*

At Modena several public sins were stamped out in the city, some feuds were brought to a peaceful resolution, the worship of the holy Sacrament was increased in the same city, the [Eucharist] was reposed where it had not usually been kept, and a continuously burning [candle] was placed before it. Christian doctrine was taught every day in public; sermons were given not only daily but sometimes twice or three times in the same day at different places. This spring [Landini] visited places where he had worked in previous years and there exercised the usual ministries of the Society, enjoying similar success. He composed constitutions for a new monastery in Casula.[5] He saw to it that some heretics were thrown into prison, so that they could not infect the Lord's flock. He took care that alms were given to the poor and assistance to the sick. He taught many people a method of prayer. Furthermore, he brought about the restoration of churches in many places, the reservation of the holy Sacrament in them, and the acquisition of the ornaments and vessels needed for divine worship. He established a Confraternity of the Body of the Lord in almost all villages and inculcated the practice of weekly or semiweekly Communion—or at least he forbade [members of the confraternity] to defer its reception beyond the first Sunday of the month. In each place he assigned two men to settle the innumerable feuds and two more to look out for the poor. He also left in each parish a method for explaining Christian doctrine on every feast day. All these things yielded wonderful fruit.

In some places, one called Castello Nuovo and the other Foiano, the townsfolk of one so feuded with those of the other that neither the bishop, as he himself confessed, nor the other important men, who made heroic efforts to accomplish this, were ever able to bring those people into harmony. By the zeal and charity of Father Silvestro, these places agreed upon mutual peace. The same occurred at two other towns, namely, San Almazio and San Levizano, that

---

[5] A later reference (§85 in year 1551) suggests that this was a convent of nuns.

no one, despite diligent efforts, had been able to reconcile. While Father Silvestro was visiting the aforesaid places, at his urging they entrusted the seeds of discord and the controversies to [the arbitration of] two good men, just as he had proposed. Almost the whole diocese was complaining that advocates of heretical depravity had fanned out from the city of Modena itself and from the town of Saxulo and had infected many others.[6]

77.   *Landini's work in the surrounding towns*

Seven or eight days before he returned to Modena, [Landini] visited almost forty places in the dioceses of Modena and Bologna and preached with considerable success in five or six or sometimes even seven different towns in one day. To be brief, I will report that the Confraternity of the Body of Christ was set up in the individual towns, [whose members] went to Communion every week or at least every month; directors were elected who were in charge of both the men and the women of such confraternities. Just as we reported had been done in other places, in this instance also two men were elected to settle vendettas.[7] So great was the discord reigning in several towns that in one place fifty, in another sixty, and elsewhere more than a hundred people had been killed. Every place was full of murders, oppression, violated young women, and robberies; and the wounds were still festering. If I may note one example from which the others may be conjectured, forty of those who had conspired to kill someone and then been thrown in jail were summoned individually by a certain Tanario; once he had them securely in his hands, he cut off their heads, sparing not even a single person, and this [he did] even though he was an old man.

To those conciliators [Landini] described this method of achieving peace that he had devised in the Lord to help them perform their task well: each feast day they were to assemble in the church with their children, so that they could teach one another Christian doctrine; for they have lived in the greatest igno-

---

[6] On Modenese Protestantism, see Salvatore Caponetto, *The Protestant Reformation in Sixteenth Century Italy,* trans. Anne and John Tedeschi (Kirksville, Mo.: Truman State University Press, 1999), 256–60. Part of the problem at Modena was that the bishop was Cardinal Giovanni Morone, who was occupied with his duties as a papal legate. Later under Paul IV he was imprisoned while being investigated for heresy. After the death of Paul IV, he was vindicated and sent to preside at Trent by Pius IV.

[7] Pacifying vendettas seems to have been a Landini specialty: see also vol. 1, §407, and vol. 2, §74 in year 1551, and John W. O'Malley, *The First Jesuits* (Cambridge, Mass.: Harvard University Press 1993), 169 f.

rance of God and of the things pertaining to their salvation. This is why such grave evils arose in those mountains. He also picked out women to take care of the sick, so that they might be protected in advance by confession and Communion; and if there were poor people, so that [these chosen women] might send some persons from the confraternity through the villages to provide necessities for the sick. Settling quarrels among women fell to the same women.

The women also were to gather on the same days to listen to lessons in Christian doctrine and to train their daughters better in chastity and modesty than they had done previously. [Landini] took care of seeing that they heard Mass, said all their prayers or rosaries, and observed the fast days of the Church. All of them promised to do all these things, and the many tears of both the priests and the laypeople demonstrated that they were speaking from their hearts. On his second visitation he noted that a remarkable change of life had taken place, and he found that both priests and the laypeople had made great progress in piety. In some places almost everyone went to Communion on Sundays. He found out that in one place almost fifteen hundred rosaries had been acquired.

81.   *Landini, a priest, and his concubine at Modena*

Such a sweet odor wafted from the convent of the converted [prostitutes] where Father Silvestro was preaching that exemplary virgins too wanted to be admitted to that convent. There was a certain priest, blessed with both wealth and a good number of relatives, who was unwilling to dismiss his concubine. Father Silvestro, by the authority granted him by the bishop, suspended the priest from [administering] the sacraments. [This priest] had five sons at home, and he severely threatened the witnesses who testified about his life. Therefore, when [Silvestro] encouraged the people in his parish to frequent confession and Communion, to the study of Christian doctrine, and to care for the poor, as we have recorded, he publicly excommunicated the concubine of that [priest]; but to avoid an uproar, he did not excommunicate that priest in public. But with the people out of earshot and relying on the testimony of many people, as we have written above, [Landini] suspended him from [administering] the sacraments. [The priest] tried to placate Silvestro by offering gifts, but [our father] would in no way accept them. But other priests were terrified by this example, and many good [priests] were greatly edified. The suspended priest came to Silvestro and confessed both that [Silvestro] had been the proper medicine for him and that no one else could have cured him. Silvestro replied that he would believe his works, not his words, and urged him to imitate the penitence of Adam, David, Magdalene, and Peter; only then he would absolve him from his suspension. He accepted that sentence with humility.

82.   *Reforming the Modenese clergy*

In short, Father Silvestro visited 120 locations or more and sowed the seed of God's word in them. In all of them he introduced frequent confession and Communion with one or two exceptions, in which people went to Communion not every week but on the first Sunday of the month. The people began to respect their priests, whereas previously they did not acknowledge them as priests. Many of these priests freed themselves from their inappropriate garb, gambling, dancing, hunting, buying and selling, running inns, carrying arms, and keeping concubines; some also began spending their time hearing confessions, administering Communion, and in pacifying disputes. A number of them also preached on feast days and taught Christian doctrine, and sometimes Father Silvestro himself did these same works either in their company or by himself. He taught the priests by both word and example how to engage in the deeds of both devotion and mercy.

They gathered every fifteen days for a disputation on cases of conscience and took notes on the matter under discussion in the presence of Father Silvestro. More than fifty churches were refurbished, and tabernacles were made for the most holy Sacrament. While he was traveling from one place to another, especially in the province of Garfagnana, he heard confessions while en route; when the confession was ended, he sat along the roadside to give absolution.[8] Among the good priests who had made the Spiritual Exercises, he found some who gave weekly Communion to all their people, with a few exceptions; day by day this holy practice was spreading to parishes in nearby localities.

85.   *Ignatius rejects unlettered priests*

[Silvestro] also went to the diocese of Sarzana, as [he had done] earlier, and visited that new convent in Casula in which several nuns had behaved badly; but when he arrived, they were so repentant that they humbly begged pardon and pleaded to be thrown into chains. He heard all their confessions to the great consolation of the whole town and gave them Holy Communion. He

---

[8] This might signify that he heard confesssions and gave absolution right where he happened to be while on the road to his next destination.

reinstated the prioress who had [held that office] previously, and put a certain priest named Francesco, who came from Garfagnana, in charge of a monastery. [The priest] wanted to enter our Society; indeed, he and many other priests hoped to live and die under the obedience of the Society and had made the usual vows of the Society, [written copies of] which Father Silvestro sent to Father Ignatius at Rome. But since they were very useful and even necessary for that province and were uneducated, withal very good priests, Father Ignatius decided against admitting them to the Society and calling them [to Rome] from there. . . .

92.   *The Jesuit college at Venice*

After Easter [Father André des Freux] decided to launch three ordinary courses in as many classes; for Father Ignatius, too, seeing that the classes would produce splendid fruit in the form of excellent training for the youth, wanted the classes at Venice to open this year. Father Cesare Helmi was in charge of one class, namely, grammar; Fulvio Cardulo was the teacher in a second on humane letters, and [des Freux] himself was planning to handle the third class in material pertaining to Sacred Scripture and Scholastic theology if some students enrolled for those courses. But shortage of space prevented these courses from starting at the same time. He decided to preach or lecture on Sundays and feast days about a subject likely to stir up people's emotions; but he was also prepared to lecture during the summer on something dealing with mathematics, such as geography or similar topics, if anyone wanted to learn such material. Since he was trained and proficient at all sorts of erudition, he could have done this without difficulty.

94.   *Gradual progress at Venice*

Father des Freux also gave the Lenten sermons at the convent of the converted [prostitutes], where almost two hundred nuns of this kind lived. He also read the notes of a certain public lecturer that religious men had brought to him, and he secretly stated his opinion that they were rife with unsound teaching, but in such a way that the one who had given this unfavorable judgment [des Freux himself] could not be identified, even though the lecturer could be convicted of erroneous teaching thereby. He also worked diligently and skillfully with the Lord Prior [Andrea Lippomano], persuading him to provide a somewhat more spacious area for classes. This objective he achieved. Thus not only could extern students be accommodated more comfortably, but the almost intolerable racket and uproar was thereby silenced to a great extent. In the home of the prior himself, he gave an exhortation to a confraternity of noblemen and citizens who were dedicated to helping poor people too ashamed to beg. In this and other ministries he was fruitfully engaged; and although the affairs of the Society made progress only gradually, still, as time went by, they enjoyed greater success.

96.   *Limits on Jesuit ministry to Venetian women*

When the question of our taking over possession of [Lippomano's] priorate was being treated, a leading man who had shown himself a friend of the Society tried to persuade Father André that Ours should not hear the confessions of any women; for seemingly he wanted to safeguard our good reputation among the senators of that republic and our security. But since this task of administering the sacraments of confession and Communion was so apposite and integral to our Institute, Father André des Freux judged that we should not follow that friend's advice, and Father Ignatius agreed with his position. From this we could still easily conclude not only how carefully we must avoid anything that militates against our good reputation, but also how we must proceed [even] in these good endeavors with caution and great skill. Therefore, Father des Freux adapted his lecturing on Saint Paul to men, so that not even one woman came to listen. But it seemed right that women could not and should not be excluded from the sermons on Sundays and feast days. Nonetheless, in these early stages there were those who complained of our initiatives and grumbled that the women were spending too much time in our church. At our house the same father [des Freux] taught readings in Greek to our scholastics and fifteen or twenty lay people.

102.   *Venetian recruits; the senate grows suspicious*

At this time, while making the Spiritual Exercises, a good priest decided to enter the Institute of the Society. Also Father André des Freux had hired a young Turk to work in our house, a man whom this priest had trained along with [a group of] orphans. He seemed apt for God's service because of his good manners, obedience, and talent sufficient for mastering writing along with some rudiments of Latin grammar. The same father was warned that the practice of writing weekly letters to Rome had already and would in the future cast a shadow of suspicion among some people [meaning Venetian senators].[9]

103. *Expurgating classical poets*

Father Ignatius wrote Father André des Freux, instructing him to draw up a plan for expurgating lascivious passages from Terence and other pagan poets, so that young men might draw [from them] a pure and elegant Latin style, while preserving untainted their moral integrity. It was not difficult to accomplish this for other poets because the salacious passages could be omitted without impairing the work. And Father des Freux did this, especially for Horace and Martial; but arriving at a rationale for removing from Terence what was improper seemed very difficult because those passages seemed integral to his plot lines. But des Freux contrived to apply what is said there about illicit love to licit and married love. Father Ignatius, however, did not approve of this method of emendation, because what is said about both married love and illicit love could in the mind's eye of the young men take on a lascivious meaning. In the end he forbade the reading of Terence in our schools for this very reason.

104. *The origin of the first Jesuit textbook*

Father Ignatius also ordered Father des Freux to write something about grammar, especially its rudiments, adapted for our schools. He recommended the grammar of Despautier [Jan Van Pauteren], or if that work seemed rather prolix, he suggested that Pelison's compendium could be taught in place of Despautier. He recommended the standard text of Donatus for the rudiments; but because Father Ignatius ordered him to harmonize these treatments, he wrote the tract that is in the hands of Ours who teach classes for beginners.

110. *The converted Jew becomes a Jesuit*

That Jew about whose conversion to Christ we just spoke conducted himself so well that he aspired not just to the Christian religion but to embracing Christ's counsels; he presented an excellent example of virtue and spirit. By a special providence of God, he was freed from the hands of the Lutherans among whom he had fallen and from whom he had begun to learn Christian doctrine, and he seemed called to the religious life. There was no difficulty that he could encounter in the religious life that he was not prepared to undergo

---

[9] Who might suspect that affairs of state were being discussed and plots hatched.

gladly for the love of Christ. Father des Freux admitted him to the Society, where he turned out to be a good worker in the Lord's vineyard. He possessed a very retentive memory and seemed gifted with judgment, talent, and good physical endowments. He had long been familiar with the Hebrew Old Testament and quickly recited from memory any passage of it. He had traveled through almost all of Palestine, Germany, and Italy; and besides Italian and Hebrew, he also knew Spanish, German, and Turkish—and he was only twenty years old.[10]

111.   *Developments in our schools*

The students who came regularly to the Venetian College went to confession almost every month, but on Friday afternoons they heard an exhortation on Christian doctrine in addition to the one delivered on Sundays. At the beginning of class and also at its end, the "Salve Regina" was recited aloud; for experience in the Roman College had taught that this was advantageous, and the same [practices] were proposed for the other colleges of Italy. Indeed, the excellent progress of the Roman College greatly consoled and inspired the other communities of the Society. Father Ignatius directed that those who could not read should not be admitted to [our] classes. Although [teaching boys to read] was an admirable work, Ours could not have handled the vast crowd of boys who would have descended upon them.

116.   *Broët becomes the first provincial of Italy*

After the college at Ferrara, which we treated earlier, was established, because the colleges at Bologna and Venice in addition to that at Padua now had to be administered and because another was to be set up shortly at Florence, Father Ignatius thought it good to designate somebody as provincial in Italy. Ours could write to him from those colleges; they could consult him as a neighbor about the things that could happen any day. And so, in the autumn of this year Father Paschase Broët was made the first provincial of Italy. Still, the college at Naples and especially those at Messina and Palermo would not be under his direction. Because Father Ignatius could easily be consulted when

---

[10] The Jewish convert was Giovanni Battista Eliano (1530–89). In 1561 Pius IV sent him to work with the Copts in Egypt. Returning to Rome, he worked as a translator. Especially notable are his translations of the decrees of the Council of Trent and two catechisms into Arabic.

anything of greater importance happened, such matters were referred to him from all over Italy.

128.   *Good deeds of our students*

Although the custom of our schools obliged students to go to confession at least once a month, still, some of them confessed every week and some every other week. Some [students] made so much progress not only in their studies but also in spirit that they drew others with them to the frequent use of the sacraments. This diligence had a happy outcome for them. Some of them were so dedicated to works of devotion that when they were released from school in the evening, they did not go to their homes until they had visited the prisoners in the jails and provided them with water and whatever else they could. Indeed, these young lads sometimes brought [the prisoners] alms that they had collected around town and urged them to go to confession and fairly often convinced them to do so; and they competed with one another in carrying out these tasks of devotion. Some of them also, without their teachers' knowing anything about it, begged for alms on behalf of the sick; this so delighted their parents that some of them, moved by the example of their sons, did the same thing.

This devotion was especially noteworthy when it extended to a poor man covered with ulcers and scabs; he could barely get out of bed and had nobody to give him even the least bit of help; it seemed certain that he would die from hunger if not from sickness. These young men made his care their main concern, so that every day they strove to bring him as much as he needed. The goodness of these adolescents helped other poor people when the price of grain was at its peak. Among them some there were who aspired to the Society's Institute, but Ours judged that only after hearing mature advice and practicing careful discernment should we admit men to probation. . . .

140.   *Helping the starving at Messina*

When the people of Messina were suffering from a great shortage of grain (including some men and women, widows and poor people, and many who were burdened with children not yet ready to go to work), our men were careful to provide for their needs; and we can believe that the alms Ours gathered for this purpose preserved many who otherwise would have perished from extreme famine.

142.　*Helping prisoners at Messina*

When some of Ours visited the prisons and brought comfort to those confined there, using alms they had gathered they freed some men who were being detained because of unpaid loans. Some of them probably would have died in prison if this subsidy had not been given them. Both they and the guard at the prison bore witness that before Ours came to Messina sometimes those imprisoned died without going to confession for lack of anyone to hear them. This is why they gave thanks to God for providing the opportunity for confession, even when they did not request it.

151.　*Setting up a convent at Trapani*

At this time, Father Nadal was at Trapani to take charge of setting up a convent for converted women that would also admit married sinners (as was done at the Convent of Saint Martha at Rome) until such time as they were reconciled with their husbands. Although this work was started with alms, those living in the convent hoped that the viceroy would soon endow it with revenues derived from taxes and allocated by the senate. Father Nadal put together some statutes that the converted nuns were to observe, and he set up a confraternity of nobles to take care of supervising material subsidies. He put a certain religious of the Order of Saint Francis, Friar Jacobo de Augubio by name, in charge of spiritual affairs. His work resulted in much spiritual fruit at Trapani. Lady Isabel [de Vega] undertook to protect the place.

152.　*Nadal works against concubinage*

[Nadal] succeeded in having effectual steps taken against men who lived publicly and notoriously with concubines, exacting from them a fine to be applied to the recently built convent for the converted. Concubines were also housed there to get spiritual help until they wished either to become nuns or really take steps toward [adopting] a respectable mode of life.

153.　*Nadal sets up a confraternity*

He also strove to set up a confraternity that initially admitted noblemen, but later commoners as well. [Members] pledged themselves to go to confession and Communion at least every month, listen to a sermon on Sundays and feast days, and devote themselves to acts of piety. Father Nadal also wrote the rules for this confraternity, and when they took them to the viceroy, he wanted to enroll in the confraternity himself; it was very advantageous that he should do so, for thus the person in charge of the confraternity could carry out its charitable works with greater authority. Hence, the viceroy sent letters to all the magistrates of the people, informing them about what we described regarding the prescribed prayers.

161.   *Nadal volunteers to accompany the fleet to Africa*

At this time, namely, the month of July, with the Turkish fleet approaching, Viceroy de Vega sent his son, Ferdinando, to Africa with a garrison of soldiers and whatever was needed for their defense, for it seemed the [Turkish] fleet would direct its attack against this area. Father Nadal, moved by God's spirit, as we believe, because Father Ignatius recommended in his letters that [Nadal] gratify the viceroy as far as possible, offered his services to the latter if he thought it a good idea for him to sail for Africa with the viceroy's son and the galleys, so that he could perform the usual ministries of the Society, both helping souls spiritually and caring for the sick. This greatly pleased the viceroy, who instructed him to be ready to sail with the galleys the following night, that is, the twenty-seventh of June.

162.   *Isidoro Bellini dies at sea*

Master Isidoro joined Father Nadal as his companion. He had taught philosophy at the college in Messina, and it seemed that he would be useful in preaching, in holding friendly conversations, and in doing other things. Ours had previously noticed how he employed those talent of his very successfully with the soldiers. Isidoro was very eager to make the voyage and prepared for it with great care. A few days earlier he gained the grace of the jubilee after making a general confession, and from that time carried out his duties with great peace of soul and consolation. As he left he said—truthfully, as it turned out; but at that moment he was unaware of the disposition of divine Providence—that he was going to turn his life completely around, adding, "When you see me, you will see a totally spiritual person." Matters unfolded differently than he had expected. . . .

He set out with Father Nadal on the fourth of July, but then a great storm blew up, sinking eight of the fifteen galleys. Because the storm struck them before dawn, for two hours it was so dark that one man could not see another even when they were very close. Among the other galleys under Antonio Doria was the *Prætoria,* upon which Ours had embarked. It went down, and almost a thousand men were killed in the shipwreck at Lampedusa between

Malta and Africa. When the men tried to swim or get to the nearby shore as best they could, Master Isidoro tried to leap from the galley onto nearby rocks but instead fell into the sea. The cruel storm shoved the galley against those rocks, trapping and shearing off Master Isidoro's arm. Then, after struggling for almost half an hour, he was pulled aboard the galley. Once aboard, even though he was in pain from his severed arm and in the greatest danger, the soldiers reported that he omitted nothing that befitted an excellent religious and a very brave man as well; and he continued to encourage the others in the galley, edifying them no end, until [the galley] sank into the sea. Eventually the soldiers and others who managed to escape reached shore safely.

172.   *The Jesuit college at Palermo*

This year the courses at the college in Palermo were divided into six grades or classes. The students made excellent progress in both their studies and their behavior. Several factors, however, prevented [the college from achieving] a sizable enrollment, especially from the ranks of the nobility. Among these problems one that was hardly trivial presented itself when a certain noble and rich young man entered the Society. His father, a baron, kidnaped his son, using a measure of force. Ferdinand de Vega, who was in charge at Palermo, took umbrage over this and threw the baron into prison. As a result, some noblemen, at once indignant at this development and fearful that their own sons might join the Institute of our Society, withdrew their sons or did not send them [to our college]. Also, the numerous [lay] teachers at Palermo tried to undermine the reputation [that our] classes [previously enjoyed] among the nobility, criticizing Ours, who were, as a matter of fact, for the most part younger men. Still, a good many came [to our college], even though fewer students were being taught in the upper classes than in the lower ones.

186.   *Should novices bring in money?*

Someone asked Ours whether the Society would be willing to admit a young man whose father wanted to give his son to the Society along with some annual income. The response was that the Society would not allow this sort of arrangement. Rather, suitable persons come to and are freely accepted by our Institute without any monetary contributions. Somebody who wanted to increase the college's income by donating alms could do so—that was up to him.

187.   *Prayer at our schools*

At the beginning of class our students observed this practice: they knelt before a picture of the Lord and said a silent "Our Father" and "Hail Mary." When class was over, one lad from each class recited aloud the "Our Father," "Hail Mary," and "Salve Regina." The other practices were similar to what was said above regarding monthly confession and so on.

188.   *Jesuits arrive at Trent*

On July 27 Fathers Diego Laínez and Alfonso Salmerón arrived at Trent, where the council had opened. Although the Cardinal of Trent had generously offered them a house and other necessities before they left Florence, and the Duchess of Florence wanted Father Diego to be [officially] sent by her noble husband, he neither should have nor could have accepted either offer, for the Supreme Pontiff had sent them as his own theologians. They, therefore, approached the legate, Cardinal [Marcello] Crescentius, who offered them lodging and his fatherly assistance. They greeted his collaborators and the other leading men, who finally expressed their belief that the council would get under way now that [the Jesuits] had arrived in Trent. For right up to this time the business of the council definitely seemed quite perfunctory, and few people were in attendance. Meanwhile, Ours heard some confessions, particularly of the poor. They heard almost everyone on the feast of the Assumption of the Blessed Virgin, and nourished many of them with the most sacred Body of Christ. Periodically they visited the hospital to help impoverished sick people, and whatever time they had left over they devoted to study, with good results. . . .

This protocol was drawn up at the council: first the theologians sent by the Supreme Pontiff would speak their mind; second came the men sent by the Emperor; third came clerics with doctorates, speaking in the order of seniority; fourth came religious in the usual sequence of precedence of their orders. Thus, on the very day of the Birth of the Blessed Virgin, speaking first of all as papal theologians, Laínez in the morning and Salmerón in the afternoon addressed their views to the electors, the legates of the princes, and the prelates, while the legates of the Apostolic See looked on. . . .

194.   *Trent's deliberations on the sacraments and the Mass*

On the feast day of Saint Catherine [November 25], a session took place at which decrees were promulgated on the sacraments of penance and the last anointing and other decrees about reformation. Later articles on the sacrament of orders and the sacrifice of the Mass were handed down. After having prepared what they had to say about this material, on September 7 Laínez discoursed on the sacrifice of the Mass for three straight hours in the morning and after lunch Salmerón held forth almost as many hours on [the sacrament of] orders. Inspired by God's grace, they satisfied their hearers in a marvelous way. By now so many doctors of theology had gathered that their number exceeded sixty, so lengthier periods of time were needed to listen to them. . . .

195.   *Cultivating friendship with the Habsburgs*

Maximilian, the king of Bohemia, traveling from Spain passed through Trent with his wife, the Spanish Infanta Maria, who is now the Empress.[11] With her was Lady Maria de Lara, who was mistress of her chambers was well acquainted with the Society. [Ours] came to her and through her assistance spoke with the crown princess and Queen of Bohemia, and they informed her about the plan of the King of the Romans [Ferdinand] to set up a college at Vienna. They recommended it to her good offices, explaining how it would serve the common good to set up similar colleges in other places in her territory as the opportunity arose. The Queen, who had known the Society well in Spain, Father [Antonio de] Araoz in particular, very kindly offered to do whatever she could and also promised her goodwill in matters relative to the Society. The Lady Maria de Lara mentioned above was the same woman who for many years not only promoted [the activities of] the college at Barcelona at her own expense but to a great extent built and endowed it.

196.   *Jesuits seek approval from the Council of Trent*

Besides these useful encounters [Ours] were quite busy in the matters that pertained to the council and were committed to them by the legate and other officials. But Father Ignatius wanted to give them an additional task, namely, that they take appropriate steps to ensure that the council give its confirmation and approval to our Society, if that were in any way possible. . . . There was no further progress on this project at that time, because several weeks ago discussions had already begun about dissolving the council. . . .

---

[11] Later Maximilian became Emperor Maximilian II, Holy Roman Emperor from 1564 to 1576.

■ **Austria**

208. *Efforts to set up a college at Vienna*

During the first months of this year, Father Claude Jay was engaged at the Diet of Augsburg and did much there to glorify Christ and to enhance the good reputation of the Society among many prominent men. Earlier, he had already labored in Germany for a long time and had expended greater effort than anyone else from our Society, traveling, teaching, preaching, and conversing; but at this meeting in Augsburg the divine Goodness wished that somehow he would reap the fruit of his previous labors and leave the princes and states of the Empire a very favorable impression of himself and the Society. In the ministry of the sacrament of penance, on the occasion of the jubilee granted to the imperial court, he reaped an abundant harvest. Canisius writes that [Claude's] contacts with the leading men at that meeting of so many German princes contributed more than anybody else from our Society had ever managed to do; neither had anybody else explained the name, origin, and progress of the Society as effectively as he had and so inculcated them in the minds of Germans that he earned for Ours the reputation and trust that were absolutely necessary for cultivating this vineyard of Christ. . . .

The representatives of the Duke of Saxony were moved by his words and arguments and devoted themselves to entering into a concord about religion; they went to the most important princes, recommended Father Claude, and strongly urged that this father travel to Saxony and confer about matters of faith with Philip Melanchthon and the other leading professors of the Lutheran sect. [They hoped that] his erudite modesty and modest erudition, which had already brought such benefit to themselves, would accomplish more among [the Lutherans] than the bitter controversies of others had achieved. Father Claude's heart did not shrink from that journey to Saxony provided, as he hoped, Father Diego Laínez could join him; but this journey to Saxony had to be canceled when one of them, namely, Father Claude himself, had to go to Vienna at the command of the King of the Romans, and the other had to stay at the council at the command of the Supreme Pontiff.

219. *Jay lectures at Vienna*

. . . Father Claude, who had thoroughly mastered the teachings of the heretics and refuted them with a certain uncommon skill, was very gratefully received and went on to labor in his task with excellent results. It is certain that the lectures and refutations of Father Claude freed from their errors many who were almost inextricably ensnared in the sophisms of the Lutherans; and so his audience was large, and very many leading men and prelates also attended his lectures assiduously.

220.   *Not all Jesuits were so successful*

This was not the case for Father Nicholas de Lanoy, whether because the Scholastic study of the *Master of the Sentences* was very distasteful to the Germans or because he, who spoke rather hesitatingly, was able to win more praise for his learning than for the attractiveness with which he presented it. Hence, when it seemed to Father Claude that [Lanoy] brought outstanding talent for governing but not much for teaching, he began to request from Father Ignatius a different professor of theology. Indeed, Ours asked for two of them, so that Father Claude himself might be better freed up for preaching in Italian and for engaging in negotiations of greater importance for the advancement of the Catholic religion. Also some Catholic noblemen began to come forward to have their confessions heard; they also wanted to take Holy Communion along with our men. It was thought that their number would grow considerably if additional priests could be found to work in this ministry.

221.   *Success and failure at Vienna*

Since the King of the Romans had decided that young boys from the provinces should be sent at his expense to study sacred theology in a place *[conventu]* devoted to the reform of religion, almost fifty of them were living in a certain house near to Ours, and their teachers and prefects discussed with Father Claude a plan for their education. All the regulations governing them were established just as Claude judged best. Once [that father] had exhorted the students to godly living, their prefects hoped that they would come to our house to make their confessions. [Claude] also had to hear the confessions of some of the professors at the university, whom he helped in the course of their discussions. Father Lanoy, too, started to have his spiritual sons, partly Italians, partly Germans, whom he instructed in [the manner of making one's] confession. Some of them took Communion along with Ours on Christmas Day at the densely crowded church of the Dominicans.

Still, at this time not much was accomplished with the Germans because of our limited skill in the language. Hence, Ours applied themselves with much greater effort to the task of studying the German language. Ours gladly continued to visit the sick and carry out other pious works, even though very many of them were suffering from fever. Two of them, one an Italian and the other a Spaniard, were always so sick that they finally had to be recalled from there, although not this year. One man of great repute and learning at the university was aroused to blazing wrath over an injury he suffered; he obstinately decided to exact revenge; but the words of Father Claude persuaded him not only to forgive the injury but also, after making a confession of his sins, to receive the most holy sacrament of the Eucharist.

222. *Differing reactions to a Jesuit college*

The people of this area reacted to the new college in different ways. One marveled at it, another ridiculed it, a third respected it. Some, infected by the poison of the heretics and hostile to the religious life, quietly denigrated and criticized it. But those who were high minded and wise showed themselves rather favorable and supportive.

Some, however, loved Ours from the depths of their hearts and showed themselves to be devoted promoters of our works; among them was the legate of the Apostolic See, Lord Abbot [Girolamo] Martinengo, who not only manifested his singular goodwill toward the college at Vienna but also, when he returned to Italy, negotiated with Father Claude about setting up a college of the Society at Brescia. He went to confession to [Father Claude], as did some noble members of his family. When he was about to leave with the King for Bohemia, at a time when Father Claude was suffering from ill health, he visited him at our house and went to confession to him before leaving and embraced all the brothers one by one with great kindness and gave them his blessing. . . .

223. *King Ferdinand finances the college at Vienna*

. . . [There were some] who predicted that our college would produce little or nothing of true worth and discouraged [the King] from building it. But he not only maintained his goodwill but increased and confirmed it. When he was setting out on a journey to Styria on the holy day of St. Catherine [November 25], he assigned to the college a revenue of twelve hundred florins, in such a way that three hundred would be paid every three months, and he sent letters to various of his counselors very sternly commanding them to pay that sum faithfully to Ours. When he returned to Vienna from the province of Styria and found out that Ours lacked the sacred priestly vestments, he sent two sets of all these garments plus a cloak that was compatible with the poverty of the Society and the generosity of the King.

A few days later the King himself came to our house accompanied by almost his whole court, in order to see the grounds, the house itself, the refectory, and the other workplaces; there it was easy to gauge, even from the expression on his face, his attitude toward Ours. When Father Claude was attempting to thank his Royal Majesty both for the revenue he had assigned and for his so graciously deigning to visit our house, [the King] would scarcely [permit him to speak] and earnestly told Father Claude that Ours should not keep silent if they needed anything, because he always wanted to be their protector in such a way that the kindness and charity of so great a prince would seem to bind Ours to him, rather than what he actually bestowed upon us.

225.   *Establishing a seminary in Vienna*

The King's purpose in establishing and endowing our college was that the study of theology might be restored at Vienna . . . [and] that a certain number of students from each province might be sent to Vienna to apply themselves to the study of theology, advance to holy orders, and then take charge of parishes. Moreover, keeping in view the same purpose, he decided to set up a college of the Society, so that from it he could have both professors of theology and students who would not only enlighten others by the example of their lives but also so that Ours might introduce the practices of Scholastic theology, such as the disputations and the exercises usually held in universities. This was the main fruit that from the start the King hoped for from the college, even though other richer fruits might come forth from it as well.

Accordingly, he wanted Fathers Claude and Lanoy to teach [theology] publicly and others of Ours to attend [these] theology classes, for he thought them suited for that. At this time there were three professors of theology at Vienna, and they had only ten students, among whom scarcely one was equipped to profit from lectures in theology. Since the professors wanted to leave their posts, our two Fathers, as we reported above, began their lectures. But because Father Claude had to preach to the Italians and hear the confessions of many people, and Father Nicholas was also assigned to other occupations, they hoped with good reason that the Society would send other professors.

227.   *King Ferdinand asks Jay to write a catechism for his lands*

The King entrusted the consistory of the University of Vienna with choosing a theologian who in the name of that university would compose a kind of compendium of the Christian doctrine that the Scholastic theologians treat at much greater length. Although none of Ours had become a member of that consistory or theological committee, the group nonetheless chose Father Claude to compose the work. When the King found this out, he encouraged Claude to take the project in hand. Doctor Jonas, his chancellor, did the same. In order to escape this [task], Father Claude called attention to various compendia that very learned men had just recently compiled right there in Germany, for example, [works] by Pedro de Soto, the Emperor's confessor, and by Doctor Johann Gropper, whose book had been printed just the previous year with the authorization of the archbishop of Cologne. Also another [book] had recently been completed in the Synod of Mainz.

But, in the end, the chancellor declared that it was the will of His Royal Majesty that another compendium should deal in more detail and explicitly with the dogmatic controversies of the present time and should emphasize those matters that every good Christian ought to know. He wanted this book to be compiled by the King's theologians and printed at Vienna by command of the King himself, and he desired the schoolmasters in all the provinces under his scepter to teach from this volume. Because Claude did not have time to devote to completing this project but it was not proper to refuse [the King's mandate] for fear the reputation of the Society would suffer harm, he wrote to Father Ignatius and requested him to recommend somebody to complete the project. Because he knew that at some point Father Ignatius had thought about freeing Father Diego Laínez from his other occupations so that he might complete a work of this sort, he reminded him that this was a perfect opportunity.[12]

228.   *Loyola's suggestions about purging the University of Vienna*

Father Ignatius wrote to Vienna about reforming its university and mentioned replacing all the professors, even of the lower faculties, that is, philosophy and literature, seeing that public professors who were not sincere about the faith did not seem likely to accomplish the task of improving the young men. Thus, he was of the opinion that theological studies could be

---

[12] Eventually the project was turned over to Peter Canisius and resulted in his enormously influential catechisms.

restored at Vienna if the young men studying that subject were well educated in letters and godliness. [Jay] showed a Latin translation of this letter to Lord Jonas, the chancellor, a man very favorable to the Society. But [the solution proposed] seemed quite harsh and would not be well received by the King and the city magistrates if such a sweeping and sudden change of professors were to take place and if the Society should substitute [its men] for those who had been dismissed. Rather, the King wanted those professors to be brought to a sounder view of things, and he wanted their faith to be examined. If some of them were unwilling to reconsider and amend [their doctrine], only as a final step did he wish them to be removed gradually from the office of teaching. Meanwhile, [he wished] humane letters and philosophy to be taught in our college, in order to stir up a holy rivalry among the lay professors, all the while having our professors available to substitute for the [lay professors] if any had to be dismissed. Thus was begun the task of setting up classes at Vienna.

229.   *King Ferdinand tries to secure key Jesuits for Vienna*

The King of the Romans had written to the Duke of Bavaria and encouraged him to found a college at Ingolstadt; but when [the King] found out from the bishop of Laibach that Fathers Peter Canisius and Nicholas [Florisz] of Gouda were not being allowed to depart from there and a college of the Society was not going to be set up, he thought they would be just right for improving things at the University of Vienna. Nor did he see any reason to go out of our way to avoid inconveniencing the duke; for [the Fathers] should be sent somewhere if a college was not going to be set up at Ingolstadt. Accordingly, he commissioned the bishop to write in his name to Father Ignatius [urging him not to] oppose this project of bringing those two doctors to Vienna. Chancellor Jonas wrote to the same effect.

Claude also asked Father Ignatius not to remove Father Nicholas Lanoy from Vienna (provided the King of the Romans was agreeable to this arrangement), because the example of his life, his learning, and his prudence seemed perfectly suited to administering that college. It seemed better to [Jay] for the one college at Vienna to be well supplied with both teachers and an administrator than for the Society to embrace many colleges that could not be staffed with men qualified to achieve the end for which the Society strives. Because they had few suitable lay brothers, they hoped that some men of this sort would be sent for household duties.

Father Claude did not willingly participate in examining the university professors on questions of faith, but he could not refuse to undertake this work, desired by the King, however odious it was to him, because it was carried out by the King's ministers in his presence. . . .

231. *Developments at Vienna*

I will not pass over [in silence] several things that Ours at Vienna, especially Father Claude, suggested to Father Ignatius. One of them was that if there was any place where hearts had to be won over and prestige gained by a demonstration of scholarship, it had to be in Germany above all because nowhere were churchmen, religious, confraternities, and external mortifications of the body more hated, scorned, and mocked than in northern countries, where they usually go out of their way to attack things of this sort. Therefore, if we are speaking about human matters, it is extremely difficult to win esteem except by demonstrating one's knowledge, especially one's erudition in the Latin, Greek, and Hebrew languages.

Hence, Ours needed greater facility in these subjects because the devil, who was irate at our founding this college in Vienna, had, even before we arrived, circulated a rumor through certain Flemish schoolmasters that the King had called in some Jesuits, hypocrites all of them, who shut people up in cells with windows closed and compelled them to make certain fasts for an unknown number of weeks so that the Holy Spirit might come upon them.[13] Thus, they seduce young men and force them to make vows. . . .

Certain people at court took umbrage that we had arrogated to ourselves the name of the Society of Jesus. After Father Claude had instructed them on the reason for this name, they became defenders of the Society. Among them was a certain doctor of theology and a count who was a leading man in the royal court.

■ Germany

232. *Preaching in German lands*

Some of the first men sent to the College of Vienna devoted themselves to preaching in the various styles customary in Italy; later they wrote to Rome

---

[13] Presumably those shut up were making the Spiritual Exercises. Note that *Jesuit* is a term applied here to members of the Society by its enemies, not by Polanco. Only later did members of the Society accept the term.

that those forms of oratory were unpopular in Germany because that nation prefers for the preacher to use a quiet voice and to avoid great changes of voice or [dramatic] gesture. Also, because they had been urged to study the German language, they warned that it was very difficult for those who had been brought up in the Italian, Spanish, or French languages to learn German because of its very difficult pronunciation. But for those whose native language was Flemish, it was rather easy, for they could read it right away and understand everything and gradually even pronounce it correctly.

233.   *Expulsions from the Society at Cologne*

Father Leonard Kessel labored this whole year at Cologne; and although he sent six young men to Rome this year, among them Baldwin Delange of Liège and William [van den Brock] of Limburg, other men who were admitted took their place without difficulty. Some men also encouraged other people to make the Spiritual Exercises and [go to] confession. In dealing with souls, Father Leonard was a master artisan and spiritually helped young students and some graduates of Louvain and Cologne so much that no few prepared themselves to hear and follow the Lord's call. In the First Week of the Exercises, they washed away the failings of their past lives with abundant tears, profiting themselves considerably.

Among them was a certain Gerard from Holland who had been sent from Louvain; after being admitted to our house, he stirred up a major conflict by arousing sedition among some of the young men who were studying in the same house. Moreover, he proceeded to render them hostile to spiritual progress and obedience to Father Leonard. When [Leonard] out of charity tried to help them, only to have them put a sinister interpretation on everything [he did], he expelled Gerard himself from the Society and the house, and eight others as well who seemed to be his supporters. He had sent away a certain Godfried previously for similar reasons. This courage in casting out the useless succeeded not only in preserving others in their purity, but in attracting good and suitable students as well to the community.

Before the expulsion of those ten, the number [of students] was fifteen or sixteen, and after their expulsion six or seven were left in the house. He sent some of them to Rome as autumn approached; nonetheless, towards the end of the year there were seventeen. Among them was a certain priest, a graduate of Louvain, who with great fervor consecrated himself to the divine service, winning the admiration of all. It became clear that in the space of twelve months [Kessel] sent twenty talented students to Rome, and it was obvious that in the case of most of them Father Leonard had made wise decisions in recognizing [their potential] and admitting them to the Society.

■ France

256. *The Jesuits at Paris*

This year, 1551, there were fourteen of Ours at the college in Paris, in addition to those who were working [for Ours], although this number was lower because [Ours] were suffering from a shortage of material resources. They sent two brothers to Rome early in the year, namely, Jean-Baptist Tavon and Master Joachim [Christiaens]. Toward the end of this year, they sent six at one time to Rome: Father Everard Mercurian, their leader, Master Adrien Candido [de Witte], Master Eleutherius Dupont, Francis Gordon, and Leonardo Massero. The sixth was the lay brother Jean Artemius. Others, though in lesser numbers, were accepted into the Society to replace those sent off. Among them was Olivier Mannaerts, a priest who for almost a year had persisted in seeking [admission to] the Society. . . . The request was made to Father Ignatius that he admit Father Olivier as a [spiritual] coadjutor of the Society, even though he was still a novice, so that he could be granted the privilege of hearing confessions and administering the sacraments, because Father Battista Viola frequently suffered from such bad health that he was barely up to the task of hearing confessions, all the more so because he had to go begging for food to sustain the brethren.

257. *Henry II grants permission for a college at Paris*

. . . Despite the opposition to our Society by many at the royal court this year, the Most Christian King granted the Society the privilege of building a college at the University of Paris. [Our opponents] also attacked the Cardinal of Lorraine, a zealous protector of our Society, hoping to deter him from carrying out his duty to promote our affairs before the King and the Royal Council. But God's providence arranged that matters would turn out quite otherwise. For setting himself as a wall protecting the house of God in this matter, the Cardinal of Lorraine secured the privilege not only from the King but also from the inner council of the King (which they call the Restricted Council); moreover, he wrung from the French chancellor a signed document granting the Society of Jesus permission to possess temporal goods for the maintenance of students. It remained for the Parlement of Paris to review this indult and list it in its register or annals, as is the custom and law of the French kingdom. Otherwise, no indult is ratified unless this Parlement judges it to belong to the [legislation] of the French state.

258.   *Opposition to the Jesuits at Paris*

When the privilege they had obtained was brought to the Parlement, the devil began to frustrate the negotiations in various ways by persuading many members of the Parlement that the number of religious orders was excessive or that the kingdom of France would derive no benefit from this Society, which seemed to have been founded not for [the purpose of benefiting] this nation [France] but for foreign nations. Nor were those lacking who thought that not only our Society but other orders as well should be driven from the country, for rumor was that the poison of heresy had infected many people and among them not a few members of the Parlement. Thus, many people would still have to undergo a good number of disputes and survive a considerable torrent of annoyances before this business was concluded. Ours believed that the Lord permitted all these trials to test their faith and patience, and they hoped that the prayers of the Society would overcome all these difficulties.

259.   *Support for the Society at Paris*

There was a great deal of goodwill toward the Society, and besides the Cardinal of Lorraine, the bishop of Bayonne [Jean Monstiers de Froissac] showed himself a great friend in obtaining that privilege and in defending the interests of the Society. The bishop of Clermont [Guillaume du Prat] also maintained his benevolence toward Ours at Paris; and when Father Everard went to Rome, he sent along with him a letter for Father Ignatius in which he expressed his heart's desire to set up a college at Billom using the services of Ours. Billom is a city of Auvergne that is subject to the bishop of Clermont in temporal and spiritual matters. To make this whole project even more explicit, he commissioned Father Everard to inform Father Ignatius that he wanted to set up a house in the same place and to support some of our brethren, just as he had also promised in another letter on June 30; furthermore, he asked to have these brethren sent to him [at Clermont] until the city itself had taken care of supplying the things necessary for setting up a college there. The good dispositions of his heart increased, and he later provided more than he had promised.

261.   *A Dominican and a Carmelite make the Spiritual Exercises*

Some people [at Paris] were very profitably engaged in making the Spiritual Exercises, and among them many were admitted to the Society; and others, although they did not enter the religious life, left their retreat greatly improved. Although Father Viola had to keep to his bed because of bad health, from there he still gave the Exercises themselves to one person. Among the others was a [former] religious of the Order of St. Dominic, who had left it with permission. Now he firmly resolved to return; and if he was not accepted back, he promised to enter the Carthusians.

There was another man, a Spaniard belonging to the Order of Carmelites, who had preached in Valencia and Barcelona and had often spoken privately and publicly against the Society. He had also tried to change the minds of those who were inclined toward it; it was his habit to dissuade people from staying with us and making the Spiritual Exercises. When he came to Paris to lay deeper foundations in theology for himself, he fell into our hands and began the Spiritual Exercises. So absorbed was he for six weeks that Ours had not witnessed such fervor of spirit in anybody else, and so abundantly was divine grace bestowed upon him that he had to prolong the Exercises beyond the usual time. He confessed to Father Viola with a flood of tears.

The religious of his community, observing a marked change in his life, were utterly stupefied by it, not knowing its cause. He said that he wanted to write to Spain to various people whom he had diverted from [making] the Spiritual Exercises, urging them to make [the Exercises] and not to allow anyone to cast aspersions on our Society in their presence. He confessed that he had never understood what it was to pray or serve God in the religious life until after these Exercises had put him into a better state of soul. Set aflame with charity, he encouraged the young men of his order to the frequent use of confession and Communion; in short, his work was considered most useful both for the order in which he lived and for others.

265.   *Efforts to get approval at Paris fail*

It is not at all easy to recount all the troubles involved in getting the privilege approved [by the council] that would allow the Society to be accepted, not indeed in the whole kingdom, but just in Paris. It seems that the complications of this business were increased because Father Viola, when he was engaged in getting the privilege, needlessly showed among other things the 1549 apostolic letter granted by Pope Paul III. When the official who had charge of this permission attached the seal testifying to the royal concession, he bundled this document along with the apostolic letter written on parchment and signed with the seal of Bishop Campeggio. Thus it happened that when the Parlement of Paris came to read the aforesaid privilege, it also had to read the faculties and exemptions that the Apostolic See had granted to the Society.

When these were shown to the King's procurator-general, he immediately began to predict what was to follow, explaining that two difficulties suggested themselves to him. One was that the King's letter declared that nothing could be found in our Institute against the holy decrees, yet these letters stated that our Society was exempt from obedience to bishops and that we were not bound to pay tithes for goods received. These and similar privileges, which should not have been disclosed at that time, rendered the negotiation so difficult that for many years Ours could not escape from the frustrations they entailed.

It is worth noting that the chancellor of the kingdom, somewhat ill disposed to the influence which the Cardinal of Lorraine had with the Most Christian King, demanded a large sum of money for the seal, perhaps because he thought that [Ours], as poor as we were, could not pay. But it happened that just then he was deposed from the office of chancellor and the seal was entrusted to the man who had interceded on behalf of the Society and had spoken in its support. Thus the seal was affixed for a tiny fee.

266.   *The poverty of Ours at Paris*

When our men at Paris described for Father Ignatius how they were suffering from poverty, he wrote that they might beg for alms in public; but at that time a public edict threatened to punish with imprisonment anybody seeking alms in public. Every day one could see people being thrown into prison on this account. Father Viola, therefore, in order to prevent the bishop of Claremont from considering himself dishonored if he beheld Ours begging (it was commonly believed that he had assumed the obligation of supporting the Society), consulted with this bishop on whether he thought it wise to send some men elsewhere because they could not be supported here. The bishop directed them to come to him when they were suffering from want, and he sent them some aid; but his enthusiasm seemed less than our needs demanded. As a result, Father Viola, with Father Ignatius's consent, sent some men to Rome, as was narrated above.

Father Ignatius did not let slip the opportunity to enkindle the heart of the bishop of Claremont. Accordingly, he had the Duke of Gandía [Borgia] send him a letter of greeting. The bishop wrote back that he had received the letter full of kindly humanity and Christian devotion; he went on to wish him well and congratulate him for his great integrity of soul. But he showed the effects of his goodwill on this matter only gradually.

267.   *The origins of our college at Billom*

This same bishop wrote about sending some scholastics to Billom and explained to Father [Viola] his intention: they should be three or four in number, should be in charge of a school at Billom, and the other lay teachers should be expelled from their teaching positions if they did not conduct themselves properly. The [Jesuits] would have to be skilled in the French language, for they would be teaching boys. One should be suited to teaching theology, a second to teaching philosophy, and a third to teaching rhetoric. The one who would be teaching theology should be prepared to preach in French. But if men like this could not be sent, Father Viola warned that nobody should be sent. And so for somewhat more than a year the Society did not undertake this work.

■ Spain

274.   *How Francis Borgia's income was devoted to the Roman College*

Before leaving Rome, the Duke of Gandía sent letters to Emperor Charles V and Prince Philip revealing to them the determinations of his soul. He also begged the Emperor's favor for the Society and for several people. The Emperor replied on March 10, 1551, while he was at Augsburg, and thanked him for communicating his firm intention to enter the Society of Jesus. He strongly approved and indicated that he valued highly the suffrages of the prayers and Masses being offered by the duke. Because the duke asked his permission to carry out what still had to be done, [the Emperor] gladly granted him this and [promised] that he would keep his house and children in mind and show them his favor, just as the merits of [the duke] and his duchess demanded. [Borgia] requested that, for five years after his explicit and public profession [of vows], he might designate for pious causes the income of twelve hundred ducats annually that the Emperor had granted for the rest of the duke's life. [The Emperor] gladly granted this, too, and gave him documents testifying to this favor. He undertook to show the Society of Jesus his benevolence because this would advance the honor of God and would be an act of kindness toward the duke. . . .

The reason that moved the duke to request those revenues for the next five years was this: he intended to give them as a subsidy for the Roman College, and he applied it thus while he could dispose of his affairs before the time expired granted him by Paul III for this purpose. The duke wanted the income earned by these six thousand ducats to be spent on building the church and then helping the college. But because he had left the disposition of [these funds] to the discretion of Father Ignatius and the number of students at the Roman College and their expenses were increasing daily, it seemed good to Father Ignatius to convert this sum of money—as each [installment of it was paid]—to the sustenance of the same collegians, and that is how it was handled.

275.   *Borgia's ordination*

During the month of May, after receiving the letter from the Emperor, the Duke of Gandía received sacred orders in our house at Oñate, having first shaved off his beard and put on a priest's cassock according to the Society's practice. He decided to celebrate his first Mass on the Feast of the Holy Trinity unless he received letters from Father Ignatius advising him to put off this celebration for a time. . . . Before receiving orders, he renounced his dukedom in favor of his son, the Marquis of Lombay, and stripped himself of all his old clothes right down to his underwear. He wanted the clothes that he had worn to be used for alms, and so Ours gave away his clothes, one man giving this part, another that part, to someone begging [alms from him]. Then joyfully putting up with his gout, he joked that this disease of the wealthy had overtaken him in a timely fashion because of his new riches of poverty. Not only in that province but at the Spanish court and the whole kingdom, his poverty and his holy actions were on the lips of everybody, and all drew inspiration and edification from them. . . .

299.   *The fruits of Francisco Estrada's preaching at Burgos*

So great was the crowd of penitents, and important people besides, that when he was about to preach, he would hear three or four [confessions] before mounting the pulpit, and he found the door wide open for serving God in that city. Sometimes he preached in the convent of the Friars of St. Augustine and in the Mercedarian convent because the Corpus Christi procession went there. There was hardly a church that did not seem to shrink [in capacity] because of the crowds who came to hear him. Many people took decisive steps to reform their lives and make frequent use of confession and Communion. Many came forward to seek advice; but although he desperately needed a priest companion and could not himself gather in such a rich harvest, still, the shortage of priests prevented Father Provincial from sending him a priest companion for almost all this year. Yet the divine Goodness increased his strength, and the unparalleled fruit issuing from his ministry of God's word and the sacraments encouraged him in his labors, as did what many were saying about him—modesty almost prevents me from reporting this—that they preferred him to all the other preachers they had seen, and similar encomiums.

300.   *Priests applying to the Society at Burgos are turned away*

Once [Estrada] did not admit two priests, and then later [turned away] two more of them who were eager to enter the Society; his reason was that they seemed not to have sufficient learning. There was one exception, whom he sent to the provincial for admission. He was the pastor in the same Church of St. Giles. His audience included many members of various religious orders, especially while the Corpus Christi processions were in progress; all of these showed him great kindness. He preached in the Convents of St. Ildefonse and of St. Dorothy as well, which are called "Huelgas." In the second convent, to which noble ladies from many provinces were admitted, many of the citizens participated. Men from the Carthusian monastery called "Miraflores" and from [convents belonging to] the Benedictines and Franciscans urged him to preach in their churches. But the religious of the Order of Preachers, when they were celebrating a feast in the Convent of St. Paul, asked him not to preach in their Church of St. Giles, so that [those who would otherwise come to his sermon would instead] come to [hear] them; as a favor to [the Dominicans], he refrained for a while from speaking.

302.   *Starting a college at Burgos*

The thinking was that setting up a college or house of the Society at Burgos would work toward God's great honor and the advancement of souls, so negotiations toward these [goals] began; and right away Lord Ferdinando de Mendoza, the brother of the cardinal, promised just under two hundred ducats annually, some of it in coin, the rest in grain. Other people also added various annual sums in the form of money and grain. Among them was Lord Benedetto Uguccioni. This seemed the sort of city that would without a doubt abundantly

supply the alms needed to support a college. Therefore, Father Francisco Estrada thought that a college should be started. When Father Provincial [Antonio de Araoz] passed through Burgos on his way from Guipuzcoa to Castile (he already knew what Father Ignatius wanted), he decided that a house should be purchased, and he promised to send some of the brethren to start that college.
. . .

309.   *Poverty of Ours at Valladolid*

Several men wanted to be admitted to the Society who would easily have increased our numbers; but housing for our men in this place was so tight that, even though Ours were so few, a single bedroom held two beds. It was not that the people were opposed to providing for more men or even to expanding the house itself, but the site itself was very confining, walled in as it was by the homes of wealthy men, so that expansion would be difficult. Still, some bedrooms were added this year. Even in that very ancient building, people of all sorts and conditions consulted [Ours] about everything affecting the salvation of their souls. [Ours] also went out frequently to people who were near death to help them and to hear the confessions of other sick people. At no hour, whether day or night and no matter however inconvenient, did they repulse people who requested their help, and they labored successfully at these and the other works of devotion.

Because Father Provincial was absent for almost the whole year, they were updated by letters sent from Rome on what the Lord was accomplishing through our men, and they were united in great consolation of heart. The apostolic letters and the other favors obtained from the Supreme Pontiff encouraged and consoled them in the Lord. Also the fruit observed both in those who came forward on the feast days already mentioned and those who frequented the sacraments, not to speak of [our own men's] eagerness for mental prayer—to which they devoted one hour in the morning and another whole hour after lunch—made them joyous, fit to receive God's grace, and eager to help their neighbors.

314.   *A bishop tries to enlist Ours for Mexico*

Many people sought out men of the Society and even entire communities of Ours, demanding to have our services, offering our men lodging and everything they needed. Among them was a bishop from New Spain [Mexico], the diocese of Mechoacan; whenever he encountered Ours, he urgently begged for some men of the Society, describing an abundant harvest along with an extreme shortage of harvesters and offering to supply everything that was needed. But that mission had not reached maturity.

318.   *An adulteress is snatched from execution at Valladolid*

When a certain prominent lady was going to undergo the extreme punishment as an adulteress, after Father Gonzales had heard her confession and before she was led away to her punishment, he arranged with her husband to spare her life on condition that she enter a convent to live there forever. Thus, just as she was about to be led from the prison, she was snatched from death under these terms.

321.   *Our ministries at Salamanca*

During the first months of this year, both Doctor Torres and the others at the College of Salamanca divided their efforts between studying and carrying out the ministries of the Society in that city. Many students endowed with special talents and gifts were carefully nurtured through the Spiritual Exercises. Some of them were admitted to the Society; others entered other religious orders. Our college's lack of space and material goods necessitated this, even though they were attracted to our Institute. Three of those admitted were priests; two of them had completed the course in theology while the third had applied himself to theology for three years. Two of them had preached in public at Salamanca. The other one was also a student at the leading college at Salamanca and had completed the course in philosophy. Martin Gutierrez, who had a licentiate in medicine, began to study theology after entering the Society.

323.   *Doctor Torres preaches at Salamanca*

Father Doctor Torres preached this Lent in the parish church of St. Benedict, where many nobles and students heard him. . . . But when a confraternity of certain leading men was set up in that church to arrange marriages for girls and young women who had no parents, they wanted Doctor Torres himself to take charge of it; and they were willing to arrange everything as he would direct, so that thus the city might be better motivated to promote this work by giving alms, [seeing that] Torres approved of it and that everything was being done with his authorization and prudent [guidance]. Thus, [they felt sure that] the project would move along more rapidly. Father Torres did not flinch from shouldering this burden, until [later] he learned the mind of Father Ignatius, who did not want either him or others of Ours to be involved in similar confraternities, although they approved of [such activities when conducted by the laity]. So then he declined this responsibility; still, he [intended to] preach about this subject whenever the marriages of such young women were being celebrated.

351.   *Amenities at the College of Alcalà*

As regards living quarters, this year two things were acquired at the College of Alcalà. The first was a garden surrounded by a wall eighteen hand-lengths high, which lay almost completely outside the boundary of the town. An opening in the wall afforded access to it from the college. This garden provided no little opportunity for healthful recreation, in that it was 730 paces in circumference; and bushes, fruit trees, various plants, and a well of very pure water rendered it beautiful and ideally suited [to our needs]. The second was a library, originally a tower forming part of the wall [around the city] that the citizens of Alcalà had modified for this new purpose. It afforded a panoramic view that delighted the eyes.

352.   *Troubles with Archbishop Silíceo*

Although these buildings were of great benefit to the college, they were also a seedbed from which sprouted considerable labor and trouble. The mayor of Alcalà came to Father [Francisco de] Villanueva on the first day of September and showed him two letters from the archbishop of Toledo in which he ordered [the mayor] (for the town of Alcalà was subject to the archbishop in temporal affairs as well) to immediately close the gate in the town wall that had been donated to our college and by which [Ours] gained access to the garden. Also, as regards the garden and the new wall surrounding it, he threatened a legal hearing and [promised that he] would then listen to what Ours would say [to defend their position against the prescriptions of] the law.

Father Villanueva was greatly distressed, wondering whether it would be better to obey the archbishop and give up possession of that gate or to appeal against the command of the archbishop, seeing that he already had tried many devices to placate the archbishop, all to no avail. Among those to whom he had appealed for help were the King and Queen of Bohemia and the Count of Malta, who had written most earnestly to the archbishop.[14] Doctor Torres too, as we

---

[14] On the Jesuits' stormy relations with Archbishop Silíceo of Toledo, see O'Malley, *First Jesuits,* 292–95.

said above, had tried in vain to mollify the archbishop on this very question. The rumor was that [the prelate] had conceived a great hostility toward our Society; not only did he ridicule it when speaking about it, but he also branded Ours with heresy. Still, because some people said that without the permission of the King or the archbishop, the mayor of Alcalá and the town magistrates could not allow our college to use that open gate, Father Villanueva decided to deprive his college of this benefit of fresh air and recreation and to close the aforesaid gate. It seemed that this submission and obedience would pacify the archbishop.

354.   *More friction with the archbishop*

That same day Father Villanueva set out for Toledo. His plan was that if he could not win the favor of the archbishop by good manners and arguments, he would go on to the Royal Council rather than allow force to be used against the Society in contravention of the grants of the Holy See. Before going to Toledo, while he was dealing with the court at Madrid, he presented the apostolic letters to the council and asked it for a document supporting his position, so that he could inform the archbishop about the apostolic letters. But because such matters were not usually dealt with so quickly by the Royal Council, following the advice of the apostolic nuncio and carrying a letter from him to the archbishop and other people, he went on to Toledo.[15]

The archbishop did not conceal his hostility toward the Society and put forward several grounds for his opposition; namely, that the Society had built our house at Alcalá without his permission, that it was called the Society of *Jesus*, that [Ours] were engaged in the ministry of preaching and hearing confessions without obtaining his permission, that the Spiritual Exercises, which he himself did not regard as in accordance with the Gospel, made people fools, with the result that noblemen did not act like noblemen; and [he leveled] other such accusations [against us]. When Villanueva tried to answer each charge at length, the archbishop resorted to threats, because his attitude was not based on reasons but on emotions. If anybody brought up the apostolic letters to him, he asserted that he would throw the person into prison. He exclaimed, "Here we don't need a Supreme Pontiff," and uttered other things that could more prop-

---

[15] Here one is reminded of the sigh of Philip II's administrators around the globe, "If death came from Madrid, we would all be immortal."

erly have been left unspoken. Finally, he said he would be coming to Alcalá—his usual response when he intended to do nothing.

356.   *Non-Jesuit use of the Spiritual Exercises*

I will not neglect to recount that Friar Luis de Avila, the master of novices in the Convent of Saint Catherine de Talavera, after he had made the Spiritual Exercises, began giving the same Exercises to his religious with great success, and he shared the Spiritual Exercises with three other convents of his order and another convent of the Cistercian Order (from which the religious were sent out to many places). He also explained the same [Exercises] to some [diocesan] clergy, hoping, as he wrote, that these good results would be spread far and wide.

362.   *Long prayers are curtailed at Gandía*

Father [Diego] Miró brought Ours a good many benefits when he returned from Rome. He not only consoled those at Gandía by talking at length about the things he had seen at Rome, but he trained them in our way of proceeding as he had observed it in Rome, and he warned them that they were adhering to practices not in accord with what was customary in Rome. Both at Valencia and Gandía the brothers used to pray together in choir and for two hours each day in chapel. As soon as he prescribed that at Valencia they should pray in their own rooms, the rector at Gandía imitated this and cut down both the practices of mortification and the time for prayer, lest their bodies be weakened beyond due measure.

376.   *Preaching and confessions at Valencia*

[Miró] writes that he found a great change in that city from the time he left there both in the frequency with which people approached the sacraments of confession and Communion and in the spiritual progress and devotion of many and their numerous works of piety. He affirmed that through God's grace the college of the Society contributed a great deal to this blessed state of affairs. Thus, that city embraced the Society, and Father Miró in particular, with great kindness and devotion, for many of the leading men made great progress thanks to his sermons and ministry of confession. . . .

377.   *Helping prisoners at Valencia*

When the grace of a jubilee was proclaimed during the last week of May, Father Miró sent three of our priests to the governor's prison to hear the confessions of those detained there. But earlier he, along with the governor, the assessor, some officials, and a large crowd of people, had gone to the numerous prisoners confined there. He exhorted them to confession with so much fervor that through God's word he softened the stony hearts of some [of these] men— who earlier had given not a thought to the grace of a jubilee—so that they wept and expressed their repentance, begging for confession at the top of their voices, so that they could obtain the jubilee [indulgence]. Because in that prison the prisoners were separated according to the gravity of their crimes, after the first exhortation he gave three separate exhortations in three other places where the prisoners had not heard his first one, making his way through the whole prison with the same loving zeal. By his exhortation and through the grace of God, he brought it about that all confessed their sins and prepared themselves for receiving the most holy Body of Christ. . . .

379.   *Preaching to prostitutes*

In the last week of Lent, as was customary in the city of Valencia, the prostitutes, who were numerous there, used to be rounded up and confined in one place, so that at least in that most sacred time they might refrain from offending God. They were allowed a preacher so that he could try to lead them back from their sins to better dispositions of soul. In this promulgation of the jubilee in gratitude for the good outcome of the Council [of Trent], after they had been herded into the place, Father Miró preached to them for three full hours, and the Lord gave him so much fervor and so much effectiveness [in proclaiming] God's word that eleven of them were rescued from a shameful sort of life, followed by four more, after listening to a sermon of equal length. Therefore, the fifteen were led to the home set up at Valencia for such penitents. . . .

390.   *Potential friction with the Spanish Inquisition*

To the colleges in Spain and other countries, Father Ignatius sent letters patent granting the faculty to absolve in cases of heresy—a faculty granted him by the Sovereign Pontiff. But prudent men thought that this authorization should be employed with great moderation in those [Spanish] kingdoms because of the prerogative of the Holy Office of the Inquisition, for the inquisitors seemed displeased that this faculty was granted to persons other than themselves. . . .

■ Portugal

398.   *Sending missionaries from Portugal to India*

This year six men were also sent to India, four of whom were priests: Melchior Nuñez (the first of all the scholastics who entered the Society at Coimbra), Fathers Gonsalvo Rodrigues, [Manuel] Morales, and [Antonio] Heredia. There were also two more who were not priests: Pedro de Almeida and Christoforo de Acosta. After being examined by the professors at Coimbra, Melchior was promoted to the grade of doctor of theology. Ten more from the orphan boys were added to these. Abbot Pedro Domenech selected them from among his orphans, judging them the most apt, so that after an orphanage was set up in India they could be admitted to the Society; for he had educated them in a way that those possessing more talent and more upright character than the others might be rendered suitable for the Society.

In addition five spiritual men, who had sold their possessions and distributed part of their goods for the use of the poor, undertook the voyage to India at their own expense, so that they might be admitted to the Society in India. They were led to hope that if they behaved well on the voyage, they would be admitted there. Fortunately, just at departure time they received a bundle of letters from Father Ignatius containing the apostolic letters of confirmation granted by Pope Julius and other items that would be most welcome to Ours in India. . . .

412.   *Ministries in the Portuguese countryside*

Father Cornelius spent Lent performing these ministries and hearing many confessions. When the daytime was too short, he spent a good part of the night reconciling penitents to God. From two [o'clock] in the morning until just before the meal after midday, he devoted himself to this pious work, and sometimes he slept barely two hours when many people were at his door waiting to have their confessions heard.

Many people wholly submitted themselves and their goods to whatever Ours might decide regarding them—they would do nothing except what Ours enjoined on them. Some clergy who were living in public concubinage left their concubines with great signs of repentance. Priests flocked to present their problems to Ours and wanted to be guided in all things by their advice.

There was a certain woman who, although she was married, had been living with someone other than her husband, even though [her lover] was himself married. Captivated by love of her, he had pretended that he wanted to live with her as her legitimate husband. Still, stricken with remorse, she left him. Another woman living in the same lustful manner could not be separated from her lover by any entreaties. The Lord separated her in a different way: for the man to whom she clung wounded her in his attempt to kill her. Thus, realizing her situation and recognizing the punishment of God, she came to her senses. This affair also terrorized the people and rendered them more responsive to the warnings of Ours. Finally, fifteen or sixteen people were banished from the town, so that the same sort of public sin might be avoided. Others married their concubines. . . .

415.   *The Spiritual Exercises at work in Portugal*

When these fathers wished to return to our college, the people on bended knees asked the bishop to keep them there; and when Ours pleaded their vow of obedience, they prepared to send one representative to the rector of the college at Coimbra and another to the Queen. . . . Thus, just after Advent not Father Alfonso but another father, whose last name was Santacruz, was sent to the same diocese with Father Cornelius, and they worked there very successfully, devoting themselves to various works of piety. They gave the Spiritual Exercises to a certain prominent nobleman, who had once led a military order in India in a laudable fashion. This man made so much progress that the changes people observed in his life moved them to admiration. By word and example he stirred other people to various good deeds; he gave considerable financial help to the poor; he wanted his wife and his entire household to be instructed in mental prayer, in which he himself made considerable progress; and he asserted that it was [only] at this time that he began to be a Christian. Many other noblemen were directed in the Spiritual Exercises, and more than forty young women from leading families were instructed in spiritual things, to which they were most receptive. Many among them decided to enter the religious life. On Christmas Day itself, after a sermon by Father Santacruz, many entered into concord who had previously been at enmity with one another.

419.   *Portugal is flooded with vocations*

Some young men adept at literary studies were admitted to the college at Coimbra, and that year the number of Ours in this college rose to 140 and more; forty of them were studying theology, and many of them possessed splendid talents. Yet, at certain times of the year their preoccupation with preaching and hearing confessions distracted the priest-theologians from their studies to some extent, especially during the time appointed for gaining the jubilee indulgence promulgated at Coimbra twenty-four days before the feast of Corpus Christi. All this time, just as in Lent, the priests were occupied with confessions; indeed, the number of penitents was even higher because almost all who wanted to gain the jubilee came to Ours for confession. These labors completely exhausted some of Ours, particularly the aforesaid Valerianus and Father Juan de San Michaele. They continued to spit up blood, so they exchanged their brief lives for eternal ones.

424.   *Formation in Portugal*

[Father Diego Miró], moreover, introduced a certain program for a house of probation: he placed thirty of those who were younger and newer to the Society in a hall similar to a dormitory and appointed Father Leo Enriquez as their first master of novices. This resulted in their making greater progress; and because the college was too small for so many men, those who stayed behind were more comfortably accommodated. Their prefect took care to demand from each of them a planned way of proceeding; he also required them to observe silence at the proper times and to adhere to the customary method for meditating and examining their consciences. They more easily encouraged one another by example, in that they lived together and had their spiritual needs taken care of. [Father Enriquez] sometimes let some of the older members mingle with them, and at night after the reading, which Father Leo outlined in brief beforehand, he proposed the subject they would meditate on the next day.

Father Miró visited with them frequently and paid special attention to their studies. He saw to it that those studying in the same faculty had rooms in the same part of the college, so that they might more conveniently be of mutual help in their work. Although the collegians had sterling talents, still they needed better organization in their studies and more practical exercises. He wanted both the theologians and the philosophers to have disputations *[conclusiones]* twice each week covering the material studied. Repetitions, however, were held daily, and Miró himself was present for them. He appointed somebody from each faculty to preside over the rest in repetitions and disputations. If anybody was observed acting negligently, he was sent to little table as punishment. Therefore, he taught them better both in spirit and in academic matters, and they began to grow more enthusiastic in both areas.

On the feast of All Saints, after having taken a flagellation, many pronounced their vows and others renewed them with great eagerness of heart. Among those who showed a fine example of abnegation and humility was Theutonius, the brother of the Duke of Braganza—would that he had persevered in that spirit to the end!

425. *New fervor at Coimbra*

Father Simão [Rodrigues] came to Coimbra on November 4—he had obtained the King's permission to stay there a fairly long time—but he left it to Father Miró to govern the college. Owing to the exertions of Father Miró and of Father Pedro Diaz, who also left Rome and came to Coimbra this year, all [of Ours] cultivated an increased disposition of charity and union toward Father Ignatius, an impulse to obey him in all things and to conform their customs to what is observed at Rome. Because each one was dealt with individually, both the graces of God at work in them and any secret temptations that needed to be overcome had suitable remedies applied to them and were cured. From this ensued a new fervor and more solid spiritual fruit among the brethren. . . .

THE YEAR 1552

■ The Society in general

1. *Overview of the Society in 1552*

At the beginning of this year, the Society had houses in forty-three places, although there were only four discrete provinces: India, Portugal, Spain, and [the rest of] Italy, excluding Rome. Governing them were four provincials, namely, Fathers Francis Xavier, Simão Rodrigues, Antonio Araoz, and Paschase Broët. Father Ignatius himself directed the other places of France, Germany, Italy, and Sicily, which had no provincial. In the previous year fourteen places were added where Ours took up residence: in India at Amanguchili and Chiorani. In Brazil, which was not yet called a province, [Ours resided] at the Port of Saint Vincent, Espírito Santo, and Santo Amari near Porto Seguro; besides these places a college had earlier been established at the city of Salvador [Bahia]; in charge of these four places was Father Manuel da Nóbrega, who bore the responsibilities of a provincial without actually having the title. To the other places in Portugal a college at Évora was added. [Houses existed] in Spain at Oñate, Burgos, and Medina del Campo; in Germany at Vienna; in Italy at Ferrara, Florence, and Naples, in addition to the Roman College. Besides these fourteen places schools were opened the same year at Bologna and Venice. Just as the Society received such a signal increase [in the number of houses] in new places such as these, so it also received an increment in the number of men that the Lord called to this Institute.

2. *Personnel changes in Iberia*

As the year 1552 began, Father Ignatius decided to name a new provincial in Portugal and to remove Father Simão [Rodrigues] from there, as will be discussed below. He divided the province of Spain into two provinces, for otherwise [it would be] too large for one provincial to direct adequately; he left one part, known as Castile, to Father Antonio Araoz, but the other part, called Aragon, also included both the kingdom of Valencia and the principality of

---

Here begins the second volume of Polanco's manuscript, which contains 1,233 pages and covers the years 1552, 1553, and 1554.

Catalonia; he assigned them to Father Simão. They had four colleges, namely, Zaragoza, Valencia, Gandía, and Barcelona.

■ Rome

4. *The Roman College*

Day by day the number [of men] at the Roman College increased because the young men who had been tested were sent there from the professed house. Hence, the great number of collegians, already great, would have increased still more had not many gone on missions. So at the start of this year there were twenty-five collegians, more or less, shortly before [men were sent to establish] the colleges at Florence and Naples.

7. *More on the Roman College*

All this year the Roman College was engaged in teaching Latin, Greek, and Hebrew literature and employed rather learned and diligent teachers for this task. One of them was Master Joachim [Christiaens], who had been sent from Paris. But there were some rather insolent men, either schoolmasters or teachers, who liked to criticize him publicly in class without having any justification for doing so, thereby giving no little offense. When this situation was brought to the attention of the Cardinal of Compostella, who had undertaken the protection of this college, he had the impudent troublemakers thrown into prison. The same week it also happened that two teenagers abandoned their family homes, and their mothers came into our church in the middle of Mass and filled the air with their screams and shouts; and both underlined their hostility by creating the same uproar in the college, and even at the homes of several cardinals. They accused Ours of having set up the college at Rome to allure the sons of local families to ourselves or, to use their own word, to plunder them. But neither of the teenagers who had occasioned this commotion had been admitted either to our house or to the college.

8. *Parents' consent needed for student to enter the Society*

Influenced by these developments, Father Ignatius ordered [a mandate] to be dispatched wherever the Society was ministering, forbidding Ours to admit [into the Society] any students from our schools without their parents' consent, because doing so would precipitate greater harm to the Society than any advantage it might afford (due to the hostility toward us stirred up by their parents), considering the greater good of all. Other ways would not be lacking for those who were called to our Institute to fulfill their worthy desires, for such men could apply for admission in other places where the Society was established. He also cautioned that if sometimes schoolmasters were to brand our teachers as ignorant, they should reply with humility that they were more ignorant than they would like to be, but still they were serving God and neighbor with the little talent that the Supreme Father had allotted to them; in short, let them strive to overcome impudence with modesty. But the number of extern students in our classes climbed and now reached three hundred.

9.   *Origins of the German College*

This year the extreme dearth of priests in the province of Germany who could benefit the people of their nation by word and example led to [the establishment of] the German College at Rome. Sizing up this state of affairs, Cardinal Morone, a man of prudence and practicality and motivated by a considerable love for that nation, in which he had long labored in the name of the Apostolic See, judged that no better plan could be conceived by which the Holy See could help those provinces than by selecting talented young Germans to be educated at Rome, in such a way that, after having grown in piety, learning, and goodwill toward that same See (which had served them well), they would return to their homelands and receive ecclesiastical benefices.

10.   *Cardinal Morone recruits Jesuit and papal support for the college*

. . . So he brought the project to Father Ignatius, who gladly approved of it as seemingly very useful for restoring discipline in many areas where it had collapsed and for upholding and propagating religion there. He readily pledged his efforts to promote such an admirable undertaking. Cardinal Morone, along with the Cardinal of the Holy Cross [Marcello Cervini, later Marcellus II], who was very enthusiastic about the project, went to the Supreme Pontiff [Julius III], who himself joyfully greeted the proposal: once a similar idea had occurred to him, but he had not developed it in sufficient detail, so now with an eager heart he welcomed this project as something that he would support. . . . Urged on by these cardinals, the Supreme Pontiff by an apostolic letter erected this college, called the "Germanicum," under the governance of our Society for the education of men in letters and morals.

11.   *Preparations to open the college*

Although the negotiations for applying ecclesiastical revenues and buying a building were in motion, rather than see this pious work delayed, it seemed a good idea to rent a building temporarily, and the Supreme Pontiff himself together with many of the Sacred College of Cardinals set down on parchment what they were willing to contribute for the support of the Germans. First of all, the Supreme Pontiff promised to give five hundred gold scudi annually, but the others promised what each one's resources and inclinations would allow, this one a hundred scudi, that one a hundred and twenty; others pledged to give more or less. Because the total amounted to almost three thousand scudi annually, the entire matter was entrusted to Father Ignatius, so that he might work out in broad outline both the requirements that the young men should meet and the means to be used in recruiting them. Although initially a hundred and [even] more students agreed to come to that college, the decision was made that while the project was in its developmental stages, no more than thirty or forty should be called there at first.

12.   *Recruiting students for the German College*

As I mentioned, the name "Germanicum" was given to the college, but Bohemia, Poland, Hungary, and other similar northern nations that lacked workers of this sort in places infected by heresy were placed in the same category as Germany. Therefore, Father Ignatius wrote both to Fathers Claude [Jay] and Canisius, and also to Fathers Leonard [Kessel] and Adrian [Adriaenssens], who were working at Vienna, Ingolstadt, Cologne, and Louvain, bidding them to send young men between the ages of sixteen and twenty-two from those nations to Rome. Likewise, even though some exceeded that age, they should be sent if they seemed good recruits on account of some outstanding mental gifts and if, moreover, they seemed amenable to being taught and deeply imbued with the education in letters and morals that they would receive. All should be of agreeable appearance, physically healthy and capable of bearing up under the labor of study. They should be endowed with talent and upright character, so that one could reasonably hope that they could emerge as reliable and strenuous workers in the Lord's vineyard. The better their education in letters when they arrive, the sooner they would seem ready to be sent back to Germany. Thus, the better educated were to be preferred; special consideration should be given to [those of] noble blood, which is much esteemed in those nations; but if they could not claim nobility by birth, certainly they should not want for nobility of heart. Later will be time enough to attract those who are noble by birth.

13. *Studies at the German College*

. . . Father Ignatius determined that not only the three languages [Latin, Greek, and Hebrew] were to be taught, as was done previously, but also the disciplines of the liberal arts; and, finally, lectures in Scholastic theology and Sacred Scripture were to be delivered at the Roman College. Although the students should live in a separate house, along with some of Ours assigned there to see to it that [the students] can more easily be kept at their studies, all should come to our college in the morning and afternoon for lectures and other scholastic exercises. Therefore, a house near our college was taken over for their use. Toward the end of this year, a fair number of young men were sent, but almost all from lower Germany; some of them had completed the arts curriculum.

■ **Spain**

17. *Toward a college at Compostella*

When the Society's reputation for skill in molding young men and teaching the disciplines was increasing at Rome, the Cardinal of Compostella [Juan Alvarez de Toledo] on his own initiative brought up with Father Ignatius the possibility of turning over to the Society a college that had been built at Compostella. So enthusiastic was he about carrying out this proposal that he said the students would gain for themselves forgiveness of their sins and mercy from God if he handed this college over to be administered by the Society. As archbishop he was the patron, but not the only one, for the Count of Monterey [Jerónimo Acebedo] was a second patron. [The Cardinal of] Compostella wrote him that, having himself observed the success of the Roman College and that of the other [colleges] elsewhere in the charge of the Society, he judged that nothing would be better for the college at Compostella than to hand it over to the Society, allowing Ours to appoint teachers in it and promote whatever would enhance both letters and good behavior. Father Ignatius agreed to the cardinal's offer; for reports [had reached him] that this was a splendid edifice, enjoying an income of two thousand ducats. Even more, the site itself in the city of St. James at Compostella swayed [Ignatius] for devotional reasons. So at the cardinal's request he wrote to Father Torres, the rector of the college at Salamanca, instructing him to handle this transaction. But how things worked out will be described later.

Rome

19. *Ignatius forbids Jesuits to accept bishoprics*

The good name and reputation of the Society, especially among important people, explain why it was almost impossible to convince several cardinals that it was not right for Father Francis Borgia to accept the cardinalatial dignity. Many were circulating their opinion that our Society should be a sort of seedbed from which many bishops and cardinals would be garnered. Taking the opposite view was Father Ignatius, who declared that our Society should at that time be a servant of God and the Church and that with the grace of God it would make some useful contributions if it was allowed to maintain its humble status. If a gate were opened to accepting this kind of dignities, the Society's ruin would be imminent. Thus, [if such a proposal were implemented, the Society] would not be useful to God's Church either as it had originally been structured or in any other way. And as for Father Francis Borgia, he dealt not only with the cardinals but with the Supreme Pontiff Julius III himself, humbly begging to be left in his present status, for which he had abandoned his dukedom in search of humility. In his kindness the Supreme Pontiff reassured Father Ignatius regarding this matter.

20. *Julius III reconfirms the Society*

This year, through an apostolic letter in the form of a brief, Pope Julius granted to our Society what he earlier had bestowed viva voce about absolving from heresy and dispensing from fasting and [eating] forbidden foods. Moreover, he confirmed the privileges granted up to that time to the Society, which were to be regarded as not rescindable. He also granted permission to anticipate and postpone the Divine Office and for Ours in universities to be promoted to master's and doctor's degrees by our own men if the rectors of universities were unwilling to promote them gratis; he granted the superior general the prerogative to freely promote Ours who were not studying at a university, granting them all the privileges that those graduating from universities enjoy. He permitted as well that with the consent of the superior general professed [Fathers] who were sick, aged, or unsuited for work in the Lord's vineyard could be provided for in the colleges.[1] I will not omit mentioning that when the Supreme Pontiff

---

[1] In Loyola's early plans for the Society, professed Fathers were to live and work in professed houses, which were bound by much stricter rules concerning poverty than were the colleges.

granted this last permission, which Father Simão [Rodrigues] had suggested to him, he jokingly added these words: "Non vorrei che si facessero questi padri poltroni con tal concessione," as if to underline that this permission should be used very sparingly and that he did not grant it very willingly.[2]

25.   *A proposed merger with the Barnabites*

The archbishop of Genoa had arranged for a letter to be sent to Father Ignatius requesting a merger of our Society with the religious men who are named after [the Church of] Saint Barnabas in Milan and who had some endowed houses in Lombardy. Father Ignatius replied to him that he loved those fathers and was aware of their virtue and integrity, but recalled that another merger with a different religious congregation of priests had been proposed once (these were the Clerics Regular, called the Theatines) and that we judged that this in no way would enhance either their service of God or ours; and that the reasons for such an important step that seemed valid to the person urging this merger did not in the least persuade him that it should take place. He wrote to that archbishop, declaring that for the reasons outlined above a merger with the religious priests of Saint Barnabas was not a wise move. . . .

26.   *Criteria for accepting new colleges*

Several colleges were accepted this year, which we will treat shortly. Because the colleges do not have endowments, it turned out that they and some others were not very well supplied with necessities. Father Ignatius wanted the other colleges also to observe what he had prescribed for the Roman College, namely, that a doctor would inspect the quality and quantity of food, sleep, and clothing and give advice as to what was necessary for protecting both health and bodily strength—advice that they were then to observe. But if resources were not equal to carrying out the doctor's recommendation, it was better to remove someone from the group of collegians and send him elsewhere, so that the remaining [collegians] could receive what was necessary for them. If the income of the college or the funds that a city, prelate, or any other person who had undertaken the responsibility of supporting the college fell short and did not suffice to supply what was needed according to the aforesaid norm, [Ignatius] ordered that Ours should have recourse to the riches flowing from holy begging, rather than allow either our ordinary benefactors to be excessively burdened or

---

[2] In English the Pope's witticism reads, "I would not like it if those fathers were to make couch potatoes of themselves through this concession."

the members of Christ to lack what they needed to preserve their health and strength. He wanted the same thing to be understood as applying to books and the other things needed for study. If even begging proved insufficient to provide necessities for everybody, at least superiors should not allow sick men to lack for these [necessities], for healthy people could better exercise patience while experiencing the effects of poverty.

27.   *Ignatius expels the disobedient*

When Father Ignatius recognized that in some places, especially in Portugal, some men become deficient in reverence and obedience, to such an extent that someone dared to answer back that he should not have been commanded [to do] this or that, or simply refused to do what had been ordered, he reproved the superior for not having hacked decaying limbs like this from the [trunk of the] Society and for not having amputated them lest this evil creep in further and infect sound members. Accordingly, he commanded the provincial of Portugal [Simão Rodrigues] in virtue of holy obedience that, if there was anyone unwilling to obey him or a superior or rector, he should dismiss him from the Society or, if he hoped a change like this could help him, he should send the man to [Ignatius] himself at Rome. [Simão] should not think that a person who is useless and harmful to himself will be useful for promoting the common good. Likewise, in virtue of holy obedience [Ignatius] ordered that wherever the Society was at work, no superior should have under him a minister or official who was unwilling to obey him. For, as they should be models of complete obedience to others, they should not be allowed to dwell where they would harm both themselves and others by their example.

28.   *Directions for the four-monthly reports*

Father Ignatius recommended brevity in the reports due every four months. He permitted them to be as copious as [their authors] wished on matters serving to edify; but for matters already discussed in the four-monthly reports, these updated reports should be kept shorter and should descend to details only when dealing with more noteworthy matters. He also [recommended] that a catalog of persons who were in every college or had been missioned elsewhere should be sent along with the four-monthly reports.

■ **Italy**

31.   *Three new colleges in Italy*

This year Father Ignatius sent out [the personnel to staff] three colleges in various places in Italy: the first [he sent] to Perugia, the second to Modena, the third to Gubbio. The Cardinal of Santa Croce [Cervini] urged that another one be sent to Montepulciano, but negotiations were so long drawn out that nobody was sent out this year.[3]

32.   *The origins of our college at Perugia*

The first colony [community to be established] this year was the college at Perugia; it drew its members from the community of the Roman College. The project was first discussed with Cardinal Fulvio Corneo, called the Cardinal of Perugia; he wanted a college of our Society to be built there to bring spiritual assistance to that noble city, his ancestral home. He held *in commendam* the bishopric of that city, and on that account was considering a subsidy for the college.[4] But before Ours were sent from Rome, the project was announced to the magistrates and other eminent private citizens in that city. They picked out a location for the college, although arrangements to acquire this property had not been concluded; but they were convinced that it could be acquired easily. Therefore, since the Cardinal of Perugia calculated that the college could be established and supported in part by a contribution from the city and its citizens and in part at his own expense, ten or twelve of Ours received the blessing of the Supreme Pontiff and were sent forth from Rome in the month of June.

38.   *Catechizing and helping the poor at Perugia*

[Ours] undertook the care of beggars also who flooded in when alms were being distributed to them. Most of the beggars, after they had been assembled and [made to] listen to frequent exhortations by the [Jesuit] brethren, confessed their sins; indeed, this was done in the main church, where there was usually a great throng of people. All these things were carried out there, arousing all the more astonishment and edification precisely because it was so

---

[3] Montepulciano was Cardinal Cervini's hometown; his nephew Roberto Bellarmino attended the college there before entering the Jesuits.

[4] An *bishop in commendam,* who could sometimes be a layman, would be entitled to much of the revenue of a diocese without having any of the responsibilities usually associated his office. He would usually appoint a substitute to care for his episcopal responsibilities in the diocese.

unusual to see [such activity]. On Sundays the poor people came to hear an explanation of Christian doctrine, for [Ours] undertook teaching this in the cathedral church. Besides the rest of the common people, the vicar, the priests, the citizens, and sometimes the nobility and male religious used to attend.

40.   *Jesuit versus charlatan at Perugia*

It happened once that a certain person of this number [of wandering performers] put up a banner in front of the doors of the main church and sold the people not just words but also harmful substances by the bottle and in powder form [*ampullatim et unciatim*]. At the time, a certain religious who was explaining a passage of Saint Paul in the same church had only about forty listeners while right outside the church doors a mountebank had [attracted] five hundred—even including priests and monks. When Father Jean Lenoir was returning by chance from the hospital, he came upon this spectacle and recognized the devil's trickery. He immediately jumped up on a heap of rocks standing next to the charlatan, and using both word and gesture he called the people to him, promising to give away free a far healthier medicine. . . .

The trickster and his companions, fearing that the stones which he had heard the bystanders mention, might replace words, quickly gathered up their belongings and fled. They left the city as soon as it was allowed, never to return, the townsfolk believed. But Father Jean continued his discourse task and denounced the people without restraint for having deserted a holy instruction to listen to the vain and worldly prate of the mountebank. Thus, after a short while he dismissed his listeners, who were as much benefited as they were filled with amazement.

41.   *Ministries at Perugia*

That good Father Jean devoted himself there vigorously to this ministry of preaching and administering the sacraments of penance and the Eucharist. Thus, many people gradually became acquainted with the Society, and in the first months [Ours] carried on these [priestly] duties mainly in prisons, hospitals, and convents. Later the vicar granted Ours their own church to use for preaching and [administering] the sacraments. . . .

45.   *The college opens at Perugia*

But a richer crop of people was harvested in the classes that Ours began to conduct from the start. Although the location was rather inconvenient, still the number of students grew day by day and reached 150 or more. The education their sons received so impressed their parents that when they encountered Ours on the public streets, they greeted them with great acclaim; and they swore that their young sons were as different from what they had been when they were initially entrusted to Ours as light itself is from darkness. Many of these parents visited our classes to observe the method that Ours used in instructing their sons (it carefully imitated the formula of the Roman College). This so pleased them, especially when they watched their sons [engaging in] the mini-disputations, that they wanted their sons to repeat them at home. At the time of the grape harvest, the parents left the city, usually taking their whole household out to the country; but now they entrusted their sons to [stay-at-home] neighbors, so that the boys would not be forced to take a lengthy vacation from acquiring learning and good manners.

48.   *Objections to our classes and methods*

But there were always some who approved of neither the subject matter at the new college nor our method of teaching young men. These tried to concoct various horror stories, attempting to turn even the vicar against Ours, who otherwise was very fair minded toward the Society. Wherefore, it seemed good to present an example of the truth, at least for the sake of our friends. . . . So Master Émond [Auger] was ordered to prepare a Latin oration that the vicar wished to be delivered in the main church in the presence of the canons, the doctors, and many leading citizens, and almost all the scholars of the Perugian Academy besides. With God's help this went off so well that not only did the oration content our friends but many scholars and men of uncommon learning repeatedly and quite earnestly demanded that it be transcribed; and even the schoolmasters, who were hardly pleased by this happy outcome, were forced to approve of the oration.[5]

---

[5] The establishment of a Jesuit college usually posed a threat to local schoolmasters, for they could lose their customers and jobs. They could hardly compete against Jesuit colleges, which did not charge tuition. Often they would have to migrate to smaller towns where there were no Jesuits, or they would have to teach on a more elementary level instead

51.   *Poverty and troubles in finding suitable housing at Perugia*

At the beginning the city magistrates sent to Rome in order to obtain from the Supreme Pontiff a site for the college.[6] They also proposed applying some three hundred florins of revenues (this sum comes close to two hundred gold scudi) for paying off the schoolmasters, who seemed to be performing their duties in an unsatisfactory manner. But this whole year neither [request] was granted, and so Ours had to live in the episcopal palace like guests. It was not that the cardinal was lacking in enthusiasm to help this college; he later proved this by taking over this whole enterprise; but he was waiting to see what the city would do. But as time passed private contributions partly ceased to flow in; and Ours, even though they did so willingly, experienced some part of the cross as they came to want for the necessities. The cardinal himself had to assume responsibility, and he did so. Nonetheless, it was always possible to witness the high esteem and favor in which the city held the Society. By their example and exertions Ours began to effect a considerable improvement in the city as regards things spiritual. The living quarters Ours occupied in the papal palace were being rearranged as far as possible while another place was being prepared for them. Still, this experience taught them clearly enough that when a few people undertook to raise funds for a college by collecting alms, in the absence of someone actually in charge, their efforts would fall short unless Ours themselves took charge of seeking the alms—something the vicar urged Ours to do.

53.   *Making do with unsatisfactory facilities*

In early fall Ours began to have cooking facilities in their quarters, whereas previously they had prepared what they needed in the same place that served the home of the vicar. A bit later they obtained a church to use for administering the sacraments; but it was distant from where they lived and it was inconvenient for our scholastics to go there for the sacraments, so a chapel was set up in a hall of that same palace. The vicar himself used to come there to receive the sacraments.

69.   *Ministries at Gubbio*

As regards people going to confessions, very few men did so, but a large number of women went to both confession and Communion every month, and

---

of conducting classes that were also offered at the local Jesuit college.

[6] Perugia was in the Papal States.

they and other people would have done so more often if Ours had had their own church; for they were embarrassed to come frequently to the cathedral church to receive the sacraments. But it was in that important church that Ours celebrated their sacrifices [of the Mass] and also administered the sacraments. Hardly a day went by in which somebody did not come for confession. . . .

72.   *The poverty of Ours at Gubbio*

As to where we lived, our quarters were rather inconvenient, although at the command of Father Ignatius and on the recommendation of the cardinal, [Ours] searched diligently for another more suitable [place] for themselves. The cardinal ordered us to be given the furniture that we needed for our use, although no revenues were applied [to the college]; Ours were allowed to take bread from a baker as they pleased, and they were given the keys to the wine cellar of the episcopal residence; from it they were also adequately supplied with oil and similar things. Next, they were provided with eighty gold scudi for clothing, and six gold scudi a month to purchase meat and other necessities. The cardinal, whose revenues paid for these expenditures, ordered that Ours should lack for nothing.

Because that city was plagued with cold weather, Ours had an opportunity, just as those at Perugia had, to exercise their patience; but by God's favor they were better able to safeguard their health than were those [at Perugia]. Both the nobility and the common people expected great things from Ours when it came to both preaching and teaching the Holy Scriptures. But Ours gave them to understand that it was not the practice of the Society to begin with these lofty ministries. Although the bishop usually had a teacher to train the clergy, as soon as Ours arrived this man was dismissed.

73.   *Details of teaching at Gubbio*

Ours took over four classes, and although the course on rhetoric had only five or six students, Father Olivier nonetheless taught the material. But there were more students in the other classes. They did not have a lay brother to do the kitchen work, and the six scholastics did not perform the task adequately. Besides, doing so detracted from their study time, so they requested that somebody be sent from Rome to cook for the community. Master Battista [Velati] gave three lectures in the morning scaled to the capacity of the three groups of boys. Afternoons, moreover, he taught a class on Greek grammar and dictated to his own students and those of Father [Bernard] Olivier a letter in the vernacular, which they then translated into Latin; he also took care of correcting those letters. Moreover, he was sub-minister of the college; and because there was nobody else to carry out this job, he performed the office of buyer and carried back [to the house] vegetables and other necessities from the marketplace. Despite this, as we reported, he preached on feast days. But when he informed Father Ignatius about all these duties, [Ignatius] wrote and ordered him to be relieved of the burden of buyer, all the more so since he wanted [Velati] henceforward to devote himself seriously to preaching. He was quite inclined to this ministry, even though he was not yet trained in either theological or philosophical studies. Even before orders had arrived from Father Ignatius, he had already been relieved of the office of buyer ever since he had [been assigned] to preach in the cathedral, ...

75.   *Helping prostitutes at Modena*

Through the efforts of [Silvestro Landini], several repentant prostitutes entered the convent for the converted, thus giving such amazing edification to the people as to defy description. Two notable ones, who had been a scandal to innumerable observers, were being led under arms to the convent when armed soldiers seemed to have the intention of blocking their entry. But these [soldiers], fearing the crowd accompanying these reformed sinners and the public authority, attempted nothing. Some virgins also entered the same monastery because they had heard good reports about the religious and spiritual life that the women led there. There was even one woman among them who, when some lay people denied her permission to enter, slipped in quietly and secretly along with officials and visitors when they entered the convent. She refused to leave later, remaining there and giving extraordinary edification to the city. Other women from the town, noticing that the convent was blessed with the preaching and sacramental ministry of Father Silvestro, wanted to enter it as well. That convent, which once suffered from bad repute, now attracted even the leading ladies by the sweet fragrance of its renown. . . .

77.   *Ignatius forbids street preaching at Modena*

Many people who were accustomed to eating meat during Lent were led by [Landini's] preaching to observe the abstinence commanded by the Church. When few people were seen coming to church and many could be found in the town squares, Father Silvestro asked Father Ignatius for permission to preach in those public areas. Because this did not seem appropriate in view of the other duties he was already performing at Modena, Ignatius did not grant this permission.

78.   *The converted prostitutes are not allowed to vow obedience to Ignatius*

Giovanni Castelvetro asked Father Ignatius in his own name and that of others who watched over the house of the converted [prostitutes] that he obtain from the Supreme Pontiff permission to reorganize that house into a convent similar to the one established in Rome under the patronage of Saint Martha and subject to the same rules. This permission Father Ignatius diligently sought and obtained. But he did not accept the vows of Girolama Pacana, the superior, and the other nuns whereby they had vowed obedience to Father Ignatius himself.

79.   *Ignatius admonishes Landini not to request a preacher*

Moved by his charity, Father Silvestro encouraged several people of Modena to try to obtain a preacher from Father Ignatius. But the latter up-braided and admonished him not to persuade or suggest to any persons that they ask for some member of the Society before previously having consulted the general and ascertaining that he would welcome this.

81.   *Landini's sermon leads a noble woman to enter a convent*

Magnificent raiment had been prepared for a certain noble young lady who was being sent off to an illustrious palace, but she was eager to decorate herself with virtues and progress in the grace of God rather than that of princes. After hearing Father Silvestro in the course of his preaching utter these words, "Mary arose and went with haste into the hill country" [Luke 1:39], she considered that they were addressed to herself and that she should resist the Holy Spirit no longer. She determined that she would not leave that church belonging to the converted nuns until she had carried out what an inward inspiration required of her. At the end of the sermon, she threw herself at the feet of Father Silvestro and begged him with tears not to exclude her from his prayers and to strive to have her admitted among the converted nuns. She also reduced to tears both the women who were in the convent and the noble men and women who heard her outside. Thus was she allowed to join the other virgins who lived with the converted nuns.

83.   *Heretics and the Inquisition at Modena*

Seeing that the depravity of heresy had infected many people at Modena, Father Silvestro was very zealous to persuade anyone at all to turn in the names of heretics to the inquisitor. This exhortation of his seemed so useful for protecting the Lord's flock that a preacher at the cathedral church declared that neither the bishop [Giovanni Morone] nor his vicar nor Father Silvestro himself had contributed so much by [hearing] confessions or preaching as [Silvestro] had by his efforts to have the errors of the heretics delated to the aforesaid tribunal. One of the group of men who were equally distinguished and devout wrote Father Ignatius that almost the entire city could in some measure have been corrupted were it not for the solicitude and charity shown by Father Silvestro. Although the mind-set of many people was not wicked, many were deceived by the heretics and imitated their lawless ways by thinking and speaking perversely about the Apostolic See.

86.   *Heretics return to the Church*

Many people who were subverted by the heretics and out of ignorance and bad will had embraced their errors were enlightened by the exertions and sermons of Father Silvestro; they returned to the bosom of the Catholic Church and directed their minds toward submission to the faith.

97.   *Our college at Modena begins*

Master Francesco Scipione gave a Latin oration in our church as classes began. In it he explained the thinking of the Society when it accepted colleges of this sort and its plan for teaching young men. He also recommended the study of humane letters and liberal arts and exhorted young people to apply themselves to them. The bishop, many canons, noblemen, and other citizens were present; the bishop was so pleased that he lamented that the entire citizenry was not present to hear the orator. Moreover, [Scipione] so pleased the citizens that some of them who were hostile toward Ours began to be friendly and supportive of the studies being imparted by Ours. One person of respectable status was so moved by this exposition that, all the while weeping for joy, he averred openly that Modena did not deserve our presence and instruction because it had not provided our men with more suitable facilities. Although Ours were not discontented with their inadequate physical arrangements, nonetheless, this man and others as well were not at all satisfied with them.

98.   *Growing piety among students at Modena*

The students were split up into four classes, and the same number of teachers were put in charge, so that they might adjust their lessons and exercises to the varied capacities of their students. In their writing, the speeches they delivered, and their other exercises, the students demonstrated now considerable had been their progress. Among them some were gifted with splendid talent and spirit, and both the little ones and those who were older behaved with humility, prudence, and modesty. All went to confession each month, as was customary in the colleges of the Society, and some went more often; and their spiritual growth seemed obvious, even though the younger generation at Modena were fairly given over to vices and made a practice of cursing, swearing, and uttering imprecations.

Those who attended our classes disdained these practices and bore themselves with simplicity and gentleness. They did not quarrel with one another and gave every indication of exerting themselves for their teachers. On Sundays and feast days they attended divine services and heard sermons, even though the cold weather was a severe trial for them. The rules were printed and even mounted on signs to inform [students] how they were supposed to behave in their literary contests as well as on the street and at home, imitating in all things what was being done at the Roman College. They were inculcated with the method and order for examining their consciences before bedtime and of praying to God when they got up, entrusting and dedicating themselves wholly to him. These techniques wonderfully inflamed our young men with zeal for virtue. Ours who devoted themselves to helping the extern students make progress strove to do so themselves while they were at home: some studied Latin literature and others applied themselves to Greek literature. Still, it was understood that Ours required a longer probation, especially those who were going to be sent to new[ly established] colleges. . . .

103.   *Both support for and opposition to our college at Modena*

The vicar of the bishop also treated Ours with great respect and confessed to one of them. The bishop treated Ours as if he were their father; sometimes in his visits to the classes, he noted that the boys were being formed in great piety and modesty, so his heart was filled with great joy. In his exhortations he encouraged them to obey their teachers and make progress in their studies and virtuous practices. Daily the reputation of the Society spread among different people; but just as [our] Institute and ministries of charity pleased all the best people, so there was no dearth of those who tried the patience [of Ours] by proclaiming that Ours were tricksters who did not teach the way they should. Among these were the school teachers who were infuriated because we were snatching their business away from them, for almost 120 students flocked to our classes. They claimed that our work was superfluous because Modena was well supplied with teachers; they hurled many accusations against Ours. Confronted with the truth, however, some began to think better of Ours and to regard them more highly.

Some young men were so impudent that they were very bothersome, displaying their unbridled insolence right at the gate to the new college. When the Duke of Ferrara, who at the time had come to Modena, learned about this, he wanted Ours to go to the governor with the request that he repress the impertinence of these cads. The rector visited him and the duke himself warmly received him. Someone then requested from his friends a subsidy for maintaining the college, and the duke offered his own good offices and assigned fifty gold scudi annually [to the college], as we mentioned earlier.

104.   *Ignatius decides against illiterate students—usually*

Parents urged Ours to accept students who did not know how to read; but after being consulted, Ignatius did not approve of the college's assuming this burden. But he judged that if an older brother brought along his younger brother to school and undertook the task of teaching him, then he thought that the person who could not read could also be admitted to the classes. The bishop, to whom Ignatius referred the problem, thought the same.

106.   *Heretical students won back to the Church*

Some of the students who were admitted were infected with heretical notions. [That they were admitted] gratified the bishop exceedingly, because this way they would progress at the same time in both good letters and in the Catholic religion. For teaching them Christian doctrine as was customary in the Society provided an opportunity to win them back from their errors.

110.   *The miserable situation in Corsica*

As we touched on earlier, [Fathers Silvestro Landini and Manuel Gomez] were sent to Corsica by the Supreme Pontiff as visitors and consultants regarding the extreme spiritual needs of that island. These were immense because for sixty or seventy years no bishop had visited any of the seven dioceses on that island. But the archbishop of Genoa, who was the pro-legate for Bologna, invoking the aid of several cardinals who were his friends, obtained the Supreme Pontiff's consent that before [Ours] sailed for Corsica they would spend a month or two in the diocese of Genoa, devoting themselves to making visitations there. Leaving Father Manuel in city itself, Father Silvestro went out to various places in the diocese; during the one month that he spent in this task, the Lord through him reaped a wondrous harvest of souls. Daily he heard many confessions and administered the Holy Eucharist to [his penitents], and he spent up to two and three hours at night listening to penitents, for he hardly had enough time to eat a morsel. Thus did he introduce the frequent use of the sacraments, so that some of the parish priests had this to say or write to the vicar: This man had to hear a hundred confessions each week and that man a hundred and fifty, when there were only a few more homes [than that] under their care.

[Silvestro] removed some apostate [priests] from the care of souls. Four of them returned to their religious orders; one among them had exercised the care of souls for twenty years after fleeing from his religious order and his convent, and another [had done so] for thirty years. He found some living in concubinage and others totally ignorant. Lastly, the sheep without a shepherd ran to him more eagerly the more they saw clearly that he was seeking their salvation and not his own comfort. They followed him around from one place to another, so that they could hear the word of God, which he preached twice each day. Some loudly cried out, "Why, O Father, did you not come here many years earlier, so that you might free us from such dense clouds of ignorance?" The vicar was greatly pleased by the Christian doctrine that [Silvestro] was teaching and saw to having it printed.

114.   *A storm at sea nearly kills Fathers Silvestro and Manuel*

Because the [apostolic] needs in Corsica and the command of the Supreme Pontiff were impelling them to do so, . . . [Silvestro and Manuel] set sail for Corsica on November 16. Rough seas made an otherwise easy voyage a rather lengthy one, but the delay worked to the spiritual advantage of many people. While the ship put in at Sestri, Castiglione, Portovenere, Lerici, Zarzane, Pisa, and Livorno many went to the sacraments. Indeed, at Livorno those in the castle and a large part of the city were helped by the holy sacraments. When the sea was hurling up towering waves, they praised God because Ours stayed there longer for this reason. [Became of their presence,] it was agreed and even stipulated in a document drafted by a notary that several churches would be refurbished. The concubines were driven out and instructions were left for both priests and lay people on how to live rightly and how to fulfill their religious duties.

Finally, when they had boarded a ship to make the transit to Corsica, during the night, the waves were surging, the mast broke. The shipmaster shouted loudly, "We are all going to die." Just then Father Silvestro finished reciting the hymn "Te Deum laudamus"; and after having spent all of that night preparing himself to pass on to a better life, he prepared to give absolution to all the people in the little ship. Onrushing waves were washing over the stern and the prow. Meanwhile, Father Manuel, took courage, cast off his coat, and climbed along on a part of the mast that was projecting into the sea. With the help of others, he pulled it out, and thus the Lord led the ship to the island of Capraia, which shortly before the pirate Dragut had devastated. Those noblemen who had come on the ship insisted that God had delivered them, thanks to Ours.

116.   *Conditions on Corsica*

Utter ignorance reigns there. The churches stand in ruins, the priest did not even remember the words of consecration and lived like a soldier, as did his sons as well. Because of their poverty practically everybody went about barefoot even in winter time. They lay down to sleep on the ground, barely throwing down a few straws. One of them who was fifty years old had never eaten his fill of bread. They ate some little fish boiled in water only and then softened with salt—a foul-smelling concoction for those who are not used to it. [The Corsicans] live so chastely that for a long time many young men abstain from approaching their wives after marriage and don't even talk to them until they bring them into their homes.

From Capraia [the priests] finally reached Corsica on December 22 and the leading town of Bastia, where the governor of the whole island resides. With great humanity he received them as his guests. From there they were transferred to a convent of the Friars Minor, where the minister of that Order treated his guests with great kindness. God willing, what they did on the island will be related next year.

135.   *Our work at Padua*

Those who made their confessions and came to our church for Communion grew more numerous. Not only Ours but also lay people received with great consolation the edifying news brought from the city of Rome and other places of the Society, especially India. Steps were also taken that some women who had occasioned great scandal by living apart from their husbands now returned to them and to a peaceful life together.

137.   *Laínez is forced to be provincial of Italy*

. . . But when Father Ignatius had listened to the arguments [of Laínez against his becoming provincial], he explained his own thinking more clearly. Then [Laínez] entered upon the office of provincial on July 15, as he had been ordered to do. Because as yet there were no written constitutions at Padua, he asked that [the rules] relating to the domestic operations of the colleges be sent to him. When several chapters that seemed very useful for this were sent to him, he set himself to coax both superiors and subjects to observe them.

149.   *Poverty at our college in Padua*

After Father Ignatius had warned the rector of the college at Padua to follow the doctor's advice about the food and clothing of Ours, [the rector] rejoined that this could not be done; for without hard cash, which he did not have, they would be forced to eat whatever meat the butcher would give [us], not to provide us with what we actually needed but to suit his own good pleasure. Ours were suffering from a shortage not just of food but also of clothing. The poverty of the living founder [of the college], even despite his charity, would allow for nothing else.

150.   *Norms for admitting candidates to the Society*

Experience also taught that those who were admitted to the Society outside Rome and the Roman house had not been examined as carefully [as they should have been]. Therefore, it seemed best that the [kind of] examination used at Rome should be sent to Padua [for use there] or that nobody should be admitted there.

157.   *Difficult cases of conscience at Venice*

Through the industry of Ours, some very difficult marriage cases were solved. Also Ours cast light on some very intricate usury cases in the course of discussing them, thus freeing the souls of some men from their snares. Some noblemen from the cities subject to the Venetian Republic were sent to Ours at Venice and received [the answers that] they were seeking to bring them peace of conscience. Some priests also were helped by confession and the advice of Ours and began to look after the salvation of themselves and of the souls committed to their care, giving much edification to others thereby.

159.   *Work with people on the margins of Venetian society*

People confined to the public prison were motivated to confess their sins; but because at that time Ours were not able to hear them, they took care through some noblemen that [the prisoners] did not lack for confessors. Previously some of the prisoners had been reduced to such desperation that they either denied God's providence or reproved [its dispositions in their own cases]. Nonetheless, before Ours left them, they promised that they would make a confession of their sins. Some people who were sick and confined to their homes were led, after making their confession, to depart piously from this life. Among them was one man [in particular]: one of our priests was summoned to hear his reconciliation and perceived that he needed a general confession of his whole life, just as if he had never gone to confession.

[Ours] also watched out for some young girls, ensuring that they were brought to a place [where they would be] safe from serious dangers. Concubines were also taken away from some priests. A certain Jew was instructed by Ours and received baptism. Another person who had denied the faith in Turkish lands and lived there sixteen years was reconciled to the Church by confession; furthermore, his wife and daughter too, who had come with him to Venice, were baptized. Afterwards, when two ships belonging to the Turks and Saracens landed at Venice, some of the passengers—and not a just few of them either— were led to the Christian faith and others who had denied the Christian faith and had lived among those Saracens were brought back to the bosom of the Church. The charity of Doctor Andrea Lippomano, the prior of the Most Holy Trinity, contributed greatly to this ministry; he used to take men of this sort into his home. Our brother Giovanni Battista [Eliano], formerly a Jew, was admitted to the Society the previous year and, with his mastery of the languages of those travelers, made himself into an instrument of divine Providence for such conversions.

163.   *Reconciling an apostate priest*

After debating religious issues with him, Father André [des Freux] through divine assistance convinced a priest who was living a very dissolute life and who declared that Masses were idolatry and the other mysteries and sacraments were nothing at all, and brought him back to a sound state of mind. He confessed his sins and went away absolved.

185.   *Candidates for the Society at Ferrara*

A good number of [applicants to the Society] possessed nobility not only of soul but also of lineage; Ours at Ferrara admitted into the Society some of them who had been better tested and were reluctant to brook any delay. Among them a man named Michele da Como from the Valtellina was admitted; soon afterwards when both his integrity and learning had been tested, he was admitted to the simple vows of the Society. He was prefect of the second class [at the school]; besides Latin, Greek, and Hebrew, he knew Chaldean and Arabic and had spent many years studying philosophy. Master Lorenzo [Tristano], an excellent stonemason, whose virtue Father Ignatius held in such esteem that, as he declared, he would not regret it if no other fruit was gathered from the college at Ferrara, seeing that it had acquired Lorenzo for the Society, a man who edified no less by the example of his life than by his craftsmanship.[7] He was famous for his work at Ferrara.

A third man of proven character was also admitted and then sent to Padua to escape his mob of troublesome relatives. Many other men at Ferrara wanted to be admitted, but the judgment came down that they should be deferred and that [instead] the desires of the young men should be fostered [by urging them] to receive the sacraments frequently, to pray, and to examine their consciences. Two or three who were closer to Ours [in spirit] notably excelled the rest of the applicants. The letters from India inflamed not only them but also many others.

---

[7] Lorenzo Tristano (1521–86) had an even more distinguished older brother, Giovanni (1515–75). Giovanni entered the Society in 1555 and became the most prominent Jesuit architect of his day. Both were lay brothers. Their careers as Jesuits are traced by Pietro Pirri in his *Giovanni Tristiano e i primordi della architettura gesuitica* (Rome: Institutum Historicum Societatis Iesu (IHSI), 1955).

186.   *Vocations to convents at Ferrara*

Many young women made so much spiritual progress by frequently approaching the sacraments and by performing other works of devotion that twenty-five of them consecrated themselves totally to God by vows of poverty, chastity, and obedience and filled the whole city with the fragrance [of their exemplary lives].

187.   *Frequent Communion at Ferrara*

The enthusiasm of many people, especially women, [to receive] the sacraments of confession and Communion so increased that they eagerly desired to go two or three times a week. Their spiritual progress was quite remarkable. A good many people did not go to confession as frequently as the others, considering how many confessors were available, and these too [who confessed relatively frequently] increased in number daily. On Christmas in the church near our residence, which was afterward handed over to the Society, four or five hundred people partook of the Body of the Lord with great devotion. This was regarded as miraculous in that city, for it was not customary there [to see so many receive the sacraments]. The example of these people later attracted other people to the same pious practice.

191.   *Jewish converts at Ferrara*

Many [Jewish] people of both genders at length accepted baptism after Ours had first taught them Christian doctrine. These people fled to Lord Agostino Mosto, who was in charge of the Hospital of Saint Anne, as if seeking a sacred asylum where he would defend them from injury at the hands of the [other] Jews. Eager to increase the Lord's flock, he welcomed such people into his home and stationed himself like a rampart defending them; he would fight legal battles for them with unconquerable spirit if they were haled into court. He availed of the good offices of the Society, of which he was always an enthusiastic supporter. Ours often had to go to the indigents in the hospital that he headed, and the throng of sick people found there offered Ours an abundant harvest close at hand. For the large garden of the hospital bordered on the garden of our house; and in order to allow Ours to enjoy its delightful surroundings and to cross over conveniently to the hospital, he allowed Ours to open a gate giving them access to the hospital through the garden.

192.   *Two bright Jewish lads*

Among the baptized Jews was a gifted young lad who made great progress in the Christian religion with the help of the rector, Father [Jean] Pelletier. A large crowd of noblemen flocked to his baptism, for he was endowed with many talents. There was another youth similar to him, from whom great things could be hoped.

224.   *Ignatius cuts back sermons to Ours at Bologna*

So that he might more diligently fulfill his duty, Father André [des Freux] daily used to give a one-hour private sermon to our brethren, and a two-hour sermon on feast days. Although the efforts he expended considerably improved the behavior of some of the men, they also hindered them from studying and, in any case, were not customary in the Society. On Father Ignatius's orders he moderated them, giving only one exhortation each week.

228.   *Ignatius moves men around*

In early autumn Master Fulvio Cardulo, who had been very successful as head of the Bolognese college as long as he was resident there, was called to Rome by Father Ignatius. It was there that Master Joachim [Christiaens], a young man outstanding for piety and learning, especially for [his knowledge of] languages, fell into a very serious sickness and gradually wasted away. Our Roman College had to be well supplied with teachers after taking over the administration of the German College and for other reasons. Before the eyes of the whole world, it had started to give classes at Rome and had been set up as a kind of seedbed from which teachers could be sent to the other colleges. As I wrote, since this was the case, it is no surprise that [Ignatius] called Father André des Freux from Venice and Master Fulvio from Bologna. At that time there was hardly anybody else equally talented who could be employed [to conduct] classes at Rome.

But the college at Bologna felt deprived when Master Fulvio departed, especially since Master Willem van den Brock, who was in charge of the first class, was unable to carry out his job properly because of ill health. Also Italian boys and teenagers found his pronunciation disagreeable, as they did that of others from north of the Alps. Regardless, those who were put in charge of the classes carried out their duties in good spirits. Still, it was obvious that the progress made by the students increased or decreased in proportion to the quality of their teachers. Thus, it was only right that an Italian should be sent to replace Master Fulvio.

233.   *The college at Florence faces problems*

Toward the end of the previous year, as has already been recounted, the college at Florence began to hold classes in rented quarters. Ours put up with considerable inconvenience at the start, but maintained their good spirits. Because they had no lay brothers, in their prayers they all competed to be assigned the task of cooking [for the rest]. Father Louis Coudret, the rector, divided all the household chores among the handful of companions at the college, and he himself served at table and acted as doorkeeper and factotum. Meanwhile, the Florentines developed a great esteem for Ours; and when at that time some heretics were thrown into prison and a preacher at the principal church fell under suspicion and was forbidden to preach, another [friar] of the Order of Saint Dominic was substituted, an excellent man and well known to Ours. A rumor circulated through the city that Ours were responsible for these developments.

243.   *Salmerón preaches at Florence*

The vicar of the archbishop, who desired to advance the spiritual welfare of women consecrated to God, persuaded Father Salmerón, who had recently come to Florence, to send some of Ours to preach God's word to them. They did this successfully, as we can hope in the Lord. But Father Salmerón himself greatly enhanced the reputation of the college and gave much edification as he delivered lucid sermons and lectures and thus reformed that city in the Lord and vivified it wondrously. Although the summer heat was rather bothersome, such great crowds came to hear him that they were said to outnumber those who usually gathered during Lent. Some in that huge concourse had reportedly been so averse to practices of devotion that they had never been seen in church before, as people averred. They paid such close attention that in that giant cathedral no noise and no coughing were heard. The faces and eyes of the congregation were so focused on the preacher that they seemed to be hanging on his lips, as the expression goes. Some bishops, canons, and members of the duke's staff were often present, spreading far and wide the good reputation of the Society. Some people requested that the lectures he gave be printed and distributed for the common good.

244.   *Laínez replaces Salmerón at Florence*

The more welcome and effective [Salmerón] was, the more the Florentines would have regretted his departure for Perugia and Rome if Father Provincial Diego Laínez, highly esteemed by all, had not come to Florence. His arrival brought great consolation not merely to Ours but to the duke, the duchess, and the whole city as well. So admirably did he proceed with the lectures begun by Father Salmerón that his hearers with good reason marveled at their spirit, wisdom, and efficacy and declared that no preacher had appeared at Florence in the last forty years who could be compared with these fathers of the Society of Jesus. Good results commensurate with the satisfaction of these people were looked for. They cast a brilliant light upon the activities of the college, begun so unpromisingly.

247.   *Laínez cultivates the Medici*

During Advent Father Laínez gave sermons in the cathedral church before a large audience, who drew much consolation from them. When requested, he gave so beneficial a sermon in a convent of nuns that they burgeoned with the perceptible fruit of a reformed spirit. The older sons of the duke indicated their favorable attitude toward the Society, as it is believed, when they visited the college to thank Father Laínez. Two short sermons were preached in their presence, one instructing the Christian prince about true happiness, the other reciting the praises of a true bishop; for it was presumed that one of them was going to become duke and the other a bishop. Between the two sermons were disputations in Greek and Latin delivered by young boys, questions asked about Christian doctrine, and poems appropriate to the situation. Everything went quite well, and the performance of some of the boys was worth witnessing and their elocution was most charming. A bishop who accompanied these princes said that he had never spent his time more profitably than he did when he devoted several hours to those literary exercises. . . .

253.   *Classes begin at Naples*

Although this college was started toward the end of the previous year, still, classes commenced only at the beginning of this year. One of the teachers, Niccolò by name, led off with an oration in which he explained our Society's objectives in its schools. Master Theodore Peltanus also gave a speech in praise of language study; Greek and Hebrew, and Latin as well, flowed quite brilliantly from his mouth, so that he more than pleased the crowd in attendance. Right from the beginning, four classes were set up, but a fifth was also added that offered instruction in the Greek and Hebrew languages. Scholastic disputations, declamations, and similar exercises quickly began to follow one another. Studies began at a higher level than in other places, but did not on that account run a more successful course later.

Therefore, five teachers began right from the beginning to teach some three hundred students, whose numbers continued to climb day by day. No meager fruit was being produced as those rather fickle young men, once they were brought to monthly confessions and other acts of devotion, made progress in good conduct no less than in learning, many going to Communion every week after they had confessed to Ours. . . .

262.   *Friction between Bobadilla and the Neapolitans*

Father Bobadilla did not think that Ours needed to observe some of the rules customary in the Society, but (as he himself kept saying) Ours should keep them with a certain Christian liberty as long as no deficiencies in solid virtues came to light. Since he was the [provincial] superior and left Father Andrea, the rector, very little scope in which to exercise his office, experience easily showed how much influence the observance of constitutions and rules exerted upon the preservation of solid virtues. First one of the teachers and then one of the scholastics (who, as we wrote a little earlier, had preached successfully in a certain convent) left the Society. But Father Ignatius mandated that the rules be observed and that the rector be given free rein to carry out his office. This man had won for himself great goodwill among not only our house staff but also the laity by the holy example he gave and his conversations.

The liberty possessed by non-Jesuits led to their requesting Father Salmerón, who was now free from the Council of Trent, to replace Father Bobadilla, even though they all had praise for the latter's solid virtue and learning. There was another cause for this development: they were still disappointed by [Bobadilla's lack of] fluency in the Italian language, even allowing for the erudition with which he expounded on the prophet Jonah and the Epistle to the Romans, giving them no end of satisfaction. Therefore, the Duke of Monteleone [Hector Pignatelli, the viceroy] in his letters began urging Father Ignatius to send Father Salmerón to Naples in accord with a promise once made, even though, as summer was approaching, Father Salmerón's arrival was postponed until autumn.

265.   *Tight finances at Naples*

We have said that the financial situation there was straitened, for [the enthusiasm of] those people who had promised a great deal grew cold, leaving the Duke of Monteleone to shoulder a heavy burden. . . . Some friends and protectors of the college undertook to merge a confraternity for the redemption of captives with our college. They were also its protectors and were content to have whatever was involved with redemption to be dealt with in one room without requiring the Society to incur any additional problems. Others also seriously discussed transferring the college to the Hospital of San Jacobo for the Incurables so that these works could be intermingled. Considering that not only would Ours earn goodwill in the aforesaid pious works but also that in this way it would become easier to support the college, they considered both of these expedients viable. Neither idea, however, seemed advisable to Father Ignatius; instead, the college exercised patience while it was supported by such alms as a procurator could solicit; moreover, he commissioned a bookseller to acquire the books Ours needed. Still, these developments taught us how much hope we should place in similar promises.

272.   *Salmerón replaces Bobadilla as provincial at Naples*

Around the middle of October, Father Salmerón reached Naples. Father Bobadilla transferred his office [of provincial] to him before leaving for Calabria. As he was departing, he made some decisions having to do with improving discipline in the house and better organizing the classes, and he imposed observance of the rules both inside and outside our house, for he recognized that the liberty reigning there previously wreaked harm both inside and outside our house. Because two or three extern students were causing harm to the rest, he saw to it that they left our school completely. Therefore, in the community and the school this change brought improvement. [Salmerón] ordered Father Andrea de Oviedo, the rector, to exercise his office to the full; and now that Father Salmerón had brought along from Rome the rules to be observed in the college, they were put into practice at the earliest opportunity and proved to be invaluable.

273.   *Salmerón's preaching at Naples*

The people welcomed Salmerón to Naples with great eagerness; the viceroy and the Duke of Monteleone especially, along with the other leaders, greeted him with tokens of great joy. Because Father Andrea had started lectures on the Sacred Scriptures and was explaining the Psalms in the cathedral church, he wrote to Father Ignatius that he did not think it right that he should be lecturing in one place and Father Salmerón in another. He should allow [Salmerón] to take his place, even though he had begun those lectures on the Psalms under obedience. This met with Father Ignatius's approval, in keeping with the view of the archbishop's vicar that Father Salmerón should lecture in the cathedral; this he did before a crowded gathering of noblemen, arousing wonderful plaudits and enthusiasm thereby. Meanwhile, Father Andrea devoted his time to visiting the public prisons and performing other works of piety; he concentrated especially on helping people whose faith was being investigated by [the Inquisition].

280. *A nobleman overcomes his hatred*

A certain nobleman had never mentioned in confession the hatred that for ten years he had harbored toward some people. These too were noblemen; one of them had cut off his thumb, another the index finger of the same hand, and a third had cut off the middle finger of his other hand. All the while, these men were in league with others who were trying to kill him. On Holy Saturday he met one of the fathers of the college in Messina, to whom he began to make his confession. Although he had begun his confession unprepared at first, his heart soon after grew warm within him; then, as a flood of tears poured from [his eyes], he promised to set aside his hatreds and to do whatever the confessor asked of him. After having completed his confession this way, he summoned a notary and witnesses and freely forgave all those people whatever they had done against him.

Among his adversaries, some of whom lived at Messina and others in exile because of this act, two of the chief ones were two brothers. He sent a written statement of forgiveness to the brother who was at Messina. Not content with this, he searched for and found [the brother] in the city. Then he kissed him with a kiss of peace and embraced him with great and pious affection. When the father of the two brothers heard about this, although he had not gone to confession for twenty years, struck with astonishment at what his adversary had done, he provided for his own salvation by receiving the sacrament of penance.

I will not omit to mention that the man whose fingers were cut off, after devoutly receiving the sacrament of Communion, that same day joyfully returned to Ours, thanking them and saying that, among other things, what he found amazing was that previously when his blood used to boil and he used to be totally distraught whenever he looked at his hands, now not only did he not experience [these emotions] but it seemed to him that his hands were almost healed and intact. He also experienced that nothing gave greater joy than worshiping God with a clean conscience. Even more, he reinforced what he said in words by his deeds: he went to confession every eighth day and to Communion every fifteenth day.

293.   *Nadal Starts a* monte di pietà *at Messina*

Father [Nadal] also saw to it that a *monte di pietà* was set up in Messina to provide for the poor of the city who had no other way of sustaining themselves.[8] Even though grave difficulties blocked carrying this out, he did not immediately surrender to them or stop demanding this project, which would be extremely helpful for the people. Father's exertions provided for many people who were ashamed to beg and tolerated extreme privation instead. Making use of his favor with the viceroy, he helped many who lacked influential advocates; otherwise, these people—who were quite numerous—would have undergone extreme hardships. Seeing that he enjoyed great prestige with the viceroy, many people sought him out, and he did not allow his efforts on their behalf to slacken.

310.   *The* monte di pietà *begins*

Finally, the *monte di pietà* that Father Nadal was striving to establish went into operation in autumn, giving rise to the reasonable hope that much good would flow from it. With Father Nadal's help, marriages were arranged for some young women bereft of money and parents.

311.   *Developments at the College of Messina*

I will also add this about the studies of Ours: since the professor of philosophy had no students, the course in philosophy was wholly discontinued. Only men in our house attended the course in Hebrew. The course in rhetoric had only four extern students besides Ours. Still there were about 270 students in the lower classes. But Ours who lived in the college and the house of probation provided Father Annibale [Coudret] with a harvest that was not to be

---

[8] A *monte di pietà* was an agency founded to make low-interest loans to people in need. It usually was associated with a confraternity or religious order.

scorned. This year eleven of the novices, according to the custom in the Society, began wearing ankle-length cassocks, winning the great approbation of the whole city and especially of their parents and even of the viceroy. His heart took great pleasure in seeing those new saplings dressed like other Jesuits. Among the novices Don Fernando de Vega, the viceroy's nephew, had already left [the novitiate]. Earlier he had indicated that he aspired to the Society and obtained admittance among the novices, but either this inclination of his heart was not judged to be genuine or perhaps Fernando abandoned it easily and returned to the court. The viceroy's daughter, Isabel de Vega, took his departure very hard.

329.   *Nadal chosen to promulgate the* Constitutions

When Father Ignatius reflected on [how best to] promulgate and reduce to practice the *Constitutions* throughout the Society, he reached the conclusion that Father Jerónimo Nadal was the ideal man to visit many places [to carry out] this task, so he wrote and directed him to terminate his commitments in Sicily in such a way that he could come to Rome at least after the feast of the Lord's Resurrection. Because Father Jerónimo Doménech was away and Father Nadal was the viceroy's usual confessor, Father Ignatius did not consider it wise to withdraw [Nadal] from there until he had performed this office just before Easter.

336.   *Ignatius seeks Nadal's advice on the* Constitutions

[Nadal] came to Rome at the beginning of spring and made his profession in the hands of Father Ignatius on March 25; he also consulted with him on many things. In turn, Father Ignatius gave him the *Constitutions* to read and asked him to make notes of anything that crossed his mind. Seeing that he was advancing in age and in poor physical health, Father Ignatius thought that, unable as he was to fulfill all his duties during the jubilee year, he should employ [Nadal] as his substitute in many things. . . .

341.   *Ignatius reacts to Turkish attacks on Italy*

Enkindled with zeal against the Turkish fleet, Father Ignatius wanted to offer several suggestions to the viceroy Juan de Vega.[9] His observations rather pleased the viceroy, in that they provided arguments confirming how advanta-

---

[9] Polanco's previous paragraph noted the Turkish raids on Calabria.

geous it would be for the Emperor to assemble a large fleet and how money for that expedition could be raised. The Emperor himself and Prince Philip had dearly hoped to carry out the first proposal; but the second one, the proposal for raising the money, seemed difficult, even though Father Ignatius's suggestion greatly delighted [the viceroy]. This he revealed in a letter he wrote to [Ignatius], in which he also urged Father to promote the scheme himself. I have included this to demonstrate that the zeal of Father Ignatius extended to public affairs, and that he did not view it as alien to his profession to deal with such matters.[10]

342.   *Nadal promulgates the* Constitutions *in Sicily*

While he was at Messina, Father Nadal, in the midst of other tasks, completed his annotations on the *Constitutions* and sent them to Father Ignatius; meanwhile, he brought [these regulations] to bear on practices at the College of Messina. Later he did this also at Palermo, where he went just before the viceroy, that is, on October 6, so that he might supervise the renewal of studies.

343.   *Nadal's good works in Sicily*

Ours there welcomed him very warmly. His coming was for them both useful and enjoyable because many things required his presence. By his diligent efforts he stabilized and strengthened the state of the college. With great application and energy, he carried out all his business, and also devoted himself to many charitable works similar to those he had engaged in earlier that year at Messina. Among his other endeavors, by his advice and appeals here too he helped the *monte di pietà* to support indigent people. Many men who had been kept in prison a long time were freed through his exertions; for as soon as he reached Palermo, he undertook to free fifteen of them, and more than fifty others at Christmas. Some of the money that he had been at pains to collect by begging he contributed to pay off the debts of these men. This work afforded singular consolation and help to many who had been reduced almost to despera-

---

[10] Here Polanco seems to have in mind Loyola's letter no. 2775, written to Nadal on August 6, 1552 (*Sancti Ignatii de Loyola Societatis Iesu fundatoris epistolæ et instructiones,* 12 vols., vols. 22, 26, 28, 29, 31, 33, 34, 36, 37, 38, 40, and 42 of the series Monumenta Historica Societatis Iesu [MHSI; Madrid, 1903–11, reprinted in Rome, 1964–68], 29:354–58). Nadal seems to have passed this letter on to the viceroy of Sicily, Juan de Vega. The letter, although largely drafted by Polanco, includes unusually detailed reflections on military questions. For an English translation, see William J. Young, ed. and trans., *Letters of Ignatius of Loyola* (Chicago: Loyola University Press, 1559), 261–65.

tion by their overwhelming miseries. He also secured help for many needy and sick people, so that with the help of God's grace twenty poor households and families were provided for each week. He also saw to it that twelve sick people were provided for every day—people who, over and above their being impoverished, were suffering from serious illness. Those who were without any human defenses and whose lives were in jeopardy began through this help to recover their strength to the extent possible.

■ Austria and Germany

356. *Cultivating rulers in Austria and Bavaria*

In his letters Father Claude [Jay] was encouraging Ours at Ingolstadt to transfer from there to Vienna, for he understood that Father Ignatius desired this. A promise had been made to Ferdinand, the king of the Romans, that after the college at Vienna had been set up, men would be sent to Ingolstadt to teach all the disciplines customary in our schools. But this is the real reason that they were summoned from [Ingolstadt]: Ferdinand, the king of the Romans, at the recommendation of Ours wrote to Father Ignatius requesting him to send those two theologians who were at Ingolstadt. Although Father Ignatius himself strongly desired to remove Ours from Ingolstadt until a fully equipped college complement could be sent there, he wanted to accomplish this without giving offense to the Duke of Bavaria; accordingly, he wanted them to be summoned by the [duke's] father-in-law, the Emperor. But because charity required avoiding any occasion of giving offense, even between son-in-law and father-in-law, he devised this plan: in the name of the King of the Romans, the Supreme Pontiff would make a request from Rome for two theologians of our Society, without specifically naming those at Ingolstadt. Because the Pope would want to satisfy King [Ferdinand], the suggestion was made to the Pope that the only two suitable ones were those at Ingolstadt, who had, however, been sent to the Duke of Bavaria to set up a college there; but His Holiness could command them to be lent to the Emperor until that college at Ingolstadt was actually established.

Through a certain cardinal the Pope requested this of Father Ignatius; and on January 28 he wrote to Ours at Ingolstadt bidding them, in the name of the Supreme Pontiff, to whom the Society owed obedience by the special vow concerning missions, to leave there for Vienna. They should begin their trip within ten days of receiving his letter. He also wrote to the Duke of Bavaria that the Supreme Pontiff had commanded him to transfer Doctors [Peter] Canisius and [Nicolas Florisz] of Gouda to his father-in-law at Vienna. . . .

■ **Austria**

360.   *Problems of teaching at Vienna*

In his lectures, which were open to the public, Father Claude [Jay] discoursed on Blessed Paul['s Letter] to the Romans before a goodly number of people. Father Nicholas of Gouda [lectured] on Genesis. But Father Canisius early in the summer began both to formulate and dictate a compendium of theology or Christian doctrine intended for the use of serious students and pastors living in the King's jurisdiction who could not remain in college any longer; this was the task that previously a mandate of the King had entrusted to Father Claude, one which those doctors of Ours began to organize.[11] In our community Master Jacob [Tsantele] of Aldenaerde [in Belgium] taught Aristotle's logic to our brethren. (He was one of those three from Louvain whom we mentioned a bit earlier.) He did this for an hour three times each day. Some young lay people were also in his class. He had all engage in disputations three times each week. Three others of Ours, namely, Masters Peter Schorich, Erard [Dawant] and Nicholas [Lanoy], taught our other men Greek and Latin literature. Some lay people joined Ours during these classes. All these students were divided into two classes, one for logic, the other for humane letters; to the latter group the three last-mentioned teachers lectured at different hours.

But this style of teaching did not please Father Ignatius, who wanted three classes divided according to the varied capacity of the students, so that one and the same student would not hear all the lectures, [some of] which were above or below their capacity. Still, at the start it seemed that this [policy] was rather impolitic and likely to turn away extern students who came to the classes of Ours and of other [teachers], just as if they were public lectures. Nonetheless, Ours made progress in these private classes, so that they also emerged from them equipped to teach this material. They made no less progress in piety than in learning.

364.   *Preparing the Canisius Catechism*

Although Fathers Claude [Jay] and [Nicholas] of Gouda by and large laid out the structure and contents of the compendium of theology mentioned earlier, still, it was Father Canisius who contributed the style imposed on the basic material. Even though it was thought that he would be sent off after Easter to

---

[11] This led, of course, to the famous Canisius catechisms.

the people at Strasbourg who were asking for him, still, he could not go there except by deferring the compendium for a long time, for he was just then putting it in its final shape. [The compendium] was awaited with the utmost eagerness; and from the time that [our three men] arrived in Vienna before the middle of March, they had ranked this in first place among their occupations.

The royal counsellors, who had been deputed to reform the university, imposed certain stipulations on this compendium: first, it must observe the order of the Master of the *Sentences;* second, it must confirm the dogmas of the Church against the heretics of the time by invoking the authority of the Sacred Scriptures and the [Church] Fathers; third, it must effectively teach the men who would be future pastors but could not study theology at the university; fourth, it must treat only theological questions and omit metaphysical ones; last of all, it was to be printed in the name of the university. Before [the compendium] was completed—indeed, while it was still in its formative stages—lectures began to be based on it and references made to it.[12]

373.   *Plague hinders our ministries at Vienna*

Just as he had begun [to do], Father Canisius continued explaining his compendium, which was elaborated in the King's name, as we have reported; he did so to the great approbation and profit of those who heard him. In the [Jesuit] community he also carried out the duties of prefect of studies. This autumn the courses could not be divided into various homogeneous classes for our extern students, as Father Ignatius had prescribed. The plague was the reason why all schools were closed just when it was time for them to open [their doors]. It began to rage, especially among students. Therefore, even though Ours were prepared to begin teaching, as we just mentioned, because of the plague we were compelled to postpone the opening until the beginning of the next year; this decision was taken not only with the consent but also with the approbation of the King, the bishop, and the magistrates. The pestilence within a few months snatched from our midst many thousands of people and put to flight from Vienna not only students but the whole court. . . .

---

[12] These references are to Canisius's *Summa Doctrinæ Christianæ,* the first edition of which was published anonymously at Vienna in 1555; later editions added new material. It was intended for priests. The children's version, the *Catechismus minimus,* only seven pages in the critical edition, came out in 1556. A third version, written for lay adults and older children, was the *Parvus Catechismus Catholicorum* of 1559; this was the most popular version.

375.   *Helping plague victims at Vienna*

Many Italian soldiers returned from Hungary, some of them severely affected with sickness, others with wounds; but still more were they afflicted with the pestilence of sin, because for many years now many of them had not yet cast off their crushing burdens of sin. These were diligently cured of their inward sickness by the holy medicine of confession, and many of them departed from this life as Christians should. Father Nicholas Lanoy took special care of the sick who were lying in the hospital and of other poor people staying elsewhere in Vienna. Showing them his fatherly heart, he not only took care of what effected the salvation of their souls but also looked out for their bodies.

His devotion and that of others of Ours were in great demand, especially on behalf of the soldiers in the places mentioned earlier. Although their nakedness, hunger, and sickness ought to have aroused sympathy in people, they received almost no assistance in that city; instead, the soldiers were allowed to lie in misery on the streets with clothes torn, exhausted by hunger and even more by their sickness. So weak and devoid of energy were they that they could not stand up or move their bodies, and hardly anybody could be found to scatter even a few straws on the bare ground for them. Seeing such a tragedy unfolding, Father Lanoy and others of Ours rightly thought that Christ had entrusted this task to them. Before the court left, he secured from the almoner of the Queen of Bohemia and from other pious people [a directive] that food, clothes, and beds would be provided for these soldiers and also for others who were impoverished. It is certain that many people in the suburbs and other parts of the city had perished from cold and other miseries before Father Lanoy came to their aid, especially after the terrible defeat the Turks inflicted on the royal army in Hungary. Father [Lanoy] marshaled some of the brothers, sending them to visit those miserable people and bring them what they needed, depending on what [afflicted them].

When death approached, the priests, especially Father Lanoy, came promptly to hear their confessions. Many of them would have died in their sins without the remedy of repentance unless his care and charity had been at hand for them. Some of these loudly professed that this Father had been sent to them by God and through him they had been delivered from death of body and soul. Alms were collected from the Spaniards who lived at the court; from the alms, in addition to the wool and linen cloth distributed to the needy, they received money with which to supply their necessities.

381.   *Successful ministry in Vienna's prisons*

Not only did the apostolic nuncio himself receive the sacraments at our house, but he wanted to celebrate Christmas by having his whole household, which was rather numerous, receive the sacred Body of Christ with Ours. Many others also came for the same purpose, bringing Ours no little consolation by their presence and devotion. But a greater change was seen among those confined to the public prison than in other people; at first they turned deaf ears to us—indeed, rebellious hearts—and seemed to mock and deride those who gave worthwhile admonitions; but in the end they put aside their hostility and obstinacy and began to listen to Ours and to love and respect them. They humbly and freely welcomed and listened to those who were sent to console them. These men collected and carried alms to [the prisoners], thus edifying not only the prisoners by their charity but lay people also. Certain noblemen sent considerable money, clothing, and similar things, which [Ours] distributed to [those confined]. Ours looked after not only the souls but also the bodies of those shut away, and the public prison took on a far different aspect than it had previously. Some [prisoners] were wholly ignorant of even the most common prayers. They used to show Ours who visited them, as a sign of their devotion, the rosaries bought for them so that they could say their prayers. They began to use these often.

■ Germany

394.   *Jesuits expelled from Cologne*

Still, [Father Leonard Kessel] found no little trouble in Cologne when he returned, One of these young men [mentioned elsewhere as having joined the Society] was seduced by a layman of learning and considerable repute. This young man then led one of his blood relatives astray, who had also taken the vow of the Society. They had been told astonishing lies against the Institute of the Society, so one of them, Johann Marbatius by name, secretly slipped out of our house. The other [scholastics], who regarded these two as paragons because they used to encourage the others to perfection, were greatly scandalized. Therefore, when Father Leonard had called in Johann and seen the perverse disposition of his heart and had observed that others as well were not treading the path befitting candidates of a religious order, he dismissed him and the others, eight or nine of them altogether. The experience taught him that even one person, once he had been tolerated more than was proper, was enough to corrupt many and draw them down to ruin along with himself. He also sent two other men off to Louvain.

395.   *More reflections on departures from the Jesuits*

During this year and the previous one, therefore, Father Leonard showed himself rather prompt to dismiss men who gave no grounds for hoping that they would improve. Father Ignatius also heartily approved of this [policy]. The experience showed as well that some of those among the new recruits who had gone back to their home regions to set their affairs in order fell from their pious resolve and returned to worldly pursuits when they had not yet sunk deep roots in the spirit.

398.   *Recruiting for the German College*

When Father Leonard received a letter from Father Ignatius about sending some young men of good character to the new German College, he showed [the letter] to the rectors of the schools so that they might pass it on to students. The good repute of the German College quickly spread through all of Cologne, and many young men with scholarly inclinations began to approach him, joyously offering to undertake the journey. A few of them were from Upper Germany. As was mentioned above, those who arrived in Rome that year were for the most part sent by Father Leonard.

■   **France**

419.   *Difficulties at Paris*

At the start of this year, Father Battista Viola was the superior of our college at Paris. So lacking were they in material resources that in the spring of this year the rector was constrained to send three more men to Rome in addition to those he had sent at the end of the previous year with Father Everard [Mercurian]. Their leader was Olivier Mannaerts. Only five of Ours remained at Paris, of whom Father Battista Viola was the only priest. Not only Paris but Louvain and Cologne as well suffered a severe lack of material necessities; but this penury served the common good, in that excellent future laborers in the Lord's vineyard had to be sent to Rome. While they themselves gained a more profound grasp of the ways of the Society, they also supplied useful services when it came to founding colleges in various places.

420.   *Broët takes charge at Paris*

Since Father Viola was constantly afflicted with bad health, Father Ignatius, who was intending to recall him to Italy, wondered whether anyone still in Paris would be qualified to assume the care of the others and improve matters at the Paris college. [Viola] wrote back to him that there was nobody, and suggested to Father Ignatius that Father Paschase Broët would be entirely suitable for both directing Ours and laboring for the good of souls in that Paris vineyard. He would also retain the goodwill of the bishop of Clermont and other friends, who would undoubtedly resent it if no professed member of our Society stayed on with the others, all of whom were young men. If somebody was to come, he should arrive there in good time, so that before Father Battista departed he could get to know the friends of the Society and learn the status of everything in which the Society was involved. . . .

■ Spain

456.   *The Spiritual Exercises at Salamanca*

One person among the colleagues who made the Spiritual Exercises with notable profit occupied a prestigious chair in the university. At his own request, seconded by the master of novices, a certain monk of the Order of Saint Augustine was trained in [the Exercises]. The hope was that through him many in his monastery could share the same Exercises. At a convent of nuns named for the Holy Spirit, a certain prominent religious devoted herself to them with great success, in the hope that through her efforts a not inconsiderable harvest of fruit would also ripen among the other nuns of the same convent.

462.   *Toward a* Ratio Studiorum

When the plan of studies that aided the lay students in the Italian colleges of the Society [to progress] in letters and spirit was sent to Salamanca, [authorities there] received it with wondrous enthusiasm. Although as regards literary studies Salamanca was blessed with an abundance of instructors, no similar method of teaching existed there that fostered virtue and spiritual matters along with letters.

■ **Portugal**

464.   *A new provincial in Portugal*

As we recorded above, Father Ignatius wanted to free Father Simão of the burden of governing the [Portuguese] Province, and so he wrote to Father [Miguel] Torres and also to Father Francis Borgia [instructing Torres] to go to Portugal. But it seemed good to Father Torres, who was closer, to send a letter to Father [Diego] Miró through a certain brother who was bound for Portugal; in it he notified [Miró] about the contents of Father Ignatius's letter about turning over the office of provincial to him [Miró], thereby freeing Father Simão. Moreover, the letter ordered [Torres] and Father Francis to go to Portugal because the King and also his brother Prince Luís seemed to want Father Francis Borgia, about whom one heard so much, to come to that kingdom. So [Torres] was now waiting for Father Francis Borgia, so that they could go to Portugal together.

But Father Miró replied that, after discussing the matter with the most important members of the Society, it was not at all advisable for him and still less for Father Francis Borgia to make their way to Portugal at that time. Rather, they should forward to Portugal the documents received from Father Ignatius transferring the office of provincial from Father Simão to Father Miró. Other Fathers, who were considered pillars [of the province], wrote in the same vein. Here is the reasoning that persuaded them: at the same time the Lord moved Father Ignatius to divest Father Simão of his burden and hand the care of the province to other men, he also moved the King of Portugal and Prince Luís to adopt the same plan and method that Father Ignatius had decided on. The King was so zealously intent upon this course that, when he was sending somebody to Rome by relay horses, he sent a message through Father Luís Gonçalves [da Câmara] recommending that Father Miró write to Rome, urging Father Ignatius to write and confirm what [the King] had already decided on; in order to expedite this matter more delicately, he sent Fathers Francis Borgia and [Miguel de] Torres to Portugal. When all these details were conveyed to Father Francis, they judged that they should not leave Salamanca. . . .

■ **Spain**

470.   *Setting up a novitiate at Salamanca*

At the college of Salamanca the function proper to houses of probation had to be implemented. As we said, in the early days of autumn there were twenty men there, and ten of them had joined the Society within the first six months of this year. A good many of them were engaged in studying theology and displayed outstanding talent therein; they were simultaneously going through their probations as novices. One of them, who was only fifteen years old, had completed his degree in liberal arts to everybody's warm acclaim, and he was noteworthy for his sound judgment, behavior, and piety as much as for his talent. During the year before he had entered, he made a weekly confession to Ours and was nourished by the Eucharist.

Two others at Medina del Campo had worked as merchants, and when Father Battista while speaking in a public square vigorously inveighed against usurers and loan sharks, these men, stricken in conscience, came to the same father pleading with him not to forbid them from doing what they earlier hoped to do, namely, enter the Society. Immediately, despite the objections of their blood relatives, they went to our college at Salamanca and along with the others performed with great zeal all the most humble tasks, and they wished that people would grind them underfoot and hold them up to ridicule. These novices devoted two hours daily to prayer, whereas the other scholastics spent only one hour in addition to the examination [of conscience] before lunch and before [going to] sleep, which was common to everybody. The same meditation on the Gospels was proposed to everybody, and after lunch, for recreation, as it were, each person shared with the others the fruit he had gathered from [his meditation]. This was quite helpful, for in this way the veterans taught the newcomers; later, however, this exercise was considered too serious for times of recreation.

481.   *The rector is thrown into prison at Medina del Campo*

Among the other things that were going well, there occurred something that I will mention now. It did not terrify Ours, but instead contributed greatly to their encouragement and consolation. The abbot of Medina del Campo (this man took the place of the bishop at Medina del Campo) on the very feast of Saint Martin sent a notary to inform Ours of a certain edict of his prohibiting any of Ours from presuming to hear confessions or preach in the churches or in the streets or in any other place unless he himself had first examined them. The notary came into the chapel of our college, delivered this edict to a priest who had finished Mass at the time, and left immediately. Therefore Father [Pedro] Sevillano together with Doctor Castillo went to the abbot to find out what he desired. . . . He had already seen the apostolic letters, and they had conducted themselves according to their terms. The moment they came into his sight, however, he did not want to listen to anything and began very angrily to call them thieves and deceivers and to heap similar insults on them. He immediately ordered his men to take them to prison in chains.

The rector then begged him to hear them out, because he had seen the apostolic letters and knew that the Holy See had approved our Society. He answered, "Your bulls are brazen forgeries and not bulls"; and in order to emphasize his words with actions, using both arms he hurled the staff he was holding at the rector. But the staff missed its mark, something that Father Sevillano regarded as a lamentable misfortune. But they departed not without some reason to rejoice, for the servants of the abbot immediately laid hands on them and threw them into prison, where they spent the whole day from morning till evening. When somebody among their friends found out what had happened, he obtained their release from the abbot. While doing this, the abbot forbade any one from hearing confessions or preaching unless he himself had examined them first. . . .

487.   *Starting a college at Burgos*

Now about the foundation of our college: some people donated money toward buying a house, first of all Don Fernando de Mendoza, brother of the cardinal, who offered fifty gold ducats in his brother's name. Others offered different amounts. But there was considerable difficulty in finding a suitable site. Didaco de Verny offered a building near a hospital he himself had built; and if Ours were willing to assume some share of his responsibilities for that charitable work, he also offered a source of income. But the site was unappealing, and it seemed even less advisable to take over care for the hospital. [Friends] had willingly purchased other houses on the street called Moneta, but we understood that several citizens were involved in litigation over them. As to the source of income, in addition to what Don Fernando was giving in the name of the cardinal, which amounted to almost two hundred ducats per year, a rich merchant added a sum of fifty gold ducats per year besides a subsidy for buying the house. Since Ours were so few at the time, supporting them was no problem, for alms were more than adequate to supply the necessities of an even greater number [of men]. . . .

489.   *Francisco Estrada's success as a preacher*

[Father Francisco Estrada] preached five times a week during Lent at set times and places, namely, on Sundays at St. Giles, on Mondays at the noble convent called Huelgas, on Tuesdays at another convent, that of St. Dorothy, on Wednesday at the convent of Saint Ildefonse, but on Fridays in the cathedral church; for in the name of their chapter several canons had requested him to preach once [a week] in their church, and they regarded it as a special favor that he scheduled those sermons for Fridays. He also delivered additional sermons at Saint Nicholas and other places; and whether he preached in the morning or the afternoon, a great crowd of the nobility and the commoners flocked to hear him. The sermon he gave on the Sunday after Easter was the last that he had promised; but regardless of this, he preached on the following Sundays.

490.   *Estrada helps the Polanco family*

My own family were among those who gained great spiritual advantage from the sermons and presentations of [Father Estrada]. Since my father and brothers were ignorant of the Society's Institute and fearful of anything innovative, they had long harbored hostility toward the Society in their hearts; and before my profession they tried as far as possible to draw me away from its Institute. Father Estrada's sermons and presentations not only mollified them, so much so that they began to deal with him in a friendly way, but my older brother also made the First Week of the Exercises and later made a general confession to Father Fernando Alvarez because Father Estrada, who had directed the Exercises, was occupied with his sermons. But later [my brother] went to him for confession and by means of letters humbly begged pardon for all the things he had said and tried to do against the Society.

My father too, who this year fell victim to a sickness that was to be his last, departed this life in the hands of Fathers Estrada and Fernando after receiving the last sacraments and being greatly assisted by them at just the right time. It happened that, as he was on the point of death, Father Estrada was celebrating Mass at his home; he said the first *memento* for him as still living, but before he came to the second one for the dead, [my father] had already died; so he said the second one for him as for a dead person. Father Francis Borgia was at that time in Burgos; he wrote that if the sickness he was suffering had not forced him to remain at home, he would not have left [my father's side] until he had completed his pilgrimage. Still, [Borgia] and others of Ours helped him by their prayers. Many others of my blood relatives were greatly improved in the Lord through the efforts of Father Estrada.

501. *More troubles with Archbishop Siliceo of Toledo*

We noted above how zealously in the name of the Supreme Pontiff his legate Cardinal Poggio dealt with the archbishop of Toledo, trying to persuade him to revoke the edict that he had promulgated against the Society, prohibiting us to exercise our ministries. Father Ignatius had also ordered that information be gathered and sent to Rome about the reproaches that he had marshaled against the Society. Father Francisco Villanova spent almost three months at this business, which forced him to make various trips; and he did not stop commending the archbishop to the Lord in his own prayers and in those of the brethren. Earlier he alone was involved in these appeals; then Doctor [Miguel] Torres joined him, as we have said; but when he returned to Salamanca, Villanova was left to carry on the task alone.

First he could not discover the reason for the edict. Earlier a general decree of the archbishop had gone out that nobody should administer the sacraments before he had been examined by [the archbishop's] visitors; accordingly, [Villanova] submitted himself and Ours to this edict rather than offend the archbishop, and requested from his visitor, one Master Palacios, faculties for Ours. Nonetheless, an edict was [later] issued specifically against the Society forbidding us to hear confessions, preach, and offer Mass and revoking all faculties given by his visitors.

503. *Siliceo's opposition to Jesuits of Jewish ancestry*

The reason for the anger of the archbishop [of Toledo] then became clear, namely, that the Society had admitted some men whom he himself had excluded from the church in Toledo by his edict. Thus the archbishop had given this reason to Prince Philip and had written that [Philip] himself should see to it that the Society would not admit that type of man that he had excluded from his church. Then he would favor the Society to the full extent of his powers. He also spoke well of the Society with other people, but he would not allow those of whom we spoke [to enter the Society].

It was understood that Cardinal Poggio had promised the archbishop two things: first, that no person of that sort would be admitted to the College of

Alcalá whom he himself had excluded in his edict from the church of Toledo; second, that the Society would conduct itself in his regard the same as did the other religious orders.[13] The cardinal then promised these two things to the archbishop without informing Ours at all. Because some scholarly and noble men excluded by some part of the archbishop's edict wanted to enter the Society, others would easily become aware of it if they were sent elsewhere to be admitted. The cardinal replied that once this storm had blown over, Ours could make free use of their privileges in [carrying out] the objectives of their Institute, seeing that the promise he had made without our consent could not be binding on us.

506.   *A noble supporter of the Society*

The Count of Melíto [Diego Hurtado de Mendoza] supported the cause of the Society just as if he had been a member of it. He came to Alcalá to listen to the sermons that Father Provincial [Araoz] planned to give that Lent; but when [the provincial's] poor physical health did not permit it and he had returned to Gandía, the count nonetheless stayed there and wanted to make the Spiritual Exercises for a second time, although he had already made them some years previously. He wrote to Father Ignatius, offered his good offices, and requested a copy of the *Exercises,* so that he could find help from them himself and do good for others. He also requested that he and his wife share in the good works of the Society and asked in a friendly manner for authorization to improve the health of Father Provincial. In his cordial response, Father Ignatius granted all his requests.

508.   *Confessions and the Exercises at Alcalá*

The arrival of [Father Villanova] prompted a good number of other respectable men to devote themselves seriously to serving God, and they were eager to make progress in the usual practices of the Society. For this purpose many of them came from the cathedral of Toledo to Alcalá. We must emphatically state that at Alcalá great advances were made in spiritual matters after this time, and many hearts were inflamed with love for the Society. Each day their desire to be helped by its ministries grew more insistent. So many people began

---

[13] The other religious orders in Spain gradually yielded to pressure from men like Silíceo and Prince Philip to refuse admittance to men of Jewish ancestry. As a result, a disproportionately large number of New Christians sought entry to the Society. The Fifth General Congregation (November 1593–January 1594) finally gave way to Spanish pressure and excluded candidates of Jewish ancestry.

to flock to the College of Alcalá either for confession or the Spiritual Exercises that during the weeks just before Lent (when more than at other times people usually indulge in corporal excesses) they surpassed the number who had come during Lent in previous years. After Lent had got underway, they had the special privilege of either confessing at our house or engaging in spiritual meditations there. The rooms that could be used by people doing such exercises at our house were always full. Some people were waiting two or three months to get a room in which to make the Exercises. To others outside our house [Ours] proposed some points for them to reflect upon, so that they could make more precise and fruitful confessions. . . .

509.   *Making the Spiritual Exercises at Alcalá*

Some professors from various faculties completed the Spiritual Exercises in a fuller form; among them was the inquisitor himself. Some of them said that they had indubitably experienced the hand of the Lord and made other assertions as well that modesty induces us to pass over in silence. Some pastors too, after making exercises of this sort, aroused great amazement in their people, who beheld the striking change in their lives. . . .

515.   *Exhortations in the community*

The style of preaching used in our Roman houses was introduced in the college at Alcalá, but Father Provincial Araoz judged it unsuited to Spain, and he ordered that [Ours] adjust themselves to the practice customary in that kingdom. As was done at Rome, every night somebody preached in the refectory, and the novices' outstanding talent in preaching was obvious [to all].

516.   *Silíceo relents*

I will not fail to report that when the archbishop of Toledo revoked that edict of his and withdrew his opposition [to the Society], beginning instead to favor us, he added these words: "because they have submitted to our jurisdiction." Although in revoking his previous statement, he seemed to have added this out of concern for his honor, still it seemed advisable that for our own part we should not simply allow these words to stand without registering some protest. So Father Pedro Tablares went to the royal court and protested before the notary of the apostolic nuncio that Ours were in no way submitting themselves to the power of the archbishop. Indeed, he did this in the presence of the legate himself and lodged an appeal against that phraseology.

I add also that the archbishop had been persuaded that all of Ours were new Christians, and he said as much to Prince Philip. But when he realized that this was not the case, the main consideration that had set him against the Society evaporated. He also was convinced—and this explains his opposition to Ours—that we had exempted ourselves from episcopal jurisdiction and that we wanted to enter the diocese of Toledo against his will. Then Father Araoz showed him the letters patent of Father Ignatius in which he specified that only with the consent and permission of the bishops would we undertake to hear confessions and preach in their dioceses.

The archbishop received and read these letters and took note of the signature of Father Ignatius; then he admitted that it surprised him to see this; he would, indeed, not have believed it without seeing it. So pleased was he by what was prescribed in those letters that he immediately ordered the governor of Alcalá to proceed no further in a suit that he had brought against the college of the Society, as an upshot of which he was about to receive a judicial mandate to tear down the walls surrounding our garden; now, as we recounted earlier, he offered to supply the needs of the Society. . . .

518.   *A generous nobleman promises support*

At this time Don Luis de Mendoza was trying to free himself [of other hindrances and was] prepared, as he himself wrote, to return to the feet of Father Ignatius at Rome. In a excellent location in that city [of Segovia] was a garden that he was making ready and that he planned to give to the Society, which he always held dear to his heart. While the college was being built, he also offered what was needed for supporting some men of the Society, and a house besides. Lastly, he asserted in his letters that he wanted to devote everything he had to the use of the Society.

519.   *A rich man plans to enter the Society*

That same year, before he left Spain Diego de Guzmán earnestly desired to be admitted into the Society, and in a letter he revealed that he was inclined to come to Italy with Doctor [Gaspar] Loarte. He also inquired into Father Ignatius's thinking regarding his patrimony, books, and the rest, so that he could dispose of everything as seemed best to [Ignatius]. The same was true of Dr. Loarte, who was his companion in everything; a master in theology, he had lectured on that subject at a college in Baeza. But Father Ignatius did not think it good [for them] to be in too great a haste to relinquish their possessions until they were better known to the Society and the Society to them.

Nonetheless, both of them were at that time already engaged in the ministry of preaching, and hearing confessions, and teaching Christian doctrine to children. In his heart and mind, Father Diego de Guzmán in particular was totally disposed to teaching children. The enthusiasm they both entertained toward the Society grew more intense after they had commended to [the good offices of] Father Ignatius a family going from Baeza to Rome. The latter cared for the family as a favor to those making the request and helped it with his influence and assistance.

537.   *Rejoicing because Borgia will not be made a cardinal*

Ours were freed from a major concern before [Nadal's] departure, for a rumor had made its way throughout the city [of Valencia] regarding Father Francis Borgia and the cardinalatial dignity; the word was that he had been forced to accept it under the pain of mortal sin. But when they received letters from Rome informing them that Father Ignatius had forestalled this business, their concern was changed to consolation. This was the reaction of Ours everywhere, although some of the blood relatives of Father Francis received the news with different emotions.

547.   *Jesuits oppose bull fighting*

I will not overlook mentioning that when this jubilee occurred close to the feast of Saint James the Greater [July 25], the patron of Spain, bullfights were to be held in accord with the ancient tradition of that country. It was decided that horsemen would also fight one another in a joust with wooden rods *[arundinum]*. Ours took exception to this event because the previous day almost everybody had prepared to obtain the jubilee [indulgence] by confessing and receiving Communion. At this time the rector at Valencia was Father Battista [de Barma]; but eight of ours, four of whom were priests, made every effort to stop those games, regarding it as inappropriate to hold [such a spectacle] in honor of God and Saint James.

With the permission of the pro-rector, four of the men just mentioned went to the bullring, the first and last with heads uncovered and feet bare, as had been done earlier at Valencia, with ropes around their necks. The first of them carried a large picture of the Crucified, the last carried a dead man's scull. The two in between had their backs and arms naked and were scourging themselves with whips. They then reached the bullring just as the first bull had been driven in and penned up. This is why Ours were able to enter the bullring safely. All the spectators, both natives and outsiders, were deeply moved by this display and shouted out for mercy with groans at the top of their voices. Climbing some steps, one of the four began to preach to the people.

Meanwhile the other four, dressed and bearing [the same sort of] penitential objects, left the college, marched down the main street, and at the top of their voices shouted a plea for mercy. The heart of a certain Ethiopian was moved, and he began shouting the same thing and asked for confession. But when they came to the bullring, the shouts and weeping began again. . . . They approached the area where the duke and duchess were, along with a big crowd of horsemen and clerics. There one of the brethren began to preach with great fervor while loud cries for the Lord's mercy went up repeatedly from the whole crowd. The wife of the duke was also weeping, as were the women attending her.

The people, however, left the stands and, uttering the cries mentioned earlier, accompanied Ours who were returning home. Some hastened to bring out whatever was needed to heal the welts caused by the whip lashes. The Lord used this occasion to stir the hearts of many people to sorrow for their sins and [the desire] to go to confession, so that people whom the jubilee did not motivate were moved by this public display to receive the holy sacraments. All the bulls were immediately driven away, and the jousting was called off, even though all the horsemen had accoutered themselves for it at considerable outlay.

567.   *Friction in Spain over the division of the province*

[Father Araoz] traveled from Valencia to Zaragoza, staying there for a time and, after dealing with matters pertaining to the small college there, he left on June 17. In a town ruled by the Count of Rivagorza, he met Don Juan de Borgia. With him [Araoz] set out for the province of Guipuzcoa, where he found letters from the Duchess of Frias summoning him to the Queen's court. There, as we said above, he found Father Francis [Borgia] and his companions; and on the very feast day of Saint Peter [June 29], he preached with great edification. From there he went back to the province of Guipuzcoa and applied himself to making peace among several who were at odds with one another. At length, during September he returned to the Queen's court to dispose of some matters of great importance.

He found out that Fathers Miró and Torres had sent Father Simão [Rodrigues] from Portugal to assume control over the colleges of the Aragon Province. He wrote that he greatly welcomed [the news that] the heasviest part of his burden had been removed from his shoulders and transferred to Father Simão; and he went on to request that the rest of the burdens [of administration] might be relegated to him as well. For, as [a] mother [would do for her child], [Araoz] hoped that the whole province would be given to one man rather than be divided up. . . . He also wrote that some men of no small authority had brought up many reasons militating against this kind of division of the province. Still, he did not want to send their arguments on to Father Ignatius. Although they judged that, as one who had borne the weight and heat of the day, he should have been forewarned about such a division, and although he considered that he had been freed in the internal forum from the remaining burden of the province, still, externally he would carry on everything as before because he thought that this was the mind of Father Ignatius or of Fathers Miró and Torres acting in his name, that is to say, that another person might take their places. Lastly, he [went on to write] that he did not seem to have regarded this division as of little consequence.

Nonetheless, Father Ignatius changed nothing in his plan, for he perhaps foresaw the growth of the Society. This required not only the present division but also greater ones in other provinces, as took place a few years later.

572.   *Provincial Araoz unhappy over being bypassed*

Araoz, the provincial, politely complained by letter that without consulting him Father Torres had moved some of Ours from one place and transferred them to a place other than the one to which the provincial had assigned [them]. Although [Torres] had done this after receiving permission from Father Ignatius, [Araoz] seems to have delicately reminded Father Ignatius himself that that Father [Torres] was not very familiar with the Society's way of proceeding, adding moreover that when a command or an assignment is given to someone, [it should specify that the person receiving the commission] should also make arrangements [for its execution] with his provincial. These things Father Araoz himself did not write, but rather his socius, Antonio Gou, who seemed, nonetheless, to have been reflecting the viewpoint and mind of his provincial when he wrote.

574.   *How should Jesuits address their superiors?*

In the name of Father Ignatius orders came down that nobody except the provincial and the general should be addressed in letters as "Very Reverend" but only as "Reverend." But people regarded this as an unheard-of novelty and did not put it into practice until Father Ignatius wrote a second time. He did not insist on this as if it were a trifle, nor did he want anybody to be addressed as "Your Paternity," not even himself. But when he learned from Father Tablares that in Spain it had already become customary to bestow the title "Paternity" on provincials, he said that each person might address [the provincial] as "Your Paternity" or "Your Reverence" as he pleased.

575.   *Winning over an opponent to frequent Communion*

The archbishop of Zaragoza did something he had never wanted to do in the past: he singled out Ours and listed them in the public catalog of confessors. The inquisitors also held Ours in high esteem. Frequent confessions and Communions did not stop even though during these days a member of the Order of Saint Augustine was preaching in the church to which Father Estrada had been invited but had been unable to [accept the invitation]. In several of his sermons the Augustinian reproached those who took Communion on certain days. He reviled them as hypocrites because in those things which pertained to God's worship, they were going beyond what was the common practice.

Sermons of this sort gave rise to rumors and scruples for those weak in faith. When Father Francisco de Rojas saw how much harm this teaching was doing to many people, he wrote to this religious about these statements and invited him to [our] college. The friar agreed to [Francisco's] interpretation in a polite and gracious way and indicated that he had something else in mind and had not wanted to criticize people who came to the sacraments frequently. Thus God changed his heart so that he gave two sermons completely contrary to the teaching he had proposed earlier—to the wonderment and edification of some people. A bit later, the Lord by a very powerful spirit moved all the preachers at Zaragoza to inflame the people with great zeal to approach the sacraments frequently.

■ **Portugal**

585.　*A Portuguese merchant repents of his price gouging*

At that time grain was in very short supply, resulting in very high prices for it. Some people sold grain at a higher price than normal because money was not paid over immediately. When Father Gundisalvo bitterly criticized this before he left the town of Lagos, one man among the other merchants was deeply moved and came to the father and stated that he had spent all his possessions to buy grain, but if he had to lose everything to gain a clear conscience, he was ready to do that. When Father Gundisalvo put off replying for two or three days, [the merchant] reported to the other merchants what the father had said. They scoffed at him: "Things would be going well for us if we left it to the apostles to set the price for our grain." But their sarcastic remarks did not deter the merchant, who immediately sold his food at a moderate price as Father Gundisalvo had advised. He viewed it as profit enough that he had decided upon frequent confession and reception of the Holy Eucharist. . . .

590.　*Reforming a small Portuguese city*

Fathers Cornelio [Gomez] and [Pedro de] Santacruz were sent to the diocese of Portalegre. Along with the episcopal officials and other respected men of that city, they wrote how rich the harvest was that the Lord gathered through them as they performed the usual ministries of hearing confessions and preaching, reconciling and establishing concord, and giving the Spiritual Exercises to various people. . . . They worked to get those people to set up a confraternity of charity, in which more than a thousand people [eventually] enrolled. They contributed alms toward arranging marriage for young women who had no parents, and other works of piety of theirs yielded alms, some of which brought in certain and fixed [sums] each year. So great was the change wrought in those people that, whereas once they had been wolves, now they seemed to have become lambs. [The Fathers] led a monastery of Cistercian nuns to the practice of prayer, thus contributing to their excellent progress. Another monastery of the Order of Saint Clare sought their services, but because the male religious of that order did not give permission, Ours did not go there. . . .

The leading men of the city made efforts to set up a college of the Society and looked around for a good site—indeed, they even found one—but Ours did not want to make any promise, being unaware of the will of their superiors. Father Santacruz was very successful at preaching, as was Father

Cornelio [Gomez] at hearing confessions; both were [skilled] in holding private conversations. Thus was a remarkable transformation of life brought about in those people, along with an intense, burning desire for spiritual progress. . . .

Others also of the leading men, after making the Spiritual Exercises, laid a solid foundation for virtues and committed themselves to seriously serving God for as long as they lived. Women, too, were taught mental prayer, a method of meditating on Christ's passion and other spiritual meditations. They pleaded for [this training] with many entreaties and, having made great progress themselves, brought along their daughters for instruction. Besides the men and the married women, almost forty reputable young women had been taught in the same way and kept growing in the spirit day by day.

According to reports, Father Santacruz preached in a way most likely to benefit his hearers, not just moving them but teaching them. He therefore compressed his sermons into three or four points, so that his hearers could fix them in their memories. If one of them forgot one of those points, they came to the hospice, so that Father Santacruz could refresh their memories. This fruit multiplied still more when one person discussed what they had heard with others. They declared that they had never heard sermons which so powerfully enticed them to acquire virtue and serve God.

596. *A Jesuit confessor for the King of Portugal?*

When the customary time approached for the King to make his confession, he called on Father Luís Gonçalves, who had recently begun to hear the confessions of the prince, and asked him to hear his confession as well.[14] Father Luís excused himself, pleading that he was young and less educated in letters than he would have to be before hearing the King's confession. But when the King pressed him with many arguments to do it, he subjected himself to whatever commands obedience might give him in this matter. Thus in sorrow he left the King and sent Father Francisco Enríquez to the provincial, Father Simão [Rodrigues], beseeching him to petition [the King] to free him of this trial out of the love of God. He also left the house lest the King's messenger find him.

Father Simão, however, did not think it possible to deny the King [his request]; for when he talked with the King, the King replied in his singular humanity and humility that just as Father Gonçalves was hearing the confessions of any number of other people, he could hear his as well. He discussed many

---

[14] He is the Luís Gonçalves da Cámara to whom Loyola later dictated his autobiography.

questions with Father Simão as a preparation for his confession; the next day he began to confess to Father Gonçalves shortly before the feast of Easter.

Father Luís wrote Father Ignatius that he was fearful that the King would choose him later as his [regular] confessor. He was young and inexperienced, however; the office [of confessor] was held in high esteem in that kingdom; everybody was convinced that the King's confessor would eventually be promoted to a prelature, as had been the case with the previous confessors, all of whom had been promoted to the episcopate. He went on to write that the King already harbored enough goodwill toward the Society, and there was no need for him to fill this office in order to win favor [for the Society]. Moreover, many numerous affairs were entrusted to the King's confessor that could not be disposed of without giving offense to many. Moreover, he was far too weak to carry such a burden and feared that he would collapse beneath it. [Hearing] the confession of the prince was already a burdensome responsibility; how much more so would it be to confess both the prince and the King? Many of his blood relatives lived at the royal court, he added; so he did not think that he should remain there also. But if obedience should command differently, he would accept it as something demanded of him by [obedience. Despite all these arguments,] Father Ignatius thought it prudent for him not to refuse this burden. But, as we will recount shortly, he found another way to escape [it].

[Luís] had been approved to make his profession, but he gladly deferred this, for he considered himself wholly unworthy; but now, recognizing the will of Father Ignatius, he made the profession the next year into the hands of Father Francis Borgia. He suggested to Father Ignatius that the *Constitutions* should be tried out experimentally for two or three years before they were printed, so that experience might better demonstrate how they were working out. . . .

606.   *Diego Miró as provincial of Portugal*

The cardinal-prince was greatly consoled that God was making use of the labors of Ours for the salvation of souls not only at Évora but also in various places in his archdiocese.[15] When others, but especially Father Diego Miró, the new provincial (his election is treated below), visited the same archdiocese [of

---

[15] Cardinal Enrique was the brother of King John III, "the Pious" (1521–57); starting in 1562, he was regent for his young nephew Sebastian. When King Sebastian was killed in the battle of Al Kassr al-Kabir fighting the Moors, the cardinal became King Henry (1578–80). The Portuguese royal dynasty died out with him, and Philip II of Spain began to reign over Portugal.

Évora] and engaged in preaching and the other usual pious works of the Society, [the archbishop] decided to provide support for ten others of the brethren there in addition to those who had begun the college. He also spurred on the work of the new college, where more than forty bedrooms besides other rooms were being built. That college in the beginning had an annual income of more than seven hundred gold pieces, used to finance construction and to provide for Ours. But from then on everything started to flourish, for the cardinal was greatly pleased that Father Miró had been chosen as provincial. Once when he saw him, he said, "Give thanks to the Lord that he has made you provincial of his religious order, through which there is hope for the reformation of Christendom."

613.   *Ours decline taking over orphanages*

According to reports, a certain Catalan priest named Pedro Domenech, after finishing the business that kept him occupied at the royal court of Portugal, aspired to [join] the Society and was closely united to the Society by the best of dispositions. He had set up several homes for orphan boys in Portugal and imbued them with the Spiritual Exercises, which he himself had learned from the Society. When he was about to return from Portugal to Catalonia, he tried to hand over to our Society the care of those homes that he had set up. It seemed, however, that we should not take over this work, even though it was very charitable and begun by a man closely linked to Ours.

614.   *Diego Miró replaces Rodrigues as provincial of Portugal*

Already in the month of May, the letters patent of our Father Ignatius arrived in Portugal which, as reported above, Father [Miguel] Torres had sent to Portugal. . . . When they were delivered to Father Simão [Rodrigues], he realized that he had been freed from the burden of governing the province. He greeted this announcement with evident manifestations of joy and consolation, asserting that when on the previous day he had fallen into a fever, the Lord was protecting him in advance, so that his sickness was now tempering his delight to be leaving office. . . .

Because Father Diego Miró, whom the fathers themselves of Portugal had suggested, had been chosen as his successor in the office of provincial, Father Simão sent him the letters patent with another [letter] to the collegians at Coimbra; in it he begged their pardon for all the defects into which he knew full well that he had fallen during his tenure as provincial. Father Miró himself accepted the letter naming him provincial. But he gave no fewer tokens of sorrow than Father Simão showed of eagerness and joy. Although he let fall many tears, still, he did not reject the burden and offered his services to each and all. . . . Father Miró strove to conform all the activities of the Society to the pattern that he had observed in Rome and to the way of proceeding of Father Ignatius, according to his understanding of it.

620.   *The crisis of the Portuguese Province*

Already at this time the waters in the fishpond [that was] the Society became extremely agitated in the province of Portugal, as we will describe a bit later. The rector of the college at Coimbra [Manuel Godinho] was greatly upset that some reports had leaked out of our college that were calculated to give little edification to the citizens of Coimbra and many others as well. He judged that he was to blame that people attributed the situation to his humility rather than to his inadequacies as a superior; so he then considered [doing] some public penance.

Therefore, after seeing to it that the sacrifice of the Mass had been offered a number of times, and prayers as well, and discussing the question with some of the fathers, on the octave day of All Saints, after celebrating Mass he urged the assembled brethren to come to the chapel and pray for strength from the Lord for a certain person in need; to beg the Lord for pardon for the sins of the whole Society, especially in Portugal, and of those who had left the Society. He commanded them not to leave the chapel until he gave them a sign. He himself went out, scourging himself with a whip through the whole city; afterwards, returning to the college and shedding many tears, he related to the brethren what he had done and what had driven him to it. They listened to this with powerful emotions of both devotion and sorrow. Forthwith, the vice-rector, Father Tiburtius, weeping profusely, begged the brethren to join him in requesting the rector's permission for him to do the same thing, because he felt that he was under the same obligation and was very fearful of God's judgment.

So they all went together to the rector and urged him to give [the vice-rector] permission [to go] through the city publicly scourging himself, and almost all requested the same permission for themselves. But Father Rector praised their desire because it was only right to make satisfaction for scandals; but because he would have to render an account to God and his superiors, he judged that their proposal demanded mature consideration. They must meet together and consult on what had to be done. Therefore, after everybody had spoken, he decided that in view of all the circumstances, the affair would have Father Ignatius's approval, so that just as the offense was public, so too the penance should be public.

He decided that everybody who, with proper dispositions, would request this and beg permission for it could do as he desired. More than sixty of Ours marched out of the college in good order to the Church of Misericordia, scourging themselves with whips. Father Rector followed them, so that he could explain his acts of penance to the people. A large image of the Crucified preceded them, and younger brothers recited the litanies in a loud voice. A great crowd of people followed; and after praying, the rector went before the onlookers and with deep emotion asked them to pardon all that our college had done to disedify them. He attributed all these misdeeds to his sins and asked the people to help him to obtain mercy from God.

His words stirred up powerful emotions of grief among the people. After returning to the church and reciting some prayers, the people asked the Lord for mercy with many tears and cries. Then they returned the same way they had come to the college, and the rector ordered that they should all go to confession and to receive Communion the next day. Some believe that on the whole the affair resulted in the edification of the people, but I do not doubt that there were those who did not particularly approve of it.

621.   *A change of heart in Portugal*

Specific action was taken to counter the defects into which almost all the collegians had fallen, resulting in a strong purpose of amendment. They learned by experience that they should take with a grain of salt the rule requiring them to put the best interpretation on things.[16] The princes themselves, who were holy and loved us, observed and sympathized with us regarding some things that Ours neither saw nor considered as wrong. These defects had to do with Ours seeming excessively delicate in their food and lodgings and similar things. Thus, they discussed whether a building should be demolished that had been built to present an attractive appearance; still, it seemed best not to do this to avoid drawing down criticism upon the person who had directed the construction of the building, namely, the provincial himself. The collegians began to work seriously at acts of humility, in which they acknowledged their deficiencies, for

---

[16] This is probably a reference to the presupposition that Loyola puts at the very beginning of the First Week of the *Spiritual Exercises.*

they had previously regarded themselves as superior to other religious orders. As their spiritual progress increased, so did their obedience and humility. On feast days when they had leisure from academic exercises, they devoted themselves to lowly tasks of service to sick paupers in the hospital. . . .

624.   *New appointments aimed at reforming the Society in Portugal*

But because in this year, as we have said, vexing problems were stirred up in Portugal, we must explain their origins and development. On the basis of letters received from men regarded as the pillars of the Society in Portugal, Father Ignatius recognized that the manner of governing was lax [in that province] and tended to foster excessive freedom of judgment. So it was necessary for him to devise a plan to lead that province back to the Society's right and authentic way of proceeding. Everybody saw that this was impossible without changing the provincial. [Ignatius], therefore, wrote letters patent to Father Simão, releasing him from his office of provincial, citing his weak bodily health and his understandable need to rest from the many labors he had expended in governing. He wrote another letter to Father Miró bidding him to accept the office of provincial.

To head off any attempts to evade [carrying out] his orders, [Ignatius] sent other letters to some of the faithful and wise sons of the Society (among whom were Father Urbanus and Father Leon Enríquez) in which he ordered them under holy obedience to present the letters patent to Father Simão and, if it seemed a good idea to talk with the King about the matter, to do so. [Ignatius] wrote also to the King himself, the Queen, and the cardinal-prince about what seemingly should be done about the situation. He also wrote privately to Father Simão himself in which he allowed him to decide whether to go to Brazil, as [Rodrigues] himself had requested with great avidity, or take charge of the new province of Valencia, Aragon, and Catalonia. In any case, he should leave Portugal, for [Ignatius] had perceived that this was very advantageous.

But he added that this change of administration would not be announced immediately but at the right place and time. Deferred also was the announcement that a master of novices would be named with the responsibility of reforming the collegians.

625.   *More reforms in Portugal*

So that all might go more smoothly, [Ignatius] wanted Father [Miguel] Torres and Father Francis Borgia as well to go to Portugal, so that the problem might be handled with greater authority and delicacy. But, as we recounted earlier, when Father Francis reached Salamanca, Father Miró and several others judged it very unwise for the aforesaid fathers, Borgia and Torres, to travel to Portugal [to deal] with this problem. Motivated by the same spirit as Father Ignatius, the King too indicated his desire to have the administration of the province transferred from Father Simão to Father Miró. The King pressured Father Luís Gonçalves to report to him about matters relative to the governance of Ours, which he had heard were going badly. He revealed to him, but not in writing, things similar to what I have mentioned; but the Queen herself and Prince Luís thought that an effort should be made to send Father Simão from the kingdom of Portugal, but in a respectful way.

Because Father Luís Gonçalves (whom the King held in high esteem) insisted that Father Miró would make a worthy successor, the King strove to arrange to have the office handed over to him. But so that the transfer might be handled in a considerate manner, [the King] thought that any implementation of it should await the mandate from Father Ignatius. Then [the King] himself would approve of what had been ordered by the superior. They requested from Father Torres the letter to this effect that had already been sent to Portugal; indeed, a [messenger] carrying the letter of Father Ignatius arrived at Coimbra right on the feast of St. Mark [April 25]. This letter was forwarded to Lisbon, and Father Luís Gonçalves was commissioned to discuss with the King the appropriate course to take.

When the letter was presented to Father Simão, as we reported above, he was very happy to be liberated [from his responsibilities]. Because his health was less than sturdy, it did not seem good for him to go to Brazil or to the province of Aragon, so he decided to go to San Fins [in Portugal]. He had not yet been notified that he was supposed to leave the kingdom.

626.   *Father Rodrigues and King John*

When Father Leon Enríquez, whom Father Simão had summoned to Coimbra, brought with him the letters patent, indicated that the King was to be given the reason for this change, he suggested that Father Simão go to the King himself. [Rodrigues] said he was not going to do so and urged Father Leon to carry out faithfully what he had been commanded. But when Father Leon was going back to the King the next day in order to inform him of these matters, Father Simão began to express some doubts and to declare that he was not yet relieved of his responsibility for the province until the King, whom he was required to obey, should say that he was pleased with [the new arrangement].

He also commissioned Father Leon to devote some study to seeing what he was bound to do [in this matter]. He began to explain to [Father Leon] the reason he thought that Father Ignatius had decided to remove him from the office of provincial, namely, that he had opposed him [Loyola] on some constitution. [Father Leon], therefore, went to the King and gave him the letter of Father Ignatius and the letters patent sent to Father Simão. After [the King] had read and praised all these documents, he ordered that [a message] in his name be taken to Father Simão expressing how gratified he was to learn how gladly [Rodrigues] had submitted in obedience to Father Ignatius. He also wanted to say to Father Miró that he was happy that the office of provincial had been entrusted to him, and that he should with full confidence ask anything from him that he would do [to advance] the good of the Society. Indeed, those were his instructions.

627.   *The painful aftermath of Rodrigues's dismissal*

Father Leon carried back to Father Simão an account of his audience with the King; then [Rodrigues] requested Father Miró's permission to go to San Fins and, if the winter was harsh, to return to Lisbon; he asked as well that Father Miró obtain [this permission] from Father Ignatius—something that seemed completely inappropriate. When these measures were communicated to the collegians at Coimbra, they seemed to listen calmly enough. Father Miró sent permission for [Rodrigues] to go to San Fins, but while en route he stopped at Coimbra. He stayed in the college three days, but did nothing that was of any use to the college. Regardless, things were moving along there much better than they had before. Still, it was necessary to dismiss many men from the Society who had belonged to it for quite a while. So that these men could give [lay people] some reason for their dismissal, they sowed slanders and gave [anyone who would listen] considerable occasion for vituperation. Still, [superiors] judged it necessary to discard this poisoned yeast rather than allow the entire batch that was the college to be corrupted.

628.   *Rodrigues's faults as a superior*

As far as [Diego Miró] is concerned, who succeeded Father Simão and was received like an angel of the Lord, as we described last year, after N. [Rodrigues] came to Coimbra with the intention, as some suspected, of pointing out that [Miró] was unsuited for spiritual or temporal governance,[17] [Rodrigues] had dealt gently with the brethren, but he urged this man to impose frequent penances. Faithful sons of the Society admonished [Miró] to put aside rigor and work at winning over hearts to himself, for the ulcer had not reached the stage where it could not be healed. Also they advised that he avoid [drastic] changes and not give the impression that he was reforming [the house].

Nonetheless, after receiving these counsels with profuse thanks, he acted exactly to the contrary; he imposed frequent rebukes and penances, he changed all the officials, and in matters that were already good as well as those that were bad, he imposed some sort of change or modification, sometimes even in matters of almost no importance. For instance, he ordered that community exhortations should take place in a different area and even that the bell should be rung for a longer period [of time]. In the course of two months he changed the method of meditation six or seven times; the result was that gradually day by day he caused the esteem with which he had been received to wither away.

He wanted to preside at theological examinations, and since he seemed little skilled in either speculative questions or cases of conscience, here too he lowered the esteem that the students had developed for the instruction [they were receiving]. When he meddled in some questions that he had not sufficiently thought through, [the community] also noticed another deficiency besides that of knowledge. Matters finally degenerated into great contempt, when his exhortations as well were so disorganized that nobody could figure out what he meant. He was also forgetful and could not keep secrets. Moreover, he showed himself utterly unsuited for dealing with lay people about practical affairs; indeed, even after many explanations he could not understand these matters. So it came about that lay people too declared that, even though he was imbued with great virtue, he was inept at getting things done. When those in whom he had more confidence than in others admonished him about these things, he utterly broke their spirits, saying that these were matters of trifling importance and that he would show that he had a talent for governing—so much so that, to someone not aware of how humble he really was, it would seem that some ambition had caused him to rush into some [form of] deception and that he possessed little self-knowledge even in obvious and evident matters.

---

[17] Polanco uses *N.* to designated persons he chooses not to mention by name, some of whom were still living when he wrote and would be offended by his remarks. Here *N.* probably refers to Rodrigues, as the editors of the MHSI point out in their footnote at this point in the text.

629.   *Torres and Rodrigues*

[The leading Jesuits in Portugal] then decided to summon Father Torres, indicating that his presence was needed in Portugal. When he had arrived during the month of August, he made some arrangements without having understood the situation very well. Still, he decided that nothing should be done until the person [Rodrigues] who had gone to San Fins had left the province of Portugal. Father Torres did not then want to show everybody his commission (although early in April Father Ignatius had sent it along with a letter to the King in which he wrote something about the college at Coimbra and asked the King to trust Father Torres); but he wanted to use the authority of Father Provincial Miró, to whom he wrote in the name of Father Ignatius urging him to command Father Simão immediately to assume responsibility for the province of Aragon and to go there directly (given that that province [which included all of Spain] stretched far and wide and, because of his bad health, Father Araoz could not minister to the whole of it). Letters patent were drawn up in the name of Father Ignatius, for he had placed his signature on these letters, and also on letters patent, to Father Torres. These were presented to him through Father Cornelius. [In them Ignatius] commanded [Rodrigues] in virtue of holy obedience to take over that province; and so that he could not plead the excuse that permission had to be obtained from the King for his departure, Ours also obtained letters from the King notifying [Rodrigues] that he should acquiesce in what obedience required of him. When he put forward the excuse that his health was too weak for him to leave that kingdom, the King and Queen in no way accepted his excuse: the King wrote a second letter commanding him to obey his superior for the edification of others, even though his health might suffer as a result. Then the letters patent of Father Ignatius together with the letters of the King were given to him; earlier he had been given only the letter of Father Miró. Father Simão obeyed these immediately and set out at once for Salamanca.

632.   *More on Portugal and Rodrigues*

Father Torres, writing about these things to Father Ignatius, asked permission for him to institute changes in both personnel and method of governance. It would not be difficult to gain the King's approval for whatever seemed good to [Ignatius] in the Lord; for both the King and the Queen and the princes gave evidence of their high esteem for the [genuine] way of proceeding in the Society and of their disapproval of [the way of proceeding] that had [recently] obtained in that province. But both Father Torres and the others judged it very advisable to recall Father Simão to Rome and not to send him back to Portugal; instead he should be put to work elsewhere, even though the King had written to request his return, for [Rodrigues's] friends could easily obtain such letters. If the reasons for not sending Rodrigues back were revealed to the princes, they would graciously accept the decision. When Father Ignatius understood how things stood, he wrote on September 24 to thank the King for acting as he had in this business, thereby winning the utmost devotion of the entire Society.

The unbridled insolence of some of the collegians increased to such an extent that they sometimes uttered [to their superiors] words betokening pride, even asserting that [superiors] should not be giving them the orders that they were. How Father Ignatius handled this matter is discussed above.

Some of them wrote libelous pamphlets and doggerel against some [of Ours]. Therefore, Father Torres judged that for the sake of keeping the rest of the body of the Society sound, he should address to them the words of Christ to some of the disciples, "Do you also want to go away?"[18] The situation being as it was, he wrote to N. [Rodrigues] at Salamanca: "The fathers and brothers of this college are going forward with great consolation and are running in the spirit of the Society. The prayers and effective dispositions of Father Ignatius have merited this quiet for us." This prompted Father Torres to suggest that assistants [so-called collaterals] be assigned to superiors similar to the person who had the duty of warning the superior general about the problems of Ours, even though assistant superiors did not have that function, which the *Constitutions* actually entrust to the consultors.

637.   *Fallout from the Portuguese crisis*

Meanwhile, people were surprised that so many [of Ours] were being scattered to various places, Father Miró being sent here, Father Gonçalves there, others to other places; and they did not understand the reason for this. Negotiations with the King that were usually expedited without delay were now sidetracked, treated as nonessential, and allowed to wend their path through the bureaucracy at a sluggish pace. Perhaps because they had sometimes spent the money unwisely that they had received from the King, purchasing superfluous things [with it], they now had difficulty obtaining [money] for necessary expenses. . . . [When Father Francis Enríquez went to the royal court] to conduct necessary business, the doors were closed in his face. The architect and

---

[18] John 6:67.

even the medical doctor proved reluctant to receive them. Here Ours were reproached for having expelled Father Simão from his lofty position of authority. Other people, seeing how many men left or were dismissed [from the Society], had doubts about who of Ours should be believed now; for those who left boasted that they were the real Society, as they continued to preach, hear confessions, and teach catechism.

638.   *The Society loses favor in high places*

The King's ministers showed a very different attitude toward Ours than they had before, and when Ours begged alms from the archbishop of Lisbon, he retorted, "What need does the King have for two hundred apostles in Portugal?" And he gave them nothing. The princes too, after they designated some men to go to the Congo, did not show them the same signs of love that they had done before. The occasion gave some [of Ours] reason to conclude that it had not been a wise move to refuse the task of hearing the King's confession; but those who looked into the matter more penetratingly and prudently judged instead that this change of our situation actually greatly benefited the Society in Portugal, giving it the opportunity to sink the anchor of its confidence not in the favor of princes but in God. At that time, they hoped to reap a more abundant harvest since Ours would plunge the roots of their self-knowledge more deeply in this frigid climate.

The bishop of Portalegre said that this was a good time to lay the foundation of the Society by not relying so much on young men, who needed to be helped so that they could make progress in spirit, letters, and maturity. What happened to Ours was exactly what a certain member of the Society used to say would benefit the Society: that he desired to see Ours hissed off the stage by worldly people rather than being puffed up by favors and praise. The cardinal-prince took no action to obtain the men whom he wanted to add to the number of Ours at Coimbra.

The Queen, when she wrote to Father Miró a commendation of Diego Viera and received an answer from him, summoned Father Urbanus, who feared [that he would receive] a strong rebuke. But since the bishop of Portalegre had previously visited with her, the audience turned out far differently than [Urbanus] had expected; for she consoled him and showed that she did not take offense that her previous request had been denied. She declared she did not want to obtain anything from the Society that would result in its harm, and she offered her help in promoting its spiritual and even its temporal welfare.

639.   *Rumors that the Portuguese Province will be abolished*

Among the common people rumors were being bruited about that the Society would be abolished in that province and that the archbishop had forbidden Ours to preach and hear confessions and say Mass; but all this was untrue. When Father Miró became aware of this troubled situation, he wrote that he did not think either Father Gundisalvus Vaz or Father Alfonso Tellez or others who were engaged on missions should be recalled to the college for fear that perchance they might leave [the Society] after being battered by this storm. Although he realized that it was a great gift of God that the Society had been purged of men unsuited to its Institute, still, he suggested to the rector of the College of Coimbra that he deal kindly with those who still remained, reminding him that Father Ignatius was accustomed to put up with imperfect men sometimes, as long as there was hope of helping them.

640.   *Charges against Father Ignatius in Portugal*

. . . They added that Father Ignatius had tried to transfer money out of the kingdom of Portugal to other provinces, but that Father Simão had blocked his effort to do so by repudiating the [Jesuit] constitution that allowed this; it was for this reason that he was deposed from office. Third, they charged, the usual intention of Father Ignatius was this: to assign elsewhere men who had already been trained in letters in Portugal and to send foreigners to Portugal for their studies. Men who seemed to be scheming to achieve the return of Father Simão to govern that province instilled calumnies such as this into the pious ears of those princes, and still other similar charges as well.

The King himself began to bring up some of these charges to Father Francisco Enríquez when he came to see him about some business. . . . Then the King added, "I hear that they send money from this kingdom as well as men, and that the Superior General had written some constitution allowing money to be transferred from one place to another." And he added, "Write to him that he must not do this; for if he does, I'll stop giving alms to the Society." Father Francisco Enríquez replied that, far from sending money from Portugal to Rome, they had refused to send the procurator general any part of what was needed for their expenses. And regarding the constitution, he explained that, as he understood it, colleges of one province that had superfluous income could help other colleges of the same province. The King approved of this, provided that [the money] was not taken out of this kingdom. And the Queen, who was present, said that "neither men nor money should be sent out of this kingdom because we have a need for them here." As regards foreigners who are sent to study in Portugal (for the King asserted that they had been sent there), he said that after Father Miró's arrival from Valencia, three gifted and learned young men endowed with superb gifts had come and had been admitted [to the Society] in Portugal, not in order to send them back to Spain but to have them stay there. "If they are going to stay, that's good." said the King and fell silent. . . .

But when [Enríquez] asked the King whether he wanted something to be written to Father Ignatius about what they had discussed, he said, "There's no need as long as the situation is as you described it." When Francisco had reassured him that Father Ignatius would do nothing in that kingdom except what [the King] himself approved of and that [Ignatius] was accustomed to write in that same vein to Ours who were working in Portugal, it pleased the King; and he said that is the way he wanted it. He also indicated that he did not want anything to be done against Father Simão, but he was aware that [Simão] was beloved by Ours.

642.   *Further conversations with the Queen and King*

[Father Gonçalves] first approached the Queen, who consoled him and related many details that could be summed up thus: the King was very solidly in favor of the Society even though others had improperly opposed him in this matter; regarding the transfer of money and men out of the Kingdom, [what the King emphasized] was that this was prohibited, not that Jesuits in Portugal should exempt themselves from Ignatius's right to govern them, as some seem intent upon doing. She also knew that the princes had been informed that N. [Rodrigues] was unfit to govern. . . . Father Luís Gonçalves himself finally spoke to the King and laid out everything necessary to disprove the calumnies, but the King indicated that he wanted still more information. At length he asked from the King himself whether he would be willing to have Father Torres come to Portugal. Although not very enthusiastically, he expressed his consent for [Torres] to be summoned. Thus [Torres] was recalled on October 13, and he was asked to bring with him all the letters and instructions of Father Ignatius; for they were hoping that solid foundations for the Society would be laid now that those earlier built on sand had crumbled away. . . .

THE YEAR 1553

■ The Society in general

1.   *Overview of the Society of Jesus in 1553*

At the beginning of 1553, the Society had five discrete provinces: namely, India, Portugal, Castile, Aragon, and Italy, not including Rome. Father Ignatius had [direct] charge of all the other colleges and houses, just as in the previous years. But in the course of this year, in July, to be exact, a sixth province was established, Brazil, that is; and through letters patent Father Ignatius appointed Father Manuel de Nóbrega as its provincial. He had already been in charge of Ours in Brazil without bearing the title of provincial. Thus, there were six provinces in the Society this year. In Italy three places where Ours had houses were added to the total, as we wrote at the beginning of the previous year. Colleges with classes have been inaugurated in Perugia, Gubbio, and Modena. One was established in India at the town of Tana. In Brazil several colleges for boys were added to those that we listed at the start of last year. . . .

■ Rome

3.   *Nadal is sent to promulgate the* Constitutions *in Spain and Portugal*

This year Father Jerónimo Nadal came from Sicily to Rome, bringing along with him Master Benedetto Palmio. He conferred with Father Ignatius about what he judged ought to be said regarding the *Constitutions* and rules of the Society. After receiving instructions from [Father Ignatius], he was sent on April 10 to Spain as commissary bearing letters patent that confirmed his assignment to present the rules and *Constitutions* to our colleges and the men of our Society, and to clarify them as well. Father Ignatius also conferred ample authority on him to handle other matters, for he had great confidence in Nadal's wisdom and knowledge of the Society's affairs.

Ignatius ordered him to go first of all to Portugal because that province was already far ahead of the others as regards the number of its members [and of] its functioning colleges, as well as the importance of its activities promoting

---

With this year *Chron.,* vol. 3, begins.—ED.

the common good. [Another reason for his visit was] the unsettled situation that had developed the previous year and now required his intervention. Moreover, the King of Portugal had requested that somebody be sent to him who understood how to organize classes [in our schools] the way they were at Rome and in Sicily, desiring as he did to have classes conducted similarly in his kingdom.

12.   *Teaching and training in Italy*

Some men were sent to various places in Italy and Sicily either to teach or to provide those who still needed training in the humanities with the opportunity to learn. This fall twelve of them were sent as a group to Sicily with Father Elpidio [Ugoletti]. At the same time, nine who were being assigned to the colleges of Italy were sent to the provincial, Father Laínez. Also when Father Jerónimo Doménech was sent to Sicily in March to satisfy the request of the viceroy Juan de Vega, he took along some companions whom Father Ignatius had assigned to this work, among whom was Father Girolamo Otello. More men presented themselves than could be accommodated outside the Roman [houses], so the Collegio [Romano] was expanded; there they could also be trained in letters and the approved methods of teaching it, so that later they could be useful in the other colleges of Italy.

15.   *New professed fathers*

. . . Therefore, now that four of the first ten [professed] fathers had passed on to a better life, namely, Fathers Jean Codure, Pierre Favre, Claude Jay, and Francis Xavier, twenty-one others were professed of the four vows to take their places; all of whom were alive this year. Together with six of the surviving First [Companions], the total number of professed reached twenty-seven. Still, Father Ignatius ordered Father Miró, the provincial of Portugal, under holy obedience to advance to profession five or six men from the more mature in the province of Portugal. This was done, as we will note later, with the advice and approval of Father Nadal after he had arrived in Portugal.

16.   *Simão Rodrigues is summoned to Rome*

When Father Ignatius found out that Father Simão had left the province of Aragon, returned to Portugal, and at that time was living at Lisbon, he did not at all approve of his conduct, so he ordered [Rodrigues] under holy obedience to come to Rome. He also conveyed expressions of gratitude to the King of Portugal for having contributed to the welfare of the whole Society when he encouraged Father Rodrigues to go to Rome, just as his superior, whom he had in the place of Christ, had commanded him under obedience to do. [Ignatius] also wanted the King himself to present the letters patent to [Simão] so that only with the King's approval would they be handed over to Father Rodrigues. . . .

19.   *Julius III sends a patriarch to the Nestorians*

When the supreme pontiff Julius sent a patriarch to the Nestorians who are in Asia, he declared in the consistory that it seemed advisable to him that some of Ours should be sent [to accompany] him.[1] And because it became known that Ours who were in India could have contacts [with them], it seemed a good plan to send men from there rather than from Europe. If a college had been established in Jerusalem, it would undoubtedly have been easier for Ours to perform the offices of charity for the Christians of that region.

20.   *Sending Jesuits to Ethiopia*

When serious attention was given this year to sending a patriarch to Ethiopia, the King of Portugal turned over to Father Ignatius the task of choosing him from among the priests of our Society. He was to select not only the patriarch but also two other bishops and a new provincial [superior] for Ethiopia, and other priests and brothers as well. Ignatius ordered all who were then living at Rome to write out a sealed document indicating whether they were inclined and ready to join this mission to Ethiopia. Each of them fervently offered his collaboration if it accorded with holy obedience. Father Ignatius chose Father João Nunes to become patriarch. He was at the time engaged in helping the Christians who were captives in Tetuán in Africa. His coadjutor bishops were Father Andrés de Oviedo, rector of the college at Naples, and Father Melchor Carneiro, who this fall had come to Rome with Father Simão [Rodrigues]. For provincial he chose Father Antonio de Quadros. He also named the other companions for this mission. The Apostolic See granted them very extensive faculties; but because the supreme pontiff Julius [III] began to notably fail in health as this year drew to a close, the completion of this business had to be deferred until next year. Finally, when Paul IV was reigning as supreme

---

[1] Here "Nestorians" seems to mean the Maronites of Syria who were in union with Rome rather than adherents of the views of Nestorius condemned at the Council of Ephesus in 431.

pontiff, what had begun under Julius was set in motion in the year 1555, as will be narrated below.

24.   *Loyola opposes Canisius's being made bishop of Vienna*

The death of Frederick Nausea, the pastor, this year left Vienna inconsolable; the question arose of conferring the episcopacy on Father Peter Canisius. When the apostolic nuncio wrote Father Ignatius . . . [a proposal] that he command one of Ours to be presented for a task of this nature, Father Ignatius wrote back to the apostolic nuncio that he was unshakably convinced that it was not appropriate for him to become involved in this question because he took it for very certain that [this proposal] in no way contributed to God's service and that Ours should be left entirely in their lowly state. . . .

27.   *Provincials should not have their own horses*

When Father Ignatius heard that too many were using horses in Portugal and Spain, something that could derogate from the poverty and humility of the Society, he wrote to Father Nadal, the commissary in those provinces, directing him to ensure that neither the provincial of Spain (even though he was not in very good health) nor the provincial of Portugal should have a horse of his own.[2] But if sometimes they needed to ride, then the colleges should provide an animal for them to ride on, lending it out or receiving it on loan as the case may be, so that the provincial could reach his destination. But if, in view of the distances to be traveled in Spain and the poor health of Father Araoz, he could not reach his destination on foot or use rented horses, Nadal judged it proper for [Araoz] to have one or another horse for his own use for a time. He could employ a sort of compromise whereby a college would have its own horse and would lend it to the provincial when he needed it. One or other horse like this could be used for other ministries serving the needs of the college when the provincial did not need it to make a trip.

29.   *Men who leave the Society should not be readmitted*

This year Master Jacobus, who after setting out for Louvain went to Vienna and then on to Rome, and the theologian Master Antonio Marin, both of whom had left the Society, returned to it fully aware of their mistake. But neither persevered in [their vocation] for very long. This experience incontro-

---

[2] Here Polanco's word is *iumentum,* which can mean "mule" and "donkey" as well as "horse."

vertibly demonstrated that there are few men who, once they have left the Society, gravely sinning thereby, can persevere in the religious life, even if they seem to have repented and returned to it.

37.   *Ignatius orders books by Savonarola to be burned*

This year Father Ignatius found two books in our house by Savonarola and ordered them to be burned because it seems [Savonarola's] spirit of rebellion against the Apostolic See should not be approved of, even though he said many good things [otherwise].

■   **Italy**

51.   *The sermons of Ours draw more women than men at Gubbio*

Master Battista [Giovanni Battista Velati] preached sermons sometimes in the cathedral church, sometimes in the monastery of the Servites, and sometimes in various [other] monasteries. Although he had a large audience of women, he drew few men. For as the cardinal said, the nature of men like this is such that they do not want to listen to a preacher unless he speaks to them about material that they have not heard discussed or understood previously, or unless the preacher who is carrying out his office among them is famous. And because Master Battista said some things in his sermons to stir up devotion to the Blessed Virgin, one of these men said it was almost an insult to the cardinal that he had preached on the "Salve Regina." . . .

52.   *Hearing confessions, especially of prisoners at Gubbio*

Regarding confessions, fifty or sixty devout women confessed to Father Alberto [Azzolini] the first Sunday of each month and went to Communion, and some of them did so once a week. Boys too, as many as 160, prepared a [spiritual] harvest by going to confession. [Alberto] made a practice of hearing sick people in hospitals and their caregivers as well. The city magistrates, who are called "consuls," manifested the benevolence that they carried in their hearts toward Ours, showing them great kindness, and they welcomed two of Ours to a dinner at the town hall as a sign of their esteem. Father Alberto wanted to visit the prison both to encourage those confined there to [go to] confession and to hear their confessions; he carried out this office of charity on Good Friday (before that time [the prisoners] could not be persuaded to receive the sacrament). When two of them were to be executed, the prefect, who is called the gonfalonier, wanted to know from Father Alberto how they had prepared themselves to do what was necessary for the salvation of their souls.

He also began to discuss his own affairs, and on the next day he sent his chaplain to request [Albert] to come and hear the confessions of all of them. Thus he heard the confessions of the consuls and of the magistrate who is called the *potestà* and of the vice-duke (that is what they call the man who serves in place of the Duke of Urbino), and of their families. They also asked Father [Albert] not to desist from the service of charity he had begun for those imprisoned, especially for those who were about to undergo capital punishment. Nonetheless, he could not obtain from [the prisoners] anything of significance except on the day before they were to be executed. Therefore, he heard their confessions at that time (for he had already heard the confessions of the other men being held in custody). Ours did not leave them until they gave up their last breath to the Lord, exhorting them and encouraging them to pass on [to the next life] as piously as they could.

63.   *Dispute over poverty in a convent at Gubbio*

On feast days Cardinal [Marcello Cervini] wanted to come to Gubbio and give exhortations to the nuns at four convents that were subject to the bishop. None of these convents lived the common life or observed perfect poverty. Father Albert had invested a great deal of effort toward remedying these defects. He talked to the nuns of one of those convents, giving them an exhortation that struck considerable fear into them. When the abbess summoned him, he found that two-thirds of the nuns were prepared to live a common life, but the remaining third clung obstinately to their own property. The cardinal thanked [Alberto] after he had visited all the convents and preached in them, seriously trying to determine whether he could in good conscience tolerate nuns who retained that sort of ownership. The practice of these nuns who did not observe the vow of poverty weighed heavily on the conscience of the cardinal, for they claimed that they had not made their profession or pronounced the vow of poverty except as matters existed at the time when they entered. Thus they thought that they had the right to retain their personal property.

Among the other considerations that moved the cardinal to call Ours to Gubbio, not the least was that he could strive to reform these convents, as they had successfully done at Reggio and elsewhere. Therefore, the cardinal wanted to ease his conscience and get a clearer grasp of his obligations. It was quite evident that most of the nuns would not give up their property unless compelled [to do so]. Indeed, some boasted that they could not be compelled [to do so], and they found supporters who agreed that they were not bound [to do so] because they had not made an explicit vow of poverty but only [vows] of chastity and obedience. Owing to a kind of negligence, they had not been required to pronounce an explicit vow of poverty when they made their profession.

77.   *The forty-hours devotion at Perugia*

It was customary near Easter for all the parishes to take turns coming to the cathedral church for [the sort of] prayer that went on continuously for forty hours, and also for somebody to be at hand not only to encourage them to pray but also to direct their method of prayer. This task was entrusted to Ours, and two of Ours carried out that office with the well-deserved plaudits of those who prayed, and brought notable benefits to them.

103.   *Troubles in the Jesuit community at Florence*

Problems in the community distressed Father Laínez no end, for some men who had not been tested very thoroughly were sent to this college, just as they were to the other small colleges. Many of them gave evidence of being deficient in humility, true obedience, and religious virtues; a few of them acted like yeast, corrupting the others. It seems that God permitted this in these early days so that the Society would adopt the practice of a lengthier probation and employ greater discernment before sending anyone to new colleges. Still in all, the attention that Father [Laínez] paid to this problem resulted in better order in the college after penances had been imposed; because [Laínez] found cop[ing] with these defects most annoying, he requested Father Ignatius to relieve him of the office of provincial. . . .

107.   *Ignatius chastises Laínez*

I will not fail to record that the liberties that Father Laínez took when writing displeased Father Ignatius. Seemingly, he took it ill when some workers who seemed essential to certain colleges that we had accepted had been snatched away from there and called to Rome. Father Ignatius wrote a letter, to be read by [Laínez] alone, in which he expressed his displeasure at what [Laínez] thought and wrote on this question, especially taking into account that in earlier letters he had conveyed to [Laínez] the argument of the universal good, which is to be preferred to the particular good.

[Ignatius] also added that he was admonishing him now to see whether [Laínez] would recognize his fault after he had reflected on the matter for a time. If he acknowledged it, he was to write back and indicate the penance he would be willing to undergo. [Laínez] replied that he had read this letter many times and had found in it grounds for personal shame [and a reason to] praise the divine mercy and to feel greater love and respect for his superior. He thanked Father Ignatius for correcting him and asked him with great humility that whenever he saw the need for correction, he would apply it.

Meanwhile, he went on to describe and acknowledge his own defects in particular. Shedding many tears, he proposed three penances, so that if the first was not given him, then the second might be; and if not the second, then at least the third. The [penances] were so severe that Father Ignatius did not allow him to do any of them or any other penance either; he accepted Laínez's own humble self-accusation as abundant satisfaction.

125.   *Copies of the* Spiritual Exercises *are to be given only to people who have made them*

When some religious and others asked for the Spiritual Exercises, and the prior of a certain monastery requested the book itself, it was made clear in the name of Father Ignatius that the book was not to be given to any one who had not already been directed through those meditations.

126.   *Financial problems at Florence*

As regards material things, the furniture of Ours was so scanty that they did even have their own beds but had to rent them. No small part of the two hundred gold ducats that the duchess assigned each year was spent on renting the house and [the beds]. They chose Lord Luis de Toledo, the brother of the duchess, as their protector, and he gladly accepted the responsibility; but he still gave only minimal temporal help, perhaps because he could not reasonably afford to [do more]. Begging was not allowed because of the princes themselves, who seemed to disapprove of it. Hence, they lacked no opportunity to suffer. When a certain friend of the Society informed the duchess about the poverty Ours were enduring, she sent fifty gold ducats with which to buy beds, and she and other citizens of both sexes sent additional alms to sustain Ours in some fashion. Rome too sent them more than a hundred gold pieces as a subsidy. . . . Sometimes Father Laínez put pressure on the duchess, and she made promises, but she did not live up to them. . . .

130.   *Teaching Christian Doctrine at Florence*

On Sundays two of the scholastics presented some [elements of] Christian doctrine at the same church in dialog form, thus enhancing the devotion and securing the admiration of their audience, who listened very attentively to what the [young men] were saying about the proper formation of a Christian person. [Father Louis de Coudret] arranged [this dialog] so that listeners might come more willingly and invite others to take in his lecture (for it seemed good to turn his sermon into a lecture). . . .

133.   *Laínez outlines a curriculum for a potential college at Compostela*

The Cardinal of Compostela, His Lordship Juan de Toledo, also wanted to learn Father Laínez's opinion about studies at the college . . . that he wanted to give to the Society at Compostela. [Laínez's] opinion came down to this: the study of law should not be allowed there, and at the start four teachers should be employed to teach grammar; a fifth should teach rhetoric, a sixth Greek literature, and a seventh [should lecture on] material necessary for hearing confessions. The curriculum in arts should begin when the students were prepared, beginning with one course each year or when the previous [course] had been completed, as the number of students and their progress demanded. Next, there should be a course in Scholastic theology according to the teaching of St. Thomas, to be completed in four years at the most, along with the more difficult books of the Scriptures and the universal rules that the doctors have handed down for understanding Scripture. Taking into account the students and their progress, at the proper time it would be possible to see if the college should be elevated to [the status of] a university. I judged that this account of his views should not be omitted, useful as they will be for similar colleges.

138.   *Laínez's ministry at Genoa*

When [Laínez] finally arrived at Genoa, as we have said, he began preaching vigorously and performing spiritual ministries. Lest his charity impel him to undertake more work for and involvement with sick people than would be compatible with his other ministries, which would be more beneficial to the people [as a whole], he was ordered not to concern himself with these sick people. When his preaching and conversations had enkindled the hearts of the citizens, the question presented itself of founding there not just one but two colleges at the same time. The first would be set up in the center of the city, whereas the other one would be in a remote part of the city called Charignani, as we reported earlier. The Sauli family wanted to establish the second college there at a site both beautiful and spacious. The family wanted to give a certain nearby monastery belonging to them as a residence for Ours while the church and college were being built. But because the building would require continual and costly expenditures, [the Sauli] asked to have someone of the Society in charge. It seemed to Father Laínez that the second of these college would serve as a villa for those of Ours who wished to get away from the city college in search of recreation and the restoration of their health.

139.   *Ignatius authorizes a college at Genoa under certain conditions*

This arrangement did not displease Father Ignatius, who let it be understood that he wanted to undertake both colleges; but in the meantime, when the second one was being fitted out, he did not think the two or three men whom they had requested should be sent. . . . The archbishop of Genoa, who was the head of the Sauli family, discussed this matter with Father Ignatius when he was at Rome; he declared that if the Society was willing to assume the burden of having twelve Masses said every day, either by Ours or by others, an annual income of a thousand scudi could be applied to the Society, provided that [Ignatius] also opened the schools in Genoa.

140.   *Difficulties in finding a good location in central Genoa*

Our Genoese friends had to admit that finding a suitable location for the college in the center of the city was more difficult than they had expected, and this college had to be functioning before the college of the Sauli [could be opened]. Father Ignatius himself wrote Father Laínez, advising him not to worry about this, but rather to leave the matter to our friends. Therefore, he devoted himself to the work of preaching both in the cathedral and in another church as well, that of Saint Columbanus. He also diligently explored questions of restitution, seeking to bring spiritual help to businessmen, and to matters pertaining to the priestly vocation, that he might look out for the best interest of these people.

148.   *Jesuits in Corsica*

Toward the end of the preceding year, Father Silvestro Landini and Manuel [Gomez] de Montemayor arrived in Corsica as commissaries of the Apostolic See. After Father Manuel had stayed fifteen days in the city of Bastia, he was sent to [the estate] of a certain Lord Jacopo Santo de Mara, a leading

man among the Corsicans, of whom even the Turks stood in fear. So successfully did [Father Manuel] begin to cultivate the Lord's vineyard at the town of
Saint Columbanus that Lord Jacopo himself confessed that he had never seen so
many people come [to listen to] sermons. In January [Father Manuel] preached
daily before dawn, so that the people could go out to their work after the
sermon. Because Lord Jacopo with his wife and whole family were among the
first to come, he encouraged his people to act as they should. Five hundred
people used to come to this predawn sermon.

Father Manuel devoted himself to hearing confessions, beginning one
hour before dawn and continuing till one o'clock the next morning without
rising from his chair. Many people who had lacked this saving remedy for many
years flocked in with great emotion to cleanse and cure the wounds of their
conscience. Many of those who had gone to confession also took Communion.
The confessions of Lord Jacopo's family also gave good example to many.

The religious of the Order of Saint Francis attended the morning sermons
of [Gomez] as well as his explanations of Christian doctrine, which took place
at evening before noblemen and a large audience of women, boys, and girls, all
of whom learned [this material] extremely well. In this area the women gave an
excellent example of their zeal by holding day-long conversations among
themselves about his teaching. Those among the people who were poor begged
him not to leave there but to continue showing them the path of salvation, from
which they had strayed far. Although people from nearby places sent him
invitations, Lord Jacopo would not as yet let him leave there. He explained that
he wanted to accompany [Gomez] throughout his whole territory, which he had
with marvelous assiduity purged of vendettas and freed from marauding Turks
and pirates.

170.   *Landini's preaching at Bastia*

[Gomez] left that domain in great peace, both interior and exterior, and
returned to Father Silvestro [Landini] toward the end of April. [The latter] had
spent this whole time in the principal town of Bastia, which was the most
important city in the whole island. Far from cutting back on his labors, he even
increased them, urged on by the fervor of his spirit. Sometimes he preached
four or five times in a single day. First he had preached very early in the
morning to the farmers and workers at the Church of Saint Francis; next, when
many others gathered at the city gate, waiting for it to be opened, he also went
there, so that such a multitude would not go out fasting without having the word

of God preached to them. He then immediately preached in another church, that of Saint Mary, to the other workers and to those who were unable to attend his first sermon. He preached a fourth time before noon to the governor, his court, noblemen, and the citizens. On feast days he also preached sermons after lunch out in the open, where five thousand people sometimes gathered; many of them came from nearby towns, so that they could provide for their spiritual salvation. Although heavy rains fell during the night and during the day itself, it never rained at the time of his sermons, so that his sermons never had to be called off. But right after it, the rain gradually returned when it no longer interfered with the devotion of those people who had gathered. More than once it happened that at one sermon many young men and women were inspired to [consider] a religious life, and some also took the habit of the Order of Saint Francis.

183.   *Ignatius intervenes to curb Gomez's zeal*

Father Ignatius considered it wise for somebody to be sent to Corsica, and for this mission he selected Sebastiano Romei, who was not yet a priest. He gave him a letter for the governor, who resided at Bastia, and ordered [Romei] to take note how the commissaries [Landini and Gomez] were conducting themselves; then he was to bring back to Rome both public and private testimonials regarding our way of proceeding. He also carried letters to Fathers Silvestro and Manuel, in which Father Ignatius admonished them to go forward in the spirit of gentleness and warned them that neither was to make decisions without hearing the advice of the other.

It was timely that Father Ignatius wrote this, not because of Father Silvestro, but because of Father Manuel. Carried away by pious zeal that drove him to assist poor people, he had laid fines on some people; rumor had it that he fined some because they had missed the class in Christian doctrine. Also, he had taught Christian doctrine to a mixed group of men and women, doing this in the castle of Lord Jacopo, and sometimes he called men away from their own work, without concern for their inconvenience, and set them to repairing the walls of churches and similar tasks. Therefore, his good intentions had to be moderated by Father Silvestro's greater experience.

190.   *Failed efforts toward establishing a college at Bastia*

Serious discussion took place about establishing a college of the Society at Bastia. A certain Juan Nadal, who was mentioned earlier, wrote Father Ignatius in May and requested that he send twelve members of the Society there. They would be provided with a house and what they needed by way of food and clothing—partly from the bishop, partly from the Genoese patricians, partly from the people in the form of alms. But later he and his wife, all of whose children had died, decided to make the college of the Society their heir. These [plans], however, never worked out, in part because of the unfortunate outcome of the actions taken during the Corsican War by the republic of Genoa against the French and the Turkish fleet this year, which cast all of Corsica into turmoil, and in part because of our Society's commitments in many other places.

198.   *Landini's ministry on the island of Capraia*

Because of its spiritual need during July, Father Silvestro went to the island of Capraia, which is near Corsica. There he worked for several days and harvested abundant spiritual fruit. He absolved several people who had incurred an excommunication reserved to the pope. He dispensed almost twenty people who had contracted marriages within the prohibited degrees, thus liberating them from grave danger [because of their reproachful] consciences. He declared eighteen others dispensed after Dragut the pirate had burned the documents communicating their dispensations and many other things besides, after he had first heard the testimony of witnesses corroborating their dispensations. As was his custom, he preached to them every morning; toward evening he taught Christian doctrine and led the crown (the rosary) of the Blessed Virgin once all had assembled in the church. He saw to it that public prayers were offered [for the needs of the people], and he rejuvenated many with the most holy sacrament [of the Eucharist].

He also brought it about that many rocks were hauled in to form a sort of bastion so that the people could defend themselves against the pirates, who a few days earlier had killed several men and had carried off into slavery twelve young women belonging to the most distinguished families. Father Silvestro arrived just at the right moment to ease the intense sorrow of those people. He did not want to send Father Manuel there, because he was in his prime and seemed suited for long labors in the Lord's vineyard; thus, he did not want to expose [Manuel] to the danger of pirates. But he himself was a sick old man, so he judged that he need not worry about falling into the hands of Turks.

199.   *Fear of the Turkish fleet leads Corsicans to prayer and the sacraments*

Right at this time and in the following month of August, the aforesaid fleet of the Turks began to swarm over those seas. When it came toward the Mountain of Christ near the shoreline of Bastia on August 7, it provided a precious opportunity for Christians: prayers were offered and every day witnessed confessions, Communions, and almsgiving, along with great contrition for sins. All the boys, women, and old men scattered in flight toward the interior part of the island. In the course of fleeing the attack of the barbarians, they spread Christian doctrine and the frequent use of confession and Communion and encouraged people to prepare themselves for death. Thus did this flight produce many preachers in Corsica. Lord Paulinus, who was in command of the fleet of the French King, warned the governor who lived at Bastia that Dragut [the pirate] planned to invade Corsica and that he [Paulinus] had tried in vain to dissuade him but [Dragut] was quite determined to avenge some damage that he had once incurred there.

211.   *The Jesuit school at Padua*

Experience also taught [Ours] that the task of teaching, although quite useful if done correctly, was very difficult unless the teachers were skilled and well balanced. If there was a rapid turnover of teachers, with some of them constantly coming and going, classes suffered considerable harm. Something like this was also the reason why the number of students at Padua lessened considerably this year. . . .

223.   *Saving a famous prostitute at Venice*

Some of those who partook of the sacraments [at the Jesuit church in Venice] entered religious life, both men and women. Some among them were prostitutes who were received into the convent of the converted and began to live chaste and holy lives there. One of them belonged to a well-known family; when she was only sixteen years old and ravishing in appearance, she seemed destined to wreak the downfall of many men in that city, as her early plunge into a disgraceful lifestyle clearly and quickly demonstrated. When this girl had been snatched from the devil's jaws and wanted to confess in our church, she had to contend with her angry lovers lying in wait for her. When she finished her confession, she tricked the men waiting for her: she was taken down to a gondola by a different door and then borne off to the convent of the converted by a rather hidden waterway. There she applied herself with great zeal to punishing her body and advancing in the spirit. Two hundred and fifty women lived in that convent; among them her zeal was outstanding, as those who had charge [of the convent] testified.

227.   *The college at Venice struggles*

As regards the classes, by order of Father Ignatius, each week a record had to be kept of the number of students in each college. When Father Battista Viola, the commissary for Italy, came to Venice, he wanted to introduce a better arrangement for the classes. He organized the students who had been taught previously into four classes under a like number of teachers. [Following] the Paris model, he ordered teachers to hold three classes in the morning and three in the afternoon. However useful this was for the students, it was a heavy burden for Ours, all the more so because they could not keep regular hours for their meals, which they took daily at the residence of the prior, Reverend Father Andrea Lippomano . . .

237.   *More problems at Venice*

Father [Lippomano], the prior of the Trinity Monastery, urged us to gradually discontinue confessing women, especially those of the nobility, who came to the sacraments on feast days. He feared that some of these women might spread false accusations against the Society. But it did not seem to contribute to the glory of God for us to leave unharvested this [sort of] spiritual fruit. Father Ignatius prescribed that if a scandal should arise, we would then reconsider the question, but he did not wish us to omit a work of piety merely out of fear. What may have influenced the prior was that the three Venetian noblemen who were in charge of all monasteries were said to be arranging to settle certain nuns on the site of our college once we had been expelled from there. It seems that some people imputed this scheme to Giovanni Lippomano, the prior's brother, who, it seemed, wanted to have Ours driven from the area.[3]

258.   *Success and failure at Bologna*

As few as eight or nine of [Ours] were at Bologna this year, with Father Francesco Palmio in charge of them. The people who frequently went to confession and Communion seemed like religious in their modesty and piety.

---

[3] Later, members of the prominent Lippomano family tried to overturn the prior's gift to the Jesuits of the monastery and its revenues, but the Venetian senate ruled against them.

There were a hundred people or more who drew spiritual refreshment from these sacraments every Sunday, and almost two hundred who did so monthly. But on the main feast days of the year, the number of penitents was so great that it was hardly possible to satisfy them all. At the feasts of the Christmas season, around seven hundred people came to Communion. Still, Father Francesco undertook other tasks besides hearing these confessions; he visited those detained in the public prison, bringing them great consolation and benefit. Sometimes private persons of great importance and others who were ailing kept him so long that he could hardly find enough time to eat. When preaching on feast days, he drew quite a large audience and did them immense good.

He took up the subject of discretion and prudence in the spiritual life by commenting on the Apostle's exhortation, "Present your bodies . . . as a reasonable worship" [Rom. 12:1]. After they returned home, many spiritual and devout persons took off hair shirts and brought to Father Francesco the whips that they had used to scourge themselves to blood. They accused themselves of doing these things without the approval of their spiritual fathers. Among these people was a woman who always wore a hair shirt, fasted a great deal, and sometimes beat herself with an iron chain for three straight hours. She would have kept going even longer had she not feared that her neighbors would hear what she was doing. There were quite a few other practices that she undertook with scant discretion, endangering her life. For all these people the advice, direction, and moderation of the confessor came at precisely the right time.

Father [Palmio] suggested spiritual readings in the convents of nuns that he visited now and then. The students being instructed in our schools customarily went to confession each month and the older ones went to Communion. At the start of this year, some of them were quite unassuming and highborn [besides], and they made gratifying progress in their behavior and education. But in this college, too, the constant substitution of teachers did considerable harm to the classes, especially when the incoming teachers were no better than the previous ones—and perhaps not even their equal. Thus, a good number of those regarded as our better students went elsewhere.

259.   *Problems in the community at Bologna*

Community affairs moved along in the face of many obstacles, in that some poorly tested young men made trouble for the rector, and three others had left the Society a short time earlier. Pedro from Gandía, one of the neophytes from that college, was admitted to the Society and sent to Italy; such was his behavior, however, that he had to be expelled from the Society and sent back to Spain. Father Francesco Palmio learned from experience that it was advantageous to keep the young men busy at their tasks except for Sundays and to hear their confessions once a week, and he made particular efforts to foster their devotion and spiritual progress.

276.   *Ignatius forbids Jesuits to inflict physical punishment on students at Ferrara*

The student body daily increased in size, reaching two hundred this year, including many of the nobility; the students advanced in learning and behavior. This year some also entered the religious life. A number of the students in the Greek course were members of different religious orders. Presenting a considerable problem for Ours was Father Ignatius's decree forbidding teachers to inflict physical punishment on the boys, yet parents resented it when laymen disciplined their sons. Father Jean Pelletier admitted [to the Society] a man of mature years who had served both as doorkeeper and disciplinarian. But because Father Ignatius did not consider it appropriate for students to be punished that way by a man who was a member of the Society, he ordered [this man] not to lay a hand on the students but to keep them faithful to their duties by intimidation alone. Besides this man, another was also admitted to the Society at Ferrara, but experience showed that the probation one received in these tiny colleges was not adequate, and so the first of them, even though he was mature in age, was dismissed [from the Society]. Elsewhere other men taught [superiors] the same lesson, although, helped by a special grace of God, some men conducted themselves well in the Lord. . . .

277.   *Older students used to administer corporal punishment at Ferrara*

The number of classes was increased since the lowest class had more than eighty students, and one [teacher] was not adequate [to handle so many]. So the class were divided into two, with two teachers in charge of them. Here is the method of punishing students that was adopted: a student of more advanced age punished younger students. Thus, the students were kept in fear, although this method of maintaining disciplinary action was not without its own drawbacks.

290.   *Jesuits who engage in gay sex are to be expelled*

Toward autumn Father Pelletier consulted Father Ignatius on what had to be done if, God forbid, one of the community should fall into an abominable sin of the flesh *[lapsum carnis nefandum]*. [Ignatius's] reply was that if—may God ward this off!—any should fall into such a sin after entering the Society, superiors should cite other [public and known] defects [of the individual] and expel him from the Society. Moreover, [Pelletier] should be warned that Father Ignatius had determined that nobody of this sort should be retained in the Society, nor did he [Ignatius] know anybody in the whole Society who was besmirched by such a stain. The offender's dismissal was to be explained by some subterfuge, either by stating that they had been sent on a pilgrimage, or by letting it be known that they were unsuitable for the Society for other reasons. Even though our confessors had very ample faculties for absolving laypeople, still, when our own men are involved, this must be a reserved case.

295.   *Language problems at Modena*

All [the students at Modena] also made progress in letters, and the students in the first class worked on writing orations in Latin, which they learned by memory and delivered on feast days in our church; thereby they gave great pleasure to the audience and succeeded in stirring up rivalry among extern students. Since many of them were endowed with excellent talents and applied themselves diligently, they made considerable progress in learning. In the lower classes it would have been most desirable to have teachers who were more skilled in the Italian language and in dealing with that tender age. The teachers there at this time were Spaniards who had an imperfect command of the Lombard dialect; still, they somehow managed to carry on in a satisfactory manner. Father Adrien de Witte, a Belgian by nationality, experienced this difficulty with the Italian language in teaching Christian doctrine. Even though he was very pious and learned and had many excellent and profitable things to say, still, he did not explain them very successfully in Italian. At this time, fewer Italians than natives of other countries joined the Society and were suited for these duties.

304.   *Reestablishing the sacrament of confession at Modena*

The fruit of the sacraments, which mounted daily, was precious indeed because some of the confessors at work in Modena were more likely to exacerbate the wounds of their penitents than heal them. There was one confessor, and a religious besides, to whom a woman confessed a certain sin of the flesh. He asked [her], "Why do you confess such things? One ought to make love [without restraint]." Driven by remorse, she had come to [what she took to be] a doctor; she then went to a [more authentic] doctor, from whom she received better care. Deceived by the heresy that was widespread then, some people of this sort tried to dissuade more than a few people from frequently going to confession. Against these false shepherds Father Adrien not only stressed the usefulness of frequent confession but learnedly proved his point as well. Many priests, even those who were not heretics, held a different opinion and argued accordingly.

There was a man who so agreed with such [priests] that he had not received Communion in forty years; there was another, almost thirty years old, who had never gone to confession. But the Lord led them back to better habits and attitudes. Although the heretics scorned and ridiculed the [papal] jubilee, not only did Ours endeavor in their sermons to persuade many to come forward and receive [the jubilee indulgence], but they also easily persuaded the bishop [Cardinal Giovanni Morone] to order pastors to promulgate [the jubilee] to their people. They went around to individual homes and invited people to [avail of the jubilee].

305. *The Jesuits gain support at Modena*

Father Battista Viola preached when he came to Modena, winning considerable gratitude and imparting consolation to the people. He strove to induce the people to live their lives as observantly as possible. As a result, even those people who earlier took pleasure in mocking us and in wintertime even hurled snowballs at Ours as they were walking by, desisted from their abuse when they observed that Ours ignored their insults and persevered in carrying on the works of the Society. Some of them began to submit to the influence of our Institute and devoted themselves eagerly to [helping us in] all sorts of ways.

315. *Ignatius refuses to worry about health costs*

The bishop [of Modena] proposed giving Ours a parish, but Father Ignatius judged that we should refuse it unless the care of souls and the revenues were transferred to a neighboring parish. At length, a rented house was accepted, and Father Jean Laurence was sent to Modena in place of Father Cesare [Aversano]. As for Father Adrien, he was sent elsewhere for the sake of his health. Father Ignatius urged that after they had consulted a doctor, if he approved [Adrien's] returning to his native air, they should spare no expense in looking after his health. [Ignatius] promised to refund whatever they spent, even though Father Adrien himself could repay what had been spent from his patrimony.

325.   *Malcontent Jesuits should not be foisted off on another community*

This year experience taught [us] that men who had caused turmoil in one college on account of their own temptations and restlessness and wished to be sent to another [college] should not readily be sent there. Aside from other inconveniences, those who had behaved badly in one place might behave even worse elsewhere. Some took their leave without a word to their superior *[insalutato hospite];* and those who were more stable in their vocation showed their rectors too little obedience when they hoped to be assigned to other colleges.

345.   *How to handle a Jesuit who accidentally stabbed another Jesuit*

At Venice one of our scholastics from Siena, not out of malice but in a spirit of frivolity, happened to pull a sword from the scabbard of a guest and, while brandishing it playfully, wounded another member of the Society on his forehead. The rector was unsure whether the man who had done something so unusual should be dismissed from the Society. But Father Ignatius thought it better not to dismiss him, for he had sinned not maliciously but only lightheartedly. Still, [Ignatius] ordered the rector not to mention that he had written to Rome, while imposing a good penance to give edification [to rest of the community].

349.   *What should be the minimum prayer time for Jesuits?*

When Master Andrea Boninsegna queried Father Ignatius whether he could curtail the prescribed time for prayer somewhat because of his heavy teaching load, the answer came back that he should not omit half an hour of prayer in the morning and half an hour in the evening.

352.   *Viola can remove rectors, but only after consulting Loyola*

When the father commissary [Viola] seemed to be dealing with certain rectors more laxly than was right, Father Ignatius wrote a letter for him to show to those rectors. In it he encouraged [Viola] to carry out energetically what he judged would advance the service of God. Furthermore, the letter stated that

[Ignatius] had given [Viola] the same authority that a provincial would have, adding that he also had the power to remove from the office of rector men who were in charge of a college and substitute in their place other men who seemed better suited, taking into consideration the universal rather than the particular good. But at the same time, Ignatius dispatched a private letter placing restrictions on this power to remove rectors and enjoined him from using this authorization without consulting him [first]. . . .

353.　*Loyola requires a scholastic to reform or leave*

After Master Antonio Marin had repented and returned to the Society, he quickly became troubled in his soul. Father Ignatius ordered him to be released from his vows and sent on a pilgrimage with the understanding that he would not return to Ours, or at least that he would not do so except with much improved and proper dispositions.

394.　*Financial help to the college at Naples*

The Confraternity of the Bianchi, which we discussed earlier, applied to the aid of the poor almost six hundred gold scudi from the alms that they used to raise. But the lord viceroy [Cardinal] Pedro de Toledo had forbidden them to raise those aforesaid alms. So friends suggested that the cardinal permit them to return to their previous practice, allowing them to apply those alms to the college. The cardinal restored their right to raise funds. Some people proposed that half the funds be given to the college for its use but the other half be given to the Hospital for the Incurables. The cardinal finally gave his approval for this, so that the alms were evenly divided between these two pious works. Accordingly, the college for some years enjoyed a subsidy of three hundred gold scudi.

395.　*Obtaining a new and better location for the college at Naples*

Some people wanted to assign to the Society a site that had a small but fairly beautiful church, but the residence was too small and the location was unhealthful and was burdened with some obligations. Therefore, Father Salmerón determined that it was quite unsuitable for our college, even though it had an income of 180 scudi. So, changing their opinion, our friends bought a palace located in the city center and enjoying healthful air. The owner was glad to sell it to Ours for five thousand gold ducats. The cardinal, however, had undertaken the responsibility of getting support from the Emperor that would cover both the purchase of the house and the foundation for its support. Thus, the city itself and the cardinal wrote a respectful letter to the Emperor in December, requesting four thousand ducats from him to purchase the house and four hundred or five hundred ducats annually for its support. They commissioned deputies from the assembly along with the Duke of Monteleone [Ettore Pignatelli] to handle this. The city itself seemed able, with the consent of the cardinal, to tap various sources and give an annual income of 150 gold ducats without any difficulty. A certain devout friend gave the college five hundred gold ducats, with which to purchase securities that would yield regular revenue, and there was hope that he would do still more.

405.   *Should a scholastic who was indirectly involved in a murder be expelled?*

A certain Girolamo, a Sicilian, was admitted to the Society at Naples and was teaching the first class in grammar; he appeared to be a good religious. But it happened that some of the brethren coming from Sicily on their way through Naples recognized him and informed the superior, and perhaps not only him, that Girolamo had been involved in someone's murder. When [Girolamo] suspected that this impediment of his, which he had not mentioned at first, had been made public, he went away quietly without a word to his superior. After learning the circumstances, Father Ignatius ordered a message to be sent to Father Salmerón, to the effect that it might easily have been those ill-considered words of one of the men who came from Sicily [that were the cause of] his departure. [Ignatius] seemed to be unhappy with developments in this case, for [Girolamo] had been setting a good example at the college. He gave it as his view that if [Girolamo] had not personally killed the man, even if he had been there when one of his companions had done it, that did not constitute one of the impediments prohibiting admission to the Society. He added that for someone endowed with rare gifts, the *Constitutions* of the Society envisioned the possibility of a dispensation when it seemed likely that the person would do above-average service for God.

407.   *The reassignment of Ours at Messina stirs resentment*

This we can say about sermons: When Father Benedetto Palmio, who was greatly beloved in that city, went to Palermo on February 11, so that he could join others on their way to Rome, initially this brought considerable anguish to our spiritual friends. They complained that, after funds had been collected for the endowment of this college, gradually all our best men left there [and went elsewhere];[4] and they tearfully begged Father Antonius [Vinck, the new rector] to address them on some topics that would be of benefit to them until Father Girolamo Otello had arrived as promised. He began to do this with the approval of the consultors, and every day of Lent he interpreted the penitential psalms from the beginning and the day's Gospel as well. We know for certain that they drew more profit than they could reasonably have expected both from his lectures and the sermons that Father Giovanni Filippo [Casini] delivered on feast days and Sundays.

409.   *The fears die down that funding for the college would be cut off*

[For that reason] the rumor that had arisen over the departure of Father Benedetto proved unfounded. It had got to the point that the city councilmen discussed forbidding the treasurer to pay funds owed to the college on the grounds that the Society did not provide the college at Messina with the high-quality workers that the amount [they were paying] warranted. But they made no such attempts, perhaps fearing to anger the viceroy. But if he left office, there were still reasons to fear [for the future]. Finally, once they got to know Father Otello, they had no excuse for discontent. . . .

421.   *What information about candidates did Ignatius want?*

Already this year, in order to exclude unsuitable men from entering the Society, [the Messina Jesuits] were enjoined from admitting anyone without first consulting Father Ignatius. Now they were given instructions regarding the qualities [in the candidates] about which they were to inform Father [Ignatius]. The first was exterior modesty and appearance; the second was temperament, judgment, talents, and aptitude for the ministries of the Society; the third was age, health, and bodily integrity; the fourth was progress in studies, the activities in which he had engaged, and any other talents he might have; the fifth was the condition of his parents, if they were still alive, [among other such contingencies], and whether they were agreeable to their son's plans. Still, if the [candidates] were not students at our colleges, the consent of parents was not considered necessary.

---

[4] It was a common Jesuit practice in the early days to send in excellent preachers and teachers to get a new college off to a good start, then gradually replace them with less-skilled men. Understandably, this caused resentment.

426.   *Our young men leave Messina for Rome*

On September 18 eleven of Ours set out from Messina bound for Rome. Among them were five young men of Messina, almost all of whom were nobles and trained in Latin and Greek literature, students of Father Annibale [Coudret]. They all went as a group to the viceroy, Juan de Vega, to bid farewell to him as they were departing. The sight of them brought him great contentment; he embraced each one of them with tears of joy and said, "These are plants that, when transplanted elsewhere, will bear even richer fruit." The previous day the viceroy attended some Latin speeches that the students from Messina delivered in our church. Other speeches were given in Greek and Hebrew. The viceroy, who delighted in keeping abreast of college activities, listened to them all with great pleasure and approval.

428.   *Vocations flourish in Sicily*

Since Father Jerónimo [Doménech] hoped to mold and conform himself and the colleges of Sicily fully to the norms of our Institute, he requested [information about] the procedures established for classes at the Roman College regarding both lectures and recitations. He also [requested information about] the method of examining those who sought to be admitted to the Society; for after consulting Father Ignatius, he had admitted several of the many men who aspired to enter it. Among them was one lad who sought [admission] with such persistence and fervor that he refused outright to leave the college until night came on and his father ordered him to come out. Father Jerónimo Doménech promised that he would admit him if he obtained permission for it from Father Ignatius.

Some parents denied permission for [their sons] to enter, and those who were attending our schools were not admitted without the consent of their parents. Ours were concerned about what should be done in such cases; otherwise (in addition to observing the ban of Father Ignatius), it was probably because they feared that their classes would very likely be disrupted that they would admit nobody without his parents' permission. Another danger to be feared was that the nobles and other citizens would remove their sons from our classes.

455.   *The viceroy de Vega and the Jesuit college at Palermo*

[The viceroy] himself urged that, before he departed for Messina, new schoolrooms should be built, so that he himself could be present at the disputations mentioned before that would be held in the new classrooms. Because the building where Ours resided was too small (for our numbers were growing day by day), yet the costs involved made Ours hesitate to build a new residence, the viceroy encouraged Ours and saw to it that they were offered financial aid. . . . He himself sometimes came over to the new college and gave his opinion on the design of the building.

456.   *Religious activities of the students at Palermo*

The students normally attended the sacrifice of the Mass daily as well as instructions in Christian doctrine on Fridays and sermons on Sundays and feast days, and they did this with such devotion that many could be called not merely hearers of the word but doers as well. Some came to confession more often than the monthly confession prescribed for all and with the advice of their confessor they went to Communion; many of them begged to be admitted to the Society. But Father Rector thought that these desires of theirs should be put to additional testing, for if [their aspirations] were genuine, the delay would increase them. They were accustomed to wait in good spirits and to participate in the usual academic and spiritual activities.

462.   *The Jesuit ministries at Palermo make parish priests jealous*

One Sunday, when more than four hundred of our people took Communion in the [Jesuit] church, not only the pastors who were in charge of the parishes but also the canons of the cathedral church fell prey to jealousy. One of the leading pastors visited Father Paolo [Achille, the rector] and asked by what authority [the Jesuits] were acting in this way and distributing Communion to people over whom they had no jurisdiction.

Two canons later came for the same purpose, and both were given the same answer: that [it was done] on the authority granted [Ours] by the Apostolic See to hear the confessions of everybody at any time, and that we are allowed to give the Eucharist to anybody except during the Easter season. They answered that the pope could not allow something that was contrary to their own legal rights. They added that if Ours did not desist of their own accord from administering Communion, they would take steps to force them to do so. The rector offered a gentle response to their words, insisting that he would in no way stop administering those sacraments and from using the faculties granted to [Ours]. From these developments one can easily conjecture how much the nascent Society, just sinking root in Sicily, needed the favor of the viceroy. This happened in July, but because of the jubilee large crowds even at that season came for the sacraments, so that sometimes more that three hundred and at other times more than four hundred took Communion the same day in our church.

483. *Rehabilitating prostitutes at Messina*

Father Provincial [Doménech], besides being in charge of our college, was constantly engaged in works of piety at Messina. Among other things, he prevailed upon the city to establish a home for those women who had led a shameful life but who could not be admitted to the convent of the converted either because the fallen women did not want to become nuns or the building could not accommodate so many. Immediately some of these women began to enter this [new] house, so that they could prepare themselves there either for marriage or for the religious life, depending on the grace God gave [them].

504. *Finding support for a convent of converted prostitutes*

So that the house for converted [prostitutes] might have more stable sources of funds, the provincial arranged that a confraternity of noblemen which had charge of an older monastery would also take charge of this house too. Thus through mutual support they might better foster those pious activities carried on in the same neighborhood. By a special gift of God, Father Giovanni Filippo, who was acquainted with the House of Saint Martha at Rome, seemed suited to help these women.

514. *Setting a spoiled lad straight*

The students [at Monreale in Sicily], meanwhile, made progress both in modesty and in putting aside their vices, and the sons corrected their own parents when they uttered blasphemies; the parents not only did not take offense [at being reproached], but ordered their sons to keep doing the same thing in the future. The town mayor had a private tutor for his sons in his home; but because they did not learn good behavior from him and the oldest son acted in such a haughty manner at home that his family could not put up with him, they discharged the tutor and sent the rascal to our school. In a few days so greatly changed was his behavior that the mayor sent his thanks to Father Bernard Olivier and let him know that his son seemed to have turned into an angel. The same thing happened to another son of a leading family of the city and to many sons of the common people.

534.   *Keeping an eye out to help younger Jesuits*

Because this year Father Ignatius had sent many men to Sicily, a good number of whom were young and had not been in the Society very long, he warned the provincial about their background, so that he would understand what sort of men they were and how he would have to govern them.

■ Austria

536.   *The community at Vienna*

The members of the community studied the German language except for a few who were deemed unsuited for [learning it]. Johann Dirsius and Jonas Adler, both young Germans, dedicated themselves to the Society; and by means of letters they earnestly asked Father Ignatius to admit them to it. One of the brothers, named Wilhelm, contracted the plague, but with God's help regained his health. That pestilence ravaged Vienna for several months, during which the court of King Ferdinand was absent. But Ours abandoned neither the place nor their duties to help both laypeople and our own men. When Father [Nicholas] Gouda could not lecture because of bad health, Father [Nicholas] Lanoy himself took over the course in logic, so that Ours would not lack instruction in this course. Ours devoted much effort to training preachers. For this reason everybody talked German in the house except when giving lectures and disputations. Daily they were engaged in delivering sermons extempore in various languages. Thus did both the younger and the older men make progress and with God's favor enjoyed fairly good health. Father Peter Canisius suffered from a rather dangerous fever, but after a short time he was restored to health and continued to carry out his usual labors.

538.   *The University of Vienna blocks the reopening of classes*

The rector, Father Lanoy, submitted a request that the consistory of the university grant us permission to open classes. [Ours] sent a list of those who would be lecturing and supervising, which was to be posted in public places. But the university, its consistory, that is, replied that Ours should refrain from opening classes until they had brought this matter before the royal council (called the Regimen). They insisted that without its consent they would not permit classes to be opened.

540.   *Jurisdictional problems at Vienna*

The governors of Austria and the royal council, to whom the university had referred the question, returned to Vienna toward the end of April. Following the advice given by a friend who was one of them, Ours presented this request [to the council]; in response they allowed Ours to begin to hold classes by command of His Royal Majesty. They did not seem to be conferring any [additional] authority, but only to be permitting [Ours] to use the authorization received from the King, now that the plague was no longer an obstacle, even though Ours had requested their authorization to teach and their approval [to exist as a university].

According to the understanding of Father Claude Jay of pious memory, our college was set up on the pattern obtaining in Paris, namely, that up to the master's degree in the Faculty of Philosophy the students were to be taught in our college and would receive the degree from the university itself along with the other students. But this was in conflict with the university's privileges and the custom of not admitting anybody to the master's degree who had not attended the classes in logic and philosophy taught by the professors of that university, who followed the same method as Italian professors. So Ours had to seek authorization from [those professors], but [the professors], assuming that Ours had secured authorization from the King of the Romans, only allowed them to teach [but not to graduate our students].

545.   *Canisius preaches in lower Austria*

[Canisius] spent the greater part of Lent traveling about lower Austria as if on a pilgrimage. From Graz (where he stayed all winter), the King of the Romans had sent four or five copies of a letter granting faculties to preach and administer the sacraments especially in these places where Christ's sheep were bereft of shepherds. Because at that time only Father Canisius among our priests was fully adept in the German language, he alone could carry out the King's behest. The godly people in those places where he was staying rejoiced because of the zeal of both their Most Christian King and of Father Canisius himself. Ignoring the depth of the snow and ice, the bitter cold, and—what was even worse—the aggressive behavior of the heretical and uncouth people whom he encountered, he traveled about performing with great diligence these sacred ministries among them.

552.   *Encouraging the reception of the sacraments at Vienna*

Even though the people had completely abandoned the custom of going to confession at the feast of our Lord's birth, the young men of our school began to introduce this pious practice. Not only did they go to confession, but many of them also went to Communion, and this with the consent of their parents. Just as this practice seemed to have resulted in a certain healthy rivalry among other students and their desire to avoid being shamed, . . . so all of them, at least on the solemn feast days, received the rich fruit of these sacraments. There is hope that the example of their sons will also soften the hearts of their parents. The number of these boys grew toward the end of the year, so that in the lowest class there were more than a hundred [pupils], so many that Ours considered adding a fourth class.

553.   *Ministries in the countryside around Vienna*

When the good reputation of the Society spread, the services of Ours were eagerly sought in the villages that surround Vienna, especially in those that were devoid of priests. Hence, some of them came to Ours on solemn feasts and humbly begged us to go there and celebrate the divine services. Although it was impossible for Ours to satisfy their godly requests as we would have wished, they nonetheless strove to do so as best they could. During the feasts of the Christmas season, Father Gouda went out with a companion to several villages and edified the people by offering the Mass and preaching.

558.   *The sorry shape of Catholicism in Austria*

. . . Not only had obedience to the Apostolic Roman See vanished [here], but it had turned into fierce hatred. It is hard to believe the extent to which the sacraments and other sacred ceremonies were despised. And this is not to be interpreted as referring only to those people who out and out rejected the Roman Church but also to those among whom the rites and ancient ceremonies were still practiced. Hence, the bishop of Laibach [Urban Weber] lamented with great sorrow that hardly one-tenth of the provinces subject to the King of the Romans were free from the stain of heresy. Others there were who calculated that a thirtieth or hardly even a fiftieth part [of the land] was free [of it]. There were practically no religious; everywhere the monasteries were empty because the monastic state was regarded with utter contempt. Hardly anybody could be found who wanted to be a religious. Indeed, even learned men shrank from taking sacred orders because of the loathing that the ecclesiastical state aroused. Hence, in that province hardly anybody could be found who wanted to go to the German College [in Rome], in part because they were ashamed of being seen as papists, in part because they viewed it as a great burden to be obliged to receive the ecclesiastical orders eventually.

573.   *Difficulties at the University of Vienna*

The advisors of King [Ferdinand] strove to their utmost to bring about some reformation at the public university, one that would include all the faculties and colleges; and in compliance with the mind of the King, they wanted to reform the Theology Faculty most of all. But while they were preoccupied with structures, they seemed to have lost sight of content, which receives the structure and is its underpinning. Our Fathers Canisius and [Nicholas Florisz of] Gouda (for he had to come back here on short notice to give his lectures) discoursed with great learning and diligence. One began with the New Testament; the other, all the while engaged in putting together his compendium of theology, explained the master of the *Sentences* [Peter Lombard].

But what was the use? They had hardly any students. It sometimes happened that not even one extern [student] attended Doctor Nicholas of Gouda's lectures, and sometimes only one came. There were at most fifteen or sixteen for Father Canisius, and sometimes only six or seven. If our scholastics had not been listening [to him teach], that [verse] of Wisdom would have been applicable, "Where there is no audience, do not pour out talk."[5] But those of Ours who were attending lectures in theology should hardly be counted among the theology students, for at that same time they were pursuing the philosophy curriculum at our college. . . . Already by the end of the year, almost 150 students were attending [the Jesuit college at Vienna]; among them the more advanced were making considerable progress in zeal for the Catholic religion. Not only did they bring their books for inspection, so that Ours could determine whether the authors were heretics, but [the students] also wanted to know about the list of those [books] that the Holy Mother Roman Church had prohibited, so that they could consign them to the flames.

574.   *The origins of the Canisius catechisms*

Our fathers at Vienna had confided to Father Laínez the task that was discussed the previous year, namely, preparing a compendium of theology. He

---

[5] The quotation is actually from Ecclesiasticus 32:6 in the Vulgate.

had begun the task imposed on him, but he gave no indications of completing it soon; the King of the Romans ordered Ours to put together at least a short catechism for the sake of the simple folk, especially in those regions. Thus did Father Canisius begin compiling his work as we know it now, even though he wanted to hand the task over to others of the Society, especially Doctor [Martin] Olave. But finally, when he could not hope to find assistance from elsewhere, he was ordered to complete it himself.

580.   *The Jesuits take over the Carmelite monastery at Vienna*

The King of the Romans himself, after recognizing this difficulty and realizing that the Carmelite monastery was readily available, wrote Father Ignatius that the large Carmelite monastery would soon be turned over to Ours, that [the King] would always be our protector, and that there would always be a way for Ours to teach the people from the pulpit or to instruct young people in that place. The King also wrote to the provincial of the Carmelites, directing him to turn over that monastery to Ours, promising that he himself would find a way to maintain those very few men [still left there]—indeed, only the prior. It seemed that old man eagerly hoped that this would happen, for he was left by himself and could not alone carry out the duties of the [monastery] church. . . . Indeed, he even asked the King to give him a parish; the King dealt with him on this matter after a letter of his provincial had called him [from the monastery] so that Ours could promptly move into that large building.

584.   *Reasons for setting up a boarding school at Vienna for young noblemen*

Toward the end of the year, negotiations got under way in Vienna about accepting a house for educating young secular noblemen under the care of the Society on the pattern of the German College. What mainly motivated Ours to agree to this was the vast lack of good training available in those places, and [Ours] hoped that this would be a excellent way of attracting some men to the Society. As experience taught, Germans found it very difficult to make the transition from the ordinary life of young Germans to the religious state. But trained at this [proposed] college, young men could be better disposed to accept the call of God.

Indeed, the thinking was that the young men already admitted to the Society should be sent to Rome, so that they could gain a better understanding of everything pertaining to the Institute of the Society. Father Ignatius was pleased that plans were underway to start such a college for lay students. The letters he had received from Ours gave him to understand that the help they received in our schools was insufficient to conserve and nourish those young men in the Catholic faith and religion, in the face of the corrupt behavior and [perverted] faith of their relatives and companions.

594.   *Parents at Cologne try to prevent their sons from becoming Jesuits*

The good reputation of the Society was daily increasing to such an extent that all the while there were many people who proved the truth of the saying of the Apostle "All who wish to live devoutly in Christ will suffer persecution" [2 Tim. 3:12]. The parents of sons who desired to serve Christ especially rose up against us like roaring lions and tried to draw their sons away from being taught a more perfect life. If neither threats nor coaxing sufficed, they called upon the secular arm, for they deemed it madness and a blot on their families' honor to renounce the things of the world and submit to the yoke of obedience.

■ **Belgium**

624.   *Priests at Louvain make the Spiritual Exercises*

Among other people, ten priests were guided through the Spiritual Exercises; not one among them would have been reluctant to enroll in the Institute of our Society, if only the circumstances and their responsibilities had allowed some of them to do this. Among them was the abbot of Liessies, a venerable person outstanding in piety, who was famous in Belgium and enjoyed great prestige with the Queen, who made use of his instruction in spiritual matters.[6] This abbot, I say, followed by five chosen religious of his monastery, including the prior, the director of the students, and the procurator, took turns in coming to Ours two by two and making the Spiritual Exercises. The abbot himself said that he and all his men were prepared to follow our Society, had the legislation of their order allowed it. What was impossible for him personally he considered encouraging others [to do]. He made serious efforts to send all the secular priests of his province to make the Spiritual Exercises. He soon sent one man who, after completing the Exercises, gave himself totally to the obedience

---

[6] The abbot was Francis Louis Blosius (1506–66), noted as a monastic reformer and spiritual writer. The queen was Mary of Hungary (1505–58), who was regent of the Netherlands from 1531 to 1552 for her brother, Charles V.

of the Society. Noble women also wanted to have the benefit of the same Exercises if Ours had had the time available for this. . . .

■ **France**

646.   *Troubles with members of the Parlement of Paris*

When on the day of the Purification of Mary [February 2], [Paschase Broët] visited many of the senators and asked them to support our cause, some of them offered their help, but some others were offended to an amazing degree [and made hostile]. One of them declared that the devil had drawn up the Institute of this Society and was its true founder. Father Paschase responded to him that he believed that the Holy Spirit was its founder, not the devil, who is not usually concerned to accomplish all the good works that the Society has undertaken throughout the whole world, even as far as the Indies. There was another, a senator, who screamed that we were superstitious, proud, and arrogant; he displayed such wrath that good Father Paschase could find no way to reply, since the senator would not listen to him. Instead of attempting a response, [Broët] armed himself with patience. But in the end, once [the senator's] anger had spent itself, the two parted as friends. In saying goodbye, Father asked him to recommend our Society as the Lord inspired him to speak.

The general procurator of the King, normally a pious Catholic, frankly confessed that he could not bring himself to support the confirmation of our privilege. By stating several reasons that seemed to affect the good of the state, he delayed the advancement of our cause. He clung to this position despite the pleas of the bishop of Claremont.

647.   *The troubles continue*

Father Paschase went to the principal president and begged him to expedite our business, for if the Parlement should decide something against our Society, we still had recourse to the King. But the president began to shout that there were more than enough religious orders and that, if we wanted to be religious, we should enter the order of Saint Francis or the Carthusians or some other one. When Father Paschase countered that the purpose of our Institute was different, he answered with great anger, "You don't perform miracles, do you, or do you think you are better than the other [orders]." . . .

Many objected that we had usurped the name "the Society of Jesus." They said, "So do we who are not members of your institute belong to the

Society of the devil?" I should add this, however: the same person who said that
the devil was the founder of the Society was not afraid to say in the hearing of
Father Paschase that the devil had been the leader of the Council of Trent. But
all those people denigrated us only with words; there was one man who thought
that Ours should be flogged with whips and banished from the University of
Paris.

648.   *The bishop and University of Paris attack the Jesuits*

Eventually the Parlement published a decision; choosing a fresh approach, it shed the entire burden from its own shoulders and transferred the duty
of reaching a judgment on this whole controversy to the bishop of Paris [Eus-
tace du Bellay] and the Faculty of Theology. It seemed quite clear that the
Parlement acted as it did to prevent the Society from gaining any advantage; for
its members could easily learn the attitude of the bishop and the doctors of
theology. Father Paschase carried the opinion of the Parlement, along with our
apostolic letters and privileges and the royal grant, to the bishop and the Faculty
of Theology. When he first came to the bishop, the latter sang the same familiar
tune as the others, that there were already quite enough religious orders—in
fact, more than enough without adding Ours to the number. When Father
Paschase said that the Supreme Pontiff had approved it and the Most Christian
King had also done so for this realm, [the bishop] answered that the Supreme
Pontiff could give his approval for territories subject to his own temporal
jurisdiction, but could not give approval for our order in the kingdom of France.
Nor could the King approve a religious order, for this was a spiritual matter.

So much for their first meeting. He added that, to the extent of his
powers, he would never allow our order to be admitted. On a second visit,
however, [Broët] found him more subdued. [Broët] had seen to it that some of
our friends enjoying considerable prestige (among them the bishop of Clermont)
would talk to the bishop. Father Ignatius at Rome also had Cardinal Maffeo
write to Cardinal du Bellay. [Maffeo] kindly performed this act of charity,
giving a glowing testimonial, as is clear from his letter.

653.   *Still more opposition in Paris*

These negotiations with the university were protracted for almost seven
months, and meanwhile the dean of the theologians tried to argue convincingly
that the Society should seek permission only to set up a college and to be able
to admit Ours to the theology curriculum and grant them the doctoral degree.

But he came to understand from Father Paschase that Ours were more interested in preaching good and sound doctrine than in taking degrees of this sort.

But when some suggested that the Society was indeed behaving itself well now, but would later become lax like the other religious orders, Father Paschase humbly responded that through God's grace [the Society] could just as well persevere in living as it should. Moreover, he went on to say, although it is still in doubt whether the Society would deteriorate in the course of time, it would be wise for the Church to use its services as long as it was behaving well. He also observed that those to whom they wanted to subject Ours could fall away themselves just as easily as we could. Nonetheless, [the authorities] gave it as their opinion that our privileges should not be approved, because the Church, [by which he meant] a council, had not approved them. The dean said explicitly that a pope could not give a privilege in contravention of the established hierarchical order, one that would impair the authority of bishops and pastors. When Father Paschase presented his own arguments, they said that what had been decreed by the sacred councils should be observed.

660.   *The generous support of the bishop of Clermont*

The bishop went down to his church of Clermont and requested that some of the Society be sent to him to help the hospital at Clermont by [hearing] confessions, preaching, and performing other charitable works there. That same autumn he wrote to Father Ignatius disclosing his often repeated prayer that, in a city of his diocese locally called Billom, [Ours] would restore the university, which was in almost total decline. Because, unfortunately, his efforts had thus far proved fruitless, he wrote that he was hoping that if Father Ignatius would send him some good and learned men, three or four in number, the divine Goodness might revive that university, which was now virtually at the point of death.

He had already taken steps to purchase buildings in the town, which he would be pleased to give to the Society. Meanwhile, he would provide for any of the brethren sent to him, ensuring that they would not be without anything that they needed. He asserted that in the meantime, judging that the [legal process] admitting the Society [to France] appeared likely to be long protracted, he was firmly determined not to wait for a favorable decision from the Parlement, but rather to donate for the use of the college at Paris the residence he used when visiting that city

■ **Spain**

676.   *Giving the Spiritual Exercises at Salamanca*

As regards the Spiritual Exercises, various fruitful results from them became obvious. Sometimes six, seven, or eight people at the same time made these meditations at our residence, and almost all of them gave evidence of a not negligible measure of progress. One man, prominent in the Spanish kingdoms, who had been separated from his wife for a long time, after having made the Exercises of the First Week and a general confession as well, abandoned the court of princes and returned to the favor and home of his wife. The bishop of Salamanca himself, who demonstrated a new love for Ours, asked to study the book of the *Exercises.* Dissensions, divorces, and quarrels among some people were set aright. After the leaders of two families that had been waging a violent feud confessed their sins at our residence, they were reconciled to one another.

683.   *The conversion of a sinful priest at Medina del Campo*

Day by day the number of those who attended such sermons increased. Among them was a certain nobleman who had taken sacred orders and been honored with a canonical dignity in the church of Salamanca. [Adopting] lay clothes to the great scandal of the people, he led a wicked life, thereby giving a terrible example—a situation that was not covert but obvious to all. On the day before the Sunday of the Incarnation [March 25], he was pierced by a dart of divine love, so he set his heart on bidding farewell to the pomps of this world and turning himself toward God with all his soul. Thus did he come to Ours, determined either to live forever with them or undertake in the future a better way of living. The sermons of Father [Juan] Bautista [Sanchez] had pleased him to a marvelous degree, even before his conversion. When somebody asked him why he did not go to hear another outstanding preacher instead who was preaching the word of God those days at Medina del Campo, he replied that Father Bautista's sermons had a signal effect on him because he knew that [Bautista] had turned his hand to [spiritual] works before he opened his mouth to speak.

699.   *Young José de Acosta moves a man to change his life*

Now that Ours were now making their way through the philosophy curriculum this autumn, Father Maximiliano Capella began lecturing to them in two courses of theology. But [Ours] also delivered lectures in two humane-letters courses. José de Acosta, the youngest of four brothers, recited some poems recounting the benefits [flowing from] Christ.[7] The Lord gave him such a powerful spiritual influence on the hearts of his audience, elevating them to the love of God, that one of those listening to him read was so moved to tears that he did not leave the gathering until he had thrown himself at the feet of a confessor and poured out the sins of his previous life; after that he began to change his conduct for the better. That same day, a larger number than usual also came to holy Communion.

719.   *The Jesuit community at Alcalá has to turn away candidates*

At the start of this year, thirty collegians were living at the College of Alcalá under their rector, Father Francisco Villanova. They kept very busy both practicing self-abnegation and pursuing their literary studies. One [of Ours] defended theses in the college three times each week, the first one in theology, the second in philosophy, and the third in logic, because some of Ours were studying in each of those faculties. Many other men wanted to be admitted to the Society; but the house was practically filled to capacity, so Father Villanova encouraged them to make progress in letters and virtue instead. Gradually he admitted some of them to replace other men who had been sent elsewhere. Sometimes, right after being accepted, those who were going to be admitted [to the novitiate] were sent away to other houses.

721.   *The Spiritual Exercises foster vocations at Alcalá*

Literary scholars and men endowed with other splendid talents were almost always making the Spiritual Exercises at our house. A certain famous man, a dignitary in one of the leading churches in that kingdom, and a good number of nobles besides garnered great spiritual advantage from such exercises. These happy results increased in number day by day, as did those who came to the house to hear us, as some encouraged others and drew them to Christ; so much was this the case that our priests could not satisfy these fervent and zealous men and their desire to go to confession, and still less could they [provide for all those desiring to make] the Spiritual Exercises.

There are many colleges at Alcalá for laymen, and previously students from these institutions had a reputation for leading very licentious lives—to the

---

[7] Acosta (1539?–1600), who had just entered the novitiate contrary to the wishes of his parents, later became the most famous Jesuit missionary and writer in Spanish America.

point that hardly anybody in the whole university seemed less studious than these. But as a result of discussions, sermons, the sacraments, and the example of others, they began to get hold of themselves; now they lived so devoutly and so many became interested in the Institute of our Society that those colleges must have seemed seedbeds for our Society, where men prepared themselves [to follow] a vocation from God to our Society by making daily progress in studies and virtues. [From] outside Alcalá also some people kept coming to make these Spiritual Exercises.

734.   *Prince Philip wants Father Araoz as a preacher*

Father Araoz could not refuse to honor the request that the legate made of him, even though he himself felt that he would be neglecting a harvest likely to become abundant. But the Lord compensated for this by offering him an equally bountiful crop at the court of the prince. The legate assigned to him the leading church at Madrid, where he began to preach on Sundays, Wednesdays, and Fridays. When Prince Philip learned from the legate that the provincial of the Society of Jesus was preaching at Madrid, he inquired whether he was Father Araoz; this was the name he knew him by and not by [the title of] provincial. When [Philip] discovered that this was indeed the case, he was delighted and directed that instructions be sent to [Araoz], warning him not to commit himself to deliver [a long series of] sermons until [the prince] decided how often he was going to preach at the palace itself. [Philip] sent the man in charge of his chapel, the brother of the Count of Luna, to inform Father Araoz that he would be preaching at the palace on Monday. . . . Lastly, the prince sent someone to notify [Araoz] . . . that he would also desire to have [Araoz] as preacher for that Lent. [Araoz] performed this to the great satisfaction of [the prince] himself and of the others. . . .

736.   *The advantage of having Jesuits at the Spanish courts*

Father Pedro de Tablares accompanied Father Araoz and helped him in tasks compatible with our Institute. Throughout the whole court, people came to hold a completely different impression of our Society than they had when there was no shortage of people intent on sowing discrediting opinions about Ours regarding several matters. God's providence [was at work], it seems, arranging that our Society had from its earliest days established its headquarters at the Roman Curia, so that it was known and approved there in the eyes of practically everybody; thus other regions paying obedience to the Apostolic See could more easily accept it. . . .

741.   *Former religious do not make good Jesuits*

Two priest were admitted to the Society who appeared to be useful workers. One was called Mendez, the other Bernardino. It seemed reasonable to grant them dispensations because they had for a time worn the habit of a different religious order. Experience in cases such as these has taught us that few such men will prove themselves suited for the Institute of the Society. Thus the first, fearing that he would be dismissed, left of his own accord, and the second was actually dismissed.

742.   *Araoz's dealings with Philip II and Nadal*

Father Araoz returned to Alcalá from the court of Prince [Philip] after having completed his duties there as preacher, having given great satisfaction to the prince and others. In private conversations the prince often listened to Father Araoz telling what the latter planned to do on matters conducive to the Kingdom's spiritual good. [Philip] showed great goodwill toward the Society. But because [Araoz] while in Madrid began suffering from a disease affecting his eyes and his heavy responsibilities did not allow him the leisure to care for [his eyes] and recover his health, he went to Alcalá, where subsequently he recuperated and regained his strength. . . .

I will not neglect to mention that among the other things he discussed privately with the prince, this important subject was included: he requested from [Philip] that bishops should not be employed in tasks outside their own dioceses. Rather, [Philip] should see to it that prelates resided in their own churches. The prince promised this, confirming this through Lord Rui Gómez, who came to Alcalá.[8]

While Father Araoz was staying at Alcalá, Father Nadal came there. He was hurrying on to Portugal, but delayed in that city three or four entire days and gave much consolation to all before resuming his journey. Before his departure, however, Father Araoz conferred with him about the methods and way of proceeding that he employed in his administration, and described the objectives that would govern him as he directed everything both in general and

---

[8] Rui Gómez de Silva was Philip II's chief minister during his years as regent and his early years as king of Spain.

in particular. Father Nadal approved everything, as he wrote to Araoz, who, encouraged by this confirmation from Ignatius himself, as it were, carried on as he had begun.

752.   *An Englishman desecrates the Eucharist in Portugal*

An incident in Portugal strongly promoted and increased a special devotion to this sacrament [of the Eucharist]. A bishop was celebrating Mass in the presence of the King and Queen, accompanied by all their children and a huge gathering of the nobility. Also present were many Spanish noblemen who had brought Juana, the daughter of Emperor Charles, to Portugal, where she was to marry the Prince of Portugal. With all of these worthies looking on, as I said, after the bishop had consecrated the blood of Christ, a certain Englishman, dressed in the garb of a nobleman, pretended to be praying at the steps to the altar; he suddenly ran up the steps, seized the chalice and host, poured out the blood, broke up the host, and threw the pieces on the ground. This mad sacrilege filled the court and Kingdom with grief. And although that deranged fellow was subjected to dire punishment, Father Francis [Borgia] thought that he should take advantage of this [incident] to exhort the people to a greater veneration of the sacred Eucharist. He did not consider that he had done enough [even] when, wherever he could go, he personally encouraged the people to pious devotion, but he also dispatched the others from the college at Oñate to various outlying regions where they could do the same for the greater honor of God and of this most holy Sacrament.

757.   *Countering Carnival at Pamplona*

In the days before Lent, many people, following their custom, ran about the city in masks, and on every hand many frivolities and unbecoming antics could be seen. Ours arranged to have some boys stage a procession with some of them in the lead carrying a crucifix; they marched through all the public streets of that city, visiting the churches on their way. In each of them they would kneel and loudly beg for God's mercy. So great a flock of people followed them wherever they went that not only did [some] boys discard their masks and silly trappings and join the procession, but people of advanced age did the same. Many let it be known that they had intended to leave their homes [wearing] masks and carrying on in bizarre ways, but they gave up their plans after they saw and heard the procession.

Some people stayed in the city that whole Lent, so that they could continue with the task of teaching Christian doctrine that had already begun. One of them was a student of Father Didaco; others were scattered through other places. On Sunday mornings and at lunch time during that same Lent, Father Miguel Navarro preached at Pamplona in addition to teaching and drilling his listeners in Christian doctrine. Uncommon indeed was the fruit for souls nurtured by his work and that of his companions. Especially the boys and girls who were learning Christian doctrine from him were attached to that father with such loving affection that when they found out that he was leaving soon, they displayed their grief with abundant weeping and tears. Many people offered money for priests to say Masses begging the Lord's grace that Ours would return there.

787.   *Francis Borgia invents a card game for the princess*

Right on the feast of the birth of the Blessed Virgin, Father Francis devised a sort of lottery that Princess Juana with her entourage learned. The names of the virtues of the Blessed Virgin were written on many cards and placed in one receptacle, while cards bearing the names of all those [in the entourage] were deposited in another one. The name of a person was picked up from one container, and the name of a virtue from another. The woman whose name was pulled out was required, during the whole octave of the Blessed Virgin, to practice the virtue on the card that she had drawn. Accompanying the virtues on these cards were brief, pious prayers that so charmed and helped those noble women that each one was careful to have her prayer transcribed into her book of hours so she could keep on saying it. The Queen herself wanted to have a copy of these cards, and the princess, Lady Maria, was so [enthralled] that this seemed to be almost the sole topic of conversation in the palace. The King was especially happy when he saw that after the arrival of Father Francis Princess Juana was very joyous when in the company of her attendants. Previously she had somehow not manifested such cheerful emotions, perhaps because of [her reaction to] the change of country and the different customs of the people.[9]

789.   *Jesuit ministries to the women of the Portuguese court*

Father Francis left Lisbon after little more than one month. In that time Princess Juana and her retainers adopted the custom of going to confession,

---

[9] Princess Juana was the sister of Philip II.

some every eighth day, some every fifteenth day; entering this palace at that time was like entering a religious house. Visitors found some women going to confession, some praying, some talking about the things of God. All exhibited great desires to serve him. Because inconstancy usually shows up in everybody, but in a special way in the female sex, Father Francis took care to ensure that this practice would be permanent by leaving someone in his place to follow up on what he had begun so admirably. Thus, he entered into an agreement first with Princess Juana and then with the Queen, in terms of which somebody from our Society would go there every Sunday and feast day afternoon to teach Christian doctrine to those noble young ladies and all the other matrons and housekeepers. After Father Francis himself had departed, this custom was put into practice for some Sundays and feast days, and everybody willingly came to these instructions rather than indulge in the other frivolities with which they used [to amuse themselves]. They seemed to bewail the time when they did not have this instruction from the fathers of the Society of Jesus, and they showed that they regarded the Society with marvelous affection.

808. *Polanco's father leaves money to the Society*

I will add a few other things written by Father Ignatius before completing my treatment of this province. When Father Francisco Estrada was transacting the purchase of a house in Burgos, he informed [Ignatius] that a certain nobleman who had a son in the Society had left in his will five hundred gold pieces or a smaller sum that his sons might dispense as they saw fit.[10] But Father Estrada arranged for Lord Benedetto Uguccioni to dispose of the funds realized from this will, feeling confident that Father Ignatius would approve of this move. But when Father Ignatius heard about this, he did not approve of it. [He was displeased] that Father Estrada, without consulting him, had urged his lay friend to write to the father and that meanwhile he had turned over the sum as if it had already been [accepted and] allocated for the use of that college. Although he objected that proper procedure had not been observed, he left the wife of the deceased testator and his eldest son free to expend that legacy on pious works. Still, it was clear that they were going to carry out the dispersal already arranged by Lord Benedetto Uguccioni.

---

[10] Polanco gives no hint in his text that he is speaking here about his father and himself, perhaps out of modesty. For a clarification of the identities, see *Chron.,* 3:368 n2.

810.   *Loyola forbids the introduction of choir at Burgos*

When some of Ours thought that [chanting the Divine Office in] choir should be undertaken in the chapel of our house in Burgos, Father Ignatius forbade it. Neither did he want it to be called a professed house until a college separate from it had been established. He did not approve of the site that had been accepted, because there was no room for expansion. Thus, in the course of time [the college would have] to be moved [to a more suitable site].

811.   *Should a Jesuit reside at the Spanish court?*

Father Araoz asked Father Ignatius whether he should reside for a time at the court of King Philip. [Ignatius] judged that this was possible when the prince showed an attitude that was kindly and supportive of the Society's works and [disposed to] using its services in important matters.

812.   *Should scholastics be pulled out of studies to staff the colleges?*

When Father Ignatius agreed to opening schools at Burgos and Medina del Campo, he recognized that in order to have a good supply of teachers available, it was necessary for some [of Ours] to interrupt their courses in philosophy and theology and take on teaching duties. But he was of the opinion that it was more important to strive for the universal good that he believed would eventually flow from the schools than it was to avoid any inconvenience that individual [Jesuit scholastics] might experience [by having their studies interrupted]. When they asked him whether they were permitted to hire a lay teacher if the Society did not have teachers available, he replied that this too could be done.

813.   *Ignatius decides tricky questions regarding benefices*

When Doctor Jerónimo de Vergara wished to put two of Ours temporarily in charge of two parish churches, so that they could later be united to the college at Alcalá or, when the occasion arose, be exchanged for unencumbered benefices better suited for such a union, Father Ignatius did not give his approval for one of Ours to accept such parish benefices even for a limited time, not even with the expectation that they could later be applied to the college. Nonetheless, if there was somebody who was not yet known to be a member of our Society, even if he desired to be admitted to it, [Ignatius] had no objections to allowing such a person to accept such benefices for the time being while [union of them with the college] was being arranged.

817.   *Should men of Jewish or Moorish ancestry be admitted to the Society?*

Because some were of the conviction that new Christians, as they were called in Spain (meaning men with Jewish or Moorish ancestry or men with some relatives of that stock), should not be admitted to the Society, an official reply was issued to the effect that Father Ignatius could not convince himself that it would be to God's honor to exclude such men.[11] Still, greater caution and perspicacity were required in testing and admitting such men. In view of the contrary attitudes of the court and of the Prince himself, however, prudence seemed to dictate that we not admit such men in that kingdom; but those who were otherwise suitable could be sent to Italy, where ancestry of this sort could do little or nothing to affect their standing [in church and state].

823.   *A candidate in Valencia refuses to be turned away*

The arrival of Father Nadal was extremely welcome to Ours and also to lay people, for the viceroy and his wife received him most warmly and deeply regretted that eventually he would depart from there. While he was in Valencia, many students begged him to admit them to the Society. Aware that the war between the Emperor and the King of France had closed [the borders], effectively preventing them from being sent to Italy or Sicily without [undue complications], he urged them to persevere [in their desires].[12]

But one young man's holy importunity is worth recording. After being rejected, he entered the house one night carrying his baggage and humbly begged [Ours] to admit him, so that he could dig in the garden, which was very large. When Father Nadal, who had recently arrived there, and Father [Pedro de] Tablares tried to send the lad away, he proclaimed that there was no way he would leave the house. When they told him the house was poor, he answered that it did not matter because he had not come to eat but to work. When they added that there was no place for him to sleep, he replied that he had not come to sleep. Moved with pity at last, Father Nadal allowed him to sleep that night in the college; the next day he could consider himself as admitted, but he should return home till an opportunity arose to send him elsewhere. He accepted this condition for staying on; but the next day he again refused to leave, so Father

---

[11] Polanco drafted Loyola's reply on August 14, 1553, and sent it to Antonio de Araoz.

[12] The need to send the candidates to Italy or Sicily suggests they were New Christians.

Nadal thought it best to have him examined. They found out that he had studied philosophy and theology and was gifted with a good head and sturdy health. Even more, he was a nobleman and the son of the regent of Aragon. His persistent desire to flee the dangers of the world and to seek asylum in the Society superseded their resolution not to admit anyone at that time. Another man also was admitted with him.

830.   *Putting a check on the Carnival at Onteniente*

Some days after Father Bautista [de Barma] had arrived in Gandía, he preached for the last time to the people on Septuagesima Sunday and greatly stirred their hearts by taking them to task for delighting in [lofty] words but never carrying them into action. Moving on toward Onteniente, on the way there he invigorated the hearts of the people of Cocentaina by [discoursing on] gospel themes. When he preached on Quinquagesima Sunday at Onteniente, he so moved the citizens that they wholly abandoned some foolishness that was everywhere a deeply entrenched custom. By public decree people were forbidden to go about in disguise or to dance to the tune of flute players, drummers, and those singing lascivious songs. They were not to follow their custom of dumping water from their windows and dousing passers-by, nor were they to play games during the entire season of Lent. Those who flouted this ban would be punished with a fine or imprisonment. When six or seven teenagers did something in contravention of the decree, they were thrown into the prison until Father Bautista pleaded for their release. Everything was silent the night [of Mardi Gras] before the first day of Lent, and it almost defied belief that so many people could have passed that night so quietly.

831.   *Old hatreds are put aside*

There was a rift between the priests and the town officials, but a single conversation with Father Bautista restored them to friendship. Two priests had disagreements with some laymen whom they had excommunicated in church for having committed some crime. By the efforts of Father [Bautista], they were reconciled amid tears on both sides, and the earlier good reputation of the laymen was publicly restored in the church.

When, in the course of one of his Lenten sermons, [Bautista] spoke at length about loving our enemies, a priest came up to him and said he wanted to make peace with his enemy. Another man, seized by even more intense emotions, went over to his enemy, fell on his knees, and asked pardon, eliciting no little amazement from the latter. Another made peace with a man whose throat he had previously wanted to slit. They both came to Father Bautista and discussed making peace with [their enemies]. Another man who for many years had treated one of his parents with hatred, inspired now [by the exhortations] of Father Bautista, converted that [hatred] into love. . . . Among those listening to his sermon was a man who for two days had lain in wait for his enemy with a pistol (commonly called a "harquebus") . . . near a path along which he thought his enemy would be passing. Overwhelmed by the word of God and bewailing his crime, he came to his senses.

836. *Liturgical changes at Gandía*

Before he left for Portugal the provincial of Aragon [Simão Rodrigues] visited the college at Gandía and gave it as his judgment that the chanting, which had become the practice in that college, should gradually be eliminated. He also thought that the brothers should go to Communion only on Sundays and the more solemn feast days. Still, he ordered the rector to consult with Father Ignatius on both these matters.

850. *The holy death of Teresa Rajadell*

The exertions of Ours were of benefit to several nuns at Barcelona; Lady Rajadell had been their leader for some time.[13] Well known to Father Ignatius, she was outstanding for her abundant gifts from God. At this time, when she was about to depart for a better life, she asked Father Jean Cheralt that in her name he ask Father Ignatius, through the wounds of Jesus Christ, not to let Ours stop helping her convent, in which many excellently disposed nuns yearned for reform. As her death drew near, speaking privately to each of them and publicly to the abbess and all the nuns, Rajadell encouraged them to this reform. She bore herself at the very end of her life with so much spirit and charity that two of Ours who were assisting her on her deathbed were in amazement. They judged that so touching an scene could have stirred even the hearts of men of faith. Hence, after her death several [nuns] yearned with fervent desires to reform their lives, and so Ours for a time extended their spiritual services to that convent.

---

[13] Rajadell was the leader of eleven nuns who desired to reform the Convent of Santa Clara at Barcelona, which originally followed the rule of the Poor Clares but later the Benedictine rule. Most of the nuns were of noble descent and were inclined to a lax observance. Loyola got to know Rajadell during his student days at Barcelona. Several of Loyola's earliest letters, rich in spiritual advice, were written to her.

■ **Portugal**

856.   *Manpower problems in the new colleges of Portugal*

Father Ignatius encouraged Ours in Portugal to devote themselves not only to opening schools but also to establishing a professed house separate from a college. Although at the start of this year teachers capable of lecturing were at hand, Father Torres was of the view that it would still be a very good idea if some men trained in teaching methods were sent there from Italy. . . . [Torres] admitted that he did not see anyone in all of Spain who was suited to establish new colleges, with the exception of the men who were already occupied in that work. He also warned Father Ignatius that because the good success of a whole college depended on its head, he should give his attention to [remedying] the scarcity of qualified men.

857.   *Problems in Portugal*

As regards a professed house, there was hope for one if people could see good results from a college. [Torres] considered that what Father Ignatius had decided would be very useful, namely, that every province should send one man a year to Rome. He explained as well his reason for being so deeply committed to choosing some of his leading fathers to be sent to India. It was that men's aspirations to go to the infidels were growing more tepid, especially among those who were talented and learned; so it seemed good to persuade [them] by [taking concrete] steps that men of this stamp were also being trained for this purpose. The cardinal-prince was also urging that he strive to persuade the Society of this truth. . . .

[Torres] himself warned that experience had taught that the devil had done the greatest harm to the houses of the Society in Portugal because some of the superiors there had not laid as deep a spiritual foundation as was needed. Also, he declared that he did not regard such men as suited for undertaking the new colleges being offered to them unless Father Ignatius sent them, after training them himself and using his own methods. Indeed, he averred that men of this stamp could not be of much use even if they were sent to already established colleges.

859.   *The King opposes Rodrigues's return to Portugal*

The King was displeased when he learned that Father Simão had come to Portugal without authorization from Father Ignatius; he made it known that he did not want [Rodrigues] to remain in the kingdom of Portugal. He also commanded the Duke of Aveiro, with whom [Rodrigues] was staying, to cease patronizing Father Simão in this realm, even if [Rodrigues] wanted [to stay] there because of his poor health and without holding any office. Thus [Rodrigues], even though he had come to Lisbon, returned to Spain and from there journeyed on to Italy, as we reported above.

860.   *The troubles in Portugal continue*

It was easy to see how necessary was the promulgation and explanation of the *Constitutions* when one considered how the scholastics interpret the vows they took in Portugal and observed the many problems associated with this faulty understanding. Some of those who had left asked to have the possessions that they had applied to the Society returned to them, and Ours thought that this should be done. During the first months of this year, many of those who had remained at San Fins left the Society. Thus, of all those who had been sent there, only one remained in the Society; although he was a scholastic, he wanted to serve the Society doing the work of the coadjutors. Melchior Ludovicus, who also had taught a course in arts and had been sent with Don Theutonius [the brother of the Duke of Bragança] to Alcalá, returned to Portugal with Father Simão, but not to the Society. Another preacher, Alfonso Tellez, who worked very successfully almost the whole year in the town of Mora, came to his mother's house but not to the college. No reason at all did he offer to explain his motivation, except that he may have feared being sent to India. Thus, those who were among us but were not of us gradually separated themselves from the others and left the Society purified.

873.   *Men return from Asia. Should Xavier return to Portugal?*

This September four ships from India reached Portugal; aboard them were two of our men sent by Father Francis Xavier. One was Andreas Carvallo, a nobleman admitted in India; the other was Andreas Fernandez, who went to Rome and later returned to India. With him was a Japanese named Bernard, sent by [Xavier] so that he might return to his people after being better trained. Later he went on to Portugal and Rome. . . . Certainly, as we will show later, no one could say that his trip to Europe was not of benefit to him. [Miró] reported [in a letter] that the King of Portugal, the cardinal-prince, and Prince Luís approved of recalling Father Francis Xavier from India because, even though he was doing very necessary work in India, one could hope that his work in these regions would yield even greater fruit. The King wrote along the same lines to Father Ignatius, while thanking him for being so energetic about fostering the spiritual welfare of his kingdoms; he also made explicit reference to the coming of Father Nadal and the foundation of schools.

874.   *The* Spiritual Exercises *are printed in Portugal*

This year the *Spiritual Exercises* were sent to Portugal and were printed there. [The Portuguese Jesuits] were forbidden to allow them to fall indiscriminately into the hands of [non-Jesuits]. Complying with Father Ignatius's desires, Father Miró saw to it that the letters from India and Brazil were translated into Spanish before they were printed.

880.   *A Jesuit confessor for the King of Portugal*

As was noted [in our account of] the previous year, when the King urged Ours to hear his confession, they refused for serious reasons and then consulted Father Ignatius. In his reply Father Ignatius criticized them for having denied the King so reasonable a request. He also bade them show this letter to the King. But when the King took on somebody else as confessor, Ours thought it was not a good idea to show this communication to the King for fear the suspicion might linger in his mind that Ours [now] wanted to hear his confession. Still, they thought the matter should be discussed with Prince Luís, who had shown himself a very close friend. When he had read the letters of Father Ignatius with the warmest affection and [observed that] Ignatius had ordered nothing in virtue of obedience, he offered as his opinion that if the King had any further desires for their services, they should not refuse him; at that time they should show him Father Ignatius's letter. But if the King asked nothing more of Ours, the letter should not be shown to him. Ours followed his very prudential advice. The King, however, who understood that our reason for not taking on the task of hearing his confession stemmed from humility and a determination to flee from honors, showed no more annoyance toward Ours on this matter.

885.   *The troubles in Portugal abate*

The great throng of young men received [into the Society] at Coimbra without careful selection made governing them difficult. Thus, when some had left freely and others who were not suited for our Institute were dismissed, only those remained who gave themselves wholeheartedly to the grace and spirit of

God. The criticisms uttered both by those who had been in the Society and by those who were linked to them by friendship or blood, reached the ears of many leading people; but now these yielded to the power of truth. After Father Simão [Rodrigues's] second departure, when the Society had been purged of those who had tainted it, the remaining members took on a new fervor for attaining perfection; now they recognized that so much perfection was contained in the newly published *Constitutions* that at last they seemed to understand the true spirit of the Society and to sense a rich and superabundant influx of divine grace. The King too is said to have been moved to great joy when he carefully examined those *[Constitutions],* and he asked for a written copy of them.

887.   *More progress in Portugal*

The order of our Society and the distinction of grades became evident this autumn in Portugal. Not only did the *Constitutions* cast [more brilliant] light but so too did actually carrying them into practice and setting up the various divisions and grades of the Society. Most important, the professed house at Lisbon was separated from the college. Residents in that house were divided into the professed and the coadjutors in matters both spiritual and temporal. There was a distinct order for novices, who lived in the house of probation; matters at the College of Saint Anthony remained as they were before. The question was raised with the King and then, at his command, with the city whether they wanted a college at Lisbon to be built similar to those of the Society in Italy and Sicily. [If so, Ours] would teach three classes of grammar and two other classes of humanities and rhetoric, besides Greek and Hebrew and another class devoted to discussing and resolving cases of conscience.

888.   *The new Jesuit college at Lisbon*

This scheme for structuring a college pleased everybody, and when they brought the matter to the King (without whose consent none of the financial resources of the city could be disbursed), he delegated his chief advisor, our very good friend, to get classes underway as soon as possible in the name of both the King and of the city. He vigilantly watched out to see that the project lacked nothing necessary for it. Thus was the college inaugurated amid the warmest applause of the citizenry. Classes began on the very feast of Saint Luke [October 18] with such a crush of students that the city imposed on the Society the obligation of admitting citizens of Lisbon to the class before outsiders. . . .

890.   *Obtaining a church at Lisbon for the professed house*

Father Nadal urged that a suitable place be sought where those who were professed in the Society might live and fittingly carry out their work. The Church of Saint Roch seemed well suited and situated, located in a fine location as it was and unburdened with parish responsibilities. The matter was brought to the King and his brother, Prince Luís. The church belonged to some confraternity members who initially proved rather uncooperative; pressure brought to bear on them by those [two] princes, in addition to the energetic support of Lord Pedro Mascarenhas, resulted in the confraternity's consenting to Ours' being sent to take possession of it.

904.   *Spiritual development of Bernard from Japan*

Paul from Hormuz grew more than a little in virtue and goodwill toward the Society, but he did not set his heart on [entering] a religious order; instead, he wished to return to India so he could be of help to others. The Japanese Bernard far surpassed him, however. He had come to Europe with the intention of returning to Japan; but later he made so much spiritual progress that he no longer had any concern about his patrimony or homeland or any created thing; instead, he was intent only on the service of his Creator, whom he wanted to serve in a religious order. If the Society did not accept him, he had decided to enter another order. He was gifted with outstanding talent but was even more remarkable for his humility and obedience. He learned to read and write virtually without a teacher. Father Nadal wanted to admit him to the house of probation at Coimbra.

905.   *Troubles at Coimbra*

At the start of this year, the rector of this college was Father Manuel Godinho, but in the course of this very year he was called to Lisbon, leaving in his stead Father Leo Enriquez. During the first months there was considerable turmoil in that college because of the many men who had left the Society, as we stated above. The departure of these men took on great significance among the laity and even among some of Ours, with the result that the devotion of many laypeople grew cold and some of Ours became afflicted in spirit. But many, including the princes, who were endowed with a more perceptive spirit judged quite otherwise, for they could understand that the excessive rigor about which those who had left complained was not [really] excessive. Rather, they called it excessive strictness when they were not permitted to do everything just as they pleased. If sometimes some mitigation of the rule was allowed, those whose imperfection had brought about the relaxation usually transformed it into something noxious. Some of those who remained did not have a completely wholesome attitude. One of these was Father Manuel Fernandez; when he was sent to Lisbon along with others, he left the group. But the next day, as if the Lord had opened his eyes, he came to himself again and poured out many tears over the dark shadows [lurking in] his heart; now he began to treat with a singular love men whom he had previously regarded with animosity.

907. *Sick Jesuits ask to be sent to Brazil*

In early spring the question arose of sending some men to Brazil. Some who were suffering from sicknesses asked to be sent there, advancing the argument that in the opinion of the doctors their malady was virtually incurable, rendering them useless in Portugal (the doctor had given up hope of healing them). In Brazil they could at least do something useful in teaching the basics of Christian doctrine. Meanwhile, according to the opinion of the doctor, a change of air could perhaps provide a remedy for their sickness. At least they hoped to die out of love for God while serving him somehow. Some of these men were sent to Brazil; after they had reached their destination, it became known that, in the course of the voyage, the supreme heavenly Doctor had restored to them the health of which the earthly doctors had despaired. . . .

909. *Improvements in Portugal*

Father [Miguel] Torres gave instructions that some of the Coimbra priests who had been dispersed to various places of the kingdom to [hear] confessions and preach should return, so that he could confer with them about their progress. Then they were to gather at the College of Coimbra. A certain letter of Father Ignatius dealing with obedience and abnegation arrived at this time and did much to console and stimulate the collegians.[14] Each week a fairly large troop of boys and older men came to Ours at Coimbra from the villages surrounding the city, for fifteen or sixteen brethren circulated through those places. Although they suppressed feuds and did many other good things, as summer approached they gave up this ministry because it was most detrimental to their studies.

---

[14] This is clearly his famous letter of March 16, 1553, on obedience, which was sent to the turbulent Portuguese Province.

914.   *New men enter the Society at Coimbra*

From this same college five men were sent to India and seven to Brazil; many others ardently begged for the same mission but were not granted their request. About this same time, four young men with excellent prospects were admitted to the Society and began to occupy the places of those who were leaving. One of them who was studying theology and was inclined to enter the Society was conversing with one of the men who had once lived with Ours. When he inquired of him why he had not persevered in the calling he had entered upon, the man replied that he found it more than he could endure to live with men who were trying to make you holy, whether you wanted it or not. The young man, who craved exactly this above all, immediately decided to enter the Society and approached [superiors to that end].

924.   *Nadal explains the* Constitutions *at Coimbra*

Father Jerónimo Nadal came to Coimbra in October; his long-awaited arrival spread great spiritual joy and enthusiasm among the collegians. On the very day he arrived, he began to promulgate the *Constitutions.* To make them all the more clearly understood, he delivered several discourses to the collegians that explained the Institute of the Society. Daily for about an hour he lectured to all the brethren gathered together, clarifying for them the end of the Society and its way of proceeding. He stayed at that college until the end of October and took pains to arrange everything both in general and in particular according to the specifications of the *Constitutions.*

940.   *Starting a new college at Évora*

Right on the day of the Beheading of Blessed John the Baptist, that is, August 29, public instruction in grammar got under way. The school had three classes of grammar and humanities, with Master Pedro Perpiña in charge of the teachers. Shortly thereafter, another of the brethren, Marco Jorge by name, began teaching cases of conscience, for he had earlier passed his examination in theology. When Perpiña gave a Latin oration to inaugurate the academic year, the cardinal wanted to be present, as did a large crowd of people. [The cardinal] was absolutely delighted at what he had heard, as he related to Father Nadal, with whom he was transacting some other business that same day. As was usually the case, [the cardinal] graciously agreed to everything that was suggested. The cardinal took care of acquiring good bookcases for the new college.

. . .

960.   *Nadal and the former Jesuits*

After Father Nadal had dealt with Ours, he wished to meet with some of the more important men who had left the Society. He spoke lovingly with them and assured them that the Society would deal with them the way God dealt with all people, namely, it would forget past faults and would remember the good things they had once done if they would seriously return to their better selves in the spirit of humility and obedience. Although he accomplished little with these men, this kindness greatly satisfied laypeople; but [awareness of his kindness] with good reason threw up a wall dividing Ours from men such as these. Also those who had left could not help but be ashamed. Father Ignatius had written that insofar as possible such men, especially those who were endowed with greater talent, should be drawn back to the Society. He also recommended that they be sent to Rome if they seemed more likely to make progress there than in Portugal.

970.   *Loyola's confidence in Nadal*

Before I cease reporting on Father Nadal and his activities, I will add this: When Father Ignatius sent him as commissary to Spain and Portugal, besides the letters sent to princes and many other people, showing how confident he was, he gave [Nadal] many blank pages to be used for both private letters and letters patent, each bearing his signature and stamped with the seal of the Society. On these blanks [Nadal] could write what he judged would be best in the Lord. [Ignatius] gave him twofold instructions, some secret and others public. As regards the proper promulgation of the *Constitutions,* imposing the proper structure on classes, and solving problems and similar matters, the letters patent could prove that Ignatius had given him authority over all these things. The secret instructions committed to [Nadal] regarded his dealings with Father Simão [Rodrigues]; but on this matter almost nothing had to be prescribed in detail because right before [Nadal] arrived in Portugal, Simão left.

[Nadal] had authority to accept colleges; but Father Ignatius warned that it seemed better to accept them [only] in the more advantageous places and in a way that did not weaken the colleges which had already been accepted. Even though Father Ignatius had commanded that five or six or more men be admitted to profession, or even more if they seemed qualified, no more than three were actually admitted, because in the judgment of Father Nadal the [usual] process had already been set in motion.

THE YEAR 1554

■ **The Society in general**

1.   *Overview of the Society in 1554*

At the beginning of this year, our Society had seven discrete provinces: the first was India, in which Ours had residences in twelve places, namely, Hormuz, Basain, Tana, Goa, Cochin, Caulan, Comurin, Saint Thomas, Malaha, Mauchum, Amagucium, and Bungo. The second was Brazil, where Ours [also] resided in four places, namely, Salvador (Bahia), Espirito Santo, Porto Securo and São Vicente. The third province was Portugal, where Ours had houses in five places: Lisbon (the professed house at St. Roch and the college at Saint Antonio) and, in addition, Coimbra, Évora, and San Fins. The fourth province was Castile, where Ours resided in seven places, namely, Oñate, Burgos, Valladolid, Medina del Campo, Salamanca, Alcalá, and Cordoba. The fifth was the province of Aragon, where four colleges had been started, namely, at Valencia, Gandía, Saragossa, and Barcelona. The sixth was the province of Italy (not including Rome), where Ours lived in eight colleges, namely, in Venice, Padua, Ferrara, Bologna, Modena, Florence, Perugia, and Gubbio. The seventh province was Sicily, where Ours carried on their ministries in three colleges, namely, in Messina, Palermo, and Monreale.

2.   *Jesuit residences directly under Loyola's control*

The other colleges and houses were under the direction of Father Ignatius without constituting a distinct province, namely, in Italy at Naples and Tivoli (besides the professed house and the Roman and German colleges), in France at Paris, in Belgium at Louvain, in lower Germany at Cologne, and in Austria at Vienna. Therefore, the Society had fifty-two residences, leaving out of consideration the gigantic Congo and Corsica and other places where Ours had not as yet a fixed residence.

With the year 1554 *Chron.*, vol. 4 begins.—ED.

3. *Overall growth*

At the start of this year, the professed [fathers] numbered thirty-three; of the ten First [Companions], six were still alive and are included in the number just given. The total number of Ours increased almost everywhere, although it was lower this past year in Portugal.

■ **Rome**

4. *Numbers grow at Rome*

The number of Ours in Rome increased greatly, in part on account of the men being admitted, who were rather numerous, and in part because of those who were sent to Rome for studies or for other reasons. In the month of May of this year, there were 120 of Ours, more or less. Many [of them], as will be noted below, were sent to new colleges, but still toward the end of the year they climbed to 140. Fewer men were sent elsewhere than were admitted.

5. *Sickness at Rome*

Almost forty of Ours, among them Father Ignatius himself, suffered from a form of catarrh accompanied by fevers, a sickness that caused a great deal of distress in Italy this year. The larger and more select group of these [140] lived at the [Roman] College, where there were seventy of Ours the aforesaid May, though later the number increased. Some worked at the German College, supervising or helping the young men; the rest lived at the professed house. Many had been sent from lower Germany, namely, Louvain and Cologne. A good number had also been summoned from Spain, so that we could carry out the many tasks already undertaken. The rest came to Rome from Italy, for at that time it was unusual to admit men for probation except at Rome.

10. *Growth of the Roman College*

This year our college flourished not only in the number and talent of our scholastics but also in the number of extern students. The classes of rhetoric, humane letters, and grammar grew in size, and the advanced classes of the college did so as well, for a good number took various courses in philosophy and those offered by the Theology Faculty, as much as the circumstances prevailing at that time would allow. It was our students at the German College—men who had laid a solid foundation in their lower courses—who brought the greatest consolation to our best teachers, proving that their hard work was worthwhile. Students like this were better equipped to make progress in the higher courses. With the passage of time, the extern students who had made progress in philosophy began to study theology, also giving promise of a rich harvest. The public disputations held in our church over a period of eight days near the end of October enhanced the good repute of the college. On three days theological theses from the Old and New Testament and from Scholastic theology were defended; on four days [theses] from natural and moral philosophy and mathematics and metaphysics were disputed. The eighth day was given to rhetoric and languages, namely, Latin, Greek, and Hebrew. . . .

12. *Progress at the German College*

At the start of this year, the German College was flourishing quite well. Pope Julius III and the cardinals paid the expenses of its sixty [students]; but Father Ignatius wrote to Louvain, Cologne, and Vienna, [asking] them to send still more students to that college, men giving evidence of being endowed with good character and suited to the regimen enforced at the college. Those engaged in both theological and lower studies notably advanced in letters by assiduously attending lectures and disputations; they made equal advances in good behavior and zeal for devout living. By giving addresses and sermons, they sharpened their skills in both Latin and the vernacular languages. They experienced not only the solicitous charity of our Society in training them but also the paternal generosity of the Supreme Pontiff toward them and that of the leading cardinals as well. To protect their health for the labors exacted by their studies, twice a week during the afternoon they were conducted out of Rome for recreation, so that after this respite they might return reinvigorated and eager for their studies.

Instructions were given that, if everybody could not be sent from Upper Germany, men could also be sent from Gelderland, Cleves, and Friesland if they possessed outstanding qualities and were schooled at least in humane letters, so that they could be quickly admitted to study logic. Men from Upper Germany were accepted even if they were less advanced in literary studies. Some men could also be sent from England, Denmark, Sweden, and other northern regions, provided they possessed good talent and character.

20. *Requests for Jesuits to work in Poland*

An earnest request came from the kingdom of Poland for a preacher from our Society to come there to preach the word of God to the Queen, who was the daughter of the King of the Romans. Also the bishop of Ermeland,

Doctor Stanislaus Hosius, a man outstanding for his learning and piety and celebrated for his writings against the heretics, urgently requested ten of Ours to start a college in Prussia (which is a province beyond Poland adjacent to the northern sea and near the Tatars).[2] Although it was impossible to satisfy his request at that time, it became feasible in later years when we accepted a college at Braniewo.

23.   *Toward a college at Prague*

In a letter to Father Ignatius this year, the King of the Romans requested that the Society undertake a new college in Prague, the capital of the kingdom of Bohemia. Although Father Ignatius could not open another college this year, in his response to the King of the Romans, he promised that within one year we would do so. And this we did. . . .

■   **Italy**

44.   *Financing a college at Genoa*

When the [government] officials grew most enthusiastic about the preliminaries to inaugurating a college and saw that many leading citizens were very well disposed toward the Society, they decreed that the council of their magistrates, who represent the republic, would discuss the allocation of fixed revenues [to this cause]. Father Laínez dissuaded them from pursuing this matter if it should seem probable that the subsidy they were requesting from public funds would be denied. Burdened by the expenses of the Corsican war, they excused themselves from providing public funding, but many private citizens and wealthy men offered everything necessary for starting and maintaining the college. Some offered money, others sources of perpetual funding. Among them was a man who offered three hundred gold scudi a year. Others offered other sums for a fixed number of years.

46.   *Laínez and the usury problem*

It also happened that when Father Laínez vigorously declaimed against contracts entailing usury, the more prominent citizens were disturbed and promised the suffragan and vicar of the archbishop that in the name of the

---

[2] It seems unlikely that the Latin *tartaris* here refers to the infernal regions. Translating it "near the Tatars" seems to lead to a geographical impossibility. "Tartary" has also in the past been used to refer vaguely to what we think of as Russia, which is a plausible meaning here.—ED.

republic they would order certain merchants to explain the rationale behind their contracts and, furthermore, that they would convoke theologians and lawyers to decide what was licit and what was not in such contracts. Moreover, [the leading citizens] decided to send these confusing cases to Bologna; then, after the theologians there had discussed the matter, they would refer the whole issue to the Apostolic See, which could authoritatively determine what was licit and what was forbidden. But they very much wanted to keep Father Laínez involved in examining these exchanges and other contracts because he seemed impervious to the deceits associated with such matters. . . .

49.   *The Milanese want a Jesuit college*

At this time several citizens of Milan wrote most earnestly to their friends at Genoa requesting that they take steps to have Father Laínez or two others of the Society come to [Milan], where they wanted to start a new college. But Father Laínez believed that this request had to be rejected for now and deferred until a more propitious time, when their petition could be granted. Father Ignatius gave his approval to this response.

88.   *The failure of Jesuit ministries at Gubbio*

Just as we spoke about [the personnel for] two new colleges being sent out from Rome this year, so we will speak also of the suppression of [the college] at Gubbio. As could be inferred from what we discussed last year, the people of Gubbio were devoted to military activities rather than to literary and spiritual pursuits. They allowed us to reap only a meager harvest for the Lord's granary [despite our labors in conducting] classes, hearing confessions, preaching, teaching Christian doctrine, and performing other pious works. Moreover, because Ours had neither their own house nor their own church, and no steady income either (although the generosity of the Cardinal of the Holy Cross [Marcello Cervini] did not allow them to lack for anything), it did not seem defensible to our father Ignatius that our exertions, which could be expended elsewhere more effectively, should be lavished upon the city of Gubbio with such a meager return. The matter was taken up with the Cardinal of the Holy Cross, who watched over the Society with paternal solicitude, and he immediately gave his permission for Ours to seek the greater service of God elsewhere once they were withdrawn from this place.

95.   *Our community at Ferrara and the boy bishop*

We have already treated the opening of two colleges [at Genoa and Loretto] and the closing of one [at Gubbio] this year. Now we will describe the early stages of the little college at Argenta. But because negotiations about Argenta hinged on Ferrara, we will deal with Ferrara first of all. There the same rector was in office [this year] as last, Father Jean Pelletier, who had with him nine and sometimes ten men of the Society. A new obligation arose at the beginning of this year. Lord Ludovico, the second son born to Duke Ercole, was still a boy when he was promoted to the bishopric of Ferrara. His father wanted Father Jean Pelletier to instruct Lord Ludovico about how to recite the [Divine] Office and to carry out whatever befitted a prelate of the Church. He insisted that instruction should begin on the first day of the year.

Accordingly, in the morning, shortly before dawn and in the evening about the fourth hour of the night [Pelletier] used to come to him; in addition to saying the canonical hours together with him, he explained in the vernacular language whatever in the Epistle and Gospel seemed to contribute to his education. The kindness, candor, and simplicity of Lord Ludovico refreshed the heart of Father Pelletier. [Ludovico] eagerly accepted all that he was being taught as if it were being stamped into soft wax. . . .

99.   *Declining enrollment at the college in Ferrara*

Gradually the classes at Ferrara began to decline as regards both the number and the noble status of the students. Three reasons for this unfortunate development were noted. The first was that teachers for whom the young men had developed an affection were sent elsewhere and their replacements were not as appreciated and sometimes were not as learned. The second was that in the lower classes the grammar of Despautier was used, which the boys seemed to find rather distasteful, whereas the [teachers] did not make use of [the grammar] of Varinus, a Ferrarese author, even though the students liked it and wore out its pages as they thumbed through it.[3] The third reason was that some young men of noble blood became attached to the Society. . . . The parents of some of these students from the nobility withdrew their sons from our school, for they feared that our classes had become like nets for trapping other young lads.

---

[3] A note by the editors of Polanco's Latin text indicates that the author had in mind the famous schoolmaster Guarino da Verona (1370–1460), also known as Varinus, who had taught at Ferrara.

100.   *Native speakers are the best teachers for the lower classes*

Experience also made manifest that in the lower classes Italian [Jesuits] should be employed rather than teachers of other nationalities because the accent of foreigners was less than pleasing. And when explanations had to be given in the vernacular, those who were unskilled in it were not too successful in their efforts [in this country]. Whereas previously there had been almost 200 students, at the beginning of this year we enrolled 140, and as the year progressed the attendance dwindled to 120. Among those who remained were fewer of the nobility, even though the students were delighted when the Varinus [grammar] was substituted for Despautier in the lower classes.

110.   *Should our lay brothers be used to punish students?*

When Ours encountered difficulties in finding a disciplinarian, the rector of the college at Ferrara consulted Father Ignatius about whether one of the lay brothers could punish the students or at least some extern could be kept on hand who would carry out this task. But Father Ignatius responded that as to Ours' having permission to correct students by laying their own hands on them, this practice was forbidden; nor might an extern be kept on staff at our house for this [purpose]. . . . Therefore, Father Pelletier arranged for one of the more mature and advanced students to discipline the others, an expedient that did not stir up the same hostility here as elsewhere.

111.   *How to handle students who cannot write*

Father Pelletier inquired of [Father Ignatius] whether we were allowed to teach boys how to write, seeing that some of them were leaving our school so that they could learn this skill elsewhere. Father Ignatius allowed what was the practice at Rome, namely, that those who had already been admitted were taught to write better; but he ordered that henceforth [students] should not be admitted who did not know how to write at least moderately well.

116.   *Loyola rejects a pious practice at Ferrara*

Before Ours had taken possession of the church, a custom common to the other churches of that city [had been observed] there, namely, that next to the door there was an box containing small wax candles. As the people came into the church in the morning, they would take one or another of these candles and drop a small coin into a receptacle in payment for them. When asked for a decision on this practice, Father Ignatius ordered the box to be removed from the church, since having one there was not the custom in our Society.

193.   *Student pranks against the Jesuits at Modena*

It is hardly a surprise that attendance at our school diminished. The youth of Modena, being rather inclined to getting their own way, preferred to go to other schools. So numerous were schools of that sort operating in Modena that, as the report went, as many as twenty-five or thirty schoolmasters were occupied there. It is from these youth who could brook no restraint that Ours suffered the troubles that we recited earlier, when impudent young scamps sometimes rang our bell, sometimes broke the rope or the chain or the door itself, and sometimes threw rocks against the door and windows and then fled in haste. Although Ours steeled themselves with patience, Lord Ludovico, the son of the Duke of Ferrara and bishop-designate, wrote to Count Ercole Rangone (to whom the protection of the college at Modena had been entrusted in the duke's name), urging him not to tolerate this insolence but to punish those who were disturbing the college and thus help and protect all of Ours.

194.   *The troublemakers at Modena are punished*

[The count] offered Ours his complete cooperation and threw into prison that miscreant who had broken our door. When the word spread that he was going to be marched out and publicly whipped, lo, some citizens rushed off to Ours and insistently begged them not to let the boy be punished in public, thus bringing shame upon his parents and relatives. The rector replied that just as Ours were prepared to suffer injuries for the honor of God, just so they would not deny forgiveness. He immediately sent those same citizens to the count-protector, so that they could petition in the name of our college that the boy be pardoned and freed. The count heeded their plea. But Count Ercole, who was the governor as well, ordered a herald to proclaim in the public square that nobody should do or say anything to annoy Ours. Thus did Ours get through the rest of this year quietly enough.

206.   *Unhealthful conditions at Bologna*

All through last year and this year, Father Francesco Palmio was in charge of this college. Ours at Bologna fell victim to serious sicknesses this year. When [Palmio] was commanded to check carefully how Ours were fed and clothed, it was discovered that the reason why sickness spread very widely among Ours and among others as well was not [food and clothing] but some kind of miasma in the air. Father [Giovanni Battista] Viola, the commissary, grew so sick that the doctors held out little hope for his recovery; but later as the year went along, he began to get better. Then (as we reported above) he was sent back to his native air, where he recovered his health.

207.   *Decline and recovery of the school at Bologna*

Regarding our school, as the year began enrollment seemed fairly low, for there were a hundred and fifteen students; but gradually this number shrank even more, and the nobility and the sons of friends of the Society dropped out of class to a great extent. Rumor had it that the reason for this was that our teachers, all of them coming as they did from other nations, were ignorant of the Italian language. Also they lacked the grace and dignity that would have enhanced their standing with the students, and some of them had need of better teaching skills. Some were of the impression that at Bologna not only the number and quality of the students but also at the same time the level of instruction in the classrooms had declined. The same general deterioration appeared to have made itself felt at Ferrara and Modena. Still, somehow both the enrollment and reputation began to be restored when Master Andrea Boninsegna was called back to Bologna, where he had worked for some time.

208.   *The Spiritual Exercises at Bologna*

Coming now to the Spiritual Exercises, we noted above that Father Ignatius wanted to receive an account of how many were directed in them. They provided Father Francesco Palmio with no trifling harvest at Bologna, where on one occasion a dozen people were making them simultaneously. Among them were one priest and two laymen, and the rest were women. But generally male religious made them, once eighteen men at the same time. Fruit of which no one needed to be ashamed was harvested this way in the hearts of many people.

229.   *Our college at Padua*

The enrollment of those who attended [our] school at the beginning of this year came to 120 students distributed in five classes. But when the enrollment declined a little bit, Rome suggested to the rector that he look into reducing the number of classes to three, so that so many teachers would not be required. He judged that the sharply divided levels of learning made this impossible, but still he reduced them to four. Nonetheless, when he could not find a teacher, he himself had to devote some of his time to that class over and above his other occupations.

234. *A bad Jesuit is sent to Padua*

I will not neglect to mention that when [Giovanni Ottilio] was admitted a second time at Rome, he was sent on to Padua (because, when he seemed to have returned to his senses, it seemed a good idea to send him back to Padua as an edifying example to [others]). He revealed to one of his companions that he had not returned to the Society with forthright intentions; indeed, even when he had entered for the first time, he had no intention to remain permanently. He merely wanted to learn what he could at the Society's expense and then leave to marry. And earlier he had encouraged others to leave. Because of his deceitful heart and deadened conscience, he behaved very badly both in and out of the house. There was even some evidence that he had done some scandalous things outside the house. Finally, when he had been tolerated longer than he should have been, Father Ignatius dismissed him. He also proved to us that men who show some talent but are without the necessary spirit and virtue do more damage to the Society the longer they are retained.

295. *Pastoral work at Perugia*

Father Everard [Mercurian] went on explaining the letters of Blessed Paul on feast days, and a good-sized audience eagerly embraced his teaching and spirit. The vicar made use of his collaboration in matters for which the former was responsible, and the Inquisitor of heretical depravity frequently referred matters to him that had to do with the censorship of books. Father Jean Lenoir also showed notable zeal in preaching, and his ministry of the word won acceptance from all. On Fridays he taught Christian doctrine to many men and women, who then used to go to Communion that same day. The same was true on Sundays. A third priest, Giovanni Castellano, lived in a separate house intended for clerics whom the Cardinal of Perugia wanted to organize there; but he also devoted his time to hearing confessions. But when he heard that Father [Jean] de la Goutte had been captured by the Turks, he felt somewhat envious of him; so he yearned for some missionary work overseas. He would preach four or five times a week and twice on all feast days.

305.   *Problems for the Jesuit college in Perugia*

When the time came for getting classes underway again, speeches, poems, and dialogs were again presented at the palace with the lord pro-legate, the senate, professors, and other leading men in attendance, all of whom were gratified. Even though our reputation for literary subjects was enhanced thereby, the number of students beginning [the school year] still declined here. One partial explanation for this may have been the change of teachers; for Master Gilberto [Pullicino] was assigned to Genoa, and his departure drew tears from his students and caused resentment in the senate. The senate then quieted down when Ours said that his successor would be Master Antonio Viperano or, if need be, Master Gilberto could be recalled. But it would only have been with much difficulty that he could have been recalled; for, after reaching Florence, he fell into a sickness from which he passed to the heavenly college, as we said above.

315.   *The Franciscan general objects to frequent Communion*

The Minister General of the Order of Saint Francis was at Perugia and rather frankly revealed to the lord vicar his reservations about the frequent reception of Communion. Partly making use of his authority and partly by adducing some arguments, he tried to implant in the vicar a scruple for having allowed lay people to receive this holy Sacrament frequently. But he did not persuade the vicar; for he perceived that the Minister [General] was jealous of the Society, as was obvious from his words, which the vicar repeated. That good religious asserted, among other things, that all the activities of the Society in the regions of India, which had won such adulation, were figments of the imagination; after all, there are few men of the Society working there, but the King of Portugal had sent hundreds of the religious of Saint Francis to those places. It is easy to figure out who this Minister [General] was and also where he was living among his own men, and so I think I should refrain from writing any more about him.

316.   *A religious attacks Mercurian*

A certain religious of another order, and a preacher besides, declared from the pulpit at Perugia that one could not readily put one's trust in all the preachers and commentators on Holy Scripture. Nor is it, he said, everybody's prerogative to interpret Scripture. According to him, once you allow one of these [preachers] to interpret Blessed Paul, they will interpret him grammatically. But nobody was interpreting Blessed Paul except [this preacher] himself and Father Everard [Mercurian], at whom these barbs seem to have been aimed. [Mercurian], who was skilled at languages, sometimes used this facility of his to arrive at the meaning of Scripture. Yet at least Ours heard these criticisms and other similar comments with profit, for they prevented them from becoming complacent over the high esteem in which others held them. The people themselves could easily conjecture in what spirit such [criticisms] were uttered, and in the end they came to recognize that for those who love God, all things work together unto good.

324.   *The Spiritual Exercises are not well received at Florence*

Father Ignatius encouraged Ours at Florence to put their efforts into giving the Spiritual Exercises when they could reasonably do so; and Father Louis de Coudret, the rector of that college, carried out this mandate with diligence, successfully proposing them to some people. But experience seemed to show us that in this city it was not easy to induce people to make those Exercises as exactly as they should, nor were the [Florentines] suited [to make them].

326.   *Food and drink at Florence*

Ours at Florence were warned in the name of Father Ignatius to cut back on some of the time they spent lecturing, especially at the time when the heat of summer was usually most intense. As for food, the bread and quantity of wine (although this was watered down) should be left to the discretion of each person. But as regards the quantity of meat, the doctor should be consulted to learn how much he would say was sufficient in that place; then that quantity should be rationed out to each one.

335.   *Jesuits should retain their family names*

Federico Manrique changed his name to Francisco Bonaventura when he made his simple vows and wanted to be addressed thus because of his special devotion to those two saints. But Father Ignatius did not agree with this and wanted him to retain his name. . . .

346.   *Mixed results at Florence*

Three Florentines who had inflicted wounds on one another put aside their hatred after listening to a sermon and made peace with one another. More than twenty soldiers were freed through the effort and influence of Father Laínez. Also some men slated for the galleys obtained pardon and liberty from the duke, partially through the good offices of Father Laínez and partially through those of Father Louis de Coudret, the rector. The city itself seemed rather favorably disposed toward the Society. But the entrance of Giovanni Ricasoli into the Society stirred up angry recriminations against our school. However, to a great extent through the good offices and support of the duchess, these died down. But because of this and some similar instances, some noblemen were less inclined to send their sons to our school.

365.   *A confraternity for men at Naples*

Two confraternities, one for men and the other for women, took root during the first months of this year through our zealous efforts. Men belonging to the confraternity were to approach [the altar] for Communion every fifteenth day. They were to work at tamping down the hatreds and vendettas that used to flare up in that city and daily result in murders. It was also their duty to encourage everybody they could to receive the sacraments and, whether by words or in any other appropriate way, to assist those confined to hospitals. They were to recall to a chaste life those living shamefully in concubinage. Lastly, they were bound by the mission of their confraternity to be of assistance to the commonwealth by word and example. To achieve this more effectively, they resolved to admit only those to membership who were leading upright lives.

326.   *A consorority for women at Naples*

The women's consorority went to the sacred Table of the Lord every month. They taught Christian doctrine only to their domestic servants. They forbade themselves [the use of] rouge and the kind of cosmetics that the women of Naples usually applied to their faces. They themselves would not admit to their consorority any woman wearing cosmetics, however insistent she was. They equaled the men in spirit and surpassed them in numbers. Just as the men had a prefect, so the women too chose one of their number whom all the other women would accept as their leader and put her in charge of the group.

382.   *Recruits at Naples*

Two Spanish soldiers were admitted to the Society at Naples; one of them, named Torres, stayed there, the other, named Juan Rodriguez, went to Rome. Lord Girolamo Vignes had wanted to serve God in the Society almost from the day the college had been founded, and wholly devoted himself to it by vow. But, following the recommendations of Ours who lived at Naples, Father Ignatius thought it more advisable for him to remain in charge of his paternal home, seeing that both his parents were very elderly and needed his help. Meanwhile, he was to hold himself in readiness to leave everything whenever the Society would summon him. Thus he labored many years at Naples and worked zealously for Ours.

387.   *The new residence at Naples*

On the vigil of the Assumption of the Blessed Virgin [August 14], Ours moved into a new house. Three hundred gold pieces had been spent in fitting it our, and much more would have to be spent later in adapting it into a college. Furthermore, Ours fell into a major controversy with some inhabitants of the neighboring houses, for some of them had schemed to snatch the house out of the hands of the Society before [Ours] moved in. When their efforts did not succeed, they secretly tried the same ploy after Ours had moved in. Other disagreements also had to be dealt with, as is usually the case with neighbors. . . .

388.   *The church and school at Naples make progress*

A certain large room was adapted for use as a chapel, with its own door opening to the public street; and in the near future [Ours] planned to add to the church a large area girded by a stone wall. On the lower floor classrooms were arranged for the use of students. The number of students usually climbed to 150 or even slightly exceeded that number. Never before had there been a more flourishing class of literature in Naples. Still, classes sometimes had to be discontinued when the days became torrid, and on those occasions classrooms were improvised in the new building. Classes were resumed on the calends of October [October 1], ushered in by many poems laudatory of literary studies.

399.   *Financial problems at Naples*

. . . The cardinal viceroy [Francisco de Mendoza] did not furnish us what he had promised, perhaps because he did not take care of it in good time, and when he was about to leave the kingdom, he did not think that he could do so; and nothing could be squeezed out of those others who had made promises; thus was verified the traditional adage in that city, "There is quite a difference between words and deeds." Also other [funding] that the [royal] court should have provided could only be exacted with great difficulty. Yet, in August of the following year the cost of house had to be paid, that is, thirty-four hundred ducats; otherwise we would have to move out of it, not without incurring shame and losing eight hundred ducats. The Emperor had promised revenues in the sum of six hundred ducats, but these had to be recovered from Prince Philip himself, because after November 25 he had taken possession of Naples with great solemnity. Therefore, Father Salmerón turned over letters from Father Ignatius to King Philip and Lord Rui Gomez [the royal favorite], urging the son to fulfill the promise of his father Charles, now that he had succeeded to his kingdom. When Lord Alvaro de Mendoza went to the court of the King, he made this negotiation his responsibility.

403. *A Japanese visits Naples*

During the Christmas holidays Bernard the Japanese, whom we described earlier as coming to Rome, stayed at Naples with two companions who were also on the way to Rome. He gave great edification by his prudence, modesty, and upright heart both to Ours and to the laypeople who talked with him and hung on his words. This disciple did not seem to be unlike Master Francis Xavier.

404. *Salmerón cannot write a compendium of theology*

When Salmerón returned to Rome, Father Ignatius instructed him to see whether in [the time he had] free he could complete that compendium of theology at Naples (since he was going to return there); but he humbly wrote back that he did not have the mastery of the Fathers nor the judgment required for such a task nor even the time for it. He admitted that even if he had a shelf filled with books and was free from all other concerns, he still would not be suited [to that task]. This is why, as we said above, this compendium was turned over to Father Laínez.[4]

405. *Jesuit contacts with devout women may give rise to scandal*

There was at Naples a poor but respectable older woman named Feliciana who kept six or seven impoverished young women at her home, instructing them [in proper living]; they all survived almost exclusively from alms. She brought the young women to our chapel for confession every week. But when

---

[4] Laínez also failed to complete the project. For the most part the *Large Catechism* of Peter Canisius served as the desired compendium.

Ours moved from a rented house to one of their own, she wanted to move to another house not far from the college—quite near it, in fact—bringing her young women along with her. Although she was cautioned that for her to rent a house easily visible from the college would stain her reputation and that of the college, she still rented a new house for three years.

When Father Salmerón observed that we could see her house through our windows and she in turn could see ours, he was greatly perturbed, aware as he was that some people in the new neighborhood were not very well disposed toward the college—actually, they had earlier attempted to take the house away from Ours; for he knew that Father Ignatius was convinced that familiarity with this sort of young ladies, even though it was a spiritual one, usually led to nothing useful. Instead, it resulted in suspicions and a blemished reputation and might even leave us with the burden of supporting the [ladies] financially. He also found out that the women were under obedience to a certain confessor [Father Giovanni Francesco Araldo], who sometimes went to their house to discuss spiritual matters. But some of our friends warned us that this was causing some scandal.

406.   *The women at Naples ignore Salmerón's opposition*

. . . Besides what has just been reported, since Feliciana was often sick, there could be danger that some wolf would invade the flock of young women and snatch off one of them. If a crime had occurred, it would undoubtedly have brought shame on those of Ours known to be directing those women. Regardless, after they had been excluded for a time from the use of the sacraments, bringing edification to those who knew about the matter, the group was later admitted to the sacraments at the intercession of Lady Pellota Spinola. But Father Salmerón looked about for a way to provide for their security; finally he arranged for them to be admitted to good convents.

411.   *A glowing tribute to lay piety at Messina*

Through our college it was evident that God was being served increasingly well at Messina. Frequenting the sacraments and attending religious lectures and sermons led to such notable progress that many of those who came to the Church of Saint Nicholas struck observers as behaving more like religious than like those living in the world. Moreover, they dealt with the affairs of worldly men in such a way that their love of heavenly things and their manner of demonstrating this love by their actions caused Ours to marvel. Some of the more important among them, both men and women, seemed endowed with such solid virtue and piety that, even though they were in the world, they could not be said to be of it; for they so spurned the allurements of the flesh and the world, riches, and lastly, their very own selves along with all their possessions, doing all this for the honor of God, that whenever it was necessary [to make a choice], they seemed disinclined to take any account of these things. There was no pious work that they omitted, whether the Holy Spirit suggested it to their minds, or whether Ours entrusted [this work to them] or recommended it. Thus did they help the poor, bury dead paupers, and try to win sinners back to the path of salvation. . . . Women, most of them from the nobility, exerted themselves similarly among the prostitutes, and their efforts were not in vain.

415.   *A convent at Messina for former prostitutes*

The Convent of the Ascension (about its establishment early the previous year we had not a little to report) was under the care of the Society for almost all of this year, and for several months it became the responsibility of Father Antoine Vinck, who also had to care for another pious work begun at the start of the previous year, namely, of young women who were turning from a disgraceful life and undertaking an upright one. He was at pains to test them at that same place until they were fit to move into a convent for the converted or undertake some other form of respectable living.

There were seventeen virgins in the aforesaid convent who suffused the city with the wonderful odor of a life more angelic than human. The fame of their holiness attracted not a few women to their convent; but at that time it seemed more prudent not to admit more women, for they had no reliable sources of income. Nor was the Cardinal of Messina [Giovanni Andrea de Mercurio] as favorable to them as he had been at first; but eventually he became more supportive once again. His own brother, who had been thrown into chains by the viceroy, had stirred up the Cardinal [against the convent]; but upon his release he wrote to his brother the cardinal, recommending this new convent.

416.   *Adjusting Jesuit relations with the convent*

Because Father Ignatius was displeased that Ours had for such a long time been responsible for the convent, arrangements were made for the Supreme Pontiff also to confirm what had already been done and to see to it that certain honorable and godly men would assume the management of its temporal affairs. Father Antoine Vinck had had to supervise not only its spiritual but also its temporal concerns until those laymen relieved Ours of this burden. But as long as Ours were in charge of these matters, they saw to it that the house was very pleasant [for the sisters] and situated where the air was wholesome, so that their quarters would not be so cramped. Fifteen prostitutes went to another godly place; twelve of them wanted to enter a convent for the converted.

437.   *The forty-hours devotion flourishes at Messina*

On the second of November continuous prayer was held for forty hours at the Church of Saint Nicholas. More than five hundred women and more than two hundred men signed up [to participate in this devotion]. It was noted that such prayer brought great profit to many people, changing their lives for the better. Although women were assigned to particular hours of the day and men to those of the night, during some periods of the day so many came to pray that the church became crowded; thus many had to stand outside a long time until those who had arrived earlier and entered had finished their prayers. There was a report that some men whose wickedness was common knowledge began to cling to God more fervently once this prayer had begun.

Some of those who used to devoutly frequent our Church of Saint Nicholas decided to petition the magistrates to take care of expanding that church of ours; and they wanted to make their contribution toward defraying the associated cost. So that the church might meanwhile be more open and accessible for people on Fridays, Father Provincial decided that Father Girolamo Otello should teach Christian doctrine once a week to the students of the advanced classes in the same classroom as the boys in the lower grades. This way, while they receiving instruction from him in their classrooms, they would leave the church empty on Fridays for the laity who came to listen.

451.   *Ignatius decides about censorship and corporal punishment at Messina*

Among other things, Father Annibale [Coudret] consulted Father Ignatius whether [the writings of Juan] Luis Vives and Terence should be excluded from our classes, considering that it was difficult to find [alternative] readings for teaching the Latin language to students in the lower grades. He also asked whether it was permitted to strike students at least on the palm of the hand, now that taking a whip to the students was forbidden; for this would seem to be useful for the students and their parents would approve. But the response from Rome was that Father Ignatius did not want the aforesaid authors to be read and that in the future those readings were going to be prohibited in the other colleges. However, they were not prohibited at the present time, so until other useful books could be found that were not written by suspect authors, Ours in Sicily could use the customary books. Father Ignatius would not permit [Ours to administer] any sort of physical punishment in the colleges of Italy, not even on the palm of the hand. Henceforth, a [lay] corrector should administer the punishment to the boys.

462.   *Providing for orphans at Palermo*

Thirty orphan boys lived in crowded quarters at Palermo. At San Jacobo Ours took charge of building on the same spot a larger and more comfortable house which could house fifty [orphans] right away and could be expanded to accommodate a hundred. There was a vineyard adjacent to the house that brought in rent amounting to 250 gold scudi annually for [the orphans]. Four priests of blameless life were in charge of the boys; they taught and educated them and held them to their duties.

463.   *Helping former prostitutes in Palermo*

Here too, just as in Messina, Ours worked at setting up a house of probation to which women might repair to recover from a shameless way of living. These were women whose hearts God had touched, even though they had not yet made so much progress that they wanted to enter a convent for the converted. So it was for such that, in addition to the ordinary house of the converted, a new sort of house was set up in which they might live temporarily until they made a firm decision about the kind of respectable life they should undertake. After that, those who were inclined to the religious life would be accepted at a convent for the converted. For those who preferred to marry, a marriage would be arranged.

Right at the beginning [the convents] had only a slender income, no more than a hundred ducats; but Ours raised so much in alms for helping the women that not only was the house supplied with operating funds, but during the first four or five months of this year, forty of its women were provided with a modest dowry and given in marriage to reputable men. A good many of these women were motivated to embrace a better way of life, to some extent by the sermons preached in our church, which they had to listen to, and to some extent by the viceroy's edict forbidding concubinage, as I mentioned a little earlier.

477.   *Problems at the College of Palermo*

In the course of the year, the student enrollment grew, although gradually, and reached almost 280 toward the end of the year. The city mayor wanted our college to offer two courses in logic; and, citing the income of 500 scudi assigned to our college, he asserted that he had been promised [the two courses]. But the provincial replied that the contract originally signed mentioned no such obligation. Regardless, the mayor kept insisting that a promise had been given in the city council. Although Father Paolo [Achille] gave a lecture course for the sake of several friends, [the mayor] pressed him to add a second course, at least in autumn; and the viceroy wished to satisfy the city's desire. This year Master Gerard Lapidius was in charge of the advanced class in rhetoric; although he was learned in Greek and Latin, he seems to have been endowed with quite minuscule skills as a lecturer, and he also failed to give his students adequate practice. Only two lay students and four of Ours remained in his class.

496.   *The viceroy pressures the Jesuits to hear nuns' confessions at Messina*

When Father Ignatius instructed Ours to cease hearing confessions at the new Convent of the Ascension, the viceroy gave them to understand that he would be displeased if Ours did not help [the nuns] at least in this ministry for a time. And as matters stood, it seemed somehow to be a violation of charity to desert the women so suddenly, before they could make other arrangements. Thus, Ours were permitted to continue this ministry of hearing confessions.

503.   *Preventing Francis Borgia from being made a cardinal*

Juan de Vega, the viceroy, learned that Father Francis Borgia was in danger of being made a cardinal, and he judged that under no circumstances should [Borgia] accept that dignity. [Borgia] consoled [the viceroy] and the provincial, assuring them that there seemed to be no possibility of his accepting it. Still, with somebody who had heard it from the Pope's own mouth as his source, Father Provincial had found out that if Father Francis himself was unwilling, the Pope would never impose this on him under holy obedience; and that if Father Francis himself were to write to the Emperor and to King Philip, insisting that he did not in any way wish to accept this dignity, they thought neither of those two princes would raise the matter [before the Pope].

■ **Austria**

523. *Canisius directs the Jesuits at Vienna to study more*

Ours did not work at their studies very hard and did not make much progress, in part because they [had to] teach, in part because they [had to] attend public and private lectures, and in part because they devoted [undue] time to spiritual matters. Father Canisius communicated his desire that the rector would give more care to [supervising their] studies. Thus did some begin to pursue their studies more diligently when they were relieved of certain of their obligations.

528. *Deplorable conditions at Vienna*

The situation at Vienna was such at the start of this year that Canisius marveled that good people were not martyred. Whatever pertained to the Catholic religion seemed to have deteriorated day by day, to such an extent that even Catholics were saying Communion should be given under both species and that the Supreme Pontiff ought to have a concern for the thousands of people who would be helped by such a dispensation. But the Hungarians and other provinces were clamoring for this so vigorously that some of them would not wait patiently until the dispensation was requested. The number of heretics at Vienna grew enormously, and nobody was punished for thus abandoning the faith. Things reached the point that when the King wanted to confer prelacies and bishoprics on carefully chosen and worthy men, he could not find any. The cathedral church at Vienna did not find ministers to conduct divine worship; the parishes were either devoid of pastors or in the clutches of apostates or men of ill repute. Young men did not want to become priests, and the report circulated that, among those who had studied at the university, not even twenty men had been ordained in as many years.

529. *Getting the Viennese to make a full confession*

As the year progressed, Father Canisius, who wrote the previous account, began to hope for improvement. For decrees enacted the previous summer and aimed at the reformation of the university were published this year with great solemnity. Still, the situation was this: so great was the dearth of good confessors in Vienna that all penitents did was confess to being sinners and ask for the consolation of God's word. [Priests] gave them absolution without asking any questions or receiving a specific declaration of their sins. Hence, Ours had less reason to wonder how so few priests could hear so many confessions. Each of those who made their confessions to Ours, however, encountered a far different technique of administering this sacrament.

Matching such [inadequate] confessors were the preachers who spoke of nothing except faith in Jesus Christ and his merits and the mercy of God, making no mention of confession or fasting and the like. Yet these men wanted to be regarded as Catholics. Father Canisius diligently and fervently kept on delivering sermons, some of them to the people, some to King [Ferdinand] himself; and a crowd of both classes of listeners followed him. He gave satisfaction to both the learned and the unlearned.

531.   *King Ferdinand moves toward enforcing Catholicism*

The most significant effects of [Canisius's] sermons was that they inspired the King of the Romans to make known his intention to officially promote the Catholic religion in his realm. This turn of events explains the King's urgent desire for Father Canisius to complete his catechism: he wanted it and it alone to be available and used to instruct the people in his provinces, and he wanted all other [catechisms] to be discarded. He also planned to promulgate a public edict to banish those who here and there in his provinces presumed to receive the Sacrament of the Altar under both species. Also owing to [Canisius's] sermons was the notable increase of those who went to confession and Communion during this Lent, far more than in the preceding Lents, especially among the Germans and Flemish. Fathers Canisius and [Nicholas Floris] of Gouda made themselves available as confessors to members of those nationalities, offering so much instruction and edification as to reinforce the hope that this manner of confessing specific sins would again become common. For the most part, the rector, Father Nicholas de Lanoy, satisfied the needs of those Italians, Spaniards, and Frenchmen who came to Ours for confession.

534.   Final steps toward the publication of the Canisius *Catechism*

Father Canisius offered to the King of the Romans the main portion of his catechism, which was largely completed, for he did not think he should apply the final touches to it until he learned what the King and his advisors thought about it. But the King, who was then staying at Bratislava, gave abundant assurance in his letter to Father Canisius that both he and the others whom he entrusted with examining it approved the catechism. [The King] went on to write that he esteemed it highly and hoped that, if it should be published, it would greatly foster the salvation of his faithful subjects. Thus, he sent the part of the catechism back that he had perused, along with the request that without delay [Canisius] complete what still had to be done and send him the completed catechism as soon as possible. He also confided to [Canisius] his carefully considered determination to have the catechism translated into German; after it had been printed in both languages, it would then be publicly prescribed for the use of the young people throughout all the Latin and German schools in the five provinces of Austria and the county of Gorizia. Anyone using other [catechisms] would incur a very severe penalty and the royal displeasure.

[The King] commanded Father Canisius to add in the margin the specific chapters and verses where the scriptural and conciliar texts and the interpretation of the holy Doctors are found to which the catechism makes reference; thus schoolmasters and other men of less profound learning could more readily consult the sources substantiating the various statements made. The King hoped that thereby many who had fallen [from the faith] because of their ignorance might be brought back to the bosom of the holy Church. Although the exacting scholarship of Father Canisius—which could barely content himself, even though it satisfied others—imposed delays [upon the appearance of the catechism], the King's insistence compelled him to bring that catechism to a conclusion at last. The intercession of the bishop of Laibach barely won the King's consent to delay its publication for a while. Thus, not once or twice but six or seven times the author himself revised it and returned it to [the printer] to be reset; finally he sent it to Father Ignatius to be inspected in accord with the [Jesuit] *Constitutions.* Thus the [catechism] was returned with [Loyola's] approval and given to King Ferdinand, who saw to its printing and distribution.

537.   *Canisius stirs up opposition by his preaching*

Canisius stirred up some persecution against himself at Vienna. Many people freely heaped criticisms upon him because a certain professor was thrown into prison for heresy. This occurred when Canisius, who along with another theologian was appointed to examine this professor's writings, carried out his duty. In the sermons he gave before the King, he argued, contrary to the common opinion held in that area, that authorities were bound to defend the Catholic religion and to punish public enemies of the faith. For this reason the students called down maledictions against Father Canisius and testified to their malice in poems and other ways.[5] It was quite clear that few of them held to the Catholic faith. Aside from Ours, not one Catholic preacher was in evidence there.

539.   *Toward a college in Poland*

During April Father Canisius, first alone and then together with Father Lanoy, held discussions with Doctor Martin Cromer, the legate of the Polish king, regarding the founding of a college in Poland. The previous year, after [Cromer] had treated this matter in a friendly manner with Ours, he returned to Poland and spoke to several bishops about [establishing] colleges of our Society; in particular he discussed with Stanislaus Hosius, the bishop of Ermeland, the foundation of a college in his diocese. [Hosius], a man of great learning, had zealously defended the Catholic religion through the spoken and written word; gladly he listened to and approved of what he heard reported about the Society. He desired to have ten men of the Society sent to him, some of them from upper and lower Germany, including two or three professors of Greek and Latin literature and at least two priests. He promised to provide a residence and the necessary income; because he possessed not only ecclesiastical but also secular jurisdiction and suffered from an incapacitating lack of workers, it seemed certain that he would carry through on his promises.

549.   *What should be the minimum age for entering the Society?*

. . . Father Lanoy inquired of Father Ignatius whether boys twelve or fourteen years of age could be admitted to the Society; for in Germany the boys had pliable dispositions and could readily reveal [their character] in our schools. If such lads were admitted, very likely we could dispatch them to assist in the new colleges about to be set up in Germany. But Father Ignatius replied that, based in part on the reasons just cited and in part on what our experience at the German College in Rome was able to teach us, [Ours in Germany] could admit men within the age restrictions spelled out in our *Constitutions;* accordingly, young men could be admitted to the Society who had passed their fourteenth year and were in their fifteenth.

---

[5] Polanco's editors here quote a letter of Canisius to Loyola in which he takes note of such poems and thanks God for being mocked for the holy name of Jesus. The editors also print eight verses of a Latin poem published in 1555 by a Lutheran minister that mocks the Jesuits for having arrogated to themselves the name Society of Jesus, when in fact they are satellites of Satan and destined for hell.

But if various reasons converged in some boy, making it seem advisable to grant a dispensation from the age requirement, the *Constitutions* permitted the superior general himself to grant such a dispensation. [Ignatius] forwarded to Father Lanoy the authority to grant a dispensation [in this matter], one that would allow him to dispense somebody from the aforesaid [minimum] age if he judged it would redound to God's glory. Still, Father Ignatius wanted to be informed about any dispensation that he might grant. He wanted this authority to be interpreted as applicable not only to Germans but also to Hungarians, Bohemians, Transylvanians, and any other northern nations.

563.   *Tensions between Viennese confraternities and the Jesuits*

There were eight confraternities drawn from among the citizens of Vienna who met at the church of the Carmelites, where it was customary according to their constitutions to celebrate some Masses each year. When Ours moved into that monastery, they threatened to go to another church and take their church decorations along with them because Ours did not promptly satisfy their request. Their threats did not in the least displease Father Lanoy, especially when he perceived that some of them cherished less-than-orthodox notions about the sacrifice of the Mass. But when Father Ignatius was consulted, he suggested that if these lay confraternities could move to another church along with their revenues and paraphernalia without detriment to the worship of God, this seemed something to hope for. He left to Father Lanoy's judgment whether or not this would detract from worship in the future.

Father Canisius was hoping to bring the college at Vienna into conformity with the other colleges of our Society, and Father Ignatius also supported this objective. Still, if it was not possible to contravene the local custom without arousing hostility, Ignatius judged that compromises would be in order and that he should not explicitly command Father Rector Lanoy to conform everything to the prescriptions of our *Constitutions* and the practices in the other colleges. Yet [Ignatius] recommended that when there is question of such departures from our Institute, [Lanoy] should be more observant of and as far as possible adapt himself to the Institute. Thus, as far as organs in church were concerned (for [Lanoy] had asked whether it was allowed to play the organ), [Ignatius] forbade him to introduce that usage, for Ours had not yet begun to do so.

564.   *Should Jesuits teaching at the University of Vienna accept salaries?*

After questioning Lanoy about the stipend that professors of theology were usually paid and accordingly were offered to Father Canisius and Father [Floris] of Gouda [in their role] as officially appointed professors, they did not accept [the stipend], in part because it was not in accord with the *Constitutions,* in part because it was equivalent to a perpetual endowment of the college, and it was not permissible for this stipend to be paid as if it were part of the endowment. When consulted later, Father Ignatius replied that for now this sort of stipend should not be accepted, but he did not want to make any universally binding decision until Ours at Vienna had written him setting forth both sides of the question.

The reason in this case why he did not openly exclude this sort of stipend was that it seemed advisable to take into account God's greater service and the common good, which would be served if we took over the whole burden of teaching theology at that university, thus snatching the teaching duties from the hands of the heretics; furthermore, [it would serve the Catholic cause] if perhaps the whole university, where the faculties in which we usually taught were in a state of almost total collapse, might come into the hands of the Society. If all the teachers were members of our Society, the students who might here and there be tainted by the corrupt doctrine of their [earlier] teachers could be educated in Catholic doctrine. Then such salaries could make it possible to support a larger number of scholastics of the Society.

567.   *Vienna was a barren field*

The status quo of the university and the local church was in utter decline, as the bishop of Laibach had demonstrated [by showing] that in the past twenty years no citizen of Vienna had wanted to be ordained a priest; thus it is less than surprising to learn that some of our teachers at Vienna were convinced that piteously little fruit could be harvested there and that a far more abundant crop could be garnered by traveling around to various places on missions.

571.   *Toward a college at Prague*

A monastery sat on the borders of Bohemia, Lusatia, Meissen, and Silesia, which are important provinces. Canisius expressed his opinion that the location did not seem suitable, far distant from cities as it was. Instead, a [college] should be set up in one of the principal cities, where there was hope for a richer harvest. But when Canisius's letter was delivered to King Ferdinand, he immediately determined to set up a college at Prague, the metropolis of Bohemia, although it would be sustained by the revenues of that deserted monastery [mentioned above]. [Ferdinand] offered to draw from his own [funds] whatever more was needed, because he hoped that from [the college] the kingdom of Bohemia would gain no small profit.

■ **Germany**

600.   *Protestant preachers at Cologne*

When [Father Leonard Kessel] returned to Cologne, he found that the city had not a single good Catholic preacher and teacher. Three preachers who were suspect and indeed were contaminated [with heresy] were preaching at Cologne before large crowds; and every day the yeast of Lutheranism was spreading more widely, but nobody was standing up to [the heretical preachers] because they enjoyed popular support. A bit earlier Father John de Catena had begun to preach at Saint Agatha's, and Father Leonard himself also continued to preach and hear confessions. Among others, a certain heretic returned to the Church of Christ this autumn, and [Father Leonard] heard the general confessions of many people, with great profit to them.

604.   *Support for establishing a Jesuit college at Cologne*

As we said, there were many—only private citizens, however—who ardently desired to have a college of the Society established at Cologne, and Father Leonard declared that the senate itself wanted our Society to carry out its mission of preaching and also of giving an education in humane letters. Having once rejected [the Society], the senate was now reluctant to request [its services] and invite it [to come]; but if it came on its own, [the senate] would show it every goodwill, especially if some of the Society came who were endowed with outstanding skill at preaching and teaching Greek and Hebrew and theology. In such a case, one could hope for considerable success from this enterprise. A certain man who had always opposed Ours and, as long as he was living, had sworn that he would always oppose us was removed from their midst at this time.

As information about the program at the Roman College spread, many people increasingly yearned to see such a college at Cologne, as did their hope that their youth would obtain a good education in letters and morality. Thus it happened that a man approached Ours at this time and showed them a very large house in the city center with salubrious air, [and suggested that] Ours judge whether it suited the Society. He indicated, moreover, that he was willing to buy it for the Society. Lord Gropper also wanted to give Ours a spacious lot in a town some nine German miles from the city of Cologne. But first the Society had to establish itself [permanently] at Cologne, where during all [these discussions] Ours were living in a rented house like transients. Still, day by day they continued to bring improvement to many people.

■ Belgium

606.   *Opposition to the Jesuits at Louvain*

[The chancellor of Liège] spelled out some of the aspects of the Society that displeased the courtiers. One [complaint] was that talented men from whom much was expected, men who would be useful for lower Germany in the future, were being sent off to foreign climes. Another objection was that [Ours] admitted sons to the Society without consulting their parents and against their wishes and then transferred them elsewhere. When Father Adriaenssens caught wind of these complaints, he informed the same Lord [Chancellor] Pictavia in writing that Father Ignatius was most inclined to help those provinces and that he would send back to Belgium those men whom [the chancellor] did not want removed from there, provided that they could be supported and carry on the ministries of the Society somewhere in that country. This was impossible unless we had colleges [in Belgium]. Second, [Ignatius promised] that parents would be informed about the admission of their [sons] when there was hope that they would not stand in the way of a call from God.

614.   *The bishop of Cambrai attacks the Society*

[Father Adriaenssens] along with Father Bernard Olivier met with [Cardinal Reginald Pole] after his return from France; they asked him for letters of commendation [addressed to] the bishops of lower Germany, so that they could exercise the usual ministries of the Society with their blessing. [Pole] composed those letters courteously and promptly. Father Bernard brought [Pole's] letter addressed to the bishop of Cambrai [Robert de Croy], among others, and showed him at the same time the apostolic letters relative to the Society. But [de Croy] exploded in wrath and assailed Ours with abusive words. He also forbade Father Bernard under penalty of imprisonment to do any preaching in his diocese. He also ordered his officials in writing that if they found anyone of the Society preaching in his diocese, they should immediately throw him into prison. He gave as his reason for this ban that all the mendicant orders had decided to bring a lawsuit against us, and that he had decided to be a party to it. Grounds for the suit were that our Society did harm to both religious and to all pastors by refusing to accept anything for [saying] Masses or preaching or hearing confessions.

660.   *Ministries at Tournai*

Tournai abounded with so many heretics that even good people were less than certain what they should believe. Therefore, Father Quintin [Charlart] began explaining the articles of the Catholic faith on Sunday afternoons. Father Bernard [Olivier] himself preached during the morning at a church that the vicar of the bishop had assigned to them for this purpose. At that time [bishops] permitted Ours to exercise these ministries of the Society at both Tournai and Cambrai. There was a church adjacent to a certain convent [of the women] they call Beguines. Father Quintin himself had cared for them before he left Tournai, and they had recommissioned him once again to hear their confessions and to preach the word of God. Since confessions occurred only rarely at that time in Tournai, Ours did not think they should withdraw from this duty until some matters of greater moment called them elsewhere.

661.   *Should a superior be elected at Tournai?*

At the beginning [Ours] lived quite peacefully, but without a superior. However, Father Ignatius inquired of them whether (as was the case at Louvain and Cologne) it would be a good idea for someone to be elected superior at Tournai; whether, moreover, someone [should be elected] provincial, with authority over Ours residing in lower Germany at Cologne, Louvain, and Tournai; and, third, whether some of those who were living in those three places should be sent to England. They responded to these questions, writing out their opinions and sending them on to Father Ignatius. Almost unanimously they agreed that a superior or rector should be appointed at Tournai; but as regards a provincial, this seemed unnecessary because so few resided in the three afore-said places (in all there were barely fifteen). There were no scholastics, for those who had been admitted were sent off to Rome or Vienna. Still, almost all thought it would be useful to have a provincial of this sort in the future.

662. *Loyola goes against the majority*

Following orders from Father Ignatius, the priests wrote their opinion of who they thought was best suited to hold the two offices. The majority voted for Father Bernard as rector at Tournai, although some voted for Father Quintin. For provincial they [voted for] Father Adriaenssens, the rector at Louvain, who was the oldest among the professed [fathers] and seemed able to conveniently direct those who were in lower Germany, Belgium, and England. But Father Ignatius appointed Father Quintin superior at Tournai instead and kept Father Bernard free for other tasks. But he did not judge that a provincial should be appointed this year. Although Father Ignatius had authority to appoint whichever superiors he wished in the aforesaid places and to designate those he considered best for those posts without consulting anybody, he sometimes chose to employ this more delicate *[suave]* method of governance.

■ **France**

677. *Broët's ministries in France*

At the beginning of this year, Father Paschase was in Auvergne, where, pressed to do so by the bishop of Clermont, he visited forty-four parishes of his diocese. He gave the Spiritual Exercises to two noblemen, one of whom renounced four or five church benefices for which he was responsible. When [Broët] gave the bishop a written summary of what he had done during his visitation, [the bishop] was overjoyed. Associated with [some] of the churches [he had visited] were hospitals and some chapters of canons, and during the little less than three weeks he spent there, he garnered considerable fruit. Father Jerome Baz, who returned to Paris, and Father Paschase himself left behind among the people of Auvergne sweet recollections of their gentleness, and the people ardently wanted to have a community of the Society sent to them.

683. *The bishop of Paris refused to ordain a Jesuit*

Father Paschase obtained [permission] to advance Jacques Morel to sacred orders. But because [Morel] was not professed, nobody was willing to ordain him. [Broët] went to the bishop of Paris [Eustace du Bellay] and displayed the privileges of our Society; but [the bishop] emphatically exclaimed that our Society was not approved in France, and that he would never ordain anyone who was not professed in an approved [religious] order or in possession of an ecclesiastical benefice.

689.   *The Jesuits and the university at Billom*

When Father Paschase said that the Society would rather assume the whole burden of the University of Billom than share the task of teaching with laymen, but that for now a good number of Ours would be needed—at least fourteen—of whom four would be teachers and the rest students, the bishop [of Billom] was greatly delighted that the Society would be willing to take on that whole task unassisted. Still, he remained convinced that at the start three good teachers of humane letters and a fourth person who would give a course in theology should be sent and that the rest of the teachers could be easily obtained for the Society at the University of Billom itself. Accordingly, Father Paschase hoped that before construction had got underway, Father Ignatius would satisfy the bishop by sending those few men, for whom [the bishop] promised to furnish a residence and all else that they needed.

690.   *More troubles with the bishop of Paris*

When the [Queen's] advisor Lord Dumont offered the bishop his services in promoting [men] to sacred orders, the bishop told him explicitly that if he admitted one of Ours to sacred orders, he would thereby seem to be approving of our Society. He added that the theologians had discovered more than forty errors in our apostolic documents; hence, he concluded that our Society was a spurious organization. It was not surprising that the apostolic letters carried so little weight in his sight, because when Father Paschase showed him the approbation of two popes, he replied that the supreme pontiffs had done many things that were not good, implying that the approbation of our Society was among them. . . .

703.   *The theology faculty at the University of Paris issues the following decree:*

This new Society claiming for itself alone the unwonted title of the name of Jesus admits anybody quite without restraint or discrimination, however criminal, illegitimate, and disreputable he may be. [Its members] cannot be distinguished from secular priests in matters of outward garb, tonsure, privately reciting the canonical hours, or chanting them publicly in church; nor do they behave differently as regards cloister, silence, their choice of foods and [observance of special] days and fasting; nor do they subscribe to various laws and ceremonies that distinguish and preserve the status of religious. Accorded very many and varied privileges, indults, and liberties, especially regarding the administration of the sacraments of penance and the Eucharist, [they function] without regard for places and persons. [These privileges] in the offices of preaching, lecturing, and teaching are prejudicial to ordinaries and the hierarchical order, as they are to other religious orders and even to temporal princes and lords. They are in contravention of the privileges of universities and finally constitute a heavy burden on the people.

[This Society] seems to violate proper monastic norms and enervate the zealous, pious, and very necessary exercise of virtues, abstinence, ceremonies, and austerity. Indeed, it even provides [authentic religious] with an opportunity to freely desert the other religious orders and detracts from proper obedience and subjection to ordinaries; it unjustly deprives both lords temporal and ecclesiastical of their rights; it promotes uprisings within both [the civil and ecclesiastical] community and induces many quarrels among the people, many legal suits, disagreements, contentions, jealousies, and various schisms.

Therefore, now that we have carefully investigated all these accusations and other ones besides, and given the question attentive consideration, we conclude that this Society seems to endanger the preservation of the faith, to disturb the peace of the Church, to undermine the monastic religious life, and to succeed more in pulling down than in building up.

Issued by the command of the Dean, the Lords, and the Distinguished Masters of the Faculty of Sacred Theology at Paris.

■ Spain

718. *Francis Borgia establishes a novitiate at Valencia*

Father Francis Borgia, whom Father Ignatius had appointed commissary (as we will report later), with good reason wanted to set up a house of probation in the province of Aragon, to which the novices would come and be tested together, seeing that many men were now entering the Society there. There was some uncertainty whether it should be set up at Gandía or at Valencia. Father Bautista de Barma was confronted with serious arguments favoring both alternatives. He would have inclined toward Gandía, except for what he had learned from experience. When intense heat waves swept over that city, Ours fell victim to various sicknesses there, whereas those sent to Valencia fared well. So he was convinced that health considerations rendered it quite inadvisable to establish a house of probation at Gandía unless [Ours] were relocated to Valencia during the three or four months of the year when summer temperatures were soaring.

722. *Jesuit students thrive at Valencia*

The number of Ours at Valencia was unusually large: there were ten at the start of the year, and as it rolled on [their number] climbed to twenty. There would have been even more except that sending men to various places had eased the burdens on the college, whose financial resources were rather meager. But those who were studying at the college, some of them in theology and others in philosophy or logic, made considerable progress in their studies because of diligent and effective [academic] exercises.

748.   *Christian-doctrine techniques at Gandía*

After returning to Gandía, [Father Bautista de Barma] wanted the people there to cling as they should to Christian doctrine, so he put one of the brethren in charge of preaching, Dionisio Vazquez, that is, who was advanced in theological studies and who had been sent from Alcalá with Doctor [Cristóbal] Rodriguez. He commissioned [Vazquez] to teach the people about the Ten Commandments, the articles of faith, and other necessary things on Sundays, adjusting the level of his instruction to the capacity of his listeners. In addition to him, when Father Bautista was absent during Lent, others of the brethren preached at Gandía to a throng so numerous that our church could hardly hold them. His efforts were very well received by the people of Gandía and no less useful [to them].

One of our brethren walked around certain places of the town at fixed hours with a bell, inviting children to [learn their] Christian doctrine. Two lads accompanied him and by their charmingly sung verses instilled in other [children] the lessons they should absorb. Hearing the bell, the children willingly followed the two singers as they headed home, or their parents brought them out of their homes and turned them over to our father. Accordingly, he returned with a large troop of children trailing him. When the church could not hold them comfortably, they had to go over to the school, which was more spacious.

One of the priests had received from God such a great talent for teaching and touching the hearts of children that he gave instruction to more than two hundred children in the course of two months; they, in turn, could then teach elsewhere what they had learned during this time. Taking into account the others who heard him, the number climbed above five hundred. Day and night adults and children sang nothing in the whole town except Christian doctrine. Indeed, the shop workers in the city and the farmers in the fields eased their toil by singing [these verses], and mothers at home were not ashamed to learn them from their children.

749.   *More fruit from teaching catechism at Gandía*

These fathers diligently helped improve the morals of youth, breaking their habits of taking false oaths and swearing improperly. So many people approached the Lord's Table weekly that our confessors were barely enough to hear their short confessions on the day they were going to Communion.[6] Many were guided through the Spiritual Exercises. Among these, a certain merchant made especially notable progress; his practice of holy meditation led him to a great knowledge of God and of himself. Some of these men were awaiting the arrival of Father Bautista so that they could plead with him to admit them into the Society. Of these he did admit some who showed greater promise; he judged that some should pursue a different kind of life; others he thought required more testing.

753.   *The Jesuits sponsor a book burning at Gandía*

While preaching on a certain occasion, a preacher at our church exhorted his hearers to burn profane books and romances or to bring them to our college to be consigned to the flames. When people heard that Ours were offering Masses and prayers and giving spiritual books to those who brought in those worldly books, more than fifty books such as *Amadis [de Gaul]* and *Orlando Furioso* and similar works were carried in, along with a large basket filled with risqué Spanish verse. All of these were burnt publicly with great joy in the middle of the university, while the children pranced about the flaming pyre chanting Christian doctrine. The same occurred on another day, when other books of a similar kind were collected.

779.   *The archbishop opposes a Jesuit college at Zaragoza*

The archbishop let Ours know that he was determined to use every expedient in his power to prevent them from starting a college and to drive them out of Zaragoza entirely. Both religious and other churchmen shared his animosity. He was convinced that Ours would not be able to obtain from the Apostolic See a clear and explicit exemption from his ban on our erecting a college. This was one of the main incidents that prompted us to request this sort of privilege from the Apostolic See, although we did not obtain it at this time, not until the pontificate of Pius IV [1559–65].

---

[6] Short in contrast to general confessions, which, naturally, took longer to make.—ED.

827.   *Nadal Proclaims the* Constitutions

On April 4 Father Nadal came to Medina del Campo and, as was his practice in the other colleges, he explained the Institute and *Constitutions* of the Society in his lectures. In his responses [to their questions] he cast light not only on matters about which [Ours] had no doubts but also resolved uncertainties that could come up in the course of time. The rector admitted that Nadal's eagerly awaited promulgation of the *Constitutions* injected into all of our hearts something like a flame and in some manner spread it to other people.

828.   *Ignatius wants three provinces in Spain*

Our professed fathers were called to assemble in a congregation [to be held] at Medina del Campo. This was the first of all the meetings to be held in Spain. Father Francis Borgia, Father Torres, Father Strada, and Father Provincial Araoz himself were summoned to participate. Aside from them, there were no other professed fathers in Spain, though some were living in Portugal. The reason for the gathering was this: at the start of this year, Father Nadal alerted Father Ignatius to the state of affairs in Spain; Ignatius judged that three changes had to be made in Spain. The first was to divide Spain into several provinces and appoint provincials over them. The second was to designate a commissary for all of them to whom the provincials and others might have recourse. The third was to limit the term of those provincials and the commissary to no more than three years.

831.   *Ignatius opposes small colleges in Spain*

Because discussions were underway at this time regarding the foundation of many colleges in Spain, Father Nadal was advised that (taking into account the workers then available in Spain and the wise principles regarding temporal matters that should regulate a foundation) [colleges] should be started in the Lord's name. But because Father Ignatius had learned from experience how bothersome negotiations were and how difficult some small colleges found it in Italy because they lacked support in temporal matters, he had decided not to allow any new ones that could not provide for at least twelve [Jesuits]. . . . He wanted Father Nadal to know his thinking on this question, so that, in view of Ignatius's opposition to accepting similar small colleges, he would see what had to be done in Spain.

847.   *Borgia and Princess Juana, the future woman Jesuit*

Afterwards Father Francis came to Valladolid, where he frequently visited the palace of Princess Juana of Portugal (when her husband died, she returned to the kingdom of Castile and took charge of the government for her brother Philip, king of Spain).[7] The noble virgins and the other women of her court approached the sacraments so eagerly and so often that they seemed to be religious rather than laywomen. . . . They supported the Society with such ardent charity that they were unwilling to confess to anybody except to Ours, even though Ours rather severely kept them away from all frivolities. Several of them made general confessions and seriously devoted themselves to reforming their lives.

856.   *Ignatius turns down care of an orphanage*

This year there was a devout man from the town of Valladolid, Gregorio de Peschera by name, who had come from New Spain [Mexico]. Twice he wrote to Father Ignatius and reported that almost twenty [orphanages] had been set up in Spain and even in India, all patterned after the school for orphan children at Rome. This outstanding work of charity had cared for a great multitude of boys [who otherwise were certain to be] lost. He asked Father Ignatius to allow the Society to take over the care and governance of such schools or homes, for they were in danger of deteriorating for lack of good management; according to [Gregorio], some of them were actually on the verge of collapse. He also reminded [Ignatius] that the apostolic letters of our Institute speak about the instruction of boys, thus allowing Father Ignatius to place such homes under the protection of the Society. . . . Because this good and devout man was all set to depart for New Spain, we conducted no negotiations with him on this matter. In any case, Father Ignatius thought that the responsibility

---

[7] Juana was the daughter of Charles V and brother of Philip II. She married Prince John, the heir of the Portuguese throne, who died on January 2, 1554. Eighteen days later Juana gave birth to his son, the future King Sebastian (1557–79), who was to have Jesuit tutors. When Philip II went to England to visit his wife, Queen Mary, and then spent time in the Netherlands, he appointed Juana regent, a post she held for five years. She had many contacts with the Jesuits, going back to sermons Antonio de Araoz preached at the Spanish royal court when she was only five. Later she had contacts with Borgia both in Portugal and Spain—these even gave rise to silly rumors that she and Borgia were lovers. To the consternation of Loyola and his close associates, she insisted on becoming a Jesuit late in 1554. Because they could not refuse the princess-regent of Spain, Loyola allowed her to take the simple vows of a Jesuit scholastic. This was kept secret even from her brother, King Philip. She was the only woman Jesuit right down to her death in 1573. See Hugo Rahner, *Saint Ignatius Loyola: Letters to Woman* (New York: Herder and Herder, 1960), 52–67.

for an institution such as this, which should be cared for and promoted by others rather than directed by Ours, must be rejected.

884. *Jesuit ministries at Alcalá*

Ours had available to them two principal means whereby they could be of spiritual assistance to their neighbors even when they did not have a [skilled] preacher at hand. One was the Spiritual Exercises. The other was the sacraments of confession and Communion, although they could give considerable help to other people by good example, private conversations, and explanations of Christian doctrine. During the first four months of this year a great throng wanted to make the Exercises at the college. It was impossible to satisfy them all, even though the house was large enough. Although there were almost always eight or nine people occupied with spiritual exercises of this sort, more than twenty others were waiting with equal eagerness for a spot to open up when somebody had finished the Exercises. Other men were likewise waiting for places to empty at the university, where students were supported *gratis*. Most of them were men who came to the sacraments often or had friendly dealings with our scholastics in the public classes.

931. *A college in Navarre is declined*

At the city of Olite in the kingdom of Navarre, . . . a certain doctor there offered some comfortable houses that he owned [in that city] for establishing a college. It seemed a good [idea] to Father Provincial Araoz to send Father Miguel [Torres] there to inspect the property and later to report back on its suitability for the establishment of a college as well as for a residence of Ours. Even though there was no college of the Society in that kingdom and the site was acceptable enough, Ours declined the houses because the local townsfolk would not supply whatever else was required.

938. *Araoz's dealings with important people*

On orders from Father Nadal, Father Araoz left Valladolid, so that he could discuss with Don Rui Gomez some matters of considerable importance at Zamora. But since he hoped that he could transact these matters more comfortably at the town of Alba [de Tormes] (Alba is about four leagues distant from Salamanca), he decided to go there; he sent Father Bartolomeo [Hernandez] ahead, so that he could summon him from Salamanca when it was opportune. Meanwhile, he brought great encouragement to our collegians at Salamanca and instructed them by holding spiritual conversations with them. He also preached in several convents of nuns, thus very much satisfying the city. Had he been able to stay there, he would probably have reaped a rich harvest in that city; but he could not remain there because by order of Father Francis [Borgia] he had to be at Valladolid [to greet] Princess Juana, who was on her way there.

941. *Ministries at the court of Princess Juana*

The good reputation of the Society was growing apace, and so many locales were requesting [the services of] Ours that our few workers would have had to be divided up into many small pieces to be able to honor all the requests. Princess Juana and her whole household made progress in things spiritual, edifying the whole kingdom thereby. Father Francis began preaching in the palace about things pertaining to Christian doctrine. When he had to leave there to go elsewhere, Father Araoz continued these sermons as well as the other ordinary ones he usually gave at the palace. Both men and women of the court began coming to confession so often that some confessors always had to be at hand to hear confessions at the palace; this was in addition to the quite numerous confessions we heard at our house. Although Father Araoz was suffering from a troublesome cough that had descended into his chest, he did not break off his usual sermons either at the palace or in the city. Princess Juana occupied so much of his time and set such a value on his opinion that she did not decide anything of importance without listening to what he had to say; she insisted upon hearing his advice. By means of his exertions and other ministries that he had to perform for various people at the court, he significantly benefited the common good and augmented the prestige of the Society.

945. *Jesuits promise to help implement the Council of Trent in Spain*

At this same time [in mid October] the Supreme Pontiff sent some apostolic letters to Spain regarding the implementation of the Council of Trent, whose effects were making themselves felt in the kingdom. Although signs of a storm had begun to appear, that kingdom was so obedient to the Apostolic See that Ours were hopeful that [Spain] would quiet down quickly. Father Araoz immediately went to the apostolic nuncio [Leonardo Marini] and dutifully offered his own full cooperation and that of the whole Society (after explaining to him the situation), if he should wish Ours to do something to render service to the Apostolic See. The nuncio set a high value on his alacrity and the service that he offered. The regent Juana always very gladly submitted herself in obedience to the Supreme Pontiff. . . . Just as Father Ignatius directed Ours to do, and Father Araoz in particular, they made every best effort to get [the Spanish] to accept in their land what the Supreme Pontiff had decided, just as they should have done.

984.   *Many at Cordoba find the rules too numerous*

The *Constitutions* as well as the Common Rules and those governing rectors and ministers had been published, but [Ours] did not sufficiently understand them. Some regarded [the rules] as [excessively] numerous—for Father [Gundisalvo] González calculated that there were more than three hundred; almost eighty concerned the rector and no fewer affected the minister and the other offices. That good father claimed that he could not find enough time even to read them, not to mention observing them. . . .

985.   *Master Juan of Avila recommends two gifted disciples to Loyola*

This summer Master Juan of Avila wrote an excellent letter to Father Ignatius expatiating on the talents of two of his disciples, whom he had sent as bearers of the same letter; they were Fathers Gaspar Loarte and Didaco de Guzman.[8] Father Torres talked with [Master Juan] and confirmed his earlier opinion regarding his excellent spirit. Evidence of this was how sincerely he embraced the spirit proper to the Society and whatever the [Society] sought in accord with its Institute. . . . [Avila] rejoiced that he had carried out the office of bridegroom for the Society; moreover, in imitation of Saint John [the Baptist], he rejoiced with gladness because of the groom. He told Father Torres that what had happened to him in relation to Father Ignatius was what happens to a boy who is struggling to move a heavy stone to its proper place but is unable to do so because he was too weak; then along comes a man possessing much greater strength, who easily lifts the stone and sets it in its place. He said that he was the boy in this parable and Father Ignatius was the man. Still, it is true that he had not made efforts to form his disciples into a congregation, even though he had a great number of them. On some things he now and then took a view different from Ours, but he based [his convictions] on his holy zeal and solid foundations of reason, according to the way he wished to proceed.

---

[8] For a description of Loarte's many spiritual writings, see J.-F. Gilmont, *Les Écrits spirituels du premiers Jésuites* (Rome: Institutum Historicum Societatis Iesu, 1961), 260–268. Months after Loarte had arrived in Rome in 1554, Loyola made him minister of the professed house; the next year he became rector at Genoa.

1041.   *No Jesuits accompany Prince Philip to England*

Father Nadal was of the opinion that Father Araoz had not acted with sufficient diligence when he neglected to see that some men of the Society accompanied Prince Philip when he set out for England, whereas several secular theologians and two or three religious accompanied him. Father Araoz replied that he was not invited to go because the [courtiers] could not find a reason or assignment to offer him [that would be] worthy of his dignity. Therefore, it seemed to Fathers Francis [Borgia] and Nadal that somehow the good reputation of the Society was being eclipsed because the prince did not take any [Jesuit] with him. When the opportunity arose, Father Francis offered a suggestion to the prince, but the latter retorted that as soon as he arrived in England, he planned to call upon the Society. . . .

1045.   *Blocking efforts to make Borgia a cardinal*

[Father Nadal] was fearful that Father Francis would be forced to accept the red hat [of the cardinalate] or be persuaded to do so, but things worked out far differently. Father Francis himself saw to it that Princess Juana wrote to Prince Philip, bidding him to take no further action along these lines or to allow the Emperor to do so. But Father Ignatius dealt with Pope Julius III in such a way that the Society was fully reassured and relieved of this fear.

■ Portugal

1047.   *Structuring the novitiate experience in Portugal*

During the first four months of this year, six men were admitted to the Society who seemed well suited to its Institute. All of them were examined and tested while they were passing through their first probation—all according to the norms of the Institute of the Society that Father Nadal had instructed them to apply. Father Ignatius believed that God had inspired this distinction of first and second probation; for the rector, Father Leo [Enriquez], declared that on the evidence of experience, this [twofold probation] assumed the greatest importance and usefulness. For in those few days it was easy to discern who of those candidates did not have a genuine vocation from God. Two or three of those admitted departed during those days, whereas no one of those who were admitted to the second probation left afterwards.

1049.   *Arrangements for the novitiate at Coimbra*

From the beginning of autumn right up to the end of the year, other men were admitted and many asked to be [admitted]. But, as the *Constitutions* themselves prescribe, the spirits [of these applicants] were carefully tested before they were admitted. Although, as we said, this house of probation was separate from the residence of the college, it was still near to it. . . .

1060.   *Preaching at Coimbra*

On Sundays and feast days so many people flocked to the sermons that were delivered in the chapel of the college and to the explanations of Christian doctrine given there during the afternoon that the chapel could not hold them, even though, on orders from Father Nadal, its dimensions had been almost doubled. Many people wanted another, still larger church to be built and promised their endeavors to initiate and support this [project]. If this was done, the people's esteem for the Society promised a more abundant harvest. Although [the chapel] was small and somewhat remote, still the people came to it in large numbers, receiving Communion even in Easter season, after they had requested their pastors' permission.

The novice master, Father [Pedro] Correa, moved the hearts of the congregation by his lectures on Christian doctrine. Father Jorge Serrano also preached on Sundays; his listeners not only praised his learning and sharp mind but were also amazed by them. Father Melchor Cotta devoted himself like a beginner to this activity, but with no less edification. Ours traveled throughout the city and ventured outside it as well, all the time preaching.

1063.   *The execution of a black slave*

When a certain black African killed the master whom be served, he was [sentenced] to be branded with red-hot tongs, and then, after his hands had been amputated, he was to be hanged. Some of Ours were summoned, as was customary, to encourage him in spirit to bear up under the tortures. They climbed into the cart in which he was being conveyed and so strengthened his heart that he no longer shrank from tortures; instead, as the red-hot tongs were approaching his body, he earnestly thanked God in a loud voice for having allowed him to do penance for his sins before he died. Certainly this greatly edified the onlookers. So tenaciously did the African fix his mind on the Passion of Christ as one of Ours was exhorting him then and there that when they arrived at the place where his hands were to be cut off, he spontaneously stretched them out.

Witnessing his extraordinary courage at his very last moment aroused great wonderment in the spectators as they beheld the grace of God at work in that man.

1089.   *Public flagellation at Évora*

Father Manuel [Fernandez] taught boys the Ten Commandments, which he had worked into a sort of pious song that so delighted the singers that it replaced their old songs. He initiated a public flagellation or discipline on every Friday as penance for sins and for God's Church. The men who did not want to be recognized came to a certain church in disguise during the evening twilight. Ours began the practice with a few participants on the first day of spring; but later such a great multitude gathered that they had to seek out a large church, and so they moved over to the cathedral. After Father Manuel had preached to the crowd, consisting partly of noblemen and partly of commoners, taking as his theme Christ's first words on the cross, he brought abundant tears to the eyes of his listeners. They recited the "Miserere mei" and "De profundis" while they were flogging themselves, all the while stirring up great edification and devotion among the people.

1114.   *The College of Saint Anthony at Lisbon*

Besides these six classes there was a seventh taught by Father Francisco Rodriguez in which cases of conscience were discussed, and many priests attended [this course] in order to learn how to hear confessions better. They wrote down accurately what the teacher had explained, and after the lecture they addressed several questions to the teacher and discussed with him the most complicated ones. Some of them went to him for confession. Because of the esteem in which they held his erudition, many others besides his students came to this father for advice when they had some more complex cases of conscience for him to dissect.

1129.   *Bernard the Japanese wants to enter the Jesuits*

At the start of this year, Bernard the Japanese also decided for the first time to enter the Society. He had a great desire to acquire knowledge, but he was so worn out from his sea voyage and the great change in climate that he had to concentrate on regaining his health rather than on studying. When he started to recover, [Ours] explained the Lord's Prayer to him. It so satisfied him that he said that he did not want to learn anything more, because that prayer contained all that he needed to learn. He merely wanted to do what the superior approved. . . . This pious man applied himself to meditation and found great treasures in it. As we noted above, he was sent this year from Coimbra through Spain and on to Rome.

1148.   *The Spiritual Exercises in Portugal*

Both men and women of considerable importance were directed through the Spiritual Exercises; it was our hope that the fruit of their progress would extend itself to many others. The thoroughly respectable young Franciscan sisters persistently pleaded for these exercises, and the Queen, who was a strong promoter of them, petitioned Father Miró to comply with their wishes. He quickly girded himself for this task, although their convent was a good distance from our house. But the progress of the nuns, who made strenuous efforts [to acquire sanctity], compensated him for his exertions. Some friars of that same order, both because of the sweet spiritual odor they detected in the nuns and because of their own humility, wanted to make the same [Exercises]. But there was no opportunity to satisfy their request. Another convent of the nuns of the Order of Christ (in which no profession is made but only a promise of obedience, poverty, and chastity as long as one lives there) demanded these Exercises. The sister of the Duke of Aveiro, a blood relative of the King, and many other noble ladies lived at that place, and Father Gundisalvo Vaz sometimes came there to assist them, not unsuccessfully, to make progress.

1150.   *A Jewish and a Muslim convert are baptized at Lisbon*

Two catechumens were under instruction for a long time in the residence of Saint Roch until they seemed to have progressed sufficiently for baptism. One was a Jew who had come overland from India with documents of great importance for the King of Portugal, who in turn entrusted him to Ours. On the day he was to be baptized, he was led from our college to another church where he could give greater edification, accompanied by many noblemen, among them the Count of Redondo. Father Gundisalvo Vaz preached in [the church]. After his baptism he was led back to Ours. The other was an African who had lived as a follower of Mohammed; he was baptized with much pomp in the presence of many onlookers. Both began to confess to Ours after their baptism.

1196.   *Loyola urges the King of Portugal to abolish dueling*

Toward the middle of July, the provincial [Diego Miró] returned to Lisbon bringing the King two letters written by Father Ignatius. The first consoled him over the death of Prince [John]; the second concerned the prohibition of duels in his kingdoms. The King observed that he had already outlawed such duels in his kingdom; but he offered his help in obtaining a similar ban, such as Father Ignatius desired, from the rest of the princes. So that he could serve as an example to those [princes], he accepted the letters of Father Ignatius and promised to reflect on them and see what he could do.

By this action Father Ignatius was striving to achieve what first the Apostolic See and then the Council [of Trent] had prescribed, namely, that those who fought such duels or freely allowed them to be fought in their domains or, even worse, were spectators at them might be liable for the most severe punishments and disgrace. The King showed himself enormously elated at matters contributing to edification that had been written from Rome, and at the favors granted for the spiritual advancement of India, at the division of the provinces in Spain, and, finally, at Father Francis [Borgia's] appointment as commissary.

1199.   *The King's support for former Jesuits*

The King showed himself inclined to favor and promote those who had left the Society, not because their apostasy had pleased him, but because he was confronted with a shortage of men adept at undertaking the care of souls. He needed many such men for ministering to the military orders, whose grand master he was. So he was happy to make use of these learned men; accordingly, he had entrusted the care of certain churches to some [of them], along with the ecclesiastical revenues associated with them. . . .

1200.   *Miró tries to change the King's mind*

Therefore, Father Provincial along with Father Gundisalvo Vaz went to the King and asserted that it did not promote the service either of God or the King himself to avail of the ministry of [Cristóbal Leiton] or other apostates [from the Society]. But the King disagreed because he saw matters differently. The Queen was also present, and strongly favored our position even though nobody had alerted her ahead of time [to take this stance]. Finally, the King was mollified and indicated that he was willing to go along with some of our petitions, promising to consider the matter [more thoroughly]. Ours went immediately to Don Luís, the prince; even though he was lying sick in bed, such was his zeal in supporting the cause of our Society that he immediately wrote to the King. Hardly had Ours returned home than the Queen sent someone to them, followed immediately by a messenger from Prince Luís disclosing that they had obtained from the King what they had requested. . . .

1209.   *Portugal will pay for the training of Spanish scholastics*

In Spain the situation was just the opposite from what obtained [in Portugal]. There [in Spain] many offered themselves to the Society, but they could not be suitably supported because of the precarious financial situation and actual poverty of the colleges. Thus Father Francis Borgia offered much consolation to Ours in Portugal when he declared that he would send many men to Portugal if that policy seemed good to them. They answered immediately that they would regard it as a great benefit, even were he to send a hundred men; for they had to provide for the colleges that were being started in India and Brazil and those that the Greater Congo was begging for. Moreover, the bishops of Portalegre and Algarve were concerned for [staffing] their colleges. . . .

1246.   *Borgia and Queen Juana*

In order to obey Queen [Catharina] of Portugal and Prince Philip, Father Francis went to the town of Tordesillas to find out if he could give some help to Queen Juana. Even though he spent two months there, his only accomplishment was to have carried out the will of the aforesaid rulers, for Queen Juana was completely bereft of reason.[9] While he was there, he received a letter from Princess Juana, who was still in Portugal; in it she requested that he await her arrival in that province of Castile, for she had been summoned to govern the kingdoms of Spain in the absence of Prince Philip.

1248.   *Borgia's work at Avila and Medina del Campo*

Father Francis traveled from this town to Avila, which was not very distant, so that he might deal personally with matters pertaining to the foundation of a college. The whole city—the clergy, the people, and the nobility, that is—were greatly delighted by his coming, and when he preached to a dense crowd in the cathedral during the octave of Corpus Christi, the whole city was deeply moved. . . . When he had dispatched the matters for which he had come, he went from there to Medina del Campo, so that he could foster in the [Jesuits

---

[9] In this sentence Polanco is talking about Queen Juana the Mad, mother of Charles V; in the next sentence he speaks about Princess Juana, the daughter of Charles V.

there] a more deeply rooted observance of the *Constitutions* and rules. After several exhortations he left behind one of his companions to act as a syndic to observe how things were going [in the aftermath of his visitation].[10]

1249.   *Borgia and Princess Juana*

At [Medina del Campo] he learned that within four days Princess Juana would be coming to Tordesillas, and he immediately set out for there. But when Lady Juana came on June 9, even though she allowed almost nobody to see her, that very day she notified Father Francis that she would be very grateful if he came to her. She received him very cordially; and she talked with him at length that day and the next about matters affecting her conscience and the principles *[ratio]* that guided her regency; she did not wish to allow external preoccupations to cause her to forget about her spiritual progress, from which she would derive the ability to govern wisely. When she was going to leave for Valladolid, she asked Father Francis to come there in fifteen or twenty days, so that they could complete their discussions about matters [pertaining] to the common good and her spiritual welfare. Father Francis did as she had requested; and on the feast of Saint Anthony of Padua [June 13], he preached to many dignitaries and members of the nobility who had gathered there at our eponymous church in Valladolid.

1256.   *Borgia and Princess Juana at Valladolid*

. . . Father Francis set out for Salamanca and Plasencia after gathering an excellent harvest at Valladolid, especially at the palace of Princess Juana, benefiting both head and members. Besides holding private conversations that very much affected the common good, he taught Christian doctrine there in the palace. Although the court, which he called Egypt, annoyed him, the progress that he observed in important people of both sexes consoled him. Princess Juana began to edify the whole kingdom by her style of governance; for besides providing an example of recollection and devotion, reports of which emanated from her palace, she saw to it that those being detained in prisons were better treated and that public business was moved along as expeditiously as possible.

---

[10] Ignatius provides for a syndic in the *Constitutions* (e.g., no. 271). This individual acted as a sort of official observer, inspector, corrector, or watchman. The function has fallen into desuetude. See St. Ignatius of Loyola, *The Constitutions of the Society of Jesus,* trans. and ed. George E. Ganss, S.J. (St. Louis: The Institute of Jesuit Sources, 1970), 160n11.—ED.

She turned her attention to the reformation of convents, especially in Catalonia, and to other things conducive to the universal good of those Kingdoms; and she was solicitous to learn what responsibilities were hers, so that she could properly execute her office of regent, so much so that she seemed to utterly surpass the limitations of her sex and age. She petitioned Father Ignatius for a share in the good works of our Society and [asked him to obtain] from the Supreme Pontiff permission for her to read the Bible in the vernacular. She preferred to obtain this faculty through Father Ignatius, although she could have [obtained it] through others.

1266.   *Borgia sets up four novitiates for Spain and Portugal*

When the question of setting up houses of probation in the individual Spanish provinces was being discussed, Gandía was designated [as the site] for the province of Aragon and Plasencia for Baetica [western Andalusia]; and for the province of Castile the choice fell upon the town of Simancas, where a college had been inaugurated this very year. Father Francis decided to send Father [Bartolomé de] Bustamante, his socius, to open the new house of probation at Simancas. To inhabit this new novitiate Father Antonio de Córdoba sent seven or eight novices from the college at Salamanca along with the money needed for their support. He was in charge of [that college] as a sort of superintendent, although Father [Bartolomé] Hernandez was the rector. After several other men had been accepted from elsewhere, he wanted twelve or fourteen novices to be assembled there who would lay the foundation of this house.

Father Francis wanted to deprive himself of his own socius both because [Bustamante] seemed strongly attracted to this work and because his heart was set on supporting any number of novices there, even by begging [for alms], and because the bishop of Plasencia, in whose diocese Simancas was, had also promised his help for [the house]. Father Francis also hoped that while training others, [Bustemante] too would grow spiritually according to the Institute of the Society—a hope that [Bustamante] himself also shared. Among others, Father Gaspar Fernandez of Toledo was admitted at this time; later he was to serve as rector of the College of Naples.

1271.   *Admitting New Christians to the Society in Spain*

. . . As regards admitting those who descended from New Christian [Muslim and Jewish] ancestry, [Antonio de Cordoba] held exactly the same view as did Father Ignatius; namely, they should not be excluded outright nor should the door be completely open to them before they had been subjected to a rigorous process of selection. Still, Father Antonio wrote what he had heard from some influential persons who were not descended from this kind [of ancestry]. They strongly hoped that this abuse of racial discrimination and other unjust norms of evaluating persons should be far removed from the Society because Christian virtues are more easily found and planted in such men than in others who hold the opposite opinion. Many of those who are descents of New Christians cease to direct their hearts to God's service when the door to serving God in religious orders is closed to them. Also not a few New Christians, seeing the opportunity of serving God in religion denied them, cease to direct their souls to the worship of God. Furthermore, some of the infidels do not come forward for baptism because they realize how badly they will be treated after receiving that sacrament. . . .

1276.   *Borgia puts the founding of new colleges in Spain on hold*

He reported to Father Ignatius his decision not to accept more colleges unless construction had already been completed and financial support guaranteed, so that workers might be trained to send to [future colleges]. Nonetheless, he intended to travel to Seville soon to make arrangements for a new college there; because of the importance of that city, we should not neglect to staff a college there.

THE YEAR 1555

■ **Rome**

2.   *The mission to Ethiopia begins*

At Rome the status of the Society—its prestige and the number of its members, that is—was growing. At a consistory held in January, the decision was made to send thirteen priests of the Society to Ethiopia. The consensus of the cardinals was to sanction what the Supreme Pontiff [Julius III] had previously done on his own authority: Father João Nunes was confirmed as patriarch and Fathers Andrés de Oviedo and Melchor Carneiro were named bishops and successors to the patriarch. At the time, the Supreme Pontiff remarked that there would be no question of greed in these prelacies at least; given the circumstances, those promoted to dignities like these should prepare themselves to undergo martyrdom and to bear crushing burdens rather than to bask in honors and wealth.

8.   *Laínez and Nadal are to accompany Cardinal Morone to Germany*

The Supreme Pontiff designated Cardinal Morone as legate to Germany; his responsibility would be to represent the Apostolic See at a diet of considerable importance that was going to take place there. [Morone] himself decided that two men of our Society should accompany him on his journey. It was Father Ignatius, however, who [specifically] chose Fathers Laínez and Nadal, and they set forth with the legate for Germany. When the Pope sent the bishop of Verona [Aloisio Lippomano], the future apostolic nuncio, to Poland, a certain cardinal of considerable authority suggested to the Pope that two of the Society should also accompany him. Although this proposal greatly pleased the Pope, he was unwilling to order it peremptorily, so he directed the cardinal to confer with Father Ignatius. Because Father Ignatius could know well enough the mind of the Pope, he was unwilling to deny the apostolic nuncio his cooperation, for the spiritual needs of that kingdom seemed to demand our help, feeble though it was. Therefore, he named Father Bobadilla to this post, who shortly before had

---

Here begins *Chron.*, vol. 5, and also the third and last manuscript of this work, which covers the years 1555 and 1556 and contains 1,255 pages.—ED.

been successfully occupied in visiting the abbacy of Farfa and other places and had now returned to Rome. Being the second companion fell to the lot of Father Battista Viola, but when the Pope expired, this and the previous mission were partly interrupted and changed.

10.   *Jesuits at Rome*

As this year began, some 160 men of our Society resided at Rome, some in the professed house, others in the [Roman] College. A few also were stationed at the German College to help the German students. More than fifty had been sent out to various places a few months ago. This college, where more than seventy of Ours were stationed, was flourishing in all respects, except that it had no financial resources, or almost none. The revenue-producing instruments purchased with money left by Father Francis Borgia were gradually sold off to support Ours. But Father Francis had taken care to write letters to Philip, the king of England and prince of Spain, and to the Pope and many cardinals, as we mentioned above.[1] . . .

12.   *The situation in France*

In some parts of France there was a strong desire for ministries of the Society, but the decree issued by the Theological Faculty of Paris that we described above was a major hindrance to the progress of the Society in that kingdom. Nonetheless, Father Ignatius decided that no steps should be taken in opposition to that illustrious university either by invoking the Pope or by employing any harsher measures; for his own part, he was content to write to Ours wherever they were, urging them to send him testimonials from princes and cities regarding the progress and accomplishments of the Society. These he could show to the University of Paris, demonstrating that our Institute did nothing to endanger the public welfare, as the [university professors] had charged in their decree, but rather served to advance the glory of God and the good of souls.

Thus, from various kingdoms and provinces came glowing testimonials of this sort sent to him by princes, universities, and a number of [ordinary] people. Cardinal [Guise] of Lorraine came to Rome this year for the papal election, bringing with him four illustrious professors of theology at Paris,

---

[1] Philip was married to Queen Mary Tudor at this time, so he held the title King of England, even though his power there was very restricted.

almost all of whom had played a part in drafting that decree. Someone averred that one of them, Master [Jean] Benoit of the Dominican Order, had composed a major portion [of the decree] himself. Some of our Society, among them Father [Martín de] Olave, whose doctorate was from Paris, went to the Cardinal [of Lorraine], who showed himself quite supportive of and favorable to the Society. He in turn summoned these [Paris] professors, with whom he intended to discuss the [University of Paris's] decree. Ours refuted the individual articles so successfully that, to put it modestly, not only did the cardinal seem quite satisfied but the professors as well. The cardinal gave indications of his desire to see to it that the Theology Faculty of Paris would completely rescind that decree. He went on to express his intentions to give our Society one of the colleges [at Paris belonging to the diocese] of Rheims—the one that was better than the others.

18.   *Good Pope Marcellus II and the Jesuits*

As for the Society, [Marcellus II] loved it with fatherly affection, and from its very beginnings he had been well informed about its activities in Europe and as far away as India and Brazil; he was familiar as well with what God was accomplishing through it. He often went to confession to Ours; and shortly before coming to Rome for the papal election, he went to confession to Father [Bernard] Olivier, who was rector of our college at Loreto. He celebrated Mass in the Chapel of the Virgin Mary in which the Word was made flesh, and distributed the Eucharist to all of Ours with his own hand; in the same place he exhorted Ours to progress in virtue.

33.   *Facilities for sick Jesuits at Rome*

This year a sunroom connected to the house called the Roscian Tower was purchased, and several rooms were fitted out to take care of the infirm. An office was prepared for the pharmacist to serve the needs of the sick, and Doctor [Baldassare] Torres, who was a physician, carefully took care to apply whatever remedies we had to the needs of the infirm. Luís, a Portuguese, was the first to fill the office of pharmacist, a trade at which he was skilled. He came to Rome with Bernard the Japanese.

40.   *Jesuit ethnic diversity at Rome*

Both in Rome and nearby, the college students were able to supply for the many spiritual needs because this year thirty priests were resident there and ten of the students were raised [to the priesthood] toward the end of this year. Many came to Rome from all the Christian nations and, once they had returned to their own people, spread good reports about us. Thus in various kingdoms colleges or universities were offered to the Society. Spaniards, Portuguese, Frenchmen, Flemish, Germans, Bohemians, Dalmatians, and Greeks could be found in the [Roman] College. and Italians besides. Many marveled when they observed the unity of spirit and the mutual love that reigned among all of them. This seemed to be a sort of seedbed [readying its sprouts] to assist all those nations at a later time. And divine Providence seemed to be calling to the Society many of those who were coming to Rome from northern countries.

41.   *Bohemian and German candidates for the Society*

Drawn by the reputation of the German College, eleven or twelve Bohemian students had come and were accepted into our house; because at that time the German College had lost its papal subsidy, it did not seem wise to readily admit so many men to the college. Meanwhile, some of Ours spoke with the men from neighboring countries; in part because Ours prompted them to do so, in part because they recognized the efforts that the Society was exerting on their behalf, and—what we must list as the most important factor of all— because the Lord had used this means to call them to a more perfect state, all of them embraced the Society at the same time. Among them were Father Baltha- sar Hostousky and Wenceslaus [Sturm] and others who later accomplished much for the Church. Six Germans also from various provinces came to the German College without having been [officially] admitted to it beforehand and, for reasons similar to those we listed above, decided to enter the Society. But some from both of these groups, perhaps because they had undertaken this Institute for human reasons rather than in response to a divine vocation, left several years later, after they had advanced in their studies.

46.   *Ignatius and Paul IV*

Meanwhile, Father Ignatius did not fail to put the attitude of the Supreme Pontiff to the test. The Pope used to utter many words of high praise about the Society and gave it much credit for its teaching and integrity. Also this pope displayed great kindness to some of Ours who came to kiss his feet, including

Father Ignatius; shortly thereafter, [the Pope] summoned him to an audience, at which he revealed that a cardinal had reported the outstanding success that Father Nadal had achieved in Germany. (Cardinal Morone had brought this report when he returned to Italy, after having spent several months in Germany, especially in Vienna). But the Pope said he did not want to grant this until he had heard Father Ignatius's opinion.[2] He spoke at length to Father [Ignatius] about his own desire to help Germany. Thus, they agreed between themselves that Ignatius would write to Father Nadal, ordering him not to leave [Germany] until October. Father Ignatius dispatched this command immediately, but the letter did not reach [Nadal] in Germany because he had already returned to Italy after completing the tasks assigned to him.

50.   *The financial crunch at Rome*

In the end, the Pope [Paul IV] approved of none of the suggestions made to him on this matter, so it could reasonably be inferred that he was unwilling to make a [financial] contribution to the [Roman] College. Thus, day by day the hope of receiving a temporal subsidy from him dwindled away. Even though the four thousand ducats that Father Nadal had sent the previous year through the Count of Malta were recovered, as was another five hundred that he or his son-in-law Lord Rui Gómez had added [to compensate] for the loss that the college had suffered while waiting many months for payment [of Nadal's contribution] to be made, the [college's] revenues were already used up and its properties had already been sold. So it was hardly surprising that our financial situation was quite desperate, for this year the price of grain had risen so high that during the month of August a bushel of wheat cost eight gold pieces. And so not only our house and college but also the German College, as we said, were almost destitute of resources and fell back on the shoulders of the Society for their support.

Almost 180 of Ours lived in the professed house and the [Roman] College this autumn and there were forty or fifty men in the German College to support; moreover, the rent for both colleges' buildings soared to almost five hundred gold pieces. Contributions from alms at Rome did not equal one-fourth of [the cost] of necessities. Thus, a loan of six or seven thousand ducats was arranged, and no human ingenuity seemed able to support these works of ours without the special help of God. But, instead of reposing our hopes in [material]

---

[2] The editors of *Chron.* suggest that the *this* referred to here was the request of Cardinal Otto Truchsess that Nadal continue to work in Germany.

resources, we placed them in God alone, whose honor we were seeking as we expanded these three houses.

51.   *Why men from many nations should not be sent home for financial reasons*

But from England and Ireland, Prussia, Sweden, Denmark, Silesia, Bohemia, Moravia, and the other German provinces, the Lord seemed to be sending many [endowed with] excellent talents either to our Society or to the German College; and we had reason to believe that Julius III would probably endow both colleges. So it was altogether reasonable for us to increase our enrollment. If only Pope Marcellus had lived, we were confident, he would undoubtedly have endowed both [colleges] generously. Without great disedification we could not have sent men back to their provinces when we had called them to Rome from there. Rather, we had to ensure that these men were well disposed toward the Apostolic See.

57.   *Ignatius enlists the support of Catholic monarchs*

At this time [Ferdinand] the King of the Romans was taking steps to set up a college at Prague, and Father Ignatius thought it would be a good idea for [Ferdinand] to write to the Supreme Pontiff, Paul IV. This was the strategy evident in similar letters that we penned: [we wished to give] the Pope an opportunity to see how the leading Christian princes welcomed the ministry of the Society; they described how their provinces needed our endeavors to establish new colleges and perform other functions. Thus it seems less than surprising that Paul IV, the supreme pontiff, would reach the conclusion that in the face of the recommendations of Emperor Charles, King Philip of England, Ferdinand, king of the Romans, and also King John of Portugal, our Society should not be so readily hampered [from carrying out its ministries]. King John, just mentioned, in his charity earnestly recommended the welfare of the Society to the Pope. Also many princes, both churchmen and laymen, communicated in numerous ways their high esteem for [the Society] and requested that some who belonged to our Institute be sent to them. The Pope himself also knew much of this from personal observation.

58.   *Heading off Paul IV regarding singing the office*

Still in all, so that Father Ignatius could forestall [Paul IV] from changing any essentials of our Institute, this year on his own initiative the former decreed that the office of vespers should be sung on Sundays and feast days in our church. Thus, it seemed the Pope would be satisfied and would not seek to introduce any further singing of the Office into the Society. However, after this matter had been discussed with some of the more important members of the Society residing in Rome, the decision was reached that a style of chanting should be introduced which was not contrary to our *Constitutions*. But Father Ignatius reserved to himself the decision on the actual style of chant to be introduced. Finally, he determined that the singing should be in figured chant (which they call *falsum bordonem*) in order to provide greater edification for the people.[3] Although this method of singing did not accord well with the *Constitutions* that he himself had drafted, Ignatius considered that there should be a dispensation from Rome [granting it]. What appealed to him about this decision was that both in our college and in the German college many students from northern countries were highly skilled in this sort of chant.

68.   *Plans for colleges in northern Europe*

Since it distressed the bishop of Strasbourg that his city was teeming with heretics, he insistently begged that a college be started there and [men] be sent to it. The bishop of Regensburg did likewise, and so did the archbishop of Esztergom in Hungary and [Cardinal Stanislaus Hosius] of Ermeland in Prussia, who was regarded as one of the pillars in the kingdom of Poland. Other men elsewhere requested colleges, but this year none of them obtained what they desired. But as far as starting one at Prague in Bohemia, the Supreme Pontiff wanted this, and Father Ignatius went along with the desires of the King of the Romans and seriously set the process in motion, even though actually sending [men] was deferred until the start of the following year.

73.   *Ignatius assigns Ribadeneira to the imperial court in Belgium*

This year Father Ignatius sent Father Pedro de Ribadeneira to the court of Emperor Charles and commissioned him to deliver and explain the *Constitutions* of the Society to Ours at Cologne, Louvain, and Tournai. Next he was to carry on the usual ministries of the Society in the Belgian vineyard of the Lord, whether in the curia of the Emperor in Brussels or wherever the door would

---

[3] In Spanish *fabordon;* in French *faux-bourdon;* in Italian *fabordone.* This seems to have been basically plain chant with harmonizing notes sung above or below it. It was an early forerunner of modern harmony. See *Chron.,* 5:33n2.—ED.

more readily open and allow him [to work] for God's honor. Besides him, Ignatius sent six other men, some to lower Germany, others to upper Germany.

94.   *Admitting Princess Juana to the Society*

[Juana, princess of Portugal], who had taken religious vows, desired to convert them into a vow of the Society and submit herself to its obedience, even though her eminent status made it mandatory that others should be unaware of this. Expediting this matter fell to Father Ignatius, requiring him to obtain this commutation from the Supreme Pontiff, while concealing the name of the petitioner. Because Father Francis Borgia doubted that this sort of obedience should be allowed (for the procedures of the Society did not allow it), Father Ignatius not only informed him that it was licit to admit her but ordered him in virtue of obedience to do so. Here he showed clearly enough that in such rare cases a dispensation from the *Constitutions* of the Society should be allowed.

95.   *Paul IV has the professed house searched for hidden weapons*

When the peaceful tranquility had begun to be disrupted, the Supreme Pontiff became suspicious, I know not why, that a great store of weapons was hidden at our house; so he sent the city governor with the fiscal agent and some of their associates to search our house. The governor, who in all other respects was a friend of the Society, left the soldiers at the door, entered the house with the fiscal agent (who is called the *Palantier*), went to Father Ignatius, and privately disclosed to him the Pope's command.[4]

96.   *The search turns up empty*

Ignatius, who always remained calm in mind and countenance, called for the secretary of the Society [Polanco himself] and in the governor's presence ordered him to lead the fiscal agent and some other officials around the whole house. This he did at once. Although from the composure of the faces and attitudes [of Ours], these otherwise upright officials recognized that the fear and suspicion were groundless, they searched the house very carefully from attic to

---

[4] Paul IV, from a leading Neapolitan noble family, resented Spanish control of the kingdom of Naples. During the sixth and last of the Habsburg-Valois Wars, he allied the Papal States with France. He was deeply suspicious of the Jesuits because of their Spanish leadership, quite aside from his religious differences with them and his long-standing animosity toward Ignatius. Any and all these factors may have motivated the search of the professed house.

cellar. They did not find even one sword, much less lances or harquebuses. They left much edified by our simplicity and obedience and by our poverty as well.

98.   *Learning vernacular languages*

This year an order was issued in the name of Father Ignatius that Ours should make a point of learning the vernacular language in the provinces where they were [residing], for instance, Italian in Italy and French in France. He ordered that at Rome Italian grammar should be taught daily, so that the men coming from many nations, especially the novices who were undergoing probation at our house, should learn that language more easily.

164.   *Attitudes toward the Jesuits in other religious orders*

The religious of some orders also showed goodwill to Ours. Both the prior of the Order of Saint Dominic and the commissary of the Inquisition showed themselves very friendly to Father Everard [Mercurian]. The vicar, however, conceived the opinion that the religious of that order were less friendly toward Ours because we seemed opposed to the activities of Girolamo Savonarola. A certain preacher of the Servite Order in his public sermon or lecture heaped considerable praise upon our college at Perugia, and on our other devout works besides.

■ **Italy**

165.   *Hostility toward the Jesuits at Perugia*

Some religious of the Orders of Saints Francis and Augustine manifested opposition to Ours, some because of the people who received the sacraments frequently at our church, others because of our academic work. In fact, a certain friar of Saint Dominic asserted that this function of imparting knowledge lay beyond the ability of Ours. The city held a far-different opinion, as we have reported.

178.   *Ending vendettas at Loreto*

In five instances peace was restored, bringing enormous consolation to the people. One case involved two prominent young men who for ten years kept the townspeople divided into two factions by their unending hostility [toward one another]. Many preachers and men of great authority had tried in vain to bring them to mutual reconciliation. Once their confessions had been heard and their hearts had been inflamed by sermons, Ours easily extracted an agreement from both parties. Right after the two noblemen had been brought together and a prayer had been offered, the two were prevailed upon to embrace one another publicly; and then each was urged to seek one another's pardon on bended knees. This they did with such heartfelt emotion that there was no one present who did not shed abundant tears. Taking a meal together afterwards, they began to love each other so ardently that they could hardly be separated from each other; frequently both came to Communion.

193.   *Pilgrims come to Loreto*

The swarm of pilgrims coming to Loreto, not only from parts of Italy but of Flanders, France, Germany, and Spain as well, kept increasing when it became known that Ours could hear confession in [the pilgrims' native] languages. When the number of priests was small, Ours were sometimes compelled to deprive themselves of the consolation of Mass and their usual prayers and even to remain in the church during mealtime. In order to satisfy the devotion and need of the penitents, they did not return home before the second or third hour of the night. They did not, however, perform this labor in hearing confessions without gaining consolation, for a very rich harvest of souls sprouted from it. Among other people, many apostates were helped to return to their religious orders; many too who had for too long slumbered in grievous sin were moved to change their lives, many imperfect people too were inspired to pursue a course that would lead them closer to salvation and perfection. The reputation of Ours glowed more brilliantly day by day.

215.   *Helping people who feared confessing to their pastor*

In a certain place almost a two-day journey from Loreto, one of our priests found that there were twenty people, more or less, who had befouled themselves with mortal sins for many years and wanted to escape from their filthy state of soul; they regretted what they had done, but they had determined they would rather die than confess to their pastor. Therefore, Father Ignatius was consulted, and with his consent arrangements were made for one of Ours to perform this office of charity.

274.   *Setting up a house for former prostitutes at Florence*

This year steps were taken at Florence to set up a house similar to the one established at Rome under the patronage of Saint Martha. Almost eighty women, many of them girls, were brought there. The woman who was the sponsor of this pious work and had done very much for us as well wanted one of Ours to undertake hearing the confessions of these women. But because the norms of our Institute did not permit Ours to take on this burden, she was able to engage Ours to hear their confessions only on the feast of Pentecost.

275.   *Eleonora de Toledo, duchess of Florence, and Laínez*

When Father Diego Laínez returned to Florence from Germany along with the legate [Cardinal] Morone, the duchess made every effort to keep [Laínez nearby]. But he obtained permission from her to go to Loreto and Rome, but then after a brief interval to return to Florence. This the duchess was more willing to permit him to do because she wanted him to visit the holy house at Loreto in her name. Because she was pregnant and physically feeble, she was very desirous that he come back right away.

276.   *Paul IV keeps Laínez in Rome; Eleonora threatens to close our*
           college

But when, as we said, Paul IV ordered him in virtue of obedience to stay in Rome, the duchess started to grow irate and threatened to close down the college unless he returned. When she was informed that Father Ignatius would gladly send him, but Ours neither could or should resist obeying the Pope, she said, " If the Pope has ordered him to stay, I also will do what I say."

277.   *The duchess punished the Jesuits at Florence*

. . . But when Father Ignatius sent Father Didaco de Guzman [to Florence], the duchess kept saying she did not want anybody except Father Laínez; and when [Guzman] came quite often to the palace, she never wanted to talk to him during the entire year. Ours experienced no small suffering from the very high price of grain because their subsidy, instead of being augmented, was reduced in part.

296.   *Preaching and teaching at Genoa*

The day after Christmas [Laínez] gave an oration on the poverty that Christ had from his tender years embraced like a daughter. So large was the crowd of listeners that it surpassed four thousand. The citizens, their support for our men ablaze, came the next day to hear a lyric poem on the Lord's birth along with some other poems. The audience listened so avidly that not even the smallest disturbance could be heard; and when the performance came to an end, they remained for a time waiting for something more. So densely packed were those present that the bishop, who wanted to attend, could not get in.

Many of the citizens were moved to entrust their sons to the training imparted by Ours. There was a man who, even though he maintained a tutor at his home to instruct his children, nonetheless sent his oldest son to Ours every day. They complained about other schoolmasters who had never been observed to produce such results as this. But some of [the schoolmasters] tried to imitate our procedures, especially by [reciting] the [same] prayers that Ours were accustomed to say at the end of class. Although some secretly but bitterly criticized Ours, still they became more diligent so that they could retain their students by exerting greater efforts.

313.   *Why Genoa produced few vocations to the Society*

Some of the young men who wanted to enter the Society were the sons of noble citizens; once aware of their desires, their parents removed them from our school, even though Father [Giovanni Battista] Viola assured parents that without their approval he would not admit anybody to the Society. Thus, he brought it about that sometimes because their parents took such an attitude toward [vocations], at other times because, after students had made some progress, [their parents] wanted to remove their sons [and put them to] work in business—for both of these reasons, then, hardly any Genoese young men, especially from the more noble families, would be admitted if this could only be done with the consent of their parents.

324.   *Difficulties with housing at Genoa*

. . . In part because it was hard to find a location in the convenient part of the city and in part because the Genoese were distracted and worried about wars and the imminent danger from the Turkish fleet, they could not easily find [Ours] another house and did not much concern themselves about the matter. But when Father Nadal came there from Rome and judged that on no account should [Ours] stay there because of the danger [the house] might collapse, Ours seemed to have been plunged into a very difficult situation, not just because of their tottering living quarters but also because of the difficulty they experienced in acquiring the costly necessities of life.

325.   *Financial difficulties at Genoa*

When Father Laínez was present, many people swore that they would certainly help; but once he had departed, they voided their promises, thus leaving the costs to be shouldered by only a few citizens. When in the course of this year [Ours] did not have in their community a man as outstanding in learning as [the citizens] had hoped for, the people seemed to grow cold; and it seemed not at all a trifling matter that our few friends had to provide for these necessities from their private patrimony, especially since they would have to cover the travel expenses of the men who were going elsewhere and provide appropriate subsidies for the sick.

343.   *Francesco Palmio works to reform the clergy at Bologna*

Owing to [Palmio's] work and advice, many priests reoriented their hearts from very serious vices to the pursuit of piety; others promised they would come back to the way of salvation. Some were so seriously repentant that, weeping profusely while saying Mass, they humbly begged forgiveness from their parishioners for having carried out their duty so [disgracefully].

355.   *A candidate for the Jesuits robs his community and flees*

When a certain Fleming, dirty and clad in tattered clothes, asked to be admitted to the Society, Father Francesco Palmio, overcome by pity, admitted him and assigned him to help the cook. He acted with circumspection, worked hard, and gave an impression of devotion and piety. [Ours] put too much trust in him; not only did they outfit him with clothes suitable for winter (for it that season of the year), but they also left him alone in the house when some were in the church and others were occupied with other tasks. The keys of the chest in which [the rector] kept the money [he] left hidden in some book. While he was making the bed of that Father, he searched all around and found the keys. After opening the chest, he found the pouch where the rector kept all the funds of the house, which did not exceed eight or nine gold pieces. But lest he leave a single penny, he also grabbed some leggings that seemed to fit him nicely and fled. In vain did two of Ours pursue him, because he turned off the highway. Thus did it cost [Ours] dearly to learn that unknown men are not to be trusted.

383.   *A Jesuit sermon gives offense to the Duke of Ferrara*

On the very feast of the Purification [February 2], something occurred in our church placing us in danger of a grave scandal. When the Duke of Ferrara accompanied by many noblemen entered the church, a certain Father Jean Jordan of French nationality, caught up by a kind of zeal and irate that there were so many wearing masks in Ferrara, arose and wanted to eject the duke along with the others from the church. He cried out in a loud voice, "Let the maskers get out."[5] It chanced that Father [Jean] Pelletier was in the company of the duke himself, and either because the crowd was so noisy or because [Father Jean Pelletier] diverted the duke's attention elsewhere, the duke did not understand what had been said or pretended not to. But some of the courtiers heard those words. But after being emphatically rebuked, Father Jordan promised that henceforward he would do nothing except what he was ordered to do under obedience.

399.   *The Duke of Ferrara defends the Society before the French king*

The duke greatly favored the works of our Society. But when he understood the terms of the Paris decree [attacking the Society], which Father Pelletier had brought to him, he wrote a letter to his ambassador to the Most Christian King [Henry II], commanding him to read it [to the King] word for word. For this was the way that that ambassador usually informed the King of the contents of the letters from his duke. The duke instructed his secretary to find out from Father Pelletier what he was supposed to write. Among other things contained in that letter was that [the duke] had known the Society for many years; that he sometimes made use of one of its members as his confessor; that he had now also assigned a confessor of the same Society as confessor for his wife and his son, a bishop; that he had seen to it that three colleges were set up in his dominions; that the other princes of Italy had the Society in their principalities and held it in high regard; that he had come to know nothing but good about the Society, and other similar points.

464.   *Why enrollment declined at the Jesuit school in Padua*

In the month of June our classes were shut down; because of the plague which was already beginning to rage, holding class was forbidden by public decree. But before this time enrollment was quite low: it declined from seventy-four students at the start of the year to sixty at this time. The explanation for

---

[5] The Latin is *larvæ*, which can mean "ghosts" but also "masks." The latter seems more likely here, because the faux pas described here took place during the Mardi Gras season. Perhaps the duke himself was wearing a sort of mask and was not recognized by Father Jordan.—ED.

this loss was not that the teachers were deficient; indeed, they were performing their tasks effectively; rather, it was that the [school] was in a remote area and most of the students were poor. After they had made a little progress, they went off to work as merchants or to take jobs as notaries, or else they attended classes open to the general public. Furthermore, some of the numerous schoolmasters at Padua strove to lure students from our school. Thus, they persuaded parents to send [their children] to public classes or to entrust their offspring to themselves for their schooling. But those who persevered in [our] classes made excellent progress in good behavior and literary studies.

468. *Nadal explains Jesuit obedience and prayer to the scholastics*

At Padua and Venice [Nadal] concentrated on explaining especially practical aspects of the *Examen* and *Constitutions,* specifically those things having to do with obedience and prayer. Thus, he reduced the time for prayer to one hour, so divided that the [community] devoted half an hour to prayer in the morning, a quarter of an hour before dinner, and another quarter of an hour after the examen [of conscience] before going to bed. The intention of Father Ignatius was that the scholastics would give only a half hour to morning prayer besides the two examens and the time devoted to attending Mass. [Nadal] also taught [them] what fruit they should derive from receiving the sacraments. After talking to [the community] privately and finding out what each one wanted to discuss with him or, on the other hand, learning what he himself wanted to find out from them, he organized their studies. Following the prescriptions of the *Constitutions,* he prescribed the renovation of vows or, if somebody had not made them at the appointed time laid down by [the *Constitutions*], he commanded that the young Jesuits do so.

469. *Nadal gets down to details on Jesuit practices*

He reviewed the rules that [Jesuits at Padua and Venice] were using and emended them as he judged proper. But he also drafted for them general regulations and some [directives] for the scholastics to follow based on Part 4 [of the *Constitutions*]: [he left behind as well regulations governing] the conduct of the master of novices and the novices themselves; moreover, he drafted rules for the rector, the corrector at table, the syndic, the buyer, the refectorian, the cook, and the doorkeeper. He inspected all the books; if he found any that were heretical, he burned them. He stored some others separately, such as those by Erasmus and Vives. Regarding other books, he acted as seemed best in the

Lord. He suggested material that would be useful when establishing colleges and that would spell out the regulations governing the distribution of a patrimony according to the *Constitutions.*

478.   *Devout women at Venice*

First [we can say this] with regard to the administration of the sacraments: many people approached the sacraments weekly. Among them were some very honorable and noble women who by the example of their devotion encouraged others of both sexes to imitate their use of confession and Communion, their devout prayers, and their pursuit of more virtuous living. Complying with the suggestions of their confessors, these women assisted the poor from their own resources and contributed money to free some who were imprisoned because of debts. . . .

514.   *Madrid's book on frequent Communion is published*

Although the Lord tried the patience of Ours in a variety of ways, still, many people came to the sacraments of confession and Communion in our church, especially on the more solemn feasts. Some men, spiritual persons in name and in the estimation of the townsfolk, opposed this frequent use of the sacraments and adduced silly arguments to deter a good many from this practice. Accordingly, Ours at Naples exerted serious efforts to print Dr. [Cristóbal] Madrid's little book on frequent Communion and took charge of its actual publication.[6]

530.   *Teaching catechism at Messina*

This year the explanation of Christian doctrine flourished at Messina. By an edict of the viceroy, all boys between six and twelve years of age had to gather in the ten parishes in that city to be instructed in Christian doctrine; noncompliance would lead to their parents' being fined) . The viceroy was convinced that any hope of achieving a well-administered commonwealth was contingent on the proper upbringing of its youth. He turned over to Father Provincial of our Society the responsibility of providing this instruction. He in

---

[6] The history of Madrid's *De frequenti usu sanctissimi Eucharistiæ sacramenti libellus* is more complicated than Polanco suggests. Loyola ordered its composition and Salmerón and Bobadilla made contributions to it. A revised version was printed at the Roman College in 1557 and went through many reprintings. See Gilmont, *Les Écrits spirituels des premiers jésuites,* 256–59.

turn appointed two of Ours for each parish to whom he delegated the task of imparting this doctrine. Ours did not undertake this assignment in a sluggish manner, nor did the people greet their efforts with indifference. On Sundays and feast days, at the sound of the bells in the main church giving the signal for this exercise, all the pastors, already alerted to their duty, sent bell ringers through the streets to summon all their boys. In this parish three hundred, in that five hundred, in another far more assembled.

531.   *Adults at Messina support and profit from catechism lessons*

The people marveled at this unusual practice and deemed this generation of boys fortunate indeed for having lived during these days and absorbed such instruction in Christian living and doctrine from teachers like this, and they wished that somehow they themselves were young again. No small number of adults listened to the same rudiments of Christian doctrine. If there was something they did not understand, after the lesson was over they asked for an explanation of it.

551.   *The Inquisition's policy discourages people from going to confession*
         at Messina

An edict of the inquisitor considerably reduced the numbers of those [going to confession]. He proclaimed that all people fell under excommunication who did not reveal the identity of persons who they knew had said or done something contrary to the faith, giving specific instances of their [offenses]; he also ordered that before hearing the confessions of any penitents, Ours must inquire of them whether they had revealed [to authorities] those who they knew had fallen into one of the enumerated categories [of heresy]. If [the penitents] answered that they had not done so, he forbade Ours to hear their confessions. Neither did he want Ours to be able to absolve anybody from that excommunication.

When the rumor spread around the city that Ours were sending penitents to the inquisitor to reveal the sins that others had committed against the faith, even those otherwise inclined to confess to Ours would no longer approach us. This was especially true of noblemen, because they were fearful of being sent to the inquisitors. Although the command of the inquisitor was general and applied to all confessors, the report had it that Ours were almost alone in observing it. The inquisitor himself said that few people came forward to denounce anything except those who went to our church for confession. This explained why even in

Holy Week, when the harvest was usually more abundant, fewer people than usual came to our church for confession.

620.   *Ignatius urges an attack on Muslim North Africa*

The viceroy [Juan de Vega] spoke amicably with Father Provincial [Jerónimo Doménech] about that worthy business that he had earnestly commended to the prayers of Father Ignatius, namely, a certain expedition against the Saracens of Africa. He indicated that there were those who did not understand the matter clearly; but Philip, the prince of Spain and now the king of England, thought differently than did those others; indeed, he strongly approved of this expedition. When the viceroy asked him for prayers, [Ignatius] showed himself very favorable to waging this African war for the glory of God. For the same purpose he wanted a college set up for Africans or those who knew their language. . . .

■   **Austria**

650.   *Progress at the college in Vienna*

This year as well Nicholas de Lanoy was rector of the college at Vienna; our situation in Austria improved considerably during this year. As regards classes, right from the start of the year the number of lay students increased; there were 250 students and more enrolled in five classes; the good reputation of our classes attracted the greatest number of them to Vienna from various provinces. They were Bohemians, Slavs, Hungarians, and Bavarians. Daily more and more came who wanted to submit themselves to the training administered by Ours. Ours were all the more inclined to admit those who they realized had the greater need for a good education. Some of the peoples from whom they came were caught up in rather barbarous and rustic customs. Since they were more involved with military matters than with anything having to do with the faith, they were easily led into dangerous errors by the ministers of the devil. In those places the heretics openly pour forth the poison of their dogmas for the ignorant people to imbibe—something Ours learned after dealing with many people. Even though they were infected by the disease [contracted from] pernicious dogmas, when Ours instructed them about the truth and Christian doctrine, both in friendly conversation and especially in the confessional, they rejected many errors and embraced the genuine Catholic faith and religion.

662.   *The generosity of women at Vienna*

Many pious and noble matrons from both the court and the city followed the example of the Queen [Anne of Bohemia and Hungary]. Although Ours did not accept all the gifts that they received now and then, not even those from the Queen herself, she embraced Ours with great respect and kindness and often sent her sacristans and secretary to inquire whether Ours or our church lacked anything. Even though we did not accept anything that she sent for the support of our house, she did not cease to decorate the church daily with precious ornaments.

670.   *The Canisius* Catechism *is rushed into print*

His Royal Majesty [Ferdinand I] urged Father [Peter] Canisius to complete the catechism that we have mentioned more than once. Nor was there any longer hope that Father Laínez—so involved was he with one demand after another upon his time—could complete the theological work that he had begun. [Canisius] finally completed that little book which goes by his name. The King was so eager to have it published that he found it impossible to wait for Father Ignatius to grant the permission [mandated] by the *Constitutions;* so he immediately had that catechism printed in many thousands of copies. The hope was that great advantages would thereby ensue, especially because several pestiferous monstrosities composed by heretics and feigning to be catechisms would thereby be wrenched from the hands of the young.

■ Bohemia

704.   *Canisius at Prague*

Father Canisius reached Prague and was accorded a very warm welcome by Prince Ferdinand and his court, and they showed him complete support for starting a college. For all the Catholics were convinced that schools conducted by Ours would yield rich fruit from all of Bohemia. Canisius himself confessed that never had he seen such propitious circumstances either in Bavaria or in Austria, so that here one could hope to lead [Hussite] schismatics back to the unity of the Catholic faith. Although the common folk in Bohemia received Communion under both species, still, they adhered to the fasts, customs, and church ceremonies better than did the Germans. Even though there was not a single bishop in all the realm, the leading clergy showed zeal for achieving religious restoration. The Hussites were split among themselves and had few men of learning. They were also not greatly concerned about the matter of John Hus. Thus, if good Bohemian preachers were performing their office well, it seemed likely that that kingdom could be greatly benefited.

718. *Jesuit prospects for taking over the University of Prague*

Canisius informed Father Ignatius that if some professors of philosophy were sent to Prague, it would be easy to amalgamate the University of Prague with our college, for only the Faculty of Arts remained in that university. The teachers there were not very competent, and the Hussites did not pay their salaries regularly, with the result that those aforesaid teachers, who were disciples of Philip Melanchthon and approved by Wittenberg, could barely make ends meet. The university student body barely exceeded two hundred.

726. *Getting the Jesuits established at Prague*

Just as many people had great expectations for the college at Prague and eagerly awaited its inauguration, so the devil also stirred up opposition through his minions. Even before Ours arrived, the devotees [of Satan] were in terror of Ours because they believed that Ours would engage in disputations and debates with the heretical teachers and easily defeat them. Wisely, Father Canisius assured the townsfolk that this was not the policy of the King of the Romans; nor did the King wish us to spend our time arguing and disputing with the Hussites. Rather, it was our objective to open a school where rich and poor alike could be educated free of charge—whether they communicated under one species or both. The chancellor [Henricus Pisek], who served in place of the archbishop, went to [Ferdinand] the King of the Romans to facilitate setting up suitable facilities at our college. Father Canisius had already spent five hundred dollars *[thalers]* on construction. He had seen to it that three new classrooms were ready, and a fourth one besides, a more private one, and eighteen rooms also for the use of our brethren. Enough room still remained that would be well suited for a house of probation. . . .

■ **Germany**

736. *On what conditions should the Society accept colleges in Germany?*

At that time the Cardinal of Augsburg [Otto Truchsess] was not thinking of handing over his college and the University of Dillingen to the Society. [Nadal] thought it would be difficult to induce both him and the other German princes to set up colleges for Ours alone, for they were convinced that seminaries for workers who would assume the care of souls and [respond to the needs] of the episcopal dioceses should be their primary concern—as the aforesaid Father Pedro de Soto[, O.P.,] had told Ours explicitly. Hence, Father Nadal, who passionately desired to help the German nation, suggested to Father Ignatius that colleges could be accepted [by the Society] where other students would be supported who had not decided to become religious; [and he insisted that this arrangement] would be in accord with the norms in the Fourth Part of the *Constitutions,* provided that governance of the institution was under the control of the Society and some of the students were members of the Society, the number of students being contingent upon how many teachers the Society was going to provide. Father Nadal was of the opinion that the acute devastation and desolation [everywhere apparent] in anything having to do with religion made it necessary to accept colleges under any conditions

749.   *The woeful condition of Catholic Germany; how Protestants saw the Jesuits*

This bishop [of Passau, Wolfgang von Salm], who was also a prince of the Empire, invited Father Nadal to his palace with much goodwill and wanted to attend his Mass. Besides the expenses of his lodging, which he paid in accord with local custom, he gave Father Nadal a boat to bring him all the way to Vienna. So well disposed toward the Society was this bishop that he thought the best remedy for the tormented and almost desperate situation in Germany would be for the Supreme Pontiff to send two men of the Society to each of the bishops in Germany, who would, by their advice and help, aid them in governing their churches. He deplored the woeful condition of his own diocese, where he was unable to replace heretical pastors and preachers or [priests] living openly with concubines or wives, for he had no one to put in their places. He admitted that he was somehow content when examining men of this sort if they knew German and said the Latin Mass. Given how great was the number of such sectarians and how tiny was the number of Ours working in Germany, it was amazing how much the heretics dreaded our Society. They seemed unconcerned about any other theologians except the Jesuits, who, as they said, were obstinate and determined not to make any concessions to them.

751.   *Nadal wants Laínez to come to Germany and write against heretics*

[Nadal] thought it would be extremely helpful if Father Laínez were sent to Germany to write against the heretics and if a suitable printing press could be available [for his use] in Vienna. [Laínez's] very presence and preaching would be of great assistance. [Nadal] disclosed that he himself was quite willing to remain in Germany, so that he could do whatever was possible both in the colleges of the Society and in other activities. There was no Catholic in Germany who was writing against the heretics; the heretics, however, never stopped writing in confirmation of their heresies.

753.   *Ferdinand I works with the Jesuits to block the spread of Lutheranism*

Steps were taken to have some new books produced. Above all, the suggestion was offered to the King [Ferdinand] that he should commission his own historian, who was a Catholic, to compose a chronicle in which he would concisely show the progress made by the Roman Church and the councils, the successes in refuting heresies; a chronicle, furthermore, that would demonstrate the progress made by the faith and doctrine, and record the obedience rendered to the Apostolic See in the German nation. Also he ordered Father Canisius to make a theological compendium based on [the Dominican Jean] Vignier and others, as he judged more useful. Moreover, [he ordered] the decrees of the Council of Trent, as well as the Gospels and Epistles for the whole [liturgical] year, to be printed in short handbook format and in the vernacular; it should feature as well argumentations, with clear references to their sources and with short explanations and annotations against the Lutherans. Furthermore, he wished to have a short book of prayers compiled, a compendium of Christian doctrine for small children, and some other works to which Father [Nicholas] Goudanus should also lend his efforts. In order to snatch children from the hands of their [Protestant] teachers, as we noted above, he ordered the schools for beginners to be set up. It was easy for the heretics to see how much the Society was thwarting their activities. Nearly everybody was admitting that almost the entire city of Vienna would soon have been Lutheran if the ministry of our Society had not prevented it.

759.   *Salmerón's trip to Lithuania with the nuncio*

[Samerón] finally reached Augsburg, where he stayed only briefly. On September 7, with the bishop of Verona, whom he met there, he set out for the

King of Poland [Sigismund Augustus], who was then staying at Vilnius, the capital of Lithuania, because at this time a plague was raging at Cracow and several other places in Poland. When he reached Prague, to his great surprise he found Father Canisius there, busy with preaching and erecting a new college. He left there on September 17 and pressed on through the whole month of October and part of November until he reached Lithuania. In the course of the journey, he had occasions enough to practice great patience, for he was passing through regions that were very barbarous and devoid of civilized amenities, especially at the inns. There was no lack of danger both from the plague and from the loathing that many of the nobility reportedly nursed against the Apostolic See. Anything that needs to be added will be mentioned in next year's account.

774.   *Good news and bad from Cologne*

At Cologne Father Leonard Kessel carried on his usual ministry of hearing confessions; sometimes he also preached and frequently visited the sick. To the extent possible, he called the attention of everybody to the jubilee [indulgence] granted by the Supreme Pontiff Julius [III], which the archbishop had not allowed to be published at Cologne. In that province the Catholics were in such a state that [the authorities] feared that any generosity of this kind shown by the Apostolic See would incite more ridicule than edification. The jubilee was, however, communicated to many people in private. The people of Cologne, who seemed to vacillate on questions of faith, now began to show better attitudes as this year went on, since the foul lives of the heretical preachers, who had all been expelled, were day by day becoming better known. The rumor circulated that any of them who did not take measures to flee would be punished in public.

785.   *The Jesuits should not expect a warm reception at Cologne*

Ferdinand, the king of the Romans, wrote to the archbishop and senate at Cologne and courteously recommended the Society to them. They willingly received the commendation, but friends warned Ours that authorities there would be swayed very little by such a recommendation and that we should not expect an invitation from the archbishop or the senate—men of this sort in those regions were emotionally too frigid to think that they should do this. Doctor [Johannes] Gropper said that if one of our Society came to Cologne and taught in public there or even preached in public, the senate or the archbishop would not prohibit them from doing this. By such tactics [the archbishop and senate] could gradually be swayed, rather than by recommendations [of King Ferdinand]. Also, right at the start the senate would show its favor, for this was how they usually spoke: "Let them come, let them come, we won't throw them out." They had heard much about the Society—more than they found credible. All that remained was for them to see how the Society behaved and its way of proceeding.

■ **Belgium**

790. *Frequent confession and Communion at Louvain*

Many were at last recalled to a healthy state of mind and a new form of life, aided by this sacrament [of confession], even after long being steeped in sin. Earlier the jubilee [indulgence] of this year (which was received and promulgated in February) induced many people to make a general confession of their whole life and to amend their lives for the better. Not a day passed without some people coming to confession who had not confessed for a long time, casting off the old man and putting on the new. Also the number of those who frequently went to confession and Communion kept increasing. Because Father Adriaenssens [de Witte, the superior at Louvain,] asked [penitents] only about the essentials and did it so speedily, he heard the confessions of many people in a short time. But if some complication arose while hearing an individual, he postponed the confession until later; then, after listening to the case, he strove to answer the penitent's difficulties and leave his soul in peace. He had to make greater efforts to dissuade some from going to Communion too frequently than to urge them to communicate.

809. *Attitudes toward frequent Communion at Louvain*

Father Adriaenssens wanted to know the thinking of Father Ignatius regarding the frequent use of the sacrament of Communion; for his own part, he believed that the people's desire to frequently communicate should be encouraged. But [he thought that only] gradually all should be admitted more frequently to this sacrament of Communion, first on solemn feast days, then once a month, then every two weeks, and finally every Sunday; [the frequency] would depend not only on how piously the individual was living but also on how deeply he had sunk roots into a godly manner of life and how frequently he experienced temptations to sin. But others were convinced that frequently approaching the sacraments [right from the start] helped the person toward [living more piously], as a good preventive medicine would do.

837.   *Sending an apostate priest back to his religious order at Tournai*

Father Antoine Buclet was completely devoted to hearing confessions and visiting and consoling the sick in both hospitals and private homes. Among others, he encountered a certain Italian priest who for three years had been following military ways and wearing the garb of a soldier, so much so that no vestige of his [belonging to a religious] order could be detected. After he had made a general confession to [Buclet] with great contrition and detestation for his past life, he returned to his homeland planning to live a life in conformity with his order; in the meantime, he began to pray the Office and wear priestly garb.

■ **France**

870.   *Living with the Sorbonne's condemnation of the Society*

Ours at Paris were tormented to an incredible degree after that edict of the Theological Faculty. On every hand they were exposed to false accusations and hardships. People who knew the Institute and customs of the Society did not run up against any stumbling block [in their confidence in Ours]; those who were superficially acquainted with the Society were persuaded to nourish hostility toward Ours; those who were wholly ignorant of Ours predicted, as if they were soothsayers, that our Society would inflict some horrible wound on the Church. Meanwhile Ours, relying on the protection of divine Providence, kept up their hopes and courage.

Because the theologians had submitted their decree to the judgment of the Supreme Pontiff, they hoped that Father Ignatius would contrive to have the Pope make a declaration that would furnish a remedy for their torments. [This did not happen], in part because in these early months, in March, that is, Pope Julius died and after a few days Marcellus was succeeded by Paul IV, from whom it did not seem possible to request an appropriate remedy; and in part because Father Ignatius believed a gentler remedy should be employed, one that would not offend the faculty or draw down upon us its censure. So instead he pursued the path we noted earlier; namely, he requested testimonials from princes, city officials, and churchmen among whom the Society had worked. The hope was that after considering these testimonials and acquiring a deeper knowledge of our Institute, the Theological Faculty, which was very wide of the mark in its factual information, would spontaneously rescind its decree. But this remedy could not be employed right away, with the result that meanwhile our men at Paris had to bear many a weighty burden.

871.   *Wild rumors at Paris against the Jesuits*

Of the four professors who accompanied the Cardinal of Lorraine to Rome, one was Master Benoit of the Order of Saint Dominic, who had written all the preliminary drafts of the aforesaid decree against the Society. Another professor was [Claude] Despence, who had demonstrated his opposition to our Institute. As we reported, these returned from Rome with their attitude completely changed. Meanwhile, some rumormongers boasted that the Society had lost its lawsuit against the theologians, yet in truth the Society had no plans to initiate a legal controversy. Some people said that our Institute was some sly contrivance and crafty deceit of the devil. The rumor was spread that the founder of our Institute had been a certain Jew who had designed this form of religious life in expiation for his dreadful crimes.

875.   *Dealing with an apocalyptic Jesuit*

On the last day of January, Father Jerome le Bas was sent to Rome along with Father Jean Arnold, who for a year and a half had been causing Father Paschase [Broët] trouble regarding a certain prophetic revelation of the Antichrist that he had uttered, according to which the Antichrist was the son of Suleiman, the king of the Turks. Within six months[, according to this prophecy,] he would crown all of Ours with martyrdom, and so they were laboring in vain to establish colleges. Also he proclaimed that the Antichrist was going to come within three months and overthrow all the lands of the Christians. But when [le Bas] could not be swayed by either prayers or arguments to believe that he was deluded, convinced as he was that his insane ideas could be deduced clearly from the prophet Daniel, [Broët] sent him to Rome. In the course of his journey, those three months had almost run out after which he had claimed the Antichrist was to come, so [Broët] thought that his error would easily be detected. But on arriving in Rome, he handed over to the superior in writing all [the arguments] that had convinced him, and then put his case in the hands of his superior and willingly accepted a remedy. [Confident that] in the future he would be more cautious—because in all other respects he was an excellent man—his superior sent him back to France, where he did splendid work in the Lord's vineyard right up to his death.

880.   *The bishop and others at Paris attack the Society*

Such contradictions infused Ours with great confidence that, if anywhere, the Society would sometime achieve renown in Paris; this was their hope because, after so much persecution, we were laying solid foundations there. But the bishop [of Paris, Eustace du Bellay], whom apostolic letters had assigned as the Society's protector and erected as a bronze wall, as it were, against all calumnies, after being informed of the censure imposed by the Sorbonne, declared his new conviction that the Society should be abolished. Furthermore, when he had Ours brought before a court of justice, after they had been indicted, his officials heaped accusations of criminal behavior on Ours and other slanders besides; they added threats; they denounced [Ours] as hypocrites, schismatics, members of secret sects, and founders of new sects; they threatened to invoke ecclesiastical censures, imprisonment, and the secular arm against Ours if in the future they observed a form of religious life in accord with our Institute. They forbade Ours to say Mass, hear confessions, or administer any sacrament. Ours appealed to the Apostolic See, thus thwarting the hope of those who were trying to hale us before the archbishop [of Lyons and primate of France]. Thus did those who were preparing crosses for Ours begin to find themselves tortured and distressed.

■ **Spain**

985.   *Saint Thomas of Villanova and the Jesuits at Valencia*

When the archbishop of Valencia, named Thomas de Villanova, was stricken by a serious illness and suspected that death was not far off, he summoned a notary and distributed in two parts the five thousand ducats that the King owed to him. He willed twenty-five hundred ducats of this sum to our college, by this action testifying to his goodwill toward Ours. He bequeathed the rest of the aforesaid sum to the hospice for the poor. He was a friar of the Order of Saint Augustine, outstanding for his sanctity and learning as well as for his singular talent as a preacher. Some permanent sources of income were purchased with this money. While the archbishop was still alive, negotiations were in progress to obtain a site for a professed house, although the matter was not brought to the hoped-for resolution.

988.　*Success of the Exercises at Valencia*

The Spiritual Exercises were presented to so many people that our college was never without someone making them, and sometimes three or four people at the same time. When some people departed, others took their places. Of this number there were hardly one or two who did not set their hearts on entering a more perfect state of life. Some of them were admitted to our Society; others were directed toward other religious orders, although some of them begged with tears to be admitted to our Society. The religious men of the monasteries to which they had been admitted were awe-struck at their spiritual progress. Some of these monks made the contemplations and exercises customary in the Society. At length men of every state in that city, not just lay people but churchmen and religious as well, held our Society in high esteem. . . .

998.　*Preaching and teaching Christian doctrine at Gandía*

This Lent [teaching] Christian doctrine was discontinued because of the need to hear confessions, but it was resumed right after Easter week. More than three hundred children and sometimes four hundred came together to listen to [the instructions] at Gandía. On feast days older people heard some other priest give an explanation of this material, for the children were gathered together every day. But after several days they too were summoned only on feast days and Sundays when those with less education now began to take lessons in Christian doctrine.

[Ours] write that anyone who did not know about the ignorance of those going to confession and about their errors in matters of faith could hardly believe how much profit people derived from this instruction. There were those who believed that no sermons had been as effective for these people as had lessons in Christian doctrine. Many did not understand even the most basic teaching of the faith. The people were grateful that now very joyous hymns about Christian doctrine had almost replaced the shameful songs which were all too popular at Gandía. Sermons on this material were preached for almost three hours after noon, to which the men flocked eagerly, and just as many attended other sermons that were preached in our church in the morning.

1002.　*Converting Muslims in the kingdom of Valencia*

Many people lived in the kingdom of Valencia, just as is the case today. Some of their fasts and their love for the Koran show clearly enough that they are followers of Mohammed, as does their heartfelt aversion to listening to, much less embracing, the things that pertain to the Christian truth, most especially when the theme of the sermon was our Lord Jesus Christ. One of our fathers began to put forth intense efforts to meet with the teachers of this pernicious sect and speak with them in secret, so that thereby he might more certainly comprehend their mentality, and could more easily call them to the true religion. These men, after discussing Christian doctrine from every angle, frankly confessed their error and freely promised to confess their sins; but they immediately forgot their promise, even though the aforesaid father never ceased encouraging and admonishing their leaders. But one of them who held the highest rank among them and taught the others came to [our] college to make his confession and did so in the proper manner, giving us reason to hope that many others would do the same thing. A very talented man among them also did this.

1030.   *Religious reform at Barcelona*

The door seemed to be opening at Barcelona, making possible a considerable improvement in the city's morals. Many people had gone not just for one year but for many years without the sacrament of confession, and they did not blush to admit this, even in public. The pastors excused themselves and threw a good part of the blame on certain apostolic letters that gave permission for everybody to choose whichever confessor he or she preferred. Thus, those who had the care of souls never saw the faces of their flock. In their judgment, this problem could be remedied by restricting the choice of a confessor to those confessors whom the bishops approved.

1031.   *The preaching of Francisco Estrada at Barcelona*

The viceroy and the royal council and many noble men and women besides listened to the first sermons of Father [Francisco] Estrada. One could observe that when he preached at the Church of our Lady del Pino, which was large and crowded with listeners, nobody seemed to stir a foot or head or hand nor even to cough or spit; as if they were hanging on his lips, they remained in place right to the end, even though he protracted his sermon for almost an hour and a half. They said that nobody had ever addressed their hearts like this. The spirits of his listeners were so touched that here and there people were talking about what they had heard in his sermon, and they were hopeful that a great harvest would burgeon if he were to preach there the following Lent.

1055.   *Siliceo keeps silent in public*

The archbishop of Toledo, even though he attempted nothing in public against the Society, showed that he was hardly a supporter of Ours; still, he did not speak against us and rather gave the outward appearance of being kindly disposed toward Ours.

1062.   *Opposition in Zaragoza*

Here is the tenor of the decree that the aforesaid vicar-general [Lope Marco] affixed to our doors: "Because some clergy, [acting] on their own authority and flouting the fear of God, have said Mass, preached, and administered the sacraments in an ordinary *[profana]* house, he was commanding all rectors and vicars to publicize this decree in their churches, forbidding anyone to go to any of the aforesaid ministries in the aforesaid house. If anybody acted otherwise, he would incur excommunication."

1068.   *The other religious orders at Zaragoza combine against the Jesuits*

When their head, the bishop, was so disposed toward Ours, all the rectors and vicars met together several times, plotting to band together in one body against our college, because Ours in Zaragoza were an annoyance to them. With this, the people began to grow extremely obstreperous. Many reported that our adversaries were stirring up the people, using both public and secret devices.

1072.   *A crowd of boys stone the Jesuit house*

That same day some gangs of boys carrying a banner on which some devils and perhaps some of Ours were painted came armed with stones against our house and began pelting it with the stones. But immediately some of the viceroy's ministers raced there and captured two or three of those boys, who confessed that some clergymen and apparently some unknown monks as well had put them up to this. The royal treasurer and city authorities brought charges against them. Immediately the monks and the pastors marched through the whole city for three days with a bell, parading along the public streets toward our house; then the mob threw stones to frighten us. They carried a crucifix facing backwards and covered with a black cloth and chanted in public from the Psalm beginning "Be not silent, O God whom I praise" [Ps. 109:1], which hurls so many curses. This business stirred up incredible hostility, and the crowd was so wrought up against Ours that the entire neighborhood rang with shouts and shocking imprecations uttered against Ours.

1073. *Aragonese versus Castilians, common folk versus noblemen at Zaragoza*

On orders from the archbishop [Hernando de Aragón], all the religious of the city (except for the [Order] of Saint Jerome) gathered together against Ours and spewed forth an endless stream of complaints, threats, and false accusations. The people were [under ordinary circumstances] fairly disorderly, but now they were driven into a fury by the archbishop, churchmen, and religious. Most of the few men we had working in Zaragoza were Castilians, against whom the Aragonese usually harbored a hostile attitude. There was reason to fear not only that the lives of Ours might be at risk but also that the nobles, who were our supporters, might be faced with a riot from the people. When the boys first attacked our house with stones, many noblemen were playing a ballgame on a nearby field or were spectators there. Half-naked they rushed to our defense, although some went to the viceroy, who himself came with a large force of nobles. There was good reason to fear a major riot.

1074. *Efforts for a compromise reach an impasse*

Before things went that far, our adversaries sought to restore order, but they would not allow us to build anything or preach or administer the sacraments or say Mass in public. Had they allowed us at least Masses and confessions, perhaps we would have agreed.

1075. *The archbishop ignores higher authorities*

Princess Juana energetically strove to secure justice for Ours and wrote the archbishop and his vicar, the abbot, ordering them to rescind whatever measures they had taken against our privileges. The Supreme Council of Aragon in its own decree ordered that our [papal] bulls be acknowledged. But the archbishop would not yield to anyone nor was he willing to obey either the apostolic letters or the brief that the apostolic nuncio sent him regarding these negotiations [with Ours].

1079. *The Jesuits leave Zaragoza*

All told, [the city authorities] were quite pleased with our [decision to leave]. However, rather than appear to be expelling Ours but to show that Ours were leaving of their own accord, one of the officials and one senator accompanied them as they left the city. But so great was the mob lining the city streets to watch Ours on their way out that they seemed to be coming to witness some public spectacular. They had done this more than once when Ours had left their house to go somewhere. The people assailed them with loud screams and even injured them, for it appeared likely that churchmen and religious had persuaded the common folk that Ours had caused this uproar in the city and the interdict, especially when they saw Ours depicted with demons looking on, as we mentioned above.[7]

1097.   *Teaching the faith to Moriscos in Aragon*

The Countess of Rivagorza requested the archbishop to grant faculties to Ours so that they could exercise their ministries there; but she did not obtain them, even though she was his blood relative. Because almost all of the inhabitants of those places were neophytes who had been converted from Islam in the past, they wanted Ours to instruct them in their [Christian] faith. Therefore, many of these neophytes came to [Ours] asking to be taught the way leading to heaven. Indeed, they even abandoned their unfinished fieldwork to come. After some hours they were told to go back; but when they returned with many others, we preached a sermon to them that flooded them with great consolation. Then they requested Ours to explain Christian doctrine to them. But because the clergy would not permit Ours to enter their churches for fear of offending the archbishop, [Ours] daily instructed them in Christian doctrine in the square right outside the count's house. Some of Ours gathered listeners from that town and another explained [Christian doctrine]; on Sundays, Wednesdays, and feast days one of Ours gave very profitable sermons on the Apostles' Creed. Almost all the people attended, and many of the neophytes from neighboring places came and attended to the word of God with great joy. We were already employing the good offices of the inquisitor to obtain permission to conduct our ministries in the churches; and now the city folk were greatly distressed that Ours were about to leave.

1099.   *The situation of the Jesuits at Salamanca*

The rector of the college at Salamanca was Father Bartolomé Hernandez, while the supervisor was Father Antonio de Córdoba. At the start of the year,

---

[7] For a more detailed and modern account of the troubles at Zaragoza, see Antonio Astráin, *Historia,* 1:438–64.

there were eighteen [of Ours] in all; but as the year progressed there came to be twenty-two, and at the end twenty-eight. Ten of them were priests studying theology, in addition to six scholastics at the same faculty; six [scholastics], however, were devoting themselves to philosophy. Many of them were sent elsewhere. . . . Otherwise, the University of Salamanca was a fertile nursery from which to pluck workers for the Lord's vineyard. Soon after the beginning of the year, six students pleaded with Ours to admit them to the Society, and many others did so in the course of the year. After Father Antonio de Córdoba came to Salamanca, more men than before, including nobles of greater authority in that city, visited our college and discussed matters with Ours that were related to making progress in their lives and other questions touching on their civil status.

1127.   *José de Acosta, the future writer and missionary, produces a school play*

A tragedy composed by one of the brethren, namely, José de Acosta, was staged [at our college at Medina del Campo] dealing with Jephthah's slaughter of his daughter [Judg. 11:30–40]. The people greeted its presentation with thunderous applause, while they also derived considerable edification and regarded the school in an even more favorable light. The amazement of the audience increased because a local young man had produced this play and at appropriate places in it interspersed norms of good living [applicable] under more ordinary circumstances.

1137.   *The palace/monastery of Princess Juana at Valladolid*

Some of our confessors were also kept quite busy at the palace of the Princess, for the Princess herself set an example for the others, so that somehow nothing was discussed among those noble women except frequenting the sacraments, making progress in virtue, and pursuing whatever pertains to the more perfect state for which many of the more prominent women yearned. We should not conceal that some of them had agreed among themselves to undertake practices common in religious monasteries, so that in this way they could test themselves (for already many were inclined toward the religious life); meanwhile, in the very palace they were imitating nuns. Accordingly, on certain fixed days and hours they went off together to a private place and elected one of their number as their superior, whom all had to obey humbly for one week. They confessed to her the faults that they had detected in themselves and then accepted a penance imposed by her; this they had to perform in the presence of the others. Indeed, some of the more noble young women sometimes obeyed their own servants when the latter were put in charge of them. Thus did they subject themselves to the test as regards their humility and obedience. Three of these noble young ladies of the royal palace, all of them with the proper dispositions and accompanied by some of their servants, entered a monastery. . . .

1140.   *Hearing confessions of wayward nuns*

Several nuns who were living outside their convent, some of them with permission from their bishop and some without it, came secretly to Ours for confession. Thereafter, they decided to return immediately to their convent. One among them who, although she had been a member of her religious institute for more than twenty years, was now living in the world with the permission of her superior, but in such a [frame of mind] that under no circumstances did she wish to return to her convent. When this woman heard that our confessors received penitents with love and gentleness, she came also. And after she had manifested all her wounds to a spiritual doctor by making a general confession, the Lord so healed her that she set about diligently getting readmitted to her convent. There she persevered, to the great consolation of her abbess and the sisters. Through the Lord's grace, other women who were not nuns were by the same sacrament freed from the very serious sins with which they had often approached [the Lord's] table. Ours heard many confessions in prisons as well, and in the same way reconciled many sick persons to the Lord.

1149.   *Princess Juana pays for a new Jesuit residence at Valladolid*

Toward the end of the year, Princess Juana gave fifteen hundred gold pieces so that Ours could purchase the house that we wrote about last year. Although a like sum was due before Easter to complete the transaction, the princess came before then and contributed what she still owed. Indeed, we understood that she had taken out a loan to prevent Ours from lacking the amenities. Her extremely favorable attitude, one befitting a queen, gave us hope that she would not withhold her alms in the future for building a church (for Father Francis [Borgia] was busy about this project). During the month of June, Ours began living in this new house; once in it, they expanded their efforts to adapt it to our purposes. They also looked into buying another small house, which was needed for the church building. . . .

1153. *Daily order in the novitiate at Simancas*

In the morning and the evening [the novices] gave two hours [meaning one hour twice a day] to mental prayer; they gave one hour to the two examinations [of conscience], two more hours to saying the Office of the Blessed Virgin Mary, and a half hour to reciting the rosary. They also heard Father Bartolomé de Bustamante deliver two instructions daily, in the morning on the beatitudes, after lunch on the *Constitutions* and Rules. They spent the rest of the hours [of the day] in pious and useful tasks. They slept for six and a half hours at night.

1208. *Confession and Communion at Alcalá*

During the first months of this year, the number of people going to confession and Communion began to grow, so that before noon on feast days, we had to keep the door of the college open because of the succession of people coming in and out. . . . Never before had anything like this been seen at Alcalá. . . . The testimony of trustworthy persons assures us that more than a thousand people came for weekly confession and Communion at Alcalá.

1215. *The Spiritual Exercises at Alcalá*

The Spiritual Exercises were presented to almost sixty people during the first four months of this year. There would have been many more if the capacity of our house and the [other] daily activities engaged in by Ours had allowed space and time for more people. Many people so hungered to make progress in things spiritual that not only those who regularly dealt with Ours informally but also more than a few others who came to Alcalá from remote places for this very purpose—all sought to profit from the Spiritual Exercises and thereby achieve interior progress. Outstanding results were observable in persons of different conditions and classes, who displayed an improvement in their lives and, in the case of hitherto abandoned people, a reformation of their conduct.

1248. *Princess Juana almost dies*

When [Father Araoz] went back to Valladolid, he was suffering from some fevers; but much more serious was the condition of Princess Juana, who was bled four times by having her veins opened. She requested that Father Ignatius be made aware of her sickness, for she was especially devoted to him. When she was in doubt about whether her sickness would be fatal, she begged Father Francis Borgia, who was present at the time, to clearly inform her about her prognosis. She gave much edification to all by her example no less in times of sickness than in times of health. She and Prince Carlos [the son of Philip II] were responsible for most of the construction of our house at Valladolid.

1275.   *The Spiritual Exercises at Plasencia*

[Ours began to] present the Spiritual Exercises to many men, indeed, to women as well, in a way that was appropriate for them. A wondrous hunger and thirst for such exercises was obvious. The women in that particular town somehow made considerably more progress in devotion and holiness than did the men. The report was that deep piety was a special characteristic of the women of Plasencia. These women urged Ours to take over responsibility for constructing a convent according to their wishes, so that they could join it. Many people of considerable importance made significant progress through the Spiritual Exercises, especially in prayer.

1276.   *Female vocations at Plasencia*

. . . Almost sixty young women whom their parents wanted to give in matrimony to respectable men decided [to direct] their lives [along a different path] and chose to serve Christ alone in perpetual chastity. Each week they confessed and went to Communion in our chapel. At first some of their parents acquiesced only reluctantly in [their religious vocation]; for some of these young women were daughters of nobles and were destined to marry rich men, and thus from childhood had been brought up in [the most elegant] finery and had virtually drunk in [the use of] such frippery with their mothers' milk. But gradually with God's help their parents granted them permission; and so, armed with their parents' consent and [arousing] the envy of other women, they proceeded to carry out their praiseworthy resolution in the Lord. I will not fail to report this about one of them: on Easter Day, the day of the Resurrection, when she was compelled to don silken raiment and golden ornaments as was the custom, she obeyed her parents as to her external dress; but under those splendid garments she put on a hair shirt; and until that glittering finery was removed from her, she continued to wear the hair shirt against her flesh.

1314.   *Francis Borgia reforms a convent of Poor Clares*

As long as Father Francis was with the bishop [of Plasencia, Gutierre de Vargas Carvajal], he devoted his efforts to reforming a certain convent to which the bishop had transferred the nuns who had been living somewhere in a deserted place. Although they were cloistered nuns, they could not be persuaded to observe the rule of their institute. The bishop, whose subjects they were, kept many of them in prison but could not overcome their resistance. But then Father Francis, in those few days he spent with the bishop in the town of Jaraicejo, by holding conversations with them and preaching sermons [to them] brought [the nuns] to such a point that they accepted constitutions from the bishop according to the rule of Saint Clare; at last they were led back to the observance of their institute just as if their convent had been newly established at that time. His work put the bishop deeply in his debt, as he beheld Borgia suavely accomplishing in a few days what [the bishop] had struggled in vain for many years to achieve.

1328.   *Preaching at Seville*

Thanks to the preaching of Father [Juan] Bautista Sánchez, some noble ladies whose hearts had long been overflowing with hostility were reconciled with one another right in the church, to the amazement of the many onlookers. Father Juan Suárez preached at the public prison once a week with considerable success. One of Ours explained the articles of the faith at the front entrance of our house every Sunday. And so large was the eager throng that came to hear him that the voice of the preacher, otherwise loud and clear, could scarcely be heard by all, even though he addressed them from an elevated platform placed next to the door.

1332.   *Founding a confraternity to help convalescents at Seville*

A certain confraternity, called the Confraternity of Charity, was set up to provide poor people with what they needed while they convalesced after being discharged from the hospital. It also provided all other needy people with aid. It occurred to some young men—and they reached consensus about this—to redirect the money that they had previously lavished on games, banqueting, and other similar or even more frivolous pursuits, devoting it instead to assisting the poor.

1339.   *A Lutheran is converted at Seville*

Father Suárez explained Christian doctrine in the public prison, preaching once a week on that subject. Over and above the many other matters he took care of there, divine Goodness availed of his ministry to convert a heretic of Flemish nationality who was confined there in chains, Peter Mendel by name. The Fleming asserted that he had sat at the feet of Martin Luther and been nourished by and imbued with his doctrines. Because he had been condemned to death, with the sentence to be executed the next day, he was advised to make his confession. Mockingly he replied: "I have already confessed to my Lord, who knows my sins. Why should I confess to a sinner like myself?" So Father Suárez was called in to help him. But he at once began shouting out his inane assertions. Very learned men of the Order of Preachers were brought in, namely, Master [Juan] de Salas and Master Vicente Calvo. Again and again they presented logical and theological arguments to him, but all their powerful exhortations were in vain.

Early the next morning Father Suárez came to him. Mendel had listened to [Suarez's] sermons and was somewhat favorably disposed toward him. [Suárez] led him to hope for and ask the Lord from the depth of his heart to [reveal] to him the true doctrine and the way of salvation. . . . The next day on a public altar he publicly renounced his errors for a second time and professed the Catholic faith; then he heard Mass and received the sacrament of the Eucharist. In the same prison a sermon of Father Juan Bautista resulted in an act of thanksgiving; for all that had just happened brought great joy and edification not only to the whole prison but to a large part of the city. Then Peter Mendel denounced to the inquisitors the accomplices of his sin; and thus one could hope that the weeds sowed by the enemy would be uprooted and culled from that field of the Lord.

1343.   *The work of the Jesuits at prisons*

Not only did Ours teach and console those detained in the public jails, but they also stood by to encourage those condemned to death and to ready them to die piously. Sometimes from this very place of punishment they also delivered sermons to the gathering. Once there was someone present among such spectators whose heart the Lord had moved, so that, putting aside the hatred and desire to kill the person by whom he had been severely wounded, he came to [our] house to confess his sins, with all thought of exacting revenge now dismissed.

1348.   *Ministry to sailors at Sanlúcar*

During the month of October, Fathers [Gonzalo] Gonzalez and Suárez traveled to the town of Sanlúcar, where a fleet of more than fifty ships were just about to sail for the Indies. They did not lack for occasions to win the gratitude of many both by preaching sermons in the church and along the seashore and by hearing the confessions of many soldiers who were on the verge of beginning that perilous sea voyage without having made their confession. [Ours] boarded the ships themselves so that they could exhort them [to confess].

1364.   *Converting Muslims at Sanlúcar*

The brethren who were in better physical health taught Christian doctrine to some Muslims whom the Duke [of Medina Sidonia] was holding captive and who had decided to become Christians. A certain free Muslim was given the same instruction in Christian doctrine; when he was living there with the King of Fez, he had been captured after committing some crime and condemned to death. When one of our brothers spoke to him and instructed him, the thought that he was going to die a Christian brought him great consolation, for he used to say that to die a Christian was not dying but passing over to a happier life.

1381.   *Why establish a Jesuit college at Granada?*

Although Seville was a very famous and wealthy city, still, Granada was an ideal location for the Society to have a residence because the royal appeals court and the university [were located there] and the city enjoyed a healthful climate and other gifts of God. Furthermore, the city was larger than most, for 130,000 families lived there; among them were an estimated 20,000 Moriscos who had converted from Islam.

1384.   *Local support at Granada for a college*

Master [Saint Juan of] Avila had also taught there with notable effectiveness, so many were eagerly hoping that Ours would come there, so that they could hear the word of God from them and receive the sacraments.[8] Many of them desired to support a college with their financial contributions, so that it could provide sustenance for more of Ours. The archbishop [Pedro Navarro] himself, delighted to have us come, also offered his help toward financing the college and strongly begged to have Father Francis Borgia come to start the college. The four [of Ours] who had already arrived were viewed as pioneers.

1402.   *Preaching to nuns at Granada*

[The archbishop] requested a good number of sermons, even though that city was already well supplied with excellent preachers. At the archbishop's

---

[8] Juan of Avila was later to be canonized.—ED.

request Ours delivered sermons rather frequently just for the nuns in three convents subject to the bishop. . . . Father Provincial [Miguel de Torres], although he stayed only a few days at Granada, nonetheless heard the general confessions of some nuns. Through their confessions the Lord wonderfully advanced their spiritual development, so much so that their superiors were astonished. But the other sisters who had not confessed, seeing the fruit that the [others] had garnered, wanted not only to imitate them but also to enter upon the Spiritual Exercises. The nun who was in charge of the others fervently hoped that the aforesaid Spiritual Exercises might be proposed to them all, and she herself determined to precede the rest by her [good] example.

1426.   *Getting the college at Cordoba started*

Right on the feast of Saint John [December 27], Ours celebrated the sacrifice of the Mass there [at Cordoba] for the first time and [further adorned the occasion] with instrumental music and excellent singing. A friar of the Order of Preachers [Pedro de San Juan], a man outstanding for his learning and piety, delivered the sermon. As others were filing out, John [of Avila] delayed a goodly number of them, including many who were religious and some who were the leaders of both senates, and invited them to be his dinner guests. Ours served these people at table in his house, even though John had prepared the feast.

When the tables were removed, a young nobleman began to chant the praises of Saint John [the Apostle] from a lectern. Four others were on the program also; the first of them announced a rhetorical topic. Each of two others defended opposing positions with strong arguments. The fourth, who had the task of pronouncing a verdict on the debate, announced his sentence in Greek and Latin; although it was after lunch, the audience still gave their full attention to [the young men].

As others were leaving the banquet, some stayed on to watch a comedy that was to be staged that evening. It was *Acolastus,* with some passages deleted that were less suited to pious ears. When news about this presentation spread through the town, many who knew Latin came [to see the play]. They asserted that never had they seen anything more delightful. It seemed to have won everyone's vote [of approval]. Verses in Spanish explained each act, and a short exhortation was delivered that flowed from the story line and inculcated good behavior.

1439.   *Should* Cristianos nuevos *be admitted to the Society?*

When Father Nadal was in Spain during the previous year, after eliciting the advice of some of the brethren, he decided that no neophyte should be admitted to the Society at Cordoba.[9] But if somebody among them was suitable [for the Society], he should be sent to Father Francis Borgia. This was why several young men of outstanding talent were not immediately admitted, among them the paramount preacher and teacher in that city. . . . Thus, upon being consulted, Father Ignatius judged that men of this sort should not be excluded. Still, he thought that Ours should have regard for the edification of others as far as possible. And so some men of this ancestry on whom God had bestowed outstanding gifts were admitted.

1443.   *Ignatius decides that few Jesuits should have faculties to absolve from heresy*

The provincial Father Torres advised Father Ignatius how essential it was for Ours to have faculties to absolve from heresy, faculties that Father Nadal had forbidden them to use. Experience has taught that there were some souls who preferred to remain in their sins rather than to admit them except in confession. After discussing this matter with the archbishop of Granada, [Torres] had come to the opinion that it was very advantageous to assign this faculty to some one of Ours. So Father Ignatius communicated this [faculty] to a very few carefully selected [priests] under certain conditions, in order to avoid any conflicts with a position taken by the tribunal of the Holy Inquisition.

1448.   *The novitiate at Cordoba opens*

And so, on October 20 thirteen novices moved into this new house of probation, and another five quickly joined them before the month was out; and hardly had three days elapsed when everything needed for this sort of probation had been arranged, with the result that in the new house of probation all was

---

[9] The neophytes, at that time called *New Christians* in Spain, were of two sorts. Some were peasants of Muslim background who seldom applied to the Society and rarely had the education that was expected of applicants. The others had Jewish ancestors who had converted to Christianity several generations previously. These candidates often came from families of successful merchants, doctors, or lawyers, whose very prosperity was resented by those whose ancestors had been Christians for generations. Anti-Semitic prejudice had led almost all the religious orders in Spain to exclude applicants of Jewish ancestry, with the result that an unusually large number of them applied to the Jesuits. On this question, see O'Malley, *First Jesuits,* 188–92.

proceeding with consolation and tranquility. All devoted themselves to mortification and abnegation, and when they requested many [spiritual and penitential] things, many [such] things were generously granted them. . . . Therefore, Father Bustamante thought it very important that two years should be spent in probations of this sort. He attested that what the Lord was accomplishing in that house was every bit as wondrous as what was occurring in the house that had been erected at Simancas. He judged that the only concern or out-of-the-ordinary precautions required of the man in charge were that he see to the perfect observance of the *Constitutions* and Rules.

1478.   *Ignatius obtains permission for Princess Juana to read the Bible in Spanish*

Father Ignatius had obtained permission for Princess Juana to read the Bible translated into Spanish. He also sent her the privilege of sharing in all the good works and merits of the Society. Father Francis [Borgia] also wrote her before he left Seville, hoping that she would draw an abundance of spiritual joy from both these favors. Still, he asked Father Ignatius for letters patent in Latin testifying to the communication of the aforesaid grace, so that Princess Juana would be more thoroughly contented.

1493.   *Jesuit clothing should follow local customs*

Father Francis [Borgia] consulted Father Ignatius whether inside the house Ours should wear their cassocks open in the Italian style or closed in the front, as is the Spanish practice.[10] Ignatius though that the local custom should not be changed.

1507.   *Ignatius seeks testimonial letters as protection against the Sorbonne and Paul IV*

Father Francis [Borgia] took pains to gather the testimonials that Father Ignatius wanted to be brought [to Rome] from Spain and Portugal. It was not only because of the decree of the University of Paris [that he had requested] these testimonials, but also so that they could be shown to Paul IV if he was hatching schemes against the Society. And so [it was for these reasons that testimonials] were obtained from princes, prelates, and other persons of high repute and forwarded from those kingdoms.

---

[10] In Latin, *tunica,* in Spanish *sotana,* here translated as "cassocks."—ED.

1509.   *Getting money for the Roman College*

[Borgia] exerted himself to aid the Roman College, and with the permission of Princess Juana he saw to it that considerable sums of money were sent, even though the difficulty of conveying such money [out of the country] was somehow no less than that of seeking it out.

1510.   *More fund raising*

As Father Ignatius had suggested, [Borgia] did not commission just one person in those provinces to be in charge of sending alms to the Roman College, but rather three men, namely, Father [Gundisalvo] González in Seville, Father Bautista de Barma in Aragon, and Father [Bartolomé de] Bustamante in the province of Castile, where he was at the time. [Borgia] judged that as long as the Roman College continued to be in need, the patrimonies of those who entered the Society in Spain and were willing to donate these resources to the use of the Society could be sent to support the Roman College. Still, he was convinced that it was necessary to insist on proceeding in a correct and balanced way in this matter, seeing that in those kingdoms a troublesome lack of money was already making itself felt.

1511.   *Ignatius rejects Borgia's plan for financing the Roman College*

Father Francis then conceived of another approach to try, namely, that each college could support some [students] in the Roman College at its own expense; but Father Ignatius did not consider this a plan to be followed. He had plenty of men, but lacked enough money to support them, so this [proposal] was never implemented.

1524.   *Abortive plans to send a Jesuit to the English court*

Father Ignatius communicated his hope to send some one of Ours to the court in England, for he was of the opinion that it would be very advantageous to have some of the Society living there; specifically, he thought about sending Father Pedro de Tablares there. But Father Francis postponed this mission because at the time there were rumors that King Philip was returning to Spain. He also thought that Cardinal [Reginald] Pole or some other dignitary should be the one who invited Ours to England, and that the manner of calling them there should be worked out in Rome. But when Philip went to Belgium and not to Spain, Father [Pedro] de Ribadeneira was sent from Rome to that court, as we noted above.

1527.   *Abortive plans for a college at Sigüenza*

During the month of October, Father Francis went to Sigüenza, where the dean was expecting him, so that they could discuss setting up a college, as we discussed above [in these notes]. Because this city already could boast of a university and colleges of arts and theology (from which four doctors of theology had entered the Society—[Marco de] Salinas, [Juan de la] Plaza, [Cristóbal] Rodríguez, and [Antonio] Sanchez—Father Francis was inclined to accept a college there. But because the source of the endowment would be ecclesiastical revenues, this could not easily be obtained during the pontificate of Paul IV; and so founding this college made no progress at that time.

■   **Portugal**

1539.   *The work of the Lisbon Jesuits at the Inquisition's prison*

When the inquisitors had obtained Father [Diego] Miró's permission to send some of Ours to [visit] their prison, so that on Sundays and feast days they could teach those who were imprisoned there the commandments leading to salvation, this task was given to some [priests] from the College of Saint Anthony; so they took turns in performing a work of charity there. The men in chains and the others detained there usually welcomed them very eagerly, although in most respects only the dregs and offscaurings of humanity could be found there. For many Jews, Muslims, heretics, sorcerers, and the like, who now repented of [the sins of] their past lives and were atoning in prison for their crimes, found their spirits elevated through our efforts. . . . The ministries of Ours not only aided the prisoners but also resulted in others' being edified no end.

1543.   *The Jesuits are accused of discriminating against the lower classes*

The Queen [of Portugal] and the princes, both the cardinal and Luís, also wanted to build these schools close to our college; therefore, they were careful about having respectable officials appointed who themselves held this project close to their hearts. Until the end of this year among the other officials was Doctor Francisco Corea, who earnestly supported our interests; but he clung tenaciously to the view that grammar should not be taught to all the common folk but only to boys who were of a higher social class. For, as he used to say, if the ordinary folk got a taste of grammar, there would not be anybody willing to work in the mechanical trades. . . . So even though he was very friendly to the Society, it did not displease Ours when another succeeded him in office, because we were ill at ease with his conviction. Indeed, from the autumn of the previous year, following the advice of the princes, [Ours] had decided not to admit more students because there were not enough classrooms or teachers to accommodate the droves of students who presented themselves; rather, they admitted only some sons of the nobility or of other persons whom they could not turn away. The people of Lisbon put the wrong interpretation on this policy; and when they saw their own sons denied acceptance, they grumbled and accused Ours of discrimination.

1544.   *The King of Portugal visits the Jesuit college*

The King wanted to watch a disputation and witness our students at Saint Anthony's in action. So Father Miró ordered the prefect of studies, Father Cyriano Suárez, to get some of the students ready. After the students had fortified themselves by the sacraments of confession and Communion, one lad undertook defending some rhetorical theses before the King. Other scholarly young men disputed against him, after [still others] had delivered some short speeches in Greek and Latin. Both sides performed excellently well, leaving the King extremely satisfied. Accompanying the King [at this event] were the Queen and Doctor Antonio Pinheiro [the bishop of Miranda do Duro]. Father Miró himself gave a full account [of the college] to them. It is quite likely that the King wanted to see this literary presentation because at the time he was holding discussions about turning his college at Coimbra over to Ours. . . .

1556.   *The Portuguese Jesuits are overworked*

Francisco Rodriquez, the province consultor, cautioned that the responsibilities Ours had undertaken exceeded what they could bear. Observing that Ours were succumbing to various ailments, he laid the blame on our workers' being too few to handle so gigantic a harvest. He also observed that our men, because they were involved in several activities, were carrying out their [principal] occupations less satisfactorily than would be the case if they were not distracted by other tasks. He also reported that, for the most part, the scholastic brothers who made strenuous efforts to progress in the spiritual life were either dead or had fallen into serious illnesses, so that it seemed unlikely that they would ever regain their strength. He admitted that he did not know the reason for this. . . .

1604.   *Many men applied to the Society in Portugal*

At this time some [forty-six] men were admitted to the Society, selected from the many who had applied. Some men sent from Lisbon and Évora resided at Coimbra in the house of probation adjoining the college. The house grew so crowded that when it would not hold [all] the [novices], some were sent to Lisbon and some to Évora to study or help with household tasks once they had laid some foundations in religious virtues. They made progress in abnegating their will and punishing their flesh and in cultivating devotion. When they saw the scholastics renewing their vows, on their own initiative they pronounced vows of their own with great fervor.

1620.   *The* Modus parisiensis *at Coimbra*

. . . Because for decades many Portuguese had studied at Paris in the College of Saint Barbara at the expense of the King of Portugal, King John III decided to establish a university at Coimbra featuring a distinguished college where philosophy and humanities courses would be conducted in many classes, all following the Paris model. By offering high salaries, the King had attracted very learned men from France and had retained their services up to this point. The King was so pleased with this college that he spared no expense, and he conferred new benefits on the teachers, in addition to the stipends he had promised. There were ten classes dealing with the Latin language, while there were four for philosophy. This curriculum in the liberal arts the students completed in three and a half years, and each year a new course began. There were four instructors, each of whom worked with his students morning and evening, either lecturing or presiding over their disputations. The fifteenth class was in Greek literature; the sixteenth taught the boys to read and write. The students who attended these courses numbered more than a thousand at the beginning of the academic year, although by this summer their number had shrunk to eight hundred, more or less. Twenty-nine or thirty boarding students lived in the college itself.

1622.   *The King considers turning the royal college over to the Jesuits*

When [the King] observed that the classes at Lisbon and Évora had made excellent progress and that the students were being admirably educated not just in letters but also in good behavior and proper mores, he thought that our Society would perform a very useful service for that kingdom if Ours would undertake the task of delivering all the lectures that were presented in the aforesaid [royal] college.

1623. *Support for the King's plan at the royal court*

The Queen and also the King's brothers, the princes, gave their approval to this plan, and Doctor Antonio Pinheiro, whom we mentioned above, was not initially opposed to it; but later, when he saw the arrangement of the classes at Lisbon, he too [actually] began to favor it. Therefore, when early this year Father Provincial Miró came to Évora, he immediately learned from the Queen that the King was awaiting his arrival, so that he could find out whether Ours were going to take over this responsibility, whether they were going to have enough teachers, and whether they would also take care of the boarding students spoken of earlier. From the Queen [Miró] also learned that the King had decided to give this college to Ours if the Society itself wanted to undertake its operation. The question seemed of great importance to Miró, for these classes were the most important at the University of Coimbra. He also took into consideration that Doctor Antonio Pinheiro, who had persuaded the King [to approve] of this plan, had once been a supporter of those who left the Society. When [Pinheiro], complying with the King's order, had discussed the question of those men with Father Miró, he completely changed his opinion and promised that in the future he would not support any of them. . . .

1660. *Renewing vows*

On the day of the Discovery of the Holy Cross [September 14], all the professed [fathers] living in the house of Saint Roch renewed their vows,]namely, Father Juan Nunez, who had not yet been consecrated patriarch [of Ethiopia], and Father Andrés de Oviedo, Fathers Gonsalvo de Silveira, and Gonsalvo Vaz, along with the provincial himself [Diego Miró], although this renewal of vows applied to the scholastics, not to the professed. The professed were only obliged to pronounce the simple vows that followed their profession [of solemn vows]. When Father Miró showed the King and the princes the constitution dealing with the simple vows, they were greatly pleased.

1661. *The Portuguese king suggests that Ignatius would make a good pope*

When the King read the letter that Father Ignatius was writing to the King of Ethiopia and the instruction he was sending the Patriarch, he gave his enthusiastic approval to both, and to the apostolic letters as well. He asserted that everything had been crafted perfectly, and he was so impressed by the work of Father Ignatius that when the news reached him that the Apostolic See was vacant and when he was discussing the election of a new pope with Father Miró, he opined that the cardinals would make a wise decision if they elected Father Ignatius as pope.

1662.   *The King wants to put a Jesuit in charge of the Lisbon Inquisition*

During the month of April, the King discussed with Father Miró appointing one or several priests of the Society to take charge of the Inquisition at Lisbon, in such a way that they would be in charge of other [lesser inquisitors] and all would be subject to the cardinal. He asked whether this task and occupations like it were in contravention of our *Constitutions*. Father Miró replied that they were not contrary to it, adding that he did not consider that a task like this should be undertaken before he had consulted Father Ignatius, unless the King commanded otherwise; for Father Ignatius had ordered [him] to obey the King's commands. And so, as the Queen had informed Ours earlier, he decided to put one of Ours in charge of the tribunal. So now the provincial had to set about finding somebody suited for that task.

1663.   *The Cardinal Inquisitor saves the Jesuits from serving as inquisitors*

The cardinal, who was the head of the Inquisition in that kingdom, told the King that it would be difficult for us to take on that the task voluntarily; and, indeed, he did the Society a great favor by preventing this from happening. Instead, a certain religious of the Order of Saint Dominic who held the office of inquisitor at Évora was called to Lisbon to take over this task. This consideration prompted the cardinal to dissuade the King from choosing one of Ours for this assignment; he realized that Ours were few in number and burdened with many weighty obligations, so that we could not simultaneously engage in so many activities.

THE YEAR 1556

■ Rome

2.   *The Roman College in 1556*

At the start of this year, there were about sixty men at our house, but about a hundred of Ours lived in the aforesaid communities [professed house, Roman College, and German College], even though beginning last September a hundred men and even more were sent to various places outside Rome. Almost as soon as men left, others were admitted to take their places, for many men were waiting [to be admitted] and actually were admitted as soon as accommodations became available [for them].

11.   *Preaching at Rome*

Father Benedetto Palmio used to preach in the morning at our church, and after lunch Father Laínez interpreted a passage of Scripture taken from the Acts of the Apostles before a large and appreciative gathering of important men, including several cardinals. Because there was no place [in the church during these lectures] for confessors and penitents, a part of our house lying between the garden and the church was added to the church and called the place of the penitentiaries.[1] There six or seven [priests] could devote their time to hearing confessions, while leaving the nave of the church free for people listening to sermons and lectures.

14.   *Singing vespers at Rome*

On Wednesday of Holy Week began the chanting of the usual [Divine] Office for that week in our church, and on the first day following Easter singing the office of vespers also began. Father Ignatius seems to have decided on this for two reasons: because the *Constitutions* suggest that this should be done,[2] and

---

With this year *Chron*, vol. 6, begins.—ED.

[1] A "penitentiary" is a confessor with special faculties to absolve from reserved sins.—ED.

[2] *The Constitutions of the Society of Jesus and Their Complementary Norms* (St. Louis: The Institute of Jesuit Sources, 1996), *Cons.* no. 587 (p. 256). Hereafter this source will be abbreviated to *ConsCN.*

in order to please the Supreme Pontiff [Paul IV], who, even though he was inclined to impose such obligation on the Society, seemed to be content with this [limited form of] chanting the Office.

36.   *Jesuits must learn the language used where they are living*

This year Father Ignatius renewed his earlier decree about learning the language of the province in which individuals were residing. He judged that it contributed to community solidarity and goodwill if everybody used the same language; furthermore, he ordered that Italian grammar classes be taught daily.

45.   *Jesuits should not be inquisitors*

As regards the office of Inquisitor, which the King wanted to entrust to Ours in Portugal, Father Ignatius forbade us to accept this function, because civil authorities wanted that official to be exempt from obedience to superiors of the Society.

49.   *Sending copies of the New Testament in Ethiopian to Ethiopia*

Our Society at Rome received as a gift from a friend a large collection of volumes of the New Testament translated into Ethiopian that had been printed at Rome the previous year. All this huge mass of books was put into two trunks and shipped to Portugal, from where they could be transshipped to Ethiopia. Just as we had received this collection of books free of change, so we gave it away free to those people.

52.   *Ignatius approves a Lower German Province*

Father Ignatius decided that it was a good idea to set up a province of Lower Germany, now that Ours were residing in Cologne, Louvain, and Tournai. But he gave orders that, in each of these three locales where Ours were laboring, two or three men were to be nominated who seemed suited to carry out the functions of provincial superior. After celebrating Mass and commending the task to the Lord, each [member of the communities] was to write down [the name of] the man whom he thought better suited to be superior than were the others. [Ignatius] wanted each person to sign these ballots, while concealing from others how he had voted, and then send them on to him, so that, after learning their views, he might decide whom to put in charge of the others. But he excluded Father Pedro Ribadeneira [from those eligible] because he was about to return to Rome.

60.   *Ignatius sends Jesuits to establish a college at Prague*

Soon after the beginning of February, the Supreme Pontiff, after receiving a letter from Ferdinand, king of the Romans, urging him to do so, ordered Father Ignatius to send twelve men to begin a college at Prague. The man appointed to lead this mission was Father Ursmarus Goisson, who made his solemn profession of the four vows on February 10 into the hands of Father Laínez. Father Cornelius Broghelmans, who also made his profession at the same time, was sent to Bohemia along with him. All those who were about to leave were sent to the Supreme Pontiff to receive his blessing. Inspiring them by an excellent exhortation in which he compared them to sheep being sent into a pack of wolves, [the Pope] bade them to offer not only their work but also, if necessary, their lives for God's honor and the common good. After receiving travel funds, they set out from Rome in the middle of February and arrived first at Vienna and then at Prague. What happened after that we will describe below.

76.   *Establishing a college at Cologne*

Although Father Ignatius had established [the principle] that colleges should not be accepted which could not support fourteen or fifteen men, still, he judged that an exception should be made on behalf of the city of Cologne and of [our] friends there. Just as he had promised, on May 11 he designated four of Ours to serve in Cologne. One of them was Father Henry Denys, who could fill the role of preacher splendidly everywhere; others were Masters Franz Coster, who could teach some sacred theology, and Johann Reidt, who could preach and teach humanities and philosophy. The fourth was Henri [Sommal] of Dinant, who was equipped to teach humanities. To these was added a fifth, Wilhelm, who was bound for Kemberg. He also decided to send Master Joachim [Christiaens] and some others from Vienna, so that, if authorities had prepared a college and classrooms in which to teach, they could begin to train young men from the first rudiments of grammar right up to upper-level subjects. Thus began classes at Cologne.

82.   *The petitions of eleven cities for colleges are turned down*

Far more colleges this year were postponed or not accepted than we reported as being accepted. Among them one was at Ancona, and another was at Macerata, a third was at Arezzo in Tuscany; to these places the customary number of fourteen or fifteen of Ours would have come if it had seemed appropriate to accept [a college]. A fourth was at Ascoli, which is a fairly large city situated on the border of the kingdom of Naples and the Papal States. This city seemed in great need of help because of civil disturbances. Lord Abbot Martinengo, who had been the nuncio to the King of the Romans, wanted to erect a fifth one at Brescia, using funds from his abbacy, whose annual revenues came to two thousand ducats. The sixth was at Genoa, [to be financed by] the Sauli family at Carignano. Cardinal Farnese was involved in a seventh at Avignon, for which two or three men were designated this year. The eighth would be supported by the archbishop of Ragusa. The ninth was at Nijmegen in Gelderland, [not] to mention another one that Lord Didaco Lasso de Castilla was in the process of erecting and endowing at Madrid. Coming nearer the City [of Rome], the town of Narni, where one of Ours was preaching, requested another [college] and offered several locations from which the Society would choose one. Partly because of the decision not to accept colleges that could not support a minimum of fourteen or fifteen men and partly because of the lack of available workers, we excused ourselves from [honoring] these requests.

94.   *Ignatius becomes ill*

On June 11 [Ignatius] began to feel indisposed, and, during the month of July, he manifested some signs of fever, in addition to his stomach ailments. Because bad health prevented him from carrying out his duties of governing (although in no way did he spare himself if he felt even a trace of energy after lunch or at any other time), he gave full powers to the secretary of the Society [Polanco himself] and Father [Cristóbal de] Madrid, so that the Society would not suffer some harm because of his feeble health. This same year he had sent fairly extensive powers to Father Commissary [Borgia] and had not revoked the powers he had given Father Nadal the previous year, although for good reasons he had suspended them while [Nadal] was in Spain.

98.   *The doctor checks Loyola's health*

Then in addition to Baltasar de Torres, a medical doctor belonging to our Society, Doctor Alexander was summoned and was informed of what Father Ignatius had said [about his health]; the secretary [Polanco] asked him to examine Father Ignatius's state of health; moreover, he requested that he notify him [Polanco] if he concluded that [Ignatius] was in danger, so that he [Polanco] could go at once to the Pope [to request the papal blessing].

99.   *The doctor finds no immediate danger*

Therefore, Alexander went in and noticed nothing in [Ignatius's condition] to suggest that death was near, so he reported to the secretary that he could make no predictions about the immediate danger; but he promised to come back the next day and observe him more carefully and form a clearer prognosis of [Ignatius's] condition.

100.   *Loyola's last meal*

Thus, toward evening [Ignatius] had his supper as usual with his close associates; among other things he discussed at some length some questions about the house that (as we said) was purchased from Donna Giulia Colonna for the use of the [Roman] College. Leaving at their post those who usually looked after his needs, the others went off, not greatly concerned about his condition. Indeed, his attendants themselves, detecting nothing unusual about Father Ignatius, fell asleep.

101.   *Loyola's last moments*

That morning [July 31] before dawn, when someone went in to Father Ignatius as usual, he noted that he was already very quietly slipping away.

102.   *His death*

Others came running to help if they could. . . . But before the secretary, who was coming back [with the papal blessing], returned to Father Ignatius, he had passed on to his Lord. We can well believe that the old man understood far better than his doctors that the death was at hand which he had long and earnestly hoped for from God. He did not summon anybody to come to his assistance all night long, for he wanted to pass [the night] with the Lord, for whom he yearned most fervently.[3]

103.   *Polanco reflects on Loyola's death*

It is worth mentioning that Ignatius did not want to name a vicar, as the *Constitutions* permitted; nor when he foresaw his death did he make known to anybody except his secretary what he had anticipated would occur; nor did he wish to talk to his companions or exhort or bless them or do anything extraordinary with them, as we read that the founders of other religious orders did so

---

[3] Many more details on the death of Ignatius are given in *Chron.*, 6:38n.

devoutly. For this humble servant attributed nothing to himself nor did he want others to attribute anything to him; rather, he wanted everything to be credited to Christ (in accord with the Society's name), who had granted them all [their gifts]. And he wanted the Society to repose its confidence in him alone and not in any human person.

104.   *Ignatius compared to other founders of religious orders*

The less he claimed for himself, the more the divine Goodness exalted him and allowed him to see some things that I do not know whether the founders of other orders were granted [to see] to such a degree.[4]

127.   *Jacopino del Ponte's portrait of Ignatius*

A certain artist [Jacopino del Ponte] after Ignatius's death made a portrait [of him], for while he was alive, out of humility he never allowed this to be done. Thus, the picture does not give an accurate impression of his face.[5]

128.   *What caused Loyola's death?*

It was discovered that his liver was the cause of his malady. It was extremely dried up and contained three stones. With good reason some of the doctors declared that only a miracle could explain how he could have lived so long in this condition.

132.   *The Jesuit reaction to his death*

Just as he himself had taught us not to be saddened over the death of their brothers whom the Lord had called to himself, so we tried to accept with equanimity and as from the Lord's hand this departure of Our Father and to give thanks for it; and the Society hoped that it would have a loving patron to advance this work of his from heaven. We observed that the men who were more closely linked to Father Ignatius experienced greater spiritual consolation. Among other things, despite the unprecedented difficulties that beset the Society—the hostile attitude of the Pontiff toward the Society, the war declared

---

[4] §§105–11 (not translated here) list seven accomplishments of Ignatius; §112 lists the eleven provinces at his death; §§113–25 list all the places where the Jesuits had houses at that time.

[5] Del Ponte's portrait may not be perfect, but it seems to be the most exact, in that del Ponte had Ignatius's death mask as a model, and Ignatius had been his confessor. On the other hand, who knew Loyola's face better than Polanco?

against King Philip, the ever-increasing number of Ours in Rome with no prospect of income or assistance from the Pope to support them—despite all this, [we perceived] that our spirits and confidence in the Lord, based on the Institute of the Society, were expanding no end, all directed toward the advancement of the glory of the Lord and the good of souls. The Society was convinced that all these good emotions were in part due to Father Ignatius's intercession before God.

134.   *Electing a vicar after Loyola's death*

When the four aforesaid men [Martino Olave, André des Freux, Ponce Cogordan, and Polanco] took up the election of a vicar[-general] according to the *Constitutions,* it seemed wise to postpone the election for several days until it was known whether it pleased the divine Goodness to keep [Laínez] in this life. While he was near death, he had been asked to declare for whom he would vote in the election of a vicar, but he replied that he approved of whomever the others would choose.

135.   *Laínez elected vicar-general*

Therefore, when after two or three days the doctors judged that [Laínez] was doing better, we unanimously elected him vicar-general. But we did not give him the news immediately—not till August 6, when several documents were brought to him for his signature, was he informed that he had been elected vicar. Although he complained about the electors because they had chosen a man who was almost dead to assume this burden, still, he accepted the election, and thus he became the first to be chosen vicar-general of the Society. He directed those two men, namely, Father [Cristóbal] Madrid and the secretary, to use the authority they had received from Father Ignatius until the Lord had restored the strength he needed to carry out his office.

150.   *Paul IV's words when Laínez visits him*

[Paul IV] changed the tone of his voice and said: "Bear in mind that you should take on no style or manner of living except as decreed by this Holy See. But if you try something contrary to that, it will not go well for you." He said that no rescript issued by earlier popes could prevent future popes from examining and then confirming or voiding any measures that they had taken. Thus did the Pope give notice that we should turn to him or to his See for guidance regarding our way of life, not relying on Father Ignatius or anybody else except

God. Finally, [he declared that] by so doing we would be placing our foundations on solid rock and not on sand; also [he admonished us that] if we had begun well, we should also persevere in [conducting ourselves] well.

152.   *Fears that Paul IV might force a union of Jesuits and Theatines*

We could easily infer from what he had said that [Paul IV] was considering changes in our Institute, as we said a bit earlier. Others also thought that it was the intention of the Pope that our Society would amalgamate with the congregation in which he himself had lived.[6] We had the impression that those same good fathers (who were popularly called the *Theatines,* but strictly speaking are called *clerics regular*) not only did not oppose such a union but indeed were quite favorably inclined to it, even though they were few in number and [had houses] only in Italy and in only a few places [there]. A good number of Ours conjectured that the Supreme Pontiff had in mind not just mixing the members [of the two orders] together but also mixing the Institutes [themselves]. But Father Ignatius regarded neither type of combination—and the second even less so than the first—as advantageous for the Society. Nor did he think it would serve the glory of God or the common good. As long as [Ignatius] was alive, the Pope made no attempt [to interfere] in this matter. It is no wonder if thoughts such as these upset our Society.

160.   *Polanco translates the* Constitutions *into Latin*

At this time when Ours were getting ready for a [general] congregation, [Polanco] translated the *Constitutions* from the Spanish language into Latin; and anything else that could ease the work of the congregation was carefully attended to.

■   **Italy**

239.   *Huge numbers flock to Communion and confession at Loreto*

Toward the end of the preceding year, in autumn and especially during September and October, such a dense a crowd of pilgrims, attracted by the plenary indulgences attached to that church, flooded in that in the space of five weeks eighty-seven hundred people had received Holy Communion, [a figure that is] based on a careful count. Amid such a huge harvest, Ours were occupied with hearing confessions not just all through the day but also during some hours

---

[6] Gianpietro Carafa (Paul IV) was cofounder of the Theatines.

of the night. Even then they were unable to satisfy the wishes of such a teeming throng.

241.   *The prestige of the college at Loreto reaches a mountain village*

The reputation of this college continued to grow, spreading day by day through the Marches and Piceno and other places; everywhere [the people] were seized by a great desire [to have the services of] the Society. If they could have one of Ours in their town even for a short time, they thought that they were fortunate indeed. This was clearly evident in a certain town they call Monte Santo. When two of our priests were assigned there, practically everybody [in the town] displayed tokens of their great joy. As soon as the Jesuits arrived there, the magistrates sent a trumpeter through the whole town and urged all [the townsfolk] to listen to the sermons and make their confessions.

242.   *The success of the town mission*

Ours stayed in that place for ten or twelve days, reaping there a rich harvest both from the sermons, exhortations, and classes in Christian doctrine that they gave and from the confessions they heard and the other works of piety they performed; for they inspired the people to eagerly drink up everything that they presented and to move forward toward genuine virtuous living with the divine help of grace.

243.   *Other ministries in the town*

They effected several reconciliations between opponents [who had been caught up] in long-lasting and inveterate hostilities; they persuaded many to make restitution; and they had a *monte di pietà* set up to help poor people. Not only did they arrange to have two convents for women assisted by badly needed alms, but they persuaded the nuns to undertake a reformation according to [the norms of] their own institute. They contrived to have a hospital on the verge of collapse restored by means of public and private alms. Many people who by their evil deeds, perpetrated [over the span of] many years, had deprived themselves of the sacraments were, with the assistance of God's grace, recalled through confession to a way of life worthy of Christians.

261.   *A mission at Macerata helps the poor*

The hospital for the poor, which through neglect was in a ruinous state and had long been closed to the sick, was restored. The leading men of that city had founded and enrolled in a certain confraternity, named after Saint Jerome, to provide generous support for those destitute in body and mind. But gradually they allowed this society of theirs to lose membership and effectiveness because there was nobody to motivate them to continue the work of charity that they had undertaken. Through the exertions of Ours, this society or confraternity, I say, began to regain its pristine zeal. At the sound of a bell, the members began to assemble for devotional prayers at fixed hours every day, to receive Communion once a month, and to exhibit generosity and devotion toward the needy.

263.   *The Forty-Hours Devotion attracts the people at Macerata*

Meanwhile, the enemy of human nature slyly composed a certain impure and obscene comedy that the young men of Macerata were going to stage before a large audience of the townsfolk. Ours searched about for ways to prevent it from being performed, but because [the producers] had already incurred considerable expenses, the Jesuits failed completely to attain their objective. But lest the devilish author triumph, Ours scheduled the forty hours' prayer for the same day on which the comedy was to be presented. So great was crowd of citizens who flocked to this prayer service and so insistent was the demand for the sacraments that the three of our priests who were carrying on the ministry here could hardly take a short break to eat and catch their breath from first light until late at night.

274.   *The Jesuit method of teaching catechism applauded at Loreto*

The method Ours employed in teaching Christian doctrine greatly pleased everybody, but above all the bishop and the mayor. They arranged for these lessons to be set in type at once and had a thousand copies of the little book printed for distribution though the diocese.

284.   *Can a man have sex with his wife and receive Communion the next day?*

. . . A certain priest raised the objection to Father Manuel [Gomez] that it was not fitting that a man who had had sex with his wife the day before should receive the sacred Eucharist. When Father Manuel asserted that this was not a sin, the monk denounced him to the vicar-general. When he also wanted to climb into the pulpit and preach the opposite [of what the Jesuit taught], the vicar forbade him to do so; then he remanded the disputed question to the bishop, [asking him] to decide what was to be preached on this matter in his diocese.

347.   *The canons at Loreto move against the Jesuit college*

The canons secretly called together a congregation or small chapter and delegated one of their number to be a procurator commissioned to go to Rome and see to it that four canonries, four dwellings for canons, and two benefices for canons were restored to the chapter. The Cardinal of Carpi, the protector [of the Society], had suppressed these benefices in order to endow the college of the Society with their revenues. The [canons'] objective was to have the college suppressed, convinced as they were that this institution could not find any other source of endowment. Very likely they were influenced by a rumor circulating among the people to the effect that our Society would at some point take control of that whole church. This, however, was far from the Society's desire, because chanting the Divine Office, which Ours would have had to do there, was contrary to our Institute.

393.   *Helping deluded nuns at Perugia*

Among the other fruits that our priests plucked while inspecting convents of nuns at the bishop's urging should be included their dispelling various errors and delusions into which the nuns had fallen after being deceived by a so-called revelation. The rector performed a very useful service, especially in weeding out these [illusions], and he saved several deluded nuns from very severe dangers.

467.   *Hearing the confessions of soldiers at Siena*

This summer 150 soldiers confessed to this same priest; some of them gave up gambling, others [dismissed their] concubines, and still others abandoned a variety of public sins. Among them was a man almost thirty years of age who had never been to confession. Still, he confessed so precisely and so contritely that he struck the confessor with astonishment.

468.   *Good relations between the Jesuits and the soldiers*

Many of these soldiers who were thus introduced to religious practices abandoned their military exploits after making their confessions and began a more worthy military career under the banner of Christ. One can easily conjecture, although [the soldiers] offered no explanation [of this phenomenon], that this was because many of them had not gone to confession for those many years. They visited our house, and both the soldiers themselves and their officers treated Ours with great kindness. Although in the course of this year there had been frequent confessions, during the last jubilee granted by the supreme pontiff Paul IV and at Christmas time such a huge throng converged on Ours that they were so occupied with hearing confessions day and night that they barely had time to eat or say their prayers.

471.   *Preaching reform to nuns*

Ours were consoled this summer by their frequent sermons at convents of nuns. Among these religious were some who had previously been at odds with one another, but they were now reconciled. Others who in contravention of their institute had been using their private resources for their sustenance turned their funds over to the community as they should have done and began to live common life.

564.   *Louis de Coudret's preaching at Florence*

The number of those who flocked to hear [Louis de Coudret's] lectures on the Canticle [of Canticles] increased to such an extent that Father Ignatius asked for and obtained permission to transfer his lectures to the cathedral, for our church could not hold such crowds of people. On the last day of May, which was a Sunday, [Coudret] began lecturing in the aforesaid cathedral and he attracted twice as many as our church could hold. He went on delivering the lectures, resulting in much profit and satisfaction [to the audience], even though his voice was not powerful enough to fill so vast a church.

570.   *Two preachers pretending to be Jesuits raise money in Tuscany*

Father Louis [de Coudret] received word that at the town of Castiglione [di Pepoli] (in which some time ago there had been some discussion about setting up a college) two Neapolitans were preaching whom the people took to be from Our Society. After their sermons, however, they asked for money and other things. Then, moving on to Arezzo, they preached on the feast of Pentecost and gave no little scandal to those people by engaging in some less-than-proper conduct. When the inquisitors were notified of this, the commissary of that holy tribunal wanted them apprehended and locked up. So he wrote to Father Louis directing that if they came to Florence, he should be sure to have them arrested. These men, who were twins, came to Florence toward the end of June and as usual began preaching. . . . The vicar had the pair cast into prison.

They were wearing the habit of protonotaries, but they removed these garments between sermons and donned ankle-length cassocks instead, deceiving the people, who believed them to be members of our Society; and the devil made use of this occasion to besmirch the reputation of the Society in several other locales. . . . Finally, when the vicar discovered several romantic novels and other disreputable material [among their possessions], he fined them, confiscated the apostolic letters [appointing them] protonotaries, and banished them from Florentine territory. They both pledged that they would not preach any more.

582.   *A student presentation of Christian doctrine draws a gigantic audience at Florence*

The usefulness of the Christian doctrine that Father Diego [de Guzman] taught the students in our church overflowed upon their brothers, sisters, and the other members of their households. Indeed, the students of the college staged a dialog conveying this instruction in the largest church, thus benefiting the people, who numbered three or four thousand. The material itself and the charm of the young men presenting it resulted in no end of wholesome recreation and wonderment, and the people called blessings upon Ours for having instructed young people in such a devout way.

583.   *Cleansing Florentine bookstores of heretical books*

When some of Ours chanced on the books of a very evil heretic displayed at a bookstore, they first obtained the gracious permission of the bookseller and then carried them home. Then they informed the inquisitors on the look-out for heresies about what they had found. He instructed Ours to use their own judgment when allowing or banning the aforesaid books and asked them to visit the rest of the bookstores and purge them of any such books that they might discover.

600.   *A public ceremony enhances the reputation of the college at Genoa*

When the bishop [Egidio Falcetta], who was an enthusiastic supporter of the Society, heard some orations being delivered by Ours, he wanted to have a public declamation presented on the proper government of a republic. In accord with his idea, on the very day of Pentecost a twelve-year-old boy, the son of a very noble citizen [Paolo Doria] (who was one of the protectors of our college), gave an oration written by Ours on the method and underlying principles [to be used in] governing a republic. The doge [Agostino Pinello] and his attendants were present in the cathedral where it was delivered, as were the bishop and other noble citizens, to say nothing of a great throng of ordinary townsfolk estimated to number over five thousand. They waited patiently for almost four hours while the Divine Office was celebrated as usual and listened very attentively to the oration. When it was finished, the citizens applauded enthusiastically and congratulated the boy's father, who was also in attendance, for having a son so abundantly endowed. As news of this oration spread through the city, many noblemen regretted not having heard it and asked repeatedly for copies. Among them was the prince, Andrea Doria, who summoned the boy (who was his blood relative) and wanted him to repeat the same oration in his presence. He too warmly applauded it. This provided noble citizens as well with powerful motivation to entrust their sons to Ours for their education, and the number of students climbed to almost two hundred and thirty.

616.   *The Jesuits at Genoa attack gambling*

Some of our brothers wanted to apply a remedy to this perverse and deep-rooted plague [of gambling], so pairs of them traversed the various neighborhoods in the city on holiday afternoons and admonished and reprehended dice players and men engaged in various [card] games. Sometimes they drew down on themselves curses and revilement, but nonetheless they did not cease from this office of charity. By the sword of God's word, they often forced such men to break off such games once they had started; and on the way home [Ours] brought along with them a number of these dice players and urged them to make their confessions. They showed them how reprehensible was their offense when they participated in such games. Each of Ours chose several of [the players] to whom he pointed out the way of Christ. Neither were their exertions in vain, for many of them, once they had amended their former misconduct, embraced a way of life worthy of Christians. After finishing their daily work, they came to our college of an evening to learn Christian doctrine, of which they were wholly ignorant. Fearing Ours, some of these gamblers stopped playing, so that now one could behold the places deserted that used to be crowded with such players. But if some kept on gambling, they took to their heels when Ours approached them.

651.   *Cases of conscience at Bologna*

Father Francisco Palmio, the rector of the Bologna college, entrusted to his companion, Doctor [Giovanni] Agostino Riva, the task of teaching cases of conscience; but because that worthy old man no longer possessed enough voice and memory and was not very acquainted with such cases of conscience, the aforesaid rector concluded that he had to take over giving these lectures himself. Meanwhile, for this reason he wanted to let the priests of Bologna who were attending the lectures get to know him better, so that he could help them in the Lord, in part by the Spiritual Exercises and in part by other means. He reaped a not insignificant harvest from this work. Because those priests were groping in dense clouds of ignorance, these lectures brought them into dazzling light and motivated them to upright behavior. The number present in this audience mounted to forty [priests], to whom he lectured twice a week. He picked out those who were better endowed than the others, so that after they had carefully studied the material, they might gather at our house once a week; then one of them who had been appointed to preside over the meeting set forth some points of doctrine. During the next meeting, each of them would present his own reflections on the subject after he had studied it. This process began to be of immense value to them; thus they escaped from the great errors in which they had previously been immersed.

652.   *Inspecting Jesuit colleges in northern Italy*

Father Francesco Palmio, the rector mentioned above, was sent to Ferrara in January to observe the condition of that college and likewise the other ones at Modena and Argenta, so that he could make a report to Father Ignatius. This he did carefully; and when he visited the Cardinal of Ferrara [Ippolito d'Este], the cardinal received him with great kindness and graciously offered his help. In his own words, "If there is any way I can help the Society," [let me know].

708.   *Saving women from suicide*

Some women in desperation decided to throw themselves into the Po River and so end their lives. But by the endeavors of some of Ours, they were restrained from this unspeakable crime and brought back to the sacraments. The women began to go to confession and to receive the most holy Body of Christ frequently.

709.   *Wild rumors at Ferrara*

As the year began, a rumor spread throughout Ferrara to the effect that one of Ours had been made a cardinal. In my opinion, the basis for this was that Father Laínez had been called to the papal palace. . . . A similar false rumor was heard that Emperor Charles V was going to enter our Society. Some conceived this idea when they observed the Emperor's friendly dealings with Father Francisco Borgia at the former's place of retirement after he had abdicated his kingdoms and emperorship.

720.   *The college at Ferrara falls into decline*

Already at the beginning of this year, Father Francesco Palmio warned that the classes at Ferrara were beginning to lack enthusiasm and that the number of students had declined sharply, down to sixty or slightly more. But after the departure of Master Ambrogio [Pullicino], the situation at the school deteriorated still more. Even though Master Giovanni Maggiori was sent to take the place of Master Ambrogio, at that time his age and learning were less impressive than [Master Ambrogio's had been], so some of the elite began to drift away from the college. It was [Giovanni's] too youthful appearance that [his classes found objectionable] rather than any lack of learning in him; but sometimes it happened that only two or three lay students in addition to some of Ours attended his lectures. Sometimes courses were dropped for lack of students. . . . Because the young people of Ferrara was more free-spirited than they should have been, Ours were disappointed when they gathered less fruit than they had expected in the form of student behavior and piety.

826.   *The poverty of the Jesuits at Venice*

During the first months, owing to the plague there were eight or nine of Ours and even fewer as the year advanced. Furthermore, they lacked sufficient food; and sometimes they went for a whole week without eating fresh meat; they had a few eggs or fish to eat, but even the bread that they needed was hard to come by. This meager fare was in no way caused by any deficiency or lack of goodwill on the part of the prior [Andrea Lippomano]; rather it sprang from the poverty that resulted from his acts of charity. Therefore, Father Ignatius decided that only those men who could endure a diet of such slender rations should be sent to Venice.

840.   *Problems in the small community*

What usually happened in our small colleges also happened in Venice this year. The novices who had not yet sunk solid roots in their vocation fell prey to various temptations. One of them had decided to leave the college; later, however, he recovered his earlier state of soul. Among them was the man who had been assigned to assist Father Simão; as we said before, he had fled from Ferrara. He was found and returned [to our house]; then he was dismissed from the Society.

927.   *Vocations to the Society at Naples*

Two more were from Cosenza, Innocenzo Spatafora and Giovanni Paolo [Mirabello], who were practicing civil law at Naples. Hardly had they spent two days making the Spiritual Exercises when, impelled by the Lord's spirit, they insisted that they wanted to join the Society. But it seemed wise to have them continue in the same meditations and confirm their decisions. Both of them were [later] admitted and went to Rome. About the same time three others decided to go from Naples to Rome for the same reason; one of them was already suitable to apply himself to God's service by reason of his age, learning, and [prudent] use of [material] things.

928.   *Two Africans enter the Society.*

Two slaves, moreover, from Africa were instructed in Christian doctrine. One of them was a slave of Lord Juan de Mendoza (about whom more will be written later). [The slave] wanted not only to become a Christian but also to enter the Society. Because he was well versed in the Arabic language and seemed to have a talent for acquiring a knowledge of literature, he gave us grounds to entertain high hopes for him.

943.   *Two priests are refused entry to the Society*

Among the others [i.e., eight men seeking to enter], one was a monk of the Order of Saint Benedict from the famous monastery of Montserrat who had come from Spain for this reason alone—to enter the Society. His superior general had granted him permission for this; moreover, he brought with him letters of recommendation from Lord Marchina. Though in all other respects he displayed good judgment and literary culture, it was easy to ward him off from the Society by demonstrating that [admitting him] was contrary to the *Constitutions.*[7] And so it turned out.

945. *The Duke and Duchess of Alba are thought to be hostile to the Society*

Soon after this year got underway, the Duke of Alba [Fernando Alvarez de Toledo] came from Lombardy to Naples [as viceroy]. The report was that he and his wife—the latter especially—were hostile to the Society. And so when Father Ignatius wrote to them offering them the assistance and respect of the Society, Father Cristóbal de Mendoza, the rector, did not believe that these [marks of honor] should be delivered, because [Alba] was said to regard us as heretics or at least as suspect because of the Spiritual Exercises. But Father Ignatius imposed a penance on that rector because he had not delivered the letters and ordered him to see to it that they were delivered immediately.

948. *The Duchess of Alba blasts the Jesuits*

That knight [Fulvio Rossi] availed himself of this opportunity to tell the duchess many things about the Society and cautioned her not to damn her own soul in her attempt to damn the Society; [he advised her] to look into the activities of the Society more carefully, lest she be blamed for letting her detestation [of the Society] impede the good that the Society could have accomplished. To that the duchess countered that there were already enough religious orders and the Church had no need of our Society. The knight said, "Do you want to be wiser than the Supreme Pontiff and the cardinals?" Nonetheless, whenever she had the opportunity, she did not refrain from venting her hostility toward the Society. Nor did Lord Francisco de Pacheco offer any rejoinder to what the duchess was saying in his presence. Perhaps he saw how fixed she was in her conviction and judged that it would be useless to say anything further.

1019. *Information from Spain hardens the heart of the duchess*

The arrival [of Salmerón at Naples] came at just the right time to stabilize the affairs of the college, restore it to a better state, and bury the rumors spread by our detractors. Yet when some of these calumnies were quashed, other sprang up and took their place. From Spain the duchess learned about the decree of the Paris professors condemning the Institute of the Society.

---

[7] See the *General Examen,* chap. 2, no. 27, in *ConsCN,* p. 29.

According to reports, the duchess was delighted to hear this and openly declared that Doctor Melchor Cano, who was such a holy and learned servant of God, had impressed upon her that she should beware of Ours. The plague afflicting the duchess regarding this question seemed incurable.

1020.   *Improving the college at Naples*

Father Salmerón found the internal affairs of the college satisfactory enough now that the rector had discontinued his preaching and was now devoting his efforts to governing the college and [hearing] the confessions of externs. He wished only for someone to teach Greek, in order to enhance the college's reputation.

1032.   *The progress of the college in Messina*

The number and progress of the students in the college kept growing daily, and the reputation and respect for its classes even increased to the point that some of the elite were prompted to remove their sons from the training provided by others and entrust them to Ours. Among other instances we might cite the case of a judge of the highest royal court who entrusted Ours with the training of his three sons in letters and morals. Another nobleman did the same with his five young sons. It was self-evident that young men with brilliant talents were emerging from those classes suited to benefit the state greatly. After these talented young men had been trained in piety and discipline, they showed themselves as eminently equipped to undertake civic responsibilities. The diligence of the professors and their skillful methods of teaching motivated parents to entrust their sons to Ours for their education when they wanted to have them carefully supervised.

1036.   *Teaching catechism at Messina*

Ten of our collegians continued to teach Christian doctrine in ten parishes of this city, something they had begun to do the previous year. But when the Cardinal of Messina [Giovanni Andrea de Mercurio], who resided at Messina this summer, transferred the function of instructing children to his pastors to find out (as he put it) whether they could carry on this task without imposing such a burden on Ours, for a time [Ours] ceased going to these parishes to perform this task. But when the cardinal discovered that in almost all the parishes the spiritual edifice that our labors had so laudably erected was on the verge of collapse, he summoned Father Provincial and asked him once again

to invest the energies of the Society in this ministry. So in the month of August
Ours began to instruct youths in the aforesaid parishes, [using] the same methods and [subject matter] as before; once again they produced not insignificant
benefits for the young people.

1038.   *A woman's prayers secure her husband's return from Turkish*
         captivity

Those of both sexes who flocked to the sacraments made zealous efforts
[to advance spiritually] and achieved no less admirable gains. To mention a few
examples in particular, there was a certain woman whose husband had been
captured by Turkish pirates and thrown into chains. When she could do nothing
else to help him, by devoting herself to frequent confession and fasting, engaging in pious works, and uttering fervent prayers she obtained from the Lord
what she hoped for: she welcomed her husband on his return.

1039.   *Her piety leads to his reform*

He observed the changed practices and spiritual state of his wife and
perceived that she was more dedicated to hearing God's word, fasting, and
praying than when he had left her. Unwisely he strove to get her to abandon
this holy lifestyle that had done her so much good. When he could not easily
persuade her with words, he added threats and blows. She sought advice from
one of Ours. He told her to go along with her husband's display of affection and
accommodate herself to him in all ways, and by her compliant attitude to win
her husband over to a better frame of mind. When she followed this advice, her
husband noted how virtuous his wife was and took to imitating her edifying
lifestyle, so much so that he seemed not just to imitate her but even to lead the
way himself. He openly proclaimed himself fortunate for having yielded to his
wife's admonitions; for if he had not happened to find a wife of this sort, he
would have been the most wretched of men.

1043.   *Helping the less fortunate*

Our priests were quite concerned not only for the people who crowded
into our church, but likewise for those in hospitals or prisons and for those who
were condemned to the galleys as well; and we wished the sick in private homes
to have a good death. I will not pass over in silence that when one of Ours
found a dead man in the street and it seemed that nobody else would take care
of burying him, he hoisted the corpse onto his shoulders and carried it to the

church for burial. The same [Jesuit found] a man half-dead, contemned by passers-by, and lying on the street; he lifted him onto his shoulders and carried him to the public hospital.

1045.   *Helping to find food for fifteen hundred poor people at Messina*

[Father Provincial] took care that the viceroy and then the city magistrates of Messina would display considerable generosity in almsgiving for the poor and unemployed; so bread, wine, and broth were distributed daily and meat twice a week to some fifteen hundred poor people. The provincial himself assisted the poor with his own hands, and some of Ours were always occupied with this pious work. Because the hospitals for the poor were already so full that they were unable to receive the throngs coming in even from Calabria, a new hospital (with one of Ours also in charge) was set up where those afflicted with disease and poverty could come for assistance.

1082.   *The Forty-Hours Devotion is repeated*

Early in November the forty hours of prayer, offered in part for the dead and in part for an end to wars, were scheduled again. Participating was an enormous crowd: on the feast of All Saints six hundred people, more or less, came to take Communion in our church, not counting the many devout women who went to Communion in another church.

1089.   *Sicilian superstitions*

Those people were quite given over to superstitions, incantations, and pagan practices. . . . They invoked blessings on silkworms and burned incense, so that the worms might produce abundant silk. For this purpose men were chosen who donned masks and belts with little bells attached. These men would enter homes on the vigil of the Circumcision and shower blessings upon the household, all the while carrying off anything edible that they could find; it was considered impious to raise any objections to this. In case of disease or urgent need, they sought out a sorceress, who would apply various remedies for these problems. If somebody died, all the blood relatives let out discordant cries; standing around the body the men plucked out their beards and the women, their hair.

1090.   *Abandoning pagan practices*

The townsfolk were brought back from these and other pagan errors, so much so that they began to detest them and to reproach others for [adhering to] them. Now those who accompanied a funeral to the church attended the Mass and also were present for the sermon. Sitting in front of the altar, Father Daniel [Paeybroeck] usually gave [his sermon] on the Four Last Things after the Gospel of the Mass for the Dead. The people rejoiced that they were no longer bound to those ancient rituals, which hitherto spelled death for them.

1114.   *Failed attempts at abortion lead a woman at Palermo to conversion*

Many other such stories [of conversion experiences] could be related, but this one was especially striking: When a certain woman attempted abortion by ingesting various medicines but failed to achieve her purpose, she determined to kill her fetus in another way. She ordered a very stocky servant girl to step on the womb as she lay supine on the floor, so that the weight of the servant might at least end the life of the child. The woman was amazed when even this did not abort the fetus; and seized by a great fear of God, she came to our church and revealed with great sorrow and weeping her cruelty in trying to conceal her sins and the miracle God worked in preserving the fetus.

1132.   *The students at Palermo take the sacraments weekly*

Many students went to weekly confession and Communion, and the happy results from receiving these sacraments manifested themselves in their virtuous behavior. This too was noteworthy: those who excelled the others in good behavior also surpassed them in learning. Even though they spent more time in matters related to spiritual progress than did the others, they wasted less time in games and relaxation and with greater diligence applied themselves to their class work.

1171.   *Hostility to the Jesuits at Syracuse*

After some of Ours were sent to Syracuse [last year] to start up a college, they had reason to exercise considerable patience in bearing injuries and contradictions with equanimity. So numerous and vexing were these that as one discharge of insults followed the previous one, it banished the earlier ones from memory. Members of religious orders, secular priests, and secular men were responsible for these assaults. In the beginning these troubles became more distressing when they were stirred up by men highly esteemed for their holiness.

1172.   *The objections against the Jesuits*

People objected that Ours were delicate since they wanted to be supported by the revenues of the college, clothe themselves in soft [garments], and to eat from the common table. They also charged that Ours were causing the shortages greatly afflicting the citizens at that time—all this they hurled at us even though we were few in number and used food and clothing frugally, whether we shared everything in common or not. Thus it came about that the townsfolk detested our men, and many looked on them with hostility and kept prating that Ours were seducing the people.

1173.   *Opposition to frequent confession and Communion*

The religious attacked Ours more than the rest of the people because Ours were encouraging people to the frequent use of the sacraments of confession and Communion. They forbade the women who wore the habit of a third order to confess to Ours. They openly called Ours haughty and hypocritical.

1175.   *Answering the criticism and winning over the people of Syracuse*

Father [Giovanni] Filippo Casini, sent as rector to this college during March of the previous year, began preaching there in order to inform the people that our college had been founded and to detail the advantages that the city would gain from it. Initially, the whole city was surprised that somebody was preaching to the people outside of Lent, because this was unheard of, even though, compared to the other Sicilians, the people of Syracuse were reputedly those most inclined to piety. But when the people began to savor the fruit coming from his sermons, such a great throng began flocking to our church that it could not accommodate them all. So many overflowed the church and were forced to stand outside on the public street that they impeded those wishing to pass that way.

1177.   *Noble women are converted to piety*

Some noble matrons drew such benefit from these sermons that not only did they lay aside their splendid garb and glittering jewelry, but also (something never seen before) some of them were not embarrassed to go door-to-door begging for alms to help the poor. They also encouraged other women to undertake the same work of mercy. In a short time such a great change in their behavior took place that, contemning worldly enticements, they could be seen zealously pursuing only what conduced to the salvation of souls.

1178.   *Casini is called in to help a soldier condemned to death*

The esteem of the citizens for the aforesaid rector increased dramatically, and they sought him out when any difficulty arose. So did the members of the organization called the Confraternity of Charity; it was normally their official duty to encourage and help persons about to undergo capital punishment. When a soldier belonging not at all to the lower ranks of society was about to undergo execution and [the members of the confraternity] could not induce him to confess his sins, they summoned Father Giovanni Filippo to help them in so critical a matter.

1179.   *Casini brings the soldier to repent*

He came to the prison and, remarkably enough, his very mien put the heart of the soldier at ease; he quickly encouraged him to make his confession and prepare for a death worthy of a Christian. He persuaded him that he was not demanding something difficult. Now the [soldier] besought [Casini] not to desert him, so he remained with the accused man in the prison throughout the night. After reciting the Divine Office with the other priests, he ordered the lights to be extinguished. He began to discourse on the Lord's Passion and the benefits for the human race flowing therefrom. His exhortation elicited so many tears from both himself and those listening to him that the accused [soldier], reflecting on how much Christ had suffered for them, determined to accept his death with a serene spirit out of love for [Christ] and in satisfaction for his crimes. Immediately he cast off his clothing and began to beat his body savagely with a whip. The others followed his example and did the same thing. But when he had persuaded Father Giovanni Filippo to celebrate a Mass for his sake in honor of the Blessed Virgin, he went on to request him to remain at his side when he was dying. [Father Casini] did not leave him till he had breathed his last.

1181.   *The activities of Ours at Syracuse*

The citizens observed that Ours were never idle. On weekdays they were busy in class; on Sundays and feast days they occupied themselves teaching catechism here and there. All boys under the age of fifteen were obliged to gather in certain designated churches at Syracuse; there Ours instructed and tested them in Christian doctrine. But besides the boys a good number of men and women were also present.

1197.   *The impact of the Spiritual Exercises on women at Syracuse*

The Spiritual Exercises were presented to some matrons who applied themselves very diligently to making them. Some widows dressed in monastic habits and dedicated themselves whole-heartedly to Christ; their great example of virtue won everybody over. Young women too who were brought to church in good numbers were so bent on spiritual progress that they amazed many observers. All the alluring pleasures that usually captivate young ladies of that age now lost their fascination for them; they spent their time in church engaged in prayer and devout exercises.

■ Germany

1390.   *The new province of Upper Germany*

At that time this province consisted of three colleges, namely, Vienna, Prague, and Ingolstadt; this year the last two colleges were separated [from the Vienna college] and designated a province. As we already reported, Father [Peter] Canisius was put in charge of it as the first provincial.

1398.   *Protestant parents send their children to the Jesuit college at Vienna*

The progress witnessed in such young people persuaded even those alien to the Catholic religion to withdraw their sons from other schools and entrust them to our supervision. Jealous men appeared, however, who opposed the pious endeavors of Ours; nonetheless, Ours carried out their ministries all the more energetically and diligently.

1415.   *The sermons of Canisius at Regensburg impress even Lutherans*

On the feast of the Assumption of the Blessed Virgin [August 15] and the Sunday following that feast, Father Provincial Canisius preached in the principal church at Regensburg before a packed audience. He so aroused his listeners that all seemed thunderstruck, even Johann Snepius, the leader of the Lutheran heretics, who was staying there. Some Lutheran women were overheard murmuring, "If this new preacher continues to preach at Regensburg, our faith is done for."

1442.   *King Ferdinand and Jesuit preachers*

The King has such an uncommon solicitude for our men and their work that he wanted those of Ours who had little experience to preach in his presence, so that he could evaluate their talent; and so on Easter Monday Father Johann Dyrsius also preached extempore before the King, fully satisfying him and the others present.

1457.   *A Jesuit in Germany is discouraged by his meager success*

Father Nicholas of Gouda labored most energetically to reap an abundant harvest of souls; but when he saw that the fruits of his preaching and lecturing were so meager (according to his own way of gauging them), he was crushed in spirit and longed to be transferred to another part of the Lord's vineyard. But on returning from Poland Father Salmerón judged that the harvest being gathered offered no grounds for lamentation, given how sterile this northern region was.

1458.   *Canisius is more optimistic*

Toward the end of last year, Father Canisius was still at Ingolstadt, engaged in negotiations aimed at reforming the University of Ingolstadt and establishing a college there. So, when he had come to an agreement with the Duke of Bavaria and his ministers, he informed Rome, as we wrote above, that certain good people were hoping for and intensely desiring some fathers of the Society from [Rome], so that, as the secretary of the duke wrote in exceedingly devout terms, they might comfort the discouraged remnants in the Catholic religion, strengthen the wavering, raise up the fallen, bring back those who had strayed, look for the lost ones if they could still be found, and, finally, send new workers to gather in the final harvest before the face of the Lord.

1465.   *Singing High Mass at Vienna*

In our church, which once belonged to the Carmelites, Father Nadal ordered Mass to be sung on Sundays and feast days, not by Ours, but by a certain priest who was living with our boarding students. Because it had once been a Carmelite church where Mass and the Divine Office were traditionally sung, continuing this practice seemed to serve for edification. Because according to [our] *Constitutions* at the time, the sung Mass was not to be introduced, Father Nadal did not think that one of Ours should sing the Mass. But when that non-Jesuit priest departed, Father Lanoy imposed that burden on Ours, fearful perhaps that discontinuing such singing might displease the people, although he suggested to Father Nadal that there was no great reason to fear this [reaction].

1473.   *The Jesuits opposed the diet's taking up religious questions*

All of Ours and many others besides were convinced that the diets previously held had almost always been detrimental to the Catholic religion. So they were of the opinion that to the extent possible such diets should be prevented from dealing with matters religious; they should concern themselves only with secular matters, such as how to resist the Turks. But if the sort of diet that also took up religious matters simply could not be avoided, then both the King and the nuncio should be present and vigorously struggle against Protestant attempts [to gain the advantage]. They should also instil confidence into princes and prelates; and to this end it would be most appropriate for the Supreme Pontiff to deliver an exhortation to this effect. The nuncio also wanted one of Ours to acquaint the Pope with that position.

1474.   *The Dominicans at Krems offer their monastery to the Jesuits*

The religious of Saint Dominic offered Ours their friary in the town of Krems, as they had done elsewhere. They foresaw the serious danger that it might fall into the hands of the citizens, who would convert it to secular uses. So [Ours] wrote to Father Ignatius to learn whether he wanted to set up a secondary school in the aforesaid monastery. . . .

■   **Bohemia**

1515.   *Canisius is needed to help found a college at Prague*

Our friends at Prague wrote that, after the departure of Father Canisius, the preliminary stages to establishing [a college] were proceeding more sluggishly than they should, and so [our friends] urged him to return, saying that it would be soon enough if these arrangements were underway before the month of May or not much later, and also if he would announce that he would be coming as the first of the Jesuits to arrive there once he had settled the matters that he had in hand in Ingolstadt. The Dominican friars who were handing over to us their monastery of Saint Clement at Prague wanted to be sure about receiving the promised revenues before they moved out of it.

1534.   *The Jesuits arrive at Prague*

Among other things, some people asked if these Jesuits expected at Prague were thieves, for the word was going around that they should be killed and stamped out.

1535.   *Problems in starting a new college*

Father Canisius welcomed them at the College of Saint Clement; his advance work was extremely necessary there. When he first arrived there in early March, he found that our expenses in remodeling the building had ballooned; also he observed that the future college lacked many conveniences and even necessities, and it was only with the greatest difficulty that he could cope with the financial demands.

1547.   *A disappointing start to the college at Prague*

Although two doctors of theology, namely, Fathers Heinrich Blyssem and Johann Tilia [van der Linden], and other learned teachers were prepared to deliver lectures in theology and philosophy, in the beginning it seemed more advisable to begin with the basic courses in humane letters because it appeared that very few would enroll for the higher disciplines, and they had not laid a foundation in the lower disciplines. Ignorance was rife in Bohemia, and books were in short supply. The patrons of the college gave indications of being quite annoyed if they witnessed only a handful of students coming to our classes. Yet if we began with the higher disciplines, we could expect only a few students.

1548.   *In Protestant Prague the Jesuits keep a low profile*

But the King, who was then at Prague, did not think he should manifest great support for Ours as they attempted to get the classes underway; rather, he directed us to begin holding class in a very modest and humble way, to avoid irritating the citizenry and the University of Prague, seeing that in Prague hardly one person in seven adhered to the Catholic religion.

1549.   *Attacks on the Jesuits at Prague*

Although Ours proceeded very cautiously, it happened that while Father Canisius was saying Mass at the high altar, he was greeted by a rock hurled through a window; and then on the feast of the Lord's Ascension, when Father Cornelius Broghelmans was celebrating Mass, a certain Bohemian came up to him after the consecration and began to upbraid him harshly and accuse him of idolatry. When the intruder ceased his tirade, the aforesaid Father went on with the Mass. The trouble maker said in Czech, "You're not answering me?" And raising his hand high, he struck [Broghelmans] with his fist. But the Lord inspired one of Ours named Gaspar, who was serving at the Mass, and another old man who was nearby, to drag that fellow, still loudly screaming, away from the altar and out of the church.

1570.   *Hussite support for the Prague college*

. . . The Hussite parents, heretics though they were, gradually came to support the school of Saint Clement more enthusiastically, admitting that their sons made more progress in one month at our school than they had made in two full years at other schools. And rather than seem ungrateful, they overwhelmed Ours with deer, wild boars, rabbits, and other gifts—all of this against our will. They compelled [Ours], though unwilling, to accept them anyway, if not as gifts, at least as alms. Many of the nobility, even some of those called barons, presented their sons not only as day students but also as boarders. Father Canisius was quite convinced that to merit the gratitude of the kingdom of Bohemia, this province of Prague also had to be won over. Although we had promised that we would house some boarding students like this, because we were so few in number (twelve were sent and roughly the same number remained there in the first months) and also because living space in the house attached to the college was ill suited for this sort of boarding college, Ours could redeem their pledge by accepting only a few boarders.

1587.   *The difficulty of finding Catholic pastors*

Ours found that nothing seemed more difficult than finding priests who wanted to settle down there. Those whom they found already there had to be ejected forcibly because they had married wives and administered the sacraments according to the Lutheran rites. The college itself did not have responsibility for souls, but it did have the jurisdictional right to approve the two parish priests of the two communities subject to the monastery. Indeed [the college] had to install them [in office]. Father Canisius held the view that it was better to have no pastors at all rather than to have heretical ones.

1588.   *Difficulties in re-Catholicizing Bohemia*

Even though Catholic pastors were found, it did not appear possible to win these people back to the Catholic way of life, so steeped were they in

Lutheranism and surrounded by Lutherans and, in any case, so given over to drunkenness. The idea occurred to him that the building at Oyb could be adapted to serve as a novitiate, but it was far from Prague, a two days' journey from it. It was an excellent place for giving the Spiritual Exercises and spending time in meditation, but [Canisius] bore witness from experience that at Prague and in Bohemia getting people to make the Spiritual Exercises carefully was extremely difficult, for their temperaments were little inclined to such pursuits.

1590.   *The sad state of Bohemian Catholicism*

It seemed to Father Canisius that people who were considered Catholics in those places were hardly such except in name, for they displayed supreme stupidity, irreverence, and negligence in their worship of God. And when he realized that this regrettable condition prevailed in both ecclesiastics and laity, sometimes it occurred to him that it was by God's righteous judgment that he had deserted those provinces and abandoned parts of them to be devoured by the Turks and heretics. The Catholic religion was declining day by day, and the Bohemian Hussites were progressively getting worse and finally becoming Lutherans.

1597.   *Should Utraquists be forced to go to confession?*

[Canisius] wondered whether the young Bohemian men who went to Communion under both species and attended our college should be given absolution. He decided against allowing them to go to confession, for they did not seem about to change their religion without the consent of their parents, who tenaciously clung to their errors. Hence, some of their parents would not send their sons to our school out of fear that Ours would lead them astray and convert them to the faith of the Roman Church. Some, however, sent their sons to the school because of their expectations of what our Institute and teaching could do for them; but they swore [their sons] not to change their religion. These people had churches and ceremonies separate from the Catholics, and sermons, priests, bishops, and judges of their own as well. So Father Canisius decided that this type of student did not have to observe the rule of going to confession once a month, even though they admitted all young men—Catholics, schismatics, or heretics—without discrimination.

1604.   *Lutheran hostility to the Jesuits at Prague*

The Lutherans continued to entertain an even-greater loathing of Ours and considered them to be the sworn enemies of their sect. Father Canisius exercised no little patience with this sort of men, whom he considered trapped in their erroneous conviction.

1638.   *Canisius does not want to serve as provincial*

When [Canisius] was notified that he was to shoulder the burdens of being a provincial, he received the news with repugnance. He humbly beseeched Father Ignatius not to impose this task on him, even though he earnestly desired to serve all the brethren of the province, just not as their provincial. To prevent it from happening, he charged all of Ours at Prague to write their opinions of him to Father Ignatius.

■ Germany

1673.   *The University of Ingolstadt*

The people of Ingolstadt seemed more moderate and cultured than were those in other parts of Germany. Report had it that the number of students was climbing to seven hundred and that the professors in all the faculties were quite learned. There were two or three professors in theology, four in law, and one in philosophy, and others as well who lectured in medicine, mathematics, Greek, Hebrew, and Latin.

1675.   *Opposition to the Jesuits at Ingolstadt*

With the exception of [Wiguleus] Hundt and Secretary Heinrich and a few others, not many in the court of the Duke [of Bavaria] were supporters of Ours. Indeed, the report was that many [of them] were disposed to heresy. The duke himself was a faithful Catholic, but [he ruled] a people who were quite infected [with heresy], and some made clear their attitude toward Ours; for on the doors of their rooms Ours sometimes found scribbled the words "You had better get out of here today." And right on the door of our house, they had written in German a word disparaging Jesus. But these things could have been the work of a few heretics.

1676.   *Amenities at Ingolstadt*

On the other hand, some people showed their goodwill even by their deeds, like a certain respectable widow who this very summer gave Ours a vineyard next to the college. Besides providing an abundance of grapes, it also featured a small fishpond. It would have been even better suited for both recreation and useful purposes if the neighbors' windows had not overlooked it.

1677.   *Salmerón finds a place to relax*

Another doctor spontaneously offered Ours a pleasant and delightful garden, and there Father Salmerón relaxed when his mind was exhausted after intense application to studies; for, he said, one could boat and fish there. Meanwhile, [workmen] were daily fixing up the rooms in our residence according to our specifications to serve our purposes. One of these rooms was a spacious dining room where the university used to host its banquets.

1770.   *Printing schoolbooks and religious writings*

When the print shop was not occupied with other projects, Father Canisius saw to having the introductory grammar, written by Father Annibale de Coudret and by now translated into German, printed for the use of our schools in Germany, with certain passages from the *Catechism* added at the back. Because the Epistles and Gospels read yearly on feast days in the churches existed only in the translation of Erasmus, he had the texts printed in Jerome's [Vulgate] translation, using an elegant typeface. He also made a point of including several beautiful prayers, because the little prayer books that people used were alien to the proper spirit of the Catholic Church. Nor did they have definitive formularies for young people to pray. The good results issuing from such little books could spread far and wide.

1775.   *The Lower German Province is established, but has no provincial*

As we said, this year a province of the Society was set up in Belgium or lower Germany, where the Society had residences in three places, namely, Cologne, Louvain, and Tournai, even though the man designated to assume the post of provincial, Father Bernard Olivier, went to the Lord before learning of his appointment. Because Father Ignatius had ended his earthly life at almost the same time, this province remained juridically in existence but without a provincial.

1786.   *The Jesuit community at Cologne*

Meanwhile, although Ours did not have a fixed residence, they did have rented quarters near the school where fourteen of them could live in reasonable comfort. And if someone was sent out to preach, he found a spacious church [awaiting him] in which to do so. If Master Johann Reidt had come, [Ours] thought that the Senate would have readily given Ours the college they call the Bursa, in which he had once taught; for the man who previously had charge of it had abandoned it. Still, we did not believe that ownership of a college of this sort would be handed over to the Society, but only permission for Ours to use it as classrooms and a residence. When the Senate first observed the works of the Society, about which they had received many reports, we heard that they were going to favor the Society exceedingly. They thought that this is the way things had to be done in Cologne if there was to be any hope for a foundation in that city. Understanding these matters, Father Ignatius judged that during May Father Henri Denys and Masters Franz Coster and Johann Reidt should be sent to Cologne. These three seemed to be suited for both preaching and teaching theology and humane letters, especially after Master Henri Sommal joined them. When this announcement reached Father Leonard [Kessel], both he and his friends were delighted; and he hoped that over and above supporting them, the Senate would soon give them [ownership] of the aforesaid college, called the College of the Crowns.

1831.   *Vocations at Cologne*

A certain other man of more than ordinary promise, recommended by the dean of Nijmegen and quite learned, was admitted [to the Society]. He was sent to Rome just before August. During July the nephew of Master Gerard, of pious memory, who was from Goldach, made much progress in the Spiritual Exercises. He was a priest, rich in material possessions but richer far in things spiritual; he had not only decided to enter the Society but had also confirmed [this pious resolution] with a vow. Toward the end of this July, he was greatly encouraged by the presence of and a conversation with Father Salmerón, who only once stayed overnight at the college. On August 24 Father Leonard [Kessel] sent to Rome four young men who in their prayers had persuasively requested this from members of the community, namely, Robert, Lawrence, and Martin (who had pronounced their vows at our house in Cologne) and Jean Bale (who just recently had arrived there with plans to devote himself to the Society).

. . .

■ Belgium

1876.   *Dealings with the court of King Philip II in Brussels*

In the court of the King, at that time residing in Brussels, Father Ribadeneira talked to Count Don Rui Gomez about admitting the Society to Belgium and about the matter of Doctor Juan de Mendoza. The Count of Feria, a faithful and fervent friend of the Society, had prepared the aforesaid Count Rui Gomez, who willingly listened to whatever Ribadeneira wanted to say. As regards the foundation of colleges, after he had listened to the reasons for and against it that Queen Mary had put forward (because she had been told many unflattering things, including the testimony sent from the University of Louvain), he judged the proposals to be discussed completely holy and advantageous.[8] But at that time the matter did not have to be pursued at Brussels but rather at Antwerp, for which the King was about to depart. It appeared that he would have more leisure there to consider this question, for he would have less to occupy his attention there. The King would let [Ribadeneira] know when he wished to hear Ours speak about this matter.

1886.   *Support at the royal court needed to counter anti-Jesuit accusations*

[The Count of Feria] could see clearly enough that if the Society had supporters enough at the King's court, it also had many enemies and calumniators there who, given the opportunity, could easily lodge many false accusations against the Society. So having a respected member of the Society at hand in the court was essential either to deter its calumniators from impudently spreading slanders against the good name of the Society or, if they did so nonetheless, to be ready to refute them with his prestige and the persuasiveness of the truth. [Feria] thought that Father [Antonio de] Araoz or Father Francis Borgia should be sent to the royal court for this purpose. And whoever [this prestigious Jesuit was who] was in residence there, he should be alerted no less to the criticisms directed against the Society than to the favorable comments made, so that knowing the full truth he may be able to counter any false rumors before they can spread like a bonfire that no water applied by human exertions can extinguish.

---

[8] Mary of Hungary (1505–58) was regent of the Netherlands (1531–55) for her brother Charles V. Although she put the dynastic interests of the Habsburgs first, her own inclinations were toward Lutheranism, so her opposition to the Jesuits is hardly surprising.

1890.   *Support for the Jesuits at the royal court from Rui Gomez and the*
       Count of Feria

    Rui Gomez replied to [Ribadeneira] that it would be most helpful if the latter himself would speak with King [Philip II]. For if the matter seemed good to the King and conducive to God's glory, neither the authority of his aunt [Mary of Hungary] nor that of his father [Charles V] would stand in its way. [Rui Gomez] showed that he had his heart set on promoting these negotiations, and the Count of Feria added his own good offices; it is amazing beyond belief how enthusiastically [Rui Gomez] embraces our activities as if they were his own. Because some friars spread some [accusations] against the Society about things that happened in Corsica, [Ribadeneira] requested from Rome the letters of Julius III, who had sent our men from Rome [to Corsica]. Even though the people at Louvain earnestly petitioned that he come and preach to them there during Lent, and the people of Tournai made the same request for Father Bernard [Olivier], still, Father Ribadeneira did not think he was justified in leaving the court until he had spoken with the King. Moreover, he decided that he should not preach at the court unless invited to do so. . . .

1944.   *Cardinal Pole does not want Jesuit help in England, other than*
       their prayers

    When Cardinal [Reginald] Pole was informed in England about Father Ignatius's death, he replied to Father Laínez, the vicar, that he mourned the Society's loss and assured him that he would warmly welcome [Laínez's] being elected to succeed him. Finally, he offered Laínez his help, but had no plans to ask the Society to assist England in any way other than through its prayers.

1945.   *Opposition to a Jesuit college at Louvain rises*

    The negotiations about founding a college began to run into considerable difficulties while King Philip was still at Antwerp, because Emperor Charles, Queen Mary, and the councils of Flanders and of Burgundy were not favorable to these negotiations.

1946.   *Ribadeneira preaches at Louvain to an enormous crowd*

    Because King [Philip] was on his way back to Brussels, Ours also had to return there; but first they traveled to Louvain, where on March 1 (which was a Sunday) Father Ribadeneira preached in the Church of Saint Michael to such a throng that no one still alive had seen such a multitude of students gathered in one place at Louvain. Although the Church of Saint Michael was vast, it was packed two hours before the start of his sermon. It was truly remarkable how delighted the audience was [with his sermon].

1959.   *Restrictive conditions on Jesuits at Louvain*

So matters seemed to be coming down to this: if the Society were to be admitted, Ours would have to promise that they would not want to use their [papal] exemption or to preach without the permission of the bishops. Accordingly, Count Feria inquired whether Ours would consent to be admitted under those conditions.

1960.   *Jesuit objection to the restrictions*

Ours, namely Father Ribadeneira and Father Bernard [Olivier], replied that Ours had no authorization to curtail the prerogatives granted by the Supreme Pontiff, which would be the case if they should promise to allow the bishops to restrict the privileges accorded the Society by the Holy See.

1983.   *Problems at a small school in Tournai*

When the canons at Tournai opened their eyes and observed that at this time none of the boys wanted to serve God in ecclesiastical ministries (for young people were perceived as being more prone to heresy than other age groups), the canons began to consider and undertake a reformation of their schools. They had a college with twelve poor boys, whose teacher was also in charge of the city's public school.

1984.   *Ignatius decides against accepting a mini-school at Tournai*

Some of these canons were hoping that Father Bernard [Olivier] would take charge of that college at least temporarily; but he consulted Father Ignatius, transmitting to him the proposal and inquiring whether a tiny college of this sort should be accepted. [Olivier] suggested in its favor that over and above the expenses of the teachers, which it seemed the canons would cover, Father Quintin [Charlat] would be able to provide for six or eight scholastics of the Society at his house. That way, seemingly, we could furnish a sample of [how] the colleges of our Society [operate], thereby inspiring some people to found a college. He concluded, if Ours were to undertake this work, two teachers, one for rhetoric and one for literature, would have to be sent from Rome. But Father Ignatius judged that this sort of college should not be accepted.

1991. *Ribadeneira preaches on frequent Communion at Louvain*

The next Sunday [Ribadeneira] preached again with excellent results about the most holy Sacrament to the usual densely packed congregation, which included the leading men of the whole university. His sermon was so down-to-earth and practical that some said that the sermon [Ribadeneira] had just delivered would be enough for ten whole years, and that in the future nobody would dare to mutter anything against frequent communicants. Many people were persuaded to receive this most holy Sacrament weekly. Some came to ask him to teach the theologians the principles that inspired his preaching and also to have those sermons printed; out of modesty, however, he declined to do this. He did say that if he had been able to continue preaching at Louvain, there would have been reason to hope for an abundant harvest [of souls], because the temperament of the Flemings was very sensitive and inclined to devotion. Some of the students reported that the few sermons delivered there had yielded a crop that was not to be scorned.

1995. *Diego de Ledesma decides to enter the Jesuits*

At Louvain Doctor Ledesma had several of his philosophical works ready for publication. But he was fearful that if he entered a religious order, he would be prevented from publishing them. He had not yet determined to enter the Society, yet he was so attracted to it that, as he said, he always wanted to be directed by the men of the Society; and from the depths of his soul he gave thanks to God for having sent Father Ignatius to the world at this time. Shortly afterwards he made such progress that, after committing everything to God's providence, he decided to turn his whole being over to the Society.[9]

1996. *Ribadeneira wants to publish the Jesuit letters from India*

Father Ribadeneira wrote to Spain asking that all the letters received from India be sent on to him. These could easily be published at Antwerp, something, in his judgment, that would result in great edification and benefit to the public. . . .

---

[9] Ledesma entered the Society on September 30, 1556, at Rome. For his career and writings, see the *Diccionario histórico de la Compañía de Jesús,* s.v. Ledesma.

2002. *The work of Father Bernard Olivier at Tournai*

Through his efforts considerable restitutions were also made. By now many people at Tournai were coming to the sacraments weekly. There would have been many more if Ours had had a church suitable for the frequent reception of the sacraments. Therefore, [Ours] thought that they should abandon the house in which Father Quintin [Charlat] was living (which they had learned from experience was unhealthful) and rent another house near a certain church whose pastor was a brother of Father Bernard [Olivier]. There they would have everything that would enhance their administering the sacraments and preaching, [conditions] that certainly did not exist in the cathedral church. Because that building was sizable, they could open a school in it and put on display in that area the [works in accordance with the] Institute of the Society. Thus would eight or ten [of Ours] have been able to live at Tournai with Father Quintin paying for their support.

2006. *Hopes for a Jesuit foothold in England*

Father Ignatius had directed the aforesaid Father [Ribadeneira] not to let slip any opportunity of entering England that might present itself. It happened that the Duke of Medinaceli, even before Ribadeneira brought this matter up, disclosed his idea that the ministries of the Society would be very useful in England. Father Ribadeneira praised his suggestion and reinforced it with additional arguments; but it was not proper for us to meddle in this mission without being invited. The duke himself, however, could suggest it to King [Philip].

2019. *Attacks on the Jesuits at Tournai*

The heretics opposed Ours in many ways, not openly but secretly, acting just like wolves. Sometimes very early or at night they painted something disgraceful on the doors of our house. Sometimes they induced boys to bring us written material full of blasphemies and insults; or during the night, when no one was looking, they pushed them into our house through some cracks [in the wall].

2020. *An example of an anti-Jesuit leaflet*

Here I am pleased to insert a summary of one of them, to give a general idea of what they were like.

All the brothers and sisters in Christ salute you, oh Fathers Bernard and Quintin. We hope that you will receive a zeal for God because you lack the true knowledge of him and preach to the people false and devilish doctrine. For example: (1) [You hold] that God instituted the Mass and that it is based on the Gospel and conforms to God's word. Check the four Gospels to see if they make mention of this teaching. We, on the other hand, confess the supper as described by Paul. (2) You claim that purgatory exists and persuade the people [of this]. We say that Christ is our purgatory. (3) You say that the saints should be adored and honored and that requests are to be made to them. We frankly accuse you of lying; we assert that Christ is our advocate before the Father. Therefore, we say that you two are false prophets and antichrists who should have been tossed out of the pulpit and classroom long ago, oh you hypocrites, oh you false prophets of the Antichrist. But we are praying that God may enlighten you. Farewell.

■ France

2034.   *Olivier preaches at Lille*

Father Bernard [Olivier] came to Lille, where he preached on the feast of Corpus Christi and during its octave. Day by day grew the number of those who heard him; and to content them he had to preach on the last day in two of the principal churches, but even so, these could hardly hold the immense congregations that flooded in. People came from Gouda, thirteen leagues away, and from many other places three, four, and five leagues away as well, to hear him proclaim the word of God.

2035.   *A farewell gift for Olivier*

The mayor sent him a token of his gratitude; and knowing that Ours did not accept money, they presented him with a quantity of wine, as was their practice, to demonstrate the love and consolation that the people drew from his sermons. But Father Bernard would not even accept the wine, alleging the practice of the Society. Because they asked him to return to them as soon as possible, for a huge harvest of souls lay ready for him to garner, he agreed to do so when the appropriate occasion arose.

2047.   *France has only two Jesuit houses*

In France our Society had residences in only two places this year, namely, Paris and Billom. Although the previous year Ours were seriously harried and those tempests had not completely subsided, still, Ours were busy as usual hearing confessions at Sainte Germain, especially in January, which was when the jubilee indulgence was promulgated at Paris; and so many begged for our ministries here and there that we could not to satisfy everybody.

2048.   *Ministries to women*

A secondary harvest was gathered in from convents, where Ours worked so effectively in instructing bevies of virgins on the use of spiritual weapons that daily they became more ready to bear the greatest of hardships for the name of Christ. About the laywomen the same could be said. Their habitual manner of living [suggested that they were already in] heaven, and they tolerated the haughtiness and turbulence of this world only reluctantly, so intently were they bent on achieving perfection.

2055.   *A Jesuit is refused ordination at Paris*

When Father Paschase [Broët] brought Master Jacques Morel, who was one of our scholastics, to the vicar-bishop (for the bishop himself was not then at Paris) with the request that he be ordained, the former refused to allow this, explaining that the Institute of our Society had not been approved by either the royal Parlement or the bishop [Eustace du Bellay].

2060.   *Broët has the letters from India published*

The letters from India were sent to Father Paschase; when they were translated into French and printed, many people read them with wonderment and edification.

2076.   *Preparing to take over the university at Billom*

When discussions were afoot about sending teachers to Billon, about accepting responsibility for the university, and about the program of studies in use there, Father Ignatius had wanted to learn which disciplines were customarily taught there; he heard that instruction was being given in philosophy and humane letters, and theology as well when there was a theologian in the faculty. Seeing that at this time Father Robert [Claysson] was present in Billom, the bishop of Clermont [Guillaume du Prat] thought that the former should lecture on theology. Father Paschase wrote to [Ignatius] that there would be three teachers for humane letters, a fourth for rhetor.c, and a fifth for logic and philosophy; [he added] that the books used there would be the ones approved by the Society, to whose judgment everything had been submitted.

2078.   *Finances and preparations at the University of Billom*

The university never had any fixed source of income: teachers received their salaries from the students. But after it was turned over to the Society, the bishop of Clermont promised to build a college and assign an endowment adequate to support twelve men of the Society; indeed, he would do so as soon as Father Battista Viola arrived with teachers from Rome. Meanwhile, he gave orders that a house was to be rented for the use of Ours and that all necessary preparations were to be made for their sustenance.

2079.   *The bishop alone finances the Jesuit college at Billom*

Other than ours, there was no other college in that nascent university, and so any possible occasion for discord and contention was precluded. The bishop decided to endow the college in such a way that no one succeeding him as bishop could meddle with or claim any prerogatives in that college. To establish this endowment he needed the authority of neither the King of France nor the Pope, because he had decided to fund the college out of his own patrimony and not from the goods of the church.

2098.   *The bishop provides for poor students*

[Bishop du Prat] had designated the house in which Father Robert [Claysson] was living at that time to serve as the residence for twelve poor students who were to be educated under the Society's direction, following the pattern of the German College at Rome; and he set aside an area for building classrooms somewhat removed from outsiders but adjacent to the aforesaid buildings. He designated another large building near to the Church of Saint Michael, which was to be under the care of the Society. He also marked off a public space that he had decided to purchase from the citizens of Billom.

2130.   *The bishop agrees to pay for the additional needs of the college at Billom*

[Father Battista Viola] also took charge of acquiring the necessary books, buying some of them at Billom, the rest at Lyons. Father Robert already had other books that he had received on loan from the bishop and friends. [Viola] ordered chairs for the professors to be prepared in the classrooms and benches for the pupils besides. Finally he departed for Paris, where he found that Father Paschase [Broët] was now convalescing. He conferred with the bishop of Clermont about all matters touching on the college at Billom—not just about necessary items that had to be purchased right away but also about money to be disbursed at set times for the expenses of twelve persons and a disciplinarian. Besides those matters, he also explored practical aspects of the perpetual endowment of the college. The bishop promised to take care of all his requests.

2131.   *Viola is dissatisfied with the Jesuit teachers at Billom*

Even though Father Viola thought that everything should be completed with great frugality, still, he convinced himself that if the college at Billom was to be quite successful, other colleges [of Ours] must be established in France. But, as he writes, our teachers were less competent than he would have wanted, especially if they were compared to the men who taught letters at Billom before Ours arrived. I mention this to highlight God's providence at work here, supplying for our defects, for the success of the studies fulfilled all our hopes, thanks to God's help.

2142.   *Winning over critics of the Jesuits*

In the beginning, when the bishop of Clermont was taking steps to transfer the University of Billom to the Society, some men opposed this plan, declaring that Ours would do everything according to their whim without concern for anyone else; but even these men, as the dean of that church related, began to approve highly of what we were accomplishing. They assured him that they were more satisfied than they ever would have hoped.

■   **Spain**

2171.   *Preaching converts prostitutes at Valencia*

Other people, detesting their vices and devoting themselves to piety and good works, regarded themselves as now changed into Christians from their previous state of wickedness. When Doctor [Juan] Ramirez preached to the women who were living shamelessly in houses of prostitution, twenty-two of the thirty-six present were converted in the course of a single sermon. Some of these married men, and the others were returned to their parents or husbands.

2176.   *Ramirez's impact on the upper classes*

The same [noblemen] wanted to agree among themselves on the formation of a confraternity of fifty men, each of whom would annually contribute twenty gold pieces to a common fund from which some income-producing instruments would be purchased for use in arranging marriages for young orphan girls without parents. Many such girls, impelled their by destitution, were giving themselves over to sinful living. But wherever Father Ramirez preached, so many noblemen and merchants rushed to hear him that, even though the church was spacious, there were fewer people within than there were standing outside in the nearby plaza because they could not get inside.

2222.   *Friendly relations with the Dominicans at Valencia*

The religious of the Order of Saint Dominic often came to see Ours and a more-than-ordinary friendship developed between the two groups. Their provincial and their superior at the Valencia monastery, who were deemed the two luminaries of that eminently laudable order, celebrated the feast of the Apostles Peter and Paul in our church with harmonious music and in the presence of a sizable host of listeners.

2223.   *The Dominicans make the Spiritual Exercises*

These same religious requested [to be directed in] the Spiritual Exercises commonly used in our Society, and they made them fruitfully. They hoped to restore one of their monasteries where discipline had deteriorated, so they sent several of their own friars to that monastery for this purpose. All of them requested to have the Spiritual Exercises preached to them; and to make this possible, they begged that one of our brethren go with them to that monastery, who could then give them the Exercises. So numerous were they that it was impossible for us to accommodate them in our college.

2242.   *Plans for converting Moriscos at Gandía*

Father [Cristóbal] Rodriguez thought that it would be worthwhile for Father Ignatius to order two of Ours to occupy their time completely in converting [the Moriscos], [thus letting them] find their India in Spain.[10] His reason was that seemingly a huge multitude of such people could be converted to the true faith if twenty or thirty of their teachers (who, as we wrote earlier, were called *alpachis*) were converted, or if some [of Ours] made a point of inviting them to become converts; for they had a love for Ours, who defended their interests in every way they could.

---

[10] The early Jesuits often spoke of working with European peasants as working in the "other Indies." The phrase applied even more appropriately to working with the Moriscos of southern Spain.

2258.   *Cutting back at Gandía*

The previous year Father Francis Borgia decided that theological studies should be discontinued at the University of Gandía, because, on the one hand, lay students did not attend these lectures and, on the other, because few of Ours could come, seeing that the college building was in need of very costly repairs; for it had been cheaply constructed and now was on the verge of collapse.

2259.   *Only a few Jesuits remain at Gandía*

There were only four priests, the same number of coadjutor brothers, and two teachers of grammar left at that college. One of the priests also lectured on cases of conscience. Those who taught humane letters carried out their assignment to the great advantage of the youth whom they instructed.

2301.   *The archbishop and Princess Juana work to return the Jesuits to Zaragoza*

During the previous year, on the day after the Birth of the Blessed Virgin Mary [September 8] and at the insistence of the archbishop and his vicar, Ours were recalled [to Zaragoza]. These worthies had been the moving force behind their expulsion. Previously that archbishop had made great efforts to settle our differences with the monks and clerics and to some extent had been successful. During this time, while some of the more stubborn were being persuaded to reconcile themselves to the policy, he earnestly entreated Ours to return to their own property. For the Princess of Portugal and Governess of Spain, Lady Juana, had very strongly argued in our defense; as was only right, she burned with zeal to achieve justice against those who had persecuted us.

2311.   *Hostility to the Jesuits continues*

But the common folk, deceived by clerics and friars who passed on false information, clung to the opinions against the Society they had absorbed from them; instead of doing them physical harm they called out one to the other the words *Ignista* or *Ignatianum.* Moreover, as Ours were walking down the streets, the passers-by accosted them with the same names, intending to heap derision upon them.

2318.   *Efforts to improve the image of the Jesuits*

The Pope and several cardinals saw to the preparation of letters commending the Society's Institute and had them delivered to the archbishop and the city, in order to dispel the hostile assessment instilled in them by [some] friars and ecclesiastics. Because a good percentage of Ours working at Zaragoza were from Castile and thus were usually irksome and hateful to the Aragonese because of their nationality, [Ours] judged that some of our members from the kingdoms of Aragon should be sent to Zaragoza; they thought that it would be very helpful if Father Francis Borgia would pay a visit to that city. Among other things, a certain well-known and rather insolent pamphlet against the Society began to circulate in public. The bishop of Gerona [Gundisalvo Arias Gallego], the inquisitor, received a copy sent to him, [urging him to] carry out the duties of his office as he should.

2323.   *A friar attacks frequent Communion and the Jesuits*

At this same time a friar of the Order of Saint Jerome, who had been the confessor of the bishop of Granada at Trent during the council, while preaching at Zaragoza had so much to say against the frequent use of the sacraments and against our Society that he managed to leave the city aroused against Ours and to instil uncertainty and scruples into the minds of those who availed themselves of our ministries. He furnished our opponents with a marvelous opportunity to slander those with impunity who were engaged in pious works; still, many in his audience easily understood that what the friar said stemmed from a mental disturbance. He left Aragon and went to Toledo; and it is said that Princess Juana put up with the seditious license of this friar only with great repugnance.

2327.   *Madrid's book answers attacks on frequent Communion*

At that time certain preachers, both in public and in private, inveighed against frequent Communion. Because of this, [Father Alfonso Roman] often requested [a copy of] the little book about frequent Communion drawn up by Father [Cristóbal] Madrid, which we mentioned above. He was delighted no end when it was sent to him. The conviction there was that it would be extremely useful against the importunate assaults of such men and in the battle waged against the people who were receiving the sacraments frequently.

2329.   *Franciscans and Dominicans make the Spiritual Exercises*

Outside our house the Spiritual Exercises were given to many people, both religious and laity. Among the religious were two friars of the Order of Saint Francis and many female religious of a famous and leading convent of the Order of Blessed Dominic. The provincial superior of that order (who regularly manifested signs of great love for the Society) had made this request. He regarded it as a signal benefit that Ours visited the nuns who were subject to him and instructed them in spiritual matters. . . .

2348.   *Previous commitments prevent Jesuits from serving as inquisitors*

The aforesaid inquisitors wanted to [confer on] some of Ours [the Inquisition's] own authority and dispatch them to other places as commissaries of the Holy Office; but the unremitting labors and limited number of our workers rendered this impossible without undue inconvenience.

2354.   *Winning over Moriscos to Christianity*

Before returning to Zaragoza, Father [Luis] Santander spent several months this year in his third missionary journey to territories [inhabited by] neophytes. He preached almost daily and sometimes twice in the same day, because the inquisitors with whom he had set out were moving in haste. Twice he taught Christian doctrine in addition. Because those people had been converted to the faith of Christ from a Muslim sect, he treated subject matters that were well suited to his listeners and he approached them with suavity, so that, contrary to their custom, they would open themselves to his instruction in a loving way. Thus, through the ministries of the Society did God enlighten them about many matters that they found entirely unfamiliar.

2416.   *The college at Salamanca*

Father Bartolomé Hernandez was superior at this college; at the start of this year there were twenty-eight of Ours [stationed there]: ten were priests, of whom nine were studying theology, and another six men were students in the same faculty but had not been ordained as yet.

2417.   *Prayer among the scholastics at Salamanca*

There were six men studying philosophy; the others were occupied in household tasks. Even though some of them had worked a long time in other faculties, they devoted considerable effort to things contributing to spiritual progress. The scholastics were less occupied in prayer and reading spiritual books. Still, they devoted one hour daily to prayer besides the examinations of conscience. In addition to Sundays, they went to Communion once every week.

2418.　*Academic exercises at Salamanca*

As regards academic exercises, every day they held discussions on both philosophical and theological questions in the college, and on every alternate Sunday and on some feast days they defended either theological or philosophical theses. Friars of Saint Dominic and important men, among them some of the lecturers in public institutions and some so-called collegians in advanced courses, came to participate in the disputation or to watch the proceedings. They came away quite content and edified; and they expressed their approval not only of the talent and devotion to study displayed by Ours but also of the methods [they followed] and their evident unpretentiousness.

2465.　*Outstanding novices at Simancas*

But when in early spring Father Francis [Borgia] sent twelve of these novices who had already completed their probation to various places, the Lord sent in a like number or even more. In April thirty of Ours were living at Simancas, some of whom were theologians who had taken a master's degree at Salamanca or Alcalá and the rest had studied law or philosophy. Father [Ruiz de] Portillo asserted that they had made so much spiritual progress that, as he was convinced, he had not seen greater perfection even in older Jesuits; he was amazed that he had not detected in them any [signs that they were assailed by] temptations of any importance.

2496.　*Teaching catechism in the prison at Valladolid*

Christian doctrine nowhere achieved more striking good results than in the public prison, as I recalled above; for in the course [of these instructions], Father Juan de Baldarrabano also held spiritual conversations. In addition to the prisoners' learning the articles of faith, the Ten Commandments, the seven sacraments, and the precepts of the Church (previously they had existed in almost total ignorance of these things), many of the men and the women as well, who were confined in separate sections of the prison, went to confession, no longer approaching this sacrament with dread, as had been the case previously.

2507.　*Devotion at the court of Princess Juana*

Almost all the noble virgins [attending] Princess Juana and the other women continued to approach the holy sacraments very frequently. When some men were called to her royal palace two or three times a week, they were struck by the wonderful purity of life, the continuous mortification of the body, the very generous alms, and the other virtues flourishing there. The Princess herself with Prince Carlos, the only son of Prince Philip, manifested abundant goodwill toward Ours in the form of generous alms and other kindnesses. Ours did not lose sight of the poor people lying sick in the hospitals; our fathers were often sent to them to impart instruction, to hear their confessions, and to exercise the other traditional works of mercy toward them.

2533.   *A Dominican attacks the Jesuits at Burgos*

Like a second Father Cano and belonging to the same order, another religious who had gained a considerable reputation by reason of his learning and eloquence now began uttering many calumnies against our Society. Two canons who were friends of the Society, one with the last name of Cuevas and the other named Jerónimo de Castro, began to counter these falsehoods and provide a remedy against them. The goodwill of many people—especially the zeal and love for Ours entertained by noble women and also by men who, treading underfoot the arrogance of the world, offered themselves totally to God—easily compensated for the opposition posed by that friar and of other people, if any such there were. . . .

2634.   *Adapting to the weather and malaria at Plasencia*

As Father Francis Borgia had decreed, studies were discontinued after the feast of Saint John [the Baptist, June 24] or, rather, they were curtailed, because the summertime heat in that place is quite intense. Nonetheless, hour-long lectures were given in three morning classes up to the feast of St. Luke [October 18]; moreover, some literary exercises were required as well, so that the students would not forget what they had learned. Even though Ours watched after their health, five or six suffered from malaria this summer.

2670.   *The goodwill of the bishop of Alva towards the Jesuits*

[Bishop Didaco de Alva et Esquievel] had known Father Diego Laínez and Alfonso Salmerón at Trent and spoke glowingly about everything they had done and about the accomplishments and the fruitful harvest that the Lord was gathering everywhere through the Society. He also spoke at length and with much energy about those opposed to us. He offered [Ours] [permission to occupy] the pulpits of the cathedral church and of other [churches]. Among other things, he approved our Society's not making use of elaborate ceremonies. He gave his enthusiastic approbation to those members of the Society with whom he was acquainted, but especially those two fathers whom he had known at Trent—he styled them Elijah and Enoch. He declared that Father Laínez was gifted enough to govern the kingdom. . . .

2697.   *Princess Juana backs papal policy*

Princess Juana, who was also the regent, seemed to exceed due measure in her affection for the Society. The ministers charged with the universal administration [of Spain] were greatly distressed that in an apostolic letter Paul IV had revoked the subsidy of one-fourth of the ecclesiastical income previously granted to the King of Spain, all the more so because at this time, when they were occupied with recovering Busia (which the Moors had recently captured in Africa) and were experiencing notable financial difficulty in building up a large fleet. Notwithstanding, Ours helped Princess Juana to remain dutiful and obedient to the Apostolic See.

2708.   *Princess Juana and the assignment of Borgia and Araoz to England and Flanders*

When Father Nadal came to Valladolid, he spoke with Princess Juana in the name of Father Ignatius about Father Francis Borgia's or Father Araoz's traveling to England or Flanders. When she was very much distressed to hear this, he assured her that, when all was said and done, [Ignatius] wanted them to make this journey only if the health of those being sent would allow it and if Princess Juana herself did not block such a trip. A message to this effect was conveyed to the Princess. She experienced a singular joy to read this and acknowledged that she ought to be grateful that [Ignatius] had left their departure to her judgment, as she testified when writing back to Father Ignatius in her own hand.[11]

2712.   *Melchor Cano returns to the attack*

[Cano] began to lecture on St. Paul's First Letter to Timothy. Rumor had it that he did this so that he would have an opportunity to speak out against the

---

[11] In the next paragraph Polanco explains that Charles V's resignation of his Spanish holdings to Philip II meant that Philip was returning to Spain; hence, the proposed journey north by Borgia and Araoz was canceled.

Society. Still, he did not enjoy so much prestige that we had reason to fear that he would alienate the court and town from their dedication to the Society.

2714. *The Spanish Government wants to investigate Cano's charges*

. . . When the regent [Juana] found out from others—not from Ours—that Father Cano was leveling many accusations against the Society, she sent the president of the Royal Council [Antonio de Fonseca] to speak to him. [Cano] answered that he would prove his statements in the presence of learned men. When Father Araoz heard of this, he took care to challenge Cano in our name to summarize in writing the doubts and objections he had against the Society and send them to the regent, who would then designate the learned men who were to hear the case. . . .

2717. *Cano applies predictions of the Antichrist to the Jesuits*

Father Cano was warned by his own provincial superior—indeed, by explicit letters patent—that if he was going to interpret a passage from Saint Paul, he should utter nothing against the Society. . . . Still, he began to interpret the aforesaid epistle in such a way as to make it evident that he regarded the signs of the Antichrist and other similar things as being realized in the Society. When some prominent men, both clergy and laymen, were troubled and disturbed by his denunciations, he modified his words so that he raved even more pointedly against the Society.

2722. *Cano's attacks backfire and attract vocations to the Society*

Just when [Cano] was lecturing on the aforesaid two chapters [of First Timothy], seven or eight men with doctorates or licentiates, some of whom were *cathedratici,* lecturers, that is, in public institutions, entered our Society. One of Ours wittily remarked that if Father Cano had discoursed on the entire epistle, our house of probation would not be capacious enough to hold the great numbers who were attracted to the Institute of the Society.

2725. *The Dominicans defend the Jesuits from Cano's attacks*

Accordingly, Ours acknowledged their great debt to the sermons and lectures of Father Cano, for they brought many prominent men to an appreciation of the Society. When these men wanted more precise information about Cano's charges, once they had grasped the truth, they either entered the Society themselves or they certainly supported and strongly favored it from then on.

Among others, Father Domingo de Soto took up the defense of the Society; and at the same time other religious of that [Dominican] Order in their public sermons mentioned the Society and defended it against all slanders, as did members of other orders.

2727.   *Where should the First General Congregation be held?*

When news of the death of Father Ignatius reached Spain, one of Ours urged that Father Araoz in particular should definitely make a point of attending the [general] congregation. [Araoz] wrote back that it had never entered his mind not to attend it. But, nonetheless, he cautioned that Father Francis Borgia was not inclined to attend if it was held in Rome. So Father Araoz proposed Avignon, which was a papal city practically on the borders of the regions in which Ours were scattered [about performing their ministries]. Other men were also of the same opinion because of the turmoil caused by the military maneuvers taking place around Rome at that time. Some suggested Nice, others Genoa.[12]

2728.   *Hostility toward the Jesuits at the imperial court*

Toward autumn the Paris decree [attacking the Society] reached the court and caused hostility to burgeon there because it seemed that both the Emperor [Charles V] and his sister, Queen Mary [of Hungary], who were ill affected toward the Society, had come to Spain from Brabant. The Emperor did not conceal his antagonism toward the Society in some remarks [that he had made]. Those unfavorably disposed toward our Society seized upon this opportunity and spoke more brazenly against it. Some also alleged that Ours had been forbidden to enter the house of Princess Juana, even though this was a falsehood. [It was true, however,] that Ours visited the palace much less frequently and that, contrary to her usual practice, she wrote nothing even to Father Francis [Borgia], who was absent; so one could [with some reason] suspect that some changes [in attitude] had occurred [at court]. Therefore, Father Araoz and some others at the court judged that his presence there was essential. Although Father Francis was of the opinion that those who were going to Rome could begin their

---

[12] As noted earlier, Paul IV hated Spaniards, who dominated Italy, especially his native Naples. Soon after his election, he went to war against Spain as an ally of the French. The Spanish army under the Duke of Alba, the viceroy of Naples, overran the Papal States. The war, which ended on September 12, 1557, delayed the First General Congregation and prevented it from convening until June 19, 1558, almost two years after Ignatius's death.

journey in January of the coming year, it seemed that traveling in the wintertime would be very difficult, especially for men whose health was precarious.

2745.   *Fund raising for the Roman College faces difficulties in Spain*

The kingdom of Spain too was in great—indeed, some might even say extreme—financial difficulty and authorities were seeking to borrow money to finance the war in Africa. So they warned Father Ignatius to proceed secretly regarding this subsidy [to the Society] and to write only to Father Francis, even though both Father Antonio de Córdoba and Father [Pedro de] Tablares were conducting themselves with propriety in this matter. They arranged that in the whole month of April Father Ignatius would have four thousand ducats available in the kingdom of Valencia and that another two thousand would be sent to Rome through other channels. The business was delayed a little longer, however, because during these months movement of currency from the kingdom of Castile to the aforesaid kingdom of Valencia and the other kingdoms of Spain was interdicted.

2746.   *Fund-Raising Details*

A certain Spanish father had let it be known that the Roman College required five thousand ducats each year, and Father Nadal [wrote] that he would keep this in mind. But because some letters sent from Rome set the number of college students [in Rome] at eighty, with forty gold ducats assigned for each of them, Father Borgia decided to send thirty-two hundred ducats.

2761.   *News of Loyola's death reaches Spain; plans for a general congregation*

Father Nadal had received news about Father Ignatius's death from a letter that Father Ribadeneira had dispatched from Belgium. He admitted that the sadness brought on when he first heard this announcement was utterly dispelled by interior consolation and joy, compounded with great confidence that the Society would grow and renew itself in whole and in its parts for the glory of God. He did not know whether the office of vicar to which Father Ignatius had appointed him in years past had been revoked (for he had not as yet received letters from Rome). And because Father Francis, the commissary, did not possess the authority to summon other men to attend a general congregation of the Society, both Father Nadal and Father Francis conferred with one another and concluded that they should write letters to the four provinces of Spain instructing all who, in accord with the *Constitutions,* were going to the congregation to make preparations [for the trip], and bidding the provincials to leave their provinces in good order.

2777.   *Princess Juana does not want Borgia or Araoz to leave Spain without her permission*

The hope mentioned above that King [Philip] was soon to return, however, deterred both of them from leaving Spain. Princess Juana herself wrote to Father Ignatius in her own hand and thanked him for having ordered Fathers Francis and Araoz not to leave Spain without her consent. She went on to request Father [Ignatius] not to permit them to make any journey without authorization from her; furthermore, she desired that by the authority of Father Ignatius these fathers would be subject to her in this regard.

2791.   *Vow ceremonies should be held in public*

Father Francis Borgia summoned Father Bautista de Barma, the provincial of Aragon, to Valladolid, because the latter was going to be admitted to profession and others [would be taking vows] as coadjutors; after [Borgia] discussed the matter with Father Nadal, it seemed a good idea to repeat in Spain what had already been done two years earlier in Portugal when some men were admitted to all the grades of the Society in public with the King and leading members of his court in attendance. [Similarly, during this ceremony,] Princess Juana herself, the regent, and the apostolic nuncio, and other leading men of her court would be present. This vow ceremony would be preceded by a sermon explaining the Institute of the Society. Father Araoz did not agree with this idea, fearing that some might find it ostentatious. But the opinion of the aforesaid [Borgia and Barma] and others prevailed, in order to clamp shut the mouths of those who were grumbling that Ours somehow carried out our own affairs in secret. Given such an occasion, we would have a chance to offer an explanation of our Institute.

2864.   *The novitiate at Córdoba*

This college was divided into two segments: one of them served men engaged in ministry, those teaching classes, and some students (toward the start of this year they numbered fifteen); the other segment was located [at some distance and functioned] as a house of probation, where eighteen men lived. Father Juan Plaza was superior of this house right from its beginning, that is, from October 20, 1555. The novices were making admirable progress in the way of the Lord. Their spirit began to expand enormously by reason of their recollection, and they devoted themselves to mortifying their bodies and subduing their emotions. When they had completed their other spiritual exercises, they applied themselves to some material tasks, this man betaking himself to books, that one plying the trade of a tailor, and others exercising other skills; and they strove with great eagerness of soul to observe the rule of obedience and all the other rules. Anyone seeking the cause of their progress would perceive that all of them devoted themselves to the observance of the *Constitutions* and the rules, totally surrendering their own wills and judgments. Everyone exerted himself with all zeal to observe these regulations after Father [Bartolomé] Bustamante, the provincial, was sent to Baetica [to assume new duties].

2865.   *Father provincial stands as a demanding model for novices*

[The novices] had a chapel, a dining room, and a kitchen at a remove from the other rooms, and the provincial lived with them. He presented to all a model and exemplar, because he surpassed the rest in prayer and in the observance of the other rules; and he exacted such a meticulous observance of the rules that, as Father [Alfonso] Zarate, the rector of the college, writes, he brought some trouble upon himself and others because he would not tolerate anyone's neglecting [to achieve] even the very peak of observance.

2900.   *Progress and vocations at Córdoba*

The number of students frequenting the classes in the humanities increased notably, climbing to three hundred, all of them making more-than-average progress in virtues and letters. Sermons stimulated and helped them to [excel in] both. Some [of the students] were devoted to prayer; moreover, not a few also whipped themselves privately of their own accord [a practice known as] taking the discipline. Many of these and other ordinary students entered the religious life. Especially after Father [Miguel] Ramirez began preaching, many of them hoped to enter the Society. . . .

2903.   *Educational standards for entering the Jesuits*

Those students who asked to enter the Society were required to wait until they had finished the arts curriculum. Other laymen who asked to enter, when they became aware that this was not a possibility because they were illiterate, gave up their former occupations and devoted themselves to getting an education. But some, as we said, took themselves off to other religious orders.

2911.   *Eucharistic celebrations for women*

Because many women had gathered there but could not enter our college because our Institute did not permit this, Father Provincial gave them a sermon on the most holy Sacrament in the church. This turned out to be more useful and pleasing to them than if they had listened to a dialog, as they had desired. Thus, to our utmost joy, we began to reserve the most holy Eucharist in our chapel.

2963.   *The archbishop of Granada encourages people to make the Exercises*

While giving a sermon to the people on the first Sunday of Lent, in order to commend our Spiritual Exercises to them [the archbishop] declared: "What purpose do you think Christ had in mind when he went out into the desert, if he didn't intend to make [spiritual] exercises? It was not that Christ needed them; but he left us an example for us to imitate. These exercises are not some new invention." At great length he demonstrated how necessary they were. The results ensuing from his sermon prove how effective it was: many people immediately pleaded for the Exercises, and others sought admission to our Society.

2971.   *Preaching to black slaves at Seville*

Christian doctrine was taught on weekdays in more than one place, but nowhere with better results than in the public prisons (where obviously it was absolutely necessary). Black slaves, who were very numerous at Seville, received the same instruction in a certain church in that city. Ours delivered the teaching leading to eternal salvation to other men of the same sort [who were] outside the city walls because they were kept there to do some kind of [manual] labor and were not allowed to come to church. Still others, summoned by the ringing of a bell, also flocked there from the river bank and other places. Ours made a practice of visiting other places as well in which crowds of lost souls and people caught up in vices in that big city used to converge. Ours gave sermons outside the city walls near the taverns and gates, rebuking the people for their sins; they spent their afternoons performing these and similar beneficial tasks.

2996.   *Getting blacks slaves to stop dancing and start studying catechism lessons instead*

Black slaves in Seville used to engage in some improper dance that they call the samba; as there were many thousands of [these slaves] at Seville, God was frequently offended. Ours made efforts to persuade them to cease wasting their time this way and to learn Christian doctrine instead, for they were utterly ignorant of such matters. Thus did they abandon these dances. Also they met to establish a confraternity for those learning Christian doctrine; moreover, the designated prefects and monitors induced the more negligent to attend the [lessons].

■ Portugal

3092.   *Disputations at Coimbra*

Shortly thereafter, on the feast of Saint Barnabas [June 11], to be exact, three scholastics who were [students in] these three courses publicly and solemnly defended theses in logic and philosophy in the chapel of our college. Reputedly these were the best [defenses] ever held at Coimbra. In attendance were the rector of the university along with many teachers and religious. The participants carried on their disputation aggressively for more than three hours in the morning and for the same period of time in the afternoon, or even longer.

3117.   *Restoring discipline at Coimbra*

Father Leo [Henriquez, the rector at Coimbra], indicated that N. [probably Diego Miró] had given great edification in that province because of his virtue and obedience. Seemingly, however, he lacked the degree of prudence in handling practical matters that his office demanded; furthermore, he had concerned himself with trifling details of administration. As a result, Ours and even lay people had realized that for these reasons he was unequal to the demands of his office. In the view of many, he was too little concerned about the observance of the *Constitutions* and rules of the Society and more ready to grant dispensations than was proper. Thus, the teachers in those colleges and especially those at Coimbra paid no attention to observing any of the rules or the examination of conscience, meditation, and readings at table. Nor were there any principals or prefects of study. But with the arrival of his successor, all these defects were remedied: almost everybody diligently observed the rules and *Constitutions,* and all administrative details were expedited with great prudence.

3219.   *The novices at Coimbra were rigidly forbidden to study*

Father Luís Gonçalves [de Câmara] discovered that those admitted to the Society had been strictly forbidden to study anything during their two years of probation, even though Father Francis [Borgia], the commissary, in some ways tempered this rigid policy, which some traced back to the *Constitutions* (although this document furnishes no explicit grounds for this interpretation). The laity, especially the students at Coimbra, found this rigidity burdensome.

3228.   *Efforts to get Portuguese Jesuits to follow Roman practices*

Father Luís requested that some rules that appeared necessary be sent to him. Among those rules being observed in Rome regarding domestic tasks, those Father Ignatius laid down for men who were staying at villa *[vigna],* and those applicable to the prefect of health. At this time, not only did he desire to return to Rome but he also thought it would be most useful for him to observe and write down many details of what he would notice was being done in Rome. . . .

3237.   *Reforms are needed among boarding students at the Royal College of Portugal*

Before the Society took charge of them, these boarders had acquired a bad reputation because of their excessive license—sometimes at night they would jump down from the windows and carry on in a very puerile way.

3238.   *The Jesuits bring reforms to the college*

Therefore, when the Society took over the college, the King earnestly entrusted these boarding students to Ours. Thus, when four of Ours were sent to them to teach their classes, the students completely modified their behavior, to the immense edification of the whole kingdom.

3239.   *Should Jesuits live together with boarding students?*

Some of Ours began to worry that if the students did something reprehensible, part of the blame would fall upon any of Ours who were living with them. So Ours were removed from students' living quarters. But a message arrived from Rome to the effect that it would be possible to make the same arrangements for the boarding students here that were made for the German students at the German College; that is, some of Ours lived with them to direct them in spiritual matters. Because experience taught that the students had behaved worse when Ours did not live with them (even if they inspected them often), Father Luís and the other fathers at Coimbra thought it advisable that from now on some of Ours should live together with boarding students of this sort. Still, it seemed wise to arrange with the King that only boys between fourteen and sixteen years of age—and no one older—would be admitted, for [boys of this age] were still capable of being trained.

3253.   *A Portuguese provincial chapter elects delegates to the First General Congregation*

After learning of the death of Father Ignatius, a provincial congregation gathered in Portugal to elect those who would be going to Rome for the general congregation. All agreed that Father Provincial himself should go to Rome, interrupting for a while his ministry of hearing the Queen's confessions. [Traveling] with him as electors were Father Luís Gonçalves [da Câmara] and Father Gonsalvo Vaz, along with Father Manuel Godinho, serving as procurator for Portugal and India.

3254.   *Getting royal permission to attend a general congregation*

When Father Luís spoke with the Queen, whose permission was required before Father Provincial could leave that kingdom, and after he had adduced the reasons proving that his departure would further God's greater glory, she gave her consent. They immediately set out with the King's approval, leaving Father Ignácio de Azevedo as vice-provincial and, in his absence, Father Francisco Enriquez. Thus on October 23 they left Lisbon for Évora; but not long after, the vice-provincial caught up with them and gave the provincial the letter of Father Francis [Borgia] instructing them to be prepared all through the month of January to begin their journey; for by that time he hoped he would have a response from the Father Vicar[-General] informing them where and when the general congregation would convene.[13]

---

[13] There remain 328 sections in this volume of the *Ratstud,* but they await their own translator.—ED.

SELECTED BIBLIOGRAPHY

Primary Sources

Bobadilla, Nicholás de. *Nicolai Alphonsi de Bobadilla . . . gesta et scripta.* Vol. 46 of the series Monumenta Historica Societatis Iesu (MHSI). Madrid, 1913.

Canisius, Peter, S.J. *Beati Petri Canisii Societatis Iesu epistulæ et acta.* Edited by Otto Braunsberger. Freiburg i. B.: Herder, 1896–1923.

Dalmases, Cándido de, S.J., ed. "De scriptis historicis P. Ioannis de Polanco, de reliquis huius voluminis monumentis." Introduction to *Fontes narrativi.* Vol. 2. Vol. 73 of MHSI, 23–39. Rome: Institutum Historicum Societatis Iesu (IHSI) 1951.

Polanco, Juan Alfonso de, S.J. *Polanci complementa.* Vols. 52 and 54 of MHSI. Madrid, 1916–17].

———. *Vita Ignatii Loiolæ et rerum Societatis Iesu historia* (generally known as the *Chronicon*). 6 vols. Nos. 1, 3, 5, 7, 9, and 11 of MHSI. Edited by D. Fernández Zapico. Madrid, 1894–1898.

> Volume 1 (569 pages) contains the *Vita* of Loyola (pp. 9–76) and the *Chronicon* for the years 1537–49 (pp. 77–569); volume 2 (820 pages) covers the years 1550–52; volume 3 (606 pages) treats the year 1553; volume 4 (760 pages) treats 1554; volume 5 (782 pages) treats 1555; volume 6 984 pages) covers 1556.

Ignatius of Loyola. *Constitutiones II.* Vol. 64 of MHSI. Rome, 1936.

> For the contributions of Polanco to the writing of the *Constitutions,* see the index of this volume, s.v. "Polanco."

———. *Sancti Ignatii de Loyola Societatis Iesu fundatoris epistolæ et instructiones.* 12 vols. Vols. 22, 26, 28, 29, 31, 33, 34, 36, 37, 38, 40, and 42 of MHSI. Madrid, 1903–11; reprinted in Rome, 1964–68.

Litteræ quadrimestres. 7 vols. Vols. 4, 8, 10, 59, 60, 61, and 62 of MHSI. Madrid, 1894–1932.

Secondary Sources

Aldama, Antonio de. *Imagen ignaciana del jesuita en los escritos de Polanco.* Rome, 1975

———. "La composición de las Constituciones de la Compagñía de Jesús." *Archivum Historicum Societatis Iesu (AHSI)* 42 (1973): 201–45.

Astráin, Antonio, S.J. *Historia de la Compagñía de Jesús en la asistencia de España.* Madrid: Razón y Fe, 1912.

Bangert, William J., S.J., and Thomas M. McCoog, S.J. *Jerome Nadal, S.J.: Tracking the First Generation of Jesuits.* Chicago: Loyola University Press, 1992.

Brodrick, James, S.J. *Saint Peter Canisius, S.J., 1521–1597.* New York: Sheed and Ward, 1935.

Constitutions of the Society of Jesus and Their Complementary Norms, The. St. Louis: The Institute of Jesuit Sources, 1996.

Diccionario histórico de la Compañía de Jesús. Edited by Charles E. O'Neill, S.J., and Joaquin M. Domíngues, S.J. 4 vols. Rome: Institutum Historicum S.I., and Madrid: Universidad Pontificia Comillas, 2001.

Dowling, Richard. "Juan Polanco S.J., 1517–1576." *Woodstock Letters* 69 (1940): 1–20.

Englander, Clara. *Ignatius von Loyola und Juan von Polanco: Der ordensstifter und sein Sekretär.* Regensburg: Pustet, 1956.

Gilmont, J.-F. *Les Écrits spirituels du premiers Jésuites.* Rome: IHSI, 1961.

Hudon, William. *Marcello Cervini and Ecclesiastical Government in Tridentine Italy.* DeKalb, Ill.: Northern Illinois University Press, 1992.

Ignatius of Loyola. *The Constitutions of the Society of Jesus.* Translated and edited by George E. Ganss, S.J. St. Louis: The Institute of Jesuit Sources, 1970.

———. *The Letters of Ignatius of Loyola.* Translated and edited by William J. Young, S.J. Chicago: Loyola University Press, 1559.

Leturia, Pedro de. " 'De constitutionibus collegiorum' Patris Ioannis A. de Polanco ac de earum influxu in *Constitutiones* S.J." AHSI 7 (1938): 1–30.

Lucas, Thomas M., S.J. *Landmarking: City, Church and Jesuit Urban Strategy.* Chicago: Loyola University Press, 1997.

Lukács, László. "La catalogue-modèle du Père Laínes (1545)." *AHSI* 26 (1957): 64.

Martini, Angelo. "Gli studi teologici de Giovanni de Polanco alle orgini della legislazione scolastica della Compagnia di Gesú." AHSI 21 (1952): 225–81.

O'Malley, John W. *The First Jesuits.* Cambridge, Mass.: Harvard University Press, 1993.

Orlandini, Niccolò. *Historia Societatis Iesu.* Rome, 1614.

Perfectæ Caritatis. In *The Documents of Vatican II,* edited by Walter M. Abbott, S.J. New York: Guild Press, America Press, Association Press, 1966.

Pirri, Pietro. *Giovanni Tristano e i primordi della architettura gesuitica.* Rome: IHSI, 1955.

Rahner, Hugo, S.J. *Saint Ignatius Loyola: Letters to Women.* Translated by Kathleen Pond and S. A. H. Westman. New York: Herder and Herder, 1960. Originally published as *Ignatius von Loyola, Briefwechsel mit Frauen.* Freiburg: Herder, 1956.

Ravier, André. *La Compagnie de Jésus sous le gouvernement d'Ignace de Loyola (1541–1556).* Paris: Desclée de Brouwer, 1991.

Roustand, François. "Sur le rôle de Polanco dans le rédaction des Constitutions S.I." *Revue d'ascetique et mystique* 42 (1966): 193–202.

Scaduto, Mario. "Uno scritto ignaziano inedito: Il 'Del officio del secretario' del 1547." AHSI 29 (1960): 305–28.

Schurhammer, Georg. "Die Anfänge des römischen Archivs der Gesellschaft Jesu." AHSI 12 (1942): 89–118.

Taylor, Larissa. *Heresy and Orthodoxy in Sixteenth Century Paris: François Le Picart and the Beginnings of the Catholic Reformation.* Leiden: Brill, 1999.

Xavier, Francis. *The Letters and Instructions of Francis Xavier.* Edited and translated by M. Joseph Costelloe, S.J. St. Louis: The Institute of Jesuit Sources, 1992.

INDEX OF PEOPLE AND CITIES

INDEX OF TOPICS AND MINISTRIES